Foundations of Library and Information Science

FOURTH EDITION

RICHARD E. RUBIN

Neal-Schuman

An imprint of the American Library Association

Chicago   2016

© 2016 by the American Library Association

Extensive effort has gone into ensuring the reliability of the information in this book; however, the publisher makes no warranty, express or implied, with respect to the material contained herein.

ISBNs
978-0-8389-1370-3 (paper)
978-0-8389-1372-7 (PDF)
978-0-8389-1373-4 (ePub)
978-0-8389-1374-1 (Kindle)

Library of Congress Cataloging-in-Publication Data

Rubin, Richard, 1949- author.
    Foundations of library and information science / Richard E. Rubin. —
Fourth edition.
        pages   cm
    Includes bibliographical references and index.
    ISBN 978-0-8389-1370-3
    1. Library science—United States. 2. Information science—United States.
I. Title.
    Z665.2.U6R83 2016
    020.973—dc23   2015024926

Cover design by Kim Thornton. Cover images © Shutterstock, Inc. Text composition in the Electra LH and Helvetica CD typefaces by Dianne M. Rooney.

♾ This paper meets the requirements of ANSI/NISO Z39.48–1992 (Permanence of Paper).

Printed in the United States of America

20 19 18 17 16   5 4 3 2 1

Contents

Figures

Foreword

by Joseph Janes

I envy you.

That may not be quite what you expected to read here, so let me explain. First and foremost, I want to congratulate you, and thank you, for choosing this profession. People come to work in library and information settings for so many reasons: getting a job in a library and discovering it's right for you, having early positive experiences in these fields, having a parent or friend who works in an information field, or just feeling an affinity, being drawn to the work, the environment, the institutions, a desire to serve. Whatever brought you here, welcome.

Surveys of our field have shown, and my own experiences and discussions with colleagues reinforce this, that the huge majority of people who do this sort of work love it, would recommend it, and would do it all over again. That's not to say there aren't challenges and frustrations—there are—but for a great many of us this is work we find nourishing, satisfying, rewarding, and enjoyable.

So, I envy you. Not only that you're joining us, but that you're joining us now. As somebody who got his library degree back in the dim dark ages of the early 1980s, I can tell you there has been no more exciting and significant time for what we do. While one still occasionally hears the old "what do we need libraries for when everything's on Google" canard, libraries of all kinds have never been in more demand, the importance of what librarians do has never been greater, and I believe the recognition and acknowledgment of that importance continues to grow as well. That's a testimony to the vision and hard work of your predecessors.

Nor have the challenges, or the opportunities, been greater. You—your generation—will get to figure out how libraries and other information organizations reenvision, reinvent, repurpose, and re-present themselves to constituencies and communities that want and need our services and collections and help more than ever, in an information environment that has never been more competitive,

Joseph Janes is an associate professor at the University of Washington Information School.

mercurial, fickle, and diverse. That may seem daunting, even burdensome, and it may well be, but it's also true, and when you succeed, the fruits will be all the sweeter.

I also envy you this book. Rick Rubin has done his usual Herculean effort to wrap his arms around the entirety and totality of our field, its history and scope. There are things talked about in this book that didn't exist a few years ago, along with ideas and practices a century old or more, and when you look back at this in a couple of decades, you'll chuckle with fond remembrance of things here that are long gone. (Oh yeah, whatever happened to e-mail, anyway?)

I know this seems like a lot to take in, and it is. You've got a sure hand to guide you through it. (And believe it or not, there's a lot more that isn't even in here! You'll get to that later.) There is so much more to what we do and how we do it than meets the eye—it ain't about reading books and shushing people, and it never was—and in the process of uncovering all that, I bet you'll find something that speaks directly to you and you'll find a career you too will love for a lifetime. Find the joy in what you do, and the rest will come.

Mostly, I envy you because it's all ahead of you. This field and profession have been very good to me, and when I see the tools and the environment and the possibilities that are available to my students, and to you, I think how wonderful it would be to start over, though I'm also quite happy I don't have to. We are waiting for you to join us, to share your enthusiasm and your creativity and your vision for a future no one else has yet imagined, for the betterment of the communities and clienteles you will serve. All best wishes to you as you make your way. Bon voyage!

Preface

Today's library and information science (LIS) professionals are experiencing both excitement and trepidation as sweeping societal, technological, political, and economic changes affect our users and institutions and transform our discipline. Today, we are part of a sophisticated knowledge infrastructure: the boundaries of knowledge creation, acquisition, organization, dissemination, use, and evaluation are rapidly blurring and creating new challenges. Similarly, we are also part of a changing environment: an aging population, a ubiquitous and evolving Internet, the proliferation of social media and mobile devices, significant financial stresses on public institutions, and changing information policies affecting creators and distributors of knowledge—print and digital. All these forces are shaping libraries and information services in various ways.

Much has happened since the third edition of *Foundations of Library and Information Science* was published. The LIS field continues to expand, the issues proliferate and grow in complexity, and the challenges we face are serious and relentless. It is daunting and delightful. Our profession demands constant growth, continuous learning, and open minds. We know that next year something new will again force us to reexamine our thinking and reassess our practices, policies, and sometimes even our purpose. We are fortunate that we have a firm foundation on which to make changes: a distinguished history, strong values, and an active profession and academic communities ready to address our challenges.

As with its predecessors, this new edition has been designed to respond to the many changes occurring in the field and the society at large. It preserves some of the content of the third edition but has been reorganized, rewritten, and extensively updated. Most important, new or enhanced discussions have been added. These include (1) the impact of digital devices and social networking, (2) the impact of digital publishing on the publishing industry and the effects of e-books on libraries, (3) the evolution of library services including virtual reference, embedded librarianship, digital access and repositories, digital preservation, and civic engagement,

(4) the new efforts to organize knowledge, including the Functional Requirements for Bibliographic Records (FRBR), the Resource Description Format (RDF), BIB-FRAME, the Semantic Web, and the next-generation catalog (Catalog 2.0), (5) the significance of the digital divide and policy issues related to broadband access and network neutrality, (6) legal developments such as new interpretations of copyright related to mass digitization of books (Google Books) and scholarly articles, (7) the continuing tensions in LIS education between information science and library science, and (8) the spawning of new initiatives to integrate libraries, archives, and museums (LAMs).

There remains an ongoing debate as to whether library science and information science are separate disciplines. There are also arguments about what constitutes the domains of each. *Foundations of Library and Information Science* is focused on the complementary nature of these disciplines using Boyd Rayward's 1983 description of the relationship between library and information science as "a disciplinary continuum . . . with no easily identifiable boundary separating them though the difference between the extreme ends of the continuum are clear and even dramatic" (p. 344). This book focuses on the points of convergence.

I. PURPOSE

The primary purpose of *Foundations of Library and Information Science* is to describe the current LIS environment and examine some of the ever-changing forces that shape that environment and the larger society. The intent is to help prepare LIS professionals to cope with and effectively manage their many complex responsibilities. Bearing this emphasis in mind, this text is designed to accomplish six objectives:

1. To provide an introduction to the field for individuals intending to work in libraries or library-like institutions, related settings, or the information field in general.
2. To identify and discuss major topics and issues in LIS that are current in the United States and that will continue to affect the profession for years to come.
3. To provide librarians and information professionals with an opportunity to refresh their knowledge through a systematic review of major issues and topics that have changed the field.
4. To introduce the profession to interested individuals or those undecided about entering the LIS field and to show its multifaceted character and possibilities.

5. To place LIS in a larger social, economic, political, and cultural context. It is too easy to view the work of LIS professionals purely within an institutional setting. Increasingly, librarians and other information professionals must negotiate and respond to a variety of political, economic, technological, and social forces.

6. To invite the interested reader to further explore topics raised in this book. Many of these topics are part of an ongoing discussion in our field that requires further reading, research, and exchange.

II. ORGANIZATION

Chapter 1, "The Knowledge Infrastructure," provides a broad overview and context for the ensuing chapters examining the infrastructure's characteristics: the devices, networks, processes, and institutions that it comprises. The interrelationship of LAMs is also explored. Chapter 2, "From Past to Present: The History and Mission of Libraries," examines the character of libraries through time with specific emphasis on their many and varied missions. Chapter 3, "The Library as an Institution: An Organizational Perspective," examines contemporary libraries, their types (public, academic, school, and special), their functions, and some of the major organizational issues and challenges that they face. Chapter 4, "Transforming the Library: The Impact and Implications of Technological Change," deals with one of the biggest areas of change in our field. The chapter addresses the topic through both a historical and a current lens, paying special attention to the growth of digital content and its impact on library services. Chapter 5, "Library and Information Science: An Evolving Profession," reviews the evolution and development of the profession. The contemporary American library and information professional is a product of more than a hundred years of growth and change. The current role of LIS professionals and the professional tensions that they experience are best understood when placed in the context of the historical development of LIS education and the profession. The chapter also addresses current issues, including the nature of the LIS labor force, gender and minority representation, and recruitment. Chapter 6 examines the intellectual organization of libraries. "The Organization of Knowledge: Techniques and Issues" discusses the organizational systems that make knowledge, in all its myriad forms, available. In spite of the vast quantities of disparate materials, our classification systems, subject headings, thesauri, databases, and powerful catalogs have enabled LIS professionals to offer effective service for many years. The chapter also addresses the impact of the dramatic increases in digital content and the evolution of the traditional catalog to the next-generation catalog. Chapter 7, "Information Science: A Service Perspective," focuses on the nature of information science as a field of study, calling special attention to those aspects of the discipline that inform the work of LIS professionals. Chapters 8, 9, and 10 deal with philosophical and policy issues affecting LIS. These include the policies, laws, values, and ethics that define our work. Chapter 8, "Information Policy: Stakeholders and Agendas," discusses the general aspects of information policy and the legal environment in which libraries and other information institutions operate. Government, business, industry, public institutions, LIS professionals, and citizens all are stakeholders in trying to shape how information will be disseminated and who will disseminate it. Chapter 9, "Intellectual Freedom," focuses on libraries. Intellectual freedom is a central value of librarianship, and this chapter examines the key policies that affect equitable and open access to knowledge resources. The factors that promote or discourage censorship are addressed. Chapter 10, "The Values and Ethics of Library and Information Science," examines the many ethical ramifications of working in the field and the values of our profession, reviewing ethical principles, codes, and situations.

To permit an examination of the same topic from different vantage points, *Foundations of Library and Information Science* addresses most topics primarily in one chapter, but some important issues are raised anew in a different context in other chapters. For example, censorship and intellectual freedom issues are discussed most thoroughly in chapter 9, but they also arise in chapter 8 on information policy and chapter 3 on the library as an institution. The Internet, because it undergirds much of our knowledge infrastructure today, is covered in multiple chapters. Similarly, because of the tremendous breadth of our field, some complementary areas are mentioned but not explored in depth, including such fields as publishing, book arts, archives, and computer science.

A list of selected readings follows each chapter. These selections provide sources of additional information and stimulate thought on the basic issues raised in this text.

Rounding out the book, three appendixes provide supplemental information on LIS associations and accredited schools of LIS in the United States and Canada, including ALA accreditation standards. A final appendix provides an example of a public library manifesto.

No burgeoning LIS professional can function unless he or she understands the importance of information, how libraries are organized intellectually and administratively, the effects of information policies, and the values and ethics of the LIS profession. The challenge of all professionals is to stay current in a world in flux. The library is a special place; LIS is a special profession. The roles of the former and latter, as well as the broader forces that shape those roles, constitute the major focus of *Foundations of Library and Information Science*. Its goal is to be a valuable resource for those entering the profession and those who have already taken their place within it.

REFERENCE

Rayward, Boyd. 1983. "Library and Information Sciences." In *The Study of Information: Interdisciplinary Messages*, edited by Fritz Machlup and Una Mansfield. New York: Wiley, 343–363.

Acknowledgments

The fourth edition of this book would not have been possible without the considerable help and support of many individuals. Thanks go to faculty members Belinda Boon, Carolyn Brodie, Greg Byerly, Kiersten Latham, David Robins, Athena Salaba, Yin Zhang, and Marcia Zeng for contributing their thoughts and carefully reviewing and commenting on the drafts of various chapters. My thanks to Ron Bammerlin, Jim Bracken, Ken Burhana, Karen Hillman, Tom Klingler, and Mark Pike for assisting me with the sections on academic libraries. Thanks must also go to the outside readers of the manuscript, whose invaluable criticisms improved the work substantially.

Special thanks go to my wife, Marcia, who in edition after edition has carefully read, edited, and improved the clarity and organization of the text. Her tireless energy, critical eye, and constructive suggestions—not to mention her endless patience—have substantially improved this and previous editions. I am truly grateful for her dedication to the cause.

1

The Knowledge Infrastructure

I. INTRODUCTION

Since the nineteenth century, American libraries have served the educational, recreational, informational, and cultural needs of their users. Libraries serve educational needs either by directly assisting schools and colleges in the formal education process or by providing individuals with an opportunity to educate themselves. Similarly, few would question the entertainment value that libraries provide through recreational fiction, newspapers, popular magazines, programming, and, more recently, by DVDs, e-books, computer games, and Internet access. The library meets informational needs through reference services either face-to-face or virtually. Cultural needs have been met by including works of great literature, music, and art in physical collections, by programs and exhibits, and by providing Internet access to cultural repositories worldwide. Of course, not all types of libraries attempt to meet all these needs. Some special libraries and information centers, for example, might focus only on information needs; nonetheless, many libraries with broader scope, such as public, academic, or school libraries, attempt to serve several or all of the needs of their users.

To function effectively, libraries and library-like organizations rely on an extensive knowledge infrastructure that supports their activities. The knowledge infrastructure is composed of the informational, recreational, educational, and cultural components of our society. The infrastructure is both a foundation and a framework, much like the infrastructure of a house. Without such a structure the house collapses. Societies have a variety of infrastructures, such as a transportation infrastructure that includes highways, train tracks, air routes, and waterways that allow people and goods to travel efficiently. It also includes the governmental agencies that regulate transportation. The knowledge infrastructure is similar, except that the traffic is knowledge rather than moving objects. This infrastructure could exist without libraries, but it is greatly enhanced by their presence.

The knowledge infrastructure integrates a variety of elements, the boundaries of which are not precise and often overlap. For example, educational resources can also be recreational; some recreational resources also have substantial educational and informational value. Understanding the components of the knowledge infrastructure highlights the interdependence of libraries with educational institutions, information producers and distributors, as well as cultural agencies and provides an understanding of the place and function of libraries in the greater society.

II. CHARACTERIZING THE KNOWLEDGE INFRASTRUCTURE

There are many ways to characterize the knowledge infrastructure. In this section it will be viewed in five ways: as processes, devices, networks, media industry, and institutions.

A. Knowledge Infrastructure as Process

The knowledge infrastructure can be viewed as a process by which knowledge and information are created, disseminated, and used in a society. Historically, the traditional process involved five actors in a linear relationship:

1. *Creators*—authors, artists, and musicians who embody their ideas in a physical form or a product.
2. *Products*—traditionally books, articles, paintings, or music and, more recently, multimedia presentations, databases, websites, and other digital content.
3. *Distributors*—publishers or vendors who make the products of many creators available, sometimes through other agencies serving as disseminators; also individuals who distribute their own digital content (e.g., blogs).
4. *Disseminators*—institutions or agencies that acquire content from distributors and make it available to users.
5. *Users*—those who consume and use the knowledge or information.

Traditionally, the role of libraries, as well as archives and museums, was as disseminator, serving as an intermediary between users, distributors, and creators. However, as technology, digitization, and the Internet created new possibilities, the linear nature of the traditional process was irrevocably and dramatically altered. Today, the ability to create and distribute digital content through the Internet blurs the relationship between creators, products, distributors, disseminators, and users. In the digital environment, creators can be distributors and disseminators. Distributors such as publishers and disseminators such as schools and libraries can also be creators (e.g., through e-sites, blogs, Twitter accounts, wikis, and digital repositories). Creators can be distributors: novelists can write a novel, put it on the Internet, and distribute it directly to consumers for a fee or for free. Similarly, musicians can distribute their own compositions online. Users can be creators: Wikipedia is a prime example. The convergence of these components creates a complex infrastructure where the actors exchange roles depending on the circumstances. Nonetheless, each of these processes must occur for the infrastructure to function effectively.

B. Knowledge Infrastructure as Devices

Another way to view the knowledge infrastructure is in terms of the devices used to transmit information and knowledge. The major devices of the twentieth century were books, periodicals, newspapers, televisions, radios, telephones, and at the end of the century, computers. Most of these devices have been commonplace in U.S. homes for many decades. For example, for many years almost all households had a telephone landline. Today, merely 8% have a landline only and 45% have a landline and wireless phone service; another 44% have wireless service only (CDC 2014). Nearly 114 million people (99% of U.S. households) have radios, and not just one; the average household has more than eight radios (U.S. Census Bureau 2012a). Similarly, nearly all U.S. households, more than 116 million, have televisions—the highest number in history; the average number of sets per household rose from 2.43 in 2000 to 3.01 in 2012 (TekCarta 2014).

By the turn into the twenty-first century an entirely new generation of devices had been developed—digital and mobile devices such as smartphones, tablets, and e-readers. The extent to which these devices can be found in U.S. households is notable. Approximately 84% of U.S. households own a computer (73% with broadband connections to the Internet). A third of American adults own tablet computers and 56% own smartphones (Rainie and Cohn 2014; Statistica.com 2014; Zickuhr 2013; Smith 2013). On a worldwide basis, 6% of the world's population owns a tablet, 20% own a PC, and 22% own smartphones (Heggestuen 2013).

Many of the most recently developed devices can access and store a range of digitally produced content that was traditionally designed for only one format. For example a television program can now be viewed on a tablet or a smartphone as well as a television set. With the proliferation of digital content, our devices make possible the convergence of knowledge resources and services. For example, a tablet can access digitally produced radio and television programs, movies, lectures, courses, digital repositories, newspapers, and magazine content. Although the utility of these mobile devices is obvious, their constant updating and alteration in addition to new, competing technologies create challenges for institutions like libraries that attempt to organize and disseminate knowledge resources to accommodate these ever-changing devices.

C. Knowledge Infrastructure as Networks

Networks perform vital interlocking functions in the knowledge infrastructure; they provide both direct access to content and enable access to other networks that provide this content. Among the types of networks that comprise the infrastructure are telephone, radio, and digital or satellite links; wireless network utilities; and the Internet. The evolution of networks has been remarkable. For example, land-based telephone networks although still in existence have been widely supplanted by wireless ones; broadcast radio remains commonplace, but satellite radio has gained in popularity; broadcast television networks, once the dominant media in American culture, encountered major competition from cable networks in the last quarter of the twentieth century, which in turn encountered competition from digital satellite networks. Additional competition now comes from digital services such as Netflix and Hulu providing streaming video content based on movies and television programs. In addition, wireless network utilities such as AT&T and Viacom enable access to digital networks and the Internet, providing a vital link to the knowledge infrastructure.

The Internet, of course, is the most prominent network of networks enabling the storage and transmission of digital content of all types from around the world. There are more than 3 billion Internet users worldwide comprising more than 40% of the world's population. In the last few years, the growth rate of Internet users worldwide was between 8% and 10% (Internetlivestats 2015). The Internet's influence, capabilities, and impact will be discussed in the ensuing chapters, but suffice it to say that it is ubiquitous and profound in its capacity to make knowledge resources available.

D. Knowledge Infrastructure as Media Industries

Libraries are dependent in large part, on the media industries that produce and distribute the knowledge and information they provide. As such, understanding the characteristics of these industries is vital to developing library collections and services.

1. Radio Industry

There are currently approximately 6,600 FM commercial stations and 4,700 AM stations. Although the number of AM stations has remained flat since 2000, the number of FM stations has increased steadily by 12% from 2000 to 2014 (U.S. Census Bureau 2012a; FCC 2014). Radio stations, both profit and nonprofit, offer a wide variety of programming, music, traditional news broadcasts and talk shows spanning the political spectrum, and educational programs informing us about issues in the community and the nation. The ubiquitous radio not only sits on our bedside tables and kitchen counters, it is affixed to our heads when we walk and run, it broadcasts in restaurants, automobiles, and other public places. But here too, the Internet has expanded people's access to radio stations. Both subscription-based and free Internet radio services provide national access to stations and are widely used.

Radio remains a heavily used medium; approximately 177 million Americans ages 12 and older listen to commercial radio including nearly 70% of individuals between the ages of 18 and 54 (Nielsen 2014). Despite its popularity, its growth rate is slightly negative losing about 2% a year since 2010. Radio listening tends to increase with level of education and income. AM/FM radio users listen to radio an average of nearly 12 hours a week. The amount of time spent per day is trending slowly downward (Statistica.com 2014c, 2014e). Radio listening tends to decline sharply for those 65 and older (Nielsen 2014).

2. Television Industry

There are more than 1,780 commercial and educational television stations in the United States. The number of commercial stations, 75% of the total, has increased modestly (8%) since 2000, while the number of educational stations has remained relatively unchanged (FCC 2014; U.S. Census Bureau 2012a).

The television industry is diversifying its delivery mechanisms. For example, in the 1960s, cable television was new and not well received. By 1980 only 15 million households (20%) had cable television. By 2000, more than 66 million households had cable television subscriptions. Since 2000, cable subscriptions have been flat as competition from satellite services and Internet access increased. Those umbrella-shaped satellite antennae once thought to be the domain of astronomers at observatories now adorn the roofs and yards of many American homes. There were no home satellite stations in 1980, but by 2013 there were more than 34 million satellite subscribers (SatelliteMarkets.com 2014). Overall, network TV stations have lost ground while cable and satellite television have increased.

The advent of digital recording devices has also changed the way people use their television. Not only can viewers fast-forward, rewind, and otherwise customize and manipulate what was before a static experience, but they can time shift, allowing them to view programs at any time and multiple times. Additionally, many people view television programs on alternative devices, such as tablets, employing Internet services like Hulu. These new services and technologies mean that people can view what they want when they want.

Television viewing has increased slightly since 2010. An average adult viewed TV in 2013 for 279 minutes (4 hours, 39 minutes) daily compared to 269 minutes in 2010. TV viewing is greatest among those 65 and over (97%), although viewing is heavy for all age groups (90% or more). Level of education does not appear to affect TV viewing except for cable viewing: those with less than a high school education view cable less often. In addition, households with very low incomes also have lower cable viewing. A substantial proportion of the TV viewing audience (18%) views free online TV, and the number of such viewers and revenue generated from such viewing is expected to increase substantially over the next few years. The most popular TV website is The Weather Channel (Statistica.com 2014d, 2014e).

3. Telephone/Smartphone Industry

In the history of communications, the importance of the telephone cannot be overestimated. Land-based telephone lines provided the crucial foundation for the computer information revolution. Although ground-based telephone networks will likely remain in some parts of the country for the foreseeable future, their importance will decline as mobile devices supplant them.

The advent of the cell phone and smartphone has had a tremendous effect on the way people receive and transmit information. As of 2014, 90% of Americans owned cell phones. As they evolved into smartphones, their uses broadened considerably, and they now take pictures, send and receive text messages, access the Internet, connect to social networks, send and receive e-mail, record videos, and download applications (Pew Research 2014; Duggan and Rainie 2012).

Libraries have responded to these developments by offering services using websites that function both technically and aesthetically on handheld devices. IM (instant messaging) and SMS (short message service) reference applications via texting have become commonplace, and such services are likely to evolve in conjunction with enabling communication technologies.

4. The Internet and Mobile Access

There are more than 3 billion Internet users worldwide and 280 million in the United States. The rate of U.S. growth is between 7% and 8% per year (Internetlivestats 2015). U.S. adults spend nearly three hours online per day. Internet use decreases with age, with 93% of those ages 18–24 accessing the Internet in a given week, compared to only 43% of those 65 and over doing so. Among GenXers, about one in four uses the Internet to watch movies, television, and video-on-demand. Internet access also increases with level of education and household income. (Statistica.com 2014e, 2014f).

The rate of growth in time spent on mobile devices now exceeds 50% annually. Smartphone use in particular is growing substantially. In 2010 the average adult used a smartphone for 32 minutes daily; in 2013 that number increased to 93 minutes, and it was projected to reach 134 minutes by 2014. Nearly a quarter of the total time spent on media in a day is now spent on mobile devices, compared to 11% on radio, 18% online, and 4% with print. Time spent on mobile devices now exceeds time spent on PCs (eMarketer 2014; Statistica.com 2014). A more detailed discussion of the impact of the Internet and mobile access will follow in the ensuing chapters.

5. Print Publishing Industry

More than 193,000 book titles were produced in 2013 (Barr and Harbison 2014). Average prices of print books have been erratic over the last several years although book publisher revenues have been relatively stable — between 26 and 27 billion from 2008–2012 (Vassallo and Maier 2014). Consumer (popular) print book sales were substantial — $13.1 billion for 2011 (not including e-books), but this is expected to decline to about $8 billion by 2018 due primarily to the rise in e-book sales. Even among children and young adult books, which traditionally have shown strong growth, sales in 2013 fell 6.6% (Milliot 2011). Only academic book sales increased, rising between 4% and 12% from 2010–2012 (Tafuri 2014).

The periodicals industry has been a mainstay of the print industry. More than 75,000 periodicals are published each year in the United States and Canada, including general interest magazines, trade publications, and scientific and other scholarly journals (LOC 2014). In the United States alone, there are more than 8,300 period-ical publishers, but the industry is heavily concentrated, with the fifty largest com-panies comprising 70% of the market (First Research 2009) (U.S. Census Bureau 2012a). A majority of the $46 billion in revenue comes from general-interest maga-zines followed by trade publications (15%). Consumer (popular) magazine publish-ing remains a stable component. Approximately 7,200 such titles are published in the United States, and many of the most popular magazines still have single copy sales in the hundreds of thousands. Revenues for such magazines were expected to exceed $25 billion for 2014–15. The size of the popular magazine audience is con-siderable: in August 2014 alone, *People* magazine had a readership of more than 70 million (Statistica.com 2014b). Of course, many popular magazines are published simultaneously in print and electronic formats and some new magazines are "born digital." Although periodicals are still widely read, scholarly publishing has experi-enced serious challenges in recent decades as the costs of publication have grown while demand has not.

About half the world's adults read a daily newspaper. In recent years, news-papers began offering digital versions often as an alternative to print or as an addi-tional format if a print subscription was purchased. Worldwide, approximately 2.5 billion people read a print newspaper and another 800 million read a digital version (First Research 2014). Despite the popularity of newspapers in some regions of the world, circulation for weekday and Sunday newspapers in the United States has been declining since 1990. Today there are approximately 1,300 daily newspapers in the United States. However, the trend for newspaper reading has been flat or declining with only 42% of U.S. adults (mainly older, more educated, with higher incomes) reading a daily newspaper either in print or online. In 2013, the average adult read a newspaper for about 30 minutes but reading time is projected to decline in the next few years possibly by as much as 15% a year. This might be due, in part to the shrinking size of the newspaper. As print advertising revenue declined, news-papers have decreased the number of pages. Although online advertising increased in the last few years, the gain has not been sufficient to offset print advertising losses (stateofthemedia 2014).

Newspapers also suffer from lack of spontaneity; a morning paper cannot com-pete with continuously updated online news websites and 24-hour cable TV news. These sources are often viewed as more interesting, timely, or appealing to a visually oriented society. By 2012, nearly three-quarters of digital device owners got their news on a desktop or laptop computer, more than half on a tablet, or on a smart-phone. In addition, an increasing number of news consumers employ a variety of platforms using desktops/laptops, smartphones or tablets, or a combination of all three (stateofthemedia 2014a).

6. Digital Publishing Industry

With the rapid rise in the ownership and use of digital devices and the ubiquity of Internet access, there has been a concomitant increase in the publication of digital content. Such content includes physical content that was subsequently migrated into digital form as well as content that was "born digital" and might or might not have a physical version.

A significant portion of the digital publishing marketplace is e-books. E-books have been around for several decades, but they expanded rapidly in the first decade of the twenty-first century with the development of the Kindle in 2007, the Nook in 2009, and the iPad in 2010 (Greco 2012). Since then, e-readership expanded quickly and broadly. Early e-book adopters tended to be dedicated readers, but today even casual readers use e-books. Although some people read e-books exclusively, many consume both print and digital books. Interestingly, as e-reading expanded throughout the population, computer tablets became the preferred e-reading device rather than dedicated e-readers (Vassallo and Maier 2014). Readers use e-books for many reasons: cost savings, readability (ability to adjust font size etc.), and portability as well as ease and speed of access (Vassallo and Maier 2014). E-books have evolved from a novelty to a maturing industry including best sellers. In fact, e-books have changed the ways books are produced, marketed, and consumed. For example, Stieg Larsson's Millennium trilogy, which includes *The Girl with the Dragon Tattoo*, sold more than one million e-copies in 2010 (Milliot 2011). The largest proportion of adult fiction is now produced in the e-book format. "Immersive" genres such as mystery, romance, fantasy, and science fiction appear to be particularly attractive to e-book users; users lose themselves in the story and the format is irrelevant to them. In contrast, growth of e-books in the K–12 and professional book categories has been slower.

In general, the publishing industry views the e-book as a "disruptive technology." Although a majority of publishers' sales still comes through physical retail stores and from print materials, by 2015 as much as 15%–25% of all book sales were from digital content (Vassallo and Maier 2014; Behar, Colombani, and Krishnan 2011). E-book prices have been somewhat erratic—declining sharply from $20 per book in 2009 to $8 per book in 2012 and then rising by 21% in 2013 (Tafuri 2014). Nonetheless, sales of e-books grew dramatically from $67 million in 2007 to approximately $2.3 billion in 2011, growing particularly fast in adult and juvenile fiction, and nonfiction. Some predict that e-sales will overtake print and audio books by 2017 (Statistica.com 2014a). Others believe that e-book sales have hit a plateau, but none can deny that they have become a substantive presence in the book publishing industry and are very likely to remain so (Vassallo and Maier 2014).

Attempting to find an acceptable economic model for e-books has been a challenge for both the publishing industry and for libraries. Only a few years ago, many major publishers denied licensing rights to public libraries (Macmillan and Simon & Schuster) or significantly limited the titles available (Penguin and Hachette). Predictably, this generated a great deal of friction and consternation that produced an aggressive action by the American Library Association in defense of libraries. By 2012 publishers provided access to libraries, although sometimes with many limitations. With e-books, rather than buying a book, libraries purchase a subscription or pay a fee through a vendor service, such as OverDrive to download copies for a limited time. The library user then can download books under varying time constraints (Vassallo and Maier 2014). Among the continuing challenges facing libraries are the higher prices (sometimes three times higher) charged for digital versions, significant limitations on the number of times an item can be downloaded through subscription services, the restriction against simultaneous use of an e-book, and sometimes restrictions against nonresident use (Vassallo and Maier 2014; Bocher and Tijerina 2012; Feldman, Russell, and Wolven 2013). The current pricing models might not be sustainable for libraries over time. Brantley (2013) suggested a possible alternative:

> What libraries need is their own cross-library open source discovery service married to an e-book file hosting and management platform that can replace OverDrive with a less intrusive, open source, interoperable system that can relieve libraries from per-loan fees and excessive setup costs. Unfortunately, this is a tall order. (p. 27)

But e-books are not the only area of digital publishing interest. To a large extent, periodicals, both popular and scholarly, as well as newspapers are now being published in digital format. Some periodicals and newspapers have converted exclusively to digital versions while others offer parallel publications in both physical and digital formats. In addition, much research and general information gathering is now conducted using digital content. Library users, for example, commonly conduct research or seek information relying on Internet access or on databases provided by subscription to libraries. The content is identified, located, accessed, and delivered digitally. The publication of some digital content, particularly articles in research-oriented databases in academic settings, has raised a variety of issues regarding who controls the content and how use might be unduly restricted. These issues are discussed in ensuing chapters.

In addition, there has been tremendous growth in self-publishing. In book titles alone, between 2007 and 2012, the number of self-published book titles increased 422% to 391,000 titles (Vassallo and Maier 2014). Although self-published books used to be considered "vanity publishing" today there is a group of well-established "indie authors" (independent authors) who publish their own works or use fee-based publishers who produce digital copies on demand for a fee. These authors often combine their distribution strategies using both a traditional publisher as well as publishing independently (Palmer 2014). As Palmer (2014) noted:

> Self-publishing has been enjoying an exceptional run in recent years, as new technologies and growing acceptance of indie books have led to an explosion of new titles and industry growth. (p. 138)

Indie publishing has substantially increased access to authors whose voices might not otherwise be heard. In addition, it encompasses more than books. Consider, for example, the creation of blogs by individuals who have readerships in the tens or hundreds of thousands.

The concept of self-publishing has also stimulated, particularly in academic institutions, the growth of digital repositories in which faculty and others deposit digital content (scholarly articles, datasets, etc.) into a database often managed by the academic library. Although there are many issues related to such repositories (discussed in subsequent chapters), they are growing in number and popularity. Libraries and bibliographic utilities have also responded to the self-publishing trend. Some public libraries, for example, provide a digital venue for local authors interested in self-publishing services. The Online Computer Library Center (OCLC) through WorldCat now lists some self-published works in its catalog, and some reviewing services now review selected self-published works (Bradley, Fulton, and Helm 2012). Digital publishing has clearly altered how content is created, edited, marketed, sold, distributed, accessed, and managed. It has also changed the relationship between creators, publishers, and end users. Today, authors and publishers might be in regular contact with consumers through blogs and websites and other social media (Huwe 2013). Digital publishing has clearly had an impact but its future for libraries is uncertain. Huwe (2013) poignantly observed:

> The way forward is not fully settled, but it promises to be exciting. Will there be creative disruption? It seems a certainty. But as users increasingly become creators, authors, and "makers," we have an obligation to provide the quality services that they need—including digital publishing. (p. 55)

E. Knowledge Infrastructure as Institutions

1. Libraries

Libraries have been an important component of the knowledge infrastructure since the seventeenth century in America, although the number and sophistication of these libraries were quite limited until the nineteenth century. Detailed discussion

FIGURE 1.1
Numbers of Public, Academic, Government, and Special Libraries*

1980–2013 BY FIVE-YEAR INCREMENTS (EXCLUDES BRANCHES AND COMMUNITY COLLEGES)					
Year	Public	Academic	Government	Special	Total
1980	8,717	4,618	1,260	8,609	28,665
1985	8,849	5,034	1,574	8,955	29,843
1990	9,060	4,593	1,735	9,051	30,761
1995	9,165	4,730	1,875	11,340	32,666
2000	9,480	3,491	1,411	9,993	31,628
2005	9,734	3,698	1,225	9,526	30,416
2010	9,744	3,745	1,113	8,476	29,329
2013	9,640	3,703	1,006	7,616	28,182

Source: American Library Directory. Medford, NJ: Information Today, 1980–2013.
*Total includes branch, departmental, divisional, military libraries, and some specialized libraries in academic institutions.

of the library as an institution will follow in the ensuing chapters. Figure 1.1 illustrates the number and growth of libraries in the United States since 1980.

Today, there are more than 120,000 libraries in the United States: more than 16,000 public libraries (including branches), 3,700 academic libraries, 7,600 special libraries, and 98,000 school or media center libraries (ALA 2014). The various libraries support primary and secondary education; higher education; business, industry and government; and the general public. They are trusted sources of information and provide a wealth of materials and services as well as access via the Internet to resources worldwide. Libraries have been an especially important channel for introducing children and adults to books and reading, literacy, and self-education. The special roles that libraries play are discussed in detail in the chapters that follow.

2. Schools and Academic Institutions

Educational institutions serve as the foundation of knowledge creation and dissemination in our society. The United States boasts one of the largest universal education systems in the world, characterized by "its large size, organizational structure, marked decentralization, and increasing diversity" (U.S. Department of State 2008, p. 2). Figure 1.2 represents the basic structure of formal education in the United States.

Primary and secondary education is offered in preschools, kindergartens, elementary schools, middle or junior high schools, and high schools. Postsecondary

FIGURE 1.2
Educational Infrastructure in the United States

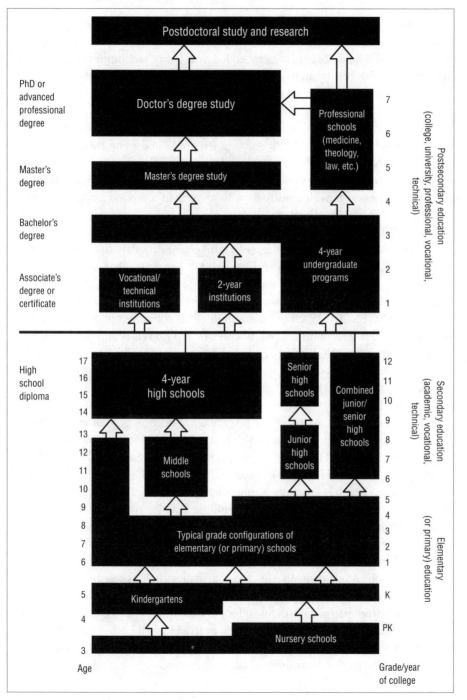

Source: U.S. Department of Education, National Center for Education Statistics, Annual Reports Program.
nces.edu.gov/programs/digest/d07/figures/fig.01.asp.

education is offered through trade schools and community colleges, and undergraduate and graduate programs offering bachelor's, master's, and doctoral degrees. Academic and school libraries are embedded as subunits within these educational agencies. In terms of educational attainment, approximately 30% of the U.S. adult population has a high school education, 19% possess a bachelor's degree, 7% have a master's, and 1% has a PhD (U.S. Census Bureau 2012b).

There are nearly 99,000 public schools in the United States, including 73,000 elementary schools, nearly 31,000 secondary schools, and more than 33,000 private schools (NCES 2012). There were approximately 3.7 million public classroom teachers serving 50 million students in 2012; similarly, approximately 440,000 private school teachers provided instruction to more than 5 million students in 2012 (NCES 2012a). Public school enrollment is projected to grow to more than 53 million by 2021 (NCES 2012b).

There are more than 4,700 degree-granting, postsecondary institutions in the United States. Most institutions are private (3,000). There are relatively few research intensive universities (~200) that offer a large number of master's or doctoral degrees. There are also more than 1,700 two-year institutions offering associate degrees and certificates (NCES 2012c). Of the more than 800,000 teachers in degree-granting institutions about three-fourths teach in colleges and university and the balance in two-year institutions (NCES 2012d). Enrollment approached 21 million in 2011 and is expected to exceed 23.5 million by 2021 (NCES 2012e). Most students are enrolled in colleges and universities while about 8 million in two-year institutions (NCES 2012f).

In terms of diversity, an increasing percentage of students of color are participating in postsecondary education. In 2000, whites represented 70% of those attending, compared to 61% in 2011. In 2000, African-Americans represented 12% of students compared to 15% in 2011. In 2000, Hispanics comprised 10% of students compared to 14% of those in 2011. Diversity is somewhat greater at two-year institutions with African-Americans representing 16% of enrollment, followed by Hispanics at 19%. In terms of gender, women have represented the majority of enrollees in higher education for many years: 56% in 2000 and 57% in 2011 (NCES 2012g).

In addition to formal postsecondary education, many Americans participate in adult education. Adult education includes activities such as technical and vocational education courses, basic skills training, work-related courses and workshops, apprenticeship programs, courses taken for personal interest, and classes in English as a Second Language (ESL). In 2004–2005, nearly 44% of the adult population was engaged in some type of structured adult education activities. In 2011, more than 1.7 million Americans took courses in adult basic education, secondary education, or English as a second language (NCES 2012h). Most adult learning is for either career/job related purposes (27%) or for personal interest (21%). Women tend to engage in adult education for personal reasons more than males. Adult learning takes place among all age groups; the highest percentages (70% or more) fall between the ages of 30 and 54. African-Americans tend to be involved more in adult education than Hispanics; those in managerial or professional positions tend to participate more than those in service or sales positions; and those with higher formal education (e.g., possessing a baccalaureate degree), participate more than those with less than a college degree (NCES 2012i).

Educational institutions are in a period of transition in how they deliver their services. New methods of delivery allow online classes and programs as a supplement to or substitute for traditional face-to-face classroom instruction. In addition, new online vendors offer college level as well as skill-based courses and programs that compete with traditional educational institutions. As online technologies increase in sophistication, instructional methods adapt to this new form of delivery, and as new economic models are created to offer courses, the nature and structure of education might well change — into what is still uncertain.

3. Nonformal Educational Units

In addition to formal educational institutions there are different types of organizations that offer nonformal education (NFE) or "informal learning" defined as "any organized, intentional, and explicit effort to promote learning to enhance the quality of life through non-school settings" (Heimlich 1993, p. 292). Examples of NFE can include "nature hikes, self-help clinics at home improvement stores, museums and historical site tours, and/or craft workshops at community centers" (Taylor 2006, p. 291). NFE usually focuses on individual needs, is less structured than formal education, and is learner centered. NFE accommodates many different learning styles and is self-paced (e.g., a guided tour through museum exhibits using a prerecorded program). It is also characterized by voluntary participation, a less formal teacher-student relationship, and teachers who are subject experts though not necessarily trained teachers. Generally, NFE is not directly associated with formal educational systems and takes place outside traditional classrooms. It serves as a complement or supplement to formal education, and sometimes as an alternative to formal education (Taylor 2006).

Although there is very little current data on the number of individuals engaged in NFE, the potential involvement is substantial. There are more than 7,000 museums, historical sites, zoo and nature parks and more than 9,000 performing arts companies (U.S Census Bureau Table 2012c). Millions of Americans participate in nonformal education. For example, approximately 5.7 million adults participated in book clubs in the United States in 2010, 20 million attended an art gallery or show, 6.4 million listened to a concert on the radio, 32 million visited a museum, 30 million attended live theater, and 28 million attended a zoo (U.S. Census Bureau 2012d). In 2013, there were more than 273 million visitors to U.S. National Parks (NPS 2014). All in all, these venues contribute considerable educational, recreational, and informational value to the society as a whole.

Libraries supplement and support these informal education experiences in a variety of ways. Many museums, for example, often have their own libraries. Educators who provide NFE often rely on libraries for their supporting materials as well as a place to offer their programs; and no doubt thousands of Americans check out their book club selections from the library.

III. LIBRARIES, ARCHIVES, AND MUSEUMS

Since the first decade of the twenty-first century, there has been an emerging consensus that libraries, archives, and museums have a special and consanguine relationship. Each institution shares a common purpose of preserving our cultural heritage:

> Archives, libraries, and museums are memory institutions . . . Their collections contain the memory of peoples, communities, institutions and individuals, the scientific and cultural heritage, and the products throughout time of our imagination, craft and learning. They join us to our ancestors and are our legacy to future generations. They are used by the child, the scholar, and the citizen, by the business person, the tourist and the learner. These in turn are creating the heritage of the future. Memory institutions contribute directly and indirectly to prosperity through support for learning, commerce, tourism, and personal fulfillment (Dempsey 1999, p. 1).

These institutions usually are either public or not-for-profit institutions that have a central purpose of serving the public (Trant 2009). Recognizing the commonality of libraries, archives, and museums has led to intense discussion within the LIS community regarding the implications for how, as a group, they can contribute to the society as a whole and to each other. Those who view these institutions as closely related often refer to libraries-archives-museums or LAMs, suggesting greater integration, but this concept sometimes rests uneasily with these institutions. As Martin (2007) observed:

> We all seem to be confident that libraries, archives, and museums collect differ-
> ent types of things—libraries collect documents of various kinds (books, journals,
> maps, and the like), archives collect documents of a specific kind (records contain-
> ing particular types of evidence), and museums collect objects and artifacts. (p. 81)

Martin noted that libraries, archives, and museums each have their own professional cultures, vocabularies, and identities as well as their own professional education programs. They also have their own distinct methods of governance and funding. In addition, the way LAMs and museums are used is distinctive: people come to libraries to have specific questions answered, to obtain a book or other informational materials, or to browse the collection for educational or entertainment purposes— emphasis is on broad-based use. Archives emphasize the preservation and protec- tion of materials. Archive users usually have a specific concern that needs to be addressed and they consult particular records or documents to address that issue. If browsing occurs at all, it usually occurs within a specific collection. People generally come to museums for education or entertainment (Trant 2009). Museum collec- tions comprise primarily unique objects. This uniqueness enables a special relation- ship between each object and each viewer—the visitor-object encounter (Wood and Latham 2014). This relationship involves much more than a transfer of information from an object to the viewer. For example, when an object is placed in proximity to other objects in an exhibition, it is intended to elicit from the viewer consideration of the particular context and the relationship among the objects in the exhibit or museum; it also stimulates the emotions, intuitions, imagination, faith, reasoning, and past experiences of the viewer—a total experience (Wood and Latham 2014). This is much more than simple consultation with a document.

At the same time, despite these real differences, Martin (2007) noted that some museums, such as zoos, aquaria, or children's museums, have strong interactive and educational components similar to libraries. Further, he observed that all of the physical artifacts and items collected in LAMs are "documents" of a type, as each item represents ideas or particular aspects of our culture. The fact that we tend to think of these institutions as separate entities is a convention that we have created (Martin 2007). While it is possible to recognize the unique contributions of each, from a cultural perspective, there is tremendous value in perceiving them from a deep collaborative, interinstitutional, integrative, and transformational perspective that sees them collectively as a common resource for the preservation and under- standing of our culture. Smiraglia (2014) argues that LAMs, by recognizing their commonalities as "information institutions," can produce a "cultural synergy" with resulting benefits greater than the sum of their individual contributions (p. 1).

The idea that libraries, archives, and museums are one entity is not new. Indeed one need only go back to ancient Greece to the Alexandrian Library, which was both a museum and a library, to see that the idea is far from novel. In fact, by the sixteenth century in Europe and the nineteenth century in the United States, individuals and institutions sponsored by wealthy benefactors assembled "cabinets of curiosities" housed in rooms or buildings containing a wide variety of items including books and manuscripts, coins, and works of art as well as natural specimens such as plants, fossils, minerals, and mechanical devices. Some even included a chemical laboratory.

During this time the division between the humanities and the sciences was minimal. Demonstrating curiosity about the natural world and being learned were admired widely (Marcum 2014; Rayward 1998). The "mixed collections" were designed as testimonies to an individual's intellectual acumen or as a demonstration of the civilized character of the cities in which they were located. They were also intended to inspire and elevate the "lower classes" (Given and McTavish 2010).

However, by the end of the nineteenth century as the sciences became more specialized and disciplines such as librarianship were professionalized, the book collections within the cabinets tended to dominate and the natural history aspects faded. By the twentieth century the library, archives, and museums performed distinct functions and were managed as separate facilities, services, and collections. Although one might consider the nineteenth century curiosity cabinets as naive attempts to bring together disparate knowledge resources, the idea behind them was sound. Today, the potential for unifying the collections, albeit not necessarily merging them, might be achievable at least in part through technology:

> . . . in a sense, our computers are cabinets of curiosities. Through their Internet-connected search buttons, we can bring to our individual inquiries multiple kinds of information from multiple sources. . . . However one reads the past, today's information technologies open opportunities never equaled before to make the world's cultural heritage accessible, usable, and valuable. (Marcum 2014, p. 86)

For years, significant portions of the physical collections of museums and archives were hidden from public view and difficult to access. With the development and widespread use of powerful search engines, people's expectations about what should be available to them increased although access to many archives and museums was limited or not available (Zorich et al. 2008). Today, local, national, and international cultural heritage collections are rapidly being digitized and archives and museums increasingly engage people through social networking sites, blogs, wikis, and mobile devices (Given and McTavish 2010). As people gain greater and greater access to LAM collections digitally, the opportunity for the reconvergence of LAM functions increases.

But as in libraries, people expect access to cultural heritage collections to mimic their search experiences using powerful search engines like Google. When people use Google they seldom care about where an item is located; they care about getting access to the content effortlessly and quickly. Similarly, people expect searching to be simple: ideally conducting one search on a given topic should be sufficient to get the information needed. Accepting the notion of LAM as an integrated institution means that libraries, archives, and museums must disabuse themselves of the view that they are "silos" of information. Instead they must recognize that people seek information on a *topic* regardless of the *location* of the content (Prescott and Erway 2011; Zorich et al. 2008).

The emerging shared model is fundamentally different from the past. In the future, from a portal in a library, archive, or museum, a person engaged in a *single* topical search should be able to easily access materials from a library, documents and records from an archive, and digital objects from a museum. It is a "user-driven perspective, where resources are evaluated based on situationally defined personal need . . ." (Trant 2009, p. 374). The new model also recognizes that it is not enough just to locate the content, it must be delivered as well. Needless to say, there are a multitude of complex issues that must be addressed for such access to be realized. These include:

- designing effective discovery systems with easy-to-use and effective search features that include not just identification, description, and location of content, but delivery of that content as well

- using consistent standards for metadata and controlled vocabularies to ensure interoperability

- harmonizing digital resource management practices including management of digital rights

- developing consensus among LAM administrators on the importance of broad access to the collections

- managing political and "turf" issues between and within institutions, for example, between IT and public service units

- determining whether the data for comprehensive search activities will be centralized or whether a federated search strategy will be employed in which users get separate sets of results from each institutions and whether the technological solutions will be open source or commercially provided (Prescott and Erway 2011)

Many of these issues present significant barriers to a vision of shared resources among LAMs. Nonetheless, Prescott and Erway (2011) argue that all LAMs have an overriding mandate to serve their users and providing powerful and simple search capabilities clearly meets that goal. Rayward (1998) anticipated the trend toward the integration of LAMs and believes that it is on an inexorable, albeit uncertain, course:

> The increasing availability in electronic form of information generally and of new kinds of information more particularly will lead to a redefinition and integration of the different categories of "information" organizations. Traditionally these have been created to manage different formats and media such as print and its surrogates (libraries), objects (museums), and the paper records of organizational activity (archives and records repositories). Differences in organizational philosophy, function, and technique have arisen from the exigencies presented by these different formats and media. These exigencies no longer apply in the same way when there is a common electronic format. It is clear that if electronic sources of information are to be effectively managed for future access by historians and others, differences between libraries, archives and museums will largely have to disappear and their different philosophies, functions and techniques integrated in ways that are as yet unclear. (p. 207)

It likely will take many years to determine exactly how technological advances and changes in the cultural milieu will ultimately affect LAMs. In the meantime, joint efforts are under way locally and internationally ranging from informal meetings, cooperation in digitizing local historical collections, partnering in the preparation of museum exhibits, or integrating information systems to provide a common portal to large scale collaborations such as merging national governmental archives and libraries (Marcum 2014; Zorich et al. 2008).

Generally, LAM initiatives are grouped into three categories: (1) collaborative programming often focused on joint topics of interest or libraries providing free access to museums, (2) collaborative electronic resource pooling in which LAMs provide common access to digital resources, and (3) joint-use/integrated facilities (Yarrow et al. 2008). Joint-use facilities have three levels: "minimal integration (collocated facilities with individual service maintained), selective integration (sharing of specific projects or departments), and full integration in which both facilities share one mission" (p. 25). Canada has embraced the joint-use concept fully. In 2004 the National Archives of Canada merged with the National Library, creating the Library and Archives Canada (LAC). This unique partnership combined their collections of documents, government records, books, newspapers, music, films, maps, photographs, family papers and painted portraits (Given and McTavish 2010).

Although LAM initiatives often require considerable coordination, they are often quite successful, especially when the joint activities

- support lifelong learning or community development
- optimize the services provided
- enable universal access to community resources
- broaden the customer base in the community for the institutions involved
- address the need for preservation of heritage materials (Yarrow et al. 2008)

Of course, aside from the technological problems noted earlier, there could be various reasons why institutions might resist LAM activities. The ability to break with cultural tradition may be the hardest. Marcum (2014) identified three particular barriers: (1) collaborations require time, money, and energy and each organization must be rigorous in assessing the value of collaborations; (2) LAMs might have different expectations of their users; some might provide much more assistance or give the user more or less freedom to use their resources; and (3) there might be insufficient communication, misunderstandings, and internal resistance.

In addition, some critics have voiced serious philosophical concerns over the fundamental rationale for LAMs and the potential for negative impacts. Cannon (2013) summarized many of these concerns:

1. There is little actual evidence that major convergence projects work.
2. There are real and important differences in the activities of libraries, archives, and museums, and these differences are often underestimated or overlooked in LAM initiatives.
3. LAM projects are most often initiated by administrators—an inappropriate, top-down management model that frequently lacks staff support. As a result they create morale problems.
4. LAM initiatives are less a result of technological developments and more a reflection of the "corporatization" of cultural institutions responding to economic and political interests rather than cultural ones.
5. LAM initiatives, because they are business-oriented and customer-driven, often cater to immediate needs rather than focus on long-term interests—this has serious ethical implications for professional practice.

In the past, some institutional staff and leaders may also have been reluctant to engage in LAM activities because of their experience in the professional programs that prepared them for their work. These programs have traditionally remained segregated for the most part. Trant (2009) observed:

> Current methods of training librarians, archivists, and museum professionals emphasize the historical difference between these types of institutions, rather than

> their emerging similarities. Conventional curricula do not support a profession
> committed to the creation of integrated, inter-institutional, inter-disciplinary infor-
> mation resources accessible to a wide public in physical and digital forms. (pp.
> 376–377)

But the situation is changing. For example, it is not uncommon today to find the distinctive coursework and curricula for archivists and museologists embedded within
forward-thinking schools of library and information science. These schools are less
likely to emphasize an institutional, library-centric focus and more likely to place
increasing emphasis on organizing information more broadly, and on the creation
and maintenance of digital content and digital libraries (Given and McTavish 2010;
Ray 2009). Quality assurance in such coursework in LIS programs is guided, at least
in part, by the LIS accreditation process which is absent in most other museum
studies programs.

Additional changes include the emergence of new professions within the
museum field. For example, the increasing demand for digital access to museum
collections coupled with a current lack of technical infrastructure to manage and
curate those resources has led to a new subfield of museum work—museum informatics and new positions such as digital curator. The content of this area is a natural
complement to informatics courses in LIS programs (Ray 2009).

Although currently there is little overlap in courses for museum studies and
LIS courses, "museum studies is gaining acceptance as an area of the LIS field
in the United States as LIS programs incorporate more museum-relevant subjects
into their infrastructure" (Kim 2012, p. 159). Trant (2009) suggested that there is
considerable room to develop future curricula that encompasses the education and
training needs of all LAMs using general knowledge categories such as management, cultural policy, creating digital representations, managing digital collections,
supporting information use, and evaluating information services. With the growth
of such programs, opportunities for greater collaboration among LAM institutions
are greatly improved.

Does this mean that libraries, archives, and museums will merge into one
memory institution? Unlikely. It is important to note that supporting the concept
of integrating libraries, archives, and museums does not mean we must reject each
type of institution as a distinct entity. In fact, it is quite possible that there might be
no true substitute for visiting a museum or being a part of an art exhibition. Similarly, sometimes it is critical to examine archival documents in-person. But there are
many situations when digital access is appropriate and sufficient and LAM activities
present new opportunities for people that did not previously exist. There are legitimate purposes for being on-site and online. As Trant (2009) observes:

> This new digital space is an adjunct to, not a replacement for, physical spaces. Dig-
> ital offerings are now available in support of, in tandem with, and before and after
> on-site services. For some users, encountering digital representations of original
> objects is exposure to a new kind of information resource, only discovered because
> it was "on the network." Sometimes, the digital surrogate fulfills all needs . . . But
> for many users of museums and archives, a digital encounter cannot replace the
> need to consult the original. Digital access facilitates—or even encourages—
> on-site consultations. (p. 375)

In today's world, libraries, archives, and museums, like many institutions serving
the public, must demonstrate that they create value for individuals and the broader
community that they serve. Martin (2007) summed up the argument for an integrative approach to LAMs nicely:

> It seems clear to me that libraries, archives, and museums are all social agencies
> that are collectively responsible for preserving the shared knowledge of humankind,
> making it available for everyone to use, and transmitting it to future generations.
> Our notions about what distinguishes one of us from the other are predicated on
> outmoded concepts of uniqueness. The impact of digital information technology
> has lifted the veil that once obscured our common mission. Now that the users of
> our collections in the digital world fail to recognize the distinctions that we have
> created, we must find ways to work together more effectively and to share our rich
> resources among ourselves and enhance public access to them. (p. 87)

It is as yet uncertain the extent to which the LAM movement will affect most libraries, archives, and museums. What is clear is that the underlying forces of digitization,
public accountability, economic challenges, and professional practice will stimulate
change in how cultural knowledge is represented, collected, organized, and disseminated. LAMs might represent a vital force in ensuring that libraries, archives, and
museums continue to make substantial contributions to our collective knowledge.

IV. SUMMARY

The role of libraries and other library-like institutions is defined by the needs of
the societies that create them. Their ability to fulfill their important missions and
roles is enabled by the capacities within the knowledge infrastructure. There are
many dimensions and pieces to this infrastructure all of them interacting and playing important, complex, and ever-changing roles.

The increasingly sophisticated knowledge infrastructure will continue to challenge us as information technologies expand and become integral to peoples' daily lives. These revolutionary new technologies provide people with new and rich opportunities for education, entertainment, knowledge creation, and culture. Individuals growing up in a digital world have new and different expectations than library users in the past. These knowledge-seekers expect to exercise more self-sufficiency in locating information, and they expect the various technologies, whether music, television, computers, or the Internet, to be integrated into one seamless "infosphere" (De Rosa, Dempsey, and Wilson 2004). LIS professionals must be at the forefront of exploring and exploiting these technologies in order to provide efficient and effective access to that infosphere for all people.

We should expect to encounter important issues that will arise in relation to the creation of an infosphere. It is likely that the following will be among them: open access, copyright protection, intellectual freedom, personal and data security, individual privacy, the costs of access, needed professional training, the library's role related to literacy and reading, and the importance of the library as a place in the community. These issues, when addressed together, reveal how important it is to assess how well libraries continue to reflect the public interest and user needs, and how well they are meeting their mission. It is a tremendous responsibility, and it becomes increasingly challenging as the social, economic, educational, political, technological, and cultural climate grows more complex. There are no simple answers to the important issues facing us. Yet it is hoped that the ensuing chapters will improve the reader's understanding of the issues involved in addressing them.

REFERENCES

ALA (American Library Association). 2014. "Number of Libraries in the United States." www.ala.org/tools/libfactsheets/alafactsheet01.

Barr, Catherine, and Constance Harbison. 2014. "Book Title Output and Average Prices: 2009–2013." In *Library and Book Trade Almanac*, 59th ed. Medford, NJ: Information Today, pp. 460–490.

Behar, Patrick, Laurant Colombani, and Sophie Krishnan. 2011. *Publishing in the Digital Era: A Bain & Company Study for the Forum d'Avignon*. www.bain.com/Images/BB_Publishing_in_the_digital_era_4_11.pdf.

Bocher, Robert, and Bonnie Tijerina. 2012. "E-Books and Their Impact on Libraries." In *Library and Book Trade Almanac*, 57th ed. Medford, NJ: Information Today, pp. 17–31.

Bradley, Jana, Bruce Fulton, and Marlene Helm. 2012. "Self-Published Books: An Empirical 'Snapshot.'" *Library Quarterly* 82 (2012): 107–130.

Brantley, Peter. 2013. "Books Going Digital: Betwixt and Between." In *Library and Book Trade Almanac*, 58th ed. Medford, NJ: Information Today, pp. 19–31.

Cannon, Branden. 2013. "The Canadian Disease: The Ethics of Library, Archives, and Museum Convergence." *Journal of Information Ethics* 22 (fall): 66–89.

CDC (Centers for Disease Control and Prevention). 2015. "Wireless Substitution: Early Release of Estimates from the National Health Interview Survey, January–June 2014." www.cdc.gov/nchs/data/nhis/earlyrelease/wireless201412.pdf.

De Rosa, Cathy, Lorcan Dempsey, and Alane Wilson. 2004. *The 2003 OCLC Environmental Scan: Pattern Recognition: A Report to the OCLC Membership*. Dublin, OH: OCLC.

Dempsey, Lorcan. 1999. "Scientific, Industrial, and Cultural Heritage: A Shared Approach." *Ariadne*. www.ariadne.ac.uk/issue22/dempsey.

Duggan, Maeve, and Lee Rainie. 2012. *Cell Phone Activities*. www.pewInternet.org/2012/11/25/cell-phone-activities-2012.

eMarketer. 2014. "Mobile Continues to Steal Share of US Adults' Daily Time Spent with Media." emarketer.com/Article/Mobile-Continues_Steal_Share_of_US-Adults_Daily-Time-Spent-with-Media/1010782.

FCC (Federal Communications Commission). 2014. "Broadcast Station Totals as of December 31, 2013." transition.fcc.gov/Daily_Releases/Daily_Business/2014/db0108/DOC-325039A1.pdf.

Feldman, Sari, Carrie Russell, and Robert Wolven. 2013. "E-Book Business Models for Public Libraries: A Response to Publisher-Library Differences." In *Library and Book Trade Almanac*, 58th ed. Medford, NJ: Information Today, pp. 3–18.

First Research. 2009. "Magazine Publishers." www.firstresearch.com/industry-research/Magazine-Publishers.html.

———. 2014. "Newspaper Publishers Industry Profile." www.firstresearch.com/Industry-Research/Magazine-Publishers.html.

Given, Lisa M., and Lianne McTavish. 2010. "What's Old Is New Again: The Reconvergence of Libraries, Archives, and Museums in the Digital Age." *Library Quarterly* 80: 7–32.

Greco, Albert N. 2012. "How E-Books' 'Disruptive Technology' Affects U.S. Book Industry, Trade." In *Library and Book Trade Almanac*, 57th ed. Medford, NJ: Information Today, pp. 530–542.

Heggestuen, John. 2013. "One in Every 5 People in the World Own a Smartphone, One in Every 17 Own a Tablet." www.businessinsider.com/smartphone-and-tablet-penetration-2013-10.

Heimlich, J. E. 1993. "Nonformal Environmental Education: Toward a Working Definition." As cited in "Making Meaning of Local Nonformal Education: Practitioner's Perspective." Edward W. Taylor. *Adult Education Quarterly* 56 (August 2006): 291–307.

Huwe, Terence K. 2013. "Digital Publishing: The Next Library Skill." *Online Searcher* 37 (September/October 2013): 51–55.

Internetlivestats. 2015. "Internet Users." www.internetlivestats.com/internet-users/#trend.

Kim, Jeonghyun. 2012. "Building Rapport between LIS and Museum Studies." *Journal of Education for Library and Information Science* 53 (spring): 149–161.

LOC (Library of Congress). "Periodicals." http://memory.loc.gov/ammem/awhtml/awser2/periodicals.html.

Marcum, Deanna. 2014. "Archives, Libraries, Museums: Coming Back Together?" *Information & Culture* 49: 74–89.

Martin, Robert S. 2007." Intersecting Missions, Converging Practices." *RBM: A Journal of Rare Books, Manuscripts, and Cultural Heritage* 8: 80–88.

Milliot, Jim. 2011. "2010: Digital Publishing's Impact Felt across Industry." In *Library and Book Trade Almanac*, 56th ed. Medford, NJ: Information Today, pp. 451–461.

NCES (National Center for Education Statistics). 2012. "Table 98: Number of Public School Districts and Public and Private Elementary and Secondary Schools: Selected Years, 1869–70 through 2010–11." Digest of Education Statistics: 2012. nces.ed.gov/programs/digest/d12/tables/dt12_098.asp.

———. 2012a. Digest of Education Statistics: 2012. nces.ed.gov/programs/digest/d12.

———. 2012b. "Table 36: Enrollment in Public Elementary and Secondary Schools, by Regions, State, and Jurisdiction: Selected year, Fall 1990 through Fall 2012." nces.ed.gov/programs/digest/d12/tables/dt12_036.asp.

———. 2012c. "Table 275. Number of Degree-Granting Institutions and Enrollment in These Institutions, by Enrollment Size, Control, and Level of Institution: Fall 2011." nces.ed.gov/programs/digest/d12/tables/dt12_275.asp.

———. 2012d. "Table 284. Employees in Degree-Granting Institutions, by Sex, Employment Status, Control and Level of Institution, and Primary Occupation: Selected Years, Fall 1991 through Fall 2011." nces.ed.gov/programs/digest/d12/tables/dt12_284.asp.

———. 2012e. "Table 224. Total Fall Enrollment in Degree-Granting Institutions, by Attendance Status, Sex, and Age: Selected Years, 1970 through 2012." nces.ed.gov/programs/digest/d12/tables/dt12_224.asp.

———. 2012f. "Table 219. Enrollment, Staff, and Degrees/Certificates Conferred in All Postsecondary Institutions Participating in Title IV Programs, by Level and Control of Institution, Sex of Student, Type of Staff, and Type of Degree: Fall 2010, Fall 2011, and 2010–11." nces.ed.gov/programs/digest/d12/tables/dt12_219.asp.

———. 2012g. "Table 263. Total Fall Enrollment in Degree-Granting Institutions, by Level of Enrollment, Sex, Attendance Status, and Race/Ethnicity of Student: Selected Years, 1976 through 2011." nces.ed.gov/programs/digest/d12/tables/dt12_263.asp.

———. 2012h. "Table 507.20. Participants in State-Administered Adult Basic Education, Secondary Education, and English as a Second Language Programs, by Type of

Program and State or Jurisdiction: Selected Fiscal Years, 2000 through 2011." nces.ed.gov/programs/digest/d13/tables/dt13_507.20.asp.

————. 2012i. "Fast Facts: Adult Learning." nces.ed.gov/fastfacts/display.asp?id=89.

Nielsen. 2014. "Nielsen Releases Radar December 2014 Network Ratings." www.nielsen .com/us/en/press-rom/2014/nielsen-releases-radar-december-2014-network-ratings.html.

NPS (National Park Service). 2014. "Frequently Asked Questions." www.nps.gov/faqs.htm.

Palmer, Alex. 2014. "A Look Ahead to Self-Publishing." *Publishers Weekly* 261 (January 27, 2014): 138–140.

Pew Research. 2014. "Cell Phone Activities." www.pewInternet.org/data_trend/mobile/ cell-phone-activities.

Prescott, Leah, and Ricky Erway. 2011. *Single Search: The Question for the Holy Grail.* Dublin, OH: OCLC Research. www.oclc.org/research/publications/library/2011/ 2011-17.pdf.

Rainie, Lee, and D'vora Cohn. 2014. "Census: Computer Ownership, Internet Connection Varies Widely across U.S." www.pewresearch.org/fact-tank/2014/09/19/census-computer -ownership-Internet-connection-varies-widely-across-u-s.

Ray, Joyce. 2009. "Sharks, Digital Curation, and the Education of Information Professionals." *Museum Management and Curatorship* 24: 357–368.

Rayward, Boyd. 1998. "Electronic Information and the Functional Integration of Libraries, Museum, and Archives." In *History and Electronic Artefacts*, edited by Edward Higgs. Oxford: Clarendon, pp. 207–226. people.lis.illinois.edu/~wrayward/museumslibs.html.

Satellitemarkets.com. 2014. "Vital Statistics." www.satellitemarkets.com/vital_statistics.

Smiraglia, Richard P. 2014. *Cultural Synergy in Information Institutions.* New York: Springer.

Smith, Aaron. 2013. "Smartphone Ownership 2013." www.pewInternet.org/Reports/2013/ Smartphone-Ownership-2013.aspx.

stateofthemedia. 2014. "The State of the News Media 2013." www.stateofthemedia.org/ 2013/newspapers-stabalizing-but-still-threatened/newspaper-by-the-numbers.

————. 2014a. "A New Era of the Digital Revolution: The Role of Mobile Devices & Social Media in News Consumption." www.stateofthemedia.org/2012/mobile-devices-and -news-consumption-some-good-signs-for-journalism/infographic.

Statistica.com. 2014. "Number of TV Households in the United States from Season 2000–2011 to Season 2014–2015 (in millions)." www.statistica.com/statistics/243789/ number-of-tv-households-in-the-us.

————. 2014a. "Consumer Book Sales Revenue in the United States from 2008 to 2018." www.statistica.com/statistics/190819/consumer-book-sales-revenue-forecast-for-the-us -market.

————. 2014b. "Number of Magazines in the United States from 2002 to 2014." www.statistica.com/statistics/238589/number-of-magazines-in-the-united-states.

————. 2014c. "Growth of Average Time Spent with Major Media Per Day in the United States from 2009 to 2012." www.statistica.com/statistics/247472/growth-of-media-use -in-the-us.

————. 2014d. "Statistics and Facts about Online TV in the U.S." www.statistica.com/topics/1514/online-tv.

————. 2014e. "Average Daily Media Use in the United States from 2010 to 2014 (in minutes)." www.statistica.com/statistics/270781/average-daily-media-use-in-the-us.

————. 2014f. "Media Consumption Habits of Generation X in the United States in 2012." www.statistica.com/statistics/300066/media-consumption-habits-of-us-generation-x.

Tafuri, Narda. 2014. "Prices of U.S. and Foreign Published Materials." In *Library and Book Trade Almanac*, 59th ed. Medford, NJ: Information Today, pp. 424–459.

Taylor, Edward W. 2006. "Making Meaning of Local Nonformal Education: Practitioner's Perspective." *Adult Education Quarterly* 56 (August): 291–307.

TekCarta. 2014. "TV Sets: Average Number of TV Sets per TV Household (68 Countries)." www.generatorresearch.com/tekcarta/databank/full/33.

Trant, Jennifer. 2009. "Emerging Convergence? Thoughts on Museums, Archives, Libraries, and Professional Training." *Archives & Museum Informatics* 24: 369–387.

U.S. Census Bureau. 2012. "Table 1132: Utilization and Number of Selected Media 2000–2009." www.census.gov/compendia/staab/2012/tables/12s1132.pdf.

————. 2012a. "Table 1128: Information Industries-Types of Establishments, Employees, and Payroll: 2008." www.census/prod/2011pubs/12statab/infocom.pdf.

————. 2012b. "Educational Attainment of the Population 18 Years and Over, By Age, Sex, Race, and Hispanic Origin." www.census.gov/hhes/socdemo/education/data/cps/2013/tables.html.

————. 2012c. "Table 1231: Arts, Entertainment, and Recreation—Establishments, Employees, and Payroll by Kind of Business (NAICS Basis): 2007–2008." www.census.gov/compendia/statab/2012/tables/12s1230.pdf.

————. 2012d. "Table 1240. Adult Participation in Selected Leisure Activities by Frequency: 2010." www.census.gov/compendia/statab/2012/tables/12s1240.pdf.

U.S. Department of State. 2008. Bureau of International Information Programs. www.amknowledgea.gov/publications/books/education-in-brief.html.

Vassallo, Nadine, and Robert C. Maier. 2014. "The Evolving E-Book Landscape: Two Perspectives." In *Library and Book Trade Almanac*, 59th ed. Medford, NJ: Information Today, pp. 24–40.

Wood, Elizabeth, and Kiersten F. Latham. 2014. *The Objects of Experience: Transforming Visitor-Object Encounters in Museums*. Walnut Creek, CA: Left Coast Press.

Yarrow, Alexandra, Barbara Clubb, and Jennifer-Lynn Draper. 2008. *Public Libraries, Archives and Museums: Trends in Collaboration and Cooperation*. IFLA Professional Reports No. 108. The Hague: IFLA.

Zickuhr, Kathryn. 2013. "Tablet Ownership 2013." www.pewInternet.org/Reports/2013/Tablet-Ownership-2013.aspx.

Zorich, Diane M., Gunter Waibel, and Ricky Erway. 2008. *Beyond the Silos of the LAMs: Collaboration Among Libraries, Archives and Museums*. Report produced by OCLC Research. www.oclc.org/content/dam/research/publications/library/2008/2008-05.pdf.

SELECTED READINGS
Books/Monographs

Behar, Patrick, Laurant Colombani, and Sophie Krichnan. "Publishing in the Digital Era: A Bain & Company Study for the Forum d'Avignon." 2011. www.bain.com/Images/ BB_Publishing_in_the_digital_era_4_11.pdf.

The Bowker Annual: Library and Book Trade Almanac. Medford, NJ: Information Today.

Feather, John P. *The Information Society: A Study of Continuity and Change.* 6th ed. London: Facet, 2013.

International Television and Video Almanac (Annual). Groton, MA: Quigley.

National Center for Education Statistics. *Digest of Education Statistics* (Annual). Washington, DC.

Prescott, Leah, and Ricky Erway. *Single Search: The Question for the Holy Grail.* Dublin, OH: OCLC Research, 2011. www.oclc.org/research/publications/library/ 2011/ 2011–17.pdf.

Smiraglia, Richard P. *Cultural Synergy in Information Institutions.* New York: Springer, 2014.

Wood, Elizabeth, and Kiersten F. Latham. *The Objects of Experience: Transforming Visitor-Object Encounters in Museums.* Walnut Creek, CA: Left Coast Press, 2014.

Yarrow, Alexandra, Barbara Clubb, and Jennifer-Lynn Draper. *Public Libraries, Archives and Museums: Trends in Collaboration and Cooperation.* IFLA Professional Reports No. 108. The Hague: IFLA, 2008.

Zorich, Diane M., Gunter Waibel, and Ricky Erway. *Beyond the Silos of the LAMs: Collaboration Among Libraries, Archives and Museums.* Report produced by OCLC Research, 2008. www.oclc.org/content/dam/research/publications/library/ 2008/ 2008–05.pdf.

Articles

Bradley, Jana, Bruce Fulton, and Marlene Helm. "Self-Published Books: An Empirical 'Snapshot.'" *Library Quarterly* 82 (2012): 107–130.

Brantley, Peter. "Books Going Digital: Betwixt and Between." In *Library and Book Trade Almanac.* 58th ed. Medford, NJ: Information Today, 2013, pp. 19–31.

Cannon, Branden. "The Canadian Disease: The Ethics of Library, Archives, and Museum Convergence." *Journal of Information Ethics* 22 (fall 2013): 66–89.

Dempsey, Lorcan. "Scientific, Industrial, and Cultural Heritage: A Shared Approach." *Ariadne* 22 (1999). www.ariadne.ac.uk/issue22/dempsey.

Feldman, Sari, Carrie Russell, and Robert Wolven. "E-Book Business Models for Public Libraries: A Response to Publisher-Library Differences." In *Library and Book Trade Almanac.* 58th ed. Medford, NJ: Information Today, 2013, pp. 3–18.

Given, Lisa M., and Lianne McTavish. "What's Old Is New Again: The Reconvergence of Libraries, Archives, and Museums in the Digital Age." *Library Quarterly* 80 (2010): 7–32.

Heimlich, J. E. 1993. "Nonformal Environmental Education: Toward a Working Definition." As cited in Edward W. Taylor. "Making Meaning of Local Nonformal Education: Practitioner's Perspective." *Adult Education Quarterly* 56 (August 2006): 291–307.

Huwe, Terence K. "Digital Publishing: The Next Library Skill." *Online Searcher* 37 (September/October 2013): 51–55.

Kim, Jeonghyun. "Building Rapport between LIS and Museum Studies." *Journal of Education for Library and Information Science* 53 (spring 2012): 149–161.

Marcum, Deanna. "Archives, Libraries, Museums: Coming Back Together?" *Information & Culture* 49 (2014): 74–89.

Martin, Robert S. "Intersecting Missions, Converging Practices." *RBM: A Journal of Rare Books, Manuscripts, and Cultural Heritage* 8 (2007): 80–88.

Milliot, Jim. "2010: Digital Publishing's Impact Felt across Industry." In *Library and Book Trade Almanac*. 56th ed. Medford, NJ: Information Today, 2011, pp. 451–461.

Ray, Joyce. "Sharks, Digital Curation, and the Education of Information Professionals." *Museum Management and Curatorship* 24 (2009): 357–368.

Rayward, Boyd. "Electronic Information and the Functional Integration of Libraries, Museum, and Archives." In *History and Electronic Artefacts*, edited by Edward Higgs. Oxford: Clarendon, 1998, pp. 207–226. http://people.lis.illinois.edu/~wrayward/museumslibs.html.

Taylor, Edward W. "Making Meaning of Local Nonformal Education: Practitioner's Perspective." *Adult Education Quarterly* 56 (August 2006): 291–307.

Trant, Jennifer. "Emerging Convergence? Thoughts on Museums, Archives, Libraries, and Professional Training." *Archives & Museum Informatics* 24 (2009): 369–387.

Vassallo, Nadine, and Robert C. Maier. "The Evolving E-Book Landscape: Two Perspectives." In *Library and Book Trade Almanac*. 59th ed. Medford, NJ: Information Today, 2014, pp. 24–40.

2

From Past to Present
The History and Mission of Libraries

I. INTRODUCTION

Not all societies can have libraries. Libraries require at least three conditions: a centralized population, economic development, and political stability (Harris and Johnson 1984). Physical libraries do not prosper in nomadic conditions; there must be a stable location for the materials. The centralization of population in cities and towns was particularly important. However, even a small stable population such as a university or monastery can serve as a sufficient concentration to produce a library. Similarly, libraries cannot prosper when the primary energies and resources of the community are devoted to subsistence; the development of libraries requires a certain level of wealth and leisure to read. Finally, libraries cannot flourish in times of revolt and political chaos. Many great libraries have been destroyed when empires fell or in times of war or other armed conflicts. Understanding how libraries emerged and the functions they served throughout history provides a basic context for understanding the current mission of American libraries and helps frame the discussion of the role of the library in the future. The discussion that follows is not a history of libraries per se, but a historical overview of the various missions of libraries with special attention to the development of libraries in the United States.

II. THE EARLY MISSIONS OF LIBRARIES

A. The Earliest Mission: Maintaining a Records Archive

No one knows when the first libraries were established, but at least two significant factors provided impetus for their creation: the rise of commerce and the invention of writing. The earliest written records date from 3000 BC and probably come from Sumeria or its environs in Mesopotamia. Sumeria was a busy commercial center. People conducted business, managed estates, and lent money in the temples which were the social and economic center of Sumerian communities. To record these transactions, wet clay from nearby river valleys was shaped into tablets and a square or triangular-tipped stylus was pressed into it producing characteristic wedge-shaped-markings. Called "cuneiform" (from the Latin *cuneus*, or wedge), the writing was both pictographic (comprising pictures) and phonographic (comprising sounds). The dried tablets were stacked on wooden shelves or in jars and baskets. Some important tablets were stored in clay envelopes.

Excavations of these ancient tablets revealed numerous insights into Sumerian society, including the holdings and sale of cattle, food, and textiles (Walker 1998) as well as important records dealing with mathematics, grammar, medicine, astrology, omens, and collections of religious prayers and incantations (Dunlap 1972). Some historical and literary works (including the *Epic of Gilgamesh*), have also been found as well as early codifications of law (Harris and Johnson 1984). Municipal and government libraries held business records as well as deeds, contracts, tax lists, and marriage records (Harris and Johnson 1984). References to small private libraries have been found as well, but little is known about them.

Reading was very rare in Mesopotamia and the culture, as it was elsewhere, was primarily oral. When reading did occur it was generally aloud. There were no librarians as we think of them today. However, an organized system for retrieving these materials was required. Evidence suggests that some of the temples had schools that taught specially qualified people how to make clay tablets, how to write cuneiform, and how to record Sumerian literature, mathematics, and accounting. These well-educated scribes or priests were known as "masters of the books" or "keepers of the tablets." These first "librarians" attached tags or marked at least some of the tablets on their edges. Sometimes a large number of tablets might be stored in a box or a series of boxes and an additional tablet was prepared summarizing the contents—a "tablet of contents," so to speak (Walker 1998). There is even evidence that there was a hierarchy among scribes with senior scribes serving as chief administrators of the tablet archives. Given the rarity of their skills, it is not surprising that these scribes were part of the elite of Sumerian society (Walker 1998).

B. The Religious and Practical Missions of Egyptian Libraries

By the third millennia BC, Egyptian society was thriving. Still primarily an oral culture, less than 1 percent of Egyptians could read and many of those were just barely literate. As with Sumeria, Egyptian temples were cultural centers that served as both historical archives and places for learning. Writing was considered a sacred activity. The temple priests trained professional scribes in a type of apprentice-master system to write a pictographic and phonographic language called hieroglyphics (Davies 1998). As clay was not plentiful, records were kept on scrolls made from flattened papyrus reeds (Jackson 1974).

The earliest Egyptian libraries probably emerged around 2400 BC The library at Edfu, known as the "House of Papyrus," had a collection of practical and spiritual materials that included writings on administration, magic, astronomy, astrology, and medicine (Thompson 1962; Shera 1976). Egyptian libraries were particularly notable for their medical collections, which included pharmacological information as well as materials on diagnosis and treatment of diseases and surgery (Harris and Johnson 1984). In addition to the temple libraries, there were also extensive private collections among royalty and individual wealthy Egyptians. Perhaps the most notable royal library was that of Pharaoh Ramses II in Thebes between 1200 and 1300 BC. This library might have had as many as 20,000 scrolls (Nichols 1964). According to the Greco-Roman historian Diodorus Siculus, the portal to the library at Thebes was inscribed with the words "Healer of the Soul," suggesting it contained both spiritual and medicinal materials, but we do not know the actual contents (Jackson 1974).

C. The Mission of Scholarship and Research

The eighth century BC Assyrian king, Ashurbanipal, was a learned man with knowledge of languages, mathematics, and astronomy as well as military strategy (Starr 1991). He believed that a library should not only maintain archival records, but should also serve as a source of current reference materials and contribute to the education of future generations (Dunlap 1972). To this end, he expanded the library at his palace in Nineveh, Mesopotamia, begun by his great-grandfather, Sargon II. Ashurbanipal directed scholars and assistants to collect clay tablets produced from other lands and the library soon had thousands of tablets on a wide variety of subjects. The collection contained Sumerian and Babylonian literary texts, history, omens, astronomical calculations, mathematical tables, grammatical and linguistic tables, and dictionaries, as well as commercial records and laws. Many of these materials were translated from their original language into Assyrian. There is also evidence of a "keeper of the books," as the collection was organized with the titles arranged by subject and listed in registers. Some of the tablets had markers to help in locating and shelving them but nothing else is known (Jackson 1974).

The library of Ashurbanipal was the greatest library of its time, providing a rich collection of materials and information on Mesopotamia and its culture. At its height, it was estimated to have as many as 30,000 clay tablets, two-thirds of which were collected during Ashurbanipal's reign (Dunlap 1972). Taken as a whole, the Royal Library at Nineveh was a remarkable achievement for several reasons:

- The collection was a concerted effort to acquire a vast amount of material on a variety of subjects.
- The holdings were developed, at least in part, for future generations.
- Many of the materials were translated to increase accessibility.
- The materials were systematically organized, marked, and arranged.
- A "librarian" played a significant role in the library's activities.

No doubt part of the reason for the library's existence was to glorify Ashurbanipal, but the characteristics noted above also suggest that the Royal Library was the first attempt to build a library for reference and research.

Advancing the scholarly mission of libraries was also one of the notable contributions of the Greeks. The values of knowledge, learning, and education were an integral part of Greek culture. Throughout much of its history, Greece, like Sumeria and Egypt, was primarily an oral culture. In the fifth century BC, a transition to a written culture began. There is some evidence that even a century earlier, the then leader of Athens, Pisistratus, had collected many works and created the first "public" library.

Written materials, whether on scrolls or clay tablets, were believed to be helpful in furthering education. Many scholars and young aristocrats established private libraries that they believed might help them obtain social and political success (Jacob 2002; Staikos 2004). Even Plato had a large library, although he believed that written materials were problematic. He was concerned that the written word would supplant memory and oral discussion which he believed were critical to understanding ideas. Plato never taught from a written text or spoke from written notes. He prized the ability to speak well above the written word (Staikos 2004). Nonetheless, spurred by the rise of the philosophical schools of Plato, Aristotle, the Sophists, and others (Dunlap 1972), Greece soon became a center for the production of written materials.

Aristotle's library, in particular, was extensive. His student, Alexander the Great (356–323 BC) played a major role in promoting libraries. Although he was not directly responsible for building libraries, by extending his empire he consequently extended the Greek values of reading and learning. Literacy, by Alexander's time, was more common compared to previous cultures and centuries—perhaps as high as 10 percent. While the wealthy could obtain a more complete education including the "classics" such as Homer, geometry, and music, others learned a basic education of writing and reading (Davies 1998; Starr 1991). In addition, Alexander might have been the first one to propose the idea of a great library in Alexandria, Egypt (Staikos 2004).

Following Alexander's death in 323 BC his conquered lands were divided among five Macedonian generals, one of whom, Ptolemy Soter (Ptolemy I), was given Egypt. Ptolemy, considered a fine diplomat, had great respect for the written word and a love for learning. He encouraged scholars and artists to immigrate to Alexandria, which in addition to a bustling port, became a center of culture, learning, and critical studies of Greek and other literatures. In order to facilitate these studies, Ptolemy and his son Ptolemy Philadelphus (Ptolemy II), with the help and encouragement of Demetrios of Phaleron, founded the Alexandrian Museum and Library.

The mission of the library was ambitious—to collect the entirety of Greek literature. The library was to be a "universal" library which promoted the Greek language but also included Near Eastern traditions. The Alexandrian, like the library of Ashurbanipal before it, aggressively collected materials. Ptolemy sent requests to the leaders throughout the known world asking them for copies of all the books they possessed in their libraries and archives so that they could be stored at the Alexandrian. Sometimes whole libraries were acquired. In some cases, the founders went to questionable lengths. Ptolemy, for example issued a royal decree that all books found on ships coming to Alexandria would be confiscated and copied. Then the *copies* would be returned to the ships! An entire annex of the Alexandrian library was created to make such copies (Staikos 2004).

The librarians organized, evaluated, classified, and maintained the materials in two buildings. A major research library called the Brucheion, was divided into ten great halls, each hall representing a separate area of learning subdivided with smaller rooms for individuals involved in special studies (Parsons 1952). A smaller library, called the Serapeum, might have provided some service to students and the public (Harris and Johnson 1984).

Many of the librarians achieved great personal fame, such as the scholar Callimachus. According to some historians, under Callimachus's guidance, the library exceeded more than a half-million items (Blackburn 2003), although the actual size of the collection relies on various accounts of questionable authenticity (Parsons 1952; Jochum 1999). Callimachus is especially known for organizing the collection. His goal was to compile a comprehensive list of authors and their works that would serve as a library catalog (Staikos 2004). His subject catalog of the library holdings, called the Pinakes, contained 120 scrolls arranged into ten subject classes. Within each class, there were subdivisions listing authors alphabetically with titles. Because some entries included historical or critical remarks, some historians regard the Pinakes as more than a catalog, suggesting that it might have also served as a history of Greek literature (Jackson 1974).

The Alexandrian possessed the characteristics of any great research institution: a comprehensive collection of materials and scholars to acquire, organize, and maintain the collection. At its height, the total collection might have amounted to between 500,000 and 700,000 items. The Alexandrian became a self-contained community of scholars that attracted other notable scholars including Euclid, Archimedes, and Galen. Many of the researchers were provided with grants and other privileges including food, lodging, and servants so that they could pursue their academic activities undisturbed (Battles 2003; Staikos 2004). Common to academic institutions even today, this was a source of much jealousy and criticism by those who were not part of the privileged community. Interestingly, Staikos (p. 167) refers to the community of scholars as a "gilded prison" because the scholars were given great freedom inside the library, but were pretty much confined to it. Arrest and imprisonment might await any attempt to leave!

In fact, the Alexandrian represented a cultural core for Greek influence on the known world. As Battles (2003) noted:

> By bringing scholars to Alexandria and inviting them to live and work, at royal expense, among an enormous store of books, the Ptolemies made the library into a think tank under the control of the royal house. The strategic implications of a monopoly on knowledge—especially in medicine, engineering, and theology, all among Alexandria's strengths—were not lost on the Ptolemies. (p. 29)

It is unclear when and how the Alexandrian was destroyed. Some historians claimed that at least part of it was set afire when Caesar invaded Alexandria in 48 BC, but there is some reason to doubt that account (Jochum 1999). Blackburn (2003) argued that the scrolls which supposedly had been destroyed had actually been removed by the librarian to protect them and still await discovery. Nevertheless, the Alexandrian deteriorated with the decline of the Greek Empire and by the third century AD suffered badly from pillaging and destruction.

D. The Missions of Personal Status and Public Use: The Roman Libraries

Around the first century BC, with the rise of the Rome as a military and cultural force, the mission of libraries appeared to shift. During the early days of Rome, the Romans possessed few, if any, libraries. Following the conquest of Greece, however, Greek libraries were plundered, and possessing a library became a symbol of status and rank as well as personal pride for many generals and the aristocracy. Rome viewed itself as the heir to Greek culture and even the Roman educational system was modeled after that of the Greeks. Many Greek philosophers and teachers migrated to Rome from the first century BC onward helping to establish a book culture among Roman patricians—keeping in mind that for the most part the "book" was a scroll. Interestingly, although owning a library provided status, knowing how to write did not. Many of those who taught, edited, and copied manuscripts, or prepared documents were educated slaves usually from Greece—quite different from earlier times, although these slaves were often prized by their owners (Battles 2003).

By the first century BC there were many libraries in Rome. Some were associated with temples, others could be found in public baths which had alcoves in which to store scrolls. Many were in the private homes of wealthy Romans. Aristotle's library, for example, was brought to Rome in the first century BC by the Roman general Sulla (Thompson 1962). Cicero had a library in each of his seven villas (Staikos 2005). Lucullus opened his libraries to others who lacked the means to have their own collections, and it was not uncommon for fellow aristocrats of similar literary interests to loan materials from their private libraries to each other (Dix 1994). Julius Caesar's imperial library contained major works in Greek and Latin along with busts of their authors (Barker 2001). Many of the library collections in Rome were known as "double libraries," that is they contained Greek materials separate from the Latin collection (Staikos 2005, p. 7). This suggests that although the Greek culture was much revered, it was distinct from Rome's.

There might have been several factors that led to the creation of the first public library in Rome. First, during the time of Julius Caesar, there was an increasing belief that works of literature were to some extent public property that should be available to all citizens, although it is likely that less than 10 percent of the Roman citizenry could read (Harris, 1989). Second, there was increasing availability of literature in both the Greek and Latin languages; there was a thriving trade in books as well. Finally, Caesar, after his conquest of Alexandria in 47 BC was affected by seeing the great library there. When he returned to Rome, he planned to build the first "public" library and he instructed the scholar Marcus Varro to begin collecting a wide variety of materials in both Greek and Latin. Unfortunately, Caesar's death delayed this project. Nonetheless, the project was continued by one of Caesar's consuls, Asinius Pollio, and it is he who is given credit for the completion of the library about 39 AD. The library was built in isolation but was connected to a group of other public buildings. Its purpose was twofold: it was a center of learning and study, and a place to serve the ever-increasing number of educated men and teachers (Staikos 2005). The emperor Augustus built two additional public libraries in Rome and by the fourth century AD there were as many as twenty-nine public libraries in the city, often associated with Roman temples (Boyd 1915). In addition to religious items these libraries also held public records and general literature, which might have been available for borrowing under rare circumstances (Harris and Johnson 1984). They also often had rooms or larger spaces that served as a public forum. It is important to remember that Roman society, like the Greeks, was primarily an oral culture, and even written works were usually spoken aloud. People, as a rule did not read silently. Instead, citizens attended special recitations at which poets or writers would recite their new works which was considered a form of publication during those times (Dix 1994; Harris 1989). The purpose of such recitations was either to obtain criticism from the listening audience, or to gain popularity and sales by entertaining fellow Romans. These public recitations evolved over time from small gatherings to much larger meetings which required larger rooms, which we now know as "auditoriums" (Staikos 2005). Although the presence of "public" libraries with public readings is a distinctive feature of the Roman achievement, one should not make too much of it. It is really unclear whether there was truly general access to these libraries; it is more likely access was still to the educated and privileged. Nonetheless, because some libraries were found in public baths, there is reason to believe that in at least some cases many Romans could partake of limited collections. Overall though, access was probably limited to an exclusive few (Dix 1994).

During most of the time of Roman domination, the Romans recorded their history and accounts using papyrus scrolls, like the Greeks before them. The scrolls, called *volumina* (volume), could be as much as 20 to 30 feet in length. There were some obvious disadvantages to the scrolls; they were bulky and it was more difficult to find one's place because there were no pages. During the first century AD, due to persecution and the need to record religious text quickly and in readily transportable form, the early Christians abandoned the scroll and replaced it with the parchment codex (book). The early Christians were the first to publish biblical manuscripts in codex form with bound pages and a wood covering (Boser 2006).

The format was a radical one because bound books were considered second class; almost all lengthy texts at the time were published on scrolls. But with its hard cover and compact size, the codex traveled better than a scroll and could be opened flat and have page numbers, which made for easier reading. (Boser 2006, p. 28)

For many subsequent centuries the papyrus scroll and the codex coexisted. During this transitional period, many scrolls deemed important by their possessors were copied into the codex format thus aiding the eventual domination of the current book form. By the fourth century AD, the codex was in widespread use and had replaced papyrus scrolls (Thompson 1962).

Also by the fourth century, the social tension between Greco-Roman "pagan" beliefs and those of the ever-growing number of Christians produced much friction and included attention to the written accounts that undergirded both pagan and Christian doctrine. The books and other writings of Greek and Roman philosophers and those of the Apostles and Church fathers drew fire from their opposing camps and produced sometimes violent forms of censorship. As political leadership ebbed and flowed in the first four centuries of the Christian era, whichever leadership dominated often attempted to censor the books and authors of the other. This was an era in which brutal and sometimes fatal punishments for authors and those who possessed their works were meted out. Book burnings as well as people burnings were not uncommon and both Christian and non-Christian leaders shared in these excesses.

As most of Western Europe plunged into political, economic, and social chaos, however, the archival and scholarly missions of libraries were sustained by Byzantine and Muslim libraries in the East, and in the monastic libraries of Western Europe.

E. Preserving Scholarship: The Byzantine and Muslim Libraries

The Middle Ages, which extended broadly from about 300 AD to 1500 AD, was a complex period. Although it is generally viewed as a period of great calamity, poverty, and chaos, this is a serious oversimplification. Generally, Western Europe in what remained of the rapidly disintegrating Western Roman Empire suffered serious political dislocations and great economic depression. Especially from 400 to 800 AD Western Europe experienced many invasions from groups outside the Empire, including the Goths, Vandals, Mongols, Visigoths, and Vikings. Political leadership in the West changed frequently and was often disorganized and fragmented. Urban areas declined and cities physically and politically disintegrated. There were essentially two classes of people: a small number of elites who dominated government, economics, and religion; and a large peasant class who provided agricultural and sometimes military labors in service of the elites (Cantor 1993). The dominant way of life was rural, provincial, impoverished, and difficult. Small villages and towns peppered large rural areas that were poorly farmed and sustained a peasant population who were poorly educated and with very low standards of living. Political control was mostly exercised locally rather than by an Emperor or King. As we will see in the discussion below, such social, political, and economic conditions were not amenable to large, universal libraries. Such conditions made it difficult or impossible for libraries to exist at all.

But while Western Europe was declining, the Eastern Roman Empire, known as the Byzantine Empire, was flourishing under the leadership of the Christian emperor Constantine and his son. This empire extended along the Mediterranean from Greece to Northern Africa, including Egypt. The empire was a center of trade and commercial activity. Constantine was the first Christian emperor of Rome and while only 10 percent of the Roman Empire was Christian at the time of his conversion, his ascension to power greatly increased Christianity's influence (Mango 2002).

The center of the Byzantine Empire was Constantinople, where Constantine's son, Emperor Constantius, strove to make the city the intellectual capital of the Empire. To accomplish this, he founded the Imperial Library in 353 AD (Jackson 1974). It appears the library operated much like a university library although it was open to the public. Like Assurbanipal and the Ptolemy's before him, Constantius sent messengers throughout the Empire to seek out Greek and Latin texts (and Christian texts as well), and to bring them to the library. Many works thus discovered were on papyrus and in serious disrepair. As a consequence, the library contained not only a large collection, but a staff of individuals and a conservation area. Here, scrolls were repaired or copied onto new parchment codices (Staikos 2005). Although the Eastern Empire was more influenced by Greek culture and traditions than Roman ones, the Imperial Library contained both Greek and Latin works organized as a "double library" (Harris and Johnson 1984, Staikos 2005). By 450 AD the Imperial Library held 100,000 items.

Constantinople was also home to private libraries and a large university library. The mission of these libraries was scholarly as well as religious, and it is impossible to overestimate their importance in preserving many Greek and Latin texts that sustained the future of Western society. As Harris and Johnson (1984) noted, "of the Greek classics known today, at least seventy-five percent are known through Byzantine copies" (p. 83). Without the preservation of these materials, the Renaissance would not have been possible.

The same can be said concerning the achievements of the Muslim Empire, which flourished from 650 AD until 1100 AD. Because of the respect afforded reading and learning in the Muslim culture, libraries were commonplace in private homes, royal palaces, and universities throughout the Muslim world. Literacy was widespread. The caliphs in many of the major cities had a deep respect for learning and some were scholars and literati (Thompson 1962). Although religion was deeply important to the culture, there were also strong secular forces that promoted learning in the sciences, medicine, and philosophy. Arab rulers built great libraries that became a critical force in fostering the translation of many materials especially classical Greek works by Aristotle, Archimedes, and Euclid. The proliferation of libraries throughout the Muslim world was impressive: Spain had seventy libraries, Baghdad thirty-six, and "every important city in Persia had its library" (Thompson 1962, p. 353).

The earliest major library was the Royal Library in Damascus, which contained materials from throughout the world on a wide variety of topics, including medicine, philosophy, history, and literature (Harris and Johnson 1984). Later, during the eighth and ninth centuries, Baghdad, under the Abbasid dynasty and the leadership of Caliph Ma'mum became the cultural center for the study of Greek medical, scientific, and philosophical works and "abounded with libraries" (Thompson 1962, p. 351). The most notable library in Bagdad at this time was the "House of Wisdom." The "House of Wisdom" was a universal library like the Alexandrian, and scholars travelled to it translating important works and studying mathematics, astronomy, and geometry. In addition, research and learning were furthered by large university libraries in Baghdad, Cairo, and Cordoba. The Cairo library might have held more than 200,000 volumes and the library at Cordoba was reported to contain between 400,000 and 600,000 volumes—larger than the Alexandrian (Harris and Johnson 1984; Thompson 1962).

With the waning of the Muslim Empire and the capture of Constantinople by the Crusaders around 1200, Muslim libraries fell into decline. Nonetheless, Muslim libraries made a substantial contribution to Western culture by preserving the central works of Western thought. The Western world owes a particular debt to the Muslims for preserving the works of Aristotle.

F. The Religious Mission: Monastic Libraries of the Middle Ages

As noted above, with the fall of the Roman Empire, social and political chaos led to economic instability throughout Western Europe. Libraries went into a similar decline, but they did not disappear. What saved libraries? During the first centuries of the Christian era, Christianity grew rapidly, even though it was viewed as an illegal activity in the Roman Empire. It is estimated that by 300 AD, nearly 25% of the Roman Empire, 15 million people, were Christians (Cantor 2003). Christianity placed considerable emphasis on education and study, and it is not surprising then that libraries would develop and prosper in some form and that reading, especially reading the scriptures would be encouraged (Staikos 2005). The form it took was the monastery library.

Monasteries, which were well established by 500–550 AD, provided a means of isolating Christian adherents, both geographically and spiritually, from the disorder that had spread and was continuing to spread across Western Europe. The mission of the monastic library was threefold: to provide a place for spiritual reflection, to archive religious texts, and to reproduce religious and sometimes secular texts.

Perhaps the best exemplar of the religious mission of the monastic library comes from the Benedictine Order, established in 529 AD in Monte Casino, Italy. According to St. Benedict, the purpose of monastic life was to concentrate on spiritual matters and to avoid secular thoughts. Much of the monk's day was spent either in physical labor, meditation, or in reading religious literature. A monk's life was to be devout and mostly silent. To this end, books were often read to monks during meals (while the monks remained silent). The purpose was less enlightenment than to keep their minds from straying to frivolous or worldly matters. Similarly, each monk was provided one book for study each year (Clanchy 1979). Other rules involved the copying of books in a special room called the scriptorium. The purpose of copying was not necessarily to create more useful and instructive texts, it was also to keep the monks busy (Thompson 1962). Sometimes copying was also used as a punishment for a recalcitrant monk, and the resultant quality of the copy often left much to be desired (Shera 1976). Nonetheless, it is clear that books, study, education, and libraries were a valued part of Benedictine life. By 800, many of the larger Benedictine monasteries had schools, substantial libraries, and scriptoria. Both literacy and publishing benefited: the scriptoria became the publishing houses of the middle ages; and a large percentage of the literate individuals in Western Europe were educated in these monastic schools (Cantor 2003).

Other monasteries founded in Ireland, Germany, Switzerland, Scotland, France, and Great Britain regarded copying in a different vein. They saw the copying of religious texts as a means to derive inspiration. Many of these monasteries produced fine, illuminated manuscripts intended to reveal the beauty of God. These works of art reflected the copyist's realization that he was representing sacred words from Scripture. Their physical beauty, however, might also have been inspirational to the laity and might even have served as an early incentive to literacy (Clanchy

1979). One other debt is due the monks, the Dominicans in particular. The Dominican friars created written guidelines related to locating the best site for a library, providing adequate shelving, organizing the library by subjects, marking the spines of the books with their titles, replenishing and weeding the collection, establishing hours of operation, and selling duplicate titles (Clanchy 1979).

Regardless of whether the purpose of reading and copying books was to learn, to inspire, or to achieve an ascetic life, the monasteries helped preserve some of the writings of antiquity. However, as Thompson (1962) observed, "it is equally true their preservation was as often due to neglect and mere chance as it was to conscious intent . . . the medieval scriptorium was more often a treadmill for meaningless labor than it was a shrine where the expiring flame of literary culture was sedulously preserved" (pp. 30–31).

G. The Educational Mission: Cathedral and University Libraries of the Late Middle Ages

The educational mission of libraries reemerged in Western Europe in the late Middle Ages (800–1200 AD). With the growth of cities and towns, improved trade and other economic and social conditions, there was a concomitant improvement in the intellectual climate. The increasing respect for learning made fertile conditions for libraries once again.

By 1100, the cathedrals in major cities served as the administrative centers for bishops and archbishops and as training centers for priests and other religious functionaries (Harris and Johnson 1984). The cathedral libraries were larger than those in monasteries and were less dominated by religious works (Shera 1976). In fact, the mission of the cathedral libraries, unlike the monastic libraries, was to support the educational program of the cathedral and encourage study. Although some of the cathedral libraries were substantial, such as those in Verona and Monte Casino, Italy, and at Rheims and Chartres in France, they still could not rival the larger libraries of the Muslim Empire (Dunlap 1972).

Although the church continued to be a vital part of the life of the late Middle Ages, it was also a period of transition. For several centuries, the societies of Western Europe were devoted to survival; energy was devoted to the most elementary forms of literacy and education. By the eleventh century, however, opportunities for more speculative, secular thinking were emerging. The monks lost their leadership in education, and a significant proportion of the laity and intellectual aristocracy placed diminishing reliance on church teaching to guide their intellectual pursuits (Cantor 2003, Hessel 1955). In the place of church teaching, there was a growing interest in classical writings as well as an interest in more contemporary studies in law, architecture, government, economics, education, arts, and sciences. A vernacular literature written in the local language rather than Latin, began to emerge with nonreligious writers creating a characteristic literature for the individual regions. This, in turn, created the foundation for the emergence of nationalism within Europe that was soon to follow (Cantor 2003).

In addition, during the late Middle Ages, European governments became more stable which in turn fostered the growth of cities, a stable middle class, and a more orderly legal system. As secular legal systems grew in importance so did the importance of those who knew the law and a new class of civil servants (secular clerks and civil lawyers) became essential to governmental functions. These developments, coupled with the dominance of less contemplative and more secularly involved religious sects such as the Dominicans and Franciscans, spawned the growth of academic centers in Bologna, Paris, and Oxford. The universities that were created in these centers supported not only theological studies, but also classical and professional instruction in law, medicine, and philosophy. Law, not theology, was the dominant discipline that was studied in these universities, and many of the civil servants needed by governments throughout Europe were educated in these universities. By the thirteenth century, the universities dominated academic activity in theology, philosophy, law, and the sciences.

Initially, these universities did not have libraries; rather, students bought their books from booksellers. The University of Paris established the first university library in the mid-thirteenth century, and Oxford and Cambridge soon followed, among others (Shera 1976). These libraries were often small, well under 1,000 items, but their mission to support and expand the educational mission of the university served as a bridge from the domination of the medieval church to the birth of the Renaissance (Harris and Johnson 1984; Shera 1976).

H. The Humanistic Mission and the Reemergence of the Library for Personal Status

The period following the Middle Ages (fourteenth, fifteenth, and sixteenth centuries) was a time of considerable economic, social, and political ferment, much of it centered in Italy, most notably Venice and Florence. Contributing factors included the rise of secular monarchies, an increased sense of nationalism, a decline in the power of the church, an increase in literacy, interest in natural sciences and secular politics, and a reawakening of the philosophical traditions of ancient Greek and Roman thinkers. This fervor for the knowledge of the ancients and for new secular knowledge, rather than spiritual enlightenment, characterizes much of what is referred to as Renaissance Humanism. The result was a cultural and educational transformation in the arts, sciences, and politics.

The Renaissance was primarily an aristocratic enthusiasm. It was a time of great wealth among the secular upper classes that now possessed considerable political and social power and who promoted a powerful and expansive city-state; its protection and beautification was paramount. The state was an end in itself. It was a time of emphasizing civic patriotism and pride and the importance of human freedom. Education for these aristocrats emphasized civic virtue, not theology (Cantor 2003).

It was also a time of great private libraries developed by leading literary figures such as Petrarch and Boccaccio, who themselves were sponsored by popes or Renaissance princes such as the dukes of Urbino and the Medici. These sponsors were passionate book collectors as both a matter of personal vanity and a genuine interest in secular learning. They sent agents throughout Western Europe to locate manuscripts in deteriorating monastic libraries. Sometimes the manuscripts were copied but often enthusiastic agents confiscated (or saved) these items for their sponsors. As a result, Renaissance libraries were richly appointed and filled with beautifully illuminated texts. They served as places for scholarship, but also as places where aristocrats could "display their sensitivity to classical Latin" (Jackson 1974, p. 107).

Although the Renaissance princes might have taken the notion of the private library as personal aggrandizement to its highest form of ostentatious display, it was hardly a new concept or new mission (remember Ashurbanipal and the wealthy Romans). Yet, the passion of these Renaissance scholars and collectors brought together entire collections of the greatest classical thinkers, including Cicero, Plato, and Aristotle (Cantor 2003). One might reasonably contend, as Dunlap (1972) did, "Had it not been for the enthusiasm of a few collectors of that age . . . we should certainly possess only a small part of the literature, especially that of the Greeks, which is now in our hands" (pp. 106–107).

I. Promoting National Pride: The Mission of the National Libraries

The growth of secular monarchies and nationalism is consistent with the emergence of a new type of library—the national library. Early examples of such libraries arose in the seventeenth century in England, France, Germany, Denmark, and Scotland. The eighteenth and nineteenth centuries saw additional national libraries in Austria, Italy, Sweden, Norway, Greece, Spain, and Ireland, among others (Gates 1976). What distinguished these libraries was not simply their large collections, but rather their special mission to preserve the cultural heritage of their countries. This meant developing a comprehensive collection of materials by and about the country, including books, manuscripts, documents, and other records.

To meet this mission, a unique collection development technique arose: the creation of a depository right. That is, some nations passed laws requiring that at least one copy of each item published within the country be sent to the national library. This was accomplished, for example, in England in 1610, when an agreement was made between the Stationers' Company (which licensed publications in England) and the Bodleian Library of Oxford University. This agreement stipulated that one copy of each book published would be given to the Bodleian in return for limited borrowing privileges (Jackson 1974). In essence, this meant that all items, or nearly all items, published would become part of the national collection. In the United States, this depository right is held by the LOC and although it is not officially our national library, it is a very close approximation.

III. MAKING MODERN MISSIONS POSSIBLE: The Printing Press

If one can identify a single historical development that profoundly affected all libraries, it would be the revolutionary invention of the printing press in 1454 in Mainz, Germany, which affected much more than libraries. Eisenstein (1979) refers to the advent of printing as "inaugurating a new cultural era in the history of Western man" (p. 33).

The printing press made books available to the masses for the first time and thus increased a desire for learning. By 1468, the church in Rome referred to printing as the "divine art." Others referred to it as the "art which preserves all other arts" (Eisenstein 1995, p. 2). It is impossible to consider the modern mission of libraries without considering the changes wrought by the printing press (Eisenstein 1979):

> **The ability to produce exact copies:** Before printing, all copies were made by hand. This laborious process sometimes produced extraordinary works of art. More often, however, copying resulted in less-than-perfect versions; copiers made mistakes or even intentionally omitted or amended text. The printing press could produce identical copies.

> **The ability to produce more titles and more copies:** The sheer volume of printed materials increased dramatically. By the sixteenth century, more

than 100,000 different books were printed in Europe alone (Harris and Johnson 1984).

The ability to cover more subjects: In the first decade of printing, ending in 1460, most of the books printed were in one of four medieval categories: (1) sacred literature (Bibles and prayer books), (2) learned literature (grammatical and scholastic works such as those of Thomas Aquinas), (3) bureaucratic literature (official documents such as papal bulls and indulgence certificates), and (4) vernacular literature (works in the language of the people, notably German readers) (Clanchy 1983). During the second decade of the press, the breadth of subjects increased and spread beyond medieval categories.

The creation of new techniques for the organization of published materials: Given the growth in size and subject diversity of library collections, new techniques for organizing and classifying materials became necessary. This eventually led to the complex systems we have today.

The stimulation of literacy and education for the general population: When books were scarce, only a few could have access to them. As more books became available, it was inevitable that more people would learn to read. This, in turn, generated a new audience for libraries.

The impact of the printing press on society was profound and rapid. By 1500, there may have been as many as 1000 printer's workshops employing 10–20,000 people; in addition, it is likely that more than 15–20 million books had been printed (Man 2002)! The most common early example of this effect was the Protestant Reformation. Martin Luther effectively disseminated his religious tracts throughout Europe using the press. The effect of the subsequent Protestant Reformation can hardly be overestimated. But there were other significant impacts as well. The printing press led to mass production of maps and navigational tables dramatically improving sea navigation and exploration, mass-produced mathematical and astronomical tables significantly enhanced scientific discoveries and their dissemination, religious knowledge found new expression through the written word rather than just through images, and the early printers' workshops became the centers for scholars, scientific thinkers, and other learned individuals (Eisenstein 1979).

For libraries in particular, the invention of the printing press, coupled with the reawakening of secular and scientific interests during the Renaissance, ultimately formed the foundation for the growth in number and in the size of libraries and consequently broadened and widened the missions of libraries.

IV. LIBRARIES IN THE UNITED STATES: New Missions

Although European libraries continued to develop in the seventeenth century and beyond, it is during this time that American libraries emerged, some with new missions. The focus of the ensuing discussion is on American library developments.

The seventeenth and eighteenth centuries were formative periods for American libraries. During the early part of the seventeenth century there were few libraries because the social preconditions were not yet in place; people were struggling for subsistence. Other than Boston there were few urban settings, and there was limited economic development or individual wealth. As an agrarian society that depended on manual labor, literacy rates in the general population were low. A few ministers, doctors, and other prominent citizens had private libraries in their homes that served as a resource for dealing with the practical or spiritual problems confronting settlers in the New World. Most of these collections were quite small.

There were also a few modest college libraries. Harvard University, founded in 1636, hired its first librarian in 1667 and by the mid-eighteenth century possessed a small library of approximately 5,000 volumes. Yale University, founded in 1700, held around 2,500 volumes by 1750 (Harris and Johnson 1984). The paucity of college libraries was a reflection of the dearth of college-educated citizens. By 1775 less than one in a thousand attended any college (Hanson 1989). By 1792, only nine colonial colleges had libraries. The size of the typical college collection was small for several reasons: the low number of book titles produced in the United States, lack of fiscal resources, and lack of recognition of the library's role in academic life. If a college had a library, it was usually open infrequently and had no librarian. When assistance was available, it was usually a faculty member who served only secondarily as a librarian (Harwell 1968). The growth of the collection depended primarily on donations. Additional book selection was accomplished usually by a committee of trustees or faculty members (Hamlin 1981; Shiflett 1994).

The religious mission of libraries was also preserved. In England near the end of the seventeenth century, an Anglican clergyman, Thomas Bray, created the Society for the Propagation of the Gospel, which advocated for establishing libraries devoted solely to religious purposes (McMullen 2000). Numerous parish libraries were established throughout England, and his teachings soon spread to America. By the early 1700s, seventy parish libraries were established, many in the south Atlantic region (Harris and Johnson 1984).

By 1876, there were more than 10,000 libraries of over eighty different types (McMullen 2000). Their variety was impressive: agricultural libraries, antiquarian society libraries, art society libraries, church libraries, county libraries, government libraries, historical society libraries, hotel reading rooms, ladies' libraries, law libraries, mechanics' libraries, medical libraries, prison libraries, public libraries, railroad libraries, saloon reading rooms, scientific and engineering libraries, sewing circle libraries, state libraries, university libraries, and YMCA libraries. Obviously, discussion of all these different types of libraries lies outside the scope of this book, but it is important to reflect on the character and purposes of some of the major types that formed the foundation of American libraries today.

A. The Mission of Self-Improvement: The Social Libraries of the Eighteenth Century

Advances in mechanical technologies during the eighteenth century led to the Industrial Revolution which, in turn, soon led to the growth of the economy with concomitant growth in individual and community wealth. This meant that some of the more fortunate citizens had more leisure time, time that could be spent pursuing self-development. These were fertile conditions for the emergence of new libraries and missions.

The social library emerged during the first half of the eighteenth century. According to Shera (1965), "the social library was nothing more than a voluntary association of individuals who had contributed money toward a common fund to be used for the purchase of books" (p. 57). There were two types of social libraries: proprietary libraries and subscription (association) libraries. Proprietary libraries operated on the principle that those who contributed money for the library actually owned the material purchased; in essence, they were stockholders. In subscription libraries, individuals paid a fee to use and circulate the collection, but they did not own the items (Shera 1965). Some social libraries were hybrids of the two models, with some members owning shares while others participated by annual subscription. Most social libraries had fewer than fifty members and consequently, the collections were often quite small, often less than 300 books.

The mission of the social library was to assist individuals' self-improvement and the search for truth. Many of the members had a genuine love of literature and believed that the sharing of books and information led to character improvement. They also believed that the members gained knowledge by discussing the ideas they found in books and newspapers. One of the earliest proponents of this mission was Benjamin Franklin, who is credited with establishing the first social library, called the Junto, in Philadelphia in 1728. The Junto was short lived, but he soon founded a second library, which he called a subscription library, in 1731. It survives today as the Philadelphia Library Company.

The social library became quite popular throughout New England in the latter half of the eighteenth century and well into the nineteenth, with its apex between 1825 and 1835. Although they were particularly popular among white, middle- and upper-class aspiring businessmen, the mission of self-improvement was not restricted to the relatively aristocratic and well-educated. As individuals migrated West, they took the social library model with them, which resulted in a wide variety of libraries—YMCA libraries, agricultural libraries, "ladies' clubs," mechanics, and mercantile libraries—all developed to meet the special interests of their particular constituencies (Arenson 2006). There were also many general interest social libraries that did not focus on one particular subject area. These collections often contained religious materials, history, travel, and literature (not to be confused with popular fiction, of which there was little). Although these social libraries might have contained materials of a more diverting nature, their purpose was still to appeal to one's "better angels."

Another important aspect of these social libraries was that although they required individuals to pay money, as institutions they had a distinctly public character. The majority was created for the general citizenry; anyone who could afford the modest fee could partake of the collection. Because there were few places other than work or home where one could occupy one's time productively, social libraries became a third place. There an individual could spend time conversing with friends, developing a sense of community, and reading newspapers or books (Arenson 2006).

However, given the voluntary nature of social libraries, their mission was deeply affected by the ability of their members to sustain the library. Often these libraries relied on one or a few benefactors, and shifting economic times, depressions, wars, and social unrest led to the relatively quick demise of many. Similarly, the rise of the public library in urban areas significantly diminished the desirability and economic soundness of social libraries. After all, why pay taxes to support a public library and provide additional funding for a private agency? Nonetheless, the legacy of the social library is significant, especially as it relates to the social nature of such institutions and the role they played as "parlors" in the public sphere (Arenson 2006). Social libraries were, in fact, an important and necessary stage for the eventual creation of tax-supported public libraries (Valentine 2011).The idea that libraries were a place to go for self-improvement became ingrained in the American psyche, and subsequently when social libraries foundered, many of these collections formed the core of new public library collections.

B. The Mission of Providing Entertainment: The Circulating Library

While the social library was attempting to meet the need for self-improvement, the mission of the circulating library (sometimes called a rental library) was to satisfy public demand for fiction and popular material intended for entertainment rather than education. Circulating libraries were well established in England and first appeared in America in the 1760s. Although there were some selections from literature, history, and theology, the majority of the collection was fiction. The popular novels of the time consisted mostly of romances (much like today), which were fairly well established in America by 1790. Although there were few romances by American authors, there was ample supply of popular foreign novels printed by American presses. As many as 350 foreign titles might have been published in America from 1789 to 1800, compared to thirty-five titles by American authors (Shera 1965).

The distinguishing feature of the circulating libraries was their profit-making character. Usually associated with a printer or bookstore, the books were rented or individuals were charged a membership fee that allowed them to borrow a designated number of books over a specified period of time. Serving mass tastes appears to have been as profitable in colonial times as it is today; many of these libraries prospered and spread throughout New England.

It is worth noting that circulating libraries often incurred the wrath of certain segments of society who were concerned with the immoral effects of popular reading. As sometimes happens today in public libraries, circulating libraries were suspected of corrupting youth, usually because of the corrupting effects of popular novels—especially the French ones (Shera 1965).

The circulating library also made several contributions to contemporary public library philosophy and service. For example, despite its profit motive, its mission to appeal to popular taste has echoes in contemporary public library service. In addition, Kaser (1980) noted, circulating libraries were the first to provide (1) service to women, (2) newspapers and magazines, (3) extended hours of service, (4) reading areas in the library itself, and (5) outreach services, including the home delivery of books. These are substantive contributions. The circulating library's survival, however, was ultimately threatened by its low status and competition from tax-supported public libraries (Kaser 1980).

C. The Mission of Providing Information: The Rise of Special Libraries

Although the circulating library as a money-making venture failed to survive, its spirit of free enterprise was certainly consistent with a capitalistic economy. Shortly after the start of the Industrial Revolution, public libraries and a few businesses started collections for factory workers, technical workers, craftsmen, and managers (Kruzas 1965). Most of the libraries associated with business and commerce were used for information and education, consultation with expert sources, or diversion. However, at the beginning of the twentieth century, American business and industry discovered the instrumentality of the library, and there emerged a new library whose purpose was the "direct application of recorded information to the practical goals of profit-seeking business enterprises" (Kruzas 1965, p. 109). The purpose of the commercial library was to promote the profitability of the company. The librarian's job was to provide reference service to the organization rather than build a collection per se. Providing information to an individual was much more important than instructing that person on where to find the information. This remains a fundamental characteristic of special libraries to this day. These libraries collected only materials that focused on the direct needs of the enterprise, many of which, such as technical records, industrial and market reports, proprietary documents, and business conference papers, were unfamiliar to many public librarians.

The unique concerns of these types of libraries led to the creation of the Special Libraries Association in 1909. Special libraries also fostered new technologies such as microfilm, which became available in the 1920s. Most significantly, the mission of special libraries to provide specific information rather than books or other materials was an important factor in the rise of information science and the exploitation of information technologies in libraries.

D. The Mission to Support Teaching and Research: The American Academic Library

Although the educational mission of libraries emerged as early as the Alexandrian library, the mission of the library as a full partner in American academic institutions did not evolve until the latter part of the nineteenth century (Hamlin 1981). There are historical reasons for this late development. From the colonial period to the Civil War, the American university curriculum followed a classical model emphasizing theology, philosophy, history, and the trivium of the liberal arts—grammar, rhetoric, and logic (Hanson 1989). The faculty taught from a single text or, at best, a few books. Classroom recitation was strongly emphasized (Hamlin 1981). Such methods produced little need for libraries, and academic collections remained small throughout this period. However, three significant events in the mid-nineteenth century substantially changed academic institutions and shifted the role of the academic libraries: changes in the academic curriculum, the rise of the research model, and the passage of the Morrill Land Grant Act of 1862.

1. Changes in the Curriculum

With the dawn of the Industrial Revolution came a need for college graduates with a practical education rather than an understanding of the classics (Hanson 1989). By the 1840s, universities began offering courses in the natural sciences. In 1850 Brown University began the first elective system including courses in the sciences and languages (Shiflett 1994). Teaching methods also changed. Seminars, laboratories, and independent study emerged as an alternative to the recitation techniques of the past (Hanson 1989). As the breadth of the curriculum expanded, access to more diverse materials became an increasingly important issue, concomitantly increasing the importance of the library. The evolution of the academic curriculum and its implication for librarianship were recognized early by Melvil Dewey (1978):

> The colleges are waking to the fact that the work of every professor and every department is necessarily based on the library; text books constantly yield their exalted places to wiser and broader methods; professor after professor sends his classes, or goes with them, to the library and teaches them to investigate for themselves, and to use books, getting beyond the method of the primary school with its parrot-like recitations from a single text. (p. 136)

2. The Rise of the Research Model

At the turn of the eighteenth century at the University of Berlin in Germany, a new model of the modern university emerged. This model envisioned faculty members as independent researchers. Objective scholarship was promoted, and an expansive faculty research agenda was encouraged (Shiflett 1994). Given the obvious need for published resources for research, the academic library played an increasingly critical role. The reforms in German higher education did not go unnoticed at some of the more prestigious academic institutions in the United States, many of which sent American students to study in Germany. Returning individuals, many of whom became professors themselves, brought the concept of research, coupled with teaching, back with them (Shiflett 1994).

Although these ideas had some effect on American higher education throughout the nineteenth century, it was not until 1876 that this model was explicitly adopted with the founding of Johns Hopkins University. Johns Hopkins placed research as a central function of the university. The seminar model of teaching was emphasized and students were encouraged to consult a wide variety of published sources. Soon thereafter, Harvard, Cornell, and Columbia adopted this teaching approach (Jones 1989). The need for a library with current and deep collections was essential to fulfill this function, and the result was to increase substantially the importance and centrality of the academic library. Although the mission of academic libraries continues to evolve, the need to support the academic curriculum and provide research support for faculty remains the academic library's primary function.

3. The Passage of the Morrill Land Grant Act of 1862

Most colleges founded before the Civil War were private and sectarian. By the nineteenth century, however, it became clear that higher education for the citizenry was also a matter for the state. Beginning in the East and South, state universities were founded in Vermont, Maine, North Carolina, Georgia, New York, Pennsylvania, Massachusetts, and Kentucky. By mid-century, the federal government recognized that it could play an important role in promoting education by providing land to states for establishing universities. This led to the passage of the Morrill Land Grant Act in 1862, which allocated 30,000 acres of public land to establish state universities promoting agriculture and the mechanical arts. The universities founded as a result of the act, including the Ohio State University and the University of Illinois, emphasized applied sciences and technology (Hamlin 1981).

E. Supporting Primary and Secondary Education: The Mission of the School Library

During the colonial period, there were few publicly supported schools, although in the mid-Atlantic states and the South there were some parochial and private schools (Hanson 1989). What schools there were provided elementary-level education, considered sufficient to create an efficient pool of agrarian labor. The few secondary schools available prepared elite students for a limited number of colleges (Hanson 1989). It was not until the second half of the nineteenth century that public schools began to emerge. In 1852 Massachusetts passed the first compulsory school attendance laws. By 1890, half of the states had such laws. At the same time, more and more schools, including secondary schools with libraries, were being built.

The earliest attempt to support public school libraries occurred in New York in 1835 when the state legislature passed a law that permitted school districts to apply some of their tax receipts to create and maintain school libraries. By 1875, twenty states had passed similar legislation (Knight and Nourse 1969). In 1892, New York again passed legislation that provided matching funds to purchase library books for school districts as long as the books were first approved by the Department of Public Instruction. Approved materials consisted of "reference books, supplementary reading books, books related to the curriculum, and pedagogical books for use by teachers" (Gillespie and Spirt 1983, p. 3). Some of them could even be taken out of the library. Unfortunately, many of these legislative efforts proved unsuccessful, often allocating money for books but not for administration and maintenance. Sometimes money allocated for books went to teachers' salaries. The result was poorly developed, poorly maintained libraries that were seldom used (Knight and Nourse 1969; Cecil and Heaps 1940). Although these libraries had great potential, they did not perform their central mission. Gillespie and Spirt (1983) have suggested, however, that these early efforts to create and maintain public school libraries established the idea that public funds were an appropriate means to support school libraries, and that school libraries could play a useful role in public school education. By the last decade of the nineteenth century, the number of school libraries, especially in high schools, increased substantially, and by 1895 it was estimated that there were from 2,500 to 4,000 school libraries (Knight and Nourse 1969).

Several groups were concerned with the development of school libraries, including the National Council of Teachers of English (NCTE), the National Education Association (NEA), and the American Library Association (ALA). In 1914 the NCTE formed a standing committee on school libraries and ALA formed a School Library Section (Cecil and Heaps 1940). In 1915 the NCTE conducted a national survey, and the findings expressed serious concern about the adequacy of school libraries. This prompted the NEA and ALA to appoint a joint committee headed by Charles Certain to study the condition of school libraries and to develop standards. Certain's first report, published in 1920, focused on high schools; the second, in 1925, focused on elementary schools. Both reports concluded that school libraries were seriously deficient.

The standards prepared by Certain's committee described the library as "an integral part of the daily life of the school" and included several significant recommendations (Certain 1925, p. 5):

- They emphasized the centrality of "materials of instruction," that is, curricular support.
- They advocated for a centralized collection. The centralization of materials in the school had been an issue for some years, with some arguing for small library collections in each classroom and others arguing for a centralized location and control of library materials.
- They promoted library instruction as a duty of school libraries.
- They recognized the integral character of the school library within the total setting of school life.

Certain's reports were significant in that they proposed the first national standards for school libraries which were endorsed by both ALA and NEA (Gillespie and Spirt 1983). One should not assume, however, that Certain's reports led to the quick development of centralized, modern school libraries, though they certainly made a major contribution. Fortunately, in addition to the reports, other significant factors contributed to progress in that direction. Among them was the educational reform movement looming on the horizon, which Certain (1925) recognized early:

> Modern demands upon the public school presuppose adequate library service. Significant changes in methods of teaching require that the school library supplement the single textbook course of instruction and provide for the enrichment of the school curriculum. (p. 1)

The decade of the 1920s was indeed an era of reform in public education. John Dewey and the progressive education movement introduced a variety of new educational theories:

- A child's growth and development, rather than subject matter, should be the central focus of the school.
- Education should involve children learning through a variety of experiences and exploring a variety of subjects.
- Children learn best when they are exploring subjects of interest to them.
- School should be a social experience that teaches children how to be self-directed. (Fargo 1930)

These "radical" ideas resulted in a more varied school curriculum requiring access to a much wider range of materials. Responding to children's interests, encouraging exploration, and providing a broad range of experiences could only increase the importance of a school library:

> With such a program, it is obvious that the library stands in a far more vital relationship to the school than before. Under the older tradition, books other than texts were desirable; in the new school they are indispensable. They are not the accompaniment of the school's activities; they are its warp and woof. (Fargo 1930, pp. 31–32)

Other influences that contributed to the emergence of the modern school library included new studies and the support of the U.S. Office of Education, NEA, ALA, the Carnegie Corporation, and the North Central Association of Colleges and Secondary Schools (Cecil and Heaps 1940; Gillespie and Spirt 1983). The combination of changing teaching philosophies and the evaluations and standards developed by NEA and ALA had a substantial impact on establishing the foundations of the school library and its mission—to support the primary and secondary curriculum by providing current and appropriate materials for students and teachers.

F. The Mission of Serving the Public: The American Public Library

The social library and the circulating library each performed a unique mission: the former to educate and enlighten, and the latter to satisfy popular taste. Both of these libraries contributed to the development of the modern public library and its very special mission—to serve the public. The term public library refers generically to libraries supported by public funds. Using this broad definition, by 1876 there were approximately 3,600 public libraries in the United States. Most of these, however, were associated with academic institutions, public schools, or social libraries. As we apply the term today, there were actually very few public libraries. By 1880 only seven of the sixteen largest cities in the United States had municipally supported libraries. The rapid growth of public libraries well into the fourth decade of the twentieth century was caused by a variety of factors. Kevane and Sundstrom (2014) have observed that among the general factors that promoted public library growth were the growth of cities and towns, the presence of an immigrant population, and the presence of state library commissions or associations.

From a historical perspective, all or most public libraries shared certain defining characteristics (see figure 2.1):

The debate as to when and where the first public library in the United States was established will continue. Some have suggested that the honor belongs to Peterborough, New Hampshire, because in 1834 "there for the first time an institution was founded by a town with the deliberate purpose of creating a free library that would be open without restriction to all classes of the community—a library supported from the beginning by public funds" (Shera 1965, p. 169).

FIGURE 2.1
Fundamental Characteristics Shared by All American Public Libraries

Supported by taxes: Public libraries are usually supported by local taxes, although over the years there have been exceptions. The notion of public support through taxation is rare before the nineteenth century. As noted earlier, prior to that time, libraries were most often sponsored or subsidized by private citizens, religious orders, or royal families.

Governed by a board: This board usually has consisted of prominent citizens appointed, or sometimes elected, to serve the public interest.

Open to all: A fundamental tenet of public libraries is that everyone in the community can access the collection. This is not to say that every group has been made to feel welcome. At different times, various subsets of the population have not found public libraries friendly or accommodating to their needs. But in principle, the libraries are open to all.

Voluntary: People are not forced to come; the use of the library is entirely voluntary. This distinguishes it from other educational institutions, such as public schools. Its voluntary nature is also part of the underlying social philosophy of the nineteenth century in which self-improvement was considered an important virtue.

Established by state law: This point is not generally well understood. During the early development of public libraries, serious questions arose concerning whether a town could create a library and tax its citizens for its maintenance without the state's approval. As a consequence, states passed enabling legislation that permitted towns and communities to establish public libraries—a key aspect of their creation. In rare instances, public libraries were not only enabled by state legislation, they were financed by state monies. Such is the case in Ohio today, where a small percentage (less than 3%) of the state's general revenue fund is earmarked for funding public libraries.

Provides services without charge: Although some public libraries charge a small fee for special services, most of the services are provided without fees.

However, there is no dispute as to where and when the first major public library was established. In March 1848, the Massachusetts legislature authorized the city of Boston to provide municipal support for a public library. The Boston Public Library, founded in 1854, receives credit for being the first major public library.

1. The Founding of the Boston Public Library

By the middle of the nineteenth century, urbanization in America had reached a tipping point. As cities matured and prospered economically, their political and bureaucratic infrastructure, including basic services such as water, sanitation, public health, fire protection, and education, also matured. Boston was typical of a prospering and stable urban environment. Therefore, when the issue of a public library was first raised, many perceived it from an administrative point of view as a logical extension of city services. The concept of a public library for Boston was first advanced more than a decade before its founding by a noted French actor and ventriloquist, Nicholas Marie Alexandre Vattemare. Vattemare was a highly successful and wealthy entertainer who also loved books and collected art. He abandoned his theatrical career and became a global philanthropist with a special interest in developing an international, reciprocal exchange of duplicate copies of books traded among major cultural institutions. He established a significant reputation among U.S. politicians with particular connections in Boston (Havens 2007). In the 1840s he proposed that several of the major private libraries in Boston combine into one public institution to facilitate this exchange. This proposal met with some favor from local officials, but the libraries resisted, and Vattemare's proposal failed. Nonetheless, numerous individuals in Boston had both the wealth and the power to generate a civic interest in libraries. Public discussion on this issue continued for some time and helped maintain the necessary political and social momentum that would ultimately produce the desired result more than a decade later. Particularly notable were the efforts of Charles Ticknor and Edward Everett. Ticknor was the educated son of a wealthy Boston merchant. He assumed that social change was possible if accomplished gradually, and he believed that public schools and libraries could improve social and political stability by promoting the education of the general population (Ditzion 1947). Everett was a Unitarian clergyman, teacher, scholar, and, at one point, governor of Massachusetts. A strong advocate of the public schools, Everett's beliefs were less populist and more academic than Ticknor's. He saw in the public library an opportunity for those no longer attending schools to continue their studies. He believed the public library could extend one's education by providing educational materials, not just for scholars, but for professionals and merchants. The efforts of Ticknor, Everett, and others finally convinced the Boston city fathers to appoint a Joint Standing Committee on the Library, which in turn recommended the appointment of a board of trustees. The Boston Public Library opened in the spring of 1854. Its mission was to serve the educational convictions of Everett and the popular needs espoused by Ticknor.

The creation of the Boston Public library is generally viewed as the result of two major factors: first, it was a natural outgrowth of urban developments in the mid-nineteenth century; and second, it was the result of prevailing social attitudes held by a small group of individuals who concluded, for a variety of reasons, that a public library was needed for the citizens of Boston. Everett and Ticknor were part of the educated elite of Boston. They believed that the responsibility to improve people lay not only with social institutions. Many members of the upper classes still believed in noblesse oblige and assumed that they, too, bore responsibility to provide the means by which others could improve themselves. This implied a duty on the part of the wealthy and better educated to improve the poor and uneducated insofar as they wanted to be improved. American philanthropy thus became one of the critical foundations for the growth of the public library for years to come. Libraries were seen as an ideal institution to help those less fortunate. This was, ostensibly, an underlying reason for the philanthropy of Andrew Carnegie, who asserted in his 1889 "Gospel of Wealth":

> This, then, is held to be the duty of the man of wealth: To set an example of modest, unostentatious living, shunning display or extravagance; to provide moderately for the legitimate wants of those dependent upon him; and, after doing so, to consider all surplus revenues which come to him simply as trust funds, which he is called upon to administer, and strictly bound as a matter of duty to administer in the manner which, in his judgment, is best calculated to produce the most beneficial results for the community—the man of wealth thus becoming the mere trustee and agent for his poorer brethren, bringing to their service his superior wisdom, experience, and ability to administer, doing for them better than they would or could do for themselves. (1962, p. 25)

The growth of libraries and librarianship during the nineteenth century was deeply rooted in these beliefs (Nielson 1989).

What can we deduce about the mission of the public library from the history of the Boston Public Library? Clearly, it shares an educational mission with American public schools. In 1876, Melvil Dewey stated that popular education was actually divided into two parts: "the free school and the free public library" (Dewey 1978, p. 5). He thought of the library as a school and of the librarian as a teacher. But in what way was the mission of the public library distinct from the public schools? First, the public library could satisfy the interest in reading and learning for all ages, not just for those who were in school; second, it was a means to self-improvement in an age when self-education was still a vital means for improving one's chances in society. Third, it was intended to produce more thoughtful people, individuals capable of making balanced and well-reasoned judgments in a democratic society that depended on their judgments at the voting booth. Such citizens would serve as a strong and stabilizing force to the democratic society. Finally, libraries were perceived as "cultural agencies." Indeed, librarians of the latter half of the nineteenth century saw themselves as agents of social improvement.

It is easy to see how many could view these objectives as noble, and those who advocated for the founding of public libraries often saw them, like museums and world's fairs, as a means to advance the cultural goals of the country. They envisioned the public library as "one cathedral more" to advance the cause of learning (McCrossen 2006, pp. 169–170). In addition, McCrossen (2006) noted that nineteenth-century public libraries provided a rare public space to use free time in healthy pursuits. Much of this same rationale is used to defend libraries today from attacks of various kinds, both fiscal and philosophical.

However, for others the library was also seen as a tool for social control. This aspect of the founding of the Boston Public Library has been examined most notably by Michael Harris (1973), whose "revisionist" interpretation provides a different perspective on the motivations of the founders. Although few of the facts are disputed, Harris challenged the notion that the founding of the public library was humanitarian, idealistic, or democratic. Rather, he reminded us that the founders were among the Boston Brahmins, a highly privileged, politically conservative, and aristocratic class that dominated the social, economic, and political life of the city. He argued that the founders were far less concerned with making educated democrats than with socializing the unruly immigrants who were subject to undue influence by political demagogues and other unscrupulous politicians who could foment political and social instability. In other words, Harris suggested that the creation of the Boston Public Library was another strategy of elitist aristocrats to maintain class stratification and ensure the social order that benefited them. If the aristocrats controlled what was taught about the social and political institutions of American society, the immigrants would accept those institutions, which were controlled and shaped by the elites. In this conceptualization, the library and librarians were seen as agents of authority and social control, implementing restrictive rules, and generally unfriendly to the *hoi polloi*. How could they be otherwise, run by board members appointed by elites, who were themselves elites? Further, Harris suggested that the public library collection was not designed for the common person, but catered to the educated and upper classes. He argued that this pattern has been repeated time and again, as evidenced by the fact that public libraries then and today are run by elites and attended by a disproportionately large number of upper- and middle-class patrons.

Harris's position has been challenged by other library historians. Dain (1975), for example, noted that there is insufficient historical evidence for some of Harris's strongest assertions. Further, she pointed out that just because elites created the first public library does not mean that other classes were not well served by them. She noted that the authoritarian nature of early public libraries reflected all public institutions of the time. She argued that public libraries made earnest efforts to attract a variety of users. Today, such efforts are evident in extended hours of operation on Sundays and evenings, information services, open stacks, classification systems, branches, children's rooms and services, meeting rooms for community groups, cooperative activities with schools, interlibrary loan, and special services for immigrants.

Although Harris's position is controversial, it reminds us that history is shaped most often by the victors and that historical interpretation varies by the position of the teller. It is true that the history of public libraries has multiple philosophical underpinnings, some of them countervailing and incompatible. Certainly, a consciousness of class was very much a part of the era from which the Boston Public Library emerged. For example, in an 1874 article titled, "Public Libraries and Fiction," the author begins with the observation: "It is worth considering that, practically, public libraries are for the benefit of and directly influence the least cultivated classes, who do not possess private collections of books" (p. 169). Consistent with Harris's notion of control, the author goes on to observe:

> [Public libraries] operate upon the very part of society where improvement is most needed. . . . The legitimate office of public libraries seems to be to aid directly in the intellectual improvement of these masses, to help them to approach the standard that is fixed above and beyond them. (p. 169)

Today, many might find such language offensive, although it was not intended as such. It reflects both a notion of noblesse oblige and a sincere belief in the improvability of one's intellectual condition.

2. The Historical Struggle over Popular Materials

If public libraries were viewed as part of a "cultural hierarchy" (McCrossen 2006, p. 173) whose primary function was the diffusion of knowledge and learning, they also were seen as purveyors of a wide range of materials, many of which were clearly not learned. From the beginning, the public library was challenged by the mission of satisfying popular tastes. Their holdings of popular novels, newspapers, and magazines were of concern to some because these materials tended to attract a clientele who were more inclined to lounge than to read—the "loafers and bummers" (McCrossen 2006). Newspapers and magazines were particularly troublesome because they potentially diverted the attention of readers away from books. Nonetheless, from the beginning, Charles Ticknor advocated that popular materials should be part of the Boston Public Library's collection for the entertainment of readers. Interestingly, the library put its newspapers and light fiction in its lower hall, with more serious reading placed in its upper hall (McCrossen 2006). The pattern of separating reading rooms in this manner still exists today. It also remains a concern that reading rooms are sometimes the source of lounging, rather than reading.

Popular fiction has a long tradition of raising concerns about lowering morals. Wiegand (1989) called this the "ideology of reading" (p. 100), the idea that there was good reading and bad reading; the former led to good conduct, the latter to unacceptable behaviors. The implication, of course, was that librarians were to buy only the "good" reading materials. It was even suggested by some that reading too much bad fiction might cause insanity. These concerns were raised soon after the creation of the Boston Public Library. In an article titled "Free Fiction" that appeared in *The Nation* in 1866, the writer expressed concern over the "light literature" available at the Boston Public Library and other circulating libraries. He admitted that there was a demand for this type of material and noted that the "leading idea of those who manage these institutions seems to be that any reading is better than no reading at all—an axiom at once false and full of mischief. . . . The value of lending libraries, if we might indulge in a truism, depends very much on the quality of the books which are lent" ("Free Fiction," p. 139). His chief concern seemed to be that such materials would deleteriously affect young minds. This is an excellent example of a certain way of thinking that seems to persist through the ages:

> Read at an age when the taste is unformed, when the passions are just developing, when the will is feeble, principles are unfixed, and resistance to temptation is difficult, if they do not utterly spoil the inquisitive minds which are attracted by their glittering mediocrity, it will be because nature is stronger than education, and original vigor more than a match for enfeebling moral influences. (p. 139)

Should library collections include such diversions? What is their effect on young people? Some early public librarians felt that popular fiction might bring less-educated readers into the library where they would then be exposed to a better quality of literature. Even among librarians with serious misgivings, most had at least some popular novels on their shelves. They realized that if they wanted library users, they would need popular fiction. Generally, their collections were not overly stocked with "cheap" novels, but offered works by Flaubert, Zola, Fielding, and Balzac. This did not protect libraries, however, from censorship attacks as the works of these masters were perceived as scandalous at the time. McCrossen (2006) nicely summarized the double edge of public library service:

> Public Libraries thus stood in the middle ground between the serious and popular—their mandate was to meet the public's demands, but their goal was to improve,

indeed to shape, its tastes. . . . Due to their inclusion of fiction, newspapers, and marginalized members of the public, public libraries occupied an ambiguous place with the hierarchy of cultural institutions. (pp. 174, 178)

The need to preserve and promote the values of literary culture while at the same time recognizing the genuine and legitimate interests of those who enjoy more common fare remains a contemporary tension with roots firmly planted in the nineteenth century.

3. Andrew Carnegie

In many ways Andrew Carnegie personified this tension. Carnegie was a Scottish immigrant who, through hard work and ingenuity, prospered in the iron and steel industry. He amassed a fortune exceeding $330 million, 90 percent of which went into charitable trusts. Carnegie's philosophy of stewardship certainly marked him as a prominent exponent of noblesse oblige, but his philanthropy served many.

From 1886 to 1919 Carnegie donated $56 million to construct more than 2,000 library buildings, many of them public libraries, in more than 1,400 communities, large and small. The communities that requested Carnegie's money viewed a library as a source of civic pride. The libraries built with Carnegie's largesse were their libraries, not his, and their shelves were stocked with materials of local interest, not his.

In fact, the specifically local character of today's public library collections and services might be a direct result of the special conditions and restrictions that Carnegie required with every donation. First, the money was for building construction only, not for the purchase and maintenance of library materials or for staff. This, in essence, guaranteed the local character of library collections. Second, all recipients had to contribute an annual sum equal to 10 percent of the money donated to build collections and hire staff. This created a tradition of shared government support of public libraries and defined local governance. The town, through its appointed board, was in control, not Carnegie. The inevitable result was that the Carnegie public library was shaped by local interest: library collections reflected the local community and popular taste. Thus one of the fundamental missions of public libraries, to meet the needs of the local community, was promoted by the Carnegie model of local taxation and local governmental control. Indeed, Carnegie might well have done more to establish this model than the Boston Public Library.

4. The Role of Women's Clubs

One cannot leave the discussion of the forces that shaped American public libraries without noting the significant contributions of women's volunteer organizations, most notably women's clubs. Such clubs became commonplace following the Civil War when it became more acceptable for women to seek an education, especially self-education. Some of these clubs were local, while others were affiliated nationally with the General Federation of Women's Clubs. Like similar organizations devoted to education, "the members were imbued with the idea of the importance of books in improving the quality of life" (Watson 1994, p. 235). Their support for improving women's education extended to developing libraries for use by members of their local community. Watson (1994) suggested that women's clubs contributed in significant ways to the development of more than 470 public libraries between 1870 and 1930. Similarly, in the same period, a large majority of public libraries in Kansas, Oklahoma, Virginia, Florida, and North Dakota were founded by them (Kevane and Sundstrom 2014). Although the exact percentage of public libraries established through the efforts of women's clubs in the early part of the twentieth century is unclear, Watson estimates that it might have ranged between 50 percent and 75 percent of the total. In some instances the clubs provided support for additional materials and club members volunteered as librarians. Some women's clubs were influential at the state level, lobbying for library legislation and the need for state library commissions (Watson 1994). Although many of the club members were aristocrats, or at least middle class, and therefore potentially subject to Harris's criticisms, their contributions to advancing the public library are substantial. Their stated mission of self-education and improvement is firmly in line with the history and values of their era, and the results were salutary.

5. A Mission of Inclusiveness

Throughout the nineteenth century American cities and towns experienced major immigrations of people from many countries, particularly from Europe. Amid this influx of polyglot peoples, there were legitimate concerns regarding education and socialization. The progressive philosophy of the times viewed the function of educational institutions, including libraries, as improving society and advancing the democratic tradition (Du Mont et al. 1994). For many, this meant that immigrant groups needed to be assimilated into the American mainstream. Because of their numbers, Europeans were considered to be a particularly difficult challenge (Stern 1991). Libraries were "to furnish fuel for the fires beneath the great melting pot" (Roberts 1912, p. 169). What better group to serve this function than libraries? Many librarians took this responsibility quite seriously and numerous articles in professional periodicals offered advice on providing services and understanding the needs of immigrants. Some librarians exhibited an almost missionary zeal in their efforts to bring the benefits of reading to the general public.

Nonetheless, it is true that the public library of the nineteenth century was used primarily by white middle and upper classes. Ethnic minorities were largely excluded from the benefits of library service (Trujillo and Cuesta 1989). Aside from the segregationist practices related to African-Americans, there is relatively limited evidence to determine whether public libraries intentionally excluded other ethnic groups, or whether librarians and trustees were simply uninformed as to how to serve them effectively.

It was not until the beginning of the twentieth century that libraries began a systematic effort to serve ethnic groups. Immigration continued, with more than 20 million arriving in the first quarter of the twentieth century (Stern 1991). Although a few librarians recognized that each ethnic group had its own literature and culture worth preserving and transmitting, the primary emphasis was on integration and assimilation. Nonetheless, library collections and services included books and newspapers written in native languages; programs on U.S. citizenship; classes in English; story hours in native languages; programs on American history and culture; supplementary materials to support school curricula; and help for immigrants in reading letters, sending messages to social service agencies, writing checks, and completing citizenship forms (Stern 1991; Du Mont et al. 1994). In 1917 ALA created a Committee on Work with the Foreign Born that collected and disseminated information on how to help educate immigrants about American values and the English language (Stern 1991). The committee produced numerous guides to assist in this process.

Perhaps the most notable service to ethnic groups and minorities was the creation of branch libraries in urban areas. Branches provided extension services that could reach special populations, especially industrial workers and those who did not speak English (Ditzion 1947). These branches also offered special services to children. By 1900 many public libraries had a separate room for children's books and services. What better place to educate the first generation of immigrant children in the ways of American life (Du Mont et al. 1994)?

Sadly, some minorities and ethnic groups did not receive much attention from librarians, most notably African-Americans and Hispanics. Although Pura Belpré provided services to Hispanics at the New York Public Library as early as 1921, this was clearly an exception (Guerena and Erazo 2000). In his study of library services to Hispanics, Haro (1981) found that libraries were often perceived as one of many Anglo institutions designed and controlled by Anglos to serve Anglos:

> While most Mexican Americans, even the poor and illiterate, aspire to better education, the public library is not seen as a vehicle to attain it. The public library is

viewed by far too many Mexican Americans, particularly within the lower classes, as an Anglo institution which has never cared about their needs, which does not hire their people, and which engages in the disproportionate distribution of resources to satisfy first the demands of an Anglo society. (p. 86)

Before the Civil War, blacks in the South were forbidden to read and it was unlawful to teach them. Illiteracy was a means to maintain the subordination of slaves; those who could read did it in secret. Nonetheless, there was, even before the Civil War, a class of well-educated African-Americans including merchants, ministers, printers, shipbuilders, physicians, and others who placed great value on education and possessed strong literary interests, living mostly in the North. In the absence of access to libraries or formal education, they created literary societies in the first part of the nineteenth century, which served as "important entry points to a literary and intellectual world otherwise inaccessible to their membership" (McHenry 1998, p. 152). Pre–Civil War societies included the Philadelphia Library Company of Colored Persons, founded by Robert Purvis, and the Female Library Association of Philadelphia (Wheeler and Johnson-Houston 2004; McHenry 1998). McHenry (1998) observed, "These societies offered a protected, collective environment in which to develop a literary background as well as the oral and written skills needed to represent themselves with confidence" (p. 157).

Throughout the nineteenth century, these societies played a vital role, especially for black women. They could read fine literature and discuss ideas that promoted eloquence and critical thinking. The societies represented a source of both intellectual challenge and emotional support (McHenry 1998).

After the Civil War, although there was a concerted push for public schooling in the South, the development of public libraries for both blacks and whites lagged by about fifty years (Fultz 2006). What libraries there were provided severely restricted or no service to African-Americans (Trujillo and Cuesta 1989). By 1900, it is estimated that 90 percent of African-Americans in the South still could not read. The first two public libraries for African-Americans followed a combined school/library pattern. In 1903, the LeMoyne Institute, a black normal school, provided space for a library and made the collection available to the citizens as well as the students. In 1904, Galveston, Texas, opened a branch of the Rosenberg Library for African-Americans as an addition to a local black high school. In 1905, two segregated reading rooms for blacks were established in the public libraries of Lexington, Kentucky, and Jacksonville, Florida.

Other early efforts by public libraries to serve African-Americans began in rented spaces, in private homes, or churches. For example, in 1905 the Western

Colored Branch in Louisville, Kentucky, opened in three rented rooms in a private home (Fultz 2006). This branch served the new, growing black middle class and was headed by a critical figure in the development of libraries for African-Americans, Thomas Fountain Blue. Blue was a graduate of the prestigious Hampton Institute and Richmond Theological Seminary. The Louisville branch was the first public library branch serving African-Americans in any American city (Josey 1994). Blue's services and library training programs for African-Americans were considered a national model (Josey 1970). His Colored Department in Louisville not only provided direct service, but also established "deposit stations" and classroom collections at various sites throughout the city and surrounding counties (Fultz 2006). Similarly, the Negro Public Library in Nashville, Tennessee, which opened in 1916 as a branch of Nashville's Carnegie Library, focused on service to children. Under the leadership of the African-American branch librarian, Marian Hadley, who studied under Blue, and the librarian of the Carnegie Library, Margaret Kercheval, a solid children's collection was developed and services such as story hours were also offered (Malone 2000). Between 1930 and 1950, Vivian Harsh, the African-American Director of the Hall Library, a branch of the Chicago Public Library, developed a rich collection of African-American resources, created a book review and lecture forum, and established the library as a community center for the African-American neighborhood. Harsh created a place for discussion of important issues to African-Americans, including their civil rights, and promoted African-American cultural history (Burt 2009).

Despite these notable exceptions, in general, public library service to people of color was poor or nonexistent. Under the "separate but equal" doctrine in operation throughout the first half of the twentieth century, services for African-Americans remained seriously deficient. In the South, there was considerable evidence that funding for library services to African-Americans was not commensurate to the proportion of African-Americans in the community (Gleason 1941).

By 1926, nationally there were perhaps forty-five public libraries providing segregated library services to African-Americans; by 1935 the number had increased to seventy-five (Du Mont et al. 1994). The establishment of branches to serve African-Americans was usually funded by the philanthropy of whites, the Carnegie Corporation, or the activities of churches or civic organizations (both black and white) (Cresswell 1996; Wheeler and Johnson-Houston 2004).

By the late 1930s, the main libraries of sixteen southern cities claimed to provide services to African-Americans. However, in reality there were few services, often offered only in segregated circumstances: separate branches, poorly funded school libraries, and restricted hours of operation, bookmobile service, and limited privileges at main libraries. Sometimes the same library served both blacks and whites but had separate entrances, collections, and reading areas. By the late 1940s, there were no more than seventeen independent black libraries in the South (Fultz 2006).

Prior to the 1960s, library service to ethnic groups and minorities was based on the perception of these communities as disadvantaged. The 1960s brought significant changes, a time of ethnic self-determination (Stern 1991). Many African-Americans and Hispanics argued for equal opportunity and equal access to the advantages that American society had to offer. The concept of a melting pot was replaced by the concept of a multicultural society.

It was during the 1960s when activist movements sponsored demonstrations, sit-ins, and "read-ins" that library services became widely available to African-Americans, especially in the South (Graham 2001). The first sit-in in Mississippi took place at the Jackson Public Library in 1961. Even then, African-Americans often paid a high price, including being beaten for attempting to apply for a library card (Wheeler and Johnson-Houston 2004). In 1963, two black ministers in Anniston, Alabama, were brutally beaten for attempting to desegregate the city's library. Nonetheless, by 1963, seventy-one of seventy-six cities in the South with populations of 50,000 or more had integrated main library facilities. Yet, the existence of integrated facilities did not mean that blacks received equal treatment. Separate restrooms, checkout desks, entrances, and age restrictions were still commonplace (Fultz 2006).

Interestingly, the desegregation of public libraries came more quickly than that of the schools, and the process began prior to the 1960s. Fultz (2006) argued that this might be because "some southerners during this period held that racial interactions in libraries were less threatening than the possibilities of social contact among children in schools or even, seemingly among strangers on buses" (p. 348). He also noted that African-American library users were perceived as predominantly middle class and therefore more acceptable.

Graham (2001) observed that even in the 1960s, white librarians in the South were ambivalent about the segregation of public libraries; they were attempting to balance their professional ethos of service to all with the powerful mores of racial segregation that permeated their communities. The end of segregated libraries in the South was much more attributable to black activists than to librarians.

This is not to say that there weren't some notable heroes among librarians. Juliette Hampton Morgan, for example, was a white reference librarian at the Montgomery, Alabama, Carnegie Library, who vocally supported the Montgomery Bus Boycott of 1955. The community reaction was so intense and vituperative that it probably contributed to her subsequent suicide. Similarly, Emily Wheelock Reed, director of Alabama's Public Library Service Division, in 1957 courageously defended the children's book, *The Rabbits' Wedding*, which had illustrations depicting the marriage of a black rabbit to a white rabbit. Notable politicians accused Reed of promoting anti-segregationist literature and race mixing. She kept the book on the shelves and was subjected to intense questioning and scrutiny by state politicians. Later, Reed was again criticized for pro-integrationist attitudes because she included the works of Martin Luther King in her collection (Graham 2001). Although Reed left public service in 1960, her fortitude was a measure of the conviction of some librarians to overcome the prejudices of the times. There was, in fact, a segment of southern librarians who endorsed the concept of racial accommodation, but who seldom confronted the powerful segregationist forces directly (Carmichael 2005).

These problems, of course, did not exist only in the South. Evidence that northern libraries also discriminated was generally overlooked. For example, communities that received Carnegie dollars often spent the money on the provision of service to whites but not to African-Americans; or far less money was spent, resulting in inferior service. As the historian John Hope Franklin (1977) observed, "one searches in vain for an indignant outcry on the part of the professional librarians against this profanation of their sacred profession and this subversion of their cherished institutions" (p. 13).

Regrettably, ALA was not outspoken on the issue of library service to African-Americans until the 1960s, when the civil rights movement made it impossible to ignore (Du Mont et al. 1994). Generally, until the 1960s the association viewed itself as representing a national constituency of librarians, including those in the South who favored segregation. ALA did not want to be perceived as judging the political or social beliefs of its members. It viewed segregationist policies as a local matter. There was also concern that too much agitation would create more resistance in the South and bring unfavorable publicity to those public libraries that were desegregating quietly (Cresswell 1996; Josey 1994). By the 1960s, a considerable number of ALA members expressed concern that the association had done little to secure open access for all citizens and to address issues of equality and social justice. In 1961 the ALA took a firm stand regarding service to African-Americans as well as all other citizens, advocating equal library service to all.

At its midwinter meeting, the association passed an amendment to the Library Bill of Rights that made clear that an individual's library use "should not be denied or abridged because of his race, religion, national origins or political views." Regrettably, many communities mounted disappointingly strong opposition. In Virginia, for example, the citizens of Danville and Petersburg voted to close their public libraries rather than to desegregate them (Cresswell 1996).

Nonetheless, the civil rights movement of the 1960s was a critical turning point in ensuring minority access. It also produced several pieces of progressive legislation affecting libraries. Most notable was the passage of the Library Services and Construction Act in 1964, a major force in developing library services and collections for ethnic, disadvantaged, and underserved groups. Similar funding was provided with the passage of the Higher Education Act for Colleges and Universities (Trujillo and Cuesta 1989). Libraries responded to these initiatives by hiring individuals from ethnic groups, collecting reference resources on ethnic cultures and experiences, creating criteria to make library collections inclusive of all members of the community, developing outreach programs to attract minorities, offering information and referral programs for minorities, and building collections that were more responsive to the needs of various ethnic groups.

In 1970 the ALA created the Social Responsibilities Round Table (SRRT). Among SRRT's purposes was "to act as a stimulus to the association and its various units in making libraries more responsive to current social needs" (American Library Association [ALA] 2009, p. 149). SRRT has been very active over the years in addressing a variety of issues, including advocating for international human rights, racial minorities and gays, and the poor and homeless, as well as promoting equal rights for women. Their focus has been both on the library profession and on policies and practices of society as a whole.

Additional organizations were established as a result of the turmoil and activities of the 1960s. One such ALA-affiliated advocacy group was REFORMA (The National Association to Promote Library & Information Services to Latinos and the Spanish Speaking), which was established in 1971. REFORMA's purpose was and is to foster the development of library collections that included materials written in Spanish as well as materials of interest to Hispanics, to encourage the recruitment of bilingual librarians and staff, to develop services and programs for Latinos, to educate Latinos about libraries, and to advocate for the information needs of the Latino community (REFORMA 2014).

Similar to REFORMA, the Black Caucus of ALA (BCALA) has worked since 1970 on behalf of African-American librarians and the African-American community. BCALA "serves as an advocate for the development, promotion, and improvement of library services and resources to the nation's African American community; and provides leadership for the recruitment and professional development of African American librarians" (BCALA 2014). BACLA became formally affiliated with ALA in 1992 and held its first National Conference of African American Librarians (NCAAL) in 1995.

The public library mission to serve all members of the community continued to grow and evolve. The 1991 White House Conference on Library and Information Services reaffirmed the need to respond to the needs of an increasingly multicultural society. Its recommendations included providing financial and technical assistance to promote service to multicultural populations and populations with disabilities, promoting outreach services to traditionally underserved populations, and encouraging support for training professionals to serve multicultural needs (White House Conference 1991).

Today, ALA has a variety of committees and round tables that monitor minority issues in addition to the ones noted above. These include the Minority Concerns and Cultural Diversity Committee, the ALA Office for Literacy and Outreach Services, the Library and Information Technology Association (LITA)/LSSI (Library Systems & Services) Minority Scholarship in Library and Information Technology Subcommittee; LITA/OCLC Minority Scholarship Subcommittee, and the Minorities Recruitment Committee of the New Members Round Table (ALA 1997).

Despite these efforts, few would argue that the problems of unequal service have vanished. Prominent issues remain, including the need for recruitment and retention of a diverse library workforce, concern for the reduction in federal funding for library services to ethnic communities, and the need for good research on the impact of the programs and services that have been developed to serve these communities (Trujillo and Cuesta 1989). In addition, new issues have arisen with the growth of computer networks, wireless communications, and mobile devices. A digital divide persists (which will be discussed in subsequent chapters) in terms of access to the digital world only part of which deals with technological access itself. Another key part is the disproportionate availability of education and training in the use and exploitation of these systems.

V. ONGOING EVOLUTION:
From Information Provision to Engagement

Traditionally libraries were recognized as a physical and cultural center for the acquisition, organization, storage, and dissemination of knowledge; they were bulwarks of books and other materials—a well-defined institution in a well-defined physical and cultural space. Over the last few decades, the world of information and the technologies that enable our access to it has changed dramatically. Since the latter quarter of the twentieth century, as the new information technologies were developing, libraries responded by promoting themselves as the "information place." This seemed appropriate at the time. The new technologies were often difficult to navigate and many information seekers and library users were unfamiliar with their design and use. Most people, including librarians, were digital immigrants, slowly, sometimes hesitantly, making the migration to the new virtual information world. The library was a needed and important intermediary—a comforting and comfortable place, assisting users to find the information they needed in a complex, but increasingly rich, virtual information environment. Although some librarians were resistant, many became enthusiastic supporters of the new virtual information environment, and libraries focused on and promoted themselves as effective navigators on the information superhighway. Soon however, important and disconcerting questions arose: if libraries defined themselves primarily as information providers, what will happen when the information technologies become so easy to use that intermediation is not needed or desired? What about the growing generation of young people, digital natives, who were quite comfortable and skilled at getting information on the Internet without help? Will they need or want us?

Today, libraries are still a respected cultural institution and a powerful physical presence, but their monopoly on knowledge is gone. The library's competitors occupy a virtual space and their products are not physical, but digital and as the Internet and digital content have grown, the role of the library has diminished as an information provider. This transition has been difficult to accept. In many ways, libraries are struggling to maintain a new equilibrium balancing their traditional missions with an environment that is placing new demands on the libraries' infrastructure and purpose. With the advent of powerful search engines and a continuous and dramatic increase in the available resources on the Internet, the questions noted above have at least in part been answered. People still come to the library for information, but in smaller numbers; students still come to do assignments, but many others find their sources on the Internet at home; people still come for books, but increasing numbers read e-books on e-readers and obtain them elsewhere or demand that libraries supply them. As a result, the library is transforming: but to what?

By the first decade of the twenty-first century, libraries, aware that their significance was being questioned, began a concerted campaign to their constituencies to remind them of all the services that they provide. In fact, it was a self-realization that the library is much more than information provision—it was a *place* in which many important things happened: informational, recreational, educational, cultural, and civic. It was a place where people met, learned, and exchanged ideas. It was a place where people got help to solve important health and other social problems. It was a place to create. In recognition of these many contributions, American Library Association created a public awareness and advocacy campaign called "'@ your library'—The Campaign for America's Libraries." The campaign was launched in 2001 with the support of then–First Lady Laura Bush. ALA characterized the underlying impetus for the program in the following way: "While libraries are popular, they are often taken for granted. While libraries are ubiquitous, they are not often visible. And, while libraries are unique, they are facing new challenges" (ALA 2014). But this was more than a PR campaign; it attempted to target specific audiences with the message that "libraries are dynamic, modern community centers for learning, information, and entertainment (ALA 2014). It was an attempt to reinvigorate interest and participation in libraries.

Although ALA focuses primarily on public libraries, the theme was taken up by other types of libraries: an Academic and Research Library Campaign was launched in 2002, and a School Library Campaign in 2003. The "@ your library" campaign emphasized that a central mission of the public library was as a "community" center, not just a place for individuals in the community to receive service. In essence, it was sending the message that the library was an integral part *of* the community, not just an entity that provides service *to* the community. Ultimately, this campaign generated a new initiative with even stronger emphasis on community-orientation: the Libraries Transforming Communities (LTC) initiative. This initiative "seeks to strengthen librarians' roles as core community leaders and change-agents" (ALA 2014). ALA describes the goal of LTC as follows:

> LTC will help libraries become more reflective of and connected to their communities and achieve a domino effect of positive results, including stronger relationships with local civic agencies, non-profits, funders and corporations, and greater community investment in civility, collaboration, education, health and well-being. ALA also hopes to shift public discourse away from past themes about libraries in crisis and toward talk of libraries as agents of positive community change. (ALA 2014a)

Such roles require much broader and deeper engagement and entanglement in the community than the traditional mission of the library requires. Indeed, LTC takes as a fundamental theme, "Turning Outward" in which the orientation of the library is expected to change from being "library–focused" to "community-focused" (ALA 2014a).

The issue of engagement with the community will be discussed further in subsequent chapters, but suffice it to say that although the library's potential power to "transform" communities has been recognized historically since Andrew Carnegie's time, in practice, such a mission was supposed to be accomplished by the mere existence of the library as an available collection of books and services to interested individuals. In the more recent sense, the library is not transforming the community individual-by-individual, but helping to transform the community itself and in doing so, affecting the individuals within it. Certainly, many types of libraries, public, school, academic and special, are focusing more and more on understanding the needs of their communities, embedding themselves in user communities outside the walls of the library and engaging many more people, agencies, and institutions, as partners and collaborators in library activities. It is unclear what the ultimate impact of this transition will be, but that this change of orientation in mission is of historical significance is undeniable.

VI. SUMMARY

Libraries over the centuries have had many missions: archival, religious, scholarship and education, self-aggrandizement, and entertainment. In each case, the library was deeply embedded in the culture that created it. It began, grew, changed, and declined in consort with the culture that produced it. That is the library's nature; it does not exist in a vacuum and its vigor grows, ebbs, and flows with its society.

It was not until the nineteenth century that libraries began to serve the broader population and developed a democratic ethic and vision. U.S. libraries (also British and Canadian ones) led the way in this regard. The significance of libraries as a democratic institution is only slightly less important than the development of the printing press. The printing press made it possible for ideas to reach many people in concrete form; democracy created the expectation that those ideas should be available to the many rather than the few; libraries in democracies helped make those expectations a reality.

The dramatic changes that have occurred in the past three decades have in some senses radically changed the way information and knowledge are acquired. But to date, it has not radically changed the modern library's mission: to inform, to educate, to entertain. What has changed in all types of libraries is the means by which libraries accomplish their missions. Perhaps the mission of the library has not changed, because people still need to be informed, educated, and entertained and although they might use other channels as well, people still see the library as a source of knowledge for themselves and their children. But if libraries are truly reflections of their societies, then the modern library's missions might well change soon, because our society is changing with each technological advance, and we see the future shape of our society only through a glass darkly.

Going forward, it is fair to ask: Will we have a mission, and what will it be?

NOTE

I am indebted to Professor Donald Krummel of the University of Illinois, whose approach to teaching library history first suggested to me the value of addressing issues in library history from the perspective of the missions of libraries.

REFERENCES

ALA. 2009. *ALA Handbook of Organization, 2008–2009.* Chicago: ALA.

———. 2014. "About @ Your Library." www.ala.org/advocacy/advleg/publicawareness/campaign@yourlibrary/aboutyourlibrary.

———. 2014a. "Libraries Transforming Communities." www.ala.org/transforminglibraries/libraries-transforming-communities.

Arenson, Adam. 2006. "Libraries in Public before the Age of Public Libraries: Interpreting the Furnishings and Design of Athenaeums and Other 'Social Libraries' 1800–1860." In *The Library as Place*, edited by John E. Buschman and Gloria J. Leckie. Westport, CT: Libraries Unlimited, 41–60.

Barker, Nicolas. 2001. "Libraries and the Mind of Man." In *A Potencie of Life: Books in Society* (The Clark Lectures 1986–1987). British Library: Oak Knoll Press.

Battles, Matthew. 2003. *Library: An Unquiet History.* New York: Norton.

BCALA (Black Caucus of the American Library Association). 2014. "BCALA's Mission, Vision and Values." www.bcala.org/index.php/about-us.

Blackburn, Robert H. 2003. "The Ancient Alexandrian Library: Part of It Might Survive!" *Library History* 19 (March): 23–34.

Boser, Ulrich. 2006. "Genesis." *Smithsonian* 37 (October): 27–28.

Boyd, Clarence Eugene. 1915. *Public Libraries and Literary Culture in Ancient Rome.* Chicago: University of Chicago Press.

Burt, Laura. 2009. "Vivian Harsh, Adult Education, and the Library's Role as Community Center." *Libraries & the Cultural Record* 44: 234–255.

Cantor, Norman F. 1993. *The Civilization of the Middle Ages.* New York: Harper Collins.

Carmichael, James V., Jr. 2005. "Southern Librarianship and the Culture of Resentment." *Libraries and Culture* 40 (summer): 324–351.

Carnegie, Andrew. 1962. "The Gospel of Wealth." In *The Gospel of Wealth and Other Timely Essays*, edited by Edward C. Kirkland. Cambridge, MA: Harvard University Press. Originally published in the *North American Review* 148 (June 1889): 653–664.

Cecil, Henry L., and Willard A. Heaps. 1940. *School Library Service in the United States: An Interpretive Survey.* New York: H. W. Wilson.

Certain, Charles C. 1920. *Standard Library Organization and Equipment for Secondary Schools of Different Sizes.* Chicago: ALA.

———. 1925. *Elementary School Library Standards.* N.p.: National Education Association.

Childe, V. Gordon. 1965. *Man Makes Himself.* London: Watts.

Clanchy, Michael. 1979. *From Memory to Written Record.* Cambridge, MA: Harvard University Press.

———. 1983. "Looking Back from the Invention of Printing." In *Literacy in Historical Perspective*, edited by D. P. Resnick. Washington, DC: LOC.

Cresswell, Stephen. 1996. "The Last Days of Jim Crow in Southern Libraries." *Libraries and Culture* 31 (summer/fall): 557–573.

Dain, Phyllis. 1975. "Ambivalence and Paradox: The Social Bonds of the Public Library." *Library Journal* 100 (February 1): 261–266.

Davies, W. V. 1998. "Egyptian Hieroglyphs." In J. T. Hooker. *Reading the Past: Ancient Writing from Cuneiform to the Alphabet*. London: British Museum.

Dewey, Melvil. 1978. "Libraries as Related to the Educational Work of the State." In *Melvil Dewey: His Enduring Presence in Librarianship*, edited by Sarah K. Vann. Littleton, CO: Libraries Unlimited, 136. (Original work published 1888.)

Ditzion, Sydney H. 1947. *Arsenals of a Democratic Culture*. Chicago: ALA.

Dix, T. Keith. 1994. "'Public Libraries' in Ancient Rome: Ideology and Reality." *Libraries and Culture* 29 (summer): 282–296.

Du Mont, Rosemary Ruhig, Lois Buttlar, and William Caynon. 1994. *Multiculturalism in Libraries*. Westport, CT: Greenwood.

Dunlap, Leslie W. 1972. *Readings in Library History*. New York: R. R. Bowker.

Eisenstein, Elizabeth L. 1979. *The Printing Press as an Agent of Change: Communications and Cultural Transformations in Early Modern Europe*. Cambridge, England: Cambridge University Press.

———. 1995. *Printing as Divine Art: Celebrating Western Technology in the Age of the Hand Press*. Oberlin, OH: Oberlin College, November 4.

Fargo, Lucile F. 1930. *The Program for Elementary Library Service*. Chicago: ALA.

Franklin, John Hope. 1977. "Libraries in a Pluralistic Society." In *Libraries and the Life of the Mind in America*. Chicago: ALA.

"Free Fiction." 1866. *The Nation* 31 (February 1): 138–139.

Fultz, Michael. 2006. "Black Public Libraries in the South in the Era of De Jure Segregation." *Libraries and the Cultural Record* 41 (summer): 337–359.

Gates, Jean Key. 1976. *Introduction to Librarianship*. New York: McGraw-Hill.

Gillespie, John T., and Diana L. Spirt. 1983. "School Library to Media Center." In *Administering the School Library Media Center*. New York: Bowker.

Gleason, Eliza Atkins. 1941. *The Southern Negro and the Public Library*. Chicago: University of Chicago Press.

Graham, Patterson Toby. 2001. "Public Librarians and the Civil Rights Movement: Alabama, 1955–1965." *Library Quarterly* 71 (January): 1–27.

Guerena, Salvador, and Edward Erazo. 2000. "Latinos and Librarianship." *Library Trends* 49 (summer): 138–181.

Hamlin, Arthur T. 1981. *The University Library in the United States: Its Origins and Development*. Philadelphia: University of Pennsylvania Press.

Hanson, Eugene R. 1989. "College Libraries: The Colonial Period to the Twentieth Century." In *Advances in Library Administration and Organization*. Vol. 8. Greenwich, CT: JAI, 171–199.

Haro, Roberto P. 1981. *Developing Library and Information Services for Americans of Hispanic Origin*. Metuchen, NJ: Scarecrow.

Harris, Michael. 1973. "The Purpose of the American Public Library." *Library Journal* 98 (September 15): 2509–2514.

Harris, Michael H., and Stanley Hannah. 1992. "Why Do We Study the History of Libraries? A Meditation on the Perils of Ahistoricism in the Information Era." *LISR* 14: 123–130.

Harris, Michael, and Elmer D. Johnson. 1984. *History of Libraries in the Western World.* Metuchen, NJ: Scarecrow.

Harris, William V. 1989. *Ancient Literacy.* Cambridge, MA: Harvard University Press.

Harwell, Richard. 1968. "College Libraries." In *Encyclopedia of Library and Information Science,* edited by Allen Kent, Harold Lancour, and William Z. Nasri. New York: Marcel Dekker, 269–281.

Havens, Earle. 2007. "The Ventriloquist Who Changed the World." *American Libraries* (August): 54–57.

Hessel, Alfred. 1955. *A History of Libraries.* New Brunswick, NJ: Scarecrow.

Jackson, Sydney L. 1974. *Libraries and Librarianship in the West: A Brief History.* New York: McGraw-Hill.

Jacob, Christian. 2002. "Gathering Memory: Thoughts on the History of Libraries." *Diogenes* 49 (April): 41–57.

Jochum, Uwe. 1999. "The Alexandrian Library and Its Aftermath." *Library History* 15 (May): 5–12.

Jones, Plummer Alston, Jr. 1989. "The History and Development of Libraries in American Higher Education." *College and Research Libraries News* 50 (July/August): 561–565.

Josey, E. J. 1970. *The Black Librarian in America.* Metuchen, NJ: Scarecrow.

———. 1994. "Race Issues in Library History." In *Encyclopedia of Library History,* edited by Wayne A. Wiegand and Donald G. Davis Jr. New York: Garland, 533–537.

Kaser, David. 1980. *A Book for a Sixpence: The Circulating Library in America.* Pittsburgh: Beta Phi Mu.

Kevane, Michael, and William A. Sundstrom. 2014. "The Development of Public Libraries in the United States, 1870–1930." *Information & Culture* 49: 119–143.

Knight, Douglas M., and E. Shepley Nourse. 1969. *Libraries at Large: Tradition, Innovation, and the National Interest.* New York: R. R. Bowker.

Kruzas, Anthony Thomas. 1965. *Business and Industrial Libraries in the United States, 1820–1940.* New York: SLA.

Malone, Cheryl Knott. 2000. "Books for Black Children: Public Library Collections in Louisville and Nashville, 1915–1925." *Library Quarterly* 70 (April): 179–200.

Man, John. 2002. *Gutenberg* (Advanced Uncorrected Proof). New York: Wiley.

Mango, Cyril. 2002. "New Religion, Old Culture." In *The Oxford History of Byzantium,* edited by Cyril Mango. New York: Oxford, 96–120.

McCrossen, Alexis. 2006. "'One Cathedral More' or 'Mere Lounging Places for Bummers'? The Cultural Politics of Leisure and the Public Library in Gilded Age America." *Libraries and Culture* 41 (spring): 169–188.

McHenry, Elizabeth. 1998. "Forgotten Readers: African-American Literary Societies and the American Scene." In *Print Culture in a Diverse America*, edited by James P. Danky and Wayne A. Wiegand. Urbana: University of Illinois Press, 149–172.

McMullen, Haynes. 2000. *American Libraries before 1876*. Westport, CT: Greenwood.

Nichols, Charles L. 1964. *The Library of Ramses the Great*. Berkeley, CA: Peacock.

Nielson, Brian. 1989. "The Role of the Public Services Librarian: The New Revolution." In *Rethinking the Library in the Information Age*. Washington, DC: GPO, 179–200.

Parsons, Edward A. 1952. *The Alexandrian Library*. Amsterdam, NY: Elsevier.

"Public Libraries and Fiction." 1874. *The Literary World: A Monthly Review of Current Literature*.

REFORMA (The National Association to Promote Library & Information Services to Latinos and the Spanish Speaking). 2014. "About Reforma." www.reforma.org/content .asp?pl=2&contentid=2.

Roberts, F. B. 1912. "The Library and the Foreign Citizen." *Public Libraries* 17: 166–169.

Shera, Jesse. 1965. *Foundations of the Public Library*. Chicago: Shoestring.

———. 1976. *Introduction to Library Science: Basic Elements of Library Service*. Littleton, CO: Libraries Unlimited.

Shiflett, O. Lee. 1994. "Academic Libraries." In *Encyclopedia of Library History*, edited by Wayne A. Wiegand and Donald G. Davis Jr. New York: Garland, 5–15.

Staikos, Konstantinos. 2005. *The History of the Library in Western Civilization*. Volume 1. New Castle, DE: Oak Knoll.

Starr, Chester G. 1991. *A History of the Ancient World*. Oxford: Oxford University Press.

Stern, Stephen. 1991. "Ethnic Libraries and Librarianship in the United States: Models and Prospects." In *Advances in Librarianship*, vol. 15, edited by Irene P. Godden. San Diego: Academic Press, 77–102.

Thompson, James Westfall. 1962. *Ancient Libraries*. Hamden, CT: Archon.

Trujillo, Roberto G., and Yolanda J. Cuesta. 1989. "Service to Diverse Populations." In *ALA Yearbook of Library and Information* Science, vol. 14. Chicago: ALA, 7–11.

Valentine, Patrick M. 2011. "America's Antebellum Social Libraries: A Reappraisal in Institutional Development." *Library and Information History* 27 (March): 32–51.

Walker, C. B. F. 1998. "Cuneiform." In J. T. Hooker. *Reading the Past: Ancient Writing from Cuneiform to the Alphabet*. London: British Museum.

Watson, Paula. 1994. "Founding Mothers: The Contribution of Women's Organizations to Public Library Development in the United States." *Library Quarterly* 64 (July): 233–269.

Wheeler, Maurice, and Debbie Johnson-Houston. 2004. "A Brief History of Library Service to African Americans." *American Libraries* 35 (February): 42–45.

White House Conference on Library and Information Services. 1991. *Information 2000: Library and Information Services for the 21st Century*. Washington, DC: Superintendent of Documents, 1991.

Wiegand, Wayne A. 1989. "The Development of Librarianship in the United States." *Libraries and Culture* 24 (winter): 99–109.

SELECTED READINGS: History and Mission of Libraries

Books

Battles, Matthew. *Library: An Unquiet History*. New York: W. W. Norton, 2003.

Cantor, Norman F. *The Civilization of the Middle Ages*. New York: Harper Collins, 2003.

Ditzion, Sidney H. *Arsenals of a Democratic Culture*. Chicago: ALA, 1947.

Josey, E. J. *The Black Librarian in America*. Metuchen, NJ: Scarecrow, 1970.

Maxwell, Nancy Kalikow. *Sacred Stacks: The Higher Purpose of Libraries and Librarianship*. Chicago: American Library Association, 2006.

Pawley, Christine, and Louise S. Robbins. *Libraries and the Reading Public in Twentieth-Century America*. Madison, WI: University of Wisconsin, 2013.

Ranganathan, S. R. *The Five Laws of Library Science*. New York: Asia, 1963. First published 1931.

Staikos, Konstantinos. *The History of the Library in Western Civilization*. New Castle, DE: Oak Knoll, 2004.

Wiegand, Wayne. *Main Street Public Library*. Iowa City: University of Iowa, 2011.

Articles

Burt, Laura. "Vivian Harsh, Adult Education, and the Library's Role as Community Center." *Libraries & the Cultural Record* 44 (2009): 234–255.

Chodorow, Stanley. "To Represent Us Truly: The Job and Context of Preserving the Cultural Record." *Libraries and the Cultural Record* 41 (summer 2006): 372–380.

Cresswell, Stephen. "The Last Days of Jim Crow in Southern Libraries." *Libraries and Culture* 31 (summer/fall 1996): 557–573.

Dix, T. Keith. "'Public Libraries' in Ancient Rome: Ideology and Reality." *Libraries and Culture* 29 (summer 1994): 282–296.

Graham, Patterson Toby. "Public Librarians and the Civil Rights Movement: Alabama, 1955–1965." *Library Quarterly* 71 (January 2001): 1–27.

Havens, Earle. "The Ventriloquist Who Changed the World: How America's French Connection Propelled the Modern Free Library Movement." *American Libraries* 38 (August 2007): 54–57.

Jones, Plummer Alston, Jr. "The Awakening of the Social Conscience: Jane Maud Campbell 1869–1947." *Library Quarterly* 82 (2012): 305–335.

Kevane, Michael, and William A. Sundstrom. "The Development of Public Libraries in the United States, 1870–1930." *Information & Culture* 49 (2014): 119–143.

Koontz, Christie M. "A History of Location of U.S. Public Libraries within Community Place and Space: Evolving Implications for the Library's Mission of Equitable Service." *Public Library Quarterly* 26 (2007): 75–100.

Leckie, Gloria J. "Three Perspectives on Libraries." *Feliciter* 6 (2004): 233–236.

Lor, P. J., and J. J. Britz. "Challenges of the Approaching Knowledge Society: Major International Issues Facing LIS Professionals." *Libri* 57 (September 2007): 111–122.

McCrossen, Alexis. "'One Cathedral More' or 'Mere Lounging Places for Bummers'? The Cultural Politics of Leisure and the Public Library in Gilded Age America." *Libraries and Culture* 41 (spring 2006): 169–188.

Pennavaria, Katherine. "Representation of Books and Libraries in Depictions of the Future." *Libraries and Culture* 37 (summer 2002): 229–247.

Prizeman, Oriel. "Function and Decoration, Tradition and Invention: Carnegie Libraries and Their Architectural Messages." *Library and Information History* 29 (November 2013): 239–257.

Rapp, David. "The Man in the Library." *American Legacy* (winter/spring 2010): 11–12.

Valentine, Patrick M. "America's Antebellum Social Libraries: A Reappraisal in Institutional Development." *Library and Information History* 27 (March 2011): 32–51.

Watson, Paula D. "Founding Mothers: The Contributions of Women's Organizations to Public Library Development in the United States." *Library Quarterly* 64 (1994): 233–269.

Wheeler, Maurice, and Debbie Johnson-Houston. "A Brief History of Library Service to African Americans." *American Libraries* 35 (February 2004): 42–45.

3

The Library as an Institution
An Organizational Perspective

I. INTRODUCTION

For decades the world in which libraries operated was predictable and stable. Diversity among library users was limited and their demands seldom varied. The library's organizational structure reflected this stability; it was a bureaucracy with well-defined departments focused primarily on internal operations and control. Today, libraries face unprecedented challenges from numerous, varied, and powerful forces including:

Increased public accountability. Funders pay much more attention to the functions and effectiveness of the organizations designed to serve them. Expectations are high.

Changing knowledge environment. The library remains a primary source of cultural knowledge but how that knowledge is packaged and delivered is increasingly important. While books, magazines and paper documents remain relevant, emphasis on information delivered electronically is growing. Even traditional materials have been converted into e-materials.

Changing technological environment. Paralleling the change in how knowledge is packaged are the ways in which knowledge is accessed. The technological environment of computers, networks, databases, and the Web has significantly altered how libraries look and how they function.

Changing financial and economic environment. Libraries have always had to budget carefully based on the fiscal resources available to them. The fiscal crisis of recent years and the changing climate toward taxes and public distrust of their institutions have made the fiscal environment less predictable. Library leaders must constantly take the temperature of their funding sources and look for new models and sources of funding. Similarly, the changing knowledge environment and increasing reliance on technology have changed how library budgets are proportioned for resources and services.

Changing human resources environment. As the environment becomes more complex, libraries need new staff with different training and skills; traditional positions often change dramatically, and some jobs are eliminated. In addition, although the traditional supervisor-supervisee relationship continues to be important, an emphasis on cross departmental work teams continues to grow. The need for a diverse workplace remains an important consideration.

There are many other forces at work. When taken as a whole, their impact is significant. If libraries are to survive and prosper, it will be essential that they respond and adapt quickly by creating new organizational structures and procedures to assure the continuation of five basic functions:

Identifying, selecting, and acquiring resources. Traditionally, print and AV materials stored physically in the library comprised the library's primary resources. Today, the collection also includes digital materials both within and outside the library.

Organizing the resources to promote accessibility. Once obtained, resources must be organized, described, and presented in such a way that users can efficiently find them. Elements that promote accessibility include high-quality bibliographic description and classification as well as efficient search tools. (See chapter 4.)

Conserving and preserving materials. Libraries have a special responsibility to ensure that knowledge and information remain available over time regardless of format. Each format brings with it special requirements for ensuring continual access and use.

Providing educational programs. As a cultural institution, libraries have long-served as a place where people come to learn. Libraries today offer a myriad of programs to meet this mission.

Maintaining effective operations. The administrative and operational activities that sustain libraries include general administration and leadership, financial management, human resources, public relations, information technology (IT) marketing, maintenance, and security. The size and complexity of the organization determine the size of the units performing these functions.

This chapter begins by briefly describing the organizational structures traditionally designed to perform these functions and then examines in greater depth the major trends affecting four major types of libraries: public, academic, school, and special.

II. ORGANIZATIONAL UNITS

It would be convenient if there was a one-to-one correspondence between the library's functions and its organizational units, but this is not the case. Further, there is little consistency in the organizational charts of different types of libraries. Nonetheless, three broad categories provide a general picture of library organization: user services, technical services, and support services.

A. User Services

The term "user services" can have different meanings depending on the organization of a particular library. It can be narrowly construed to include reference, subject area units, and subdivisions such as branch libraries, or it can be broadly construed to include reference, interlibrary loan, circulation, media services, and in academic and special library settings, reserves and e-learning services (Su 2008). In addition, when considering the list of user services below, many of the services described are duplicated in public libraries in separate units, for example: "Adult Services" and "Youth Services."

1. Information Services

When an LIS professional assists someone seeking information, the process has been referred to as "reference service." The Reference and User Services (RUSA) division of ALA refers to "reference and user services librarians" as those professionals "that assist, advise, and instruct users in accessing all forms of recorded knowledge" (ALA 2014b). This includes answering user-initiated queries, whether face-to-face or electronically, using print, nonprint, and digital sources; selecting and/or helping users select information in print or electronic environments; interpreting resources; preparing guides that assist patrons to find what they're looking for; providing direct instruction in how to use the library's materials and services, including Internet instruction; maintaining information files in print and electronic formats; creating websites; developing and conducting tours in person or digitally; creating and delivering programs; and evaluating information sources and services. Depending on its size and service philosophy, a library might have one or several information services units. Larger libraries often have units subdivided by subject (history, science, business), by age (children, adults, young adults), by characteristics of the user (visually or hearing impaired), or by geography (branches or decentralized libraries).

2. Circulation or Access Services

The term "circulation" suggests the flow of materials in and out of the library; more recently, the department has also been called "access services." Traditionally, its primary task has been dispensing or receiving library materials and collecting fines for late or lost materials. Staff might also answer basic questions about library hours and coordinate shelving activities. Access services also oversee periodicals, interlibrary loans, and materials held for restricted use (e.g., reserve files in an academic library). Sometimes, it might also control audiovisual materials. Today, with automated circulation systems, users check-out and renew their own materials (Su 2008). Access services might also participate in evaluating and selecting digital resources.

3. Audiovisual Services

As the name implies, the audiovisual (AV) department provides various media and equipment, and sometimes advisory services. Organizationally, however, not all AV materials are necessarily included in this division. For example, although DVDs might be found in AV, music compact discs might still be found in a music or fine arts department. In other cases, because the primary activity of AV departments is dispensing or receiving items, it is sometimes located in the circulation unit.

4. Archives and Special Collections

Archives or special collections deal with records of local or general historical importance or with materials that are considered rare or especially fragile. The size and scope of special collections departments vary tremendously. Research libraries (special, public, or academic) are more likely to house, manage, and preserve materials in special collections. Traditionally, access to such collections was restricted on-site and great care was taken in the handling of the materials and in supervising their use. However, the ability to digitize archival and special collections has dramatically changed their character and availability. When digital collections are made available on the Internet, their reach is worldwide.

5. Special or Outreach Services

Some libraries have departments that serve special clientele such as people with visual or hearing impairments, or people who are physically unable to come to the library such as prisoners, nursing home residents, or those who are homebound. Bookmobile service remains a common form of outreach in public libraries.

B. Technical Services

Historically, catalogers in technical services were responsible for applying and implementing complex rules and practices for the bibliographic description of materials. Evans, Intner, and Weihs (2011) identified nine functions performed by technical services. The first five considered "traditional":

1. *Identification:* Locating potentially worthwhile items to add to the collection(s);
2. *Selection:* Deciding which of the identified items to add;
3. *Acquisitions:* Securing the selected items;
4. *Organization:* Indexing and cataloging the items acquired in a manner that will help the end-user locate materials;
5. *Preparation:* Labeling and otherwise making the items ready for easy retrieval;
6. *Storage:* Housing the prepared items in units that consider the long-term preservation of the items while allowing staff and end-users easy access to the material;
7. *Interpretation:* Helping end-users locate appropriate materials;
8. *Utilization:* Providing equipment and space to allow staff and end-users to more effectively use the retrieved items;
9. *Dissemination:* Establishing a system that allows patrons to obtain and use items without coming to the library.

Many of the traditional functions of technical services are now performed by vendors and bibliographic utilities through Web-based ordering, bibliographic description, and cataloging techniques and procedures. Mackenzie and Aulich (2009) suggested that the effectiveness of these external services might forever change technical services. They asserted,

> Technical Services Departments are part of the twentieth-century library, not the twenty-first. The days of every library having its own catalogers and processers are surely numbered, as library managers look for smarter ways of allocating resources, both human and fiscal. (p. 1)

Fessler (2007) stated the issue even more succinctly: "today's library technical services face the most significant changes since the invention of moveable type" (p. 139). Surely some traditional roles will diminish, but equally important roles will emerge and evolve. For example, considered a "backroom" operation in the past, in contrast to user services (Evans, Intner, Weihs 2011, p. 8), today's technical services staff ensure that users can easily understand the organization and the means of access to all information available in the library. Given this "front room" interface with users, technical service librarians have been renamed "metadata librarians" who are familiar with the Web-based approaches to identifying, describing, and making accessible electronic resources. Digital Resource Management (DRM) is another technical service area that requires special training and expertise including familiarity with a plethora of vendors and their products, digital collection development, contract negotiation, licensing, e-books and e-journals, collecting and analyzing data from electronic systems, conducting database trials, database maintenance, and digital preservation (Leffler and Newberg 2010). Responsibilities assigned to DRM librarians continue to expand and include exploring and evaluating catalog alternatives, working with electronic resource management systems, working with vendors on producing high-quality exchanges of information, working with reference staff on the selection and management of e-journals and providing training and education on the systems implemented. Increasingly DRM librarians collaborate with public service staff (Burke and McConnell 2007). Whether DRM librarians operate in distinct units or continue as part of technical services will likely depend on the size of the library. Nonetheless, these new responsibilities will "challenge librarians to develop new policies, apply new technologies, develop new competencies, and to take risks for making improvements" (Fessler 2007, p. 139). The goal for technical services, as always, will be to ensure high-quality service for all library users.

C. Support Units

Support units provide services that enable the library to perform the essential functions of the organization. These units include administration, information technology and systems (ITS), facilities maintenance, and security.

1. Administration

Under the broader category of administration fall the Director's Office, Treasurer's Office, Human Resource Management, and Marketing and Public Relations.

a. Director's Office

The Director is the Chief Executive Officer of the organization responsible for ensuring that the central mission, goals, and operations are executed and achieved in a lawful, efficient, and sound fiscal manner. The Director is often supported by an Assistant or Associate Directors who assist in carrying out these functions. Director positions in some types of libraries, such as academic or school libraries, are actually imbedded in much larger hierarchies and control is limited.

b. Treasurer's Office

The Treasurer's Office is responsible for the fiscal operations of the organization. It is usually staffed by a chief financial officer who ensures legal compliance with all fiscal operations. The Office is also responsible for assisting in the preparation of budgets, projecting current and future revenues and expenses, and for properly maintaining the fiscal accounts.

c. Human Resources

Human Resources (HR) ensures that all library practices related to library personnel are carried out in conformance with the policies and procedures of the library and are consistent with all applicable local, state, and federal laws and regulations. Among the practices administered by HR are recruitment and selection of staff, evaluation, discipline and termination of staff, collective bargaining, health plan administration, and employee motivation.

d. Marketing and Public Relations

Marketing and Public Relations (MPR) is responsible for assuring that the user community and other stakeholders view the library as a positive entity, for communicating to the relevant constituencies the services and resources available at the library, and for reporting the library's accomplishments, goals, and mission to the user community and to funding bodies. MPR staff prepares promotional materials for library programs and activities; develops PR plans for major projects; writes grants; manages communication with the media, as well as political, civic, and religious leaders; and manages crises when controversies arise. MPR assists in the development of the library's Web presence and contributes content to it.

2. Information Technology and Systems (ITS)

Given the fiscal and human resources now devoted to information technologies, systems, and networks, and their critical role in providing the library's essential services, ITS executes an increasingly important function. ITS advises and collaborates with staff and vendors on the acquisition, implementation, and use of new technologies and systems; provides system maintenance, repair, and updating as needed; trains staff on new or updated systems and technologies; assists in the measurement and evaluation of systems and technologies; and ensures network security to prevent viruses or inappropriate or unauthorized use of the system.

3. Facilities Maintenance

People expect a clean, attractive, well-maintained facility that is well lighted and comfortable to work in. Facilities Maintenance ensures that the buildings and grounds are effectively maintained. In smaller libraries, maintenance staff might also perform some security functions and build displays.

4. Security

Both library staff and users expect and deserve a safe library. Security needs vary depending on the size and location of the library and can range from dealing with minor nuisances to significant criminal behavior. Security staff patrol the premises, monitor security devices, guard entrances and exits, deal with difficult or problem patrons, advise administration on security processes and procedures, and contact additional safety forces if needed.

III. ORGANIZATION OF LIBRARIES BY TYPE

A useful way of understanding libraries as organizations is to examine them by type. There are more than 120,000 public, academic, school, and special libraries in the United States (figure 3.1) (ALA 2014). Although there are substantial variations within each type, many similarities also exist. This section reports on the mission of each type of library, provides some pertinent background, followed by identification and discussion of some of the major issues confronting each type.

FIGURE 3.1
Numbers of Libraries in the United States

Public Libraries (administrative units)		8,956
Academic Libraries		3,793
School Libraries		98,460
Special Libraries**		7,616
Armed Forces Libraries		265
Government Libraries		1,006
Total		120,096

* The number of central buildings is different from the number of public libraries because some public library systems have no central building and some have more than one. Public Libraries in the United States Survey: Fiscal Year 2011 (2014) specifically explains in a footnote to table 3, "Of the 8,956 public libraries in the 50 States and DC, 7,227 were single-outlet libraries and 1,729 were multiple-outlet libraries. Single-outlet libraries are a central library, bookmobile, or books-by-mail-only outlet. Multiple-outlet libraries have two or more direct service outlets, including some combination of one central library, branch(es), bookmobile(s), and/or books-by-mail-only outlets."

** Special libraries include corporate, medical, law, religious, etc.

NOTE: From *American Library Directory 2011–2012* (page viii): "Branch records for academic and government libraries are no longer counted within these breakdowns, causing some discrepancy when comparing figures with previous editions. This does not affect the total number of libraries listed in the *American Library Directory*™." Please contact Lauri Rimler at Information Today, Inc., with any questions regarding this. This difference was initially reported and took effect in the 2010–2011 edition.

A. Public Libraries

There are nearly 9,000 public libraries in the United States. According to the most recent data published by the Institute for Museum and Library Services (Swan et al. 2014), public libraries with 17,000 branches and outreach bookmobile services served nearly 300 million individuals in a service area that covered 95 percent of the country. Three-quarters of the nation's public libraries serve populations under 25,000, while about 6% serve populations of more than 100,000.

Most public library revenue comes from public sources with 85% coming from local government, 7.5% from the state, and less than 1% from federal sources. Other revenue (about 7%) comes from gifts, fees for library services, fines, interest, and grant income. Expenditures exceeded $10.5 billion dollars in 2011, an increase of 9% over 10 years, with 67% spent for staff salaries and benefits. Remaining funds were spent primarily on the 950 million items in public library collections. Although declining as a percentage of the overall collection, 80% of the materials were print, while 14% of funding was spent on electronic materials including digital, downloadable materials, as well as CDs and DVDs. Over 35 million e-books were purchased, an 89% increase in just 12 months; but still comprising less than 4% of the collections. Internet access was substantial with libraries providing more than a quarter million public-access Internet computers, an 86% increase over a ten-year period. In 2012, there were more than 92 million attendees at four million public library programs (ALA 2015).

The library director or chief administrator reports to a board of trustees. The board has statutory authority to operate the library. Members can be elected or appointed. The board's primary purpose is to establish policies, plan strategically, set goals and directions, and ensure fiscal accountability.

1. Mission

Most public libraries state their mission simply as striving to meet the educational, informational, recreational, and cultural needs of their communities. Some mission statements also include the desire to advance knowledge, strengthen communities, enrich lives, or serve diverse segments within communities. Increasingly, public library missions recognize their broader obligation to participate in civic engagement: to inform the citizenry about social and political issues, and to encourage and facilitate participation in democratic processes.

The Public Library Association (PLA) emphasizes a strategic planning process to help libraries determine their mission, goals, objectives, and desired competencies. During this process, libraries are expected to involve the community in identifying the needs to be met and the goals to be achieved (Nelson 2008). Emphasis on long-range planning has diminished with more emphasis placed on responding to local community needs. "What a library does for, or offers to, the public in an effort to meet a set of well-defined community needs" (Nelson 2008, p. xi) are considered "service responses," and public libraries today recognize that their plans must be flexible and adaptable to meet rapidly changing conditions.

2. Use

The use of the American public library is not dependent on any one characteristic; it is complexly related to other aspects of one's life. As Zickuhr, Rainie, and Purcell (2013) have observed:

> . . . Americans' relationships with public libraries are part of their broader informa-
> tion and social landscapes, as people who have extensive economic, social, tech-
> nological, and cultural resources are also more likely to use and value libraries
> as part of those networks. Deeper connections with public libraries are also often
> associated with key life moments such as having a child, seeking a job, being a
> student, and going through a situation in which research and data can help inform
> a decision. (p. 2)

It is clear, nonetheless, that Americans use their libraries well. A 2013 Pew study (Zickuhr et al. 2013) found that

- More than half (53%) of Americans used a public library in the past 12 months, and 72% lived in a household with a library user.
- 44% of individuals 16 and older visited a public library website, with 30% doing so in the last 12 months.
- Among parents with minor children, 70% say at least one child visited the public library (or bookmobile) in the last 12 months.

The Pew study (2013) also revealed what people do when they come to the library. The most frequent activity was borrowing print materials (73%), browsing the shelves for books and other media (73%), researching topics of interest (54%), and getting help from a librarian (50%). Other common activities were sitting or reading print materials, watching or listening to media, using a research database, attending or bringing a younger person to a program, and borrowing a DVD or video (40%–49%) Using the Internet in public libraries was also substantial. One study by IMLS (Becker et al., 2010) found,

> Internet access is now one of the most sought after public library services, and it is
> used by nearly half of all visitors. Over the past year, 45 percent of the 169 million
> visitors to public libraries connected to the Internet using a library computer or
> wireless network during their visit, even though more than three-quarters of these
> people had Internet access at home, work, or elsewhere. (p. 1)

The Pew Center (2013) found that 80% of Americans indicated that borrowing books and reference librarians were "very important"; while 77% also said that free access to computers and the Internet was also "very important." Pew concluded that

FIGURE 3.2

Typology of Public Library Engagement

PUBLIC LIBRARY ENGAGEMENT TYPOLOGY: GROUP OVERVIEWS			
Level of engagement with public libraries	Group name	% of U.S. population ages 16+	Major characteristics
High engagement ~80% used a public library in the past year	*Library Lovers*	10%	Members of this group report frequent personal use of public libraries, along with high levels of household library use. This group includes many parents, students, and job seekers; members tend to be younger, with higher levels of education.
	Information Omnivores	20%	This group has the highest rates of technology use, as well as the highest levels of education, employment, and household income. They have high levels of personal and household library use, but their visits to library are less frequent than Library Lovers.
Medium engagement ~50% used a public library in the past year	*Solid Center*	30%	Centered in smaller towns, this group is similar to the general U.S. population in most measures. About half have used a public library in the past year; most view libraries positively.
	Print Traditionalists	9%	This group contains the highest proportion of rural, Southern, or white respondents. It is similar to Solid Center in many measures, except that its members tend to live farther away from libraries. They also have positive views about libraries' roles in communities.
Low engagement ~30% used a public library in the past year	*Not for me*	4%	This group is distinguished from other low engagement groups by its members' strikingly negative views of libraries. In particular, they are far *less* likely than most other groups to say public libraries are important to their communities.
	Young & Restless	7%	This is a relatively young group, and few of its members have lived in their neighborhoods for very long. Their most striking feature is that only 15% know where the nearest public library is located.
	Rooted & Roadblocked	7%	This group generally views public libraries positively, but many face hurdles in their lives that may prevent them from engaging with libraries. They tend to be older, and many are living with disability or have experienced a recent illness in their family.

PUBLIC LIBRARY ENGAGEMENT TYPOLOGY: GROUP OVERVIEWS			
Level of engagement with public libraries	Group name	% of U.S. population ages 16+	Major characteristics
None Have never personally used a public library	*Distant Admirers*	10%	Though members of this group have never personally used a public library, they view libraries quite positively—perhaps because many say other family members use them. Many also say that various library services are important to them and their families. They tend to be older and are often living in lower-income households.
	Off the Grid	4%	Members of this group tend to be disengaged from their communities and social life in many ways. Many live in rural areas, and just 56% use the internet. Most have very low household incomes, as well as low levels of education—only one in ten has graduated from college.

Source: Pew Research Center's Library Services Survey of 6,224 Americans 16 & older conducted July 18–September 30, 2013.

"the availability of free computers and Internet access now rivals book lending and reference expertise as a vital service of libraries" (p. 3).

Another Pew study (2014) characterized library users ranging from highly engaged—"library lovers" and "information omnivores"—to those individuals who were totally disengaged—"distant admirers" and "off the grid." The typology illustrated in figure 3.2 represents a more sensitive profile than simply user/nonuser. Pew found that 30% of library users were highly engaged, while 40% were more moderately engaged. Engaged library users were also connected to other social, technological, and cultural resources in their communities.

3. Attitudes toward Public Libraries

A 2011 Harris poll of library users found that people valued library services. They believed that such programs provided educational support for family members, high-quality health and financial information, and opportunities for lifelong learning. A significant majority also valued the library as a community center, a place for cultural programming, and an aid for finding jobs. The 2013 Pew study also reported that a large majority of Americans (90%–94%) believed that the public library performs several critical functions, including giving people a chance to succeed, promoting literacy and a love of reading, and improving the quality of life in the community. Americans also believe that public libraries provide services that people would not otherwise have. Similarly, people expressed positive feelings based on their own experience; a large majority (94%) indicated they never had a negative experience. Many described it as a welcome, pleasant, and friendly environment; more than 70% felt that the availability of books and media, librarian assistance, a quiet safe place, and research resources were either "very important" or "somewhat important" to them. Sixty-nine percent felt the same about programs for youth, and a majority believed that Internet and computer-access programs for adults, assistance in applying for government information, and help in finding and applying for jobs were important as well. It is instructive, however, that although some valued these services, 30% indicated that they actually knew little or nothing about the many services provided and only 23% indicated that they knew about all or most of the services available (Zickuhr et al. 2013).

Overall, it appears that the citizenry remains very pleased with the public library. The situation is not all salutary, however, particularly in the area of new technologies and easy access to information in other venues. In the 2013 Pew study, more than one-third (34%) thought that public libraries were not keeping up with new technologies and more than half (52%) believed that they did not need public libraries as much as they used to because they could locate the information they needed on their own.

4. Major Developments and Challenges

a. New Information Technologies

New information and communication technologies, the Internet, and the World Wide Web have dramatically redesigned all library services, physical structures, and organizational charts. A more detailed discussion of the impact of these technologies is discussed in the chapter—"Transforming the Library." However, a brief overview here highlights some the changes wrought by rapidly changing technology. According to 2012–2013 data released by the Pew Research Center,

- Ninety percent of American adults have cell phones, while adults older than 65 are slightly less likely to own a cell phone (74%). Fifty-eight percent of cell phone owners own a smartphone. Among 18–29 year olds, 83% own a smartphone, while adults older than 65 have a 19% adoption rate.
- Fifty-two percent of cell phone owners sent or received e-mail on their cell phones, 50% downloaded a software application, 60% accessed the Internet, 21% participated in a video call, and 81% sent or received text messages.

- A large portion of the population now has broadband/wireless access; 70% of adults have a high-speed wireless connection at home.

- Eighty-seven percent of American adults use the Internet. Of the 14% not online, they are disproportionately African-American and Hispanic/Latino, age 65 or older, lack a high-school diploma, have lower incomes, or live in a rural area. There are few if any gender differences.

- Ninety-five percent of teens between the ages of 12–17 are online. Of those, 78% own a cell phone, 80% own a desktop or laptop computer, and 23% have a tablet computer.

- Three in four teens access the Internet on cell phones, tablets, and other mobile devices regardless of gender, ethnicity, level of education of parents, income, or urbanity.

- Seventy-five percent of all Internet users use social networking sites regardless of gender, level of education, or income. Forty-two percent use multiple sites.

- Eighty-one percent of teens use some kind of social media, and 89% of adults ages 18–29 use them, compared to 49% of older adults.

- Thirty-two percent of adults own an e-reader, and 42% own a tablet computer (Pew Research Center 2013).

Public libraries are now part of this evolving technological environment. According to the data from the Library Research Service (Wanucha and Hofschire 2013),

- Most public libraries now have websites. All libraries serving populations of 25,000 or more have them, as do 98% of those serving 10,000–25,000 and 83% of those serving fewer than 10,000.

- A majority of libraries now have social media accounts, the most popular being Facebook, followed by Twitter, YouTube, Flickr, Foursquare, Pinterest, Google, and Tumblr. Nearly all the largest libraries (93%), a substantial percentage of midsized libraries (83%), and a majority of smaller libraries (54%–69%) are using social media.

- Three-fourths of the largest libraries, three-fifths of the midsize, and between one-third and one-fifth of the smaller libraries offer some type of access through mobile devices.

- Forty-one percent of the largest libraries and a fourth of the midsized libraries provide for mobile versions of their sites.

- More than four out of five libraries offered online access to a patron's library card account, and a very large percentage of all but the smallest libraries offered online card sign-up as well.

- Nearly two in three of the largest libraries and four in ten of libraries serving 100,000–500,000 have blogs and RSS feeds, but these services decline rapidly as the size of library decreases.

- More than half of libraries serving 100,000 or more offer virtual reference services (VRS) with nearly 80% of the largest libraries offering it.

In addition, some public libraries are creating "digital branches." A digital branch is

> a branch library, delivered digitally, on the Web. It offers much more than a traditional library website in many ways, because a digital branch has a real staff, a real building, a real collection, and real community happening on and around it. (King 2009, p. 8)

The digital branch, when properly created and implemented, becomes an actual "destination," much like Amazon can be seen as a bookstore. It provides access to library resources and databases, allows for circulating, reserving, and downloading resources, including e-books and audiobooks. It is a community in that people can interact with other members of the community through social media, attending digital meetings, and interacting with library staff.

b. Changing Fiscal Realities

There can be little doubt that a major source of financial stress for public libraries has been the cost of electronic access, including the subscription costs to the ever-increasing number of electronic information databases, maintenance costs of system access, and the costs of operating and maintaining a next-generation catalog. In addition, the costs of new materials such as e-books and the costs of redesigning library spaces all add to fiscal burdens.

To pay for these ever-increasing costs, libraries traditionally relied on local tax dollars, often property taxes. However, given the precipitous decline in housing values in some areas, and a concomitant decline or flattening of government revenue at all levels, many public libraries experienced significant financial declines. Efforts to supplement income through additional levies sometimes were resisted as part of general antitax movements which also questioned whether libraries were appropriate institutions for tax support in general.

In a few instances, some communities even attempted to outsource or privatize their public libraries. Outsourcing involves the transfer of certain library responsibilities to a third party. An outsourcing contract was usually quite narrow, involving only a small portion of library services. Privatization, on the other hand, is an extreme form of outsourcing involving the transfer of entire library operations to a third party. According to ALA (2011), "privatization is the shifting of library service from the public to the private sector through transference of library management and operations from a government agency to a commercial company" (p. 3). The major commercial vendor currently providing this service is Library Systems & Services, LLC (LSSI). As of 2014, LSSI had 21 public library clients stretching from California to Florida (LSSI 2014). Understandably, ALA has raised serious concerns about this practice regarding quality of service, loss of local community control, governance, loss of control of tax dollars, intellectual freedom, collection development, and potential loss of community involvement from foundations and Friends organizations (ALA 2011).

The attitude of the citizenry toward library support cannot be described simply. OCLC studied public attitudes and found that:

- A large percentage of voters (75%) claimed they would support library funding, but for half of them, the commitment was not particularly strong.
- Public awareness of library services was often limited to the provision of books and other materials; the public was less aware of such services as teen programming, computer training, or ESL classes.
- The public was not aware of how libraries were funded and did not know that libraries were financially stressed.
- Public officials had a positive attitude toward libraries but were not necessarily supportive of additional funding.
- Not all library users supported additional funding; those who believed that libraries transform lives were more likely to support additional funding.
- Library supporters were involved generally in their communities, considered librarians as advocates of lifelong learning, and perceived the library as a vital part of their community (De Rosa and Johnson 2008).

Continuing financial strains have forced libraries to become active in both the political and marketing arenas. If libraries are to make their case that they deserve public support, they must engage their communities, provide services valued by community members, and continuously inform the community of their contributions and successes using both qualitative and quantitative measures.

c. Assessing Value

Although few doubt that public libraries greatly benefit their communities, those benefits are sometimes hard to define or quantify. Nonetheless, in a climate of taxpayer reluctance to fund public services, it is crucial that libraries explain why they make a difference. Based on social marketing principles, the language used should resonate with issues that the community cares about. For example, a report by the Urban Libraries Council (20011) found "that the return on investment in public libraries not only benefits individuals, but also strengthens community capacity to address urgent issues related to economic development" (p. 1). The study went on to say that libraries provide early literacy services that contribute to long-term economic success; their employment and career resources help prepare a workforce able to deal with new technologies; library support to small business through resources and programs contributes to development and stability; and the library bolsters cultural and commercial activities and provides a stable, safe, and high-quality environment for community activities.

In addition to such explanations, libraries in the twenty-first century will need to be able to demonstrate the library's value in dollars and cents. The Americans for Libraries Council (2007) identified several reasons for conducting quantitative evaluations, including the need for accountability and providing evidence to gain support from advocates and elected officials. Quantitative studies generally employ two basic research techniques: (1) the analysis of comparative data and (2) economic valuation methods such as cost-benefit analysis, contingent evaluation, and studies that measure the indirect impact of libraries (secondary economic impact analysis) (Imholz and Arns 2007).

There are several sources for comparative data. Hennen's American Public Library Ratings (Hennen 2010) uses a fifteen-item scale to assess public libraries in five areas: circulation, staffing, materials, reference service, and funding levels. Some of the weighted measures are expressed in *per capita* population terms such as circulation ratios (number of books circulated divided by the population served). Additional measures that might be expressed in *per capita* include expenditures, volumes, and reference questions. Other measures might be expressed *per hour* such as number of visits and number of hours open. In 2009, *Library Journal* implemented the LJ Index of Public Library Service, created by Ray Lyons and Keith Curry Lance, which identified "star" libraries in the United States. The index, sponsored by Baker & Taylor's Bibliostat, rates more than 7,000 public libraries using four *per capita* output measures: circulation, visits, program attendance, and public Internet use. Highly ranked libraries receive three, four, or five stars (*Library Journal* 2014).

Holt and Elliott (2003) suggested that with increasing accountability pressures, cost-benefit analysis will become more common, although the emphasis should shift from outputs to outcomes. That is, the focus will shift from what libraries do, to what tangible benefits they provide to their communities. Their proposed cost-benefit measures include (1) consumer surplus, which is "the value that library users place on separately-valued library services" (p. 429); and (2) contingent valuation, which measures how much an individual would be willing to pay rather than lose library service, or how much an individual would be willing to pay in taxes to maintain current services.

In general, quantitative studies of the return on investment (ROI) of public libraries both locally and statewide have produced positive results. For example, a study of nine libraries in southwestern Ohio reported operating costs of a little more than $74 million, but the direct economic benefit exceeded $238 million or $3.81 for every dollar expended (Levin, Driscoll & Fleeter 2006). A study of Pennsylvania public libraries found an ROI of $5.50 for every dollar tax support (Pennsylvania Library Association 2009). A study in Suffolk County, New York, found similar results: every dollar spent on the public library yielded $3.87 in economic benefit (Americans for Libraries Council 2006). Additional state studies include Vermont, $6.96 ROI; Florida, $6.54 ROI; Wisconsin, $4.06 ROI; Indiana, $2.36 ROI; South Carolina, $4.48 ROI; and Minnesota, $6.62 ROI. A study of eight libraries in Colorado produced an ROI of $4.99 (Steffen et al. 2009).

Unfortunately, the study methodologies cited above were not consistent. There is a critical need for consistent data standards and valuation techniques, greater national coordination, and greater awareness of appropriate valuation techniques (Imholz and Arns 2007). In addition, although such measures are often undertaken to maintain or secure funding, they should also be directed toward helping the library fulfill its purpose. As Rodger (2002) reminded us, the key question should not be, "How can we get more money?" but rather "How can we become more valuable to the community?"

d. The Political Climate

Public library funding is inherently a political issue and public libraries exist in an inherently political environment—a fact often overlooked and greatly underestimated. The library's role in the community is increasingly political as the library actively promotes civic engagement. The library acts politically when it encourages people to vote, assists in voter registration; provides programs on issues on which voters decide; or offers job training that might help ameliorate challenging economic and social conditions.

Public libraries build their collections and provide their services and programs without regard to any particular political party; they support no particular candidates or issues, or advance particular political agendas; their role is nonpartisan rather than apolitical. The library does not take sides, rather it represents both sides. Books and other materials advancing both liberal and conservative viewpoints should be part of the collection; LIS professionals have an obligation to ensure that the library collection is balanced.

The library is political in another sense; library administrators and library boards must establish and preserve effective working relationships with all segments of the community and particularly with individuals whose financial support is needed, including individual voters. In addition, they must maintain good relationships with local, state, and federal officials and with legislators and their staffs. Library board members are often appointed by elected officials or legislative bodies. If the library is supported by a local tax levy, boards must be particularly sensitive to the needs of the citizens who support it.

Similarly, when library leaders participate in the advocacy activities of their professional associations, such as the American Library Association or the Association of Research Libraries, they are acting politically. Sometimes this advocacy involves testifying in front of legislative bodies on the association's behalf or preparing briefing documents or programs to inform others about library issues.

Although public libraries cannot lobby for particular candidates or issues, the library can actively make its case based on its accomplishments and the benefits of library service. By keeping the public library visible to political bodies and officials, the library is more likely to receive support when issues come up that affect it. The library has a complex relationship to the political process and balancing the many political interests is a challenging task. Library leaders must be well-informed, deliberate, and sensitive to the many political forces that shape their communities: local, state, and national.

e. Civic Engagement

For many decades, the public library has focused on satisfying the information and reading needs of individual users. That is not to say that libraries were unwelcoming to groups, but rather that their energies and resources were primarily directed toward individuals. With the growing dominance and convenience of Google and other search engines, LIS professionals became increasingly concerned that providing information to individuals might no longer be the library's primary function. They recognized that because convenience is so important, more people would seek information using the Internet and fewer would come to the library even though the authority of other sources might be less valid. At the same time, concerns were also increasing about peoples' lack of civic engagement and lack of trust in government. There is a disconcerting pattern of declines in voting, in participation in service organizations and community meetings, and reductions in charitable giving

(Kranich 2012). All of these issues led LIS professionals to identify an opportunity consonant with their mission to reemphasize the role of the library as an essential community institution. As Kranich (2012) observes:

> . . . libraries uphold and strengthen some of the most fundamental democratic ideals of our society; they not only make information freely available to all, but also foster the development of a civil society. They also provide comfortable, inviting, neutral, safe civic spaces conducive to democratic discourse—spaces where citizens can work together to solve public problems. (p. 75)

The Urban Libraries Council (ULC) (2011) identified five civic leadership roles for public libraries:

Civic Educator—raising awareness of civics, civic engagement, and civic responsibility;

Conversation Starter—identifying challenging community issues, creating forums for sharing opinions, and developing action strategies;

Community Bridge—bringing diverse people—including local government officials—and organizations with different perspectives together to build stronger communities;

Visionary—leading efforts to develop a broad and inclusive community vision;

Civic Forum—walking, talking, thinking, and acting as **the** place where democracy, civic engagement, and public discourse happen—the realization of democracy in action.

To achieve these ends, libraries will need to reach beyond the building, identifying key leaders in diverse segments of the community, contributing the library's expertise and resources in the engagement process; making the library building central to engagement activities, creating a culture of engagement in the minds of staff, and developing activities and programs that improve the community (Urban Libraries Council 2011).

On the national level, increased community engagement has been recognized and strongly supported by ALA in its "Libraries Transforming Communities (LTC)" initiative in partnership with the Harwood Institute for Public Innovation, a non-profit, independent organization that assists organizations to "address community challenges, improve their own effectiveness, and do their work in a way that make communities stronger" (Harwood 2014). The Initiative emphasizes a theme of "Turning Outward," reflecting a need for libraries to shift from a library-focused, internal perspective to an external, community focus. Among several strategies, ALA suggests that libraries develop and implement a team-based community engagement training program for library staff. According to ALA:

> LTC will help libraries become more reflective of and connected to their communities and achieve a domino effect of positive results, including stronger relationships with local civic agencies, non-profits, funders and corporations, and greater community investment in civility, collaboration, education, health and well-being. ALA also hopes to shift public discourse away from past themes about libraries in crisis and toward talk of libraries as agents of positive community change. (ALA, LTC 2014, n.p.)

IMLS also recognized community engagement as a major goal in its 2012–2016 strategic plan: "IMLS promotes museums and libraries as strong community anchors that enhance civic engagement, cultural opportunities, and economic vitality (p. 5). As a trusted and stable institution, IMLS perceives the library as a central community "convener" that can serve as a community anchor. IMLS supports projects that position libraries as a core institution in the community learning infrastructure, and partners with other federal agencies that support libraries in advancing national priorities such as education, health, economic development, and disaster preparedness (IMLS 2012). In addition, IMLS has promoted libraries and museums in the area of early learning particularly in regard to providing opportunities for children who are often deprived of library and museum exposure. Among the ways libraries and museums can make a difference are (IMLS 2012)

- improving the quality of early learning experiences
- making libraries and museums safe places for families to learn together
- promoting seamless learning activities from kindergarten to preschool to the third grade
- supporting education in basic literacy, reading, and the sciences and supporting the development of social, emotional, and cognitive growth
- providing educational support during the summer months
- developing partnerships with schools, public broadcasting, health facilities, government agencies, and corporations
- providing access to digital technologies that promote digital literacy and access to digital media

In many ways, civic engagement returns the public library to its historical roots as critical for an informed democratic conversation. Budd (2007) reminds us,

With regard to the democratic mission of public libraries, *a primary responsibility is to provide communities with the apparatus of democratic deliberation—ideas that gird the foundations of democracy along with the contemporary statements, claims, and discussions about the issues that arise in a democratic society.* (italics the author's, p. 2)

f. The Growth of Makerspaces

The increased emphasis on engaging the community has also led to the creation of makerspaces in public libraries. Makerspaces are part of the "maker" culture that emphasizes the value of creating and learning through "hands-on" activities. A makerspace, sometimes referred to as a "hacker space," is "a physical location where people gather to share resources and knowledge, work on projects, network, and build" (EDUCAUSE 2013). The library, or other community center, provides space, tools, and sometimes expert assistance. What people make depends on how the space is designed, but generally, makerspaces emphasize new technologies such as 3-D printers, engineering, and testing new ideas in group discussions, informal classes, and self-directed learning (EDUCAUSE 2013). Britton (2012) noted that there are numerous benefits of makerspaces for public libraries, because they

- foster play and exploration
- facilitate informal learning opportunities
- nurture peer-to-peer training
- work with community members as true partners, not as users or patrons
- develop a culture of creating as opposed to consuming (p. 20).

Makerspaces are, at their heart, social places where people can explore, share, create, and solve problems together. Instead of simply receiving knowledge, people learn by doing. Makerspaces can transform the act of learning into peer-to-peer teaching; teens seem naturally attracted to them. IMLS has supported a variety of makerspace initiatives in libraries. Makerspaces open new possibilities for libraries. As Britton (2012) observed, "maker spaces provide libraries with an opportunity to reimagine how they engage with community members" (p. 23).

g. The Rise and Popularity of the Graphic Novel

Most of the innovations in publishing relate to the digital world. But there is a notable exception in the popularity of the graphic novel. A graphic novel "is a self-contained story that uses a combination of text and art to articulate the plot. It is equivalent in content to a long short story or a short novel . . ." (DeCandido 1990, p. 50). The first graphic novels appeared in the late 1970s. Although their roots are in comics and comic books, the often serious themes, extended story development, and complexity visually and texturally distinguish graphic novels from these roots.

The genres of graphic novels are varied and reflect both traditional literary genres and those of the comic book. Among the genres are the super hero, fantasy, crime and mystery, horror, action and adventure, science fiction, contemporary life, and nonfiction works—historical, educational, and biographical. Perhaps, the best known of the nonfiction graphic novels is *Maus: A Survivor's Tale* by Art Spiegelman, which won the Pulitzer Prize in 1992 (NCAC 2006; Pinkley and Casey 2013).

Graphic novels have been criticized for containing violence, explicit sexuality, and sexism; additionally, critics claim that they contribute to delinquency, which is rooted in claims about the effects of comic books as early as the 1950s. Librarians have expressed concern about the books' lack of physical integrity. Nonetheless, libraries are building collections of graphic novels for all ages, and the novels are among the fastest growing areas in publishing. Today the graphic novel is viewed by many as an important literary contribution, especially for its capacity to encourage young people to read and think critically. Graphic novels have been especially useful for stimulating reading among students who are reluctant readers (Crawford 2004). Gavigan (2011) notes that graphic novels may also be useful for promoting reading among reluctant young males—a group particularly reluctant to read. Interestingly, although teens are enthusiastic readers, graphic novels are especially popular among those in their twenties because of the sophisticated themes in many of them (DeCandido 1990; Pinkley and Casey 2013). There is also a growing supply of graphic novels for young children. The ALA provides a list of "The Best Graphic Novels for Children" to provide readers' advisory for parents and librarians in this area (ALA 2014d). There is little doubt that graphic novels are a permanent and growing part of the publishing landscape, and LIS professionals need to keep up-to-date to maintain strong collections in this area.

h. Persistence of the Digital Divide

As library services and resources rely more and more on digital access, the fundamental problem of making sure all people can access library services and resources must be addressed. The term "digital divide" describes the gap between those who have access to, and can use, the Internet and those without access or skills. In the twenty-first century, such knowledge is critical for success in education, finances, health, employment, and participation in a democratic society (IPAC 2014). Despite rapid gains for the population in general, those who still lack communication technologies, skills, and access tend to share characteristics such as low socioeconomic status, low level of education, isolated geographic location, and senior citizen status.

"Digital literacy generally is used to refer to an individual's ability to locate, evaluate, and use digital information, encompassing both technologies (e.g., computers) and services . . ." (Jaeger et al. 2012, p. 5). Hildreth (2013) estimated more than 100 million people, one-third of the population, is digitally illiterate. Horrigan (2014) reported that 29% of Americans have low levels of digital skills, 42% have moderately good levels of digital skills, and 29% have high levels of digital skills.

A solution to digital illiteracy is "digital inclusion." It is a commitment by the society and its institutions (including libraries) to bridge the digital divide for all who suffer from it. The Information Policy & Access Center (IPAC) (2014) described digital inclusion in the following way:

- All members *understand* the benefits of advanced information and communication technologies.

- All members have *equitable and affordable access* to high-speed Internet-connected devices and online content.

- All members can take *advantage* of the *educational, economic, and social opportunities* available through these technologies.

The American Library Association, IMLS, and IPAC are enthusiastic supporters of digital inclusion. They suggested a number of ways that libraries can help create digitally inclusive communities:

- by providing free access to public access technologies (hardware, software, high-speed internet connectivity) in their communities

- by providing access to a range of digital content to their communities

- by providing digital literacy services that assist individuals to navigate, understand, evaluate, and create digital content using a range of information and communications technologies

- by providing programs and series around key community need areas such as health and wellness, education, employment and workforce development, and civic engagement (ALA 2014c)

In fact, evidence suggests that libraries have already made significant contributions toward a digitally inclusive society. A 2014 IPAC study found that all the libraries surveyed offered access to online databases, virtual reference, homework help, and e-books either directly or through licensing arrangements. Similarly, nearly all surveyed libraries offered some type of formal or informal technology training; urban libraries were more likely to offer formal training.

Even as the digital divide lessens, new digital issues arise. Horrigan (2014) argued that next-generation Internet applications allow people to access, analyze, and repurpose vast amounts of data in areas such as government and health, but most people lack the knowledge and skills to exploit these applications. Horrigan believes public libraries should pay less attention to digital literacy and concentrate more on "digital readiness," which he defines as "the capacity for people to engage with online resources with full information about service attributes and use of personal and household data" (p. 3). A digitally ready population will help ensure intelligent consumers and an informed citizenry. The role public libraries will play in promoting this level of knowledge and skills is as yet unclear; but that it will play a role is certain.

i. Censorship Issues

The public library has a long history of individuals, groups, and governments trying to limit or restrict access to materials in its collection. The trend is unabated. Special focus continues to be on youth and the possible effects that certain books or other library resources might have on them. In addition, materials about, or of interest to, lesbian, gay, bisexual, and transgender (LGBT) individuals are also a focus. Restrictive state and federal legislation continues to be a factor as well, especially the Children's Internet Protection Act (see discussion below).

Censorship attacks on libraries extend well beyond the libraries themselves to the American Library Association and to its most important intellectual freedom policy expressed in the ALA Library Bill of Rights. As a result, public librarians have been forced to defend not only their own libraries, but also their professional association and its tenets. Complaining patrons have led some librarians to compromise their professional standards by restricting access or eliminating controversial materials. A detailed discussion of censorship and intellectual freedom issues is found in chapter 9.

j. Serving All Segments of the Community

As the U.S. population becomes increasingly diverse, libraries must ensure that they provide effective access to their physical and electronic resources, and provide services that respond to the needs of all community members. Public libraries are used by a diverse population. Pew, for example, found that substantial percentages of people of all ages, household incomes, and educational attainment used the library. If there is a trend it would be that users tend to be younger, female, and have higher educational attainment than nonusers. Income does not seem to affect library use except that those earning less than $30,000 annually use it somewhat less.

ALA has made strong recommendations to encourage and promote library service to all segments of the community. Its policy on diversity makes clear the breadth of diverse groups that must be considered and issues that they face:

> The American Library Association (ALA) promotes equal access to information for all persons and recognizes the ongoing need to increase awareness of and responsiveness to the diversity of the communities we serve. ALA recognizes the critical need for access to library and information resources, services, and technologies by all people, especially those who might experience language or literacy-related barriers, economic distress; cultural or social isolation; physical or attitudinal barriers; racism; discrimination on the basis of appearance, ethnicity, immigrant status, religious background, sexual orientation, gender identity, gender expression; or barriers to equal education, employment, and housing. (ALA (Policy) 2014)

ALA suggested a variety of strategies to serve diverse populations, including the purchase of materials and resources for diverse populations, providing training and development on diversity for library staff, providing adequate and secure funding for the purchase of diverse materials and resources, developing and promoting public awareness of the library's programs and resources of interest to diverse groups, and promoting career advancement for diverse personnel.

i. Service to Ethnic Populations

Pew (2013) found that African-Americans and Hispanic/Latino communities place great value on libraries; 55% of adult African-Americans and 46% of Hispanics/Latinos visited the library or bookmobile in the last 12 months, compared to 54% of whites. More than 80% of the African-American and Hispanic/Latino respondents felt that the library was important to them and their families, and more than 90% felt the library was important to the community as a whole (Zickuhr et al. 2013). In addition, Pew found that African-Americans and Hispanics/Latinos said they were more likely than whites to use new services that might be offered, including (1) online reference services, (2) apps that locate library materials and instructional programs on apps and other electronic devices, (3) e-book services and classes on e-book downloading, and (4) kiosks that would dispense books and movies in the community.

ii. Service to Those with Low Income

Service to the poor has been a matter of great concern to public librarians for decades. ALA has promulgated a number of policies addressing this issue, most notably "Library Services for the Poor" (ALA 2008), which describes the urgency of responding to the needs of "poor children, adults, and families" (p. 55). The recommendations include the removal of all barriers to library services, including fees, the provision of funds for programming to people with low income, increasing materials and services that realistically address the issue of poverty and homelessness, and more training for library staff.

Despite these encouragements, some believe that the profession has not been sufficiently aggressive in reaching out to low-income communities. For example, Gieskes (2009) reported that the poor "appear to be an invisible population among library potential constituencies" (p. 55). She found that few libraries consult with ALA divisions or resources in seeking ways to serve people with low incomes and many were uncomfortable identifying poor people as a distinctive group due to reluctance to label them. Nonetheless, she recommended that libraries and the ALA take a more proactive approach.

iii Service to the Elderly

As the baby-boom generation ages, the need to develop responsive collections and services for them is becoming increasingly important. In 2000 individuals over 65 represented 12.4% of the population; in 2009, 12.9%; by 2030, they will represent nearly 19% or nearly one in five (HHS 2015). Generally, most library services are geared to populations such as children and youth, although large-print collections and outreach services through nursing homes, bookmobiles, and homebound populations are common (Bennett-Kapusniak 2013). The American Library Association (ALA (RUSA) 2008) has established guidelines for services to the elderly and includes the following recommendations:

- Acquire current data about the older population and incorporate it into planning and budgeting.
- Ensure that the special needs and interests of older adults in your community are reflected in the library's collection, programs, and services.
- Make the library's collection and physical facilities safe, comfortable, and inviting for all older adults.
- Make the library a focal point for information services to older adults.
- Target the older population in library programming.
- Reach out to older adults in the community who are unable to travel to the library.
- Train the library's staff to serve older adults with courtesy and respect.

Regrettably, there is some evidence that public libraries are not meeting the desired goals. Bennett-Kapusniak (2013) after examining more than 50 public libraries found that few of their programs (8%) actually targeted older adults and that less than 50% provided assistive technologies to aid older library users. Computer literacy programs were also found lacking with many having no lab to practice skills and less than half offered assistance from a librarian. In addition, only 22% of the libraries had websites on which font-size could be increased.

The ensuing years will likely see increased pressures on libraries to respond to the library needs of the elderly, and libraries should be planning and budgeting for these developments.

iv. Service to Rural Communities

Although rural residents comprise only 17% of the U.S. population, they live on four-fifths of the land area. Nearly 50 million people reside in nonmetropolitan areas in the United States. The Hispanic/Latino population has doubled in rural areas since 1980 (Economic Research Service 2004). Rural libraries serving fewer than 25,000 people typically have a book collection of approximately 26,000 volumes, and an operating budget of $155,000 (Vavrek 2003). States differ widely in terms of the percentage of libraries that are rural, but in ten states, rural libraries comprise 70% or more of the libraries in the state. When taken as a whole, rural libraries have a service population of over 37 million people, which is over 12% of the population in the United States.

In terms of collections and library use, rural libraries mirror libraries in urban and suburban areas although their collections and services are often more limited. In 2011, there were more than 167 million visits to rural libraries circulating 242 million items. Hours of operation in rural libraries tend to be on average somewhat less than city libraries: 33.5 versus 42.7 hours respectively. Many rural libraries offer electronic resources like their urban counterparts, but they have less access to Broadband. When electronic resources are available they are well used. More than one-third of rural libraries offer e-books; total collection size of e-books for rural libraries exceeded 10 million in 2011 (Swan, Grimes, and Owens 2013).

There are a number of challenges that are unique to rural libraries. The rural library workforce accounts for approximately 12% of the total library workforce and nearly 16% of all LIS positions in public libraries. Only about one-third of rural librarians hold a master's degree, and attracting and retaining well-trained staff is an on-going problem (Swan, Grimes, and Owens 2013). Other challenges for rural LIS professionals include

- decreasing per capita revenue coupled with rising visitation and circulation rates
- utilities and connectivity issues
- lack of expertise to support electronic networks
- significant geographic barriers
- supporting schools and homeschoolers
- providing reading, information, and computer literacy instruction for recent immigrants
- serving as a community center (Vavrek 2003; Johnson 2000)

Despite these challenges, rural librarians find their work very satisfying and believe that they play a vital role in their communities, that they support economic development, and that they make a difference in people's lives (Flatley and Wyman 2009).

v. Service to Individuals with Disabilities

The Passage of the Americans with Disabilities Act of 1990 (ADA) was intended to ensure equal opportunity for people with disabilities. It also raised the consciousness of Americans regarding the number of people with disabilities and the everyday struggles they face. It is estimated that more than 56 million Americans (19%) have disabilities. More than half of these have severe disabilities (U.S. Bureau of the Census 2012).

Adults with disabilities ages 21–64 had median monthly earnings of $1,961, compared with $2,724 for those with no disability. They are less likely to be employed (41%), compared to individuals with no disability (80%). They are more likely to be economically disadvantaged; more than 10% experience persistent poverty compared to 4% of those with no disability.

The nature of people's disabilities varies considerably. According to the U.S. Bureau of the Census (2012),

- About 8.1 million people have difficulty seeing, including two million who are blind or unable to see.
- About 7.6 million people experience difficulty hearing, including 1.1 million with severe impairment. About 5.6 million use a hearing aid.
- Roughly 30.6 million have difficulty walking or climbing stairs, or use a wheelchair, cane, walker, or crutches.

- About 19.9 million people have difficulty lifting and grasping.

- About 9.4 million noninstitutionalized adults cited difficulty with at least one activity of daily living. These activities include getting around inside the home, bathing, dressing, and eating. Of these people, 5 million needed help to perform daily activities.

- About 15.5 million adults have difficulties with one or more instrumental activities of daily living, such as doing housework, using the phone, and preparing meals. Of these, nearly 12 million require assistance.

- Approximately 2.4 million have Alzheimer's disease, senility, or dementia.

- Seven million adults reported being frequently depressed or anxious to a degree that it interfered with ordinary activities.

Individuals with disabilities often have increased and particular information needs that create special responsibilities for libraries. Further, individuals with disabilities are often part of the digital divide; they are less likely to have Internet access in their homes and thus have less access to information. The library community has responded in many ways. The ALA, for example, approved a "Library Services for People with Disabilities Policy" in 2001. The policy recognizes that "people with disabilities" are "a large and neglected minority" and that libraries "play a catalytic role in the lives of people with disabilities." The ALA policy urges libraries to ensure that their library services, facilities, and collections are accessible to all. Ensuring accessibility might require remote electronic access to the catalog or reference services, extended loan periods, multiple formats for materials, assistive technologies, training for librarians on working with people with disabilities, and modifications to facilities to make sure that access to the building, parking lot, information desks, physical and digital collection, and restrooms is unimpeded (ALA (Policy) 2014).

People with disabilities have mixed perceptions of public libraries. About two-thirds perceive the facilities as accessible, a slight majority believes that the library has sufficient materials for them, and about the same proportion think the library has sufficient assistive devices (Burke 2009). These findings suggest that libraries are not doing enough. Lewis (2013) suggested several ways libraries can improve their services to the disability community, including improved communication on what services are available, ensuring that assistive technologies are easily available and well-maintained, and that all staff are appropriately trained on them, surveying or otherwise asking the disability community directly about its information needs, providing inclusive programming (e.g., book discussion groups using alternative formats amenable to people with disabilities), and engaging in community outreach. The ultimate goal is universal access through universal design of library resources. Universal design means that "rather than design your services and facility for the average user, you design them for people with a broad range of abilities and disabilities" (Do-It 2014). As Lewis (2013) observed,

> Remarkable advances in technology have made it possible for individuals with disabilities to independently access information they want and need. Individuals with disabilities have always wanted the same access to information that their family members and friends have at libraries. Now, because of adaptive technology, the Internet, and e-books, they know they can get more from our libraries. Individuals with disabilities are hungry for more information, and they deserve to get it. (p. 230)

vi. Services to Native Americans (Tribal Libraries)

Tribal libraries, although unique in many ways, are best understood as public libraries. In serving their constituents they face many of the same challenges experienced by other public libraries, in addition to several distinct issues (ATALM 2014). The Association of Tribal Archives, Libraries, & Museums (ATALM), a native-led advocate for tribal libraries described some of their distinguishing features and the issues that confront them:

- Tribal libraries do not have the same funding sources as public libraries . . . Tribal libraries are funded primarily through the Institute of Museum and Library Services and tribal governments.

- When all sources of funding are considered, it is estimated that tribal libraries, on average receive less than $3 per capita per year. In contrast, public libraries receive an average of $45 per capita.

- Tribal libraries often are not eligible to receive services from state library agencies.

- Tribal libraries generally serve large and geographically diverse areas, some of which are as large as many states.

- Tribal libraries often are incorporated into council houses, schools, tribal government complexes, and other facilities that serve community needs. They are not always dedicated stand-alone facilities, but are located in areas that are most accessible to tribal citizens.

- Locations may be in remote areas where access to training and resources, including Internet access, are not readily available.

- Tribal libraries' collections may include sacred materials to which culturally appropriate access must be assured. These materials are in addition to public access materials that are available to everyone.

- Staff members of tribal libraries are often knowledgeable "culture keepers," but may have limited experience or professional training in traditional library sciences.

- Tribal libraries are responsible for addressing needs not traditionally associated with public libraries (for example, the preservation of a tribe's language and life ways). (ATALM 2014, pp. 3–4)

Among the most prominent challenges for tribal library services are their underfunding, and the great distances people must travel to receive service. Technological issues are particularly problematic. A recent study on digital access in tribal libraries by ATALM and the Institute for Museum and Library Services (2014a) revealed a variety of troubling findings including the following:

- At least 40% of tribal libraries did not have broadband Internet connection—the actual figure might be as high as 89%.

- Only 89% of tribal libraries offered Internet access, and only 86% provided public computer workstations, compared to 100% of public libraries.

- Only 68% of tribal libraries provided Wi-Fi, compared to nine in ten rural public libraries.

- Three-quarters of public libraries offered e-books, compared to 36% in tribal libraries; only 11% offered remote e-book access.

- Nearly all rural public libraries offered licensed access to electronic databases; less than half of tribal libraries provided such access.

- Almost 90% of public libraries offered some type of technology training, compared to 42% in tribal libraries.

- Only a third of tribal libraries had a website, and only 45% had a Facebook presence, compared to nearly two-thirds of rural public libraries.

Contributing to these significant disparities in technology and technological access, only 15% of tribal libraries participated in the E-Rate program, a primary means of federal subsidy to help public libraries connect to the Internet. As of 2013, fewer than half had even heard of E-Rate funding (ATALM 2014, 2014a).

Despite these disadvantages, tribal libraries make a difference. Given the considerable poverty of many tribal citizens, it is not surprising that nearly

20% of tribal library users had no broadband access at home, others had poor access, and nearly a third had no free Wi-Fi access within a ten-mile radius of their home. But it is also clear that tribal libraries require additional broadband access, trained staff, and funding for equipment, software, and database access (ATALM 2014a).

vii. Services to Children and Youth

a. Services to Children

Providing service to young people remains an important library role. Although there are many reasons for this, of primary importance is the promotion of reading and literacy. When Americans are asked about the role of the public library, one of their highest priorities is providing library services to children and encouraging literacy (Swan et al. 2014). Pew (Miller et al. 2013) found that 94% of parents felt that "libraries are important for their children" and 79% said it was "very important." Further, 84% of these parents said the library was important because "libraries help inculcate their children's love of reading and books" and 81% said because "libraries provide their children with information and resources not available at home." Such findings are a clear indication of the centrality of the public library in the educational lives of children. In fact, there is strong evidence that exposure to reading even in the very early years of a child's life has a substantial effect on the subsequent cognitive development of a child; strong reading skills have significant impact on a child's success in school and in life.

In addition to providing reading materials, public libraries provide many more services and resources, such as answering parents' reference questions, helping to locate and recommend age-appropriate reading, and providing programs, including story hours, homework support, and makerspaces for teens. Children's materials represent nearly 35% of total circulation, a percentage that has remained stable over the last ten years (ALA 2014). Similarly, attendance at children's programs accounts for 70% of all library program attendance; this is logical because 60% of all programs are designed for children and 9% for teens (Swan et al. 2014). Youth use of the Internet in libraries is difficult to document. One survey by Pew (Zickuhr et al. 2013) found that 39% of the respondents 16–17 years of age who had used the library in the last twelve months had used a computer, the Internet, or the Wi-Fi provided by the library. According to one Pew study (Miller et al. 2013) 70% of parents indicated that their child had visited the library in the last twelve months. It is informative to discern the reasons:

- 87% visited the library to *borrow books*
- 55% went to do *school work*—77% of youth ages 12–17
- 46% went to *borrow DVDs or CDs*
- 46% went to *attend a library event*—53% of children under age 12
- 37% went to *use the Internet*—43% of youth ages 12–17
- 37% went to *socialize with their friends*
- 32% went to a *library-sponsored book club or program* (pp. 3–4)

Although traditional book borrowing and school work were the most common, it is also clear that events, Internet use, and opportunities for socialization are also important. A complementary finding of the above study was that the library benefits from increased parent engagement when their children use the library. Parents browse shelves, borrow books, attend library classes or events, borrow DVD/CDs, use the library computer and Internet, borrow e-books, and use new library services (e.g., online reference) at substantially greater percentages than other adults. Library services for children will continue to grow and engage young people and their parents.

b. Outreach to Very Young Children

The changing U.S. family structure has resulted in increased numbers of working parents and a proliferation of day care and preschool programs. Children's and YA librarians collaborate with schools, Head Start programs, day care centers, and other organizations serving very young children. Many develop special library programs for infants (lap-sit programs), toddlers, and students in preschools. Some libraries also prepare kits of print materials, AV materials, and lists of appropriate websites that can be borrowed by groups serving children at remote sites. Some public libraries send their librarians into these establishments to provide programs. Although clearly important, this type of outreach is costly in terms of personnel and time. Nonetheless, children's need for library materials is critical. If children cannot come to the library, many librarians have committed to take materials and services to them.

Underlying this attention to the youngest children is the concept of emergent literacy. Historically, studies on reading tended to focus on children in the early years of schooling. We now know that a child's reading habits are affected by experiences from birth; the ability to read has its origins in a child's early nonverbal and verbal interactions with others and the environment. Early experiences with language and books build the foundation for literacy skills (Stratton 1996). Informal literacy activities, even as an observer, can have substantial effects on the development of reading skills. Justice and Kaderavek (2002) found that children acquire literacy skills at different rates. For example, it is not surprising that children with disabilities such as autism or other mental impairments experience delays in acquiring literacy skills. Others at risk are children in poverty, those with limited English proficiency, and those with limited access to literacy materials.

Byrnes, Deerr, and Kropp (2003) suggested four critical services that public libraries can provide to develop literacy skills: "age-appropriate spaces, materials, programming, and the opportunity for parents to gain skills through modeling" (p. 42). In addition to modeling, librarians also help them better utilize the library's resources and encourage them to read to their children at home, incorporating such activities as reciting and singing nursery rhymes together.

In response to the recognition of the importance of emergent literacy, the ALA and the Public Library Association (PLA) created in 2004 the "Every Child Ready to Read @ Your Library program. Early literacy programming requires the cooperation, and often the presence, of a parent or caregiver. And this program is an outreach literacy program intended to provide support for parents and caregivers. It focuses on at-risk families or families who are not likely to come to the public library. The program encourages adults to engage their children in five practices: singing, talking, reading, writing, and playing and provides resources to implement these practices in the home (ALA (Every Child) 2014).

c. Outreach to Teens

Attracting teens to the library can be challenging, but their use is greater than one might think. Individuals between 14–24 make up 25% of all public library users, and nearly three in four teens between 16–17 used the public library in 2012 (Braun et al. 2013). As noted above, teens use the library to accomplish school-related activities, explore personal interests or hobbies, maintain social relationships, or access the Internet. Factors that can inhibit attendance include poor relationships with library staff, lack of comfortable places to sit, inadequate technology, or poorly designed websites. Some adolescents find the organization of the collection confusing. Some are unaware of the library's services and programs (Howard 2011). Young adult (YA) librarians reach out to youth in a variety of ways. As of 2012, 82% of American public libraries offered specialized YA services, 65% dedicated parts of their websites to young adults, and 40% had Facebook pages specifically designed for teens (Agosto 2013).

The challenges for public libraries to adapt to the needs of teens are considerable for a variety of reasons. Teens reflect the growing diversity of the population in general: there are increasing numbers of children of color and significant numbers of children are from immigrant families. In addition, many teens face social challenges: many come from families with poverty level incomes, have dropped out of school, are homeless, or suffer from depression or violence. But they are also tech-savvy, deeply engaged in social networking and expect 24/7 digital services from a responsive librarian (Braun et al. 2013).

Gaming is a particularly interesting growth area in YA services. An increasing number of libraries now offer services to gamers, including special events or gaming tournaments (Levine 2006). Some libraries incorporate video games into summer reading programs or community programming, while others offer dedicated gaming workstations and MMPOGs (massively multiplayer online games) (Ward-Crixell 2007; Levine 2006). Although aimed primarily at young people, gaming crosses many socioeconomic and demographic categories. For example, a large number of individuals who play games online, especially word and puzzle games, are women over the age of 40. In fact, women make up 38% of all gamers, a larger fraction than teenage boys, who make up 30%. Similarly, some libraries are attracting older adults to their libraries to play Wii or other electronic games using teens as coaches (Lipschultz 2009). Nicholson reported that 80% of public libraries permitted patrons to play games on library computers, 20% of libraries circulated games, and 40% used in-house gaming programs (Nicholson 2007).

With the increasing sophistication and collaborative nature of electronic games, educators and sociologists have investigated the effects of gaming on young people. Although there is some evidence that repeated use of violent video games can have an adverse effect on behavior, it is important to remember that 85% of all games are appropriate for children under 17 (Levine 2009). In addition, numerous studies (Levine 2006, 2009) found that games offered a variety of benefits including the following:

- stimulate problem-solving skills
- facilitate learning
- provide fields for practice of leadership and team skills
- allow teens to try on roles and behaviors in a safe environment
- improve visual/spatial skills
- provide a source of self-esteem and self-confidence
- provide practice in planning and anticipating consequences

In addition, Faris (2007) observed that gaming promotes literacy skills by helping preschool children acquire pre-reading skills and older children acquire logic skills, including hypothesis testing. Because some games require teamwork and a community, some believe that gaming creates a "participatory culture." Games "break down barriers between the library and community and make the library a welcoming place for a whole new group of users" (Ward-Crixell 2007, p. 38).

In November 2009, ALA launched its first National Gaming Day @ Your Library. Libraries across the country offered a variety of games, including modern board games, traditional games such as chess and checkers, and two national video game tournaments. Fifteen hundred libraries participated. The annual games attracted international interest, and in 2012 it evolved into the International Games Day @ Your Library. From the program's inception, over a six-year period, more than 132,000 individuals from 7,400 libraries and 43 countries have participated (ALA (News) 2010; ALA (International Gaming) 2014).

Although some believe that gaming diverts attention from the basic mission of libraries, there is little doubt that young people find gaming attractive and that it is likely to grow in the future:

> Playing games in today's public and school libraries is a profoundly social experience for library patrons both young and old. . . . What matters is the opportunity for play, a willingness to learn, the supportive presence of experts and novices, and the library as the setting for learning, playing, and gaming. (Lipschultz 2009, p. 40)

The opportunities for public libraries to serve teens are many and varied. Braun et al. (2013) note that libraries can encourage the development of multiple literacies helping students to think critically, use digital resources and media effectively. They can also serve as safe places to go after school or during the summer, provide an informal learning environment that builds on their own interests, provide workforce training, and connect teens with other community agencies. Interestingly, the space allocated for teens and the quality and types of services provided to them are related to some extent by the amount of participation teens have in the design of library spaces for them. Similarly, the greater the participation of teens, the fewer the subsequent behavioral problems (Bernier, Males, and Rickman 2014).

d. Intellectual Freedom Issues, Children, and Youth

Censorship and intellectual freedom issues are often at the forefront of library services to children and young adults. With the passage of the Children's

Internet Protection Act, children's and YA librarians faced new challenges to abide by the law and still protect the information access rights of the young (see School Library Media Centers). In terms of intellectual freedom, a public library differs fundamentally from a school library in at least two important ways. First, public libraries contain a great quantity of materials primarily published or produced for adults; school libraries seldom have adult materials, except those for teachers. Second, unlike schools, public libraries do not serve *in loco parentis*, that is, in the place of the parent, although some parents and political groups want the library to act as a monitor and censor. Given ALA's policy on open access, there is considerable discussion regarding children's exposure to materials aimed at adults, which will likely increase, not only because of the increasingly graphic nature of violence and sexuality in visual and audio materials, but also because access is expanding through the Internet. The resulting political and legal tensions will require ever more vigilance on the part of LIS professionals to protect the rights of minors. To some extent, ALA has tried to accommodate the concerns of parents and other adults by establishing websites that link to numerous educational and recreational sites. The issue of censorship and intellectual freedom as it relates to children and youth is also discussed in chapter 9.

viii. Cooperation between Public Libraries and School Library Media Centers

Public libraries cooperate with numerous agencies in the community, particularly school library media centers. Cooperative programs can include class visits by public librarians, extended borrowing periods for teachers, compiling information on Web resources for teachers, coordinating public library materials to coincide with curriculum units, providing bibliographic instruction and library tours to students, and participating on education-related committees. Nonetheless, 85% of the population believes that public libraries should coordinate even more closely with local schools (Swan et al. 2014). Despite the obvious benefits, a number of factors tend to limit cooperation:

- Schools and public libraries are usually separate political subdivisions. There is often little or no administrative or board support for cooperation.
- Teachers, school librarians, and public librarians have little free time; they tend to focus their time and attention primarily on the duties within their own institutions.
- Limited fiscal resources reduce the time and staffing available for cooperation.

- Public librarians are often wary that their cooperation is being used as an inappropriate subsidy of the school budget. That is, the public library budget is being used for services that should be in the school budget.
- There is insufficient expertise to develop effective cooperation.

A recent development, although somewhat controversial, which might help stimulate cooperation is the adoption by numerous states of the Common Core State Standards (CCSS). Although these standards apply much more directly to school library media centers, they provide a significant opportunity for public libraries to enrich their own programs and collections while supporting the CCSS at the same time. For example, the CCSS emphasize nonfiction, providing a great opportunity to enhance the narrative and informational nonfiction collection of the library. Because critical thinking skills are emphasized as well, the library could consider starting a nonfiction book club (ALA (ALSC) 2012). Strong collaboration and cooperation on CCSS could enhance public libraries' reputation, support teachers as they transition to the Common Core, and improve educational opportunities for students.

Perhaps the ultimate exemplar of cooperation between schools and public libraries is the combined school–public library facility. In hard economic times, citizens want their public institutions to cooperate to maximize fiscal efficiencies. Combining libraries is, at least on the surface, attractive. There are significant advantages to students who, in one place, have librarians trained to assist them and a collection that is usually much larger than a typical school library. On the other hand, there are a number of challenges. For example, who will manage the library? How will use of the facility be determined? Who determines policies related to materials access? How are costs allocated? Who is expected to perform cataloging and processing functions? Who has priority during certain times of day? Are there two separate staffs? How will conflicts between school library and public library staff be handled (Owens 2002; Casey 2002; Blount 2002)? Despite these problems, the advantages of shared resources, expanded hours, increased economies, shared technologies, shared expertise, and potential community approbation make this a tempting alternative.

5. The Digital Public Library of America and the World Digital Library

New technologies allowed many of our libraries, archives, and museums to digitize at least parts of their collections, including books, images, audiovisual materials, documents, and other historical records. Unfortunately, accessibility was often limited by local search systems and unique interfaces, depriving others of remote access (Cohen 2014). In 2010 scholars, library leaders, foundation representatives, and others began serious discussions to create "an open, distributed network of comprehensive online resources that would draw on the nation's living heritage from libraries, universities, archives, and museums in order to educate, inform and empower everyone in the current and future generations" (DPLA 2014, n.p.). These early efforts led to the creation of the Digital Public Library of America (DPLA). DPLA was not created to replace public libraries but to provide unique opportunities to exploit the potentialities of the Internet. DPLA's mission is to

> . . . bring together the riches of America's libraries, archives, and museums, and makes them freely available to the world. It strives to contain the full breadth of human expression, from the written word, to works of art and culture, to records of America's heritage, to the efforts and data of science. DPLA aims to expand this crucial realm of openly available materials, and make those riches more easily discovered and more widely usable and used . . . (DPLA 2014, n.p.)

DPLA is less a repository of digital items than an aggregator of digital items. Participating partners, known as digital hubs, digitize their items in a standardized fashion that makes them accessible through the DPLA. The DPLA in turn aggregates the metadata assigned to these items so they are searchable and discoverable by users anywhere (Cottrell 2013). When the DPLA began on April 18, 2013, 2.4 million items were available; by the end of the year 7 million items were logged. Continued annual growth is anticipated. As of April 2014, more than 1 million unique visitors used the library. As of 2014, there were 1,200 participating partners.

Among the challenges facing DPLA are digital rights and international copyright issues; providing the necessary training to LIS professionals to make the needed connections; and sustainable funding for DPLA (Cohen 2014). Despite these challenges, there has been a tremendous growth in the interest of cultural heritage materials. People want to see the documents, photographs, moving images, books, and other materials that are part of our archives, museums, and libraries. DPLA is an important step in making such items truly available to many individual who would appreciate them, but up to now have had no opportunity to access to them.

On the international level, the LOC with the support of UNESCO has developed a similar effort—the World Digital Library (WDL). The emphasis of the library is on primary source materials of historical or cultural importance. The WDL "makes it possible to discover, study, and enjoy cultural treasures and significant historical documents on one site, in a variety of ways. Content on the WDL is provided on the Internet free of charge and includes books, manuscripts, maps, newspapers, journals, prints and photographs, sound recordings, and films" (WDL 2015). Contributing partners include libraries, museums, archives, and other cultural institutions. The digital objects are accompanied with multilingual explanations and interpretations (Oudenaren 2013).

6. Models of the Future: Four Dimensions

It is useful to conclude the discussion of public libraries by considering briefly their future character—not so much as a form of prediction, but as a glimpse of possibilities. Levien (2011) noted that public libraries are at a critical point where they must make a variety of strategic choices, and by those choices, they will create libraries placed on a continuum along four specific dimensions.

Dimension 1: Physical to Virtual Libraries. It is highly unlikely that any public library will not have any electronic access or content, but at one end might be a library that emphasizes strongly its physical place and content with a minimal Web presence. At the other end would be a library that is almost entirely virtual in which all library services are provided in a digital environment.

Dimension 2: Individual to Community Libraries. On one end of the dimension, a library might continue to focus almost entirely on service to individuals, satisfying them on a one-on-one basis. Such a library would be designed to provide maximum privacy and the staff would be oriented to serving individual needs. On the other end, the library emphasizes the needs of groups and the community-at-large. Group and community activities, events, and programs would be commonplace; meeting rooms for groups and makerspaces would be provided along with collaborative technologies. There might be frequent displays of items and materials of local interest.

Dimension 3: Collections to Creation Libraries. On one end of the continuum, a library emphasizes its traditional role as a collection of information and knowledge, virtual or physical. The collection is intended to satisfy a wide range of needs: educational, informational, recreational, and cultural. On the other end is a creation library where, as Levien puts it:

> . . . media conveying information, knowledge, art, and entertainment are created. Such a library houses a range of specialized equipment and facilities to help authors, editors, performers, and other creators prepare new works, alone, or in groups, in new or old media, for personal use or widespread distribution. (p. 5)

Dimension 4: Portal to Archive Libraries. In a portal library most of the information and knowledge gathered by the library patron are actually owned and hosted by other agencies. Although the library as a physical place might persist, it primarily contains the technologies needed to access the external sources. Library staff help people locate the appropriate gateways and resources. Such "portals" might be distributed throughout a community in offices, commercial properties, or schools. On the other end, the library possesses the content itself; emphasis might be on local materials both physical and virtual; they might collect rare materials or materials on highly specialized topics.

Levien offered a useful orientation to how we might discuss the future of public libraries. In doing so, he reminded us that there is no one way to deal with the changes faced by public libraries. By the same token, some choices might be better than others in the dynamic environment in which public libraries now exist.

7. Public Libraries: A National and International Purpose

The activities of the public library will certainly evolve as our communities and society as a whole evolve. But the many significant contributions of the public library are likely to remain. The public library has been recognized as a positive instrumental force both nationally and internationally. The national role is succinctly stated by the American Library Association's document, Declaration for the Right to Libraries (figure 3.3).

FIGURE 3.3
Declaration for the Right to Libraries

LIBRARIES CHANGE LIVES

Declaration for the Right to Libraries

In the spirit of the United States Declaration of Independence and the Universal Declaration of Human Rights, we believe that libraries are essential to a democratic society. Every day, in countless communities across our nation and the world, millions of children, students, and adults use libraries to learn, grow, and achieve their dreams. In addition to a vast array of books, computers, and other resources, library users benefit from the expert teaching and guidance of librarians and library staff to help expand their minds and open new worlds. We declare and affirm our right to quality libraries—public, school, academic, and special—and urge you to show your support by signing your name to this Declaration for the Right to Libraries.

Libraries Empower the Individual

Whether developing skills to succeed in school, looking for a job, exploring possible careers, having a baby, or planning retirement, people of all ages turn to libraries for instruction, support, and access to computers and other resources to help them lead better lives.

(cont.)

FIGURE 3.3
Declaration for the Right to Libraries (cont.)

Libraries Support Literacy and Lifelong Learning

Many children and adults learn to read at their school and public libraries via storytimes, research projects, summer reading, tutoring, and other opportunities. Others come to the library to learn the technology and information skills that help them answer their questions, discover new interests, and share their ideas with others.

Libraries Strengthen Families

Families find a comfortable, welcoming space and a wealth of resources to help them learn, grow, and play together.

Libraries Are the Great Equalizer

Libraries serve people of every age, education level, income level, ethnicity, and physical ability. For many people, libraries provide resources that they could not otherwise afford—resources they need to live, learn, work, and govern.

Libraries Build Communities

Libraries bring people together, both in person and online, to have conversations and to learn from and help each other. Libraries provide support for seniors, immigrants, and others with special needs.

Libraries Protect Our Right to Know

Our right to read, seek information, and speak freely must not be taken for granted. Libraries and librarians actively defend this most basic freedom as guaranteed by the First Amendment.

Libraries Strengthen Our Nation

The economic health and successful governance of our nation depend on people who are literate and informed. School, public, academic, and special libraries support this basic right.

Libraries Advance Research and Scholarship

Knowledge grows from knowledge. Whether doing a school assignment, seeking a cure for cancer, pursuing an academic degree, or developing a more fuel-efficient engine, scholars and researchers of all ages depend on the knowledge and expertise that libraries and librarians offer.

Libraries Help Us to Better Understand Each Other

People from all walks of life come together at libraries to discuss issues of common concern. Libraries provide programs, collections, and meeting spaces to help us share and learn from our differences.

Libraries Preserve Our Nation's Cultural Heritage

The past is key to our future. Libraries collect, digitize, and preserve original and unique historical documents that help us to better understand our past, present, and future.

While the history of public libraries in the U.S. is a long one, the promotion of public libraries on an international level is much more recent. Much of the impetus for worldwide public library development stems from the efforts of United Nations Educational, Scientific and Cultural Organization (UNESCO) beginning around 1950. At that time, the public library was seen as a way to promote peace, mutual understanding, and democracy through popular education. Over the years, UNESCO has worked with the International Federation of Library Associations and Institutions (IFLA) on a variety of projects (Laugesen 2014). UNESCO and IFLA jointly recognize the critical role that public libraries play around the world in its "Public Library Manifesto" (Appendix D) which states in part,

> This Manifesto proclaims UNESCO's belief in the public library as a living force for education, culture and information, and as an essential agent for the fostering of peace and spiritual welfare through the minds of men and women. (IFLA 2012, p. 1)

B. School Library Media Centers

School library media centers (SLMCs) in the United States have nineteenth-century origins, but few existed until the twentieth century when the National Education Association's (NEA) Committee on Library Organization and Equipment published the first standards for junior and senior high schools in the early 1920s (Woolls 1994). In 1925 NEA created standards for elementary schools. The first comprehensive standards for K–12 were published in 1945 (Brodie 1998). Major improvements in American school libraries occurred after the Soviet Union launched the Sputnik satellite in 1957. This event triggered considerable social and political upheaval as Americans feared they would fall behind their cold war adversary. In response, the federal government increased funding for elementary and secondary education, especially to improve curricula and teacher training. For example, the National Defense Education Act of 1958 was intended to strengthen mathematics and science. Title III of the act provided money for books, other print materials, and AV materials. Later changes to Title III provided funding for equipment in school libraries. Political support for education continued well into the 1960s, resulting in the passage of the Elementary and Secondary Education Act in 1965, which provided additional funding for materials for schools and libraries. At the same time, standards for SLMCs were updated to emphasize the importance of a strong collection and resulted in increased materials, particularly in AV formats (Brodie 1998).

Ninety-seven percent of Americans believe that "school library programs are an essential part of the education experience because they provide resources to students and teachers." Similarly, 96% believe that school libraries are important "because they give every child the opportunity to read and learn" (ALA 2009, p. 4). Today, there are an estimated 116,000 K–12 schools in the United States; of which approximately 73% are traditional public schools, 4% are public charter schools and 23% are private schools. There are approximately 90,000 public schools and more than 81,000 SLMCs.

The following data are for public schools; there is little current data on private schools (ALA "State of" 2014; Bitterman, Gray, and Goldring 2013; Bitterman and Goldring 2013). The average size of the book collection in SLMCs is a little over 12,700 titles, with much smaller AV collections, less than 500 items. The average school library spends about $12,000 on books and an additional $2,500–$3,000 on periodicals, database licensing, and software. SLMCs are bureaucratically embedded in their school systems, and the school board's policies ultimately govern their activities. Although board members seldom supervise or control libraries, they often become involved when there are complaints about materials.

The size of the school library workforce is considerable: more than 88,000 school librarians or state certified library media specialists and 55,000 library media center aides or clerical staff. Most workers are concentrated in the primary grades and in cities and suburbs. Only 28% of school librarians are employed in rural areas. Among the professional staff, more than half have a master's degree in librarianship or closely related field, and 83% were certified as library media specialists by their state; 63% were certified classroom teachers. Two-thirds of SLMCs have at least one full-time person who is state certified, although one in five school libraries have no full- or part-time certified school librarian.

The degree of autonomy and authority of SLMC librarians varies greatly. In some cases, a school librarian exercises considerable autonomy, but more often control and supervision often rest with a school principal or a district's curriculum director or district librarian who might be responsible for selecting or approving materials for all of the district's SLMCs. Shontz and Farmer (2007) reported that 92% of SLM specialists communicated regularly with their principals and 42% served as mentors for new teachers or other SLM personnel. In addition, 60% served on school leadership teams or educational committees at the building, district, or state level. SLMC specialists were also active in reading motivation programs, providing book talks, storytelling, and read-aloud programs, as well as popular materials such as graphic novels. SLMC specialists played major roles in crafting board policies for selecting and reevaluating library media resources, with 84% indicating that their policies had been approved.

The American Association of School Librarians (AASL) has taken an active role in shaping the character of SLMCs. The mission of an SLMC is

. . . to ensure that the students and staff are effective users of ideas and information. The school library media specialist (SLMS) empowers students to be critical thinkers, enthusiastic readers, skillful researchers, and ethical users of information. (AASL 2009a)

AASL's (2009a) publication *Empowering Learners: Guidelines for School Library Media Programs*, identified five ways that SLMCs accomplish their mission:

(1) collaborating with educators and students to design and teach engaging learning experiences that meet individual needs; (2) instructing students and assisting educators in using, evaluating, and producing information and ideas through active use of a broad range of appropriate tools, resources and information technologies; (3) providing access to materials in all formats, including up-to-date, high quality, varied literature to develop and strengthen a love of reading; (4) providing students and staff with instruction and resources that reflect current information needs and anticipate changes in technology and education; (5) providing leadership in the total education program and advocating for strong school library media programs as essential to meeting local, state, and national education goals. (p. 8)

As a companion to *Empowering Learners*, AASL issued *Standards for the 21st-Century Learner* (AASL 2014), which identified specific skills, responsibilities, and self-assessment strategies students need to be effective learners and to develop four abilities: (1) inquire, think critically, and gain knowledge, (2) draw conclusions, make informed decisions, apply knowledge to new situations, and create new knowledge (3) share knowledge and participate ethically and productively as members of our democratic society, and (4) pursue personal and aesthetic growth. The standards were based on nine beliefs:

- Reading is a window to the world.
- Inquiry provides a framework for learning.
- Ethical behavior in the use of information must be taught.
- Technology skills are crucial for future employment needs.
- Equitable access is a key component for education.
- The definition of information literacy has become more complex as resources and technologies have changed.
- The continuing expansion of information demands that all individuals acquire the thinking skills that will enable them to learn on their own.
- Learning has a social context.
- School libraries are essential to the development of learning skills.

The implications of these standards are many and varied. Among them are that school libraries need to adapt both their collections and physical facilities to new learners. The school library has evolved from books on shelves to new digital formats, from physical access to access to information on the Internet, and from locating specific information to providing mediation that promotes critical thinking skills (AASL 2014a). It also means the creation of new spaces. Libraries are no longer just shelves and tables; they are places for performances and activities, for creating class projects; for facilitating communication and self-expression; for blogging and use of other social media (AASL 2014b).

Public schools and, by extension, school library media centers face many challenges. The discussion below highlights some of these critical issues.

1. Achieving the Educational Mission of Schools

If SLMCs are to thrive, parents and taxpayers must recognize their substantial contribution to academic achievement. Too often, the SLMC is considered an expensive appendage rather than integral to the educational process. This viewpoint is especially troubling given the evidence. In one study, Lance, Welborn, and Hamilton-Pennell (1993) found that students who scored higher on norm-referenced tests tended to come from schools with larger library collections and trained librarians. In addition, high academic performance was correlated with SLMCs in which librarians served in an instructional and collaborative role. The size of the library staff and the collection were, in fact, the best predictors of academic performance, with the exception of at-risk conditions such as poverty. This study was later repeated with similar findings (Lance et al. 2000). In Ohio, Todd (2003) surveyed more than 13,000 students in grades 3–12 and interviewed more than 870 teachers. More than 90% of the students felt that the school library helped them find information, work on school topics, locate different sources of information, or find different opinions about topics. Overall, the study concluded that "an effective school library, led by a credentialed school librarian who has a clearly defined role in information-centered pedagogy, plays a critical role in facilitating student learning for building knowledge" (p. 6). A later Colorado study confirmed the significant relationship between students' advanced reading levels and the presence of state endorsed (certified) school librarians (Lance and Hofschire 2012). In addition, there appears to be a significant correlation between the number of SLMS in a SLMC and reading level; declining numbers of SLMS were negatively correlated with poorer reading scores. These findings highlight the need for school librarians to regularly communicate and cooperate with teachers, principals, and administrators. By demonstrating the library's ability to contribute to the school's mission, greater political and fiscal support is more likely to follow.

2. The Common Core

The Common Core State Standards (CCSS), known more popularly as "The Common Core," are a "set of clear college- and career-ready standards for kindergarten through 12th grade in English language arts/literacy and mathematics" (Common Core, p. 1). Governors and education commissioners initiated the development of the standards, and several organizations including the National Governors Association Center for Best Practices and the Council of Chief State School Officers pushed for their adoption. The initiative was stimulated, in part, by the fact that many students entering college required remedial attention before taking regular college courses. Input into creating the standards was broad-based including teachers, administrators, parents, and national experts.

Similar to traditional standards, the CCSS established learning goals and indicated what students should be able to do in each of the content areas. However, whereas traditional standards focused on high school completion; the Common Core standards implied that students should be *ready* to enter college or career. The intent was to set high standards that could be consistently applied nationwide so that all students had similar skills and the knowledge needed for academic, career, and life success. Common standards also provided an opportunity to produce common texts and other digital resources, evaluation systems, and instructional and teacher support tools (Common Core 2013). Although meant for all American students, adoption and implementation resided at the state and local level. As of 2014, 43 states voluntarily adopted the standards and are engaged in implementing them (Common Core 2013).

With the development of the CCSS, AASL recognized the need for library media specialists to integrate their own standards into those of the Common Core. To accomplish this, AASL created a "Standards Crosswalk." The Crosswalk identified each of the AASL standards and mapped them to the Common Core standards in the areas of English language arts; and reading and writing standards for literacy in history/social studies, science, technical subjects, and mathematics (AASL 2014a).

School library media specialists can play a significant role in implementing the CCSS in their schools using a three-step process recommended by AASL: understand the standards, create a plan, and act on the plan. Schools adopting the CCSS might need to reconceptualize the library's space and rethink how they use it. Merely providing a larger collection and more computers is not enough; the school library will need to evolve and SLMSs will need to actively participate in the following activities:

- building reading, writing, speaking, and listening skills together across the curriculum
- building appreciation of the best literature and informational materials together across the curriculum as part of a literate culture
- creating a school-wide participatory culture
- building co-taught research projects in blended learning experiences
- promoting interdisciplinary real-world problems, projects, and learning experiences that take advantage of rich information resources and useful technology tools
- using technology to boost teaching and learning together
- creating cultural experience across the school, community, and across the world
- fostering creativity, innovation, play, building, and experimentation
- assessing the results of collaborative learning experiences
- managing the integration of classroom, school library learning commons, and technology tools (AASL "Implementing . . . ," p. 12)

Pursued collaboratively with teachers and school administrators, the Common Core presents a great opportunity for school librarians to play a critical role in materially improving student achievement.

3. Information Technologies and Information Literacy

The technology available in SLMCs varies widely but generally includes automated circulation systems (90%), automated catalogs (88%), and DVDs and VCRs (83%). Most school libraries provide laptops for staff (54%) and students (40%). Only 31% have assistive technology for those with disabilities. On average, SLMCs have 17 computer workstations with Internet access although suburban schools, high schools, and schools with large enrollments can have more (Bitterman and Goldring 2013). School libraries face the same issues as public libraries in trying to maintain traditional services while budgeting for new technologies and access to digital content. This problem is exacerbated by the public's reluctance to support additional taxes for schools, and school boards' and administrators' tendency to allocate resources to the classroom rather than the SLMC. Nonetheless, with the increased use of technologies, generally, there is a clear need to teach students how to locate and evaluate valid information. Although students born after 1990 (Generation Z) tend to be technology savvy because they grew up with Web browsers, wireless access, video games, and multitasking wireless devices, this does not mean that they know how to access information efficiently or evaluate it critically. The new AASL *Standards for the 21st-Century Learner* (2014) integrates computer literacy into its broader standards. Among the specific technologically oriented standards are the following:

1.1.8   Demonstrate mastery of technology tools for accessing information and pursuing inquiry.

1.3.5   Use information technology responsibly.

2.1.4   Use technology and other information tools to analyze and organize information.

2.1.6   Use the writing process, media and visual literacy, and technology skills to create products that express new understandings.

3.1.4   Use technology and other information tools to organize and display knowledge and understanding in ways that others can view, use, and assess.

3.1.6   Use information and technology ethically and responsibly.

4.1.7   Use social networks and information tools to gather and share information.

4.3.1   Participate in the social exchange of ideas, both electronically and in person.

4.3.4   Practice safe and ethical behaviors in personal electronic communication and interaction.

These ambitious standards must be seen in the broader context of creating lifelong learners, and meeting them implies that the traditional role of the SLMC librarian will continue to evolve. Ideally, SLMCs will play a crucial role as Johnston (2012) noted:

> Technology integration is the seamless infusion of technology as a resource to enhance the learning in the content areas. School librarians have a vital role to play in integrating technology to help students develop 21st-century skills to enable them to use technology as a tool for learning and ensure they are prepared to succeed and participate [in] a digital society. (p. 2)

Success in this role means that librarians must be strong advocates for students and believe that they can make a difference (Johnston 2012). Johnston found that the single most important factor for success was having a supportive principal. Other factors included supportive teaching colleagues, an institution that facilitated staff leadership, and opportunities for professional development. Barriers included resistance from instructional technology staff who perceived competition, lack of time, and failure of teachers to perceive the school librarian as competent to fulfill this role. If SLMC librarians want to be seen as critical resources for student academic success, they must be familiar with new technologies and their value to the educational process, and they must be active participants with their teaching colleagues.

4. Diminished Funding, Diminished Staffing

Federal aid to education diminished in the first decades of the twenty-first century. State funding levels for schools, which comprise approximately 44% of total education spending, as well as funding support from property taxes, experienced similar declines. Adding to these financial strains were the increased costs of technology and general operational expenses (Leachman and Mai 2014). In tough financial times, not surprisingly, school administrators are reluctant to reduce teaching staff but as a consequence, SLMCs often become a target for budget cuts. The financial impact on SLMCs has been considerable: the total number of school librarians has declined by at least 1% annually since 2008 and in 2011 the number declined more than 4%. (ALA "State of" 2014). As noted above, the disturbing result of eliminating trained LIS professionals and reducing the size of the SLMC is likely to be lower levels of student achievement (Lance and Hofschire 2012). Barbara Stripling, the 2014 President of ALA characterized the irony well:

> On the one hand, budget and testing pressures have led to decisions to de-professionalize or eliminate school libraries. On the other hand, the increased emphasis on college and career readiness and the integration of technology have opened an unprecedented door to school librarian leadership (Stripling, 2014, p. 9).

In the current political and economic climate, SLMCs will need to take a more active role in the life of their schools, join forces through their advocacy organizations, and regularly communicate their worth to their colleagues, parents, and taxpayers.

5. Censorship

Few issues in librarianship generate so much heat and so little light as censorship. A more detailed discussion of general censorship issues can be found in chapter 9 on intellectual freedom. Generally we believe that parents have an obligation to protect children and adolescents from unhealthy and corrupting influences. Similarly, by law, schools serve *in loco parentis*, in the place of the parents, and therefore have a special duty to ensure their students' safety, both physical and emotional. However, there are often two conflicting issues that arise regarding censorship attempts in schools. The first issue involves differences in how people view the purpose of schools and the role of SLMCs; and the second concerns the rights and powers of school boards versus the rights of students and parents. Both of these issues have been disputed in court for years, but with often unclear or contradictory outcomes.

a. The Purpose of Schools and the Role of School Library Media Centers

How one defines the purpose of schools profoundly affects how one perceives the role of SLMCs. There are two fundamentally different viewpoints. Some people believe that schools should inculcate particular values. These individuals believe that students should not be exposed to unorthodox points of view unless such exposure occurs under tightly controlled conditions to ensure that the views are not mistakenly understood as acceptable or reasonable. This perspective would require that SLMCs restrict the materials in the collection to only those that promulgate the accepted values or that access to unorthodox materials would be highly controlled. An alternative perspective believes that schools should teach students to think critically, expose them to many ideas, and develop students' judgment skills. From this perspective, the role of the SLMC is to contain materials reflecting many perspectives, some unorthodox as well as orthodox, and the librarian's role would be less supervisory and controlling. Access might be guided, but unrestricted. These two views have been painted here as polar opposites, although there are certainly many gradations between them. For example, all schools promulgate values, and all try to get students to think, more or less. But beliefs about its primary purpose are likely to affect attitudes toward the role of the SLMC, particularly when books about suicide, revolution, or sexuality are part of the collection.

Yet a third perspective is to believe that the function of the school is different from that of the SLMC. One might argue, for example, that it is appropriate for schools to inculcate certain values while also believing that the SLMC's purpose is different. Within this framework, the SLMC serves as a special forum, where many different, even controversial and subversive, ideas might be considered. Obviously, if the library is a special forum for ideas, its collection would be more catholic in perspective, no matter what the defined purpose of the classroom.

b. The Rights of School Boards, Students, and Parents

In general, states have delegated considerable authority to local school boards to establish policies, hire teachers, approve curricula, and select materials. From time to time, school boards discover that some materials in the SLMC are unacceptable to some parents. Problems usually arise when parents complain but objections can also come from principals, teachers, students, or school board members themselves. Many boards respond to these complaints by restricting access or discarding the disputed material. Such actions, in the absence of formal policies regarding selection or reconsideration of disputed materials, do not resolve the problem, however. Although the rights of young people might be less than those of adults, the courts have recognized that minors retain First Amendment and due-process rights. As one court decision noted:

> A library is a storehouse of knowledge. When created for a public school it is an important privilege created by the state for the benefit of the students in the school. That privilege is not subject to being withdrawn by succeeding school boards whose members might desire to "winnow" the library for books the content of which occasioned their displeasure or disapproval. (*Minarcini v. Strongsville City School District* 1977)

One of the most important SLMC cases was brought by a student, Stephen Pico (Board of Education 1982). We cannot review all the details of *Island Trees* vs. *Pico* here, although this Supreme Court case illustrates some of the key issues surrounding censorship issues in schools. In the *Island Trees* case, the Supreme Court decided that school board members "possess significant discretion to determine the content of their school libraries" but they cannot exercise that discretion in a "narrowly partisan or political manner" (*Board of Education* 1982, p. B3922). In other words, a school board violates the constitutional rights of students when they attempt to restrict access to ideas just because the board doesn't like those ideas. At the same time, the Court left open the possibility that a school board could remove materials that were "pervasively vulgar" or educationally unsuitable, if they followed a well-structured procedure to review and evaluate those materials. This case highlights the dynamic tension between the rights of school boards to run a community's schools and the rights of citizens, including young people, to First Amendment and due-process protection. Coupled with conflicting views on the role of schools and SLMCs, this tension will likely ensure that these issues will arise again and again, particularly as SLMCs provide students with greater access to the Internet. The challenges of protecting the intellectual freedom of students in schools are increased further because school districts have reduced or eliminated school librarian positions. In their absence, it is not likely that library assistants or volunteers will be able to resist censorship attempts or articulate succinctly the professional principles that underlie that resistance (Adams 2011).

C. Academic Libraries

Academic libraries have existed in the United States since the seventeenth century, beginning with the library at Harvard. By 1792, nine colonial colleges had libraries, though the collections were quite small due to the emphasis on religion, rhetoric, and the classics which required little library study (Jones 1989). Well into the nineteenth century, academic collections were too small to require a separate structure and there was little linkage between the library collection and academic instruction. In fact, many professors, academic departments, and college debating societies often maintained their own collections which were superior to those of the academic library (Jones 1989). It wasn't until the latter half of the nineteenth century that academic libraries began to prosper, following a shift away from the classical model of education toward education emphasizing professional and technical training; and the physical and social sciences. This change was heavily influenced by industrialization and the German model of the university, which identified research as a central function. As more American universities adopted this model, the library grew in status; it was a logical place to centralize research collections and provide a place for study.

Following the passage of the GI Bill after World War II, academic libraries grew and flourished at universities, four-year colleges, and community and junior colleges. The GI Bill allowed nearly 12 million veterans to attend institutions of higher education, some of whom went on to graduate programs in the 1960s, when research libraries became the hub of academic life (Churchwell 2007). Other factors that contributed to expansion included the use of universities to conduct military research; the reaction to Sputnik and the cold war in the 1960s; and the higher education initiatives of the Kennedy administration which provided an infusion of funds for the necessary facilities and equipment to educate millions of baby boom students. The combination of these factors resulted in significant growth in library collections and reference, cataloging, and acquisition departments. It also led to the development of separate graduate and undergraduate libraries, increases in subject departments, the creation of a collection development office, and the development of area studies departments specializing in specific regions such as the Middle East, Africa, Eastern Europe, and Asia. Over the years, support for academic libraries also came from the American Library Association and its divisions, the Association of College and Research Libraries, and the Association of Research Libraries.

Like SLMCs, the academic library does not have an independent purpose; its functions reflect the mission of the host institution. Major university libraries, for example, tend to serve research and graduate programs. While supporting undergraduate programs, much of the library's financial resources are devoted to research journals, special collections, rare materials, dissertations and theses, data sets, and monographs. Four-year liberal arts colleges, on the other hand, tend to emphasize teaching and a well-rounded undergraduate education, and the libraries' collections provide curricular support primarily. Insofar as the college expects research and publication from its faculty, the library provides access to appropriate research resources, but the bulk of the funding supports teaching. Community and junior colleges devote almost all of their energies to teaching and continuing education, and their collections and services reflect this emphasis.

Recent data compiled by the National Center for Educational Statistics for fiscal year 2012 provide an overview of academic libraries:

- There were slightly less than 85,000 full-time staff (FTE) working in academic libraries, 26,600 of which were librarians, 7,800 were other professional staff, and another 50,000 were support staff and student assistants.

- Approximately 2,000 libraries had expenditures under half a million dollars; more than 1,000 had expenditures above $1 million. Salaries and wages accounted for 49% of expenditures, approximately $3.4 billion. Information resources accounted for $2.8 billion, half of which went to electronic serial subscriptions. An additional $123 million paid for bibliographic utilities, networks, and consortia.

- More than one billion volumes are held by academic libraries as a whole, 60% of which is in public institutions; 223 libraries had more than a million volumes.

- Academic libraries added more than 52 million e-books in 2012 with total e-book holdings exceeding 250 million.

- There were more than 22 million visits to the library in a typical week; two-thirds of those visits were in public institutions.

- Academic libraries' general circulation approached 117 million items, public institutions accounting for 64% of the total. Institutions with 5,000 or more FTE accounted for 72%; institutions with 20,000 or more accounted for 38%. More than 10 million items were interlibrary loaned overall.

- In terms of providing information or otherwise assisting individuals, there were more than 28 million information contacts during the year.

- Seventy-seven percent reported providing library reference service by e-mail or the Web. One-quarter of academic libraries use short message services or text messaging (Phan et al. 2014).

Despite what appears to be robust activity, this brief statistical snapshot does not begin to describe the changing realities of academic libraries today. Consider just three observations:

> Research libraries have entered an era of discontinuous change—a time when the accumulated assets of the past do not guarantee future success. (Calhoun 2013, p. 143)

> The environment of the second decade of the 21st century is changing so rapidly that it seems as if higher education has been struck by a fast-moving tsunami filled with obstacles as well as with potentials, a tsunami that is striking so forcefully and so quickly that often it is difficult to find safe ground for an opportunity to reflect on what being in that storm of whirling ideas and concepts might mean for us in the future. (Kaufman 2012, p. 54)

> Shifts in the higher education environment continue to have an impact on libraries in terms of collection/content development, access to and curation of new and legacy resources, and service for extended audiences. As parent institutions redefine themselves, libraries must evolve and continue to demonstrate value in terms of contributions to the effectiveness of their parent institution. (Association of College and Research Libraries 2013, p. 2)

As noted in our discussions of other libraries, the changes affecting academic libraries are part and parcel of much broader changes occurring in the information environment and in higher education as a whole. Academic libraries can no longer rely on the practices of the past to ensure their continuation in the future. The list below illustrates just a few of the issues affecting higher education and academic libraries:

- increasing costs of scholarly publications and a growing interest in open-access resources and local digital depositories
- a focus on retention of students to preserve and protect the fiscal stability of the institution, including activities that improve student achievement, redesigns in spaces such as the learning commons, enriched information-literacy programs, a computer interface, and a catalog that provides one-stop access
- an ever-increasing emphasis on access to digital collections and resources, including e-books and remote access through a variety of digital devices; the attendant increases in costs and legal entanglements because of copyright issues will place new fiscal burdens on the library.

- a decreasing emphasis on physical book and journal collections with concomitant concern that large print collections are underutilized and not cost-effective
- the decreasing use of the traditional desk reference function
- the expectation that academic libraries, like other non-revenue-generating parts of the academic institution, demonstrate that their value is greater than their cost
- the growth of online courses and curricula that create new demands for online access to resources with concomitant need for monitoring copyright and intellectual property rights
- the changing expectations of the role of the librarian and increased emphasis on providing personalized services to faculty, departments, and students
- greater collaborations with outside agencies and institutions to improve productivity and reduce redundancy of services and collections

The complexity and number of issues facing academic librarianship are great, and it is not possible to address them all here, but below is a brief discussion of some major challenges and opportunities.

1. The Crisis in Scholarly Publishing

As noted earlier, there were tremendous increases in federal support to higher education in the 1960s to ensure American scholars and researchers could compete in the international arena. There was also an explosion of scholarly and scientific publication in academic journals, the backbone of research. By the end of the twentieth century, however, the majority of scholarly journals were owned by commercial publishers and in some cases, especially in the areas of science, technology, and medicine, a very small number of publishers. The resultant monopoly led to substantial, repeated hikes in subscription costs, often as large as 10% annually. The strain on the budgets of academic libraries was significant and monies shifted to periodicals resulted in declining budgets for books and other monographs. By the end of the twentieth century, this situation, popularly known as the "crisis in scholarly publishing," was intolerable (Yiotis 2005).

The Association of Research Libraries, Johns Hopkins University, Indiana University, Pennsylvania State University, and numerous other research and academic institutions met in March 2000 to discuss the crisis. Concluding that the current

FIGURE 3.4
ARL's Principles for Emerging Systems of Scholarly Publishing

1. The costs to the academy of published research should be contained so that access to relevant research publications for faculty and students can be maintained and even expanded. Members of the university community should collaborate to develop strategies that further this end. Faculty participation is essential to the success of this process.

2. Electronic capabilities should be used, among other things, to provide wide access to scholarship, encourage interdisciplinary research, and enhance interoperability and searchability. Development of common standards will be particularly important in the electronic environment.

3. Scholarly publications must be archived in a secure manner so as to remain permanently available, and in the case of electronic works, a permanent identifier for citation and linking should be provided.

4. The system of scholarly publication must continue to include processes for evaluating the quality of scholarly work, and every publication should provide the reader with information about evaluation the work has undergone.

5. The academic community embraces the concepts of copyright and fair use and seeks a balance in the interest of owners and users in the digital environment. Universities, colleges, and especially their faculties should manage copyright and its limitations and exceptions in a manner that assures the faculty access to and use of their own published works in their research and teaching.

6. In negotiating publishing agreements, faculty should assign the rights to their work in a manner that promotes the ready use of their work and choose journals that support the goal of making scholarly publications available at reasonable cost.

7. The time from submission to publication should be reduced in a manner consistent with the requirements for quality control.

8. To ensure quality and reduce proliferation of publications, the evaluation of faculty should place a greater emphasis on quality of publications and a reduced emphasis on quantity.

9. In electronic as well as print environments, scholars and students should be assured privacy with regard to their use of materials.

system was simply too costly, they produced nine Principles for Emerging Systems of Scholarly Publishing (Case 2010). These principles (figure 3.4) go beyond the fiscal issues to examine the entire process of evaluating and refereeing scholarly works, preservation issues, the assignment of publishing rights, and individual privacy rights.

a. Demand for Open Access (A Response to the Crisis in Scholarly Publishing)

One response to the crisis in scholarly publication was open access (OA). OA "refers to full-text scholarly articles made completely free and unrestricted to all users to read, copy, download, and distribute over the World Wide Web" (Schmidt et al. 2005, p. 407). An underlying principle of OA is that scholarly research is a public good that should be shared unfettered by economic or intellectual property constraints.

OA is usually achieved in two ways: self-archiving or publishing in open-access journals. When self-archiving, scholars place their refereed articles in open electronic archives and configure them so they are easily searched. Open-access journals are either new journals specifically designed for OA or existing journals willing to make the transition to OA (Bailey 2007).

There are three basic models for providing open access:

Green open access: An article is published by a conventional subscription journal, and a copy is archived in a freely accessible source, usually an institutional repository.

Gold open access: An article is published in a conventional journal but is available freely; either the journal makes all articles OA, or just allows access to some without subscription (this, of course, is only possible in a digital environment). Authors of articles are charged for publication.

Platinum open access: Articles are published in fully open-access journals, with no charge to the author (Bawden and Robinson 2014, p. 220).

One major force promoting OA in academia is the Scholarly Publishing and Academic Resources Coalition (SPARC), which began in June 1998 as an initiative of the ARL. SPARC (2014) describes itself as

> an international alliance of academic and research libraries working to create a more open system of scholarly communication . . . SPARC believes that faster and wider sharing of the outputs of the scholarly research process increases the impact of research, fuels the advancement of knowledge, and increases the return on research investments. (n.p.)

SPARC's membership is now international and includes approximately 800 members. Financing is through member fees and grants. SPARC focuses on three areas: (1) open, barrier-free access to scholarly and scientific research articles and the rights to reuse articles in the digital environment, (2) open access to the data that supports scientific and scholarly research so that the data can be reused, mined, and extended, and (3) promotion of open, digital teaching and learning materials, referred to as open educational resources (OER). Such materials promote a culture of sharing and collaboration in teaching. SPARC also engages in education and advocacy activities to advance OA (SPARC 2014).

The Coalition of Open Access Policy Institutions (COAPI) complements SPARC's activities. Established in 2011, COAPI now has more than 200 members in Canada and the United States who have committed to the following four principles:

- the immediate and barrier-free online dissemination of scholarly research resulting in faster growth of new knowledge, increased impact of research, and improved return on public research investment
- developing and implementing institutional open-access policies
- sharing experiences and best practices in the development and implementation of open-access policies with individuals at institutions interested in cultivating cultures of OA
- Fostering a more open scholarly communication system through cultural and legislative change at the local, national, and international levels (COAPI 2014).

Although the goal of both of these groups is free and open access, even in the open-access world, someone has to pay for the costs associated with digital publication and for administration of the digital items. Some publishers make their articles available at no cost only after an embargo period, thus making a subscription desirable. Other publishers make the article freely available but defray the publication costs by charging authors a publication fee, which can amount to a considerable sum. Recently a group of universities joined together in the Compact for Open-Access Publishing Equity to ameliorate the costs of such fees by agreeing to pay all or most of the fees for scholars participating in open-access publishing (Compact for . . . 2014).

The future of OA is still clouded, but it is clearly gaining substantial momentum. Renfro (2011) outlined several alternatives that could advance OA:

- Funders recognize scholarly publication as part of the cost of research and include it as an allowable expense on grants.
- Universities also view publication costs as an integral part of research and defray any publication charges for non-grant-funded research.
- All research institutions adopt open-access policies.
- All funders adopt policies that require the deposit of all research into public access repositories.

A recent investigation by The Advisory Board (2011), a nonprofit agency established to study trends in academic libraries, summarized the current situation in scholarly publishing:

> Public access mandates from federal research funders and increasing opposition to rising journal prices have begun to push publishers to make more content available on the Web at no cost. While a complete transition to open-access publishing is unlikely to occur, many experts believe that the traditional business model undergirding scholarly communication will begin to unbundle as faculty embrace alternative modes of discourse and information consumers demand greater access at lower cost. Most faculty, however, are more concerned with publishing in prestigious journal than in supporting open access. (Advisory Board 2011, p. x)

The Advisory Board (2011) also identified four ways institutions divert emphasis from traditional library collections and services to open access initiatives:

Open-access fee subsidies—Institutional funds help underwrite publication by students, faculty, or staff in open-access journals.

Open textbooks—Faculty create digital textbooks for introductory undergraduate courses, published by the institution, and made freely available to students or charge a small fee for access.

Disciplinary repositories—Hosted by libraries and run by faculty and scholarly societies, these Web portals host and disseminate relevant scholarship and provide free public access.

Institutional repositories—Often run by the university library, these portals provide a publicly accessible home for faculty research, data, and copies of published articles (typically one year after first publication).

The open-access movement is not just a national one. Broad international support has been a part of it since 2000. In 2002 supporters of OA met in Budapest and adopted the Budapest Open Access Initiative (BOAI), which recommended two strategies: (1) self-archiving and (2) creating new open-access journals and assisting current journals in transitioning to OA (BOAI 2002). This was followed in 2003 by the "Berlin Declaration on Open Access to Knowledge in the Sciences and Humanities," which encouraged researchers and grant recipients to publish their findings in open-access journals and repositories. The declaration also recommended that universities ensure that open-access publications are properly evaluated in promotion and tenure processes (Max Planck 2003). Ten years after the BOAI statement, in recognition of the maturation and growing support of OA, a second statement (BOAI10) was created reaffirming the two strategies and addressing in greater detail issues related to policies, licensing, technological infrastructure, and advocacy of high-quality open-access publications and standards (BOAI 2012).

b. Institutional Repositories

As the relationship between publishers and academic libraries eroded, universities and their faculty began to consider aggregating scholarly content at a university or multi-university level. These discussions led some institutions to create digital repositories, "digital collections capturing and preserving the intellectual output of a single or multi-university community" (SPARC 2002, p. 4).

> Institutional repositories centralize, preserve, and make accessible an institution's intellectual capital, at the same time they will form part of a global system of distributed, interoperable repositories that provides the foundation for a new disaggregated model of scholarly publishing. (SPARC 2002, p. 6)

Hosted by the academic library, these repositories generally include only peer-reviewed articles and conference papers. LIS professionals provide access support.

Despite their potential, there is a variety of factors that inhibit wider adoption of institutional repositories. For example, faculty can be a source of considerable resistance due to the amount of work required to prepare an electronic document for submission, lack of clarity regarding the advantages of participating in a repository, fear that deposited work will be plagiarized, lack of technical knowledge on how to deposit, fear of violating copyright constraints of the publisher, fear that early deposit would disqualify the work for publication elsewhere (Quinn 2010). Each of these issues must be addressed if repositories are to succeed. In addition, there is a variety of institutional responsibilities that must be considered, such as long-term maintenance of digital resources, sustainable budgets, and appropriate system design to ensure efficient access, administration, and security; methods for effective system evaluation; and adoption of effective policies and practices that can be routinely evaluated (RLG 2002). Nonetheless, with the growing costs of journal access and the growing interest in the academic community for open access to knowledge, digital repositories might well become an integral component of academic libraries in the years to come.

2. Increased Attention to Student Success and Student Retention

Public institutions today must demonstrate their value to citizens and to funders if they expect support. Public universities are no exception. Their survival is threatened if they cannot demonstrate that they prepare students for future careers at a reasonable cost. The need to meet parental expectations is even greater because state governments provide a smaller percentage of the revenue needed to support academic institutions: the result is a growing reliance on student tuition and student retention to support the costs of providing a higher education.

Similarly, units within the institution that do not generate revenue are under special pressure to demonstrate their value. Although there is a reservoir of good will extended to the academic library based on its long tradition of supporting faculty and students, that goodwill alone cannot maintain the budget, services and staff. Similarly, libraries cannot rely on traditional measures of value, such as number of books circulated or programs offered, but now must focus on outcomes—how does the library really make a difference? Although we assume that academic libraries improve student achievement, retention, and later success, the research on the relationship is modest. Mezick (2007) found a positive relationship between total library expenditures, total materials expenditures, serial expenditures, the size of the professional staff, and student retention at the baccalaureate level. Zhong and Alexander (2007) queried students about which aspects of the library they felt most affected academic achievement and the most cited features (in descending order) were facilities, website, electronic periodicals and databases, areas of quiet, library seating, groups study areas, off-campus electronic access, library hours, computer workstations, and research assistance at the reference desk. Positive relationships were also found in relation to library instruction and positive perceptions toward the library, and library resources that integrate the student into the broader academic community (Zhong and Alexander 2007). More recent studies continue to support these findings: Haddow (2013) found that students who took out library materials and logged into the library electronically were more likely to stay. Soria et al. (2013) found that first-year undergraduates who used the library had a higher GPA for their first semester and higher retention from fall to spring than nonusers. Bowles-Terry (2012) found a positive correlation between upper-level library instruction and GPA among seniors.

In the last few years, the Association of College and Research Libraries of ALA has undertaken a systematic effort to measure the impact of academic libraries on student learning and success. Its *Assessment in Action* (AiA) initiative begun in 2012 has been supported with a three-year grant by a National Leadership Demonstration Grant from the Institute of Museum and Libraries Services (IMLS). In the first year alone, more than 70 higher education institutions in North American conducted team-based assessment projects. The results were salutary. Among the findings was that:

- Library instruction builds students' confidence with the research process.
- Library instruction contributes to retention and persistence, particularly for students in first-year experience courses and programs.

- Students who receive library instruction as part of their courses achieve higher grades and demonstrate better information literacy competencies than students who do not receive course-related library instruction.
- A library's research and study space fosters social and academic community among students.
- Library instructional games engage students, enhance information literacy skills, and increase positive attitudes toward the library and its staff.
- The library's use of social media promotes awareness of the library and builds academic community among students. (ACRL 2015)

It is well-established that a major reason students remain with an academic institution is people: that is, students develop relationships with one or more individuals—faculty, administrators, staff—who encourage and support them. Isolated students tend to disengage and drop out (Bell 2008). Academic libraries employ a number of strategies to build relationships and engage students. These include (1) offering programs on information literacy, on how to prepare research papers and on how to improve writing skills, (2) embedding librarians into the academic units of the university, and (3) providing physical spaces for students to collaborate on projects. In addition, Connaway et al. (2013, p. 295) note that in the digital era encouraging use of library reference services requires engaging faculty and students in a variety of ways. Libraries need to

- market and promote library services
- create simple and convenient interface designs
- provide a broad range of tools
- remove the barriers between discovering and accessing information

3. Creating Collaborative Spaces: the Information Commons

Providing collaborative or customized spaces has become particularly important in recent years. Historically, libraries were places where students came to study quietly alone, or to seek a piece of information or item, and leave. Although this still occurs, of course, academic libraries in the twenty-first century are emerging as centers for collaboration—for group work and group production of learning projects. In fact, in the last few years, more than 60% of academic libraries have reported "repurposing space for group study, student success areas (writing/tutoring centers), quiet study space, technology learning spaces, and additional seating (ALA 2015, p. 7). This change reflects corresponding changes in classroom pedagogy, including greater emphasis on active learning, cooperative or collaborative learning in groups, and changes in learning styles, mainly stemming from increased reliance on electronic resources. Academic libraries have consequently created spaces known alternatively as information commons (IC), information centers, learning commons, or instructional commons, configured to offer a variety of library services and emphasizing digital resources. Located in the IC are computer workstations (including multimedia workstations) with access to the Internet and local databases, the online catalog, and software to prepare assignments. Reference materials, and computer and reference staff are located nearby for consultation and support. Tutoring and writing support might also be available, and spaces for group work are provided. The creation of an IC requires careful planning, significant resources, and adequate staffing, training, and funding. It also requires a productive liaison with faculty whose assignments and attitude toward the IC must encourage its use (MacWhinnie 2003).

4. Embedded Librarianship

Embedded librarianship is most commonly associated with undergraduate and distance education. Drewes and Hoffman (2010) explained that "embedded librarian programs often locate librarians involved in the spaces of their users and colleagues, either physically or through technology, in order to become a part of their users' culture" (p. 76). In other words, the LIS professional becomes an extension of the teaching function of an academic department or unit and part of its social structure. The unit might even share or cover salary expenses. Embedded librarians might contribute to the creation of instructional modules for either face-to-face or online courses, provide in-depth research assistance to students or faculty, and hold office hours (Schulte 2012). In some instances the librarian is available electronically through the course management system. Embedded librarians might also provide personalized functions in-person or online, including tutorial services, produce interactive guides and links, and perform chat functions. In order for such programs to succeed, the participating LIS professionals must have excellent communication and interpersonal skills, a strong service ethic, a flexible and creative disposition, and enjoy collaboration (Drewes and Hoffman 2010). By becoming part of the local or online community, the academic librarian is more likely to be perceived as part of the learning team, a faculty collaborator, and instrumental in the academic program's success. Hamilton (2012) summarized the significance of embedded librarianship well:

> As information literacy becomes an essential literacy and form of cultural capital in today's world, embedded librarianship offers exciting possibilities for teaching

these processes and skills within content area study over an extended period of time . . . By integrating the librarian into projects that meet people at their points of need, librarians and those with whom librarians are collaborating cultivate a more authentic and meaningful relationship, as all stakeholders, learn from the transactions occurring in the project, course, or unit of study. (p. 6)

5. *Preservation, Digital Preservation and Digital Curation*

The need to preserve physical materials, both print and audio-visual, continues as many disciplines still depend on them for scholarship. But, as with almost everything else in academic libraries, the digital world has substantially altered the focus and techniques of preservation. Digital data bring new and difficult challenges that have significantly broadened the range of preservation activities. Meyer (2009) in a report on preservation challenges to the Association of Research Libraries noted four important aspects of the current situation:

- Research libraries have been profoundly affected by digital technologies that have influenced user expectations and behavior;
- Libraries must continue to balance the preservation needs of physical collections and digital content;
- Funds are insufficient to address all preservation needs in a research collection; and
- Collaboration and the creation of shared community resources and preservation strategies are essential, particularly for digital content.

In the past, the academic library was the preeminent source for research information for scholars and therefore it had great control over the organization of the items within its collection. In the digital environment, a large portion of information is owned and controlled by third parties such as Google or JSTOR. Control, therefore, is shared. As a consequence, as libraries seek to preserve digital knowledge, they often need to collaborate and partner with commercial, nonprofit organizations, governmental agencies, and other research universities. This collaboration can be mutually beneficial as academic libraries have been dealing with vast amounts of digital information for some time: information in digital repositories and archives, virtual communities, digital learning resources, electronically published documents and articles, and research datasets. Their experience in managing digital knowledge can make a substantial contribution to ensuring access for scholars in the future (Walters and Skinner 2011).

a. The Problem with Paper

Academic libraries' physical collections are particularly vulnerable to deterioration because they are generally held for long periods of time. The primary culprit is acid paper. Since the 1860s, most books and other resources were printed on acid paper. Over a period of years, the acidity dries the paper until it is brittle. Simply touching or turning the pages can crumble the paper. Brittle books are an immense problem in research libraries. The Council of Library Resources estimated that there are more than 75 million brittle books in American research libraries alone, and to preserve just 3 million of them would cost millions of dollars (Byrnes 1992). Given the fiscal constraints imposed by today's economic environment, few dollars are available for conservation; instead many libraries simply use protective enclosures to stabilize print materials (Meyer 2009). Other factors exacerbate degradation, including improper handling of materials, improper heating and air conditioning, improper lighting, poor plumbing, fire hazards, insects, insufficient security to prevent mutilation, and the lack of disaster planning. To mitigate these threats, libraries provide professional development for staff and educational programs on proper handling for students, use proper storage facilities, implement effective environmental controls, use reformatting and migrating techniques such as microfilming and digitization, and physically treat materials in need of repair and restoration, including deacidification (Cloonan 2001). Although many academic libraries provide most of these services, disaster recovery plans are often missing. One need only think of recent hurricanes to realize that natural disasters can wreak havoc on valued library collections (Silverman 2006).

In response to these serious problems, major universities and the federal government have increased their efforts to digitize significant and important print materials. Priority has been given to research collections but there have also been cooperative efforts among smaller academic libraries. In truth, however, these efforts are more access initiatives than preservation efforts. Smith (1999) noted ironically that providing greater access through digitization often increases demand for the original items, thus risking further deterioration. Similarly, Cloonan (2001) expressed concern that emphasizing digitization might, in fact, divert attention from important physical preservation initiatives. Given that research libraries possess rare and unique artifacts, this would be a regrettable outcome.

b. Digital Curation and Preservation

Access to digital content has been a boon to scholarship worldwide and there is no doubt that as this content expands it will play an even greater role.

> Digital information is a vital resource in our knowledge economy, valuable for research and education, science and the humanities, creative and cultural activities, and public policy. But digital information is inherently fragile and often at risk of loss. Access to valuable digital materials tomorrow depends upon preservation actions taken today; and, over time, access depends on ongoing and efficient allocation of resources to preservation. (Blue Ribbon Task Force 2010, p. 1)

The need to preserve digital resources has spawned a new and growing field, digital preservation, which the LOC describes as the "active management of digital content over time to ensure ongoing access" (LOC 2014, "Digital Preservation"). Digital preservation is sometime referred to as "digital curation" though some argue that curation is a broader concept. Meyer (2009), for example, referred to digital preservation as a subset of digital curation which she defined as "all the activities that relate to the creation, capture, description, use, preservation, and re-use of a digital resource, be it a simple digital object (e.g., a sound file) or a set of interrelated digital resources" (e.g., a website) (p. 29).

What constitutes digital information has broadened to include not only digital versions of books and journals, but also blogs, Web pages, and datasets. The formats are also broad: sound, moving image, and text. Preservation efforts have traditionally focused on two areas: preservation of physical materials through digitization (the creation of "surrogates") and the preservation of "born digital" resources that were originally created in a digital format. Born digital resources might not be part of the library's collection, but owned by third parties. In this case preservation efforts require collaboration with outside partners in order to prevent redundancy of effort (Meyer 2009). Unfortunately, once the digital content loses its commercial value, third-party owners have little incentive to retain it (Blue Ribbon 2010).

Another challenge is that although preservation responsibilities for academic libraries have increased, library budgets have not. Libraries must balance their need for current digital resources with the need to protect and preserve the digital resources they already own. Since it will not be possible to preserve all digital content, libraries will have to create criteria for making decisions as to which digital resources will survive and which will not. The balance will be difficult to maintain as demand for current resources is great and expectations high.

D. Special Libraries and Information Centers (SLICs)

The origin of the special library began in the eighteenth century with the founding of the library at the Military Academy at West Point in 1777. The Special Library

Association (SLA) was founded in 1909 when there were about a hundred special libraries. By 1920 this number had grown to about 1,000. Major growth occurred after World War II, and by the 1960s there were over 10,000 special libraries, many of them in scientific and technical laboratories (Mount 1995). Today there are more than 7,600 special libraries in the United States whose heterogeneous nature is revealed in the various divisions of the Special Libraries Association, including Biomedical & Life Science, Business & Finance, Chemistry, Engineering, Government Information, Insurance & Employee Benefits, Knowledge Management, Legal, Military, Museums, Arts & Humanities, Petroleum & Energy, Science-Technology, Social Science, and Transportation (SLA 2014).

Mount (1995) defined special libraries as "information organizations sponsored by private companies, government agencies, not-for-profit organizations or professional associations" (p. 2). Information centers are "special libraries with a very narrow scope" (p. 3). For example, there might be an information center on aluminum within a special library devoted to metals manufacturing. White (1984) identified a number of characteristics of special libraries and information centers:

- They tend to emphasize the provision of information for practical purposes rather than instruction on how to find information or a physical document.

- They generally involve the librarian researching and finding the answer for a client, rather than the client expecting to locate the answer with the librarian's assistance.

- They tend to give librarians a great deal of autonomy because those requesting the information are unfamiliar with the function of information centers.

- They tend to have a relatively small number of users and restricted access to relatively small, but highly specialized collections.

- They are directly and narrowly related to the mission of the organization in which they are located, and must regularly demonstrate their usefulness to survive.

- They involve management oriented to the goals of the larger organization rather than the library, and the library staff itself represents only a small fraction of the total organizational workforce.

As individuals recognized quick access to up-to-date information as a cornerstone of a competitive intellectual and economic society, the role of special libraries and information centers became obvious. Their growth is attributable to at least three factors: ever-increasing amounts of information, continued development of information technologies, and recognition of the critical role of information for organizational survival (Christianson et al. 1991). In fact, special libraries and information centers tend to operate in a more entrepreneurial environment, often within private, profit-oriented organizations—quite different from most other types of libraries. They serve only their special clients or sponsors and market themselves as "knowledge services" or "content management services." "Knowledge services is about establishing social communities; about creating the social infrastructure, a foundation of trust, and a collaborative environment in which all stakeholders contribute to the successful achievement of the parent organization's mission" (St. Clair et al. 2003, p. 11). Reflecting this perspective, although referring to corporate libraries in particular, Felix and Dugdale (2011) describe the situation for nearly all special libraries:

> At a crossroads in their evolution, corporate libraries and knowledge centers have been regarded as places centered on information storage and retrieval within environments of quiet, individual contemplation. However, these libraries have the opportunity to become true "hubs' within the workplace—fostering collaboration, facilitating discovery, fueling innovation, and expressing the organization's culture and brand. (p. 25)

Knowledge access is now mobile; people can access it from many locations rather than having to visit a library. Rather than the special library serving as simply a physical place where information is stored, the special library today reflects a more a dynamic process; the library is an activity that focuses on meeting users' information needs. The special librarian is less a selector and organizer of materials and more a facilitator and collaborator (Felix and Dugdale 2011).

Most of the trends discussed in relation to other library types also apply to special libraries, many of which, unsurprisingly, are related to the growth of digital knowledge. For example, funds are being shifted from print collections to electronic collections and to the technology that provides access to them. As a consequence, there is increased used of Web portals to gather information and an increasing use of electronic journals and electronic document delivery (ALA 2009b). Zeeman et al. (2011) noted a variety of important changes affecting special libraries in this new environment. Five of these changes are briefly noted below:

1. The Emergence of the E-library

Special librarians now think of themselves as "stewards of content" in a digital age (p. 8). They both deliver information and provide digital access to their clients.

They manage digital collections and negotiate and administer third-party contracts for access to information. In some cases they digitize special collections or create new ones and make them available for use.

2. The Addition of Value-added Services

The current trend in special libraries places less emphasis on the physical library and more on distributed services. Special librarians now deliver their services virtually using a variety of devices and channels such as e-mail, texting etc. Sometimes, LIS professionals are embedded directly into the workflow so that they become members of work teams and can tailor their services to the specific needs of that team. Similarly, because clients desire self-service access to information, LIS professionals in special libraries offer training and create interfaces to increase usability. Special librarians might feel that they have lost their reputation as the "expert," but "the impact that information professionals can have today, through networking and social interaction tools, is much broader than in the past (Ard and Livingston 2014, p. 57).

3. Changes in physical space

Because the physical collections are shrinking, space in special libraries is being reconfigured as places for collaboration and training that include videoconferencing, collaborative meeting spaces, comfortable reading areas, and places for clients to use new technologies. In other instances, the actual physical library may be significantly reduced in size or disappear as the librarian, linked almost exclusively to digital resources and applications merge with IT (Swanson 2014).

4. New Technologies Enabling E-services

Convenience is a key component in information seeking and delivery. The introduction of Wi-Fi in many SLICs has enabled effective delivery of digital documents. Similarly, the computer search systems are being configured so that only one sign-on is needed to access and receive the needed information.

5. The Growth of Licensed Content

The age when the special librarian depended on the physical collection inside the organization to satisfy information queries is over for most special libraries. Although the physical collection might still be used, much of the information that might be needed is owned and controlled by third parties. As a consequence, special librarians also negotiate and administer licenses and contracts.

All the changes noted above both physical and professional are evidence of a dynamic and demanding environment. There are additional challenges; for example the next generation of SLIC librarians will have to manage both a physical and electronic space—a virtual collection and a centralized space for collaboration. They will have to be familiar with digital resources, integrated videoconferencing, Webinar technologies, and advanced technologies that analyze data in 3D displays. They will also need skills in such areas as data analysis, marketing strategy, patent research, and project management (Swanson 2014). In addition, special librarians will need to enhance their expertise in data curation. Most special library users focus on their immediate need for information; the special librarian, on the other hand, can provide additional value by focusing on future use of the data through its preservation (Goldstein 2013). Still, some traditions will endure. Ard and Livingston (2014) point out that SLIC librarians, even in this new environment, must ensure that the service they provide is both timely and of good quality.

> Now, with access to the Internet, open access resources, and the ever growing commercial research sources as well as traditional print information, quality reference service requires the application of more complex analytical skills. This is especially true for corporate and special libraries where often time is money and mistakes are costly. (p. 519)

As with all libraries, scarce resources create challenges. Shrinking budgets mean fewer personnel and often a single person might need to perform multiple functions. Less staff makes it difficult to maintain adequate hours. With fewer professional colleagues, continued professional education and training must be found outside the organization (Murray 2013). Further, the SLIC is always competing with other units for a share of the larger corporate or organizational budget. SLICs are generally viewed as cost centers rather than profit centers. Again, LIS professionals must justify their existence or be trimmed from the budget. This is why engagement is so important: the more special librarians are actively part of the workflow process; actively delivering timely and valued information or making the valued information accessible, the stronger the library's position is. As Cromity and Miller (2009) observed:

> Over time, especially in tough economic climates, their roles come to be perceived by some as less than a critical part of the core competencies necessary for the

operation of the business. In fact, in many cases, information departments are identified as a disposable cost center and not a vital component of the decision-making process that can ultimately lead to generating the revenue needed for the business to function . . . Info pros and librarians must change this perception. (p. 29)

In the current economic climate units considered "overhead" will be carefully monitored. It is critical that special libraries demonstrate their tangible contribution to the bottom line. Ard and Livingston (2014) suggested that the communication of value must be done continuously using both statistics and qualitative findings, and using verbal and visual language that reflects the culture of the organization. The communications should also be broadly distributed in meetings, briefings, and to all personnel from new employees to senior executives. In this way, the SLIC can demonstrate the material contribution it makes to the survival of the organization and to its organizational mission.

Matarazzo and Pearlstein (2013) express deep concern that the number of special libraries are declining and many of those that remain are being reduced in terms of space. As the competitive fiscal environment grows, and as faith (often undeserved) in the Internet grows as a substitute for the special library and librarian, so will the challenges facing the existence of the special library. In response, Matarazzo and Pearlstein exhort special librarians to be thought-leaders and clear communicators of the library's value. — to become such they must—

- Understand your customers
- Know how management defines success
- Refine the services offered
- Be client-centered
- Provide leadership (pp. 5–6)

At the heart of all the challenges facing special librarians is the issue of alignment. Special libraries must align closely with the goals of the larger organization and its units. Special librarians must position themselves effectively within the organization as a whole. They must develop strong personal relationships with each of the libraries' clients. They must know their clients as individuals and engage them. They cannot simply be invisible staff within the library: they must be perceived as respected, trusted, influential, and making substantial contributions to their organization. As best as they can, they must be able to demonstrate their personal contributions to the productivity and advancement of organizational goals (Abrams 2013).

IV. SUMMARY

Libraries of all types serve a critical function in our society. Lankes et al. (2007) have observed that libraries are a critical nexus for the exchange of ideas over time, place, and people. They promote and enhance a conversation with humanity:

> Knowledge is created through conversation. Libraries are in the knowledge business. Therefore, libraries are in the conversation business. Some of these conversations span millennia, while others only span a few seconds. Some of these conversations happen in real time. In some conversations, there is a broadcast of ideas from one another to multiple audiences. Some conversations are sparked by a book a video, or a Web page. Some of these conversations are as trivial as directing someone to the bathroom. Other conversations center on the foundations of ourselves and our humanity. (p. 17)

How we organize our libraries and develop our services determines how effective we are in promoting these conversations. In the past, conventional bureaucracies and hierarchical administrations served libraries well. However, today's environment presents new challenges caused by situations and events that lie outside LIS professionals' direct control. A few challenges are unique to particular types of libraries but far more common are shared stressors including decreasing budgets, the rapid expansion of knowledge, the growth of new technologies, and changes in user expectations. Regardless of the source of these challenges, libraries as organizations must maintain clarity of mission while rapidly adapting their organizational structures to ensure they continue to function effectively.

REFERENCES

AASL (American Association of School Librarians). 2009. *Empowering Learners: Guidelines for School Library Programs.* Chicago: ALA.

———. 2013. *Implementing the Common Core State Standards.* www.ala.org/aasl/sites/ala .org.aasl/files/content/externalrelations/CCSSLibrariansBrief_FINAL.pdf.

———. 2013. *Library Spaces for 21st-Century Learners.* Chicago: AASL.

———. 2014. *Standards for the 21st-Century Learner.* Chicago: ALA. www.ala.org/aasl/sites/ ala.org.aasl/files/content/guidelinesandstandards/learningstandards/AASL_Learning Standards.pdf.

———. 2014a. *Learning Standards & Common Core State Standards Crosswalk.* www.ala .org/aasl/standards-guidelines/crosswalk.

———. 2014a. *Developing Collections to Empower Learners.* Chicago: AASL.

Abels, Eileen G. 2011. "Transforming the Internet Public Library into the ip12 Virtual Learning Laboratory." *The Reference Librarian* 52: 284–290.

Abrams, Stephen. 2013. "We're Different: Influencing Skills and Special Librarians." *Information Outlook* 17 (November/December): 25–26.

ACRL (Association of College and Research Libraries). 2013. *Environmental Scan 2013.*

———. 2015. "Academic Library Contributions to Student Success: Documented Practices from the Field: Executive Summary." www.ala.org/acrl/files/issues/value/contributions _summary.pdf.

Adams, Helen R. 2011. "Fewer School Librarians: The Effect on Students' Intellectual Freedom." *School Library Monthly* 27 (March): 52–53.

The Advisory Board Company. 2011. *Redefining the Academic Library: Managing the Migration to Digital Information Services.* Washington, DC.

Agosto, Denise E. 2013. "The Big Picture of YA Services: Analysing the Results of the 2012 PLA PLDS Survey." *Young Adult Library Services* (spring): 13–18.

ALA. 2008. *Handbook of Organization 2008–2009.* Chicago: ALA.

———. 2009. *The Condition of U.S. Libraries: School Library Trends, 1999–2009.* www .ala.org/research/sites/ala.org.research/files/content/librarystats/librarymediacenter/ Condition_of_Libraries_1999–20.pdf.

———. 2009a. *Libraries Connect Community: Public Library Funding and Technology Access Study.* Chicago: ALA.

———. 2009b. *Trends in Special/Government Libraries & Nonprofits/Associations: Report for ALA Planning Retreat.* September 11–13, 2009. Power Point Presentation.

———. 2011. Keeping Public Libraries Public. Chicago: ALA.

———. 2014. "Number of Libraries in the United States: Fact Sheet 1." Chicago: ALA. www.ala.org/ala/tools/libfactsheets/alalibraryfactsheet01.

———. 2014a. "Library Operating Expenditures: A Selected Annotated Bibliography: Fact Sheet 4." Chicago: ALA. www.ala.org/ala/tools/libfactsheets/alalibraryfactsheet04.

———. 2014b. "Professional Competencies for Reference and User Services Librarians." www.ala.org/rusa/resources/guidelines/professional.

———. 2014c. "Digital Inclusion Builds Communities Today (and Tomorrow). Chicago: ALA. www.digital.inclusion.umd.edu.

———. 2014d. "The Best Graphic Novels for Children." www.atourlibrary.org/ connectwithyourkids/reading-together/best-graphic-novels-children.

———. 2015. The State of America's Libraries: 2015. Digital Supplement. American Libraries (April 2015): 1–28.

ALA (ALSC). 2012. "The Public Library Connection: The New Standards Require that Public and School Librarians Pull Together on Common Core." www.slj.com/ 2012/12/opinion/on-common-core/the-public-library-connection-the-new-standards -require-that-public-and-school-libraries-pull-together-on-common-core.

ALA (Every Child). 2014. "Frequently Asked Questions." www.everychildreadytoread.org/frequently-asked-questions.

ALA (International Gaming). (2014). "International Games Day @ Your Library." http://igd.ala.org/faq.

ALA (LTC). 2014. "About LTC." www.ala.org/transforminglibraries/libraries-transforming-communities/about-ltc.

ALA (News). 2010. www.ala.org/news/press-release/2010/11/more-1800-libraries-celebrate-national-gaming-day-nov-13.

ALA (Policy). 2014. "B.3 Diversity (Old Number 60)." www.ala.org/aboutala/governance/policymanual/updatedpolicymanual/section2/diversity.

ALA (RUSA). 2008. *Guidelines for Library and Information Services to Older Adults.* Chicago: ALA.

———. 2014. *Guidelines for Implementing and Maintaining Virtual Reference Services.* Chicago: ALA.

Americans for Libraries Council. 2006. "Long Overdue: A Fresh Look at Public and Leadership Attitudes about Libraries in the 21st Century." Public Agenda.

Ard, Constance. 2012. "Beyond Metrics: The Value of the Information Center." Information Outlook 16: 16–18.

Ard, Constance, and Shawn Livingston. 2014. "Reference and Research Services in Special Libraries: Navigating the Evolving Riches of Information." *Journal of Library Administration* 54: 518–528.

ATALM (Association of Tribal Archives, Libraries, & Museums). 2014. "The Disconnect between the FACC's Schools and Libraries Universal Service Program (E-Rate) and Tribal Libraries." www.atalm.org/sites/default/files/ATALM%20E-Rate%20Brief.pdf.

———. 2014a. *Digital Inclusion in Native Communities: The Role of Tribal Libraries.* www.atalm.org/sites/default/files/REport%20for%20Printing.pdf.

Bailey, Charles W., Jr. 2007. "What Is Open Access" www.digital-scholarship.org/cwb/WhatIsOA.htm.

Bawden, David, and Lyn Robinson. 2014. *Introduction to Information Science.* Chicago: ALA.

Becker, Samantha, Michael D. Crandall, Karen E. Fisher, Bo Kinney, Carol Landry, and Anita Rocha. 2010. *Opportunity for All: How the American Public Benefits from Internet Access at U.S. Libraries.* (IMLS-2010-RES-01.) Institute of Museum and Library Services. Washington, DC.

Bell, Steven. 2008. "Keeping Them Enrolled: How Academic Libraries Contribute to Student Retention." *Library Issues: Briefing for Faculty and Administrators.* 29 (September): 1–4.

Bennett-Kapusniak, Renee. 2013. "Older Adults and the Public Library: The Impact of the Boomer Generation." *Public Library Quarterly* 32: 204–222.

Bernier, Anthony, Mike Males, and Collin Rickman. 2014. "'It Is Silly to Hide Your Most Active Patrons': Exploring User Participation of Library Space Designs for Young Adults in the United States." *Library Quarterly* 84: 165–182.

Bitterman, A., L. Gray, and R. Goldring. 2013. *Characteristics of Public and Private Elementary and Secondary Schools in the United States: Results from the 2011–12 Schools and Staffing Survey.* (NCES 2013–312.) U.S. Department of Education, Washington, DC: National Center for Education Statistics. http://nces.ed.gov/pubs2013/2013312.pdf.

Blount, Patti. 2002. "Double Your Fun with a Combination Public-High School Library." *Public Libraries* 41 (September/October): 254–255.

Blue Ribbon Task Force on Sustainable Digital Preservation and Access. 2010. *Sustainable Economics for a Digital Planet: Ensuring Long-Term Access to Digital Information.* http://brtf.sdsc.edu/biblio/BRTF_Final_Report.pdf.

BOAI (Budapest Open Access Initiative). 2002. "Read the Budapest Open Access Initiative." www.budapestopenaccessinitiative.org/read.

———. 2012. "Ten Years on from the Budapest Open Access Initiative: Setting the Default to Open." www.budapestopenaccessinitiative.org/boai-10-recommendations.

Board of Education, Island Trees Union Free School District v. Pico. 1982. 42 CCH S. Ct. Bull.

Bowles-Terry, Melissa. 2012. "Library Instruction and Academic Success: A Mixed-Methods Assessment of a Library Instruction Program." *Evidence Based Library and Information Practice* 7 (2012): 82–95.

Braun, Linda W., Maureen L. Hartman, Sandra Hughes-Hassell, and Kafi Kumasi. 2013. *The Future of Library Services for and with Teens: A Call to Action.* (IMLA/YALSA.) www.ala.org/yaforum/sites/ala.org.yaforum/files/content/YALSA_nationalforum_final.pdf.

Britton, Lauren. 2012. "The Makings of Maker Spaces." *Library Journal* (October 1): 20–23.

Brodie, Carolyn. 1998. "A History of School Library Media Center Collection Development." In *The Emerging School Library Media Center: Historical Issues and Perspectives,* edited by Kathy Howard Latrobe. Englewood, CO: Libraries Unlimited, 57–73.

Budd, John. 2007. "Public Library Leaders and Changing Society." *Public Library Quarterly* 26: 1–14.

Burke, Leslie, and Stephen McConnell. 2007. "Technical Services Departments in the Digital Age." *Against the Grain* 19: 57–64.

Burke, Susan K. 2009. "Perceptions of Public Library Accessibility for People with Disabilities." *The Reference Librarian* 50: 43–54.

Byrnes, Marci, Kathleen Deerr, and Lisa G. Kropp. 2003. "Book a Play Date: The Game of Promoting Emergent Literacy." *American Libraries* 34 (September): 42–44.

Byrnes, Margaret M. 1992. "Preservation and Collection Management: Some Common Concerns." In *The Collection Building Reader,* edited by Betty-Carol Sellen and Arthur Curley. New York: Neal-Schuman, 57–63.

Case, Mary M. 2010. "Principles for Emerging Systems of Scholarly Publishing." www.arl .org/bm~doc/principles.pdf.

Casey, James. 2002. "The Devil Is in the Details." *Public Libraries* 41 (September/October): 252.

Christianson, Elin B., David E. King, and Janet L. Ahrensfeld. 1991. *Special Libraries: A Guide for Management*, 3rd ed. Washington, DC: SLA.

Churchwell, Charles D. 2007. "The Evolution of the Academic Research Library during the 1960s." *College and Research Libraries* 68 (March): 104–105.

Cloonan, Michèle Valerie. 2001. "W(h)ither Preservation?" *Library Quarterly* 71: 231–242.

COAPI (Coalition of Open Access Policy Institutions). 2014. "COAPI." www.sparc.arl.org/ COAPI.

Cohen, Dan. 2014. "The Digital Public Library of America: Collaboration, Content and Technology at Scale." *Educause* (July/August): 56–57.

Common Core State Standards Initiative. 2013. "Frequently Asked Questions." www.corestandards.org/up-content/uploads/FAQs.pdf.

Compact for Open-Access Publishing Equity. 2014. "Frequently Asked Questions." www.oacompact.org/faq.

Connaway, Lynn Silipigni, Donna Lancois, and Erin M. Hood. 2013. "'I Find Google a Lot Easier than Going to the Library Website.' Imagine Ways to Innovate and Inspire Students to Use the Academic Library." Proceedings of the ACRL Imagine, Innovate, Inspire Conference, April 10–13, Indianapolis, IN.

Cottrell, Megan. 2013. "A Digital Library for Everybody." *American Libraries* (March–April): 44–47.

Crawford, Philip. 2004. "Using Graphic Novels to Attract Reluctant Readers." *Library Media Connection* (February 2): 26–28.

Cromity, Jamal, and Barry Miller. 2009. "Reinventing Ourselves for Success." *Information Outlook* 13 (December): 29–31.

DCC (Digital Curation Centre). 2014. "What Is Digital Curation?" www.dcc.ac.uk/ digital-curation/what-digital-curation.

DeCandido, Keith R. A. 1990. "Picture This: Graphic Novels in Libraries." *Library Journal* (March 15): 50–55.

De Rosa, Cathy, Lorcan Dempsey, and Alane Wilson. 2004. *The 2003 OCLC Environmental Scan: Pattern Recognition.* Dublin, OH: OCLC.

De Rosa, Cathy, and Jenny Johnson. 2008. *From Awareness to Funding: A Study of Library Support in America.* Dublin, OH: OCLC.

Do-It. 2014. "Universal Access: Making Library Resources Accessible to People with Disabilities." www.washington.edu/doit/UA/PRESENT/libres.html.

DPLA (Digital Public Library of America). 2014. "History." www.dp.la/info/about/history.

Drewes, Kathy, and Nadine Hoffman. 2010. "Academic Embedded Librarianship: An Introduction." *Public Services Quarterly* 6: 75–82.

Economic Research Service, Department of Agriculture. 2004. "Briefing Room: Rural Population and Migration." www.ers.usda.gov/briefing/Population.

EDUCAUSE. 2013. "Makerspaces." net.educause.edu/ir/library/pdf/eli7095.pdf.

Emmons, Mark, and Frances C. Wilkinson. 2011. "The Academic Library Impact on Student Persistence." *College & Research Libraries* (March): 128–151.

Evans, G. Edward, Sheila S. Intner, and Jean Weihs. 2011. *Introduction to Technical Services*, 8th ed. Santa Barbara, CA: Libraries Unlimited.

Faris, Crystal. 2007. "Game On! Research into Children and Gaming." *Children and Libraries* 5: 50–51.

Felix, Elliot, and Shirley Dugdale. 2011. "Libraries as Hubs in the New Workplace." In *Best Practices for Corporate Libraries*, edited by Sigrid E. Kelsey and Marjorie J. Porter. Santa Barbara: ABC-CLIO.

Fessler, Vera. 2007. "The Future of Technical Services (It's Not the Technical Services It Was)." *Library Administration and Management* 21 (summer): 139–145.

Flatley, Robert, and Andrea Wyman. 2009. "Changes in Rural Libraries and Librarianship: A Comparative Survey." *Library Quarterly* 28: 24–39.

Gavigan, Karen. 2011. "More Powerful than a Locomotive: Using Graphic Novels to Motivate Struggling Male Adolescent Readers." *The Journal of Research on Library and Young Adults.* www.yalsa.ala.org/jrlya/2011/06/more-powerful-than-a-locomotive-using -graphic-novels-to-motivate-struggling-male-adolescent-readers.

Gieskes, Lisa. 2009. "Why Librarians Matter to Poor People." *Public Library Quarterly* 28: 49–57.

Goldstein, Steven. 2013. "Adding Value through Data Curation." *Information Outlook* 17 (March/April): 10–11.

Haddow, Gaby. 2013. "Academic Library Use and Student Retention: A Quantitative Analysis." *Library and Information Science Research* 35: 127–136.

Hamilton, Buffy J. 2012. "Introduction." *Embedded Librarianship: Tools and Practices.* Chicago: ALA.

Harris Interactive. 2011. "January 2011 Harris Poll Quorum." Available at: www.ala.org/ research/sites/ala.org.research/files/content/librarystats.

Harwood Institute for Public Innovation. 2014. "About." www.harwoodinstitute.org/about.

———. 2008. "American Public Library Ratings 2008." *American Libraries* 39 (October): 57–61.

Hennen, Thomas J., Jr. 2010. "Hennen's American Public Library Rating." www.haplr -index.com/rating_methods.htm.

Hildreth, Susan. 2013. "Inspiring Libraries as Community Anchors." *National Civic Review* (winter): 44–47.

Holt, Glen E., and Donald Elliott. 2003. "Measuring Outcomes: Applying Cost-Benefit Analysis to Middle-Sized and Smaller Public Libraries." *Library Trends* 51 (winter): 424–440.

Horrigan, John B. 2014. *Digital Readiness: Nearly One-Third of Americans Lack the Skills to Use Next-Generation "Internet of Things" Applications.* http://jbhorrigan.weebly.com/uploads/3/0/8/0/30809311/digital_readiness.horrigan.june2014.pdf.

Howard, Vivian. 2011. "What Do Young Teens Think About the Public Library?" *Library Quarterly* 81: 321–344.

IFLA. 2012. "IFLA/UNESCO Public Library Manifesto." www.unesco.org/webworld/libraries/manifestos/libraman.html.

Imholz, Susan, and Jennifer Weil Arns. 2007. *Worth Their Weight: An Assessment of the Evolving Field of Library Valuation.* New York: Americans for Libraries Council.

IMLS (Institute for Museum and Library Services). 2012. *Creating a Nation of Learners: Strategic Plan 2012–2016.* www.imls.gov/assets/1/AssetManager/StrategicPlan2012–16_Brochure.pdf.

———. 2013. *Growing Young Minds* (Executive Summary). www.imls.gov/assets/1/AssetManager/GrowingYoungMinds_Exec_Sum.pdf.

Internet Public Library. 2003. www.ipl.org/div/about.

IPAC (Information Policy and Access Center). 2014. *2013 Digital Inclusion Survey: Survey Findings and Results Executive Summary.* http://digitalinclusion.umd.edu.

Jaeger, Paul T. et al. 2012. "Describing and Measuring the Value of Public Libraries: The Growth of the Internet and the Evolution of Library Value." www.firstmonday.org/ojs/index.php/fm/article/view/3765.

Johnson, Linda. 2000. "The Rural Library: Programs, Services, and Community Coalitions and Networks." *Rural Libraries* 20: 38–62.

Johnston, Melissa P. 2012. "School Librarians as Technology Integration Leaders: Enablers and Barriers to Leadership Enactment." *School Library Research* 15. www.ala.org/aasl/slr.

Jones, Plummer Alston, Jr. 1989. "The History and Development of Libraries in American Higher Education." *College and Research Libraries News* 50 (July/August): 561–564.

Justice, Laura M., and Joan Kaderavek. 2002. "Using Shared Storybook Reading to Promote Emergent Literacy." *Teaching Exceptional Children* 34 (March/April): 8–13.

Kaufman, Paula. 2012. "Let's Get Cozy: Evolving Collaborations in the 21st Century." *Journal of Library Administration* 52: 53–69.

King, David Lee. 2009. *Building the Digital Branch: Guidelines to Transform Your Website.* *Library Technology Reports* 45 (August/September 2009).

Kranich, Nancy. 2012. "Libraries and Civic Engagement." In *Library and Book Trade Almanac,* 57th ed. Medford, NJ: Information Today, pp. 75–97.

Lance, Keith Curry, and Linda Hofschire. 2012. *Change in School Librarian Staffing Linked with Change in CSAP Reading Performance, 2005 to 2011.* Denver: Library Research Service.

Lance, Keith Curry, Marcia J. Rodney, and Christine Hamilton-Pennell. 2000. *How School Librarians Help Kids Achieve Standards: The Second Colorado Study.* Castle Rock, CO: Hi Willo Research and Publishing.

Lance, Keith Curry, Lynda Welborn, and Christine Hamilton-Pennell. 1993. *The Impact of School Library Media Centers on Academic Achievement.* Castle Rock, CO: Hi Willo Research and Publishing.

Lankes, R. David, Joanne Silverstein, and Scott Nicholson. "Participatory Networks: The Library as Conversation." In *Information Technology and Libraries* 52 (December 2007): 17–33.

Laugesen, Amanda. 2014. "UNESCO and the Globalization of the Public Library Idea." *Library & Information History* 30 (February): 1–19.

Leachman, Michael, and Chris Mai. 2014. "Most States Funding Schools Less Than Before the Recession." Center on Budget and Policy Priorities. www.cbpp.org/cms/?fa=view&id=4011.

Leffler, Jennifer J., and Pamela Newberg. 2010. "Re-Visioning Technical Services: A Unique Opportunity to Examine the Past, Access the Present, and Create a Better Future." *Cataloging & Classification Quarterly* 48 (August): 561–571.

Levien, Roger E. 2011. *Confronting the Future: Strategic Decisions for the 21st Century Public Library.* Policy Brief No. 4. Chicago: ALA Office for Information Technology Policy.

Levin, Driscoll & Fleeter. 2006. *Value for Money: Southwestern Ohio's Return from Investment in Public Libraries.* Columbus, OH: Levin, Driscoll & Fleeter, June 22.

Levine, Jenny. 2006. "Gaming and Libraries: Intersection of Services." *Library Technology Reports* 42 (September/October): 1–80.

———. 2009. "Gaming and Libraries: Learning Lessons from the Intersections." *Library Technology Reports* 45, no. 5. Chicago: ALA.

Lewis, Jill. 2013. "Information Equality for Individuals with Disabilities: Does It Exist?" *Library Quarterly* 83: 229–235.

Library Journal. 2014. "The LJ Index: Frequently Asked Questions (FAQ)." http://lj.libraryjournal.com/stars-faq.

Lipow, Anne Grodzins. 2003. "The Future of Reference: Point-of-Need Reference Service: No Longer an Afterthought." *Reference Services Review* 31:31–35.

Lipschultz, Dale. 2009. "Gaming." *American Libraries* 40 (January/February): 40–43.

LOC. 2014. "Digital Preservation." www.digitalpreservation.gov/about.

LSSI. 2014. "Communities." www.google.com/?gws_rd=ssl#q=lssi.

Mackenzie, Christine, and Michael Aulich. 2009. "Technical Services—Gone (and Forgotten)." In *More Innovative Redesign and Reorganization.* Westport, CT: Libraries Unlimited, 1–9.

MacWhinnie, Laurie A. 2003. "The Information Commons: The Academic Library of the Future." In *Portal: Libraries and the Academy.* Vol. 3. Baltimore: Johns Hopkins University Press, 241–257.

Matarazzo, James M., and Toby Pearlstein. 2013. *Special Libraries: A Survival Guide.* Santa Barbara: ABC CLIO.

Max Planck Institute. 2003. "Berlin Declaration on Open Access to Knowledge in the Sciences and Humanities." http://openaccess.mpg.de/286432/Berlin-Declaration.

Meyer, Lars. 2009. "Safeguarding Collections at the Dawn of the 21st Century." Association of Research Libraries. www.arl.org/storage/documents/publications/safeguarding-collections.pdf.

Mezick, Elizabeth M. 2007. "Return on Investment: Libraries and Student Retention." *Journal of Academic Librarianship* 33 (September): 561–566.

Miller, Carolyn, Kathryn Zickuhr, Lee Rainie, Kristen Purcell. 2013. *Parents, Children, Libraries, and Reading.* Washington DC: Pew Research Center.

Minarcini v. Strongsville City School District. 541 F.2d 577 (1977).

Mount, Ellis. 1995. *Special Libraries and Information Centers: An Introductory Text*, 3rd ed. Washington, DC: SLA.

Murray, Tara E. 2013. "What's So Special about Special Libraries?" *Journal of Library Administration* 14: 274–282.

NCAC (National Coalition Against Censorship). 2006. "Graphic Novels: Suggestions for Librarians." www.ncac.org/resource/graphic-novels-suggestions-for-librarians.

Nelson, Sandra. 2008. *Strategic Planning for Results.* Chicago: ALA.

Nicholson, Scott. 2007. "The Role of Gaming in Libraries: Taking the Pulse." White paper. http://boardgameswithscott.com/pulse2007.pdf.

Oudenaren, John Van. 2013. "The World Digital Library." Proceedings of the Memory of the World in the Digital Age: Digitization and Preservation Conference, edited by Luciana Duranti and Elizabeth Shaffer. September 26–28, 2012. Vancouver, BC.

Owens, Margaret. 2002. "Get It in Writing!" Public Libraries 41 (September/October): 248–250.

Pennsylvania Library Association. 2009. "Return on Investment (ROI) Materials." www.palibraries.org/displaycommon.cfm?an=1&subarticlenbr=23.

Pew Internet Research Project. 2013–2014. "Internet User Demographics." www.pewInternet.org/data-trend.

Pew Research Center. Library Services in the Digital Age. http://libraries.pewInternet .org/2013/01/22/library-services.

Phan, T., L. Hardesty, and J. Hug. 2014. *Academic Libraries: 2012* (NCES 2014–038). U.S. Department of Education, Washington, DC: National Center for Education Statistics.

Pinkley, Janet, and Kaela Casey. 2013. "Graphic Novels: A Brief History and Overview for Library Managers." *Library Leadership & Management* 27: 1–10.

Quinn, Brian. 2010. "Reducing Psychological Resistance to Digital Repositories." *Information Technology and Libraries* (June): 67–75.

Renfro, Patricia. 2011. "Open Access within Reach: An Agenda for Action." *Journal of Library Administration* 51: 464–475.

RLG. 2002. *Trusted Digital Repositories: Attributes and Responsibilities: An RLG-OCOC Report.* Mountain View, CA: RLG.

Rodger, Eleanor Jo. 2002. "Values & Vision." *American Libraries* (November): 50–54.

Schlachter, Debbie. 2009. "Adjusting to Changes in User and Client Expectations." *Information Outlook* 13 (June): 55–57.

Schmidt, Krista D., Pongracz Sennyey, and Timothy V. Carstens. 2005. "New Roles for a Changing Environment: Implications of Open Access for Libraries." *College and Research Libraries* 66 (September): 407–416.

Schulte, Stephanie J. 2012. "Embedded Academic Librarianship: A Review of the Literature." *Evidence Based Library and Information Practice* 7: 122–138.

Shontz, Marilyn L., and Lesley S. J. Farmer. 2007. "Expenditures for Resources in School Library Media Centers, 2005." In *The Bowker Annual: Library and Book Trade Almanac 2007*, 52nd ed., edited by Dave Bogart. Medford NJ: Information Today, 445–458.

Silverman, Randy. 2006. "Toward a National Disaster Response Protocol." *Libraries and the Cultural Record* 41 (fall): 497–511.

SLA (Special Library Association). 2014. "Divisions." www.sla.org/get-involved/divisions.

Smith, Abby. 1999. *The Future of the Past: Preservation in American Research Libraries*. Washington, DC: Council on Library and Information Resources.

Soria, Krista M., Jan Fransen, and Shane Nackerud. 2013. "Library Use and Undergraduate Student Outcomes: New Evidence for Students' Retention and Academic Success." *Portal: Libraries and the Academy* 13 (2013): 147–164.

SPARC. . 2002. "The Case for Institutional Repositories: A SPARC Position Paper." Prepared by Raym Crow. Washington, DC: SPARC.

———. 2014. "About Us." www.sparc.arl.org/about.

Special Libraries Association. 2009. "Divisions." www.sla.org/content/community/units/divs/index.cfm.

St. Clair, Guy, Victoria Harriston, and Thomas A. Pellizzi. 2003. "Toward World-Class Knowledge Services: Emerging Trends in Specialized Research Libraries." *Information Outlook* 7 (July): 10–16.

Steffen, Nocolie, Zeth Lietzau, Keith Curry Lance, Amanda Rybin, and Carla Molliconi. 2009. *Public Libraries—A Wise Investment*. Denver: Library Research Service.

Stratton, J. M. 1996. "Emergent Literacy: A New Perspective." *Journal of Visual Impairment and Blindness* 90 (May/June): 177–183.

Stripling, Barbara K. 2014. "Advocating for School Librarians." *American Libraries* (January/February): 9.

Su, Mila. 2008. "Beyond Circulation: The Evolution of Access Services and Its Relationship to Reference Librarianship." The Reference Librarian 49: 77–86.

Swan, D. W., J. Grimes, T. Owens, K. Miller, J. Arroyo, T. Craig, S. Dorinski, M. Freeman, N. Isaac, P. O'Shea, R. Padgett, P. Schilling, and J. Scotto. 2014. *Public Libraries in the United States Survey: Fiscal Year 2011*. (IMLS-2014-PLS-01.) Institute of Museum and Library Services. Washington, DC.

Swan, Deanne W., Justin Grimes, and Timothy Owens. 2013. *The State of Small and Rural Libraries in the United States*. Research Brief No 5. Washington, DC: IMLS.

Swanson, Jennifer. 2014. "The Future of the Corporate Library." *Information Outlook* 18 (July/August): 10–24.

Todd, Ross J. 2003. "Student Learning Through Ohio School Libraries: A Summary of the Ohio Research Study." www.oelma.org/studentlearning.htm.

Urban Libraries Council. 2011. *Library Priority: Community-Civic Engagement.* www .urbanlibraries.org/filebin/pdfs/ULC_Leadership_Brief_II_Full_4Pages.pdf.

U.S. Bureau of the Census. 2012. "Nearly 1 in 5 People Have a Disability in the U.S., U.S. Census Bureau Reports." www.census.gov/newsroom/releases/archives/miscellaneous/ cb12–134-html.

Vavrek, Bernard. 2003. "Rural Public Library Services." In *Encyclopedia of Library and Information Science*, 2nd ed., edited by Miriam Drake. New York: Marcel Dekker, 2550–2555.

Wanucha, M., and L. Hofschire. 2013. *U.S. Public Libraries and the Use of Web Technologies, 2012.* (Closer Look Report.) Denver, CO: Colorado State Library, Library Research Office.

Ward-Crixell, Kit. 2007. "Gaming Advocacy: New Ways Librarians Can Support Learning and Literacy." *School Library Journal* 53 (September): 36–38.

WDL (World Digital Library). 2015. "About the World Digital Library." www.wdl.org/en/ about.

White, Herbert. 1984. *Managing the Special Library.* White Plains, NY: Knowledge Industry.

Winter, Michael F. 1988. *The Culture and Control of Expertise: Toward a Sociological Understanding of Librarianship.* Westport, CT: Greenwood.

Woolls, Blanche. 1994. *The School Library Media Manager.* Englewood, CO: Libraries Unlimited.

Yiotis, Kristin. 2005. "The Open Access Initiative: A New Paradigm for Scholarly Communications." *Information Technology and Libraries* 24: 157–162.

Young, Peter R. 1994. "Changing Information Access Economics: New Roles for Libraries and Librarians." *Information Technology and Libraries* 13 (June): 103–114.

Zeeman, Deane, Rebecca Jones, and Jane Dysart. 2011. "Assessing Innovation in Corporate and Government Libraries." *Computers in Libraries* (June): 6–15.

Zhong, Ying, and Johanna Alexander. 2007. "Academic Success: How Library Services Make a Hamilton, Difference." *ACRL Thirteenth National Conference Proceedings.* Chicago: ALA.

Zickuhr, Kathryn, Lee Rainie, and Kristen Purcell. 2013. "Library Services in the Digital Age." http://libraries.pewInternet.org/2013/01/22/Library-services.

———. 2013a. "Younger Americans' Library Habits and Expectations." http://libraries .pewInternet.org/2013/06/25/younger-americans-library-services.

Zickuhr, Kathryn, Lee Rainie, Kristen Purcell, and Maeve Duggan. 2013. "How Americans Value Public Libraries in Their Communities." www.libraries.pewInternet .org/2013/12/11/libraries-in-communities.

Zweizig, Douglas L. 1982. *Output Measures for Public Libraries.* Chicago: ALA.

SELECTED READINGS (By Type of Library)

Academic Libraries

Books/Monographs

ACRL (Association of College and Research Libraries). *Academic Library Contributions to Student Success: Document Practices from the Field.* Prepared by Karen Brown. Contributions by Kara J. Malenfant. Chicago: ACRL, 2015.

———. ACRL "Environmental Scan 2013." Chicago: ACRL, 2013.

The Advisory Board. *Redefining the Academic Library: Managing the Migration to Digital Information Services.* Washington DC: Advisory Board, 2011.

Allen, I. Elaine, and Jeff Seaman. *Opening the Curriculum: Open Educational Resources in U.S. Higher Education, 2014.* Babson Survey Research Group, 2014.

ARL Digital Repository Issues Task Force. *The Research Library's Role in Digital Repository Services.* Washington, DC. ARL, 2009.

Blue Ribbon Task Force on Sustainable Digital Preservation and Access. Sustainable Economics for a Digital Planet: Ensuring Long-Term Access to Digital Information. 2010. http://brtf.sdsc.edu/biblio/BRTF_Final_Report.pdf.

Dugan, Robert E, Peter Hernon, and Danuta A. Nitecki. *Viewing Library Metrics from Different Perspectives: Inputs, Outputs, and Outcomes.* Santa Barbara, CA: Libraries Unlimited, 2009.

Gregory, Vicki L. *Collection Development and Management for 21st Century Library Collections.* New York: Neal-Schuman, 2011.

Hernon, Peter, and Joseph R. Matthews. Editors. *Reflecting on the Future of Academic and Public Libraries.* Chicago: ALA, 2013.

Leeder, Kim, and Eric Frierson. Editors. *Planning Our Future Libraries: Blueprints for 2025.* Chicago: ALA, 2014.

Oakleaf, Mega. *Value of Academic Libraries: A Comprehensive Research Review and Report.* Chicago: ALA, 2010.

Shorley, Deborah, and Michael Jubb. Editors. *The Future of Scholarly Communication.* London: Facet, 2013.

Articles

ACRL. "2014 Top Trends in Academic Libraries: A Review of the Trends and Issues Affecting Academic Libraries in Higher Education." http://crln.acrl.org/content/75/6/294full.pdf+html.

Allner, Irmin. "Managerial Leadership in Academic Libraries." *Library Administration and Management* 22 (spring 2008): 69–78.

Connaway, Lynn Silipigni, Donna Lancois, and Erin M. Hood. "'I Find Google a Lot Easier than Going to the Library Website.' Imagine Ways to Innovate and Inspire Students to Use the Academic Library." Proceedings of the ACRL Imagine, Innovate, Inspire Conference, April 10–13, Indianapolis, IN.

Drewes, Kathy, and Nadine Hoffman. "Academic Embedded Librarianship: An Introduction." *Public Services Quarterly* 6 (2010): 75–82.

Franklin, Brinley. "Surviving to Thriving: Advancing the Institutional Mission." *Journal of Library Administration* 52 (2012): 94–107.

Gregory, Cynthia L. "'But I Want a Real Book': An Investigation of Undergraduates' Usage and Attitudes toward Electronic Books." *Reference and User Services Quarterly* 47 (2008): 266–273.

Haddow, Gaby. "Academic Library Use and Student Retention: A Quantitative Analysis." *Library and Information Science Research* 35 (2013): 127–136.

Hamilton, Buffy J. "Introduction." In *Embedded Librarianship: Tools and Practices.* Chicago: ALA, 2012.

Kaufman, Paula. "Let's Get Cozy: Evolving Collaborations in the 21st Century." *Journal of Library Administration* 52 (2012): 53–69.

Mercer, Holly. "Almost Halfway There: An Analysis of the Open Access Behaviors of Academic Librarians." *College & Research Libraries* (September 2011): 443–453.

Neal, James G. "Raised by Wolves: Integrating the New Generation of Feral Professionals into the Academic Library." *Library Journal* 32 (February 2006): 443.

Paulus, Michael J., Jr. "Reconceptualizing Academic Libraries and Archives in the Digital Age." *Portal: Libraries and the Academy* 11 (2011): 939–952.

Quinn, Brian. "Reducing Psychological Resistance to Digital Repositories." *Information Technology and Libraries* (June 2010): 67–75.

Renfro, Patricia. "Open Access within Reach: An Agenda for Action." *Journal of Library Administration* 51 (2011): 464–475.

Schulte, Stephanie J. "Embedded Academic Librarianship: A Review of the Literature." *Evidence Based Library and Information Practice* 7 (2012): 122–138.

Simmons-Welburn, Janice, Georgie Donovan, and Laura Bender. "Transforming the Library: The Case for Libraries to End Incremental Measures and Solve Problems for Their Campuses Now." *Library Administration and Management* 22 (summer 2008): 130–134.

Soria, Krista M., Jan Fransen, and Shane Nackerud. "Library Use and Undergraduate Student Outcomes: New Evidence for Students' Retention and Academic Success." *Portal: Libraries and the Academy* 13 (2013): 147–164.

Zemon, Michkey, and Alice Harrison Bahr. "Career and/or Children: Do Female Academic Librarians Pay a Price for Motherhood?" *College and Research Libraries* 66 (September 2005): 394–405.

Public Libraries
Books/Monographs

ALA. *The State of America's Libraries* (various years). www.ala.org.

Battles, David M. *The History of Public Library Access for African Americans in the South, or, Leaving Behind the Plow.* Lanham, MD: Scarecrow, 2009.

Becker, Samantha, Michael D. Crandall, Karen E. Fisher, Bo Kinney, Carol Landry, and Anita Rocha. *Opportunity for All: How the American Public Benefits from Internet Access at U.S. Libraries.* (IMLS-2010-RES-01.) Institute of Museum and Library Services. Washington, DC, 2010.

De Rosa, Cathy, and Jenny Johnson. *From Awareness to Funding: A Study of Library Support in America: A Report to the OCLC Membership.* Dublin, OH: OCLC, 2008.

De Rosa, Cathy, et al. *Perceptions of Libraries and Information Resources: A Report to the OCLC Membership.* Dublin, OH: OCLC, 2005.

Horrigan, John B. *Digital Readiness: Nearly One-Third of Americans Lack the Skills to Use Next-Generation "Internet of Things" Applications.* 2014. www.jbhorrigan.weebly.com/uploads/3/0/8/0/30809311/digital_readiness.horrigan.june2014.pdf.

Howard, Mary Lynn. *Growing Young Minds.* Washington, DC: IMLS, 2013.

Imholz, Susan, and Jennifer Weil Arns. *Worth Their Weight: An Assessment of the Evolving Field of Library Valuation.* New York: Americans for Libraries Council, 2007.

Lankes, David R. *The Atlas of New Librarianship.* Cambridge, MA: MIT, 2011.

Levien, Roger E. *Confronting the Future: Strategic Decisions for the 21st Century Public Library.* Policy Brief No. 4. Chicago: ALA Office for Information Technology Policy, 2011.

Miller, Carolyn, Kathryn Zickuhr, Lee Rainie, Kristen Purcell. *Parents, Children, Libraries, and Reading.* Washington, DC: Pew Research Center, 2013.

Pew Research Center. *From Distant Admirers to Library Lovers—and Beyond: A Typology of Public Library Engagement in America.* Washington, D.C. March 2014. Available at http://libraries.pewInternet.org/2014/03/13/typology.

Pew Research Center. *Library Services in the Digital Age.* 2013. http://libraries.pewInternet.org/2013/01/22/library-services.

Zickuhr, Kathryn, Lee Rainie, Kristen Purcell, and Maeve Duggan. *How Americans Value Public Libraries in Their Communities,* 2013. http://www.libraries.pewInternet.org/2013/12/11/libraries-in-communities.

Articles

Bennett-Kapusniak. "Older Adults and the Public Library: The Impact of the Boomer Generation." *Public Library Quarterly* 32 (2013): 204–222.

Bernier, Anthony, Mike Males, and Collin Rickman. "'It Is Silly to Hide Your Most Active Patrons': Exploring User Participation of Library Space Designs for Young Adults in the United States." *Library Quarterly* 84 (2014): 165–182.

Britton, Lauren. "The Makings of Maker Spaces." *Library Journal* (October 1, 2012): 20–23.

Budd, John. "Public Library Leaders and Changing Society." *Public Library Quarterly* 26 (2007): 1–14.

Fultz, Michael. "Black Public Libraries in the South in the Era of De Jure Segregation." *Libraries and the Cultural Record* 41 (summer 2006): 337–359.

Gavigan, Karen. "More Powerful than a Locomotive: Using Graphic Novels to Motivate Struggling Male Adolescent Readers." *The Journal of Research on Library and Young Adults.* (2011). www.yalsa.ala.org/jrlya/2011/06/more-powerful-than-a-locomotive -using-graphic-novels-to-motivate-struggling-male-adolescent-readers.

Gieskes, Lisa. "Why Librarians Matter to Poor People." *Public Library Quarterly* 28 (2009): 49–57.

Hamada, Dalia, and Sylvia Stavridi. "Required Skills for Children and Youth Librarians in the Digital Age." *Future Libraries: Infinite Possibilities Conference.* IFLA WLIC 2013. www.library.ifla.org/70/105-mhamada-en.pdf.

Hightower, Jim. "Why Libraries Matter." *American Libraries* 35 (January 2004): 50–52.

Howard, Vivian. "What Do Young Teens Think About the Public Library?" *Library Quarterly* 81 (2011): 321–344.

Jaeger, Paul T., et al. "Describing and Measuring the Value of Public Libraries: The Growth of the Internet and the Evolution of Library Value." 2012. www.firstmonday .org/ojs/index.php/fm/article/view/3765.

———. "The Intersection of Public Policy and Public Access: Digital Divides, Digital Literacy, Digital Inclusion, and Public Libraries." *Public Library Quarterly* 31 (2012): 1–20.

Kelly, Betsy, et al. "Applying Return on Investment (ROI) in Libraries." *Journal of Library Administration* 52 (2012): 656–671.

Kranich, Nancy. "Libraries and Civic Engagement." In *Library and Book Trade Almanac.* 57th ed. Medford, NJ: Information Today, 2012, pp. 75–97.

Lankes, R. David, Joanne Silverstein, and Scott Nicholson. "Participatory Networks: The Library as Conversation." In *Information Technology and Libraries* 52 (December 2007): 17–33.

Laugesen, Amanda. "UNESCO and the Globalization of the Public Library Idea." *Library & Information History* 30 (February 2014): 1–19.

Leckie, Gloria J., and Jeffrey Hopkins. "The Public Place of Central Libraries: Findings from Toronto and Vancouver." *Library Quarterly* 72 (2002): 326–372.

Lewis, Jill. "Information Equality for Individuals with Disabilities: Does It Exist?" *Library Quarterly* 83 (2013): 229–235.

McCrossen, Alexis. "One Cathedral More or 'Mere Lounging Place for Bummers'? The Cultural Politics of Leisure and the Public Library in Gilded Age America." *Libraries and Culture* 41 (spring 2006): 169–188.

Pinkley, Janet, and Kaela Casey. "Graphic Novels: A Brief History and Overview for Library Managers." *Library Leadership & Management* 27 (2013): 1–10.

Scott, Rachel. "The Role of Public Libraries in Community Building." *Public Library Quarterly* 30 (2011): 191–227.

Swan, Deanne W., Justin Grimes, and Timothy Owens. *The State of Small and Rural Libraries in the United States.* Research Brief No 5. Washington, DC: IMLS, 2013.

Taylor, Natalie Greene, Paul T. Jaeger, Abigail J. McDermott, Christie M. Kodama, and John Carlo Bertot. "Public Libraries in the New Economy: Twenty-First-Century Skills, the Internet and Community Needs." *Public Library Quarterly* 31 (2012): 191–219.

Urban Libraries Council. 2007. "Making Cities Stronger: Public Library Contributions to Local Economic Development." www.urban.org/uploadedpdf/1001075_stronger _cities.pdf.

Zickuhr, Kathryn, Lee Rainie, and Kristen Purcell. "Younger Americans' Library Habits and Expectations." 2013. http://libraries.pewInternet.org/2013/06/25/younger-americans -library-services.

School Libraries

Books/Monograph

American Association of School Librarians. *Developing Collections to Empower Learners.* Chicago: American Association of School Librarians, 2014.

———. *Empowering Learners: Guidelines for School Library Media Programs.* Chicago: American Association of School Librarians, 2009.

———. *Library Spaces for 21st-Century Learners.* Chicago: American Association of School Librarians, 2013.

———. *Standards for the 21st-Century Learner in Action.* Chicago: American Association of School Librarians, 2009.

Lance, Keith Curry, and Linda Hofschire. *Change in School Librarian Staffing Linked with Change in CSAP Reading Performance, 2005 to 2011.* Denver: Library Research Service, 2012.

Rosenfeld, Esther, and David V. Loertscher. Eds. *Toward a 21st Century School Library Media Program.* Lanham, MD: Scarecrow, 2007.

Squires, Tasha. *Library Partnerships: Making Connections between School and Public Libraries.* Medford, NJ: Information Today, 2009.

Woolls, Blanche, and David V. Loertscher. *The Whole School Library Handbook 2.* Chicago: ALA, 2014.

Articles

Adams, Helen R. "Fewer School Librarians: The Effect on Students' Intellectual Freedom." *School Library Monthly* 27 (March 2011): 52–53.

Ballew, L. M. "The Value of School Librarian Support in the Digital World." *Knowledge Quest* 42 (2014): 64–68.

Cooper, O. P., and Marty Bray. "School Library Media Specialist-Teacher Collaboration: Characteristics, Challenges, Opportunities." *TechTrends* 55 (July/August 2011): 48–54.

Ewbank, Ann Dutton. "Values-Oriented Factors Leading to Retention of School Librarian Positions: A School District Case Study." *School Library Research* 14 (2011): 1–15.

Heindel, M. C., K. R. Roberts, and A. J. Southworth. "Demonstrating the Essential Role of the School Librarian." *Knowledge Quest* 42 (2014): 74–76.

Houston, Cynthia R. "The Use of Reading Levels as Alternative Classification in School Libraries." *Cataloging & Classification Quarterly* 45 (2008): 65–80.

Johnson, Linda, and Jean Donham. "Reading by Grade Three: How Well Do School Library Circulation Policies Support Early Reading?" *Teacher Librarian* 40 (December 2012): 8–12.

Johnston, Melissa P. "School Librarians as Technology Integration Leaders: Enablers and Barriers to Leadership Enactment." *School Library Research* 15 (2012): 1–33.

Jones, Mai L. "Dropout Prevention through the School Library: Dispositions, Relationships, and Instructional Practices." *School Libraries Worldwide* 15 (July 2009): 77–90.

Kaser, Linda R. "A New Spin on Library Media Centers: The Hub of the School with the Help of Technology." *Library Media Connection* 24 (August/September 2005): 64–66.

Kemps, N. M., M. Marhefka, and A. Rominiecki. "Revisiting the Common Beliefs." *Knowledge Quest* 43 (2014): 74–77.

Kimmel, Sue C., Gail K. Dickinson, and Carol A. Doll. 2012. "Dispositions in the Twenty-First Century School Library Profession." *School Libraries Worldwide* 18 (July): 106–120.

Lance, K. C., and D. Kachel. "Achieving Academic Standards through the School Library Program." *Teacher Librarian* 40 (2013): 8–13.

McGrath, K. G. "School Libraries & Innovation." *Knowledge Quest* 43 (2015): 54–61.

Sensing, Victor. "Reading First, Libraries Last: An Historical Perspective on the Absence of Libraries in Reading Education Policy." *Journal of Education* 191 (2010/2011): 9–18.

Small, R. V., K. A. Justus, and J. L. Regitano. "ENABLE-ing School Librarians to Empower Students with Disabilities." *Teacher Librarian* 42 (2014): 18–22.

Stephens, W. S. "The School Librarian as Leader: Out of the Middle, into the Foreground." *Knowledge Quest* 39 (2011): 18–21.

Special Libraries

Books/Monographs

Corporate Libraries Metrics Task Force. *The Search for the Value of the Corporate Library:* A *Compendium of SLA-Funded Studies.* Alexandria, VA: SLA, 2013.

Kelsey, Sigrid E., and Marjorie J. Porter. Editors. *Best Practices for Corporate Libraries.* Santa Barbara: ABC-CLIO, 2011.

Matarazzo, Jame M., and Toby Pearlstein. *Special Libraries: A Survival Guide.* Santa Barbara: ABC-CLIO, 2013.

Articles

Ard, Constance. "Beyond Metrics: The Value of the Information Center." *Information Outlook* 16 (2012): 16–18.

Ard, Constance, and Shawn Livingston. "Reference and Research Services in Special Libraries: Navigating the Evolving Riches of Information." *Journal of Library Administration* 54 (2014): 518–528.

Brenneise, Philip. "Practical E-Book Solutions for Information Professionals." *Information Outlook* 17 (September/October 2013): 22–24.

Browne, M. "Communicating Value through Strategic Alignment." *Information Outlook* 15 (July/August 2011): 25–29.

Felix, Elliot, and Shirley Dugdale. "Libraries as Hubs in the New Workplace." In *Best Practices for Corporate Libraries*, edited by Sigrid E. Kelsey and Marjorie J. Porter. Santa Barbara: ABC CLIO, 2011.

Hiller, S. "What Are We Measuring, and Does It Matter?" *Information Outlook* 16 (2012): 10–12.

Keiser, Barbie E. "Competitive Intelligence for the Information Center." *Information Outlook* 6 (December 2002): 32–35.

Lastres, Steven A. "Aligning through Knowledge Management." *Information Outlook* 15 (June 2011): 23–25.

Murray, Tara E. "How Much Is a Special Library Worth? Valuing and Communicating Information in an Organizational Context." *Journal of Library Administration* 53 (2013): 462–471.

———. "What's So Special about Special Libraries?" *Journal of Library Administration* 14 (2013): 274–282.

Schachter, Debbie. "Creative Chaos: Innovation in Special Libraries." *Information Outlook* 9 (December 2005): 10–11.

Shumaker, David, and Mary Talley. "Models of Embedded Librarianship: A Research Summary." *Information Outlook* 14 (January–February 2010): 26–28.

St. Clair, Guy, Victoria Harriston, and Thomas A. Pellizzi. 2003. "Toward World-Class Knowledge Services: Emerging Trends in Specialized Research Libraries." *Information Outlook* 7 (July): 10–16.

Stamison, Christine. "Developing a Sound E-Book Strategy." *Information Outlook* 15 (July/August 2011): 10–12.

Swanson, Jennifer. "The Future of the Corporate Library." *Information Outlook* 18 (July/August 2014): 10–24.

Zeeman, Deane, Rebecca Jones, and Jane Dysart. "Assessing Innovation in Corporate and Government Libraries." *Computers in Libraries* (June 2011): 6–15.

4

Transforming the Library
The Impact and Implications of Technological Change

I. INTRODUCTION

People have been using technology to solve practical problems ever since they created tools from stones. When it comes to new technologies, LIS professionals historically have been quick to see their possibilities and to experiment with their use. For example, shortly after electric lights were invented, libraries installed them in library stacks in the nineteenth century, allowing librarians to quickly locate materials without burning down the library. Librarians have also created important intellectual technologies such as the Dewey Decimal Classification System. As early adopters, libraries were one of the first places to use computers. Today we can be certain of only two things: technological changes will continue unabated, and they will occur at an accelerated pace. Each time a library adopts a new technology, the functions and the culture of the library evolves in some way. Consider some of the changes the Internet has wrought on technical services and on the way librarians identify and deliver information to library users. It has changed the physical facility, the nature of the library's collection, and the roles of the library staff. It has changed the users themselves in terms of what they expect and how quickly they expect it. There can be little doubt that technology brings both exciting possibilities and complex problems associated with change and adaptation.

This chapter begins with a review of how new technologies affected libraries historically. The remainder of the chapter discusses some of the major issues and current challenges facing libraries.

II. TECHNOLOGICAL DEVELOPMENTS AFFECTING LIBRARIES FROM 1900

A. Developments in Microphotography

The first half of the twentieth century was a fruitful period for technological development. Major improvements in communications and transportation were especially notable, including the growth and expansion of telephone services, improvements in airplanes and automobiles, and development of the cathode ray tube and photoelectric cells. Perhaps the most notable developments for libraries were related to new photographic technologies, especially microphotography, which permitted the reproduction of print documents (reprography) onto film (microforms). The physical format was usually a roll of film, the microfilm, or a rectangular card, the microcard. As an alternative to paper, microphotography had advantages: it provided a significant amount of information in a compact medium and it was lighter and easier to store. It also proved to be an exceptional medium for the preservation of materials likely to deteriorate over time, such as newspapers, magazines, and documents. By the 1920s most libraries were using microforms.

Reprography saw additional advances in the 1960s with the development of duplicating machines, most notably the photocopier. Photocopying profoundly affected the dissemination of knowledge (as well as paper consumption). Although not as dramatic as the invention of the printing press, photocopying revolutionized communications because it permitted greater flexibility in the distribution of published materials. In essence, "libraries became publishers of single copies on demand" (De Gennaro 1989, p. 42).

B. First Application of Computer Technologies in Libraries: The 1960s

In the nineteenth century, libraries adopted new, mechanical sorting techniques using punch cards, an early precursor to computers (Buckland 1996). These early efforts at "mechanization" evolved into "library automation" in the 1960s as computers became more sophisticated. Bierman (1991) defined automation as "the application of computer and communication technologies to traditional library processes and services" (p. 67). The rationale for automation was based on reasonable assumptions that these new technologies increased efficiency, produced costs savings, and reduced the size of staff.

The first significant application of computer technologies in libraries was the creation of Machine-Readable Cataloging (MARC), which became the standard for the creation of bibliographic records. MARC allowed librarians to enter, store, and disseminate bibliographic data electronically on computer tapes (see chapter 6). Library support agencies, known as bibliographic utilities, quickly recognized MARC's potential. One of these, the Ohio College Library Center (OCLC) was incorporated as a not-for-profit corporation serving academic libraries in 1967. OCLC loaded the MARC tapes created by individual OCLC member libraries. The member libraries then examined the centralized bibliographic records, edited them for their local institutions, and ordered tailored catalog cards electronically. The cards arrived quickly, ready for filing, in effect creating an online, shared cataloging network. The advantages quickly became clear to other libraries, and in 1972 OCLC opened its membership to nonacademic libraries (Grosch 1995). This led to tremendous growth in membership and increased cooperation among different types of libraries and among regional library networks. Consequently, in 1981 OCLC changed its name to the Online Computing Library Center. Over the decades, OCLC services grew, offering interlibrary loan and document delivery, acquisition systems, serials control, electronic publishing, and access to electronic databases. Major research libraries formed another bibliographic utility called the Research Libraries Group (RLG) that created the Research Libraries Information Network (RLIN), now a part of OCLC. RLIN offered access to bibliographic databases containing thousands of research records. It is difficult to overestimate the major changes created by MARC. The impact on cataloging departments, for example, was substantial, resulting in a significant reduction in the number of catalogers.

The 1960s was also when the first applications of online information retrieval systems developed. Initially these were prototype systems, usually consisting of a small database and one terminal. In 1966, the Lockheed Missiles and Space Company, working primarily with government agencies such as NASA, developed the earliest form of the Dialog system, containing over 200 bibliographic and reference databases (Summit 2002). Today, ProQuest owns the Dialog system and provides access to 90,000 authoritative sources and 6 billion digital pages, spanning six centuries of information. During this same period, the National Library of Medicine, one of the great special libraries in the world, was confronted with a rapid expansion of scientific and technical knowledge. It quickly became obvious that they could no longer continue manually indexing the medical literature. By recording all bibliographic citations on computer tapes, Index Medicus became a searchable database, one of the great achievements of the decade.

The decade ended with even more far-reaching developments that would significantly affect libraries several years later. In 1969 the Defense Advanced Research Projects Agency within the Department of Defense developed at the University of California at Los Angeles a computer network called ARPANET. ARPANET was

created to improve government-sponsored research by electronically linking organizations with defense-related contracts at different sites and allowing them to share
research and data (Tennant 1992). One of the innovations of this system was the
first practical use of a new technology that allowed discrete packets of information
to be sent independently of one another across "packet-switching" networks. The
discrete packet transfer increased reliability and speed, thus substantially improving
the transmission of research data and analysis. Although ARPANET membership
was restricted to government-funded institutions, this network was the genesis of
what would become the Internet. ARPANET significantly advanced development
of key Internet features such as file transfer, remote access of data, and electronic
mail (Bishop 1990).

Although libraries were quick to adopt MARC records for creating catalog cards
and to use computers to generate purchase orders, there remained considerable
skepticism that automation could be applied practically to most library functions
and services (Grosch 1995). Nonetheless, a new era had begun.

C. Use of Online Information Retrieval Systems for Reference: The 1970s

The increasing sophistication of computer technologies, including the development of the minicomputer, made online interactive capabilities a reality (Grosch
1995). Major information-dependent institutions such as the military, and business
and industry, quickly recognized their potential, and commercial vendors rapidly
developed a variety of databases that could be accessed through telephone lines.
Although these vendors did not necessarily design their services for libraries, it was
clear that libraries would be substantial users. However, due to the technical and
scientific nature of the databases, academic and public libraries often created separate facilities and assigned a specially trained librarian to conduct online searches
because the cost of a search was calculated based on the time it took to perform it.
Even then, libraries often had to pass on at least part of the costs to the individual for
whom the search was conducted—a disconcerting practice that ran counter to the
normal practice of providing free services.

Online access also required search strategies that could exploit the unique flexibility of computerized systems. Perhaps the most prominent development in this
area was Boolean searching, based on the nineteenth-century logic theory of George
Boole. Its application in the online environment permitted searching using logical
connectors such as "and," "or," and "not," which narrowed the search and yielded
more precise access to large bodies of knowledge in a much shorter period of time.

Another strategy involved searching for a particular key word or phrase anywhere in the bibliographic record, including an abstract. This strategy differed significantly from traditional searches using subject terms, titles, or authors.

The 1970s also saw the beginning of early attempts to automate library circulation, serials control, cataloging, and acquisition systems. However, these systems were far more complex than anticipated, and they did not reach maturity until a decade later.

D. CD-ROMs and Integrated Library Systems: The 1980s

1. The CD-ROM

No less remarkable than online searching was the revolution in information access provided by the development of the Compact Disk–Read Only Memory (CD-ROM). One 4½" disk could contain all, or most, of the contents of standard reference tools such as the *Reader's Guide to Periodical Literature*. CD-ROMs had several distinct advantages over online searching because they were held locally and required no telephone line. Librarians could search vast databases directly using Boolean tools as well as by author, title, and subject. Libraries subscribed to vendor services that provided the CD-ROMs, thus offering a fixed-cost alternative to variable online computing costs. Information vendors sent the software and disks to load onto library computers, along with periodic updates.

2. Integrated Library Systems

a. The Development of Online Public Access Catalogs (OPACs)

Online public access catalogs (OPACs) allowed patrons to directly access the library's computerized bibliographic records using a variety of search tools, including the familiar author, title, and subject search, as well as keywords, call numbers, and ISBNs. There was no longer any need for libraries to buy catalog cards or hire individuals to file them. These savings, however, were offset by major investments in hardware, software, computer maintenance, and construction costs to change the library's physical environment and infrastructure.

Although OPACs were helpful, Borgman (1996) noted that much of the improvement in user interfaces was superficial. Library users experienced persistent problems related to their lack of knowledge of (1) the conceptual and semantic framework of OPACs' specific terminology, (2) the basic search strategies such as "browse" or "keyword" searching, (3) how to search fields other than author, title, or subject, and (4) Boolean searching. Today, as more people are familiar with the functionalities of search engines and the Internet, they will demand the same flexibility from the online catalog (Novotny 2004). Markey (2007) noted that although online catalogs used to be where people started searching for information, Google now takes precedence. He suggested that online catalogs need to be redesigned with similar retrieval capabilities, with improved subject searching and metadata, and with the ability to return precise search results.

b. The Linked System Project: Linked Systems Protocol (LSP)

As online catalogs proliferated, the advantages of linking computers in various libraries and organizations became obvious. Unfortunately, at the time, computers could not "talk" to each other because different developers had created incompatible systems. The Linked System Project, funded by the Council on Library Resources, which involved the American Library Association, OCLC, the Research Libraries Information Network, the Western Library Network, and the LOC, sought to solve this problem. The project's solution was the linked systems protocol (LSP), also known as the Z39.50 standard (NISO 1994) which became a national standard for bibliographic information retrieval. By linking automated systems, authorized users could consult the OPACs of countless libraries and information organizations (Buckland and Lynch 1987, 1988). Realization of this goal wasn't achieved until the 1990s, with major improvements in telecommunications technologies.

c. Online Circulation Systems

Once OPACs were linked, the next logical step was automating circulation. Initially attempted in the 1970s, it wasn't until the 1980s that commercial vendors developed practical automated circulation systems. Although these "turnkey" systems were relatively inexpensive, it took considerable time for staff to bar-code the materials and convert records into machine-readable format (retrospective conversion). Additional time was needed to weed the collection to avoid spending money to input old, unused materials. Public library staff generally continued to process the materials while many academic libraries enabled "self-initiated" systems that allowed patrons to check out their own books. These more computerized systems could track overdue items, send out recall notices, produce circulation reports, and analyze how the library collection was being used and, therefore, could assist in planning.

d. Automated Acquisitions and Serials Systems

The 1980s also saw the burgeoning of systems designed to help libraries acquire materials. Some of the larger book vendors, such as Blackwell North America and

Baker and Taylor, were quite active in developing these systems. Other vendors such as Innovative Interface developed acquisitions systems for serials. All of these systems were directly linked to the vendors and the library ordered its materials online. The system could set limits so that a particular department could not exceed its budget, and produced reports for analysis and evaluation. Some systems included a serials check-in system to save labor on the cumbersome tasks of checking in magazines and other periodicals. They could also create an electronic profile of the library based on its purchases. The vendor could then automatically send materials that matched the profile without the library ordering each item, saving time for both the library and the vendor.

3. The Growth of the Internet and the World Wide Web: The 1990s

a. Growth of the Internet

Auspiciously, the birth of the Internet occurred in 1984, the result of a mutually beneficial arrangement between the Department of Defense (DoD) and the National Science Foundation (NSF). At a time when government funding for ARPANET was declining, the NSF was establishing supercomputing centers at major university research centers to support some of the most advanced research in the world. NSF needed a "high-speed telecommunications backbone" to facilitate communication among the centers. NSF negotiated with DoD to use the ARPANET technology. The NSF later invited other universities to join the network for a flat, reasonable fee and encouraged faculty and students to participate. Every linked computer used a standardized communication protocol, the Transmission Control Protocol/ Internet Protocol (TCP/IP), which provided a unique, numeric IP address (e.g., 121.123.46.22) for every computer. Because most people are better at remembering names than numbers, the Domain Name Service (DNS) translated the IP address into a name (e.g., www.slis.kent.edu).

The resulting NSF-linked network formed the foundation of what was to become the Internet. The growth of the Internet brought increased attention to national productivity issues and international competitiveness. During the George H. W. Bush administration, Democratic Senator Al Gore introduced legislation to develop a national "information highway." The National High Performance Computing Act of 1991 ensured an efficient national communication system and mandated the creation of the National Research and Education Network (NREN) to increase electronic access to federal agencies, industry and business, libraries, and educational institutions. While moving toward this goal, however, a significant shift in political attitudes occurred during the Clinton administration. Private groups with a significant stake in the Internet's development advocated for greater privatization, less reliance on government financial assistance, and regulatory relief (Gomery 1994). At this critical juncture, the telecommunications industry (e.g., telephone, television, and cable industries) and private enterprises, as well as literally thousands of interested individuals and organizations, became the primary developers of the Internet.

The involvement of all of these varied participants created a network of networks with an open architecture, the Internet we have today. In an open-architecture structure, individual networks can be designed for specific environments and user requirements, with their own unique interface, but which can be available to other users and/or providers (Leiner, et al. 2010). This open structure produces tremendous flexibility, a concept Zittrain (2006) referred to as "generative capacity."

> Generativity denotes a technology's overall capacity to produce unprompted change driven by large, varied, and uncoordinated audiences. . . . The Internet is built to be open to any sort of device: any computer or other information processor could be part of the new network as long as it was properly interfaced, an exercise requiring minimal technical effort. (pp. 1974–1976)

The Internet is an especially generative technology because it is highly adaptable, relatively easy to use, makes a variety of difficult tasks easier, and is accessible to a wide audience using many applications. The fact that developments and innovations were not controlled by a small number of proprietary interests or governed by a centralized unit created tremendous potential for growth and creativity:

> The design of the Internet also reflects both the resource limitations and intellectual interests of its creators, who were primarily academic researchers and moonlighting corporate engineers. These individuals did not command the vast resources needed to implement a global network and had little interest in exercising control over the network or its users' behavior. . . . The resulting Internet is a network that no one in particular owns and that anyone can join. (Zittrain 2006, pp. 1989, 1993)

Librarians quickly recognized its values. Kuttner (2006) observed, perhaps somewhat romantically, "In some respects the Internet is just an extension of the physical library, the Enlightenment dream of a universal encyclopedia" (p. 13).

i. Early Features of the Internet

Electronic Mail: First introduced in October 1972, electronic mail (e-mail) allowed individuals and organization to quickly communicate locally or worldwide. Groups of individuals could subscribe to a mass e-mail list known as a

"Listserv" and post information to the list, usually on a particular topic or area of interest. A Listserv allowed a common message to be sent to thousands of individuals, promoting further discussion and responses from Listserv members. Some Listservs were open; others had restricted membership and there was usually an administrator who handled membership and other administrative functions.

Remote Login: Remote login allowed an individual to access thousands of computer systems located anywhere in the world. Tennant (1992) identified the significant advantage of remote login:

> What makes this application truly remarkable is that ease and speed of access are not dependent upon proximity. An Internet user can connect to a system on the other side of the globe as easily as . . . he can connect to a system in the next building. In addition, since many Internet users are not at present charged for their network use by their institutions, or at least are not charged by the level of their use, cost is often not a significant inhibitor of usage. Therefore the barriers of distance, time and costs, which are often significant when using other forms of electronic communication, can be reduced in the Internet environment. (p. 2)

File Transfer: The File Transfer Protocol (FTP) allowed the transfer of electronic files (reports, numerical data, sounds, and images), including large amounts of data referred to as archives, from one computer to another. This function still occurs as an integral part of other, more sophisticated, services.

b. The World Wide Web

The development of the World Wide Web was closely related to, but distinct from, the development of the Internet. The Web's technology was developed for CERN (European Organization for Nuclear Research) in 1989 under the direction of Tim Berners-Lee. In one of the most extraordinary acts of public generosity, Berners-Lee placed this technology in the public domain making it openly and freely available worldwide (Pew Research "World Wide . . . 2014). The World Wide Web Consortium (W3C), created in 1994, established working groups to develop Web protocols and guidelines. Since then W3C working groups have produced technical reports and open source software; promoted standardization by making recommendations regarding social, legal, and public policy concerns; and addressed accessibility issues related to usability for people with disabilities (World Wide Web Consortium 2010).

The Web created exciting new possibilities. Using a variety of protocols including HTML (hypertext markup language) and HTTP (hypertext transfer protocol), Web designers could embed sound, video, graphics, and illustrations in documents.

When the document was accessed, the embedded images and sound were also available. In a hypertext environment, these documents have visible (highlighted) links to other documents, which allow ideas or terms to be connected. A user can move from one part of a text or document to another merely by clicking on the highlighted term. Navigation between documents is accomplished by graphical Web browsers. In the 1990s, Netscape and Internet Explorer were popular browsers that displayed Web documents and enabled the hyperlinks (December and Randall 1995).

Establishing standards and consistency on the Web was one of the goals of its early developers. W3C was created in 1994 to develop common protocols and guidelines that would enable long-term growth of the Web (World Wide Web Consortium 2010). Over the years, W3C working groups produced technical reports and open source software and promoted standardization by making recommendations regarding the architecture of the Web. They also addressed features that affect interaction with Web users, including social, legal, and public policy concerns, and accessibility issues related to usability for people with disabilities.

Finding information on the Web requires the use of search engines. Fielden and Kuntz (2002) describe a search engine as "an automated software that matches a searcher's topic terms (keywords) with an indexed list of documents found on the Web . . . arranges that list according to some order of relevancy, and provides hyperlinks to those documents so that they might be visited" (p. 13). Search engines do not search the entire Web, but rather a particular database or specific collection of documents, which can be composed of millions of websites and documents. Google, for example, indexes billions of Web documents.

Search engines in the 1990s performed many of the functions they do today. They compiled collections of websites by sending out what are called spiders, robots, bots, or crawlers to locate as many seemingly relevant documents as possible. Located documents were then scanned by software that created an index based on the keywords in each document. Some crawlers might scan entire documents, or just the title and certain segments. When someone typed a query, the search engine related the search terms to the index and produced the relevant pages. Each search engine was unique and therefore the results might vary substantially. For example, some but not all search engines ranked the contents from most relevant to least relevant. Ranking might be influenced by the tags assigned to a particular Web document, or the frequency of keywords or phrases. By the late 1990s and into the early twenty-first century a number of search engines existed, including Google, Yahoo, Mozilla, and Bing.

For LIS professionals, the proliferation of websites and their growing use was a mixed blessing. Despite the volume of information available, there was serious concern about its quality and trustworthiness. The traditional methods librarians' used to evaluate and select informational materials did not apply to the search-engine process. Librarians' worst fears were realized in a study by Pew (Associated Press 2005), which reported that one in six adult users could not tell the difference between unbiased search results and paid advertisements. Thirty-eight percent of adults searching the Web did not know the difference between sponsored links and regular ones and less than half could indicate which links had been paid for. Librarians began to address this issue by establishing their own Web pages that guided users to specific sites that had been vetted like other library materials.

III. TECHNOLOGY AND LIBRARIES IN THE TWENTY-FIRST CENTURY

A. The First Decade: 2000–2010

1. Web 2.0 and Social Media

As the Internet continued to evolve, dramatic improvements in applications increased the potential for social interaction and the creation of online communities. The Internet became a dynamic network where the users added to the online content—in effect creating an "architecture of participation" (O'Reilly 2005, p. 7). The participatory nature of this activity prompted a new phrase—Web 2.0 or "social media"—to describe the evolution from consultation with Web pages to social interactions among Web users. Curtis (2014) characterized social media in the following way:

> Social media are Internet sites where people interact freely, sharing and discussing information about each other and their lives, using a multimedia mix of personal words, pictures, videos and audio. At these Web sites, individuals and groups create and exchange content and engage in person-to-person conversations. (p. 1)

A variety of new social media formats appeared: blogs, wikis, and social networks.

a. Blogs

A blog or Weblog "refers to a category of Website where the content is presented in a continuing sequence of dated entries. Put simply, 'a blog is an online diary'" (Kajewski 2006, p. 157). Blogs permit an individual or a group to post their ideas on a website, permit others to respond and link to other websites. Users can react to the content, contribute their own content, and see others' comments as well. Blogs can be highly personal—of interest primarily to one's family or friends—or they can disseminate information on a broad scale; some report or analyze current news or political events. During national or international crises, blogs have been a major source of news when traditional sources were either unavailable or suppressed by authorities. Libraries used blogs to communicate news or information to the public about new services, new books, and AV materials, and to stimulate discussion, as well as to promote the library and its services (Kajewski 2006).

b. Wikis

The wiki, derived from the Hawaiian word for "quick," was designed in 1994 by Ward Cunningham, an Oregon-based computer programmer, for the purpose of collaborative development (Stephens 2006). A wiki differs from a blog in that the content is created without any defined owner or leader, and wikis have little implicit structure, allowing structure to emerge according to the needs of the users (Mitchell, 2008). Chawner and Lewis (2006) described a wiki as "a server-based collaborative tool that allows any authorized user to edit Web pages and create new ones using nothing more than a Web browser and a text entry form on a Web page" (p. 33). The term wiki can refer to a website or the software that runs it. Wikis do not require knowledge of coding or programming languages; rather they use a "simple text-based markup language that is easy to learn" and allow any user with a Web browser to insert new pages, enter new content in existing pages, or delete information (Cochenour 2006, p. 34).

Perhaps the best-known application of the wiki technology is Wikipedia, a massive, dynamic, ever-expanding, and changing reference tool. Rather than relying on a limited number of "experts" to create the tool, thousands of contributors and reviewers collaboratively contributed to its creation, what O'Reilly (2005) referred to as harnessing a "collective intelligence" (p. 9). Underlying this revolutionary approach was the belief that the community of users could also be creators and contributors to the content. Wikipedia has editors and several hundred experienced users, designated as administrators, with the authorization to regulate content and users (Binkley 2006). Because users also "vet" the encyclopedic entries, some critics argued that Wikipedia's approach invited inaccuracies or fraud, but to date there is little evidence that it is less accurate than other similar tools (Eiffert 2006):

> Bottom line: Subject to ongoing critical review, Wikipedia articles are generally well-researched and substantiated by footnoting and linking to sources, allowing readers to judge the quality of information being used. Moreover, Wikipedia entries often have more and more current information. (p. 83)

In fact, Wikipedia's breadth of coverage and constant updating made it one of the most consulted sites on Google (Crovitz 2009).

c. Social Networks

Although first launched in the late 1990s, social networking found its first success in Friendster, a site created in 2002 for people to connect with their friends, make new friends, and date (Digital Trends 2014). The site was tremendously popular: in three months Friendster had more than 3 million users (Curtis 2014). The following year, a professionally oriented site, LinkedIn, was introduced, and a new social network, MySpace, competed directly with Friendster. For a time, MySpace was a favorite among young people who were attracted by

> . . . music, music videos, and a funky, feature-filled environment. It looked and felt hipper than major competitor Friendster right from the start, and it conducted a campaign of sorts in the early days to show alienated Friendster users just what they were missing. (Digital Trends p. 7)

MySpace declined in popularity, in turn, as a newer social media tool, Facebook, founded in 2004 at Harvard University, gained exposure. Facebook's highly attractive features led to its quick expansion and in 2006 it was open to public access. Facebook launched its open platform in 2007 which permitted third-party developers to create applications that operated within Facebook itself. Facebook also introduced the "Like" button which engaged its users in a unique way and which was quickly appropriated by other social networks, like Twitter (Digital Trends 2014). In 2008 Facebook overtook MySpace in number of visitors, and by 2009 it was recognized as the most widely used social network around the world with more than 200 million users—twice that of MySpace (Curtis 2014).

Librarians noticed that young people and students were frequently using the library's computer terminals for access to social networking sites. The issue for LIS professionals was how to exploit the popularity of social networking to benefit the library. Could the library create its own social presence? Perhaps social networking was an opportunity for libraries to communicate with users, promote library services, and strengthen their relationship with users. Among many discussions on these issues, there was particular concern of the potential misuse and victimization of library users by online predators (Chu and Meulemans 2008).

2. Really Simple Syndication (RSS) and Podcasting

Really Simple Syndication (RSS) is "an XML-based document format for the syndication of Web content so that it can be republished on other sites or downloaded periodically and presented to users" (RSS Advisory Board 2010, p. 2). A "feed" is the stream of content from an RSS account. Feeds allow online sources to send information to users in real time once the user subscribes to the feed and possesses the necessary software (Wikipedia 2009). This is a highly valuable medium to maintain awareness of current events. Users might receive messages about news, events, and activities sent to their designated communication devices. Commercial enterprises can inform customers about sales and new product developments; libraries can push announcements to patrons about upcoming activities, the latest services, or newest materials being acquired by the library.

RSS technology was the foundation for "podcasting." Podcasts were "audio files that [could] be downloaded and played either through a computer or an MP3 player such as an iPod" (Balas 2005, p. 29). With the RSS technology people no longer had to access the Web each time they wanted certain information; rather, once they subscribed to a particular feed, new files were downloaded automatically. It was the syndication aspect that made podcasts unique. Podcasts became quite popular for news updates and music downloads. They contained video as well as audio content and could be sent to phones and other communication devices as well as computers. In 2013, 27% of Internet users listened to podcasts (Pew Research, 'Over a Quarter" 2013). LIS professionals have used podcasting for training and development for patrons and staff, book reviews, updates on the library, a source of presentations or lectures, and library tours. The library became not only a place to access podcasts (some libraries loan iPods), (Stephens 2005; Kajewski 2006) but a content creator as well.

3. Internet2

Although originally designed for research and development, the Internet evolved to serve popular and commercial purposes. Nonetheless, the original purpose remained critical for academics and scholars. Consequently, in 1996, more than 200 U.S. universities and other institutions of higher learning, seventy corporate partners, and forty-five government agencies and laboratories as well as fifty international partner organizations collaborated to found the Internet2 Consortium. Its purpose was not to replace the Internet but to enhance and improve it and share new developments with others in the educational community (Internet2 2009). To that end, members promoted "leading-edge network capabilities and unique partnership opportunities that together facilitate the development, deployment, and use of revolutionary Internet technologies" (Internet2 2009, p. 1). Ultimately, their goal was "to accelerate research discovery, advance national and global education, and improve the delivery of public services (Internet2 2014). The Internet2 network is now in its fourth generation with 8.8 Terabits of capacity; providing an advanced platform for U.S. researchers and educators to share greater quantities of data over a 100 gigabit-per-second network. As of 2014, there were more than 500 members including 250 U.S. universities, 82 major corporations, 68 affiliate members including government agencies, 41 regional and state education networks, and more than 65 national research and education networking partners representing over 100 countries. The members of Internet2 collaborate on a variety of initiatives and technical issues through working, special interest, and advisory groups. Initiatives such as its "K20-Initiative" extended technologies, applications, and content to a wide range of educational and cultural institutions including colleges, universities, primary and secondary schools, libraries, and museums (Internet2 2014). As a vital and continuing force, innovations produced by the Internet2 community have transformed higher education and extended its influence beyond its members, affecting more than 93,000 institutions both in the United States and around the world.

4. The Growth of Google

In the first decade of the twenty-first century, search engines became everyday information tools for millions of people around the globe, including LIS professionals. Yahoo, Mozilla, and Bing were household names, but Google ruled. Google began as a research project of Sergey Brin and Larry Page. The company incorporated in September 1998 and its first location was a garage in Menlo Park, California. Once online, within a few weeks, Google was conducting 100,000 searches a day. Quickly recognized as a state-of-the art search engine, venture capitalists clamored to become a part of the enterprise. By June 2000, Google was indexing 1 billion pages, handling 18 million search queries a day, accepting advertisements, and generating more than $19 million in revenue. It was the largest and busiest search engine on the Internet. The next year, Google indexed 3 billion pages and generated more than $86 million in revenue (Robison 2007). Google continued to grow, adding Gmail, Google Scholar, and Google Books (see discussion below). By 2010, Google was indexing one trillion sites (Curtis 2014).

LIS professionals closely monitored Google's rise, often feeling somewhat overwhelmed by what was happening in the online environment. OCLC reported survey findings in 2005 that convey some of the reasons:

- Seventy-two percent of the respondents had used a search engine at least once, and among people who used online sources for information, 84% started with search engines. Sixty-two percent indicated that Google was the most frequently used search engine, more than 40 percentage points ahead of the nearest competitor—Yahoo.

- Search engines were viewed more favorably than libraries as a place to get information, although both were favorably viewed: 88% viewed search engines favorably compared to 79% for libraries.

- Ninety-three percent believed that Google provided worthwhile information compared to 78% for a library's website.

- When compared to the library, people reported that they thought search engines were much faster, more convenient, easier to use, cost effective, and available. Libraries were viewed as more credible, trustworthy, and accurate.

- When comparing the information provided by a search engine and the information received from a librarian, people were equally very satisfied from both sources, although they received the information from the search engine more quickly. In general, they felt that search engines were equally trustworthy when compared to library sources. (De Rosa et al. 2005)

5. Mass Digitalization and Google Books

Libraries and other institutions have digitized materials for years, but the scale of such efforts accelerated with Google Books. In December 2004, Google entered into a partnership to digitize and index more than 10 million unique titles with five major research libraries known as the G5: the University of Michigan, Harvard, Stanford, Oxford, and the New York Public Library. The goal was formidable: "Our ultimate goal is to work with publishers and libraries to create a comprehensive, searchable, virtual card catalog of all books in all languages that helps users discover new books and publishers discover new readers" (Google "Books" 2015).

The project had two parts: a "Partners Program" and a "Library Project." The Partners program allowed publishers to enter their books, with embedded features, called "snippets" such as previews, into the Google Books database. A visitor to Google books could browse the publishers' content that would help foster book sales. To protect the book from inappropriate copying, publishers could limit the amount of content available. Google Books also provided links to bookstores and online retailers (Google "Google Books Library Program" 2015). Because publishers were voluntarily making their copyright materials available, there was no significant controversy over this aspect of Google Books.

The "Library Project" was an entirely different matter. In this case, major libraries permitted Google to scan significant portions of their library collections. Google did not seek permission to scan copyrighted works owned by the libraries. In exchange for scanning, Google provided the libraries with digital copies of their scanned books. Google also stored a digital copy of these works. Using metadata, the book was indexed and digital copies were then made available, allowing an individual to search the extensive database of scanned titles by word or phrase. As of 2013, more than 20 million copies had been scanned and the number of library partners increased to forty, including several institutions from other nations. A Google Books search was similar to a typical Google search: searchers designed their own queries and Google returned a list of books fitting the query. As Google described it,

> When you click on a search result for a book from the Library Project, you'll see basic bibliographic information about the book, and in many cases, a few snippets—a few sentences showing your search term in context. If the book is out of copyright, you'll be able to view and download the entire book. In all cases, you'll see links directing you to online bookstores where you can buy the book and libraries where you can borrow it (Google "Books" 2015).

From the perspective of a typical user or researcher, this was a wonderful tool. A vast number of books could be searched and accessed to determine the relevance of the title and whether purchasing the title or borrowing the title was merited. If a book was out of copyright, the entire title could be downloaded.

From a publisher's perspective, however, Google Books represented a significant copyright violation. Consequently, in 2005, the Authors Guild brought a class action suit accusing Google of copyright infringements. Google responded that their activity fell under "the doctrine of fair use" which permits an individual or organization to make a single copy of a work without the permission of the copyright owner. A protracted series of negotiations led to a proposed settlement early in 2011. However, the judge overseeing the case, Judge Chin, rejected the proposed settlement "on the grounds that is was not fair, adequate, and reasonable" (U.S. District Court 2013, p. 13). Despite further efforts to reach a settlement, an agreement could not be reached. On November 14, 2013, Judge Chin issued a ruling in favor of Google (U.S. District Court 2013). The judge acknowledged that on the face of it, Google made copies of copyrighted works with intent to make a profit. However, the judge also noted that Google did not sell the digitized books. As a result, the judge ruled that the use of the copyrighted works was "transformative," that is, the scanned text was used in a manner and for a purpose that was fundamentally different from selling the book to a prospective reader. The use was "transformative" because (1) the texts were repurposed as part of a comprehensive index intended to aid the discovery of the books by scholars and others, (2) the "snippets" provided were used to facilitate the search process, and (3) the texts were transformed into a format that allowed for significant research purposes such as data mining which supported new fields of research (U.S. District Court 2013). The judge concluded,

> In my view, Google Books provides significant public benefits. It advances the progress of the arts and sciences, while maintaining respectful consideration for the right of authors and other creative individuals, and without adversely impacting the rights of copyright holders. It has become an invaluable research tool that permits students, teachers, librarians, and other to more efficiently identify and locate books. It has given scholars the ability, for the first time, to conduct full-text searches of tens of millions of books. It preserves books, in particular out-of-print and old books that have been forgotten in the bowels of libraries, and it gives them new life. It facilitates access to books for print-disabled and remote or underserved populations. It generates new audiences and creates new sources of income for authors and publishers. Indeed, all society benefits. (U.S. District Court 2013, p. 26)

Interestingly, while the Google Books case was going through the courts, in 2011 the Authors Guild also sued the HathiTrust. The HathiTrust described itself as "a partnership of major research institutions and libraries working to ensure that the cultural record is preserved and accessible long into the future." The trust had more than ninety partners, and membership was open to institutions worldwide. The focus of the trust was to build comprehensive and widely accessible digital archives from materials that originally appeared in print. The HathiTrust Digital Library combined in digital form the scholarly collections of the partner institutions, securing the digital content, making it accessible to the partners through keyword searching, and preserving the content for future generations (HathiTrust 2014). The trust did not, in general, deliver the digital content, but delivered titles and page numbers to help researchers locate and acquire the desired materials. However, it did provide full-text content to individuals who were blind or otherwise print disabled (Barclay and McSherry 2012).

As in the Google case, the guild claimed that the digitization of the materials was a copyright violation. The judge at the federal district court level supported the HathiTrust, declaring the creation of a searchable database for scholarly purposes was a transformative use and a significant contribution to the advancement of science and the arts—a fundamental reason for copyright regulation (Barclay and McSherry 2012). The guild appealed and the appellate court again supported the HathiTrust's transformative use of the database and the provision of full text to the visually disabled (EFF 2013). In the future, it will be important for LIS professionals to stay up-to-date on any new rulings that might arise from these or other cases that could limit access to scholarly knowledge.

6. Preserving Digital Content

Digital preservation is addressed from the academic library's perspective in chapter 6 on library organization. This section discusses digital preservation issues generally.

Historically, the purpose of preservation was to protect an item. Use of the item, in fact, was often perceived as one of the threats to preservation: using rare and fragile paper documents, for example, might cause them to deteriorate further. In contrast, preserving information in a digital format increases access; fragile documents could be converted to a digital format so that millions can access them. Digital preservation is a "series of managed activities necessary to ensure continued access to digital materials for as long as necessary" (DPC 2012). It can take many forms, including making a "digital double" of a paper document or a physical object.

Candidates for digital preservation include cultural objects such as artworks that are difficult to access due to their remote location or fragility; scientific data both current and historical; and books, journals, and other paper records for educational, business, and governmental purposes. The need for digital preservation also extends to Web pages and datasets that were born digital; that is, they were originally created digitally and might not have a representation outside the digital environment. As more and more information appears on the Web, how do we preserve Web content? It is now common to search for a website and see the familiar message: "File Not Found." A significant proportion of sites can disappear from the Web in just a few years, and there are billions of sites.

Caplan (2008) identified at least three functions of digital preservation: (1) protecting materials against unauthorized alterations, (2) conserving storage media to avoid deterioration, and (3) maintaining digital materials so they can be used over time. This third function suggests a larger notion that Caplan referred to as "digital curation," which takes a "life-cycle approach focusing on the ongoing use and re-use of digital materials" (p. 38). In other words, digital information originally created and stored in a now-obsolete format should be able to migrate to a new format, thus restoring access. This concept revealed a new perspective: the importance of preserving access (Zeng 2008):

> The survival of a document is not dependent on how long the medium carrying it will last, but on the capacity of that document to be transferred from one medium to another as often as possible. . . . The most significant threats to digital continuity concern loss of the means of access. (p. 8)

Access and preservation are related but distinct activities. Failure to recognize this distinction was a serious problem at the end of the twentieth century because often the medium employed to store content, such as magnetic tape and CD-ROMS, was not particularly stable, certainly not as stable as paper. In our rush to provide access, LIS professionals must remember that in order to preserve the content, the access medium must be stable. This problem is referred to as "fixity." That is, print materials have some permanence, but electronic text is impermanent. The ease with which digital material can be altered also raises serious questions about its capacity to serve as a preservation technique. Regardless of format or medium, eventually all electronic data will need to be refreshed or transferred to a new technology; otherwise, the content might be lost.

With the continued trend of digital collections residing in the hands of commercial vendors rather than libraries, the preservation of data might rely on the commitment of those vendors to preserve their data. Unlike libraries, one of whose traditional missions is to preserve access to cultural data, vendors are driven by the commercial value of the data they possess; as soon as the data loses its revenue-generating potential, there is little incentive for them to retain it or make it accessible. In 2010, the Blue Ribbon Task Force on Sustainable Digital Preservation and Access (BRTF) (2010) attempted to address these issues and made a series of recommendations designed to foster sustainable digital preservation. They include:

- providing financial incentive to commercial owners of digital content to preserve materials that are in the public interest
- issuing governmental mandates when appropriate
- revising copyright laws to permit archiving of some commercial digital content by stewardship organizations acting in the interest of long-term preservation
- developing agreements among relevant parties to implement policies and procedures that preserve digital content throughout its life cycle: creation, selection, preparation, and secure transfer of the content
- creating policies and processes to transfer commercial digital content to public stewardship for preservation after the content has lost its market value but is still of value for research, cultural, or other public purposes
- developing techniques that significantly reduce the costs of digital preservation, including storage, energy consumption in system maintenance, preservation/curation strategies, and access
- creating both market-based and public-good-based funding models for producing and preserving digital content

These recommendations highlight what LIS professionals have realized for some time: that the magnitude of the digital preservation challenge cannot be met by individual libraries or singular organizations alone. Rather, the stakeholders who produce and distribute digital content must collaborate with libraries and other public institutions in order to maintain our cultural heritage and traditions. The LOC National Digital Information Infrastructure and Preservation Program's National Digital Stewardship Alliance (NDSA) is one example of such a partnership. The mission of NDSA is "to establish, maintain, and advance the capacity to preserve our nation's digital resources for the benefit of present and future generations" (NDSA 2014). The alliance has more than 160 partners including universities, businesses, professional associations, and governmental and nonprofit organizations. NDSA has three primary objectives related to preservation:

- identifying, communicating, and advocating for common needs of member organizations
- convening and sustaining a national community of practice for digital stewardship
- providing professional development opportunities for staff at member organizations (NDSA 2014)

Despite these collaborative efforts, it is difficult to see a truly national coordinated plan for the preservation of digital content coming to fruition in the near future. Some organizations might wish to centralize particular content and provide access to it; others might adopt a distributed approach assigning distinct preservation responsibilities to various participant institutions. Some entities will have a commercial purpose in preserving content; others will offer its content openly for the public good.

Efforts at digital preservation are also occurring at the international level as awareness grows that sharing digital knowledge can produce economic and political stability. On an international level, however, several barriers present themselves: (1) digital preservation has not been a development priority as other more pressing needs are often present, (2) there is a lack of awareness of the importance of digital preservation for social and economic development, (3) there is a lack of appropriate laws, standards, and critical technologies, and (4) there is a lack of competent professionals to manage preserved records (Thurston 2012). As a consequence of these factors, in 2012, UNESCO sponsored an international conference on "The Memory of the World in the Digital Age" in Vancouver, British Columbia. One result was the "UNESCO/UBC Vancouver Declaration." The declaration emphasizes the need to make digital preservation a priority and to establish models for trustworthy digital preservation techniques that provide long-term preservation solutions. It also recommends collaborations among UNESCO, members of the archive, library, and museum communities, and governments to protect, preserve, and devise methods of effective dissemination of digital documents (UNESCO 2012).

One thing is certain: the volume of digital content that will need to be preserved will continue to grow rapidly as will the magnitude of the institutional, national, and international challenges to preserve it for future use.

B. The Second Generation: 2010–

Today, it is no longer feasible to discuss the development of technologies without also discussing their societal impact. Computer networks, which we thought of as simply ways computers were linked, have now become social networks composed of people using technologies to create human networks. One enables and fosters the other. The result is that our focus turns less to the devices themselves and more to their uses, their social potential, and their consequent impact on traditional institutions—in our case, libraries.

1. The Pervasive Use of Technology and the Internet

Most Americans are now online. Eight-seven percent of the adult U.S. population use e-mail or accesses the Internet using a mobile device. The percentages are over 80% for men, women, urban, suburban, or rural dwellers, whites, African-Americans, and Hispanics, at all educational levels except high school or less, and for all age groups except those over 65. The percentages exceed 90% for many of these groups (Pew Research "Internet Users" 2014).

What do most American adults use the Internet for? Figure 4.1 provides a list of the most frequent uses and the percent of use (Pew Research "Trend Data" 2013). Using a search engine as an information-seeking tool is at the top of the list (91%), using e-mail follows at 88%. Eighty percent or more of adults seek information on a hobby, search for a map or driving directions, and check the weather. A quick review of the entire list indicates the considerable depth and breadth of Internet use.

Among teens, the findings are even more pronounced. Ninety-five percent of teens are online and the percentage has been this high since 2007. Ninety-three percent of teens either own a computer or have access to a computer at home. Black teens are less likely to have a desktop or laptop at home than white teens; older teens (14–17) are more likely to have them than younger teens (12–13). Similarly, 78% of teens own cell phones, 47% own smartphones, and nearly a quarter (23%) own a tablet computer. Nearly three in four teens indicate that they access the Internet on their cell phones, tablets, or other mobile devices, and a quarter, compared to only 15% of adults, indicate that cell phones are their preferred means of Internet access. Predictably, a major destination for teens is social networks. Older teen girls with smartphones (34%) use them almost exclusively to access the Internet (55%) (Madden et al. 2013).

Generally, people believe that the Internet has been a benefit. Ninety percent of adult users believe that it has been a good thing for them personally; only

FIGURE 4.1
Adult Internet Use

(Use 50% or greater)	
Use a search engine to find information	91%
Send or read e-mail	88%
Look for information on a hobby or interest	84%
Search for a map or driving directions	84%
Check the weather	81%
Look for information online about a service or product	78%
Get news	78%
Go online just for fun or to pass time	74%
Buy a product	71%
Watch a video on a video-sharing site	71%
Visit a local, state, or federal government website	67%
Use a social networking site	67%
Buy or make a reservation for travel	65%
Do any banking online	61%
Look online for news or information about politics	61%
Look online for information about a job	56%
Look for how-to, do-it-yourself, or repair information	53%
Look for information on Wikipedia	53%
Use online classified ads or sites	53%
Get news or information about sports	52%
Take a virtual tour of a location online	52%
Search for information about someone you know or might meet	51%

Source: Pew Research Center. 2013. "Trend Data (Adults)."
www.pewinternet.org/Static-Pages/Trend-Data-(Adults)/Online-Activities-Total.aspx.

6% believe that it has not been helpful. Three-quarters (76%) also believe that it has been good for society. Similarly, the value people place on the Internet has increased over time; more than half (53%) believe that it would be very hard for them to give it up, an increase from 36% in 2006. Approximately 39% of adults believe the Internet is essential to them for work or other reasons. Compare this to only 35% who say that it would be very hard for them to give up television or 28% who would find it hard to give up their telephone. Many Internet users (67%) also believe that their online activities with family and friends have generally strengthened their relationships, while only 18% believe it has weakened them. Internet use, by those who use it, seems to have substantial, salutary effects. The perceived social benefit cross all demographic characteristics: race, income, educational level, and age (Pew Research "The Web" 2014).

These data make it abundantly clear that Internet access and use is now ubiquitous. Going forward, LIS professionals must focus less on the technologies themselves and more on their social effect and the consequent impact on libraries. Three issues are likely to be prominent in such discussions: broadband access, mobile devices, and social media

a. Broadband Access

Broadband access to the Internet remains an issue although access is clearly increasing. In fact, the number of individuals without broadband access (the digital divide), dropped from 270 million in 2000 to 86 million in 2012. As of September 2013, 70% of American adults had high-speed connections in their home, compared to only 3% in June 2000. Currently about 74% of whites, 62% of African-Americans, and 56% of Hispanics have broadband connections. There appear to be no gender differences. Not surprisingly, broadband use increases with income and level of education: 90% of college graduates, and 91% of those earning more than $75,000 use broadband compared to 52% of those with incomes less than $30,000 or those with no high school diploma (28%). Older people over age 65 are less likely than younger people ages 18–29 to use broadband access (47% vs. 81%, respectively) (Pew Research "Mobile Technology" 2014). People residing in rural areas also have less access.

The primary reasons given by individuals without broadband access at home appear to be cost of the service and computer equipment; lack of digital literacy and comfort with computers; and the belief that online access is not useful or worthwhile (Horrigan 2013). Interestingly, the Pew Internet Project ("Three Major" 2014) found that as people adopted higher-speed, always-on connections, they became different Internet users: they spent more time online, performed more activities, watched more video, and became content creators themselves. Horrigan (2013) suggested that LIS professionals focus less on the lack of access to broadband technology and refocus attention on increasing digital literacy and skills so people can be effective in using it.

b. Mobile Devices

Mobile devices have revolutionized the daily lives of almost every American. Digital Trends (2014) characterized this change:

> Over the course of the past two years, "Fourth screen" technology—smartphones, tablets, etc.—has changed social networking and the way we communicate with

one another entirely. What used to sit on our desks now conveniently fits in the palm of our hands, allowing us to effortlessly utilize functionality once reserved for multiple devices wherever we go. (p. 9)

The following discussion briefly examines three of these devices: cellphones, smartphones, and tablets.

i. Cell Phones

As of January 2014, 90% of Americans owned cell phones and used them not just for making phone calls: 82% took pictures, 80% sent or received text messages, 56% accessed the Internet, 50% sent or received e-mail, 44% recorded video, and 43% downloaded apps (Pew Research, "Mobile Technology" 2014). Picture taking tends to rise with income and educational level and declines with age. More than 90% of cell phone owners under the age of 35 take pictures. A similar pattern emerges with texting and e-mail activities. Gender and ethnicity do not seem to play any role in these activities. Accessing the Internet, however, is another matter. A typical pattern emerges for age, income, and level of education, but whites use cell phones less than African-Americans and Hispanics. Young people ages 18–29 are substantially more likely to download apps than any other group, 65% compared to individuals 30–49 (53%). Twenty percent or less of individuals over 50 download apps (Duggan and Rainie 2012).

ii. Smartphones

As of January 2014, a majority of adult Americans (58%) owned smartphones, up from 35% in 2011 (Pew Research "Mobile Technology" 2014). Like many of the new devices, ownership is greater among young people; about 80% under the age of 35 compared to 18% over 65. Ownership consistently increases as educational attainment and income increases and the differences are considerable. For example between 60%–70% of individuals with some college or a college degree own smartphones while percentages among individuals with a high school education or less vary between 36% and 46%. Individuals in urban and suburban areas have substantially greater ownership than in rural areas (59% vs. 40%). Similarly individuals earning $75,000 or more have much higher rates of ownership than those earning $30,000 or less. The iPhone and Android platforms dominated (Smith 2013).

iii. Tablets

As of January 2014, 42% of adult Americans owned a tablet computer compared to 3% in May 2010 (Pew Research "Device Ownership" 2014). Although there are no differences by ethnicity or gender, owning a tablet is positively related to increasing household income and level of education. Households earning more than $70,000 are much more likely to own a tablet than those with incomes under $50,000 (56% vs. 28%). Similarly, 49% of college-educated individuals have a tablet, compared to 26% of those with a high school education or less. Of particular note is that contrary to typical patterns related to adoption of other new technologies, adults between the ages of 35–44 (49%) are more likely to own a tablet than young people. This pattern has emerged only in the last few years and might reflect a major increase in ownership among parents with minor children at home (Zickuhr 2013).

c. Social Media

Social networking comprises the largest block of time spent on the Internet. People spend 20% of their PC time and 30% of their mobile time on social networks. Young adults (25–34) were most likely to use social media in the office; and nearly a third of young people (18–24) use social media in the bathroom! As of September 2013, among individuals using the Internet, 74% of adults used some type of social networking site. Of those, 71% used Facebook, 19% used Twitter, 21% used Pinterest (an online visual pin board), and 17% used Instagram (taking and sharing pictures) (Pew Research "Social" 2014). Many different groups use social networks but generally, they appeal most to women and to adults between the ages of 18 and 29—the same group most heavily using Facebook. Adults between 18 and 29, African-Americans, and urban dwellers use Twitter. Women, adults under 50, whites, and those with some college education use Pinterest; and adults 18–29, African-Americans, Latinos, women and urban residents primarily use Instagram (Duggan and Brenner 2013). More than three-fourths of people who use social media feel connected and informed as a result, a positive feeling. Staying in touch with friends and maintaining professional connections are the most often cited reasons for using social media. Among individuals who "dual screen" that is, use a mobile device such as a smartphone or tablet while watching TV, more than 40% say they visit social networking sites (Neilsen and NN Incite 2012).

As noted earlier, teens, particularly African-American teens, were the largest users of social networking sites. Eighty-one percent of teens ages 12–17 used social networking sites, compared to 67% of adults. Twenty-four percent of teens used Twitter, compared to 16% of adults. Older female teens (14–17) were much more likely than younger teens or older male teens to use social networking sites. Three-fourths of teens who visited social media sites visited them on a daily basis. Facebook dominated teen use (93%), compared to MySpace (7%) (Madden et al. 2013).

Although privacy continued to be a concern among most adults, it did not appear to be of much concern to teens. Older teens were likely to share even more personal information than in the past: 92% posted their real name, 91% posted a photo of themselves, 84% posted personal interests, 82% posted birthdates, 71% posted their school's name and city or town where they lived, and 53% posted their e-mail address. One in four posted a video of himself or herself. On the other hand, younger teens tended to accept as friends only those people they knew or members of their extended family. Only a third were friends with people they had not met (Madden et al. 2013).

C. Technological Innovations Transforming Library Functions

It is informative to turn now to some of the technological innovations that have had a direct impact on libraries. Almost all the basic functions of libraries have been affected in one way or another and it is not possible to address all the technological developments and their implications. Rather, the examples below are suggestive of the breadth and magnitude of the changes that have occurred or are now occurring in four areas: the evolving collection, the evolving search process, the evolving space, and the evolving technological infrastructure.

1. The Evolving Collection

a. Digital Libraries

Although the traditional concept of a "library" remains firmly fixed in peoples' minds, a new type of library emerged with the growth and expansion of the Internet—a "digital library." Digital libraries began in their most primitive form in the 1990s as collections of photos posted on local Web homepages. At that time there were no standards for their creation, no way to effectively search them, no way to support the wide variety of digital materials—photos, images, documents, books— and few of these collection were sustainable over time (Zick 2009).

With the development of metadata standards, additional software advances, and increasingly sophisticated search engines, these issues were soon resolved, and digital libraries grew rapidly in the first decade of the twenty-first century, particularly in response to the growth of distance-learning opportunities at universities. In the absence of a physical library, students taking courses online required access to a virtual library (Fox and Urs 2002; Wright 2002). Since the environment was electronic, the format of the collection could include text, graphics, video, audio, images, data sets, and software (Fox and Urs 2002). Calhoun (2014) described some of the characteristics of mature digital libraries:

> systems and services, often openly available, that (a) support the advancement of knowledge and culture; (b) contain managed collections of digital content (objects or links to objects, annotations and metadata) intended to serve the needs of defined communities; (c) often use an architecture that first emerged in the computer and information science/library domain and that typically features a repository, mechanisms supporting search and other services, resource identifiers, and user interfaces (human and machine). (p. 18)

This characterization notes that most digital libraries are open to all members of the community for which it was designed, which might be the general population or a specialized group such as scientists. Similar to public libraries, they should provide democratic and egalitarian service, usually free or at little cost, and their organization and structure should be similar to traditional library databases. The repositories for content can range from file systems to distributed storage systems. Indexing and metadata support the search functions along with systems for locating digital objects. Finally, the user interfaces allow users to perform searching, browsing, visualization, and delivery (Calhoun 2014).

Despite the obvious potential, the challenges for creating successful digital libraries are considerable. In 2007, the NISO Framework Working Group, under the sponsorship of the Institute for Museum and Library Services, developed guidelines or principles for creating good digital library collections—the *Framework of Guidance* (figure 4.2).

In their short history, digital libraries have been collections of digital content, much like traditional libraries have been collections of print materials. But just as traditional libraries have evolved, the same forces driving those changes—the growth of social networks and the increasing involvement of users (or citizens)—have led to the creation of *social* digital libraries. These libraries also emphasize participation and involvement of the users, and focus on the social usefulness of the digital content. Calhoun (2014) identified a variety of contributions such digital libraries make, including increasing access to digital content on an international, national, and local level; promoting the free flow of ideas through crowdsourcing, blogs, and wikis; empowering and informing the citizenry as a whole through virtual public libraries, mobile interfaces, and online exhibits and archives; making formal online educational opportunities available; assisting in the archiving and preservation of content; and providing economic benefits by improving access to technical, scientific, and cultural content.

FIGURE 4.2
Nine Principles for Building a Digital Collection

1. A good digital collection is created according to an explicit collection development policy.
2. Collections should be described so that a user can discover characteristics of the collection including scope, format, restrictions on access, ownership, and any information significant for determining the collection's authenticity, integrity, and interpretation.
3. A good collection is curated, which is to say its resources are actively managed during their entire life cycle.
4. A good collection is broadly available and avoids unnecessary impediments to use. Collections should be accessible to people with disabilities and usable effectively in conjunction with adaptive technologies.
5. A good collection respects intellectual property rights.
6. A good collection has mechanisms to supply usage data and other data that allow standardized measures of usefulness to be recorded.
7. A good collection is interoperable.
8. A good collection integrates into the user's own workflow.
9. A good collection is sustainable over time.

Source: NISO Framework Working Group 2007, p. 4.

Regardless of type, successful digital libraries provide quality content, ease of use, sustainable funding, an enthusiastic audience, a quality brand, and an excellent discovery system (Calhoun 2014). Among the larger digital libraries with broad scope and appeal are Europeana, JSTOR, Project Gutenberg, American Memory, and Internet Archive.

With the development of the semantic Web and linked data, the potential to create a network of digital libraries capable of integrating into a larger digital library infrastructure becomes possible. Calhoun (2014) identified four key elements required for achieving this lofty goal:

1. *They must be interoperable.* It is critical, if sharing of digital content is desired, that the computer systems be able to communicate with each other effectively. This is particularly challenging because most libraries remain "hybrid"—combinations of digital and non-digital items—the non-digital content being inaccessible by search engines. The systems must be able to share syntactic structures so that navigation, querying interfaces,

and viewing interfaces are compatible across systems. Common metadata formats, protocols, and standards are needed to ensure interoperability.

2. *There must be community engagement.* Digital libraries are designed to serve specific communities; these communities can be highly focused or very broad. Regardless, creators of successful digital libraries must thoroughly investigate the needs and practices of the audience being served. Developers must be deeply committed to the library's success and ideally are credible and respected members of the community.

3. *Intellectual property issues must be addressed.* To the extent possible, digital library creators must be active proponents of open access and the integrity of public domain; the new frontier might require a total rethinking of intellectual property. For example, digital libraries raise a host of new issues: "What constitutes the public domain?" "How can we prevent the public domain from shrinking?" "How can we promote mass digitalization of the world's knowledge and insure access to all?" "How can we ensure that libraries lawfully digitize content for the purpose of preservation?" "How can we protect scholarly communication?" "How do we develop expertise concerning licensing, authentication and authorization to access licensed scholarly content?" "Who can best develop models in the linked data world to lawfully exploit the semantic Web, digital library, and other online information services?"

4. *The library must be sustainable.* Sustainability has been a major problem for digital libraries: some have succeeded while many others failed. Sustainability requires answers to questions in three core areas: economic, social, and ethical:

> *Economic:* "Does it have ongoing funding and a successful business model"? "Does it have measurable standards to determine effectiveness?"
>
> *Social:* "Is the content valuable and relevant to the intended audience?" "Are members of the audience aware of the library?" "Does the library have the ability to preserve its content and provide long-term access?"
>
> *Ethical:* "Can the library insure the broadest possible access?" "Does it promote the free exchange of ideas?" "Are intellectual property rights respected?"

It is certainly possible that, if these questions can be successfully answered and intellectual property issues can be ameliorated, in the near future, many or most of the successful digital libraries will be linked together. The vision of a national or even worldwide digital library will become a reality. All types of traditional libraries are likely to benefit from such an achievement.

b. The Rise of Electronic Books (E-books)

Although adoption was initially slow, electronic books grew rapidly and were a substantial part of the book market by the middle of the second decade. In 2014, e-books made up 30% of all U.S. book sales; more than 19% of all books sold in the United States were Kindle titles (Quora.com 2014; Bercovici 2014). There were many good reasons why e-books became popular: searchable text, cross-referencing with hyperlinks, compact size, adjustable fonts and text size, and e-readers with sufficient memory to store hundreds of books (Castro 2007).

Readership of e-books also rose steadily. In 2011 17% of the U.S. adult population read an e-book in the previous year, in 2012 that number jumped to 23%, and a 2014 study by Pew revealed that 28% were reading e-books (Pew Research "E-Reading" 2014). Interestingly, parents of minor children were more likely than nonparents to read e-books (38% vs. 27%). From this, we can deduce that children's exposure to e-book reading was growing as well.

This is not to say that Americans stopped reading print books. A 2013 study found that 70% of adults had read a print book in the last twelve months, an increase of 4% over the previous year, and that parents still believed that it was important for their children to read print books (Pew Research "In a Digital" 2013). The initial fear that e-books might replace print books was allayed by Zhang and Kudva (2014), who found that only a very small percentage of e-book users restricted their reading solely to e-books. They also concluded that

> e-books have firmly established a place in people's lives, due to their convenience of access, but e-books are not yet positioned to replace print books. Both print books and e-books have unique attributes and serve irreplaceable functions to meet people's reading needs. . . . (p. 1695)

Nonetheless, use of e-books is expected to grow. This growth will be enabled in part by the fact that ownership of either a tablet or an e-reader continues to grow: 24% of American adults owned an e-book reader, 42% owned a tablet (Pew Research "Device Ownership" 2014), and 43% had either one or the other (Pew Research "Tablet" 2013). Pew found that 57% used a specifically designed e-reader (Kindle or Nook), 55% used a tablet to read e-books, 29% used a computer, and 32% used a cell phone. With the exception of computers, there have been substantial increases in the use of these devices for reading e-books since 2011 (Pew Research "E-Reading" 2014).

The implication of the Pew data for libraries is significant. Their findings revealed that 12% of e-book readers borrowed an e-book from the library over a recent twelve-month period. Although this suggests substantial use of the library for this purpose, Pew also found that many people (58%) were unaware that their library provided access to e-books. Identifying a substantial marketing gap, 48% of owners of e-book reading devices did not know, and 47% of people who read an e-book in the past year were unaware of the library's e-book services. Among the borrowers of library e-books, more than half criticized the library for not having the e-books they wanted or complained about being on waiting lists. Nearly one in five expressed concern that the e-books available were not compatible with their readers. Despite these criticisms, nearly half the people surveyed expressed interest in borrowing readers with desired books already loaded on them, and about one in three indicated an interest in receiving library instruction on e-books and how to download them. Of those who regularly borrowed e-books, about four in ten indicated that the library was their starting point for accessing e-books.

As noted earlier, adopting new technologies changes libraries—providing e-book services changes the character of library use, library holdings, and LIS professionals' roles. Pew found that e-book patrons used branch libraries less and the library website more, that funds for the purchase of e-books reduced the amount available for print materials, and that librarians provided more technical support to assist people accessing e-books and less time performing traditional reference functions (Zickuhr et al. 2012).

E-book services generate a variety of new complexities for libraries. Initially, many major publishers were reluctant to make e-books available to libraries. Some were willing to make them available but only after an embargo period during which time only a print version was available to libraries. After considerable negotiation, by the end of 2013, all major U.S. publishers, including Macmillan, Simon & Schuster, and Penguin Book Group, agreed to some type of e-book lending to libraries (ALA 2014). Polanka (2011) identified several other issues. For example, e-books are priced differently than print materials. The negotiated price depends on the vendor's selected business model; some vendors assess annual fees, others charge per-use fees. E-book purchases generally involve licensing agreements with use and restriction requirements related to intellectual property issues and questions of ownership. That is, do libraries own the items or just the right to access them? Polanka suggested that libraries concerned about ownership issues might acquire items mostly in the public domain or only those subject to open access. Widdersheim (2014) believes there is a deeper problem with e-books because, at least in the current market, e-books are embedded in a highly commercialized environment;

major corporate interests are involved in their development and distribution. For example, e-book readers are provided by only a few vendors and each reader restricts the content that can be downloaded on them reflecting individual vendor's proprietary interests. He observes, "Binding libraries to specific technologies is a central marketing strategy for e-content and e-vendor manufacturers" (p. 105). By determining what content is available and by licensing rather than selling that content, the vendors and developers create an artificial scarcity that they control, including subsequent denial of access to that content.

Although print collections will remain an integral part of library collections, there is no doubt, however, that e-books will be an increasingly important part of many library collections going forward, and libraries will be struggling with establishing economic models that work for them and for e-book publishers. Libraries will need to provide online resources in an intuitive, easy-to-use, one-stop shop. Given the ever-expanding marketplace, librarians might increase their flexibility and responsiveness by continual beta testing of new services and functions (Emery and Stone 2013). How libraries will balance shifting format demands with often-declining budgets represents a major challenge in the years to come.

c. Electronic Resource Management Systems (ERMS)

As digital content proliferated, librarians quickly recognized that managing digital content required significantly different strategies than managing print collections. Anderson (2014) noted that

> . . . the very physicality of the book makes its management simpler; the book is on order, then it is in processing, then on the bookshelves, checked out, returned, repaired, and finally discarded. Electronic resources have no such simple life cycle. (p. 6)

Traditional integrated library systems were insufficient to manage electronic resources. In response, librarians initially developed a variety of techniques, procedures and workflow schedules on an *ad hoc* basis. As online resources gained traction, the Digital Library Foundation of the Council on Library and Information Resources urged vendors to develop software systems that included functionalities to deal with e-resources. The first commercially produced electronic resource management systems were developed between 2003 and 2005 (Emery and Stone 2013; Anderson 2014). ERMS were simply "any software that helps to manage electronic resources" (Anderson 2014, p. 9). Open source ERMS are now available as well.

ERMS manage digital content throughout the life cycle of the resource. Pesch (2008) identified six major phases: acquiring, providing access, administering, supporting, evaluating, and renewing (or discarding). Each phase has several steps: acquiring requires attention to titles, prices, licensing and invoicing; providing access includes attention to cataloging, registration, searching and linking; administering involves use rights, check-in, claims, and title changes; support involves contacts and troubleshooting; evaluation analyzes usage and cost data; and renewing includes renewal orders, invoicing and title lists. More recently Stone and Emery (2013) organized these six phases into what they called "TERMS": Techniques for Electronic Resource Management. The TERMS workflow included investigating new content, acquiring new content, implementation, ongoing evaluation and access, annual review, and cancellation and replacement review (Emery and Stone 2013).

Some ERMS were designed to be used independently; others could be integrated into an existing library system. Different ERMS often could not "talk" with each other. In fact, they were implemented in only a limited number of libraries. Many libraries kept their homegrown systems. Although Anderson (2014) noted that the National Information Standards Organization developed an "open URL" standard that created a "durable, flexible link between citation and full text, a link that is sensitive to the library holdings to ensure that patrons are linked to subscribed content" (p. 7), he further noted that "no system is perfect, and each one, be it homegrown, commercial, or open-source, has its own complexities and idiosyncrasies" (p. 5). Among the more notable complexities are the cost and difficulty of implementing them, including significant adjustments to workflow in technical services. In addition, the platforms and models for some digital content, such as e-books, remain in flux. Implementation is particularly challenging when technological and business models are unstable. Consequently, before acquiring an ERMS, the advantages and disadvantages should be weighed carefully. Anderson (2014a) raised several issues that should be explored, including how well the system will integrate disparate electronic databases within the library and between vendors, and to what extent it can connect the knowledge databases to other critical functions such as budget, subscription, and purchasing, management, administration, licensing, and reporting. "How well does the system execute budgetary, subscription, and purchasing functions?" "How well does it store administrative information such as publisher and vendor contact information, pricing, usage data, invoice data, and journals held by the library?" "How well does it track licenses for e-content?" "Can it maintain all the necessary terms of each license and track it against the relevant digital resources?" Finally, how well can it produce necessary reports such as budget, check-in, and usage data?

The need for ERMS will persist and grow. The issues of flexibility, standardization, and interoperability of such systems will be of primary importance as well as the cost and complexity of implementation and operation. LIS professionals will need to keep abreast of developments in both the commercial and open-access arenas.

d. Demand Driven Acquisitions (DDA)

The concept of Demand Driven Acquisitions, also known as patron-driven acquisitions, is not new. DDA has been part of library practice since LIS professionals began monitoring interlibrary loan requests and selecting materials based on those requests. When patrons requested individual titles that were then evaluated and potentially selected for inclusion, DDA was operating. It was also an aspect of ordering materials based on the number of holds placed on a particular title. Nonetheless, although historically present, these practices generally played only a small role in developing print collections. Selecting materials for the library traditionally has been the bailiwick of librarians and subject specialists. Even with automated systems, it was still LIS professionals who created the computer profiles, and defined and limited the domain of materials to be selected. Following this practice, referred to as a "just-in-case" model, the librarian attempted to anticipate the needs of users. In fact, there was no guarantee the selected items would be used; a certain percentage of materials were never used. In today's fiscal environment, this is a serious problem.

The National Information Standards Organization (NISO) defined demand-driven acquisition as "acquisition of library materials based on patron use at the point of need" (NISO 2014, p. 3). Although the definition applies to print and audio-visual materials as well as digital content, it has been only since collection development budgets have shrunk and demands for digital content have increased, that DDA has evolved to become a serious factor in selection practices. Today, DDA refers to a "just-in-time" model. Vendors or aggregators prepare library e-content profiles, often based on previously ordered print materials, and provide these records to the library that are then up-loaded into the library's catalog. Users peruse these records in the discovery process in the same way they would look for an item on a commercial site like Amazon. Once selected, access to the e-book is immediate (Caminita 2014). In some business models, whether a library subsequently purchases that e-book is based on "trigger activity," how a particular e-book is being used by a patron. For example, when a user accesses a particular e-book, the first few minutes of use are usually free (Cramer 2013). According to Downey (2014) although triggers can vary, "purchase triggers commonly consist of 10 page views, 10 consecutive minutes of use within a title, or one page (or portion thereof) copied or printed" (p. 108).

Many librarians remain skeptical about allowing patrons to determine acquisitions. Among their concerns are the following: users will add only popular items, not necessarily high-quality materials; users are only interested in their own needs, not the broader needs of the community; the collection will be skewed by a small number of heavy users; individual items might be of interest to only a narrow segment of the population; and users are not aware of the budgetary constraints facing libraries. Bushman (2014) further warned that DDA generally promotes the acquisition of e-books, and although understandable in terms of responding to user demand, there might follow unintended consequences. For example, promoters of DDA, especially commercial vendors, have reason to overplay its futuristic aspects and play down the fact that many people, both children and adults, still prefer to read print. LIS professionals must resist vendors' strong marketing seduction and remain deliberate in their choices. They must be wary of skewed collections that meet individual's immediate needs but no longer meet the library's mission to promote learning and inquiry. Bushman argued that the environment created by reading print is more conducive to learning and permits the reader to get more deeply involved in the text. Another concern is that costs will no doubt grow as demand grows; how libraries will fund these spiraling costs over time is uncertain.

In contrast, NISO (2014) stated that increased use of DDA will rebalance libraries' collections "away from possible use toward immediate need" (p. 1). Other benefits of DDA systems are that they

- provide users with immediate access to a wide range of titles to be purchased at the point of need
- present many more titles to their users for potential use and purchase than would ever be feasible under the traditional purchase model
- make it possible, if implemented correctly to purchase only what is needed, allowing libraries to save money or to spend the same amount as they spend on books now, but with a higher rate of use (p. vii)

DDA is still in its infancy in terms of widespread library adoption but growing steadily, particularly among academic libraries. Recent studies in academic libraries found that as much as 40% of the print collection never circulated (Caminita 2014; Downey et al. 2014). As a result, many academic libraries adopted DDA as a complement to traditional selection practices. Brigham Young University found that their DDA program was 94% cheaper and materials circulated 1,300% more on average than the traditionally selected electronic items! Further, after the first month of purchase, more than two-thirds of the traditionally selected items were not used compared to only 30% of the DDA-selected items (Howland et al. 2014). Downey et al. (2014) reported similar findings at the University of Vermont. After implementing a DDA program, the user-selected books had better circulation rates than the traditionally acquired books. In another study of academic librarians with DDA programs, Nixon et al. (2014) found most of the librarians surveyed were highly supportive of the program and believed that the users selected appropriate materials used by both faculty and students.

The weight of the evidence to-date is that library users are in fact better predictors of subsequent circulation than either librarians or vendor profiles (Tyler et al. 2013). These findings suggest that DDA will become more widespread, fostering yet another library transformation in which users will play an important role in building the library's collection: both print and electronic. Complementing traditional acquisition practices, Harrell et al. (2014) concluded,

> As libraries of all types struggle with the ability to meet the needs of their customers while managing with lower budgets and space constraints, patron-driven acquisitions can be used to supplement a balanced collection. (p. 155)

e. Radio Frequency Identification (RFID)

RFID is among the many technological developments affecting circulation and control of the library collection. According to Caldwell-Stone (2014) RFID

> enables the tracking and monitoring of physical items by attaching an RFID tag or transponder to an item. Each tag consists of an internal antenna and a computer chip that stores data. When the tag is scanned or interrogated by a reading device equipped with its own antenna, the tag communicates its data wirelessly via radio waves to the reader.

RFID has been used in libraries since 1999 and its most common use was for self-check-out machines and security gates as well as for inventory, shelf-reading, weeding, and locating misplaced or incorrectly shelved materials (Ayre 2012; Singh and Mahajan 2014). RFID tags are easier to use than bar codes because they don't need to be aligned, and, depending on the type of tag, can be read from considerable distances. There are two types of RFID tags: active and passive. Passive tags "have no power source and no on-tag transmitter" (BISG 2004, p. 3). The tags themselves are relatively inexpensive and rely on an external reader to activate them. Active tags have "both an on-tag power source and an active transmitter. . . . They are usually used in manufacturing, such as tracking equipment and other high value assets, and toll collections systems" (BISG 2004, p. 3). Libraries generally employed passive tags.

Caldwell-Stone (2014) identified several advantages to RFID:

> Because RFID tags do not require a clear line of sight and allow multiple items to be read in a stack, far less time and human effort are spent on processing materials.

> Patrons using RFID-enabled self-check stations and automated sorting equipment further free up library staff for essential work. Handheld RFID readers can be moved along the shelving units to read the tabs attached to books on the shelves, allowing for more efficient and frequent inventory of the library collection. And by eliminating the need for the repetitive movements required by traditional barcode scanning technology, RFID can help reduce the incidence of repetitive stress injuries among staff and the costs associated with lost time and worker's compensation payments. (p. 39)

These substantive benefits contributed to broader adoption, particularly in academic and special libraries (Ayre 2012; Handy 2014). Despite these advantages, emphasis on RFID slowed as attention has shifted to digital content (digital libraries) and digital access of materials such as discovery systems. Another barrier to adoption was cost: tagging, equipment, software, and staff time can represent substantial initial and ongoing expenditures. Ayre (2012) speculated smartphone technology might overcome some of these costs and enable increased use of RFID technologies.

Despite its usefulness, a persistent concern with RFID has been its potential to violate patrons' privacy rights. Warfield (2005) noted that "RFID's fundamental privacy threat comes from the fact that the tags reveal their information to any compatible reader" (p. II). For example, readers could link a borrower's name to a particular book title. Privacy advocates and the ALA advocated for establishing a taskforce with the Book Industry Study Group (BISG), a trade association involving publishers, manufacturers, and book distributors. The final report, issued in 2004, incorporated many of ALA's concerns and offered a variety of guidelines and four principles:

1. Implement and enforce an up-to-date organizational privacy policy that gives notice and full disclosure as to the use, terms of use, and any change in the terms of use for data collected via new technologies and processes, including RFID.
2. Ensure that no personal information is recorded on RFID tags which, however, might contain a variety of transactional data.
3. Protect data by reasonable security safeguards against interpretation by any unauthorized third party.
4. Comply with relevant federal, state, and local laws as well as industry best practices and policies. (BISG 2004, p. 2)

In addition, ALA created its own policy *RFID in Libraries: Privacy and Confidentiality Guidelines*, which was adopted by the Intellectual Freedom Committee (IFC) in June 2006. The essence of the policy states:

> Because RFID tags might be read by unauthorized individuals using tab readers, there are concerns that the improper implementation of RFID technology will compromise users' privacy in the library. . . . Libraries implementing RFID should use and configure the technology to maintain the privacy of library users. (ALA 2006, p. 1)

The IFC also advised libraries to make sure that information stored on RFID tags was kept to a minimum and that the library's privacy and confidentiality policies were reviewed and updated regularly to ensure that the rights of their patrons were protected. Similarly, the IFC recommends that patrons should be clearly informed regarding the RIFD technologies used by the library.

2. The Evolving Search Process

a. Discovery Systems

Historically, the technical functions of the library and the public service functions were separate. With the application of computers to these functions, many of the processes and practices were changed and streamlined, but the distinctions between public service and technical departments remained. With the advent of integrated library systems (ILS) and online-computer-access catalogs, discussed earlier, the integration of internal processes began in earnest. A remaining barrier was the fact that the catalog remained focused on print holdings, notably books, while other materials such as periodicals, digital repositories, and information on the Web were accessed using electronic and manual indexes and independent Internet access. The consequence of these silos was that library users still had to use multiple access points to obtain the knowledge they required. As the powerful search engines of the Internet gained wider usage, the inefficiency of the library's search process became increasingly obvious. Libraries lost their competitive position as a provider of information and content. Libraries and library vendors have been struggling to catch up ever since. In the first decade of the twenty-first century, libraries began to reconfigure and redesign their websites into what is referred to as next-generation library catalogs. Breeding (2014) noted,

> These products included search and retrieval technology and modern interface conventions and were generally designed to work independently from any given integrated library system. The search capabilities of these products were based on the creation of a new index, populated by exporting records from the ILS and from repositories maintained by the library. This approach allowed them to use more

> modern and powerful search and retrieval technologies . . . open-source products widely used in all information technology sectors with very advanced capabilities.

This innovation was known as a "discovery system," a "discovery layer," or a "discovery platform." Vendors as well as practitioners adopted this terminology for the next generation of library interfaces. Discovery interfaces generally exceeded the capabilities of traditional ILSs, but also relied on information contained in them, so integration of the systems was needed. The term "discovery" is now generally applied to the process of identifying, locating, and delivering content to a user.

Current discovery products focus on a level termed "Web scale." Web scale generally applies to "the discovery services that, usually through massive indexes, aim to represent the full body of library content . . . these discovery services aim to address the full breadth of content resources relevant to libraries" (Breeding "Discovery . . ." 2014, p. 13). In other words, "Web scale" discovery layers maximize the ability of the user to identify, locate, and receive delivery of any content regardless of format or location. This includes access to the library's book collection, DVDs, local electronic content, digital image collections, institutional repository materials, content from full-text and abstracting and indexing resources including e-books, and licensed content available by remote access (Vaughn 2011). Among the vendors offering Web-scale discovery services are OCLC's WorldCat, ProQuest's Summon, Ex Libris Primo and Primo Central, Innovative Interfaces Chamo Discovery, and Ebsco's Discovery Services. Some open source ILS/Discovery systems are now emerging and growing in popularity, representing about 12% of the market in 2014. Koha and Evergreen are two examples (Breeding 2014, 2015).

OCLC WorldCat Discovery Service is the oldest and largest of Web scale discovery systems and provides an instructive example. OCLC (2014) describes WorldCat Local in the following way:

> WorldCat Local is a Webscale discovery solution that delivers single-search-box access to more than 1.8 billion items from your library and the world's library collections. It connects people to all your library's materials—electronic and digital and physical—as well as to the delivery services that get them what they need.

According to OCLC, WorldCat Local locates quickly and easily the materials needed; connects the users to those materials; and provides the means for the user to explore those materials—at last achieving a "one-stop" shop for information seekers (OCLC 2014, under "Overview"). Among its features are the following (OCLC 2014):

- Search results include multiple formats of materials such as electronic materials, digital items, databases, music, video, maps, journals, theses, and print.

- Users can quickly link to online resources, place hold or request items, and borrow materials from other libraries.
- A locally branded search box that can be placed on any Web page.
- Link resolution and an A to Z list built on the WorldCat knowledge base connects users to articles and synchronizes electronic resource holding with records in the WorldCat dataset.
- Branch-level holding displayed when Local Holdings Records (LHRs) are present.
- Social networking tools allow users to create and share lists, write reviews, rate items, and more.
- Faceted browsing by author, format, year, audience, topic, and more.
- Ten interface languages include: Czech, Dutch, English, French, German, Italian, Korean, Portuguese, Simplified Chinese, and Spanish.
- Detailed usage statistics through a hosted tracking/metrics tool.
- Browser-based, mobile-specific version compatible with almost any phone.

Despite the attractiveness of discovery systems they are still very much in the development phase. Particularly many public and school libraries, in contrast to academic libraries, remain satisfied with their ILS systems and have not implemented discovery software. Vendors, therefore, will continue to offer newer and enhanced ILS versions for the foreseeable future that include the management of e-books and demand-driven acquisitions (discussed above) (Breeding 2014, 2015). Nonetheless, Breeding (2014) observed,

> Discovery services continue as a major area of activity, seen by libraries as especially critical given their intimate connections with customers, serving as one of the main delivery vehicles for access to collections and services. (p. 1–2)

There is little doubt that as time passes more and more libraries will adopt such systems. The most compelling reason is that most users, socialized to the expectations of information access on the Internet, will expect the same efficiencies with library services and resources. Libraries contain many resources that remain for the most part unsearchable—part of the "deep Web." Libraries have an opportunity through discovery systems to offer their unique resources and at the same time make the needed connections to the vast information world outside. The extent they are able to do so easily, quickly, and reliably might determine if they will thrive in the future. In this sense, the discovery systems might well help them compete and survive in a dynamic information environment.

b. Virtual Reference Service (VRS)

In the past, people often began their search process at the library reference desk. Today, the ubiquity of the Internet, the proliferation of websites, the growth of digital libraries, and the rise of social networks have all combined to make information access easy and convenient for millions of people. One consequence of these changes has been the decline in face-to-face reference services in both public and academic libraries. In academic institutions alone, reference use has dropped 25% annually since the late 1990s (Henry 2011; Tyckoson 2011; Zhang and Deng 2014). In response to these changes, LIS professionals developed new VRSs that could exploit the new technologies and continue to serve their constituencies in the new electronic environment. VRSs have many names, including "digital reference" and "Ask-a-Librarian," but the Reference and User Services Association (RUSA 2010) of the ALA, defined them in the following way:

> Virtual reference is reference service initiated electronically where patrons employ computers or other technology to communicate with public service staff without being physically present. Communication channels used frequently in virtual reference include chat, videoconferencing, Voice-over-IP, co-browsing, e-mail, and instant messaging. (p. 1)

Early forms of VRS usually took the form of e-mail. This is usually considered an "asynchronous" form of virtual reference in that the queries came in at one point in time and the answers were provided later. Although e-mail was a useful mechanism that is still employed today, it has at least two drawbacks: the response was not immediate, and it was not possible to see or hear the patron. As a consequence, the reference librarian was not able to take full advantage of the reference interview (Arya and Mishra 2011). As early as 1995 the "chat" facility was used by the Internet Public Library. Now, with the development of social media, chat, instant messaging, and other forms of synchronous communication, VRS has moved to an entirely new level and the immediacy of the face-to-face interview has been effectively, albeit not perfectly, simulated. The size of the library often determines which technique is used. A study by Wanucha and Hofschire (2013) found that among large libraries serving 500,000 or more, nearly 80% employed e-mail, a majority used chat services, and 40% provided text services. Among libraries serving 100,000 to 500,000, 63% used e-mail, but only 38% provided chat. In libraries serving 25,000–1000, nearly a majority (48%) used e-mail VRS. Some libraries collaborate with other libraries to provide VRS and some states provide virtual reference service on a statewide level. For example, Ohio offers the KnowItNow 24X7 reference service which in 2013 conducted more than 40,000 chat reference sessions, and handled more than 2,000 text messages and 870 e-mails (Boozer 2014). The benefits of collaboration include increased hours of availability, shared staffing responsibilities, increased availability of expertise, and cost savings from vendors (ALA 2014).

There are many considerations in the design and implementation of a VRS. RUSA (2010) identified many of them in its "Guidelines for Implementing and Maintaining Virtual Reference Services" (2010). Among the issues addressed by these guidelines are the following:

1. VRS needs to be carefully integrated into current reference service as a long-term commitment.
2. The audience for the service needs to be identified;
3. Appropriate institutional policies need to be adopted and levels of service defined. These include standards and expectations of behavior of staff, policies regarding privacy and confidentiality of user queries, and hours of service.
4. There needs to be a meaningful commitment in terms of budget, equipment, staffing, and maintenance.
5. The appropriate software must be selected.
6. The library's digital collection must be evaluated and if necessary enhanced.
7. An ongoing evaluation of VRS must be implemented.

There are many reasons that VRS is desirable. The strongest motivation is convenience. People do not have to travel to use the service, and VRS is often provided well after closing hours, sometimes 24/7. In addition, VRS can take advantage of multiple social media channels for communication such as chat, e-mail, and Facebook.

However, even when implemented well, VRS presents significant challenges. Connaway and Radford (2011) conducted a series of research studies on the factors that promote or dissuade people from using VRS. Resistance to using VRS can come from a variety of sources. For example, older users tend to be resistant because the new technologies can be unfamiliar and frustrating. Millennials, on the other hand, are less resistant than baby boomers, but they still prefer face-to-face contact. Their resistance stems less from the technologies, with which they are generally comfortable, but more from personal issues such as the need for reassurance from librarians.

Connaway and Radford (2011) argue that there needs to be a fundamental reconceptualization of reference service in the virtual environment. They noted that to an ever-increasing extent, people's virtual lives are entangled in their "analog" lives—their everyday life of work, play, and friendships. They refer to this entanglement as "synchronicity" (p. 2). They believe that if virtual reference is to succeed, it must do more than provide information; the service must establish strong relationships with potential VRS users. A successful VRS program not only attracts a user the first time, it stimulates the desire to use the service again and again. If the information obtained is accurate and users are comfortable with the service, they likely will return. Comfort is important: many people prefer face-to-face relationships in the reference process because the user can build a relationship with the librarian. Establishing this interpersonal connection in the online environment is particularly important for VRS to succeed. If users feel the librarian abrupt or disinterested, they are not likely to return. Similarly, if the librarian closes the interview poorly or abruptly, users will not be attracted to VRS.

Interestingly, another reason why people in general do not use VRS is that they are simply unaware that the service exists. Libraries have not done the job they need to do to make the service widely known. Based on these findings and others, Connaway and Radford made many suggestions to improve the chances of VRS success. These are summarized below:

1. Aggressively market and promote VRS services. Create an awareness of the service through face-to-face opportunities in the library. For example, when a user is at the reference desk, remind them of the VRS. At library training sessions on VRS or other library resources, make sure that the attendees are aware of the service.

2. Ensure that there is sufficient support to assist patrons in using the VRS.

3. Provide 24/7 service if possible; respond quickly and efficiently.

4. Design catalog interfaces and databases to mimic popular Web browsers.

5. Provide access from mobile devices.

6. Increase convenience by integrating other library services and tools into the VRS site.

7. Be especially sensitive to teenagers and assure them their questions are welcome.

8. Make sure during appropriate library training and programs that VRS is mentioned.

9. Use clarification techniques to ensure the right question is being addressed. Employ open-ended questions and determine question type: is it for a school assignment, or what they might be using the information for?

10. Provide specific and accurate answers, always act with courtesy, be patient and do not appear hurried, close the session making sure the information need was satisfied, and provide a pleasant "goodbye."

As with any new and developing service, a variety of challenges arise, including administrative, start-up, and maintenance costs; selecting appropriate software; availability and licensing of electronic resources; policies for provision of services; staffing and scheduling; marketing issues; impact on facilities; and negotiating collaborative activities with other libraries. Nonetheless, use of these services is expected to grow and will likely be heavily used. In a study of U.S. adults, Pew (Zickuhr 2013) found that 37% were "very likely" and another 36% were "somewhat likely" to use an online "Ask a Librarian" service if a library provided it. Many people enjoy their contact with librarians and insofar as libraries can create a VRS service that is convenient, personal, welcoming, accurate, and efficient, including such a service is likely to become a staple of the library and a significant benefit to its users. In such an environment, the very nature of reference service will continue to change: the physical reference desk staffed by reference librarians will likely persist but decrease in importance and use.

c. Social Question & Answering Services (SQA)

When people search for information online, their first choice is usually a search engine, but an alternative growing in popularity is the use of social question and answering services, sometimes referred to community-question answering (CQA). These sites often compete with VRS. Radford et al. (2012) described SQA in the following way:

> Social Q&A services are community-based, and purposely designed to support people who desire to ask and answer questions, interacting with one another online. People ask questions to the public and expect to receive answers from anyone who knows something related to the questions, allowing everyone to benefit from the collective wisdom of many.

SQA is a peer-to-peer public forum in which all users potentially participate as information seekers and information givers. SQA exemplifies the collaborative and egalitarian spirit of social networks. Participants not only answer questions, but they can evaluate and rank responses and comment on them as well. Some SQA services also encourage collaborative problem-solving in which multiple members attempt to address a problem posed by another participant. One example of SQA service is Yahoo! Answers, which as of August 2014 had more than 6.1 million visitors per month (Quantcast.com 2014). SQA is low cost and response time for answers is usually short (Shah and Kitzie 2012). In addition, users appear satisfied overall. Zhang and Deng (2014) reported that 70% of users were satisfied or very satisfied with the answers they received from Yahoo! Answers and only 18% were dissatisfied.

Students, overall, prefer SQA to VRS, but they also indicate that they test the veracity of the answers they get through SQA by consulting external sources (Radford et al. 2012). Interestingly, the credibility of an SQA service for students increases, if the student locates the site though a Google search. Google lends credibility (Shah and Kitzie 2012). In general, the quality of the answer is not related to how fast the answer is provided (Chua and Benerjee 2013).

As might be expected, some librarians have substantive concerns about SQA especially in regard to the questionable authority and accuracy of the answers given. Despite librarians' suspicions, however, some have chosen to participate in SQA services by providing high-quality answers and then identifying themselves as librarians to educate participants about the expertise of librarians and the usefulness of VRS (Radford et al. 2012). Interestingly, in exploring the relationship between SQA use and VRS use, Zhang and Deng (2014) found that 70% of the Yahoo! Answer respondents indicated that were not aware that libraries even had VRS services.

When comparing VRS and SQA services, Shah and Kitzie (2012) note that both have their strengths and weakness. Based on their review of the research, the strengths of each are summarized below:

VRS outperforms SQA on

1. *Customization:* VRS services tend to identify both the specific question *and* contextual factors such as intended use.
2. *Quality:* The quality of answers tends to be higher.
3. *Relevance:* VRS tends to minimize irrelevant information.
4. *Accuracy:* VRS focuses more attention on accuracy of the answer even if it takes long to answer the query.
5. *Authoritativeness:* Answers are generally more authoritative because of the subject and information-seeking expertise of the librarian.
6. *Completeness:* Librarians tend to exert extra effort to ensure that the answer addresses the need in its entirety.

On the other hand, SQA services tend to outperform VRS on the following characteristics:

1. *Cost:* With no forms to complete and immediate, free access to a large community, there are few if any real costs to the service.
2. *Volume:* Because answers are saved for others to consult, popular SQA services such as Yahoo! Answers have a vast collection of answers for consultation. These answers are indexed by Google, which makes the site easy to access.

3. *Speed:* SQA sites provide answers more quickly than VRS.
4. *Social aspects:* Popular SQA services frequently provide easy connections to other external social media sites such as Facebook.
5. *Engagement:* While VRS sites are used to ask a question and obtain an answer, SQA sites invite exploration and interaction beyond the answer itself.
6. *Collaboration:* SQA services invite interaction and information exchange and discussion.

Given the advantages of each, it is likely that both SQA and VRS will persist and users will determine which service is selected for a given question. Nonetheless, the evolution of SQA services will need to be monitored to determine their future impact on library services, including VRS.

D. The Library's Evolving Space

A library building is more than a container for content, digital or print. It is a cultural space recognized as a place of learning. Its presence in a community is both practical and symbolic:

> The library has often, and for obvious reason, become synonymous with reading and literacy, but the true definition of the library has always been ideological and transcendent of format: to inspire, facilitate learning, to advance knowledge, and to strengthen the community. In this, a library's space is different from that of a warehouse, as it has values, a philosophy, a spirit, and a soul. Not just a personalized space, it is personified as a lexicon of local culture and the human experience. (Malczewski 2014, p. 37)

How library spaces are changing is more than a reflection of changes in technology; they are an expression of how the library adapts to changes in the larger culture—how patrons see the library, and how the library views itself and its mission. Changes in a library's physical spaces are less about changes in blueprints and floor plans and more about ensuring that the library remains relevant and continues to accomplish its critical mission.

Historically, library space was primarily devoted to two aspects of library service: (1) the physical collection and access to it and (2) reference services. Today's libraries recognize that spaces emphasizing book collections and the reference desk do not reflect the changes in how twenty-first-century users seek and use information. The new information technologies create a culture of self-sufficiency among many information seekers, and although the library remains an important provider of information, its role and centrality in this area have declined. But the cultural significance of libraries remains: to educate, to promote an informed citizenry, and to disseminate knowledge. As a response to the change in information-seeking behavior of users, the library must refocus its attention to other critical functions and in doing so, reimagine its space. We examine three such spaces below.

1. *Spaces for Learning*

   While libraries continue to provide space that supports individual learning, many libraries also create places where people can use appropriate technologies to work collaboratively to complete school assignments or personal projects. These spaces reflect the greater emphasis now placed on collaborative learning in schools and higher education. For example, public libraries establish "homework help" centers that assist students with assignments and instruct them on learning strategies. They also offer classes on computer use and computer coding. Many academic libraries create learning commons where students can interact, use search engines, and complete assignments and presentations, often with the aid of multimedia production software. Academic libraries also incorporate various centers that improve students' skills in math or "writing centers" that help them prepare papers and improve general writing skills. Space might also be devoted to online classrooms for in-house and university-wide classroom education or training.

2. *Spaces for Creating*

   As library patrons became creators of content, libraries provided spaces and resources. These "makerspaces" provide tools, often state-of-the-art technologies such as 3-D printers, laser cutters, and advanced video and audio production software, as well as traditional technologies such as sewing machines. Malczewski (2014) referred to these resources as libraries' *dynamic content*, in contrast to passive, traditional materials such as books, and they are yet another way libraries actively engage with the community.

3. *Space for Engagement*

   Library spaces today focus less on internal operations and more on the needs of their communities. While many of these needs remain informational, they might also be social. Library space that helps people accomplish social tasks or cope with social challenges is becoming more common. For example, libraries help people register to vote, complete forms and applications for jobs, sign up for health insurance or Social Security, and provide shelter and support to cope with disasters such as hurricanes or floods. Many libraries offer retail spaces to sell discarded books, Internet cafes, dedicated spaces for teens and for parenting classes, spaces for business meetings, digital labs, and community collaboration spaces. Some libraries even offer their land for community gardening (ALA "State of" 2014). A particular focus remains on literacy with libraries providing programming for adult literacy, information literacy, and emergent literacy. Academic libraries provide spaces for collaborative research activities and discussion rooms such as a "faculty commons" (Maloney 2014). Both individuals and groups benefit from these activities, but their focus is on service to the community of users rather than just on one individual.

As libraries design and redesign their spaces, they are cognizant of the ever-changing environment in which they operate. Flexibility is a high priority; classrooms can be reconfigured into meeting rooms or collaborative learning centers; tables, chairs, even walls are moveable; equipment and technologies are portable and wireless. It is not clear that all libraries have actually obtained equilibrium in attempting to deal with emerging space needs; it is probably best to describe the current situation as a *dynamic equilibrium*; an ever-changing environment as library users place new demands and expectations on a critical cultural institution. In these new spaces, LIS professionals and the public engage in new ways that foster relationship-building, human interaction with technology, and collaboration.

E. The Evolving Technological Infrastructure: Cloud-Based Computing

As noted throughout this chapter, libraries continually adopt new technologies to improve their internal operations and to provide enhanced services to their users. Some of the adopted technologies have included integrated library systems, Web portals, websites, digital libraries, and institutional repositories. Each new innovation resulted in significant costs to the library for hardware, software, and trained staff to maintain and upgrade these services as needed (Bansode and Pujar 2012). Cloud computing represents a significant advance in network access and has the potential to help libraries control some of their costs while continuing to provide enhanced services to users as well.

The National Institute of Standards and Technology (NIST) defined cloud computing as

A model for enabling ubiquitous, convenient, on-demand network access to a shared pool of configurable computing resources (e.g., networks, servers, storage, applications, and services) that can be rapidly provisioned and released with minimal management effort or service provider interaction. (Mell and Grance 2011, p. 2)

Breeding (2012) identified some of the defining characteristics:

- An abstract technology platform that involves generalized access to remote computing resources rather than locally owned and managed discrete services

- A utility model of computing involving fees charged for levels of use rather than capital investment in hardware or permanent software licenses

- Computing that's provisioned on demand, with resources allocated as needed

- Elastic quantity and power of the computing resources that increases at times of peak use and scales down when demand is lower

- Highly clustered and distributed computing infrastructure that spreads computing tasks across many devices to maximize performance with high fault tolerance for the failure of individual components. (p. 2)

More simply, Corrado and Moulaison (2012) applied the concept directly to libraries: "it is enough to think about cloud computing as library data and services hosted beyond the library's walls and accessible via the Web" (p. 49).

There are actually several different types of "clouds." Beaty (2013) identified five types: the "public" cloud, the most common and the one used by the public for Web-based applications such as e-mail, social media, YouTube, iTunes, and so on; a "private cloud" owned by a particular user or a third-party cloud provider; a "community cloud" used by groups of users with a common purpose or interest such as several like-minded businesses, departments within a corporation or governmental agency, or a parent company and its partners or subsidiary companies; a "hybrid cloud" in which some of the applications are located in a public cloud and others in a private cloud; and finally a fifth type of cloud recently emerged, the "federated cloud," in which users obtain cloud services from a provider who in turn might contract with other cloud providers to broaden the reach of the users (much like cellular phone services that create agreements with other services to expand coverage).

Cloud-based computing in libraries is based on a model known as "Software-as-a-Service" (SaaS). Libraries use a vendor's cloud applications, infrastructure, and hardware to provide the needed library services. This model, according to Breeding (2014a),

. . . trades higher upfront costs, incurred by libraries for equipment and software licenses, for a comprehensive annual subscription fee. Leveraging economies of scale, SaaS providers have the potential to enable savings for libraries over time compared with direct and indirect costs of maintaining local servers and related infrastructure. (p. 3)

SaaS allows simultaneous access to multiple applications on the Web, providing numerous benefits to the library, including

> *Efficiency:* cloud computing maximizes use of server time, energy, and results in minimal downtime;
>
> *Flexibility:* services can be expanded immediately to meet changes in demand;
>
> *Cost savings:* the computing time is paid for incrementally on an as-needed basis; staff is not needed for implementation, maintenance and upgrading of equipment and software;
>
> *Mobility:* cloud-base systems can be accessed by mobile devices;
>
> *Storage:* storage capacity can be increased on demand;
>
> *Ease of operations:* IT responsibilities are shifted to the cloud provider;
>
> *Mission focus:* cloud-based activities reduce the time spent on IT activities and allow staff and administration to focus on meeting the goals and mission of the organization. (Bansode and Pujar 2012; Corrodo and Moulaison 2012; Han 2010)

Rather than taking on the responsibility and costs for hosting, maintaining, and upgrading multiple servers and applications over the library's own network, these responsibilities and costs are moved to the cloud provider.

The array of services that can be moved to the cloud is considerable and includes both administrative and service functions such as the library's website, integrated library systems, digital repositories, learning object management systems, ILL, and public and private storage systems including backup and file-sharing activities (Han 2010). Cloud-based discovery services allow access not only to the catalog, but to a wide array of information resources the library holds or has access to, including special collections, digital repositories, journal databases, citation management systems, and e-books (Bansode and Pujar 2012; Corrodo and Moulaison 2012).

Although the advantages of cloud computing appear considerable, they must still be weighed against fees and other costs including transition costs and backup storage costs. Other concerns relate to the reliability of the cloud service, maintenance quality, and amount of down time; the capacity of the service to ensure data security and confidentiality; and effective management of the data in the system. Once the data is in the cloud, who owns and controls it? Can the data be mined by the vendor? What happens to the data if the vendor goes bankrupt or if the library is not timely in its payments—can the library lose access to its data? (Bansode and Pujar 2012; Breeding 2012; Corrodo and Moulaison 2012). Acquiring cloud-based services is also likely to increase the library's dependence on Internet access and greater bandwidth, and will have substantial impact on the library's IT department and staff (Breeding 2012).

The development of cloud-based services is still in its early stages, and few libraries have adopted it. But as vendors develop more sophisticated cloud-based systems, such as OCLC's WorldShare, ExLibris Alma, Amazon Web Services (AWS), and Google Apps, it is inevitable that a large number of libraries will eventually move in this direction.

IV. SUMMARY

Libraries in the United States have been adapting to changing technologies since the nineteenth century. But the changes incurred by the introduction of computers, the Internet, digitalization, social networks, and mobile devices have created true transformations in library services, collections, and facilities. In a real sense, these transformations have just begun. Physical collections remain important, but they play a decreasing role as access to digital content ascends in importance. As library users grow accustomed to the convenience of Google and other powerful search engines, their expectations about the convenience of library service have risen as well. Users want their library search experience to have the look and feel of Google while at the same time they also want the diversity of services and personal touch that libraries provide. Libraries have worked hard to satisfy these demands. Electronic catalogs have evolved into discovery services that bring the library collection, access to digital content far beyond the walls of the library, and access to LIS professionals' expertise to the users' fingertips. The focus today is on the user—whether it is providing virtual reference service or demand-driven acquisition.

Increased information access is just one part of the library's transformation. The relationship of the library to its community is shifting as well with increased outreach and engagement. While serving individuals remains important, LIS professionals are interacting with groups in new ways. They create makerspaces within the library so that users can contribute content. They are more civically involved in their communities and help people trying to navigate government and other online services. They promote digital literacy and work to embed the library in the fabric of an electronically connected society. The end result of these transformations is unknown. One thing is clear: LIS professionals will need to be flexible and open-minded about these transformations. The stakes are high, but the results might again demonstrate the centrality of the library in the lives of those they serve.

REFERENCES

ALA. 2014. "The State of America's Libraries: A Report from the American Library Association." Chicago: ALA.

Anderson, Elsa K. 2014. "Introduction." In *Electronic Resource Management Systems: A Workflow Approach. Library Technology Reports* 50 (April): 5–10.

———. 2014a. *Electronic Resource Management Systems: A Workflow Approach. Library Technology Reports* 50 (April).

Arms, William Y. 2000. *Digital Libraries*. Cambridge, MA: MIT Press.

Arya, Harsh Bardhan, and J. K. Mishra. 2011. "Oh! Web 2.0, Virtual Reference Service 2.0, Tools & Techniques (I): A Basic Approach." *Journal of Library and Information Services* 5:149–171.

Associated Press. 2005. "Users Confuse Search Results and Ads." www.msnbc.msn.com/id/6861158.

Ayre, Lori Bowen. 2012. *RFID in Libraries: A Step toward Interoperability. Library Technologies Reports* 48 (July).

Balas, Janet L. 2005. "Blogging Is So Last Year—Now Podcasting Is Hot." *Computers in Libraries* (November/December): 29–32.

Bansode, S. Y., and S. M. Pujar. 2012. "Cloud Computing and Libraries." *Journal of Library and Information Technology* 32:506–512.

Barclay, Michael, and Corynne McSherry. 2012. "Digitizing Books Is Fair Use: *Author's Guild v. HathiTrust*." Electronic Frontier Foundation. www.eff.org/deeplinks/2012/10/authors-guild-vhathitrustdecision.

Bearman, David. 2007. "Digital Libraries." In *Annual Review of Information Science and Technology*, edited by Blaise Cronin. Medford, NJ: Information Today, 223–272.

Beaty, Donald I. 2013. "Cloud Computing 101." *ASHRAE Journal* 55 (October): 88–93.

Bercovici, Jeff. 2014. "Amazon vs. Book Publishers, By the Numbers." www.forbes.com/sites/jeffbercovici/2014/02/10/amazon-vs-book-publishers-by-the-numbers.

Bierman, Kenneth J. 1991. "How Will Libraries Pay for Electronic Information?" *Journal of Library Administration* 15: 67–84.

Binkley, Peter. 2006. "Wikipedia Grows Up." *Feliciter* 52: 59–61.

BISG (Book Industry Study Group). 2004. *BISG Policy Statement POL-002: Radio Frequency Identification*. New York: BISG.

Bishop, Ann P. 1990. "The National Research and Education Network (NREN): Promise of a New Information Environment." *ERIC Digest* (November): EDOIR–90–94.

Blue Ribbon Task Force on Sustainable Digital Preservation and Access. 2010. *Sustainable Economics for a Digital Planet: Ensuring Long-Term Access to Digital Information*. http://brtf.sdsc.edu/biblio/BRTF_Final_Report.pdf.

Boozer, Don, to Richard Rubin. (E-mail.) November 13, 2014. "KnowItNow."

Borgman, Christine L. 1996. "Why Are Online Catalogs Still Hard to Use?" *Journal of the American Society for Information Science* 47: 493–503.

Bradford, Jane T., Barbara Costello, and Robert Lenholt. 2005. "Reference Service in the Digital Age: An Analysis of Sources Used to Answer Reference Questions." *Journal of Academic Librarianship* 31 (May): 263–272.

Brantley, Steve, Annie Armstrong, and Krystal M. Lewis. 2006. "Usability Testing of a Customizable Library Web Portal." *College and Research Libraries* (March): 146–163.

Breeding, Marshall. 2012. *Cloud Computing for Libraries*. Chicago: ALA.

———. 2014. "Discovery Product Functionality." In *Library Resource Discovery Products: Context, Library Perspectives, and Vendor Positions. Library Technology Reports* 50 (January): 5–32.

———. 2014a. "Library Systems Report 2014." www.americanlibrariesmagazine.org/article/library-systems-report-2014.

———. 2015. Library Systems Report 2015. *American Libraries* (May): 28–41.

Buckland, Michael K. 1996. "Documentation, Information Science, and Library Science in the U.S.A." *Information Processing and Management* 32: 63–76.

Buckland, Michael K., and Clifford A. Lynch. 1987. "The Linked Systems Protocol and the Future of Bibliographic Networks and Systems." *Information Technology and Libraries* 6:83–88.

———. 1988. "National and Linked Systems Protocol for Online Bibliographic Systems." *Cataloging & Classification Quarterly* 8:15–31.

Bushman, John. 1990. "Asking the Right Questions about Information Technology." *American Libraries* 21 (December): 1026–1030.

———. 2014. "Seven Reasons to be Skeptical about Patron-Driven Acquisitions." In *Customer-Based Collection Development: An Overview*, edited by Karl Bridges. Chicago: ALA.

Caldwell-Stone, Deborah. 2014. "RFID in Libraries." In *Privacy and Freedom of Information in 21st Century Libraries. Library Technology Reports*. 48, no. 8. Chicago: ALA.

Calhoun, Karen. 2014. *Exploring Digital Libraries: Foundations, Practice, Prospects*. Chicago: ALA.

Caminita, Cristina. 2014. "E-book and Patron-Driven Acquisitions in Academic Libraries." In *Customer-Based Demand Driven Collection Development: An Overview*, edited by Karl Bridges. Chicago: ALA, pp. 1–12.

Caplan, Priscilla. 2008. "Digital Defense: A Primer for the Preservation of Digital Materials." *American Libraries* (May): 38.

Carr, Nicholas. 2008. "Is Google Making Us Stupid?" *Atlantic Monthly* 302 (July/August): 56–63.

Castro, Kimberly. 2007. "The Future of E-books." *Business Week Online* (October 29). www.businessweek.com/investor/content/Oct2007/pi20071026_777647.htm.

Chawner, Brenda, and Paul H. Lewis. 2006. "WikiWikiWebs: New Ways to Communicate in a Web Environment." Young Adult Library Services 4 (March): 33–43.

Chu, Melanie and Yvonne Nalani Meulemans. 2008. "The Problems and Potential of MySpace and Facebook Usage in Academic Libraries." Internet Reference Services Quarterly 13: 69–85.

Chua, Alton Y. K., and Snehasish Banerjee. 2013. "So Fast So Good: An Analysis of Answer Quality and Answer Speed in Community Question-Answering Sites." Journal of the American Society for Information Science and Technology 64:2058–2068.

Cochenour, Donnice. 2006. "Is There a Wiki in Your (Library) Future?" Colorado Libraries 32 (winter): 34–36.

Connaway, Lynn Silipigni, and Marie L. Radford. 2011. Seeking Synchronicity: Revelations and Recommendations for Virtual Reference. Columbus, OH: OCLC.

Corrado, Edward M., and Heather Lea Moulaison. 2012. "The Library Cloud." Library Journal (March 1): 49–51.

Cramer, Carol Joyner. 2013. "All About Demand-Driven Acquisition." The Serials Librarian 56: 87–97.

Crovitz, L. Gordon. 2009. "Wikipedia's Old-Fashioned Revolution." Wall Street Journal (national ed.) 258 (April 6): A13.

Curtis, Anthony. 2014. "The Brief History of Social Media." www2.uncp/home/acurtis/ NewMedia/SocialMediaHistory.html.

December, John, and Neil Randall. 1995. The World Wide Web Unleashed 1996. Indianapolis: Sams.

De Gennaro, Richard D. 1989. "Technology and Access in an Enterprise Society." Library Journal 114 (October 1): 40–43.

De Rosa, Cathy, et al. 2005. Perceptions of Libraries and Information Resources. Dublin, OH: OCLC.

De Rosa, Cathy, Lorcan Dempsey, and Alane Wilson. 2004. The 2003 OCLC Environmental Scan: Pattern Recognition: A Report to the OCLC Membership. Dublin, OH: OCLC.

Digital Trends Staff. "The History of Social Networking." www.digital trends.com/features/ the-history-of-social-networking.

DMR (Digital Marketing Ramblings). 2014. "By the Numbers: 170 Amazing Facebook User & Demographic Statistics." www.expandedramblings.com/index.php/by-the -numbers-17-amazing-Facebook-stats/.

———. 2014a. "By the Numbers: 50 Amazing Facebook Mobile & App Statistics." expandedramblings.com/index.php/Facebook-mobile-app-statistics/#.VEOa _7DF98F/.

Downey, Kay. 2014. "Technical Services Aspects of Demand-Driven E-book Acquisitions." In Customer-Based Demand Driven Collection Development: An Overview, edited by Karl Bridges. Chicago: ALA, pp. 103–113.

Downey, Kay, Yin Zhang, Cristobal Urbana, and Tom Klinger. 2014. "A Comparative Study of Print Book and DDA E-book Acquisition and Use." *Technical Services Quarterly* 31: 139–160.

DPC (Digital Preservation Coalition). 2012. "Introduction—Definitions and Concepts." www.dpconline.org/advice/preservationhandbook/introduction/definitions-and -concepts.

Duggan, Maeve, and Joanna Brenner. 2013. The Demographics of Social Media Users—2012. www.pewInternet.org/Reports/2013/Social-media-users.aspx.

Duggan, Maeve, and Lee Rainie. 2012. Cell Phone Activities 2012. www.pewInternet.org/ Reports/2012/Cell-Activities.aspx.

EFF (Electronic Frontier Foundation). 2013. "*Authors Guild v. HathiTrust.*" www.eff.org/ cases/authors-guild-v-hathitrust.

Eiffert, Robert. 2006. "Wikipedia, the Review." *School Library Journal* 52 (March): 82–83.

Emery, Jill, and Graham Stone. 2013. "Introduction and Literature Review." In *Techniques for Electronic Resource Management. Library Technology Reports* (February/March): 5–9.

Fielden, Ned L., and Lucy Kuntz. 2002. *Search Engines Handbook.* Jefferson, NC: McFarland.

Fox, Edward A., and Shalini R. Urs. 2002. "Digital Libraries." In *Annual Review of Information Science and Technology.* Vol. 36. Medford, NJ: Information Today, 503–590.

Gomery, Douglas. 1994. "In Search of the Cybermarket." *Wilson Quarterly* (summer): 9–17.

Google. 2015. "Books." www.google.com/googlebooks/library.

———. "Google Books Library Program." www.google.com/googlebooks/library.

Greenstein, Daniel. 2000. "Digital Libraries and Their Challenges." *Library Trends* 49 (fall): 290–303.

Grosch, Audrey N. 1995. *Library Information Technology and Networks.* New York: Marcel Dekker.

Hahn, Trudi. 1996. "Pioneers of the Online Age." *Information Processing and Management* 32: 33–48.

———. 2006. "Impacts of Mass Digitization Projects on Libraries and Information Policy." *Bulletin of the American Society for Information Science and Technology* (October/ November). www.asis.org/Bulletin/Oct-06/hahn.html.

Han, Yan. 2010. "On the Clouds: A New Way of Computing." *Information Technology and Libraries* (June): 87–92.

Handy, Stephanie. 2014. "Considering RFID? Consider This." *Computers in Libraries* (November): 19–22.

Harrell, Jeanne, Carmelita Pickett, Simona Tabacaru, Jeannette Ho, Ana Ugaz, and Nancy Burford. 2014. "PDA in a Multi-Library Setting: Challenges, Implementation, and

Outcomes." In *Customer-Based Demand Driven Collection Development: An Overview*, edited by Karl Bridges. Chicago: ALA, pp. 139–158.

HathiTrust. 2014. "Welcome to the Shared Digital Future." www.hathitrust.org/about.

Henry, Jo. 2011. "Death of Reference or Birth of a New Marketing Age?" *Public Services Quarterly* 7: 87–93.

Horrigan, John B. 2013. *Adoption of Information & Communications Technologies in the United States: Narrowing Gaps, New Challenges.* knightfoundation.org/media/uploads/media-pdfs/DigitalAccessUpdateFeb2014.pdf.

Howland, Jared L., Rebecca Schroeder, and Tom Wright. 2014. "Brigham Young University's Patron-Driven Acquisitions." In *Customer-Based Demand Driven Collection Development: An Overview*, edited by Karl Bridges. Chicago: ALA, pp. 115–138.

Internet2. 2014. "Internet2." www.Internet2.edu.

———. 2009. "About Internet2." www.Internet2.edu/resources/AboutInternet2.pdf.

Kajewski, Mary Ann. 2006. "Emerging Technologies Changing Public Library Service Delivery Models." *Aplis* 19 (December): 157–163.

Kuttner, Robert. 2006. "In Defense of Books." *Oberlin Alumni Magazine* (spring): 13–15.

Lankes, R. David. 2000. "The Foundations of Digital Reference." In *Digital Reference Service in the New Millennium: Planning, Management, and Evaluation*, edited by R. David Lankes, John W. Collins III, and Abby S. Kasowitz. New York: Neal-Schuman.

Leeder, Kim, and Eric Frierson. 2014. "Introduction." In *Planning Our Future Libraries: Blueprints for 2025*, edited by Kim Leeder and Eric Frierson. Chicago: ALA, pp. vii–xiii.

Leiner, Barry M., et al. 2010. "A Brief History of the Internet." www.isoc.org/Internet/history/brief.shtml.

Madden, Mary, Amanda Lenhart, Maeve Duggan, Sandra Cortesi, and Urs Gass. 2013. *Teens and Technology 2013.* www.pewInternet.org/Reports/2013/Teens-and-Tech.aspx.

Madden, Mary, Amanda Lenhart, Sandra Cortesi, Urs Gasser, Maeve Duggan, Aaron Smith, and Meredith Beaton. 2013. *Teens, Social Media, and Privacy.* www.pewInternet.org/Reports/2013/Teens-Social-Media-And-Privacy.aspx.

Malczewski, Ben. 2014. "Meaningful Space in a Digital Age." In *Planning Our Future Libraries: Blueprints for 2025*, edited by Kim Leeder and Eric Frierson. Chicago: ALA, pp. 29–40.

Maloney, Krisellen. 2014. "The Faculty Commons: Reimagining the Intellectual Heart of Campus." In *Planning Our Future Libraries: Blueprints for 2025*, edited by Kim Leeder and Eric Frierson. Chicago: ALA, pp. 41–54.

Markey, Karen. 2007. "The Online Library Catalog: Paradise Lost and Paradise Regained?" *D-Lib* 13 (January/February). http://dlib.org/dlib/january07/markey/01markey.html.

Mell, Peter, and Timothy Grance. 2011. *The NIST Definition of Cloud Computing: Recommendations of the National Institute of Standards and Technology.* Special Publication 800–145. (September).

Mitchell, Scott (July 2008), *Easy Wiki Hosting, Scott Hanselman's blog, and Snagging Screens*, MSDN Magazine, retrieved March 9, 2010, for Wikipedia, retrieved December 19, 2014.

Mutch, Andrew, and Karen Ventura. 2003. "The Promise of Internet2." *Library Journal* 128 (summer): 14–16.

NDSA (National Digital Stewardship Alliance). 2014. *2015 National Agenda for Digital Stewardship.* www.digitalpreservation.gov/ndsa/documents/2015National AgendaExecSummary.pdf.

Neilsen and NN Incite. 2012. "The Social Media Report 2012." Posted by Jasmine Jaume. www.brandwatch.com/2012/12/how-we-use-social-ghlights-from-the-social-media.

NISO (National Information Standards Organization). 1994. *Information Retrieval: Application Service Definition and Protocol Specification.* Bethesda, MD: NISO.

———. 2007. *A Framework of Guidance for Building Good Digital Collections*, 3rd ed. NISO.

———. 2014. *Demand Driven Acquisition of Monographs: A Recommended Practice of the National Information Standards Organization.* (NISO RP-20–2014). Baltimore, MD: NISO.

Nixon, Judith M., Suzanne M. Ward, and Robert S. Freeman. 2014. "Selectors' Perceptions of E-book Patron-Driven Acquisitions." In *Customer-Based Demand Driven Collection Development: An Overview*, edited by Karl Bridges. Chicago: ALA, pp. 27–47.

Novotny, Eric. 2004. "I Don't Think I Click: A Protocol Analysis Study of Use of a Library Online Catalog in the Internet Age." *College and Research Libraries* (November): 525–537.

OCLC. 2014. "WorldCat Local at a Glance." https://oclc.org/worldcat-local/overview.en.html.

———. "Overview." https://oclc.org/worldcat-local/Webscale.en.html.

Olsen, Florence. 2003. "Internet2 at a Crossroads." *Chronicle of Higher Education* 49 (May 16, 2003).

O'Reilly, Tim. 2005. "What Is Web 2.0." www.oreilly.com/pub/a/web2/archive/what-is-web -20.html.

Pesch, Oliver. 2008. "Library Standards and E-Resource Management: A Survey of Current Initiatives and Standards Efforts." *The Serials Librarian* 55: 481–486.

Pew Research. 2013. "In a Digital Age, Parents Value Printed Books for Their Kids." www.pewInternet.org/fact-tank/2013/05/28/in-a-digital-age-parents-value-printed -books-for-their-kids.

———. 2013. "Over a Quarter of Internet Users Download or Listen to Podcasts." www.pewresearch.org/fact-tank/2013/12/27/over-a-quarter-of-internet-users-download -or-listen-to-podcasts.

———. 2013. "Tablet and E-Reader Ownership Update." www.pewInternet.org/2013/10/18/ tablet-and-e-reader-ownership-update.

———. 2013. "Trend Data (Adults)." www.pewInternet.org/Static-Pages/Trend-Data -(Adults)/Online-Activities-Total.aspx.

————. 2014. "Device Ownership over Time." www.pewInternet.org/data-trend/mobile/devices-ownership.

————. 2014. "E-Reading Rises as Device Ownership Jumps." www.pewInternet.org/2014/01/16/e-reading-rises-as-device-ownership-jumps.

————. 2014. "Internet Users in 2014." www.pewInternet.org/data-trend/Internet-use/latest-stats.

————. 2014. "Mobile Technology Fact Sheet." www.pewinteret.org/fact-sheets/mobile-technology-fact-sheet.

————. 2014. "Social Networking Fact Sheet." www.pewInternet.org/fact-sheets/social-networking-fact-sheet.

————. 2014. "Three Major Technology Revolutions." www.pewInternet.org/three-technology-revolutions.

————. 2014. *The Web at 25 in the U.S.* www.pewinternet.org/2014/02/27/the-web-at-25-in-the-u-s.

————. 2014. "World Wide Web Timeline." www.pewinternet.org/2014/03/11/world-wide-web-timeline.

"Playing with Technology—Meredith Farkas." 2006. *Library Journal* (March 15). www.libraryjournal.com/article/CA6312495.html.

Polanka, Sue. 2011. "Purchasing E-books in Libraries: A Maze of Opportunities and Challenges." In *The No Shelf Required Guide to E-book Purchasing*, edited by Sue Polanka. Chicago: ALA, pp. 4–13.

Quantcast.com. 2014. "Yahoo! Answers." www.quantcast.com/answers.yahoo.com.

Quora.com. 2014. "How Many E-books Are Available on Amazon." www.quora.com/How-many-e-books-are-available-on-Amazon.

Radford, Marie L., Lynn Silipigni Connaway, and Chirag Shah. 2012. "Convergence and Synergy: Social Q&A Meets Virtual Reference Services." www.asis.org/asist2012/proceedings/Submissions/111.pdf.

Rider, Freemont. 1944. *The Scholar and the Future of the Research Library: A Problem and Its Solution.* New York: Hadham, 99.

Robison, Richard. 2007. "Google: A Chronology of Innovations, Acquisitions, and Growth." *Journal of Library Administration* 46: 5–29.

RSS Advisory Board. 2010. "Really Simple Syndication Best Practices Profile." www.rssboard.org/rss-profile.

RUSA (Reference and User Services Association). 2010. "Guidelines for Implementing and Maintaining Virtual Reference Services." www.ala.org/rusa/sites/ala.org.rusa/files/content/resources/guidelines/virtual-reference-se.pdf.

Shah, Chirag, and Vanessa Kitzie. 2012. "Social Q&A and Virtual Reference—Comparing Apples and Oranges with the Help of Experts and Users." *Journal of the American Society for Information Science and Technology* 63: 2020–2036.

Singh, Meeraj Kuman, and Preeti Mahajan. 2014. "RFID and It's (sic) Use in Libraries: A Literature Review." *International Journal of Information Dissemination and Technology* 4 (April-June): 117–123.

Smith, Aaron. 2013. *Smartphone Ownership2013 Update*. www.pewInternet.org/Reports/2013/Smartphone-Ownership-2013.aspx.

Stephens, Michael. 2005. "The iPod Experiments." *Netconnect* (spring): 22–25.

———. 2006. "Web 2.0 & Libraries: Best Practices for Social Software." *Library Technology Reports*. https://publications.techsource.ala.org/products/archive.pl?article=2580.

Stone, Graham, and Jill Emery. 2013. "Developing TERMS: Techniques for Electronic Resource Management." *Library Faculty Publications and Presentation*. Paper 70.

Summit, Roger. June 2002. "Reflections on the Beginnings of Dialog: The Birth of Online Information Access," Chronolog. The Dialog Corp. ISSN 0163–3732.

Tennant, Roy. 1992. "Internet Basics." *Eric Digest* 18: EDO-IR-92-7.

Thurston, Anne. 2012. "Keynote: Digitization and Preservation: Global Opportunities and Cultural Challenges." Proceedings of the Memory of the World in the Digital Age: Digitization and Preservation. 26–28 September 2012, Vancouver, British Columbia, Canada, edited by Luciana Duranti and Elizabeth Shaffer.

Tyckoson, D. A. 2011. "Issues and Trends in the Management of Reference Services: A Historical Perspective." *Journal of Library Administration* 51: 259–278.

Tyler, David C., Christina Falci, Joyce C. Melvin, Marylou Epp, and Anita M. Kreps. 2013. "Patron-Driven Acquisition and Circulation at an Academic Library: Interaction Effects and Circulation Performance of Print Books Acquired via Librarians' Orders, Approval Plans, and Patrons' Interlibrary Loan Requests." *Collection Management* 38: 3–32.

UNESCO. 2012. "UNESCO/UBC Vancouver Declaration." www.unesco.org/new/fileadmin/MULTIMEDIA/HQ/CI/CI/PDF.

U.S. District Court (Southern District of New York). *The Authors Guild, Inc. vs. Google Inc.* 05 Civ.8136 (DC). Case 1:05-cv-08136-DC. Document 1088. Issued November 14, 2013.

Vaughn, Jason. 2011. "OCLC WorldCat Local?" *Library Technology Reports* 47 (January): 12–21.

———. "WebScale Discovery Services: What and Why?" *Library Technology Reports* 47 (January): 5–11.

Walters, Tyler, and Katherine Skinner. 2011. *New Roles for New Times: Digital Curation for Preservation*. Washington, DC: ARL.

Wanucha, M., and L. Hofschire. 2013. *U.S. Public Libraries and the Use of Web Technologies, 2012*. (Closer Look Report.) Denver, CO: Colorado State Library, Library Research Office.

Warfield, Peter. 2005. "RFID: More Worrisome than You Think. *Public Libraries* 44 (November-December): ii.

Webster's Third New International Dictionary. 1970. Springfield, MA: G & C Merriam.

Widdersheim, Michael M. 2014. "E-Lending and Libraries: Toward a De-commercialization of the Commons." *Progressive Librarian* 42 (summer): 95–114.

Wikipedia. 2009. "RSS." http://en.wikipedia.org/wiki/RSS.

World Wide Web Consortium. 2010. "Mission." www.w3.0rg/Consortium/Mission.

Wright, Cheryl D. 2002. "Introduction." In *Digital Library Technology Trends.* www.google .com/webhp?sourceid=chrome-instant&ion=1&espv=2&ie=UTF-8#q=digital%20 library%20technology%20trends.

Zeng, Marcia Lei. 2008. "Digital Preservation: For the Future of the Past." [Unpublished Presentation Overheads]. Kent State University.

Zhang, Yin, and Shengli Deng. 2014. "Social Q&A Versus Library Virtual Reference: Evaluation and Comparison from the Users' Perspective." (Manuscript): 1–42.

Zhang, Yin, and Sonali Kudva. 2014. "E-books Versus Print Books: Readers' Choices and Preferences across Contexts." *Journal of the Association for Information Science and Technology* 65:1695–1706.

Zick, Greg. 2009. "Digital Collections: History and Perspectives." *Journal of Library Administration* 49:687–693.

Zickuhr, Kathryn. 2013. Tablet Ownership 2013. www.pewInternet.org/Reports/2013/ Tablet-Ownership-2013.aspx.

Zickuhr, Kathryn, Lee Rainie, Kristen Purcell, Mary Madden, and Joanna Brenner. 2012. Libraries, Patrons, and E-books. http://libraries.pewInternet.org/2012/06/22/libraries -patrons-and-e-books.

Zittrain, Jonathan L. 2006. "The Generative Internet." *Harvard Law Review* 119 (May): 1974–2040.

SELECTED READINGS: Impact of Technology
Books/Monographs

ALA. *Electronic Resource Management Systems: A Workflow Approach. Library Technology Reports* 50. Chicago: ALA, April 2014.

Blue Ribbon Task Force on Sustainable Digital Preservation and Access. *Sustainable Economics for a Digital Planet: Ensuring Long-Term Access to Digital Information.* 2010. brtf.sdsc.edu/biblio/BRTF_Final_Report.pdf.

Breeding, Marshall. *Cloud Computing for Libraries.* Chicago: ALA, 2012.

Bridges, Karl, ed. *Customer-Based Demand Driven Collection Development: An Overview.* Chicago: ALA, 2014.

Bushman, John. *Information Technology in Librarianship.* Westport, CT: Libraries Unlimited, 2008.

Calhoun, Karen. *Exploring Digital Libraries: Foundations, Practice, Prospects.* Chicago: ALA, 2014.

Cloonan, Michèle Valerie, ed. 2015. *Preserving Our Heritage*. Chicago: ALA,

De Rosa, Cathy, Lorcan Dempsey, and Alane Wilson. *The 2003 OCLC Environmental Scan: Pattern Recognition: A Report to the OCLC Membership*. Dublin, OH: OCLC, 2004.

Dempsey, Lorcan. *The Network Reshapes the Library*. Chicago: ALA, 2014.

Leckie, Gloria J., and John E. Buschman, eds. *Information Technology in Librarianship: New Critical Approaches*. Westport, CT: Libraries Unlimited, 2009.

Thomsett-Scott, Beth C., ed. *Implementing Virtual Reference Services*. Chicago: ALA (LITA), 2013.

Articles

Arya, Harsh Bardhan, and J. K. Mishra. "Oh! Web 2.0, Virtual Reference Service 2.0, Tools & Techniques (I): A Basic Approach." *Journal of Library and Information Services* 5 (2011): 149–171.

Barjak, Franz. "The Role of the Internet in Informal Scholarly Communication." *Journal of the American Society for Information Science and Technology* 57 (August 2006): 1350–1367.

Bearman, David. "Digital Libraries." *Annual Review of Information Science and Technology* 41 (2007): 223–272.

Burke, Leslie, and Stephanie McConnell. "Technical Services Departments in the Digital Age: The Four R's of Adapting to New Technology." *Against the Grain* 19 (November 2007): 58–64.

Bushman, John. "Seven Reasons to be Skeptical about Patron-Driven Acquisitions." In *Customer-Based Collection Development: An Overview*, edited by Karl Bridges. Chicago: ALA, 2014.

Caldwell-Stone, Deborah. "RFID in Libraries." In *Privacy and Freedom of Information in 21st Century Libraries. Library Technology Reports*, 48. no. 8. Chicago: ALA, 2014.

Carr, Nicholas. "Is Google Making Us Stupid?" *Atlantic Monthly* 302 (July/August 2008): 56–63.

Downey, Kay, Yin Zhang, Cristobal Urbana, and Tom Klinger. 2014. "A Comparative Study of Print Book and DDA E-book Acquisition and Use." *Technical Services Quarterly* 31 (2014): 139–160.

Horrigan, John B. *Adoption of Information & Communications Technologies in the United States: Narrowing Gaps, New Challenges*. 2014. knightfoundation.org/media/uploads/media-pdfs/DigitalAccessUpdateFeb2014.pdf.

Levine, Jenny. "The Gaming Generation." *Library Technology Reports* 42 (September–October 2006): 18–23.

Luther, Judy, and Maureen C. Kelly. "The Next Generation of Discovery." *Library Journal* 136 (March 15, 2011): 66–71.

Madden, Mary, Amanda Lenhart, Sandra Cortesi, Urs Gasser, Maeve Duggan, Aaron Smith, and Meredith Beaton. 2013. *Teens, Social Media, and Privacy.* www.pewInternet.org/Reports/2013/Teens-Social-Media-And-Privacy.aspx.

Malczewski, Ben. "Meaningful Space in a Digital Age." In *Planning Our Future Libraries: Blueprints for 2025*, edited by Kim Leeder and Eric Frierson. Chicago: ALA, 2014, pp. 29–40.

Maloney, Krisellen. "The Faculty Commons: Reimagining the Intellectual Heart of Campus." In *Planning Our Future Libraries: Blueprints for 2025*, edited by Kim Leeder and Eric Frierson. Chicago: ALA, 2014, pp. 41–54.

Phillips, Angus. "Does the Book Have a Future?" LOGOS: *The Journal of the World Book Community* 19 (March 2008): 26–33.

Polanka, Sue. "Purchasing E-books in Libraries: A Maze of Opportunities and Challenges." In *The No Shelf Required Guide to E-book Purchasing*, edited by Sue Polanka. Chicago: ALA, 2011, pp. 4–13.

Radford, Marie L., Lynn Silipigni Connaway, and Chirag Shah. "Convergence and Synergy: Social Q&A Meets Virtual Reference Services." 2012. www.asis.org/asist2012/proceedings/Submissions/111.pdf.

Shah, Chirag, and Vanessa Kitzie. 2012. "Social Q&A and Virtual Reference—Comparing Apples and Oranges with the Help of Experts and Users." *Journal of the American Society for Information Science and Technology* 63 (2012): 2020–2036.

Singh, Meeraj Kuman, and Preeti Mahajan. "RFID and It's (sic) Use in Libraries: A Literature Review." *International Journal of Information Dissemination and Technology* 4 (April–June 2014): 117–123.

Tyler, David C., Christina Falci, Joyce C. Melvin, Marylou Epp, and Anita M. Kreps. "Patron-Driven Acquisition and Circulation at an Academic Library: Interaction Effects and Circulation Performance of Print Books Acquired via Librarians' Orders, Approval Plans, and Patrons' Interlibrary Loan Requests." *Collection Management* 38 (2013): 3–32.

Vaughn, Jason. "WebScale Discovery Services: What and Why?" *Library Technology Reports* 47 (January 2011): 5–11.

Widdersheim, Michael M. "E-Lending and Libraries: Toward a De-Commercialization of the Commons." *Progressive Librarian* 42 (summer 2014): 95–114.

Zhang, Yin, and Shengli Deng. 2014. "Social Q&A versus Library Virtual Reference: Evaluation and Comparison from the Users' Perspective." Manuscript. (2014): 1–42.

Zhang, Yin, and Sonali Kudva. "E-books Versus Print Books: Readers' Choices and Preferences across Contexts." *Journal of the Association for Information Science and Technology* 65 (2014): 1695–1706.

Zittrain, Jonathan L. "The Generative Internet." *Harvard Law Review* 119 (May 2006): 1974–2006.

5
Library and Information Science
An Evolving Profession

I. INTRODUCTION

Since the late nineteenth century, librarians in the United States have established a solid professional identity and developed important values to guide their actions and goals. In the past, changes in the profession occurred slowly and incrementally and consequently the role of the librarian remained relatively constant. One of the most stable elements, historically, was the association of the librarian with the physical library; one does not usually think of librarians without also thinking of the place where they ply their trade. But is the identity of today's LIS professional inextricably linked to this physical entity? The profession is now in the midst of a revolutionary—and for some, disconcerting—change. The stable condition of the past has been replaced by a dynamic environment in which the content and functions of libraries are being revised and modified by technological, political, and economic changes. In the new world of digital access to information, will the library disappear? Will there be librarians without libraries? Will the term *librarian* disappear like the passenger pigeon or simply be transformed into information consultant, information specialist, information manager, or knowledge manager (as it already has in some libraries)?

Despite some distress, there is no evidence that libraries or librarians will vanish in the near future. The modern American library might still have its quiet spaces for contemplation and study, but today's library—academic, public, school, and special—is a vital and dynamic place. The library professionals required to serve in them have many names reflecting the need for generalists and specialists. They are reference librarians, catalogers, and serials librarians, and they are also systems librarians, metadata librarians, project coordinators, e-resource catalogers, digital librarians, repository managers, informatricians, research data managers and curators, information literacy educators, knowledge managers, and Web managers (Park et al. 2009; Cox and Corrall 2013). Those considering LIS as a career will need to be adaptable, patient, constant in times of uncertainty, and amenable to acquiring new knowledge and skills throughout their career. How the profession evolves in the next decades will be determined by the essential worth of our foundational values, by our capacity to adapt, and the new or modified missions required by our society. This chapter focuses on four aspects of the profession: the historical forces that shaped education for librarianship; contemporary issues facing the field; the nature of the LIS workforce; and the challenges facing LIS professionals in the future.

II. HISTORY OF LIBRARY EDUCATION AND THE PREPARATION OF LIBRARIANS

As noted in chapter 2, American libraries in the eighteenth century were small; if librarians existed, they functioned primarily in a custodial capacity. By the middle of the nineteenth century, a few librarians, invariably male, could be found in more sophisticated academic institutions. These individuals were described as "bookmen" by Pierce Butler (1951) because they were scholars, not custodians. Before 1850, there was no training to speak of for those who worked in a library except trial and error. Librarians were self-taught or followed the example of others; a novice librarian often contacted other librarians for advice and counsel. Between 1850 and 1875, a more formal apprenticeship emerged. Sometimes a librarian would recruit an interested individual and train that person under close observation.

During the 1870s, another route for training began to emerge with the appearance of instructional publications from private publishers and the U.S. government. *Publishers Weekly* began in 1872 and although it focused on the publishing industry, there were small sections devoted to librarians. Another significant source of information was the U.S. Office of Education, which produced publications for educators. The most significant publication affecting library education was the landmark study issued in 1876, *Public Libraries in the United States of America: Their History, Condition, and Management*, which presented substantial statistical data on more than 3,600 public libraries, and data on other types of libraries as well. As part of this work, the bureau issued a manual including articles written by noted authorities on librarianship. The topics included such areas as management, administration, history, cataloging, popular reading, and library buildings. In essence, it was the first authoritative library reader (U.S. Office of Education 1876). The period from 1876 to 1923 marked a critical time in the development of library education. A variety of forces discussed below created the foundations for the professionalization of librarianship during this period.

A. The Decline of the Classical English and Apprenticeship Models and the Rise of the Technical Education Model

American education during the nineteenth century was generally shaped by the dominant immigrant population: the British. The British model of education emphasized the study of classical languages, religion, literature, and grammar. The traditional British apprenticeship model trained individuals for a craft; only a few individuals could be trained at a time for a specialized, narrowly defined job. With industrialization, many people had to be trained for positions that might be quite similar from factory to factory. A classical education was inappropriate, and apprenticeship was too inefficient. It was during this period that many educators and some library leaders were exposed to the European technical education model at various international fairs and expositions in Europe and the United States. The resulting rise of technical schools in the United States and the vocational emphasis of these educational institutions fit well with the needs of American libraries (White 1976).

B. The Influence of Andrew Carnegie

The latter half of the nineteenth century saw tremendous growth in the number of libraries. Between 1825 and 1850, 551 public libraries were founded; in the next twenty-five years, more than 2,200 were established (U.S. Office of Education 1876, p. xvi). There were many reasons for this rapid increase, including increased recognition of the important role of libraries in research and teaching. But it was Andrew Carnegie who, from the end of the nineteenth century to the first two decades of the twentieth, financed the construction of nearly 3,000 libraries throughout the world, a large proportion of them public libraries in the United States. This proliferation had the inevitable effect of increasing the demand for library workers and establishing a permanent workforce.

C. Melvil Dewey and the Professionalization of Librarianship

There is little dispute that Melvil Dewey was a prime force in the professionalization of American librarianship and in library education during the latter part of
the nineteenth century. Interestingly, Kendall (2014) argued that Dewey, like many
other highly successful innovators (Charles Lindberg, Steve Jobs, Henry Heinz),
had obsessive compulsive personality disorder (OCPD), a form of highly productive obsessive behavior; in contrast to OCD (obsessive compulsive disorder) which
generally inhibits life functions. Certainly, Dewey's energy and passion produced
many library innovations and significantly advanced the profession. He believed
that books had considerable power to shape a community's thinking, a power that
could be used for good or evil. He also believed that a librarian's duty was to provide
the public with "better" books that could improve people.

Discussed below are four of Dewey's accomplishments that were clearly important in establishing the professional foundations of the field: his decimal classification system, his role in establishing the American Library Association, his role in
creating *Library Journal*, and his influence on library education.

1. The Dewey Decimal Classification System

While a student at Amherst College, Dewey worked in the college library. After graduation, he remained at Amherst and served as the librarian. He was excited by the
possibilities arising from the Industrial Revolution and was fascinated with labor-sav-
ing routines and devices. He belonged to a number of organizations promoting the
use of metrics and simplified spelling (hence, Melvil rather than Melville). As the
Amherst librarian, he quickly recognized that the existing classification system was
inflexible and he set about to find a new, more efficient way to organize materials.
He heavily promoted his new classification system, and it grew in popularity over
the years. In terms of the profession, the Dewey Decimal System (discussed in more
detail in chapter 6) provided a fundamental and important theoretical principle by
which professional skills and responsibilities could be organized.

2. The American Library Association

Although discussions of the need for a professional association for librarians began
as early as the 1850s, it took time to bring the idea to fruition. During that time,
Dewey was a guiding force. In 1876, he organized a national meeting of librarians
in Philadelphia. On the final day, the ALA was founded with Dewey as its secretary.

The creation of a national professional association was an important benchmark. It substantially increased professional identity among the practitioners, helped identify important issues, and established standards of service and conduct. The first national conferences, for example, provided a common forum for the discussion of ideas and issues such as classification, indexing, and protecting materials from abuse. The founding of ALA elevated librarianship and provided national visibility and recognition to the field.

3. American Library Journal

Dewey was also instrumental in creating the *American Library Journal*, the first major professional publication devoted solely to the interests of librarians. Dewey and the other editors intended the journal to assist librarians in their daily work. For example, in the first issue, Justin Windsor (1876), associate editor and director of the Boston Public Library, advised new librarians on management:

- Locate whatever printed materials on librarianship are available.
- Locate similar libraries and ask for their rules and reports.
- Study the materials received.
- Evaluate the extent to which other libraries are good comparisons to the library in question.
- Contact an experienced librarian.
- Do what seems to come naturally. (p. 2)

He also warned the novice who did not have time to do this research and analysis to "resign your trust to someone who has" (p. 2). The value of such a publication was not lost on the ALA, which in 1877 adopted the journal as its official organ and shortened the name to *Library Journal*. Subsequent issues included articles, summaries of ALA conference proceedings, and a section titled "Notes and Queries" that responded to questions and comments from librarians, many of which concerned cataloging and classification, circulation, library buildings, equipment, and funds.

4. Library Education

Until the latter part of the nineteenth century, institutions such as the Boston Athenaeum, Amherst, and Harvard University offered traditional apprenticeships, as did major public libraries in Boston, Los Angeles, Denver, and Cleveland. Some academic or technical institutes offered special classes in library techniques. All of this training, however, was usually of short duration and idiosyncratic in terms of curriculum.

In 1879, Dewey promoted systematic training for librarianship. He envisioned a knowledgeable faculty: experienced librarians in major libraries who would advise apprentices on library matters, suggest readings, and identify areas of study worth investigating (Vann 1961). It is important to note that Dewey did not believe that just anyone could be a librarian. Rather, he thought that only people with the appropriate "character" should be accepted for training; character in this nineteenth-century sense meant a "moral potential" for self-refinement and improvement (Wiegand 1999). This first proposal, however, was not well received at ALA.

Then a fortuitous event occurred in 1883. By this time, Dewey's reputation had grown considerably and he was recruited for the head librarian's position at Columbia University. During his interview with the president, F. A. P. Barnard, he discussed his desire to establish a school for formal training. President Barnard was enthusiastic and the trustees were supportive, although perhaps naive about what would be involved. Dewey accepted the appointment in 1884, and the first library school, the Columbia School of Library Economy, opened on January 1, 1887, with a class of twenty students: three men and seventeen women (Vann 1961). The course of study was pragmatic and included selection, readers' aids, bibliography, repair of materials, administration, and cataloging. The training took three months and required an internship that could take as long as two years, so that the students were exposed to their professional tasks (Vann 1961).

Unfortunately, Dewey's relations with the university's officials were tense. Some of the trustees felt that he had not been completely forthcoming, especially in regard to the problematic presence of women in the school. Indeed, when the trustees discovered that women were accepted, they voted to deny Dewey the use of Columbia's classrooms. The students met across the street from the Columbia campus in a converted storeroom, which Wiegand (1999) called a "bootleg operation" (p. 18). By 1888 it was clear that Columbia would close the school.

Dewey, anticipating this event, accepted a position as head of the New York State Library in Albany, which agreed to have the school transferred there, thus preserving the only formal education program for librarians in the country. Dewey remained director, but the daily operations became the responsibility of Mary Salome Cutler Fairchild, who served as the vice director and taught there for sixteen years (Maack 1986). Fairchild had worked both as a cataloger and a cataloging instructor under Dewey at Columbia.

Fairchild's view of library education differed in some significant ways from Dewey's. As a student of the Industrial Revolution, Dewey saw libraries as businesses and he emphasized the practical aspects of running an institution. Fairchild broadened this perspective by emphasizing more theoretical and cultural aspects. For example, Dewey recommended book selection using standard reviews, while Fairchild believed that a librarian should have personal knowledge of books and an understanding of people's tastes (Wiegand 1996). Fairchild gave "form and substance to the Dewey dream" through her able administration and inspiring pedagogy (Gambee 1978, p. 168). Gambee also noted that she commanded considerable loyalty from her students and alumnae, and was credited with establishing selective admission criteria and maintaining a quality education that made Albany the standard of library education.

D. The Growth of Library Schools

The success of the Albany program inspired additional programs. By 1900 there were four major library schools: Albany, Pratt Institute, Drexel University, and the Armour Institute, which became the Library School at the University of Illinois in 1897 (Vann 1961). Among the directors of these schools were some of the future leaders of the library profession—women who helped shape library education and librarianship for years to come.

1. Pratt Institute

Pratt's school was established in 1890, originally to train staff for the Pratt Institute library. Mary Wright Plummer, a member of the first class at Columbia and one of its best students, became the director in 1895. She was an ardent advocate for professional training. Under her leadership, the school broadened its purpose, extended the program from six months to two years, and enriched the curriculum, making the education equivalent to the best training available (Brand 1996; Vann 1961). In 1896, Plummer offered a specialization in scholarly libraries, adding special courses in bibliography, advanced cataloging, and courses on the history of books, bindings, and engravings. Three years later, she launched a specialization in children's librarianship (Karlowich and Sharify 1978; Maack 1986). Despite the difficulties women generally encountered as leaders and administrators, Plummer became the second female president of ALA and director of the library school of the New York Public Library (Weibel and Heim 1979).

2. Drexel

Alice Kroeger, another Dewey protégé of the Albany school, directed the Drexel library and their training program. Kroeger's program mirrored Dewey and

Fairchild's, including course work in cataloging, literature, bibliography, the history of books, and library management (Vann 1961; Grotzinger 1978a). In addition to serving as faculty, Kroeger was a prolific author and presented at numerous ALA conferences. At a time when there were few texts for the library student, she published the first major text on reference materials as well as a work on book selection.

3. Armour Institute/University of Illinois

The Armour Institute, established in Chicago in 1893, was the first library school in the Midwest. Under the leadership of Katharine Lucinda Sharp, another Dewey graduate, the basic program took one year, with the possibility of a second year of advanced work. The advanced training included courses in bibliography in specialized areas, the history of printing and libraries, and a specialized children's program (Vann 1961).

Sharp adopted Dewey's view that librarians were powerful because they could influence people's access to ideas (Grotzinger 1966). She was not satisfied with the existing admission requirements for the program and wanted to award a degree, rather than a certificate, for library training. She established such a notable program that both the University of Wisconsin and the University of Illinois courted her. She successfully negotiated a transfer of the Armour program to the University of Illinois, where she served as director of the University Library, head of the school, and a full professor. This unique position allowed the library students to use the university library as a laboratory (Grotzinger 1978b; Maack 1986).

In terms of academic requirements, the Illinois program was comparable to the Albany training (Vann 1961). Sharp was an innovative curriculum designer, adding courses on documents, extension work, and research methods (Grotzinger 1978b). She also involved students in the life of the community; they created traveling collections, conducted public story hours, and organized collections (Grotzinger 1966). Sharp did much to advance the academic credibility of library education and, although the Illinois program was a four-year program leading to a bachelor's degree, she was an early proponent of graduate-level library education. During her tenure, the school at Illinois was "constantly the center of experimentation and innovation" (Grotzinger 1966, p. 304). As a consequence, Sharp was highly respected as both a library educator and a librarian and was twice elected ALA vice president.

4. Continued Expansion of Schools

By 1919, there were fifteen programs, ten of them founded by women (Maack 1986). They varied by length of program, type of degree or certificate awarded, and requirements for admission. Most of the schools awarded a bachelor's of library science (BLS) degree after one year of library education following the regular baccalaureate degree, sometimes referred to as a fifth-year degree (Robbins-Carter and Seavey 1986). The MLS was not awarded, except at Albany, until the 1920s. The master's at Albany was given after two years of education beyond the baccalaureate (sometimes referred to as a sixth-year degree).

E. The Role and Influence of the ALA Committee on Library Training

As the number of library schools grew, ALA took a greater interest. Apprenticeships and other methods of library training coexisted uneasily with the emerging library schools up until the end of the nineteenth century. By that time, the library schools wanted ALA to recognize and endorse them as the only appropriate forum for library training. Instead, ALA created the Committee on Library Training and in 1902 asked the members to review the various library training programs. This led to ALA's "Standards for Library Education" in 1903. These standards reflected no commitment to any particular source of professional preparation but established separate standards for the different types of training programs. Subsequent standards issued in 1905 and 1906 again equivocated. Tensions between academic institutions and "practical" schools became acute between 1910 and 1920. During this period, ALA established a Section on Professional Training that conducted additional reviews of the programs being offered by various organizations.

ALA's reluctance to endorse the academic schools as the only appropriate form of library education pushed the schools to create their own organization, the Association of American Library Schools, in 1916. Establishing the association unified the schools and helped them establish a separate identity. As a result, library school educators were no longer concerned about the political value of ALA endorsement. Instead, they focused on administrative and curricular issues such as establishing consistent admission standards, faculty requirements, course content and program length, the types of degrees awarded, the proper balance between practical and theoretical approaches, and developing a system for transferring credits from one school to another (Vann 1961).

F. The Williamson Report

In the end, it was neither ALA nor the American Association of Library Schools that most profoundly influenced the direction of library education. Rather, it was the Carnegie Corporation, established by Andrew Carnegie to administer his philanthropic activities after his death. The corporation continued to fund library construction but suspected that the resulting libraries were often inadequately staffed and supported. In 1915, the corporation appointed Alvin Saunders Johnson to investigate the status of Carnegie libraries. Johnson's 1916 report revealed serious problems; in particular, he found that library staff members were often poorly trained. The corporation, concerned about Johnson's report, subsidized a major study of library education that investigated library schools in particular.

The corporation appointed C. C. Williamson to undertake this study. Williamson was ideally suited for the task; he was a political economist, a graduate of Columbia, and had been a professor of economics at Bryn Mawr. He had served as head of the Economics and Sociology Division at the New York Public Library, and at the time of his appointment was head of the Municipal Reference Library in New York. Williamson conducted a close examination of fifteen library schools and issued a final report in 1923 with numerous critical recommendations (figure 5.1). Referred to as the "Williamson Report" (1923), its historic importance to library education is unquestioned.

The Williamson Report represented a significant breakthrough and turning point for library education. Although many of the issues raised were not original with Williamson, his report represented a culmination of the historical forces working to define library education. The imprimatur of the Carnegie Corporation could not be ignored. He criticized the quality of many programs and suggested that the corporation assist by offering scholarships to recruit better-qualified individuals, and by providing financial assistance to library schools and summer school programs. As a result, the corporation shifted its emphasis from construction to library service (Vann 1961).

The Williamson Report articulated the theoretical and professional nature of the discipline and designated the university as the appropriate provider of professional preparation. Other forms of library education did not immediately disappear, nor did the profession uncritically accept all of the recommendations, most notably the certification of librarians. Likewise, only a few library schools adopted a two-year program of study. In addition, some felt the report would adversely affect the proportion of female library educators because at the time, most academic institutions did not consider women for faculty positions (Maack 1986). But the report marked the eventual death knell of all other forms of professional education. Because Williamson regarded a college degree as an entrance requirement, he advocated professional preparation in librarianship as a graduate degree (Williamson 1923). In a broader sense, the Williamson Report affirmed that a substantial part of librarianship was, or should be, advanced education rather than simply training. Further, it

FIGURE 5.1
The Williamson Report: Major Findings and Recommendations

1. There is a difference between clerical and professional work. Professional work deals with theory and the application of clear principles. It requires a broad education including four years of college. Clerical work requires far less education and largely involves following task-specific rules rather than application of theory. Library schools should provide professional, rather than clerical, instruction.

2. The library schools did not agree on which subjects should be taught or emphasized; certain schools devoted much more time to particular subjects than to others.

3. The curricula must undergo constant reexamination so that the most current and relevant practices can be taught rather than merely traditional practices.

4. The breadth of content required for graduate professional preparation cannot be realized in only one year of education.

5. There is considerable inconsistency in entrance requirements. Library schools should require a college education (or its equivalent) for admission.

6. Many library school instructors lacked college degrees themselves and were therefore not adequately prepared to teach college graduates. Many lacked experience in teaching, and nearly one-third had no library experience.

7. Instruction relied too much on lectures, and there were too few good textbooks.

8. Faculty salaries were too low and must be adjusted to recruit teachers of better quality.

9. Schools must provide financial incentives for faculty to produce texts.

10. To recruit students, schools should maintain high educational standards and provide fellowships and scholarships to make library training more attractive.

11. Library schools should be part of a university, conforming to the model followed by other professional schools. Universities are better situated to maintain academic standards and increase the status of the graduates; public libraries cannot devote the resources necessary to maintain these standards.

12. Professional preparation should consist of two years of schooling. The first year should follow a general program of study; the second year should be highly specialized. This might involve cooperative efforts with other local educational institutions.

13. There was little incentive for employed librarians to seek continuing education. Generally, the focus was on clerical workers. Schools should redirect their attention to the enrichment of professional education. Correspondence schools should be considered.

14. There were no standards for professional preparation. Librarians should establish the standards, which once established, should eventually be made part of the law.

15. The American Library Association should create a system of voluntary certification of librarians regulated by a national certification board, which should also accredit library schools. (Williamson 1923)

forced the profession to consider the importance of consistency and high standards for quality of curricula, administration, and teaching.

G. Response to and Effects of the Williamson Report

ALA responded to the Williamson Report by creating the Temporary Library Training Board in 1924, which soon became the Board of Education for Librarianship (BEL). The BEL established additional standards for library education in 1925 and 1933, including the need for one year of postgraduate education in librarianship (Robbins-Carter and Seavey 1986). By the early 1950s, most library schools granted the fifth-year master's degree.

The Carnegie Corporation's response to the report was even more dramatic. There was obviously a considerable need for library schools to improve. In the ensuing fifteen years, the Carnegie Corporation gave nearly $2 million to seventeen library schools to that end. One of the corporation's most notable achievements was its special attention to the lack of research and quality instructional texts. The corporation determined that the best solution was to support a doctoral program for librarians. In response, the Graduate Library School was established at the University of Chicago in 1926 and a doctoral program began in 1928. The doctoral degree was granted for "library science" as opposed to librarianship, because the course work emphasized theoretical approaches and the application of the scientific and research tools of other disciplines to library work (Rayward 1983).

In addition to establishing the notion of library science, the Graduate Library School made many other contributions. First, its faculty was diverse, drawing instructors with expertise from a variety of fields including sociology and history. Second, because the faculty were primarily scholars rather than practitioners, they produced a considerable body of research, which formed the foundation for further research. Finally, the school sponsored many conferences and programs on major issues in the profession, which drew practitioners and other library school faculty together and resulted in numerous publications, which also served as texts.

Another notable Carnegie achievement following the Williamson Report was the establishment in 1925 of the Hampton Institute Library School, the first school specifically established to train African-American librarians. Prior to that time, Emory University in Atlanta was the only accredited library school in the South, but it did not admit African-Americans until 1962 (Campbell 1977; McPheeters 1988). Professional preparation available to African-Americans was primarily through training programs in libraries, education supported by organizations such as the Julius Rosenwald Fund, which focused on library services in the South (Campbell 1977).

In very rare instances, a few African-Americans were able to attend a library school in the North. Edward Christopher Williams, a graduate of the New York State Library School, became director of the library at Howard University in 1916 (Campbell 1977). The founder and first director of the Hampton Institute Library School, Florence Rising Curtis, also played a significant role in advancing professional librarianship for African-Americans. Curtis was also a graduate of Dewey's school in Albany. Before coming to Hampton, she had a distinguished career, teaching at the University of Illinois for twelve years, and serving as vice director at Drexel. She played a major role in establishing the Association of American Library Schools and served as its first secretary (Davis 1978). At Hampton, she was not only largely responsible for developing a quality library school program, but was devoted to improving library service for African-Americans throughout the South.

The Hampton Institute produced some notable graduates including Virginia Lacy Jones, who became dean of the Atlanta University School of Library Service, and Wallace Van Jackson, library director at Virginia State College and a teacher at Hampton Institute, who made substantial contributions to academic library service for African-Americans (Campbell 1977). Unfortunately, the Depression led to a decline in philanthropic resources, and the Hampton Institute Library School closed in 1939. However, two years later its mission was revived at Atlanta University under the urging of its president, John Hope (Davis 1978).

H. Library Education from the 1930s to 2000

The Depression and World War II placed severe burdens both on the development of libraries and on librarianship. Library educators were especially concerned that many schools' curricula still emphasized routines rather than theory, and that there was considerable variation in quality among the schools. In 1951 the ALA Board of Education for Librarianship issued a new set of standards that finally required five years of post–high school education (in other words, a master's degree) as the standard for professional education. This ended once and for all the alternative forms of library education. In 1956 the ALA Committee on Accreditation was formed and given the responsibility of reviewing and accrediting library school programs, a task it holds to this day.

1. The Ebb and Flow of Library Schools

The 1950s and 1960s might be considered the heyday of library schools. The expanding economy, the baby boom, and the important federal legislation supporting the development of elementary, secondary, and higher education institutions and their libraries all led to a significant expansion of libraries and collections. This concomitantly resulted in an increased need for librarians, which, in turn, spawned new library schools. By the 1970s there were more than seventy accredited library schools with master's programs in the United States and Canada. Also, during this time, library school curricula evolved significantly due to the influx of new computer technologies. Aside from traditional courses in reference, cataloging, and children's and school library work, the curricula included courses in library automation and database searching. There was a concomitant influx of new faculty with computer technology backgrounds to teach these courses.

The next two decades, however, saw a significant decline in the number of schools, including closures of several prominent library schools—the University of Chicago and Columbia among them. By 1999 there were only fifty-six ALA-accredited library school programs in the United States and Canada. There were many reasons for this decline. The recession of the 1980s resulted in deliberate efforts to reduce costs at universities. Taxpayers, politicians, and trustees became more reluctant to finance higher education. Library schools were never high-profile departments; they were rarely mentioned when speaking of the reputation of an academic institution, nor did they produce many major donors in comparison with law or medical schools. Many of these library schools failed to develop an energetic alumni network to defend them. The result was that they were vulnerable targets for closing (Paris 1988). Boyce (1994) suspected that an additional one-third to one-half of the remaining library schools might close. Some library educators recognized the lessons inherent in the closings and saw the need to improve the quality of their academic programs and set higher standards (Boyce 1994). By the end of the twentieth century the decline had ended.

2. The Emergence of i-Schools

During this same period, reflecting the dramatic changes occurring in information technologies not only in libraries but throughout society, some schools of library science transitioned from an emphasis on libraries as institutions to information access in general. At first, the change manifested itself by changing the school's name. In 1964, for example, the University of Pittsburgh's program became the Graduate School of Library and Information Sciences. In 1974 Syracuse University renamed its school the School of Information Studies. In 1996 the University of Pittsburgh again renamed its program as the School of Information Sciences; in the same year, the University of Michigan's program became the School of Information (Olson and Grudin 2009). The increasing number of I-schools gradually led to the creation of an international organization (although most members are from the United States) called the "iSchool Caucus," which started sponsoring conferences devoted to I-school issues.

By the beginning of the twenty-first century, ten schools referred to themselves as "I-schools" and as of 2012, "among the ALA-accredited LIS programs, over 30% use the general School of Information or Information Studies names, with the majority of these having dropped the word "'Library' at some point in the last two decades" (Dillon 2012, p. 267). Dillon (2014) identifies three "defining characteristics" of I-Schools:

> A recognition that no existing discipline has a monopoly on appropriate theory and method for studying information, hence any genuine information school must contain an intellectually diverse faculty willing to engage collectively in shared problems;
>
> An understanding and treatment of information that conceives of it as mediated by people and technology across multiple environments, rather than one based on the practices of traditional agencies of collection (libraries, archives, museums, etc.)
>
> A commitment to research activities that seek answers to fundamental and pressing questions about information in all human endeavors. (p. xviii)

As might be expected, the name changes caused consternation among some because the removal of the word "library" from the schools' names suggested a fundamental change in philosophical perspective: that library education was moving from being library-centered to being information-centered with the inevitable changes in curricular content and faculty composition. A 2001 study of twenty-five I-schools by Wu et al. (2011) found faculty representing diverse disciplines with a core faculty focus on the relationships between information, technology, and users. Wiggins and Sawyer (2012) reported that most I-school faculty came from computer science, followed by information science, library science, and the social and behavioral sciences. Additional faculty came from management, science and engineering, education, humanities, and communications.

Although the interdisciplinary nature of I-school faculties and curricula could yield significant benefits, they tend to suffer from problems related to academic focus, problems that can be quite challenging within a traditional academic culture. Dillon (2012) described the I-schools' particular perspective as "a more contextual analysis of information use in the lives of people, organizations and cultures" (p. 272). Others were not convinced of the distinctiveness of I-schools compared to their non-I-school brethren. Chu (2012) examined I-schools and non-I-schools in relation to programs, curricula and research found that the schools were very similar except that I-schools conducted more funded research. The research distinction however might arise from the membership requirement in the I-School Caucus that an I-school member have significant funded research, rather than from a difference in the nature of the programs. Wallace (2009) suggested that at least one major motivation for becoming an "I-school" was branding; becoming an I-school was seen as a way of attracting students and improving the school's position within its local institution.

Needless to say, by the end of the twentieth century, LIS education was in considerable flux. In 1998, in an attempt to understand the state of LIS education and its future prospects, the W. K. Kellogg Foundation joined with the Association for Library and Information Science Education (ALISE) to launch the KALIPER Project. Its purpose was "to analyze the nature and extent of major curricular change in LIS education" (ALISE 2000, p. 3). Led by an advisory committee, five scholar teams were created, comprising primarily faculty and doctoral students from schools of LIS. Using a variety of data collection techniques, the KALIPER Advisory Committee concluded, based on studies of twenty-six schools, that LIS was a "vibrant, dynamic, changing field that is undertaking an array of initiatives" (ALISE 2000, p. 1). The report identified six trends that continue to reflect developments in LIS education today:

Trend 1　In addition to library-specific operations, LIS curricula address broad-based information environments.

Trend 2　While LIS curricula continue to incorporate perspectives from other disciplines, a distinct core has taken shape that is predominantly user centered.

Trend 3　LIS schools and programs have significantly increased their investment and infusion of information technology into their curricula.

Trend 4　LIS schools and programs continue to experiment with the structure of specialization within the curriculum.

Trend 5　LIS schools and programs offer instruction in multiple formats to provide students with more flexibility.

Trend 6　LIS schools and programs have expanded their curricula by offering related degrees at the undergraduate, master's, and doctoral levels. (ALISE 2000)

Conrad and Rapp-Hanretta (2002) identified a number of internal and external forces contributing to these trends. Among the external forces were advances in technology, changing employer expectations, need for ongoing training, changing patterns of educational financing (including reduced governmental funding), and increasing corporate funding. Internal factors included changing modes of information access and dissemination, the increasingly entrepreneurial culture of universities, shortages of faculty, and trends toward reorganization. Taken together, these trends characterize a dynamic field that must respond not only to the demands of the LIS environment but the greater demands placed on it by the many social, political, economic, and educational forces at work. What kind of skills and training will the twenty-first-century LIS professional require and who will prepare them for those roles?

III. CONTEMPORARY ISSUES FACING LIS EDUCATION

The debate over the role of the library in the new information environment is complex and intricately bound up in the historical roots of the field, beliefs about the purpose of libraries, the nature and centrality of information in our society, and the role of LIS professionals. These issues can only be addressed briefly here.

A. The Library Paradigm and the Information Paradigm

In 1995 Cronin suggested that "library and information science is certainly not a marriage made in heaven" (p. 897) and that the removal of the word *library* from many LIS programs "is a clear indication of mounting dissatisfaction with what the label connotes" (p. 898). Cronin argued that "library science" is an oxymoron, what is referred to as library science is really librarianship—a profession associated with a particular physical structure. Information science, on the other hand, involves emerging methodologies and models that are not bound by a particular institution. Campbell (1993) took a different view but raised the same issue. He argued that the computer revolution created the need for greater technical proficiencies and that the failure to alter library education significantly might lead to its obsolescence. He noted that "the MLS might no longer be a viable credential given the nature of the technological and practical challenges we face in everyday library work" (p. 560). These comments illustrate some of the sticky issues in the discussion about the relationship between library science, libraries, information scientists, and information science.

1. Two Paradigms

Some people characterize the library versus information debate as a collision of two paradigms. The *library service paradigm* stems from the long-held belief that the library is an educational institution. As Apostle and Raymond (1997) commented, "In terms of larger social purpose, libraries perform such socially necessary functions as encouraging reading, literacy, and the diffusion of commonly-held cultural values" (p. 5). These functions coupled with the obligation to conserve the graphic record represent a primary purpose of libraries. If one accepts the library service paradigm, it then follows that the LIS curriculum should reflect an emphasis on educational theory, library service, literacy, and reading.

On the other hand, Apostle and Raymond (1997) noted that the twentieth century introduced increased industrialization, major scientific and technological advances, and the growth of both business and government, which in turn required significantly more information. This need spawned special libraries. By the second half of the century, with the rise of computer technologies, the importance of information provision as a vital societal function was manifest. By the 1970s, most libraries had, at least in part, begun to reposition themselves as information centers based on an *information paradigm*. This paradigm was based on several assumptions (Apostle and Raymond 1997):

- Postindustrial societies are information societies.
- A merger of library and information sciences was already occurring.
- Information technology was the driving force that would determine the future functions of libraries as well as the information professions.
- The needs of library users and the functions of libraries should be reformulated in terms of information needs.
- The ideas of an information industry and an information professional were interdependent.
- A convergence of library education and information science education was necessary and inevitable.
- Employment prospects for LIS graduates in the emerging information market were optimistic.

Van House and Sutton (2000) argued that LIS education needed to change from a traditional orientation to an information focus:

> The LIS profession's focus on libraries has been challenged by a fundamental shift from the Ptolemaic information universe with the library at its center, to a dynamic, Copernican universe with information at its center and libraries playing a significant, but not necessarily central, role. (p. 55)

Van House and Sutton saw two broad forces shaping the future of LIS education: the rapidly changing information landscape and the shifting university environment in which LIS programs were housed. In particular, they argued that as the value of information became increasingly clear, other disciplines, such as computer science and business administration, would become powerful competitors with LIS schools, threatening the traditional jurisdiction of library and information science. This competition, in turn, would produce an unstable university climate, with various disciplines competing for students and university resources. They warned that LIS schools must make substantial adaptations to survive and suggested that, while not abandoning a focus on libraries, LIS education must broaden its niche, making the curriculum less library-centered and more information-centered.

Wiegand (2001, 2005) agreed that one function of libraries was to make information accessible. However, he expressed concern that some library educators appeared to define libraries and librarianship solely in terms of technological capabilities, which resulted in curricula that ignored a central and essential purpose of libraries to serve as a "cultural agency in the everyday life experience of ordinary people" (Wiegand 2005, p. 58). According to Wiegand (2001), an information orientation resulted in an emphasis on information seeking while a significant body of research on the importance of reading and its significance in everyday life was ignored. He argued that much of the activity in libraries dealt directly with reading and that the LIS curriculum should emphasize the importance of reading and the library as place, rather than information that could be gained on a computer. He advocated for a curriculum that included research in reading, including literacy studies, the social history of books and reading, reader-response theory, and the ethnography of reading (Wiegand 1997).

The strength of both arguments in this debate led Gorman (2004) to contend that there was a crisis in library education:

- What we used to call library schools have become hosts to information science and information studies faculty and curricula. These disciplines (if they exist at all) are, at best, peripheral to professional library work.
- Some prestigious universities in the United States have given up on LIS education. This has led to a diminution of research into library topics (in quality if not quantity).
- Many of the topics historically regarded as central to library education (cataloguing, reference, collection development) are no longer central or even required by today's LIS curricula.

- Many library educators (whether librarians or information scientists, but especially the latter) have lost faith in and regard for the traditional mission, policies, programs, and value of libraries and are more interested in research in their areas of interest outside librarianship or in equipping their students to take jobs in other areas of work.
- There is a dearth of research in U.S. LIS schools dedicated to the real needs of real libraries.

Based on these observations, he advocated for a nationally recognized core curriculum that included collection development, cataloguing, reference and library instruction, circulation, systems, management, and types of libraries. He also recommended substantial reform of the ALA accreditation process to ensure national standards for curriculum and an emphasis on research and practice directly related to libraries and librarianship. He also speculated that if the male-dominated information science faculty increased in power, the gender composition of the LIS professorate would shift in favor of males.

Shortly thereafter, Crowley (2008) confirmed that adopting the information paradigm did, in fact, lead to a dominance of information scientists, shifted a school's orientation toward libraries as information providers, and characterized LIS professionals as intermediaries rather than educators. He expressed concern that as schools embraced an information orientation, the traditional values of library education—to promote lifelong learning, reading, and education—were subjugated and diluted. He advocated for a reorientation to ensure that LIS education continued to emphasize learning theory, programming, and education—that literacy and reading return as a central focus. Crowley's argument was not based on quaint nostalgia for the past, but on the strong conviction that adopting an information perspective threatened the very survival of libraries and librarians. He felt that by focusing on information access, the library would compete with the ever-increasing sophistication of technologies and information providers such as Google, a competition he believed libraries would have great difficulty winning. On the other hand, by focusing on socially critical cultural values and activities such as reading, literacy, and lifelong learning, libraries and LIS professionals could continue to make valued contributions to individuals and to the society as a whole, a concept Cowley refers to as "life-cycle librarianship." He strongly believed that these contributions could not easily be made by technologies whose primary purpose was simply to provide information.

Another view, expressed by Dillon and Norris (2005), challenged the notion that there were two competing paradigms. They noted that the entire LIS community recognized the important responsibilities of libraries as stewards of the cultural record of human knowledge. At the same time, they pointed out that LIS educators must recognize that libraries are but "one part of the system" (p. 283) and that the introduction of information technologies has, in fact, radically changed not only how people seek information, but how libraries provide their services. They challenged the claims that there was a dearth of research on library issues and cited numerous journals and a substantial body of research—including award-winning doctoral dissertations. They also found that although there were significant variations in course-work offered by LIS programs, there was actually fairly close agreement concerning requirements. In addition, they examined concerns about the gender of faculty by analyzing teaching assignments and found that "females are contributing to the development of LIS education by teaching both library science-oriented courses and information science-oriented courses" (p. 291). In sum, they argued that the term "crisis" overstated the situation, although they acknowledged some legitimate concerns about the impact of emerging information technologies on recorded knowledge and hence, on libraries:

> When the Internet has given rise to easy access to previously unimaginable amounts of information from one's own location; when cheap, widely available information and communication technologies are used by everyone across multiple task domains; and when students arrive in LIS programs familiar with and skilled in the use of such routine technologies, it would seem difficult to justify any other response from LIS programs than one of embracing the tools and opportunities for study and use they enable. That LIS programs seem to have managed this transition gracefully speaks volumes. (p. 294)

The notion of a crisis was also challenged by King (2005), who observed that such a claim has been a persistent theme at least since the Williamson Report of 1923. He noted that the elements that cause anxiety in LIS education are similar in other fields: lack of funding, lack of respect, and disagreements between practitioners and educators about what should be taught. King noted that the L-school/I-school debate "has all the markings of a Hatfields and McCoys cartoon" (p. 15). He argued that whether a school has the word *Library* in its title says little about what goes on inside and observed that the deans of the various schools appeared to work quite well together. Both I-schools and library schools belong to the Association for Library and Information Science Educators (ALISE) and there was little evidence that I-schools were abandoning LIS traditions.

Estabrook (2005) suggested that those who claimed there was a crisis were crying wolf, although she exhorted LIS programs to make clear the reasons for any changes in their programs. She noted that LIS education needs both an understanding of technology and core library principles and felt that "the beauty of our LIS programs is the way in which many of them have been able to marry the two" (p. 299). Further, she argued that faculty research cannot strictly be confined to solving immediate, practical library problems—that would reduce scholarship to consultancy.

Stoffle and Leeder (2005) suggested that misunderstandings between practitioners and LIS educators exacerbated the situation:

> The greatest problem with LIS programs is the fact that many practitioners do not understand the goals of library education, the demands under which these programs operate, or the standards to which they are held. Practitioners want to dictate a curriculum based on their interests or the hiring needs of their particular libraries, without acknowledging the tremendous range of subject matter that these schools must address in only 36 to 42 hours of coursework. (p. 315)

2. Finding Common Ground

It is not likely that the library versus information debate will dissipate soon. However, the notion of two competing paradigms is more likely to confuse, rather than facilitate, the discussion. Miksa (1992) analyzed the debate from the perspectives of the "library as a social institution" versus the "information movement as a system of human communication" and found significant conceptual defects in both. He argued that what was needed was "a more essential approach to what is involved in the work of the field, one that conceptualizes the processes in a more thoroughgoing but unitary manner" (p. 243). An attempt to unify, rather than divide, seems desirable since it has been hard to determine what constructive end the debate over competing paradigms has achieved.

The notion of a paradigm as it is generally used today was based on the work of Thomas S. Kuhn (1970) in his groundbreaking treatise on the history of science, *The Structure of Scientific Revolutions*. Kuhn illustrated a paradigm shift in science using the example of the change from the Ptolemaic view of the universe with the earth at its center to the Copernican conception with the sun at its center. Kuhn's notion of paradigm shift was not merely an adjustment in perspective or emphasis; it was a change so great that one paradigm could not be held at the same time as the other. As he stated, "scientific revolutions are here taken to be those non-cumulative developmental episodes in which an older paradigm is replaced in whole or in part by an *incompatible* new one" (p. 92, italics added). Although Kuhn offered numerous examples in the sciences, he questioned whether there were any social science paradigms.

In terms of LIS education, isn't it reasonable to believe that both information and education are critical—that the two perspectives are not incompatible? Indeed, don't our everyday conceptions of information and education assume that they are closely related—that information is a necessary part of learning? Isn't the promotion of reading as a central function of libraries quite compatible with and complementary to finding information for people? Certainly, over the years, the mission statements of public libraries have declared a desire to meet the educational, recreational, and informational needs of their communities. Shouldn't LIS programs reflect these same multiple goals? Exploring the potentialities of a unitary vision, as Miksa (1992) suggested, would seem to have many happy prospects.

B. Continuing Education

Continuing education (CE) has been a part of LIS education since the turn of the twentieth century when a small number of public libraries and some academic institutions offered "institutes" for library workers. The Higher Education Act of 1965 offered funding for CE, which led to the founding of the Continuing Library Education Network and Exchange (CLENE), whose purpose was to improve the quality of CE. CLENE assessed the needs of practicing librarians around the country and provided opportunities for CE. In 1983, CLENE became a Roundtable of the American Library Association (Roberts and Konn 1991). CLENE subsequently changed its name to Learning RT.

Although the ALA Code of Ethics requires librarians to update their professional skills, CE remains for the most part a voluntary activity. Unlike the teaching profession, where licensure often requires it, most library positions have no CE requirements, nor do employers offer monetary rewards as incentives. A few employers implement competency-based performance evaluation systems that provide financial rewards and job opportunities for those acquiring new skills, but these are still rare. Nonetheless, there is considerable interest in CE and recognition by LIS professionals and library administrators that professional learning must be continuous and should be integrated into the organizational culture (Blakiston 2011). Among the areas of special interest are management training and training in knowledge organization such as cataloging, RDA, and metadata management and quality control (Boyd 2012; Park et al. 2010; Matteson et al. 2013). Leong (2014) recommended that organizations take a new systematic look at CE and create a "purpose-driven" learning strategy that aligns organizational goals with structured, continuous, experience-based education and training for staff.

Continuing education is available for LIS professionals from a variety of sources. Schools of LIS offer a variety of courses and workshops for practitioners; national and state associations, and state libraries provide special programs individually or at their state and regional conferences; local libraries and consortia provide workshops and other forms of training to meet their local needs. The digital world, including webinars, blogs, and Twitter feeds from associations and nonprofit providers, adds a new dimension to CE. Among the notable nonprofit providers is WebJunction®, a collaboration of OCLC with the Gates Foundation, in cooperation with many state library agencies. WebJunction began in 2003 and by 2014 provided self-paced courses to more than 80,000 library staff. Courses were provided in such areas as customer service, library management, library services, and marketing (WebJunction 2014). Other sources of Internet-based education include U.S. government agencies such as the LOC as well as library-related organizations such as the Copyright Clearance Center and OCLC (Keiser 2012). Schools of LIS are also exploring digital access to CE including the use of MOOCs (massive open online courses). Recently, Stephens and Jones (2014) reported on the successful delivery of a non-credit MOOC through San Jose State University's School of Library and Information Science. Such courses could make CE available to a much wider audience.

C. Distance Education

With developments in telecommunications, it is now possible to deliver high-quality LIS education to remote sites using interactive video and Web-based instruction. As of 2014, there were twenty-eight accredited LIS programs offering a complete MLIS program online (ALA 2014a). Online LIS education matured in 2004 with the creation of the Web-Based Information Science Education (WISE) Consortium which began with funding from an Institute of Museum and Library Services (IMLS) grant to Syracuse University and the University of Illinois at Urbana–Champaign. The vision of WISE (2014) was to provide a collaborative, cost-effective distance education model that could increase quality, access, and diversity of online education opportunities in Library and Information Science. It had three guiding ideals: quality, pedagogy, and collaboration. As of 2014, there were sixteen consortium members that benefitted from administrative and technical support. Students have access to online courses taught by the member schools, and faculty can participate in workshops and training through the consortium. WISE also makes some of its training available to nonmembers and has developed principles and metrics for effective online instruction.

Distance learning is appealing for a number of reasons, foremost among them the advantage of not having to travel or relocate, thus relieving stress on family and finances, and students don't have to quit their jobs to enroll in a quality program (Wilde and Epperson 2006). Scheduling flexibility is also a significant advantage in that students don't have to be at a particular physical location each week or several times a week, and students can participate in class activities at times more convenient to them. Carey and Gregory (2002) surveyed participants in Web-based distance learning at the University of South Florida. Respondents found the experience satisfying and equivalent or sometimes even superior to face-to-face classroom experiences. Logan, Augustyniak, and Rees (2002) found that in the online environment some students appeared to take increased responsibility for their education. Wilde and Epperson (2006) surveyed distance learning alumni from ALA accredited programs with strong reputations that did not require travel (Wilde and Epperson 2006). They found that 90% of the respondents believed that the distance program was comparable to a degree program delivered on-site, although there was a general feeling of being disconnected from other students and faculty.

Despite its many benefits, distance education brings its own set of issues. Lester (2011), for example, reported that the faculty composition of distance learning programs was different from face-to-face programs. Online programs relied more heavily on part-time faculty drawn from academic libraries, compared to the tenured teaching faculty in the face-to-face programs. Other issues that must be continuously addressed include:

- How do we ensure that the quality of distance education is equivalent to that provided in traditional classrooms?
- How do we provide a comparable variety of courses and specialties that are currently offered face-to-face?
- How do we create a sense of community for students who might have little face-to-face contact with faculty members and other students?
- How do we train full and part-time faculty to use effectively the new, instructional technologies such as learning management systems?
- How do we administer and evaluate online programs effectively?
- How can we best assess student academic performance in the distance-learning environment?
- How do we ensure compliance with federal and state laws and regulations regarding financial aid and authorization to offer programs in other states?

Despite these questions, distance learning has become an integral part of LIS education and will remain so. The adoption of LIS online programs comports with the trends in higher education overall as many universities create online programs as part of their broader educational mission (Stephens 2011). No doubt part of the reason for this trend is that competition for students and fiscal resources is increasing and the stakes—institutional survival—-are high. Well-designed online LIS programs can be a valued part of universities' attempts to adapt to this new and highly competitive environment.

D. Competencies and the Evolving LIS Curriculum

Competencies generally refer to the necessary knowledge, skills, and abilities required to perform professional tasks. Ostensibly, academic coursework was the preferred avenue to gain competence. Unfortunately, for a long period there was little agreement in LIS programs regarding the necessary core courses for specialization (Lynch 1989). For example, in 1994 Marco found that none of the U.S. library schools required students to take courses in each of the seven major subject areas considered core at the time: "book selection, cataloguing and classification, reference work, administration and management of libraries, history of books and libraries, research methods, and libraries in society" (p. 182). In fact, he concluded that only two subjects were universally required: cataloging and reference.

Although there was widespread recognition that general competencies for librarians were needed, it was not until 2009 that the ALA approved its "Core Competences of Librarianship" (figure 5.2) intended to define "the basic knowledge to be possessed by all persons graduating from an ALA-accredited master's program in library and information studies" (ALA 2014).

FIGURE 5.2
Core Competences of Librarianship

ALA's Core Competences of Librarianship (Final Version)
Approved by the ALA Executive Board, October 25, 2008
Approved and adopted as policy by the ALA Council, January 27, 2009

This document defines the basic knowledge to be possessed by all persons graduating from an ALA-accredited master's program in library and information studies. Librarians working in school, academic, public, special, and governmental libraries, and in other contexts will need to possess specialized knowledge beyond that specified here.

CONTENTS
1. Foundations of the Profession
2. Information Resources
3. Organization of Recorded Knowledge and Information
4. Technological Knowledge and Skills
5. Reference and User Services
6. Research

7. Continuing Education and Lifelong Learning
8. Administration and Management

A person graduating from an ALA-accredited master's program in library and information studies should know and, where appropriate, be able to employ:

1. FOUNDATIONS OF THE PROFESSION

1A. The ethics, values, and foundational principles of the library and information profession.

1B. The role of library and information professionals in the promotion of democratic principles and intellectual freedom (including freedom of expression, thought, and conscience).

1C. The history of libraries and librarianship.

1D. The history of human communication and its impact on libraries.

1E. Current types of library (school, public, academic, special, etc.) and closely related information agencies.

1F. National and international social, public, information, economic, and cultural policies and trends of significance to the library and information profession.

1G. The legal framework within which libraries and information agencies operate. That framework includes laws relating to copyright, privacy, freedom of expression, equal rights (e.g., the Americans with Disabilities Act), and intellectual property.

1H. The importance of effective advocacy for libraries, librarians, other library workers, and library services.

1I. The techniques used to analyze complex problems and create appropriate solutions.

1J. Effective communication techniques (verbal and written).

1K. Certification and/or licensure requirements of specialized areas of the profession.

2. INFORMATION RESOURCES

2A. Concepts and issues related to the lifecycle of recorded knowledge and information, from creation through various stages of use to disposition.

2B. Concepts, issues, and methods related to the acquisition and disposition of resources, including evaluation, selection, purchasing, processing, storing, and deselection.

2C. Concepts, issues, and methods related to the management of various collections.

2D. Concepts, issues, and methods related to the maintenance of collections, including preservation and conservation.

3. ORGANIZATION OF RECORDED KNOWLEDGE AND INFORMATION

3A. The principles involved in the organization and representation of recorded knowledge and information.

3B. The developmental, descriptive, and evaluative skills needed to organize recorded knowledge and information resources.

3C. The systems of cataloging, metadata, indexing, and classification standards and methods used to organize recorded knowledge and information.

4. TECHNOLOGICAL KNOWLEDGE AND SKILLS

4A. Information, communication, assistive, and related technologies as they affect the resources, service delivery, and uses of libraries and other information agencies.

4B. The application of information, communication, assistive, and related technology and tools consistent with professional ethics and prevailing service norms and applications.

(cont.)

FIGURE 5.2
Core Competencies of Librarianship (cont.)

4C. The methods of assessing and evaluating the specifications, efficacy, and cost efficiency of technology-based products and services.

4D. The principles and techniques necessary to identify and analyze emerging technologies and innovations in order to recognize and implement relevant technological improvements.

5. REFERENCE AND USER SERVICES

5A. The concepts, principles, and techniques of reference and user services that provide access to relevant and accurate recorded knowledge and information to individuals of all ages and groups.

5B. Techniques used to retrieve, evaluate, and synthesize information from diverse sources for use by individuals of all ages and groups.

5C. The methods used to interact successfully with individuals of all ages and groups to provide consultation, mediation, and guidance in their use of recorded knowledge and information.

5D. Information literacy/information competence techniques and methods, numerical literacy, and statistical literacy.

5E. The principles and methods of advocacy used to reach specific audiences to promote and explain concepts and services.

5F. The principles of assessment and response to diversity in user needs, user communities, and user preferences.

5G. The principles and methods used to assess the impact of current and emerging situations or circumstances on the design and implementation of appropriate services or resource development.

6. RESEARCH

6A. The fundamentals of quantitative and qualitative research methods.

6B. The central research findings and research literature of the field.

6C. The principles and methods used to assess the actual and potential value of new research.

7. CONTINUING EDUCATION AND LIFELONG LEARNING

7A. The necessity of continuing professional development of practitioners in libraries and other information agencies.

7B. The role of the library in the lifelong learning of patrons, including an understanding of lifelong learning in the provision of quality service and the use of lifelong learning in the promotion of library services.

7C. Learning theories, instructional methods, and achievement measures; and their application in libraries and other information agencies.

7D. The principles related to the teaching and learning of concepts, processes, and skills used in seeking, evaluating, and using recorded knowledge and information.

8. ADMINISTRATION AND MANAGEMENT

8A. The principles of planning and budgeting in libraries and other information agencies.

8B. The principles of effective personnel practices and human resource development.

8C. The concepts behind, and methods for, assessment and evaluation of library services and their outcomes.

8D. The concepts behind, and methods for, developing partnerships, collaborations, networks, and other structures with all stakeholders and within communities served.

8E. The concepts behind, issues relating to, and methods for, principled, transformational leadership.

Various divisions within ALA such as the Young Adult Library Services Association, the Association for Library Service to Children, the Reference and User Services Association, and the Public Library Association have developed their own competency statements. Additional competencies have been promulgated by the Special Libraries Association, the Medical Library Association, the Music Library Association, and the Society of American Archivists. Certain states, including Arizona, California, Connecticut, and Ohio also produced competencies (Van Fleet and Lester 2008).

Markey (2004) examined the websites of fifty-six schools and suggested that programs should consider expanding their curriculum and offer certifications, specializations, or concentrations in such areas as knowledge organization, content creation, authoritative information, and collection preservation. Chu (2006), in an analysis of nearly 3,000 courses from forty-five accredited U.S. programs, found that a wide range of subjects was covered and that curriculum changes reflected not only technological developments but also social and cultural ones. For example, elective courses included digital libraries, website design, networks, digitization, information architecture, cyberspace law, and knowledge management. At the same time, Chu also found that the number of core courses had contracted: the mean number of required courses was five or six, although in some cases only two were required. The most commonly required courses were in traditional areas: foundations, reference, organization of information, and management.

The lack of consistency in LIS curricula echoes the historical and ongoing debate over the right proportion of theory to practice in course content. For example, Main (1990) suggested:

> There is no longer a need to be concerned with theoretical and philosophical issues. What we must be concerned with is what enables us to survive in a competitive world, namely information technology. And information technology is a practical discipline. (p. 228)

On the other hand, others argued that the challenges and issues raised by information technologies make understanding the philosophical issues even more important today. Their argument was that LIS professionals will need *increased* theoretical understanding in order to perform the planning, evaluation, and decision-making functions so vital in the rapidly evolving information environment. Lynch (1989), for example, believed:

> The shaping of the future of librarianship rests not on the vocational skills necessary to the time, but on the principles common to all specialization in the field. The professional expects library education to be built on a solid intellectual foundation. (p. 81)

LIS programs continue to strive toward a balance between theory and practice. Most provide practicums or internship programs usually for academic credit that allow students to perform professional work in a library or other information organization. Such experiences provide a real-life context, improve the student's self-confidence, and provide important future contacts for employment and professional development. Ball (2008) recommended that coursework should include greater opportunities for "service learning," a related but distinct form of experiential learning. He felt that service activities tied to specific learning objectives could be reflected upon throughout the semester "in order to enrich student appreciation of course content" (p. 71). More recently, Kelley (2013), Editor in Chief of *Library Journal*, suggested that apprenticeship might be a better model for educating librarians instead of an "overreliance on an expensive and unnecessarily exclusionary credential." At the least, Kelley recommended a rational discussion on the topic. There remains considerable debate as to the proper balance between theory and practice and no doubt these different perspectives will continue to generate discussion for years to come.

E. The Role of the Master's Degree in Library and Information Science

As the notion grew in the twentieth century that substantial theoretical knowledge and principles should form the foundation of professional practice, the importance of the master's of LIS degree also grew. The American Library Association (1996) recognized the importance of graduate education in one of its policy statements:

> The American Library Association supports the provision of library services by professionally qualified personnel who have been educated in graduate programs within institutions of higher education. . . . The American Library Association supports the development and continuance of high quality graduate library/information science educational programs of the quality, scope and availability necessary to prepare individuals in the broad profession of information dissemination. The American Library Association supports education for the preparation of professionals in the field of library and information studies (LIS) as a university program at the master's level. (p. 137)

This supporting statement was strong but not unequivocal. It does not, for example, insist that all professional librarians possess a master's degree from an accredited program. Nonetheless, it was clear that graduate library education at the master's level was the accepted norm for entry into the library profession. Others asserted that the body of theoretical knowledge was insufficient to require graduate academic training. For example, Hauptman (1987) stated:

> There is not even any mandatory a priori knowledge necessary to function effectively as a librarian of any persuasion. Any intelligent college graduate can begin working in a special, public, or academic library and quickly learn the skills necessary to catalog, do reference work, manipulate overrated computer systems, or even administer. (pp. 252–253)

Hauptman described the work of a librarian as 90% clerical and claimed that librarians created a mystique regarding their work; that patrons could often learn to perform some library functions in only a short time. Campbell (1993) took a different view but raised the same issue. He argued that the computer revolution created the need for greater technical proficiencies and that the failure to alter library education significantly might lead to its obsolescence. He noted that "the MLS might no longer be a viable credential given the nature of the technological and practical challenges we face in everyday library work" (p. 560).

Others disagree. For them, library and information science, like many professions, combines routine elements as well as considerable theoretical and conceptual knowledge and judgment. As a profession, it provides an essential social and political function that demands a broad understanding of the nature of knowledge, of information, of people, and of society. That understanding allows LIS professionals to evaluate, make judgments, and set future courses of action. For example, knowing the name of a particular source might be useful for answering a specific query, but understanding people's information needs and how to identify and evaluate them requires a different type of knowledge. This type of understanding helps LIS professionals design information systems, select areas of emphasis, and implement strategies that enable and encourage people to use such systems. The same might be said for understanding the principles of selection, the effects of information policy, the uses of technology, the manner by which knowledge is organized, and the principles that guide the operation of information-giving institutions. White (1986) noted that the master's degree is a qualification not so much for a particular position as for entry into the profession.

The importance of the master's degree became the focus of a significant court case when a legal challenge was lodged against its use as a criterion for hiring a librarian at Mississippi State University in the 1980s. Title VII of the Civil Rights Act protects various classes from discrimination by age, race, color, religion, or disability. The act extends to protecting individuals from being discriminated against in the hiring process, especially when an irrelevant characteristic or qualification is considered in that process. In other words, employers are obligated to use only those selection criteria that directly relate to an individual's ability to perform a job. Glenda Merwine sued Mississippi State University when she was not hired for a librarian's position at the Veterinary Medicine Library. Although the case, *Glenda Merwine v. Board of Trustees for State Institutions of Higher Education* (Holley 1984) had many complications, one of Merwine's arguments was that she was denied employment because she did not possess a master's degree from a program accredited by ALA. Interestingly, ALA did not take a stand on the issue, but several prominent library educators testified. The court found that no reasonable alternative to the master's degree had been provided and that the master's degree was both relevant and broadly accepted as the professional degree. Despite the supportive decision, it has not inoculated the profession from attacks from other sources, most notably the Office of Management and Budget of the federal government, which challenged the need for a master's degree from an accredited LIS program for some government positions that previously required it. Such actions put the profession on notice that it must be able to articulate clearly the nature of its professional responsibilities and the need for formal graduate education to meet them.

Although many support the need for the master's degree, there remains a concern as to whether the education and training provided by the schools match the needs of the library community. Job requirements for positions in libraries are changing significantly and demanding new knowledge and skills. This includes expertise in such areas as digital content and collection development, website management, usability, information literacy instruction, community and civic engagement, and metadata creation and management. Bertot and Sarin (2015) suggest that the schools of LIS need to develop MLIS programs that provide broad-based skills to enable LIS professionals who can:

> *Inform,* by serving as vital conduits to the information resources that people need when they need them.
>
> *Enable,* by actively providing their communities with tailored opportunities to succeed through the resources and services provided.
>
> *Equalize,* by ensuring that—regardless of background, ability, means, or any other factors—their communities have access to the information resources, services and skills necessary for today and tomorrow
>
> *Lead,* by taking leadership roles in their communities around access to and the availability, dissemination, and preservation of information. (p. 41)

They believe that such professionals will need to be adaptable, creative, and tech-savvy. If LIS schools are to prosper, the MLIS must be responsive to the rapidly changing social, technological, and information environment.

F. Standards for LIS Education

Standards for accreditation in LIS have a variety of purposes. Among those is helping to maintain quality and consistency of the education delivered across many programs and providing quality assurance to potential students that the programs they are considering are recognized by institutions who hire librarians. In other words, that their education, if completed successfully, is a good investment.

Since the 1950s, the ALA Committee on Accreditation has been the formal mechanism for ensuring quality in professional preparation. Only master's-level LIS programs are accredited. The ALA accreditation standards have changed as the field evolved (ALA 2014b). Currently they address five areas considered essential to a quality program: systematic planning; curriculum; faculty, students, and administration; finances; and resources. These standards employ qualitative rather than quantitative measures and are intended to provide guidance rather than prescribe particular practices. The standards place strong emphasis on a school's ability to articulate its own mission; develop a comprehensive curriculum to reflect that mission; develop and execute systematic, active, and ongoing planning processes and outcome assessment mechanisms; and provide high-quality faculty and facilities for students. The standards acknowledge that education can be delivered through a variety of mechanisms, such as interactive video or online. The standards, however, remain the same regardless of the delivery technique (ALA COA 2015).

Although support for accreditation remained strong historically, not all LIS educators have been satisfied with the standards and approaches. For example, in 1994 Saracevic (1994) suggested that allowing schools to set their own missions was illogical and focused too much attention away from developing a basic curriculum centered on essential competencies and the theoretical foundations of the field. His concern was prompted by the observation that too often, university administrators viewed LIS programs as vocational rather than academic. Without clarity about theoretical underpinnings, schools were vulnerable to closing.

More recently, the accreditation process and standards have been subject to additional criticism. Mulvaney (2014) suggested that there was not enough emphasis on determining the quality of schools and their graduates. He suggested, for instance, that admissions standards should be raised significantly, and output measures should be employed to measure the productivity of students as alumni. He also suggested that a certification exam might prove beneficial. Other criticisms came from some LIS educators and librarians who believed that the standards should increase their emphasis on librarianship and reduce their focus on information science. As a result of these concerns, in 2006 ALA appointed a President's Task Force on Library Education to identify the core knowledge that all programs should provide and make recommendations. The Final Report (ALA 2009c) identified a variety of concerns including a perceived misalignment between what was taught and what was actually needed for work in libraries, a lack of emphasis on values and ethics, and an overemphasis on information in some schools. Among the task force's recommendations were the following: the accreditation standards should be more prescriptive; the ALA statements on core values and core competencies should be incorporated into the standards; and a majority of faculty should be grounded in librarianship. Not surprisingly, the American Society for Information Science and Technology had a different perspective. In a recent white paper (ASIS&T 2007), the authors asked: "Is ALA the appropriate agency to review for accreditation those programs that do not have a library focus?" (p. 3). The society proposed new accrediting standards in collaboration with a variety of information-related partners but no formal actions have been taken.

The accreditation standards promulgated by ALA and its Committee on Accreditation remain the basis for quality assurance in schools of library and information science. No doubt the accreditation debate will continue, and LIS professionals should understand the issues and follow evolving developments, as they will affect the type of graduates that enter the workforce.

G. Diversity among LIS Students

Total enrollments in schools of LIS have remained stable over the last decade. In 2011, more than 18,000 students enrolled in accredited MLIS programs in the United States and Canada. About 80% of enrollees were female. Reflecting a youthful library labor force, in 2011 17% of the enrollees were between 20 and 24; an additional 48% were between 25 and 34. Less than 6% were over 54. The number of new professionals graduating with master's degrees in LIS from schools accredited by the ALA has increased steadily over the last decade. For example there were 4,877 graduates in 2000; 6,502 in 2005; and 8,227 in 2011. The population of graduates remains predominantly female and white: comparing the 2005 and 2011 cohorts, both cohorts were 79% female; while the percentage of whites has declined somewhat from 76% in 2005 to 70% in 2011 (ALISE 2009, 2012).

In terms of racial and ethnic diversity, the situation is problematic. The American population is becoming increasingly heterogeneous; today, the four major minority populations—Hispanics, African-Americans, Asians, and Native Americans—comprise approximately one-third of the U.S. population. Currently in many large cities, minorities comprise the majority, or at least a very substantial proportion, of the urban population. Ethnic and racial diversity in LIS does not reflect this trend. For example, African-Americans comprise about 4% of enrollees for both the 2005 and 2011 cohort; there has been only a slight increase over the same period for Hispanics from 4% to 6%. In terms of MLIS degrees awarded, only 4% were Hispanic and 4% African-American (ALISE 2009, 2012).

ALA has been proactive in attempting to increase the diversity of the library profession. The dearth of African-American librarians and their lack of involvement at the higher levels of ALA were among the main reasons for the creation of the ALA Black Caucus in 1970 under the chairmanship of E. J. Josey. In 1997, ALA launched the Spectrum Initiative to correct the underrepresentation of people of color. The Initiative recruited and supported approximately fifty students of color annually with the objective of doubling the number of librarians from minority groups. Subsequent support from ALA presidents led to the creation of a permanent scholarship fund that extended the initiative indefinitely. As of 2014, more than 800 Spectrum Scholars have matriculated (ALA 2014c). Other groups, such as the ARL and the Asian/Pacific American Library Association, also have outreach programs.

The challenge of recruiting nonwhite individuals into LIS has been recognized for decades. Davis-Kendrick (2009) examined this issue in relation to the career selection and recruitment of African-American males. She found that a majority of African-American librarians learned about librarianship from a librarian (51%) or from a friend of family member (20%). The primary reason these librarians entered librarianship was to help people. More than two in five indicated that they "fell into" the career. Interestingly, a large majority (81%) indicated that financial aid in the form of scholarship or grants was very important to their successful completion of their library program, followed by assistance with job placement (71%). She noted that most were not actually recruited for a position (57%). Finally, most were pleased with their career choice and more than 80% planned to stay in librarianship and retire from it. Davis-Kendrick suggested that the problem of underrepresentation was not so much that African-American males were unaware of the profession, but that they are not sufficiently recruited for it.

Retention is another important aspect of maintaining diversity in the profession: it does little good to hire for diversity only to find that the people hired leave. Damasco and Hodges (2012) studied academic librarians of color who were seeking tenure or promotion and observed that they were often burdened with teaching and service responsibilities to the detriment of research; were asked to assume roles such as "diversity specialist" that were not respected in the tenure and promotion process; and often struggled to fit in with the organizational culture of their department and institution.

Diversity has many dimensions and all should be considered when recruiting individuals into the field. Jaeger et al. (2013) urged LIS schools to develop "culturally competent" librarians and make concerted efforts to attract and retain a diverse body of new librarians who can reflect and respond to the diverse character of our society. In 1993, McCook and Geist suggested a variety of ways to increase diversity broadly, including establishing cooperative partnerships between LIS schools and employers, providing greater monetary support, increasing recruitment activities in undergraduate and secondary education programs, recruiting in nontraditional settings such as military and community colleges, and improving the cultural climate of colleges and universities. Greiner (2008) argued that the largest barrier facing minorities interested in LIS programs was not discrimination but the financial burden. Clearly, the need to recruit members of minority groups into the profession will grow as the population becomes increasingly diverse.

IV. THE TWENTY-FIRST-CENTURY LABOR FORCE: Composition and Issues

A. Composition

Estimates of the labor force working in libraries vary, but the Bureau of Labor Statistics (BLS 2014) placed the number at approximately 148,400. ALA estimates were somewhat larger at nearly 166,000 (ALA 2014). The labor force is broken down by type of library in figure 5.3.

FIGURE 5.3
Numbers Employed in Libraries by Type of Library

LIBRARY EMPLOYEES BY LIBRARY TYPE			
	Librarians	Other Paid Staff	Total Paid Staff
Academic Libraries	26,606	59,145	85,751
Public Libraries	46,630	90,473	137,103
Public School Libraries	78,570	47,440	126,010
Private School Libraries	14,090	3,770	17,860
Bureau of Indian Education School Libraries	90	80	170
Total	**165,986**	**200,908**	**366,894**

Source: American Library Association. 2014. *Number Employed in Libraries.*
www.ala.org/tools/libfactsheets/alalibfactsheet02.

Schools employ the largest number of people, followed by public libraries and then academic libraries. The number of library support staff (library assistants, clerks, and technicians) was estimated at approximately 200,000. Combined, the size of the total library work force exceeds 350,000 (ALA 2014). However, compared to the number of people working in education or the computer industry, library workers represent a small fraction (figure 5.4).

For example, there were approximately 4.3 million primary, secondary, and elementary school teachers, 520,000 computer systems analysts, 343,000 computer programmers, 174,000 computer network support specialists, and 332,000 computer information systems managers. (U.S. Census Bureau 2012). BLS (2014) projected that the library workforce will grow approximately 7.4% by the year 2022. Although this reflects a lower-than-average growth rate, it is a higher rate than was projected previously—3.6% through 2016. Growth for library assistants (14.7%) is also above previous estimates (7.9%) while the growth for library technicians (8.4%) has not changed significantly (8.5%). Not surprisingly, the projected growth of LIS professionals is slower than those entering computer-related occupations, for example, the need for computer systems analysts is expected to grow by 24%; and a 50% growth rate was expected for computer and information systems managers,

Judging solely from the projected growth rate, it might appear that job prospects for new librarians might be poor. That is not necessarily the case when one considers the significant aging of the current library labor force. The median age of librarians working today is 50.5 with 36% over the age of 55. Only 18% are between 20 and 34. Compare this to computer occupations overall: the median age is 41.5; 15% are over the age of 55; and 31% are between 20 and 34 (BLS 2014a). The truth is that there will be many more opportunities for replacement in the library work force than in computer-related fields. BLS (2014) estimated that approximately 44% of librarian openings are expected to come from replacement needs through 2022.

B. Issues

1. Persistently Low Numbers of Minority Librarians

Attention to diversity is important: diversity increases the number of perspectives in an organization, might well increase organizational performance, and increases the quality of service to diverse populations. Diversity in its broadest sense includes gender, age, years of education, income, religion, nationality, ethnicity, race, and types of life experiences. For LIS professionals, a central focus has been on gender, race, and ethnicity particularly historical inequities that deprived women and a variety of ethnic and racial groups from access to valued jobs. Figure 5.5 illustrates the representation of ethnic groups in librarianship.

FIGURE 5.4
Selected Occupational Projections Data: Employment

| | | Employment (in thousands) | | Employment change, 2012–2022 | | Percent self-employed, 2012 | Job openings due to growth and replacement needs, 2012–2022 (in thousands) | 2012 median annual wage (in dollars) |
| | | 2012 | 2022 | Number (in thousands) | Percent | | | |
Occupation Title	Code							
Total, all occupations	00-0000	145,355.8	160,983.7	15,628.0	10.8	6.5	50,557.3	34,750
Elementary school teachers, except special education	25-2021	1,361.2	1,529.1	167.9	12.3	99.9	467.4	53,400
Secondary school teachers, except special and career/technical education	25-2031	955.8	1,008.7	52.9	5.5	99.9	312.6	55,050
Computer user support specialists	15-1151	547.7	658.5	110.8	20.2	0.8	196.9	46,420
Computer systems analysts	15-1121	520.6	648.4	127.7	24.5	4.0	209.6	79,680
Computer programmers	15-1131	343.7	372.1	28.4	8.3	5.1	118.1	74,280
Information and record clerks, all other	43-4199	188.9	172.2	-16.7	-8.8	99.9	40.8	37,240
Computer network support specialists	15-1152	174.6	186.8	12.1	6.9	0.8	39.6	59,090
Librarians	25-4021	148.4	159.4	11.0	7.4	99.9	44.4	55,370
Library assistants, clerical	43-4121	110.4	126.6	16.3	14.7	0.2	64.4	23,440
Library technicians	25-4031	106.2	115.2	9.0	8.4	99.9	66.3	30,660
Social workers, all other	21-1029	61.2	67.0	5.8	9.5	0.6	18.8	54,560
Museum technicians and conservators	25-4013	11.3	12.1	0.8	7.1	3.0	3.3	38,220

EMPLOYMENT PROJECTIONS: 2012–2022

Source: Bureau of Labor Statistics. 2014. "Employment Projections." http://data.bls.gov/projections/occupationProj.

FIGURE 5.5
Selected Occupations by Sex, Race, and Ethnic Origin

Occupation	Female (%)	African-American (%)	Asian (%)	Hispanic (%)
Librarians	82.6	9.2	1.7	5.2
Social workers	80.8	22.8	3.3	11.3
Library assistants, clerical	77.1	5.9	3.2	12.3
Secondary school teachers	57.0	8.0	1.6	6.7
Computer systems analysts	30.5	7.3	14.9	5.1

Source: U.S. Bureau of the Census. 2012. "Table 616: Employed Civilians by Occupation, Sex, Race, and Hispanic Origin: 2010." www.census.gov/compendia/statab/2012/tables/12s0616.pdf.

Underrepresentation of various ethnic and racial groups is broad-based: African-Americans make up approximately 13% of the U.S. population but comprise only 9% of the library workforce; Hispanics comprise 17% of the population but only 5.2% of the librarian workforce; and Asians comprise 5.3% of the population but only 1.7% of the library workforce (U.S. Bureau of the Census 2012, 2014). Among academic librarians, underrepresentation is even more problematic. Only 5.4% of the higher education librarian workforce is African-American and only 2.6% are Hispanic. Among ARL libraries only 4.3% are African-Americans and 2.8% are Hispanic. (This is only a 1% rise among African-American ARL librarians since 1981.) The percentage of Asians in academic libraries however is greater than in libraries as a whole, 7% (ALA 2012; ARL 2014; Chang 2013).

Recruitment of underrepresented groups has been among the major objectives of a variety of professional associations, including the ALA, the Black Caucus of the American Library Association, REFORMA, and the Asian/Pacific American Librarians Association. The fact that underrepresentation persists despite these efforts suggests strongly that structural barriers exist that tend to discourage minorities from applying to schools or being retained by libraries. For example, it might be that LIS programs and employers do not devote enough energy to recruitment or there might be insufficient academic and financial support for minority students. There might, of course, be other factors as well. The master's degree requirement might disproportionately screen out minorities, who, for a variety of reasons including discrimination, have been unable to obtain higher academic degrees. Additionally, members of some ethnic and racial groups might not consider librarianship simply because they have not been introduced to it as a career option.

Finally, the work experiences of underrepresented groups in libraries might not promote retention, or they might have access to more highly paid career options. There are a number of organizational characteristics that can make a substantial difference in retention. For example, African-Americans value salary and benefits; challenge, encouragement, and support on the job; opportunities to work with computers; and opportunities for advancement (Morgan et al. 2009).

2. Gender Discrepancies

Historically, women were only allowed to work in fields considered gender-appropriate. These fields—teaching, social work, nursing, and librarianship—tended to emphasize nurturing. In librarianship women still comprise 83% of the library labor force (U.S. Census Bureau 2012).

Salary disparities have been a particular concern and inequities have been found in numerous studies. A 2007 survey of recent library school graduates revealed that men were paid 7.7% more on average. Higher salaries for male librarians were found among public, school, and academic libraries, but not special or government libraries. More recently, a 2014 annual salary survey by *Library Journal* compared the salaries of men and women overall and on five library job titles among all types of libraries (Grimscheid and Schwartz 2014). Overall, women made 89 cents for every dollar made by men. Among reference/information librarians, women made 94 cents; among adult/public service librarians, 85 cents; for directors—women made only 74 cents on the dollar compared to male directors. Interestingly, there was pay parity for library/branch managers, and women actually made more than men for positions in technical services ($1.06).

The situation in academic and research libraries (ARL) has been particularly problematic, but it has been improving. The number of female librarians working in university libraries remains disproportionately low: 64% compared to the general library workforce of approximately 83% (ARL 2014). However, the proportion of female managers and administrators in ARL libraries has risen significantly. Morgan et al. (2009) studied the representation of women in administrative positions in academic libraries from 1972 to 2004. They found substantial increased representation over the years. In ARL libraries for example, in 1972, only 2% of the directors were women; by 2004 61% were women. In 2013, 59% were women (ARL 2014). Over the same period, representation at the department head level increased from 51% in 1972 to 64% (ARL 2002, 2008). There have also been some salary improvements. In 1980, women working in ARL libraries made 87 cents for every dollar earned by males. In 2013 that improved to 96.3 cents (ARL 2014). But problems persist. ARL in 2014 reported that . . .

> . . . there are seven categories where women, on average, have more experience and less pay: Associate Director, Administrative Specialist, Digital Specialist; Head,

Rare Books/Manuscripts/Special Collections; Head, Library Technology; Department Head-Other, and Public Services . . ."(ARL 2014, p. 13)

Interestingly, information technology positions may be a promising place for women in terms of pay equity. Lamont (2009) reported that, in general, IT positions were compensated at higher rates than other library positions but that men disproportionately occupied those positions. Lamont noted that in 2008, in academic libraries, nearly two in three computer systems department heads were men. Despite the disproportionality of distribution, the average salaries of men and women in IT positions in libraries were nearly identical suggesting that IT positions might achieve pay parity in libraries. Given the fact that IT positions were relatively highly compensated and pay equity was present, Lamont urged libraries to create a welcoming culture for women in IT to increase their numbers.

3. Generational Issues

For the first time in history, the library workforce includes a substantial number of workers from four generations despite the fact that there is some disagreement about when each generation begins and ends. The four generations include traditionalists (b. 1925–1942), baby boomers (b. 1943–1960), generation X (b. 1961–1981), and generation Y, otherwise known as millennials (b. 1982–2002). Although baby boomers are often considered the largest generation (80 million), in fact, the millennials constitute the largest cohort (88 million) (Graybill 2014).

Much attention has been paid to the differences among these generations: for example traditionalists' values stress hard work within a bureaucratic organization and strong loyalty to the organization. Baby boomers are more attentive to the political aspects of organizational life, have a strong work ethic, tend to stay with their employer, and place less emphasis on work/life balance. GenXers are skeptical of organizational politics and hierarchies, are conversant and comfortable with new technologies, tend to be independent learners, and are less likely to stay with one employer. They are also the obvious candidates to benefit from the transfer of institutional knowledge and power as baby boomers retire (Munde 2010). Managing millennials has received considerable attention in the library literature. Fine (2008) noted that millennials grew up relatively sheltered by their parents. They are a relatively altruistic group who believe they can make the world better; they believe in causes. Their work style is collaborative. In addition, they are "digital natives," fluent in the use of information and communication technologies and familiar with social networking activities. Millennials like to multitask, stay connected, and use technologies in a novel manner. They have grown up with highly advanced video games, the Internet, smartphones, and iPads/tablets. In addition, millennials do not consider their jobs as lifetime employment, and they are not particularly comfortable in hierarchies

The potential for generational clashes are obvious. Downing (2006) for example reported that one-third of respondents in one survey indicated that they had often been offended at work by someone from another generation, and that individuals in one generation believed that they were not viewed positively by individuals from other generations. Munde (2010) noted that some of these clashes might be based on generalities that sometimes amount to stereotypes of the young and old. Munde (2010) profiled these stereotypes in the following way:
Older workers

- are resistant to change, especially change suggested by younger workers;
- initiate more internal conflict;
- are not as energetic or ambitious;
- cost more to insure;
- are harder to train;
- are uncomfortable with technology;
- are more reliable;
- miss fewer days of work;
- are willing to work harder;
- are more loyal to the organization than younger workers.

Younger workers

- have highly developed technology skills;
- learn faster;
- are more innovative, but don't work as hard as their older counterparts;
- miss more days of work;
- require high levels of autonomy and control;
- are less professional in dress and manner;
- complain more than their older counterparts. (p. 95)

Munde noted that contrary to the stereotype, resistance to training was not linked to generations but more to the content of the training. Munde (2010) suggested that some of the clashes between groups might be related to differences in power within library hierarchies as genXers and millennials attempt to wrest power from baby boomers who currently hold the senior positions and are reluctant to retire.

There is no doubt that a multigenerational workplace is complex as each group attempts to navigate their place. Franks (2012) reminded library administrators that they cannot focus on any one group. Instead, libraries will need to accommodate baby boomers who might need flexibility to care for elderly parents while providing opportunities for those traditional workers who might still want to grow and adapt to the new information environment. Interestingly, Murray (2011) proposed a form of "reverse mentoring" in which millennials mentored and trained older workers on new technologies. Millennials want a flexible work environment that promotes a healthy work/life balance. For them, the organizational culture should encourage collaborative rather than hierarchical communication and decision-making. At the same time, they want regular feedback. GenXers want mentoring from the baby boomers as they assume leadership roles, but they also want independence to learn and be creative while still receiving regular feedback. To be a library administrator under such conditions is truly a challenge.

V. LIBRARIANSHIP: MODELS AND PERCEPTIONS

American librarianship has been developing for more than 150 years. However, what constitutes a profession and how society views our particular profession has been subject to considerable modification over the years. Below is a brief discussion of three ways professions might be distinguished from other occupations, how LIS professionals are viewed by others, and how they see themselves.

A. Professional Models

The first professionals were members of the clergy. Professions in their modern sense (law, medicine, nursing, teaching, librarianship) emerged in considerable numbers during the Industrial Revolution in the later nineteenth and early twentieth century. The following is a brief discussion of three models used to recognize professions and how librarianship might be characterized within those models.

1. The Trait Model

One way to characterize a profession is by determining whether or not a particular occupation exhibits certain traits such as the following:

- The occupation is service-oriented and altruistic in its orientation rather than profit making.

- Members of the occupation belong to associations that hold conferences, produce publications, promulgate codes of ethics, accredit educational institutions, and provide for licensure of idividuals.
- Professional associations possess normative and sometimes legal authority to control conduct.

Some of these traits are evident in LIS but not all. For example, the power of LIS professional associations is limited; they cannot sanction practitioners whose conduct violates professional codes. Librarianship exercises no monopoly, and a license to practice is not required. In addition, the one year of formal graduate training is not equal to the extensive training required in other professions. Others have proposed different traits to satisfy the requirements of a profession:

- Commitment to serve the interests of clients, in particular, and the welfare of society, in general
- A body of theory or special knowledge with its own principles of growth and reorganization
- A specialized set of skills, practices, and performances unique to the profession
- A capacity to render judgments with integrity under conditions of both technical and ethical certainty
- An organized approach to learning from experience both individually and collectively, thus growing new knowledge from the context of practice
- A professional community responsible for the oversight and monitoring of quality in both practice and professional education (Gardner and Shulman 2005, p. 14)

LIS fits more easily under this trait model primarily because the concepts of enforcement and monopoly are missing.

2. The Control Model

An alternative approach for distinguishing professions was suggested by Winter (1988), who proposed a model based on power or control. In this model, a professional's power comes from higher education and possession of intellectual and theoretical knowledge in contrast to occupations that rely on work experience and manual skills. He identified three ways librarians exerted power: classifying knowledge as a means of organizing it, indexing knowledge so it can be accessed, and understanding the formal and informal organization of various bodies of knowledge.

These functions cannot be accomplished without considerable knowledge and training, both theoretical and practical.

In the past, librarians achieved their power partly because the library itself was unique. It was, after all, often the only publicly accessible place with a substantial collection of well-organized materials and people who knew how to locate the desired materials. This gave the librarian, if not a monopoly, at least significant control over some types of knowledge. This type of special status was referred to as "asymmetry of expertise" and described the special trust that a client or patron placed in the knowledge of a professional (Abbott 1988, p. 5). Abbott (1988) labeled the type of knowledge controlled by librarians as "qualitative information" (p. 216). Librarians "had physical custody of cultural capital" (p. 217) which they organized and disseminated to everyone for education or entertainment, but not profit.

The control model, however, did not assume that all control was vested with the professional. In Winter's conceptualization there were other types of control: collegial control, client control, and mediated control. In collegial control, professional practice was controlled by those who provided the service. For example, doctors and lawyers determine their practice in regard to their patients. In a client-controlled situation, the individuals who use the services determine their wants, their needs, and the means by which they are satisfied. In mediated control, there is a balance between collegial and client control. Winter suggested that almost all professions were moving toward mediated control. Even in medicine, for example, patients exercise a great deal more control over their medical treatment than in the past. Traditionally, LIS professionals fit into the mediated control category but there is a high probability that in the twenty-first century, the client-controlled model will dominate. Birdsall (1982), suggested that new information technologies stimulated a trend toward de-professionalization by making expert knowledge more widely available. He argued that professions will no longer be characterized by a monopoly over special knowledge, but will instead encourage and teach clients to become more self-sufficient. Birdsall's speculations appear to fit for all of today's helping professions.

3. The Values Model

A fundamental value of all professions is the value of service. The original professions (clergy, lawyers, doctors, teachers, nurses, and social workers) were dedicated to the betterment of people and the improvement of society and "stood outside the new commercial and industrial heart of society" (Abbott 1988, p. 3). LIS professionals serve the public good by bringing people in contact with knowledge. In doing so, LIS professionals also support fundamental democratic values by ensuring that all people have equal access to that knowledge. Under this view, the professional foundation of LIS is not its knowledge or techniques, but its fundamental values. The significance of LIS lies not in mastery of sources, organizational skills, or technological competence, but in *why* LIS professionals perform the functions they do. The fact that modern LIS encompasses knowledge in all formats (e.g., print, audiovisual, and electronic) increases the importance of these underlying values.

B. Perceptions of Librarians

1. Stereotypes

> Librarians are in the business of presentation. Whether we are presenting information or presenting ourselves to the public, it is a constant of the profession. And all of our constituents—especially our served communities—judge our presentation, consciously and subconsciously, as to whether they can see us reliable, authoritative, approachable source of information. (Pagowsky and Rigby 2014, p. 1)

How does society view LIS professionals and do the perceptions match the reality? Generally, female librarians have been most often portrayed negatively: they are spinsters, wear their hair in a bun, buy sensible shoes and glasses, look stern, act like policemen—authoritarian and controlling—and are quick to say "shhussh" at the slightest disturbance. They are afraid of life, socially inept, and more interested in reading a book than experiencing life. More recent interpretations using a cultural studies approach suggested that librarians can use such stereotypes to their advantage. Adams (2000) and Radford and Radford (2003) argued that rather than objecting to the persistent image of the "old maid," librarians should transform the stereotype into a positive, using such techniques as parody, mimicry, and humor. They saw the 1995 film *Party Girl*, in which a young woman was transformed from a self-centered, fun-obsessed individual into a serious-minded librarian as a good example of how stereotypes can be used to librarians' advantage.

Male librarians had other concerns: they assumed that they were perceived as working in a "woman's profession" and therefore feared being seen as ineffectual or effeminate. This concern was sufficient to inhibit many men from admitting that they were librarians; instead, they were more likely to identify themselves as "information scientists" (Morrisey and Case 1988). But how accurate were those perceptions? Morrisey and Case (1988) examined college students' perceptions of male librarians and found that they were often quite positive. In fact, the most common terms used to describe male librarians were "organized, approachable, logical, friendly, patient, and serious" (p. 457). Their conclusion was that male librarians perceived themselves in a much more negative light than others did.

Not all stereotypes have been negative; sometimes librarians are perceived as smart, like Kathryn Hepburn in *Desk Set*, or heroic and sexy like *Batgirl*. Schuman (1990) pointed out that such notable writers as Sinclair Lewis, Sherwood Anderson, Henry James, and Edith Wharton depicted librarians in positive terms. Furthermore, the media's occasional portrayal of librarians in a negative light is consistent with portrayals of other professions; lawyers and politicians certainly receive their share of disrespect.

Nonetheless, the negative stereotypes persist. Peresie and Alexander (2005) studied the portrayal of librarians in young adult literature and found that the majority (70%) portrayed the librarian as a female with negative characteristics such as being overweight, wearing glasses, having white hair, and wearing outdated clothing. They were often described as cold or stern, or timid and shy. In only a few cases were the librarians beautiful, stylish, intelligent, and well informed. If young people perceive librarians in a poor light they are not likely to consider it as a career in adulthood. On the other hand, Attebury (2010) compared 100 YouTube videos produced by librarians and nonlibrarians. She found that the videos from nonlibrarians tended to focus on the old maid stereotype as an enforcer of rules or inept. Librarian's videos on the other hand portrayed the librarian as a hero. Vassilakaki and Moniarou-Papaconstantinou (2014) examining numerous research papers on librarians' image and found that, in general, the negative image had not changed — the "old maid" was the dominant theme, although male librarians received more positive characterizations.

Although some might suggest that it is within librarians' powers to change the dominant negative stereotypes through changes in their appearance and behavior, others contend that the stereotypes are deeply ingrained in the culture — a function of the historical roots of the profession and the racial, gender and class injustices which depreciate the value of activities such as library work (Keer and Carlos 2014). Certainly, the negative stereotypes can have pernicious effects: they can impede recruitment into the field, affect an individual's willingness to seek service from a librarian, affect user expectations of librarians, adversely affect the willingness of citizens to fund the library, and affect the status and growth of the profession as a whole (White 2012). Obviously, there is still much work to be done in educating the public about what LIS professionals do today and who they are.

2. Personality Types

The first major study of librarians' personalities was conducted by Alice Bryan in 1948 as part of a large study called the Public Library Inquiry. She found that the mostly female librarians were submissive and lacked qualities of leadership (Bryan 1952). Later studies summarized by Agada (1984, 1987) found that, in general, both male and female librarians exhibited personality traits of deference, passivity, and self-abasement.

Scherdin (1994), using the Myers-Briggs Type Indicator, suggested that most librarians fell into one of two typologies: introversion: sensing, thinking, judging or introversion: intuitive, thinking, judging. Among the characteristics associated with these types were determination and perseverance, independence, a drive to work hard, the desire to innovate, and placing a high value on competence. Interestingly, despite the stereotype, there was little evidence that librarians were authoritarian. One should also hasten to add that none of these traits were considered abnormal. One should, of course, be careful about trying to extrapolate from these findings. Fisher (1988) reviewed a number of these personality studies and concluded that many of the personality tests were flawed, and overall there was no one distinct personality type for librarians.

Williamson, Pemberton, and Lounsbury (2008) attempted to analyze more than 2,000 librarians' personalities by their choice of library specialization using the Personality Style Inventory. Among the traits measured were adaptability, assertiveness, autonomy, conscientiousness, customer service orientation, emotional resilience, extraversion, openness, optimism, teamwork, tough-mindedness, work drive, and operational work style. Their findings suggested that different specialties attracted people with different personality traits. When taken together, they concluded:

> High extraversion, low tough-mindedness, and high teamwork (among other variables . . .) characterized person-oriented academic reference librarians, special librarians, public librarians, school librarians, distance education librarians and records managers. For the technique-oriented specialties, operational work style and low customer service orientation characterized catalogers, and high assertiveness and high tough-mindedness characterized the archivists and systems librarians. (pp. 5–6)

3. Gender Perceptions

The first female clerk was hired by the Boston Public Library in 1852; by 1878 two-thirds of the library workforce was female, and by 1910 more than 75% of library workers were women (Garrison 1972–1973). From a historical perspective, the numerical dominance of women in American librarianship, especially public librarianship, might explain the perception of passivity among librarians, since passivity was a normative expectation of women well into the twentieth century.

The rapid expansion of public libraries in the nineteenth century increased the need for library workers, but as these libraries were often poorly funded, they needed staff members who were willing to work for low pay. Male library directors openly acknowledged the desirability of hiring talented women because they worked for half the pay. In addition, librarianship fit the values of work for women at the time. There was a narrow range of jobs outside the home that were considered acceptable for women, mostly related to children or caregiving, such as teaching and nursing, that capitalized on women's homemaking and child-raising skills. Because libraries were seen as civilizing and nurturing, they were acceptable places for women to work (Garrison 1972–1973). In addition, the nineteenth-century values of personal improvement and the belief that books and reading could improve morals also drew women into librarianship. Indeed, it was sometimes described as missionary work. The fact that librarianship still draws at least some individuals who share these convictions is, in part, a legacy of these historical forces and confirmation that its service aspect is still deeply ingrained.

Garrison (1972–1973) suggested that the feminization of public librarianship in the nineteenth century created an inferior image for the profession that it might not have had if it remained the domain of male scholars. In other words, an occupation that once had considerable status lost ground as it became dominated by women. Although women outnumbered men in libraries, they were not perceived as potential leaders or heads of libraries. Women were perceived as more delicate and unable to tolerate the rigors of administration. Indeed, some believed that administrative responsibilities might even lead to mental illness. This perceived passivity led Garrison to lament that librarianship failed to engage those with the necessary leadership or assertiveness (meaning men) to establish it in the pantheon of professions:

> Specifically lacking in the librarian's professional service code are a sense of commitment, a drive to lead rather than to serve and a clear-cut conception of professional rights and responsibilities. The feminization of library work is a major cause of these deficiencies. (pp. 144–145)

The legacy of this attitude persists particularly in public libraries where women occupy a disproportionately low percentage of leadership positions. There are several possible explanations. Women tend to have more career breaks due to family and marital responsibilities, although a study by Zemon and Bahr (2005) found that the choice of parenthood, which often created additional burdens and barriers for women, did not appear to have a significant deleterious effect on library careers.

Women often began their library careers later than men and tended to remain within the same organization longer than men, effectively reducing the number of promotional opportunities. When women do move, they are more likely than their male counterparts to relocate because of a spouse. As a result, they often take the only positions available rather than positions involving promotion.

Image and status problems also persist. For example, women are more likely to serve as children's librarians or in cataloging positions; men are more likely to seek technology-oriented and managerial positions, despite the fact that male librarians have no greater motivation to manage than females (Swisher et al. 1985). The former categories reflect values of nurturance or attention to detail, while the latter reflect technical competence, leadership, or managerial skills. The dominance of men in technical and managerial categories further supports the theory that many men are uneasy working in a field perceived as feminine. Assuming that certain library positions are more suited to one gender further also serves to depress the status and pay of women. As Hildenbrand (1989) observed, librarians in children's services and cataloging generally receive lower pay than those in other basic service positions. Male children's librarians are a rarity and raise eyebrows, no matter how undeservedly. These inequalities are yet another example of the persistent messages that women's work is of less value and status.

The underrepresentation of women in administrative positions, however, is not fully explained by the reasons noted above—sex discrimination still appears to play a role. Hildenbrand (1996) argued that to fully understand the status and place of women in librarianship requires an appreciation of the historical, political, and social relationships between men and women, especially in terms of how power is distributed. She argued that the traditional analysis of library history is biased (Hildenbrand 1992). She believed that important women have largely been ignored while prominent males, such as Dewey, have been studied in detail. She criticized Garrison for holding women responsible for their poor status (blaming the victim), rather than attributing it to the pernicious attitudes of the times. She believed that a reanalysis of the history of women in librarianship would reveal that they were responsible for its rapid growth, the increase in the quality of library workers, and the growth of a national purpose for public libraries.

Consistent with Hildenbrand's position, Harris (1992) argued that librarians' self-consciousness about their image was counterproductive, especially when it led to self-deprecation. Such self-criticism leads to blaming the victim and denigrating worthy "feminine" traits rather than focusing on why society gives nurturing activities such low status. For Harris, disparaging caring attitudes and lionizing management, research, and technical expertise (considered male traits) was tantamount to endorsing and perpetuating the suppression of women. That both men *and* women deprecate these traits was particularly disturbing.

Maack (1997) suggested that striving for a status traditionally associated with male-dominated professions such as law and medicine was misdirected. Rather, she argued that there was a need to reconceptualize the professions into three categories: high-authority professions, such as law and medicine; indirect or product-oriented professions, such as engineering and architecture; and empowering professions, such as education, social work, and library and information science. In empowering professions, "the professional shares expertise with the goal of enabling clients to use knowledge in order to take control of their own lives or their own learning" (p. 284). It is a collaborative, client-centered activity in which sharing and facilitation are fundamental activities of the professional. Such a profession contrasts clearly with high-authority professions in which "the professional offers prescriptions, directives, or strategies that the client must follow" (Maack 1997, p. 284). As noted earlier, in the client-centered model of the professions, it was not power and authority that dominated, but the desire to help others develop their own abilities and confidence so that they can deal with their own problems and challenges. Accepting LIS as an empowering profession eliminates the need to strive to be like law or medicine and recognizes the vitality of a profession that increases the independence and abilities of others.

VI. THE FUTURE ROLES OF LIS PROFESSIONALS

There is much that is unknown about the role LIS professionals will play in the future, in large part, because the information and technological environment in which we operate is uncertain. Most likely, some of the traditional roles will remain or expand while others will diminish. For example, a 2001 *Library Journal* survey of 1,000 librarians reported that they perceived their most significant roles as instructing patrons in navigating the Web, directing patrons to appropriate information resources, evaluating collections, organizing resources, creating programs, creating e-resources, and establishing digital archives. Interestingly, although the respondents believed that many of those functions would persist, only creating e-resources and establishing digital archives were seen as increasing in importance ("Projecting Librarians' Roles" 2002).

Baruchson-Arbib and Bronstein (2002) conducted a survey of LIS experts that seemed to confirm that whatever changes will occur will proceed in an evolutionary, rather than revolutionary, fashion. The experts perceived that the traditional library model would not be replaced by a virtual one, but would undergo significant changes, especially in regard to accessing information outside the library. Similarly, they saw the role of LIS professionals as increasingly user-centered rather than organization-centered and that there was greater need to understand how individuals seek and use information. In addition, they saw a need for LIS professionals to be more aggressive in marketing and promoting their services to the community, and to develop the skills needed to accomplish these activities. For the most part, these findings were confirmed a decade later.

Lankes (2011) describes the emerging role of the librarian as "participatory" and argues for a reconception of our profession as "new librarianship": librarianship that promotes conversations that produce and infuse knowledge. (p. 2). He observes:

> Be it in practice, policies, programs, and/or tools, librarians seek to enrich, capture, store, and disseminate the conversations of their communities. (p. 2)

The roles fulfilled by LIS professionals might involve different means from the past, but they are likely to fall into three well-established categories:

A. The Educational Role

Since the mid-nineteenth century, the library, whether public, school, or academic, was characterized as providing critical support not only to students, but to all individuals who desired to continue their education informally. LIS professionals foster people's understanding and judgment. They educate, enriching the lives of others through their advice and guidance. They promote a love of reading, promote intellectual stimulation, provide access to knowledge, offer instruction so that everyone can continue to grow and develop intellectually throughout their lives, and provide entertainment and diversion from an often wearying world. The intimate relationship of libraries with learning, literacy, and reading remains strong, and the public continues to expect libraries to play a role in each of these areas. People will continue to expect the library to be a place, both physical and virtual, where they can find books and programming that stimulates reading among people of all ages, but particularly among the young. In many instances, it is this educational function that "sells" the library as an institution deserving of public support. Books, including e-books, remain the library's "brand" for many people (De Rosa et al. 2005). The public's perception of the LIS professional as an advocate for lifelong learning strongly influences their support for the library (De Rosa and Johnson 2008). In an age when many believe that schools have failed in their role, the perception of the library as a learning place can go a long way toward securing its future. There is a clear need for LIS professionals to continue in this role.

B. The Information Role

While people expect LIS professionals to play an educational role, they also see them "as a provider of practical answers and information" (De Rosa and Johnson 2008, pp. 4–9). With the expansion of the digital information world and the plethora of potential sources for information, LIS professionals have significant competitors for information access and provision, especially powerful search engines. Nonetheless, LIS professionals have been enthusiastic participants in making digital resources available. They have adapted their databases, catalogs, and services to effectively exploit the digital world and they have remained a trustworthy source of information for their users. To accomplish this, LIS professionals have had to (1) develop new skills in evaluating and selecting digital resources and providers of these resources, (2) create new services such as digital reference to reach users outside the physical library, (3) adopt new organization of knowledge practices, (4) develop broad-based collaborations with other libraries and nonprofit organizations, and (5) engage user communities to determine and satisfy their information needs. Suffice it to say that these activities have increased access but also brought new challenges for LIS professionals. The implications of these emerging roles will be discussed in more detail in the ensuing chapters.

C. The Social/Cultural Role

A common perspective is that LIS professionals serve individuals or small groups (e.g., families). But librarianship has always had a cultural significance as well. Butler (1951) referred to the field's humanistic values as the "cultural motivation" to promote "wisdom in the individual and in the community" (p. 246). It was not technological competence that formed the basis of the profession; it was service to people and the community. What makes LIS attractive as a profession is not merely that we satisfy a person's information needs but that we care about people, about solving human problems, and about improving lives. LIS professionals help people by assisting them to obtain social services; by helping them access critical government agencies; by providing quality information for decision-making; by providing a space for social interaction and a forum for discussion of important issues. Today, we recognize that the library's role is much more than educational, much more than information provider; it is a place that improves civic and social life. In truth, it is a role that helps hold the social fabric together.

Can LIS professionals effectively navigate the eddies generated by these three strong currents? Certainly, they are part of the same stream; for the most part, they are complementary forces. We must steer a central course, respecting the potential of each to influence our direction. It is a difficult task. Perhaps, the key question for the future is whether the traditional cultural values of librarianship should form the context for the exploitation of information technologies, or whether those information technologies will create a new social context that changes the meaning and significance of libraries and LIS professionals?

REFERENCES

Abbott, Andrew. 1988. *The System of Professions.* Chicago: University of Chicago.

Adams, Katherine C. 2000. "Loveless Frump as Hip and Sexy Party Girl: A Reevaluation of the Old-Maid Stereotype." *Library Quarterly* 70 (July): 287–301.

Agada, John. 1984. "Studies of the Personality of Librarians." *Drexel Library Quarterly* 20 (spring): 24–45.

———. 1987. "Assertion and the Librarian Personality." In *Encyclopedia of Library and Information Science.* New York: Marcel Dekker, 128–144.

American Library Association. 1996. "ALA Policy Manual: Policy 56.1." In *ALA Handbook of Organization, 1995–96.* Chicago: ALA.

———. 2009b. "Number Employed in Libraries: Fact Sheet 2." Chicago: ALA. www.ala .org/ ala/aboutala/offices/library/libraryfactsheet/alalibraryfactsheet1.cfm.

———. 2009c. *President's Task Force on Library Education: Final Report.* Chicago: ALA.

———. 2012. "Table A-5: Number of Higher Education Credentialed Librarians by Characteristic, 2009–2010." ala.org/offices/sites/ala.org.offices/files/content/diversity/ diversitycounts/diversitycountstables2012.pdf. Accessed February 13, 2015.

———. 2014a. "Searchable DB of ALA Accredited Programs." www.ala.org/cfapps/lisdir/ lisdir_search.cfm.

———. 2014c. "Spectrum-Scholarship Overview." www.ala.org/offices/diversity/Spectrum/ scholarshipinformation.

———. 2014b. 2008 *Standards for Accreditation of Master's Programs in Library and Information Studies.* Office of Accreditation. www.ala.org/accreditedprograms/sites/ ala.org.accredited programs/files/content/standards/standards_2008.pdf.

———. 2015. "Standards for Accreditation of Master's Programs in Library and Information Studies." www.ala.org/accreditedprograms/sites/ala.org.accreditedprograms/files/ content/standards/Standards_2015_adopted_02–02–15.pdf.

ALA COA (Committee on Accreditation.) 2014. *Standards for Accreditation of Master's Programs in Library and Information Studies.* www.ala.org/accreditedprograms/sites/

ala.org.accreditedprograms/files/content/standards/Standards_2015_adopted _02-12-15.pdf.

ALISE (Association for Library and Information Science Education). 2012. *Library and Information Science Education Statistical Report 2012*, edited by Danny P. Wallace. Chicago: ALISE.

———. 2009. *Library and Information Science Education Statistical Report 2006*, edited by Jerry D. Saye. Chicago: ALISE.

———. 2000. *Educating Library and Information Science Professionals for a New Century: The KALIPER Report: Executive Summary*. Reston, VA: ALISE.

American Society for Information Science and Technology (ASIS&T). 2007. *ASIS&T White Paper: Accreditation of Programs for the Education of Information Professionals*. October 20.

Apostle, Richard, and Boris Raymond. 1997. *Librarianship and the Information Paradigm*. Lanham, MD: Scarecrow.

ARL. 2013. (Association of Research Libraries.) "Minority Representation in the 2012–2013 ARL Annual Salary Survey: Taking a Closer Look." www.arlstatistics.org/news/1367.

———. 2014. *ARL Annual Salary Survey 2013–2014*. Washington, DC: ARL.

Attebury, Rmirose Iliene. 2010. "Perceptions of a Profession: Librarians and Stereotypes in Online Videos." *Library Philosophy and Practice* (October). www.Webpage.uidaho .edu/~mbolin/attebury.htm.

Ball, Mary Alice. 2008. "Practicums and Service Learning." *Journal of Education for Library and Information Science* 49 (winter): 70–81.

Baruchson-Arbib, Shifra, and Jenny Bronstein. 2002. "A View to the Future of the Library and Information Science Profession: A Delphi Study." *Journal of the American Society for Information Science and Technology* 53 (March): 397–408.

Bertot, John Carlo, and Lindsay Sarin. 2015. "The Future of the MLS: Rethinking Library Education." *American Libraries* (March/April): 40–41.

Birdsall, William F. 1982. "Librarianship, Professionalism and Social Change." *Library Journal* 107 (February 1): 223–226.

Blakiston, Rebecca. 2011. "Building Knowledge, Skills, and Abilities: Continual Learning in the New Information Landscape." *Journal of Library Administration* 51: 728–743.

BLS (Bureau of Labor Statistics). 2014. "Employed Persons by Detailed Occupation and Age, 2013 Annual Averages." www.bls.gov/cps/occupation_age.htm.

———. 2014a. "Selected Occupational Projections Data." data.bls.gov/oep/noeted? Action=empoccp.

Bonnet, Jennifer L., and Benjamin McAlexander. 2012. "Structural Diversity in Academic Libraries: A Study of Librarian Approachability." *The Journal of Academic Librarianship* 38 (September): 277–286.

Boyce, Bert R. 1994. "The Death of Library Education." *American Libraries* (March): 257–259.

Boyd, Morag. "2012. "From the Comfort of Your Office: Facilitating Learner-Centered Continuing Education in the Online Environment." *Cataloging & Classification Quarterly* 50: 189–203.

Brand, Barbara B. 1996. "Pratt Institute Library School: The Perils of Professionalization." In *Reclaiming the American Library Past: Writing the Women In*, edited by Suzanne Hildenbrand. Norwood, NJ: Ablex, 251–278.

Bryan, Alice. 1952. *The Public Librarian.* New York: Columbia University.

Butler, Pierce. 1951. "Librarianship as a Profession." *Library Quarterly* 21 (October): 235–247.

Campbell, Jerry D. 1993. "Choosing to Have a Future." *American Libraries* 24 (June): 560–566.

Campbell, Lucy B. 1977. "The Hampton Institute Library School." In *Handbook of Black Librarianship*, edited by E. J. Josey and Ann Shockley Allen. Littleton, CO: Libraries Unlimited, 35–46.

Carey, James O., and Vicki L. Gregory. 2002. "Students' Perceptions of Academic Motivation, Interactive Participation, and Selected Pedagogical and Structural Factors in Web-Based Distance Learning." *Journal of Education for Library and Information Science* 43 (winter): 6–15.

Chang, Hui-Fen. 2013. "Ethnic and Racial Diversity in Academic and Research Libraries: Past, Present, and Future." Presentation, ACRL Conference, April 10–13, 2013, Indianapolis, IN.

Chu, Heting. 2006. "Curricula of LIS Programs in the USA: A Content Analysis." In *Proceedings of the Asia-Pacific Conference on Library and Information Education and Practice* 2006 (A-LIEP 2006), Singapore, 3–6 April 2006, edited by C. Khoo, D. Singh, and A. S. Chaudhry. Singapore: School of Communication and Information, Nanyang Technological University, 328–337.

———. 2012. "iSchools and non-iSchools in the USA: An Examination of Their Master's Programs." *Education for Information* 29: 1–17.

Conrad, Clifton F., and Kim Rapp-Hanretta. 2002. "Positioning Master's Programs in Library and Information Science: A Template for Avoiding Pitfalls and Seizing Opportunities in Light of Key External and Internal Forces." *Journal of Education in Library and Information Science* 43 (spring): 92–104.

Cox, Andrew M., and Sheila Corrall. 2013. "Evolving Academic Library Specialties." *Journal of the American Society for Information Science and Technology* 64: 1526–1542.

Cronin, Blaise. 1995. "Cutting the Gordian Knot." *Information Processing and Management* 31 (November): 897–902.

Crowley, Bill. 2008. *Renewing Professional Librarianship: A Fundamental Rethinking.* Westport, CT: Libraries Unlimited.

Damasco, Ione T., and Dracine Hodges. 2012. "Tenure and Promotion Experiences of Academic Librarians of Color." *College & Research Libraries* 73 (May): 279–301.

Davis, Donald G., Jr. 1978. "Curtis, Florence Rising." In *Dictionary of American Library Biography*, edited by Bohdan S. Wynar. Littleton, CO: Libraries Unlimited, 108–109.

Davis-Kendrick, Kaetrena D. 2009. "The African American Male Librarian: Motivational Factors in Choosing a Career in Library and Information Science." *Behavioral & Social Sciences Librarian* 28: 23–52.

Debons, A. 1985. "The Information Professional: A Survey." In *The Information Profession. Proceedings of a Conference Held in Melbourne, Australia (November 26–28, 1984)*, edited by James Henri and Roy Sanders. Melbourne, Australia: Centre for Library Studies.

De Rosa et al. 2005. *Perceptions of Libraries and Information Resources*. Dublin, OH: OCLC.

De Rosa, Cathy, and Jenny Johnson. 2008. *From Awareness to Funding: A Study of Library Support in America*. Dublin, OH: OCLC.

Dewey, Melvil. 1989. "The Profession." *Library Journal* 114 (June 15): 5. Reprinted from *American Library Journal* 1 (1876).

Dillon, Andrew. 2012. "What It Means to be an iSchool." *Journal of Education for Library and Information Science* 53 (October): 267–273.

———. 2014. "The Emerging Discipline of Information." In David Bawden and Lyn Robinson. *Introduction to Information Science*. Chicago, ALA, pp. xvii–xix.

Dillon, Andrew, and April Norris. 2005. "Crying Wolf: An Examination and Reconsideration of the Perception of Crisis in LIS Education." *Journal of Education for Library and Information Science* 46 (fall): 280–298.

Downing, Kris. 2006. "Next Generation: What Leaders Need to Know about the Millennials." *Leadership in Action* 26 (July/August): 3–6.

Estabrook, Leigh. 1981. "Productivity, Profit, and Libraries." *Library Journal* 106 (July): 1377–1380.

———. 2005. "Crying Wolf: A Response." *Journal of Education for Library and Information Science* 46 (fall): 299–303.

Fine, Allison. 2008. "It's Time to Focus on a New Generation." *Chronicle of Philanthropy* 20 (August 21): 22.

Fisher, David P. 1988. "Is the Librarian a Distinct Personality Type?" *Journal of Librarianship* 20 (January): 36–47.

Franks, Rachel. 2012. "Grey Matter: The Ageing Librarian Workforce, with a Focus on Public and Academic Libraries in Australia and the United States." *Aplis* 25 (September): 104–110.

Gambee, Budd L. 1978. "Fairchild, Mary Salome Cutler." In *Dictionary of American Library Biography*, edited by Bohdan S. Wynar. Littleton, CO: Libraries Unlimited, 167–170.

Gardner, Howard, and Lee S. Shulman. 2005. "The Professions in America Today." *Daedalus* 134 (summer): 13–18.

Garrison, Dee. 1972–1973. "The Tender Technicians: The Feminization of Public Librarianship." *Journal of Social History* 6 (winter): 131–156.

Gorman, Michael. 2004. "What Ails Library Education?" *Journal of Academic Librarianship* 30 (March): 99–100.

Graybill, Jolie O. 2014. "Millennials among the Professional Workforce in Academic Libraries: Their Perspective on Leadership." *The Journal of Academic Librarianship* 40: 10–15.

Greiner, Tony. 2008. "Diversity and the MLS." *Library Journal* 133 (May 1): 36.

Grimscheid, Laura and Meredith Schwartz. 2014. "Payday: LJ Salary Survey 2014." *Library Journal* (July 3). www.lj.library.journal.com/2014/07/careers/payday-lj-salary-survey-2014/#_.

Grotzinger, Laurel A. 1966. *The Power and the Dignity: Librarianship and Katharine Sharp.* New York: Scarecrow.

———. 1978a. "Kroeger, Alice Bertha." In *Dictionary of American Library Biography*, edited by Bohdan S. Wynar. Littleton, CO: Libraries Unlimited, 295–298.

———. 1978b. "Sharp, Katharine Lucinda." In *Dictionary of American Library Biography*, edited by Bohdan S. Wynar. Littleton, CO: Libraries Unlimited, 470–473.

Harris, Roma M. 1992. *Librarianship: The Erosion of a Woman's Profession.* Norwood, NJ: Ablex.

Hauptman, Robert. 1987. "Iconoclastic Education: The Library Science Degree." *Catholic Library World* 58 (May–June): 252–253.

Heim, Kathleen, and Leigh Estabrook. 1983. Career Profiles and Sex Discrimination in the Library Profession. Chicago: ALA.

Hildenbrand, Suzanne. 1989. "'Women's Work' within Librarianship." *Library Journal* 114 (September 1): 153–155.

———. 1992. "A Historical Perspective on Gender Issues in American Librarianship." *Canadian Journal of Information Science* 17 (September): 18–28.

———. 1996. "Women in Library History: From the Politics of Library History to the History of Library Politics." In *Reclaiming the American Library Past: Writing the Women In*, edited by Suzanne Hildenbrand. Norwood, NJ: Ablex, 1–23.

Holley, Edward G. 1984. "The Merwine Case and the MLS: Where Was ALA?" American Libraries 15 (May 1984): 327–330.

Jaeger, Paul T., John Carlo Bertot, and Mega Subramaniam. 2013. "Preparing Future Librarians to Effectively Serve Their Communities." *The Library Quarterly* 83: 243–248.

Karlowich, Robert A., and Nasser Sharify. 1978. "Plummer, Mary Wright." In *Dictionary of American Library Biography*, edited by Bohdan S. Wynar. Littleton, CO: Libraries Unlimited, 399–402.

Keer, Gretchen, and Andrew Carlos. 2014. "The Stereotype: Our Obsession with Librarian Representation." In *The Librarian Stereotype: Deconstructing Perceptions and Presentations of Information Work*, edited by Nicole Pagowsky and Miriam E. Rigby. Chicago: ALA, pp. 63–83.

Keiser, Barbie. 2012. "Professional Development and Continuing Education." *Online* (May–June): 20–27.

Kelley, Michael. 2013. "Can We Talk About the MLS?" *Library Journal* 138 (May 1): 8.

Kendall, Joshua. 2014. "Melvil Dewey, Compulsive Innovator." *American Library* 45 (March/April): 52–54.

King, John Leslie. 2005. "Stepping Up: Shaping the Future of the Field." Plenary Address, Association for Library and Information Science Education Conference, Boston, MA, January 11–14, 2005. http://dlist.sir.arizona.edu/739.

———. 2006. "Identity in the I-School Movement." *Bulletin of the American Society for Information Science and Technology* 32 (April/May): 13–15.

Kuhn, Thomas S. 1970. *The Structure of Scientific Revolutions*, 2nd ed. Chicago: University of Chicago Press.

Lamont, Melissa. 2009. "Gender, Technology, and Libraries." *Information Technology and Libraries* (September): 137–142.

Lankes, David R. 2011. *The Atlas of New Librarianship*. Cambridge, MA: MIT.

Leong, Julie. 2014. "Purpose-Driven Learning for Library Staff." *The Australian Library Journal* 63: 108–117.

Lester, June. 2011. "Use of Adjunct Faculty in Delivery of Distance Education in ALA-Accredited LIS Master's Programs in the U.S. and Canada." *Journal of Education for Library and Information Science* 52 (summer): 212–237.

Logan, Elisabeth, Rebecca Augustyniak, and Alison Rees. 2002. "Distance Education as Different Education: A Student-Centered Investigation of Distance Learning Experience." *Journal of Education for Library and Information Science* 43 (winter): 32–42.

Lynch, Beverly P. 1989. "Education and Training of Librarians." In *Rethinking the Library in the Information Age*. Washington, DC: US GPO, 75–92.

Maack, Mary Niles. 1986. "Women in Library Education: Down the Up Staircase." *Library Trends* 34 (winter): 401–431.

———. 1997. "Toward a New Model of the Information Professions: Embracing Empowerment." *Journal of Education for Library and Information Science* 38 (fall): 283–302.

Maatta, Stephanie. 2007. "What's an MLIS Worth?" *Library Journal* 132 (October 15): 30–38.

Main, Linda. 1990. "Research versus Practice: A 'No' Contest." *RQ* 30 (winter): 226–228.

Marco, Guy. 1994. "The Demise of the American Core Curriculum." *Libri* 44: 175–189.

Markey, Karen. 2004. "Current Educational Trends in the Information and Library Science Curriculum." *Journal of Education for Library and Information Science* 45 (fall): 317–339.

Matarazzo, James M., and Joseph J. Mika. 2006. "How to Be Popular." *American Libraries* (September): 38–40.

Matteson, Miriam L., Elizabeth Schleuter, and Morgan Hidy. 2013. "Continuing Education in Library Management: Challenges and Opportunities." *Library Management* 34 (2013): 219–235.

McCook, Kathleen de la Peña, and Paula Geist. 1993. "Diversity Deferred: Where Are the Minority Librarians?" *Library Journal* 118 (November 1): 35–38.

McPheeters, Annie L. 1988. *Library Service in Black and White: Some Personal Recollections, 1921–1980.* Metuchen, NJ: Scarecrow.

Miksa, Francis L. 1992. "Library and Information Science: Two Paradigms." In *Conceptions of Library and Information Science: Historical, Empirical and Theoretical Perspectives,* edited by Pertti Vakkari and Blaise Cronin. London: Taylor Graham, 229–252.

Morgan, Jennifer Craft; Brandy Farrar and Irene Owens. 2009. "Documenting Diversity among Working LIS Graduates." *Library Trends* 58 (fall): 192–214.

Morrisey, Locke J., and Donald O. Case. 1988. "'There Goes My Image.' The Perception of Male Librarians by Colleague, Student, and Self." *College and Research Libraries* 49 (September): 453–464.

Mulvaney, Phil, and Dan O'Connor. 2014. "Most Likely to Succeed: Opinion: Rethinking How We Rate and Rank MLIS Programs." *Library Journal.* 139: (June 15): 37.

Munde, Gail. 2010. "Considerations for Managing an Increasingly Intergenerational Workforce in Libraries." *Library Trends* 59 (2010): 88–108.

Murray, Adam. 2011. "Mind the Gap: Technology, Millennial Leadership and the Cross-Generational Workforce." *The Australian Library Journal* 60 (February): 54–64.

Olson, Gary M., and Jonathan Grudin. 2009. "The Information School Phenomenon." *Interactions* (March–April): 15–19.

Pagowsky, Nicole, and Miriam Rigby. 2014. "Contextualizing Ourselves: The Identity Politics of the Librarian Stereotype." In *The Librarian Stereotype: Deconstructing Perceptions and Presentations of Information Work,* edited by Nicole Pagowsky and Miriam E. Rigby. Chicago: ALA, pp. 1–37.

Paris, Marion. 1988. *Library School Closings: Four Case Studies.* Metuchen, NJ: Scarecrow.

Park, Jung-ran, Caimei Lu, and Linda Marion. 2009. "Cataloging Professionals in the Digital Environment: A Content Analysis of Job Descriptions." *Journal of the American Society for Information Science and Technology* 60 (2009): 844–857.

Park, Jung-ran, Yuji Tosaka, Susan Maszaros, and Caimei Lu. 2010.; "From Metadata Creation to Metadata Quality Control: Continuing Education Needs Among Cataloging and Metadata Professionals." *Journal of Education for Library and Information Science* 51 (summer): 158–176.

Peresie, Michelle, and Linda B. Alexander. 2005. "Librarian Stereotypes in Young Adult Literature." *Young Adult Library Services* (fall): 24–31.

"Projecting Librarians' Roles." 2002. *Library Journal* 127 (February 1): 48.

Radford, Marie L., and Gary P. Radford. 2003. "Librarians and Party Girls: Cultural Studies and the Meaning of the Librarian." *Library Quarterly* 73: 54–69.

Rainie, Lee. 2006. "Digital 'Natives' Invade the Workplace." www.pewresearch.org/pubs/70/digital-natives-invade-the-workplace.

Rayward, W. Boyd. 1983. "Library and Information Sciences: Disciplinary Differentiation, Competition, Convergence." In *The Study of Information: Disciplinary Messages,* edited by Fritz Machlup and Una Mansfield. New York: Wiley, 343–363.

Rice, James. 1989. "The Hidden Role of Librarians." *Library Journal* 114 (January): 57–59.

Robbins-Carter, Jane, and Charles A. Seavey. 1986. "The Master's Degree: Basic Preparation for Professional Practice." *Library Trends* 34 (spring): 561–580.

Roberts, Norman, and Tania Konn. 1991. *Librarians and Professional Status: Continuing Professional Development and Academic Libraries.* London: Library Association.

Saracevic, Tefko. 1994. "Closing of Library Schools in North America: What Role Accreditation?" *Libri* 44 (November): 190–200.

Scherdin, Mary Jane. 1994. "Vive la Difference: Exploring Librarian Personality Types Using the MBTI." In *Discovering Lib*rarians, edited by Mary Jane Scherdin. Chicago: ACRL, 125–156.

Schuman, Patricia Glass. 1990. "The Image of Librarians: Substance or Shadow?" *Journal of Academic Librarianship* 16: 86–89.

Stephens, Michael. 2011. "Online LIS Education—or Not." *Library Journal* (October 15): 36. lj.libraryjournal.com/2011/10/opinion/michael-stephens/online-lis-education-or -not-office-hours/#_.

Stephens, Michael, and Kyle M. L. Jones. 2014. "MOOCs as LIS Professional Development Platforms: Evaluating and Refining SJSU's First Not-for-Credit MOOC." *Journal of Education for Library and Information Science* 55 (fall): 345–361.

Stoffle, Carla J., and Kim Leeder. 2005. "Practitioners and Library Education: A Crisis of Understanding." *Journal of Education for Library and Information Science* 46 (fall): 312–318.

Swisher, Robert, Rosemary Ruhig DuMont, and Calvin J. Boyer. 1985. "The Motivation to Manage: A Study of Academic Librarians and Library Science Students." *Library Trends* 34 (fall): 219–234.

U.S. Census Bureau. 2012. *Statistical Abstract of the United States: 2012.* www.census.gov/ compendia/statabs/2012/tables/12s0616.pdf.

———. 2014. "State & County QuickFacts." quickfacts.census.gov/qfd/states/00000.html.

U.S. Office of Education. 1876. *Public Libraries in the United States of America: Their History, Condition, and Management: Special Report.* Washington, DC: GPO.

Van Fleet, Connie, and June Lester. 2008. "Is Anyone Listening? Use of Library Competencies Statements in State and Public Libraries." *Public Libraries* (July/ August): 42–53.

Van House, Nancy, and Stuart A. Sutton. 2000. "The Panda Syndrome." *Journal of Education for Library and Information Science* 41 (winter): 52–68.

Vann, Sarah K. 1961. *Training for Librarianship before 1923.* Chicago: ALA.

Vassilakaki, Evgenia and Valentini, Moniarou-Papaconstantinou. 2014. "Identifying the Prevailing Images in Library and Information Science Profession: Is the Landscape Changing?" *New Library World* 115: 355–375.

Wallace, D. 2009. The iSchools, Education for Librarianship, and the Voice of Doom and Gloom. *The Journal of Academic Librarianship* 35, no. 5 (September): 405–409.

Web-Based Information Science Education. 2009. *Strategic Plan.* Syracuse, NY: WISE.

Weibel, Kathleen, and Kathleen M. Heim. 1979. *The Role of Women in Librarianship 1876–1976: The Entry, Advancement, and Struggle for Equalization in One Profession.* Phoenix: Oryx.

White, Ashanti. 2012. *Not Your Ordinary Librarian: Debunking the Popular Perceptions of Librarians.* Oxford: Chandos.

White, Carl M. 1976. *A Historical Introduction to Library Education: Problems and Progress to 1951.* New York: Scarecrow.

White, Herbert S. 1986. "The Future of Library and Information Science Education." *Journal of Education for Library and Information Science* 26 (winter): 174–181.

Wiegand, Wayne A. 1996. *Irrepressible Reformer: A Biography of Melvil Dewey.* Chicago: ALA.

———. 1997. "Out of Sight, Out of Mind: Why Don't We Have Any Schools of Library and Reading Studies?" *Journal of Education for Library and Information Science* 38 (fall): 314–326.

———. 1999. "The Structure of Librarianship: Essay on an Information Profession." *Canadian Journal of Information and Library Science* 24 (April): 17–37.

———. 2001. "Missing the Real Story: Where Library and Information Science Fails the Library Profession." In *The Readers' Advisors' Companion,* edited by Kenneth D. Shearer and Robert Turgin. Englewood, CO: Libraries Unlimited.

———. 2005. "Critiquing the Curriculum." *American Libraries* 36 (January): 60–61.

Wiggins, Andrea, and Steven Sawyer. 2012. "Intellectual Diversity and the Faculty Composition of iSchools." *Journal of the American Society for Information Science and Technology* 63: 8–12.

Wilde, Michelle L., and Annie Epperson. 2006. "A Survey of Alumni of LIS Distance Education Programs: Experiences and Implications." *Journal of Academic Librarianship* 32 (May): 238–250.

Williamson, Charles C. 1923. *Training for Library Service: A Report Prepared for the Carnegie Corporation of New York.* Boston: Updike.

Williamson, J. M., A. E. Pemberton, and J. W. Lounsbury. 2008. "Personality Traits of Individuals in Different Specialties of Librarianship." *Journal of Documentation* 64: 273–286.

Windsor, Justin. 1876. "A Word to Starters of Libraries." *American Library Journal* 1 (September): 1–3.

Winter, Michael F. 1988. The Culture and Control of Expertise: Toward a Sociological Understanding of Librarianship. Westport, CT: Greenwood.

WISE. 2014. "What Is Wise?" www.wiseeducation.org/students/whatiswise.aspx.

Wu, Dan, Daqing He, Jiepu Jiang, Wuyi Dong Kim Thien Yo. 2011. "The State of iSchools: An Analysis of Academic Research and Graduate Education." *Journal of Information Science* 38: 15–36.

Zemon, Mickey, and Alice Harrison Bahr. 2005. "Career and/or Children: Do Female Academic Librarians Pay a Price for Motherhood?" *College and Research Libraries* 66 (September): 394–405.

SELECTED READINGS: The LIS Profession

Books

Abbott, Andrew. *The System of Professions.* Chicago: University of Chicago, 1988.

Bobinski, George S. *Libraries and Librarianship: Sixty Years of Challenge and Change, 1945–2005.* Lanham, MD: Scarecrow, 2007.

Budd, John. *Self-Examination: The Present and Future of Librarianship.* Westport, CT: Libraries Unlimited, 2008.

Crowley, William A. *Renewing Professional Librarianship.* Westport, CT: Libraries Unlimited, 2008.

Greer, Roger C., Robert J. Grover, and Susan G. Fowler. *Introduction to the Library and Information Professions.* 2nd ed. Westport, CT: Libraries Unlimited, 2013.

Harris, Michael H., Stan A. Hannah, and Pamela C. Harris. *Into the Future: The Foundations of Library and Information Services in the Post-industrial Era.* 2nd ed. Greenwich, CT: Ablex, 1998.

Harris, Roma M. *Librarianship: The Erosion of a Woman's Profession.* Norwood, NJ: Ablex, 1992.

Lankes, R. David. *The Atlas of New Librarianship.* Cambridge, MA: MIT, 2011.

Leckie, Gloria, and John E. Buschman, eds. *Information Technology in Librarianship: New Critical Approaches.* Westport, CT: Libraries Unlimited, 2009.

Pagowsky, Nicole, and Miriam E. Rigby. *The Librarian Stereotype: Deconstructing Perceptions and Presentations of Information Work.* Chicago: ALA, 2014.

Vann, Sarah K. *Training for Librarianship before 1923.* Chicago: ALA, 1961.

White, Ashanti. *Not Your Ordinary Librarian: Debunking the Popular Perceptions of Librarians.* Oxford: Chandos, 2012.

Winter, Michael F. *The Culture and Control of Expertise: Toward a Sociological Understanding of Librarianship.* Westport, CT: Greenwood, 1988.

Articles

Adams, Katherine C. "Loveless Frump as Hip and Sexy Party Girl: A Reevaluation of the Old-Maid Stereotype." *Library Quarterly* 70 (July 2000): 287–301.

American Libraries. "Forecasting the Future of Libraries: 2015." *American Libraries* (March/April 2015): 28–45.

Bertot, John Carlo, and Lindsay Sarin. 2015. "The Future of the MLS: Rethinking Library Education." *American Libraries* (March/April): 40–41.

Bonnet, Lennifer L., and Benjamin McAlexander. "Structural Diversity in Academic Libraries: A Study of Librarian Approachability." *The Journal of Academic Librarianship* 38 (September 2012): 277–286.

Cox, Andrew M., and Sheila Corrall. "Evolving Academic Library Specialties." *Journal of the American Society for Information Science and Technology* 64 (2013): 1526–1542.

Cronin, Blaise. "The Sociological Turn in Information Science." *Journal of Information Science* 34 (2008): 465–475.

Crowley, Bill, and Bill Brace. "The Control and Direction of Professional Education." *Journal of the American Society for Information Science* 50 (1999): 1127–1135.

———. "Lifecycle Librarianship." *Library Journal* 133 (April 2008): 46–48.

Danner, Richard A. "Redefining a Profession." *Law Library Journal* 90 (1998): 315–356.

Dawson, Alma. "Celebrating African-American Librarians and Librarianship." *Library Trends* 49 (summer 2000): 40–87.

Dillon, Andrew. "What It Means to be an iSchool." *Journal of Education for Library and Information Science* 53 (October 2012): 267–273.

Dillon, Andrew, and April Norris. "Crying Wolf: An Examination and Reconsideration of the Perception of Crisis in LIS Education." *Journal of Education for Library and Information* 46 (fall 2005): 280–297.

Dowell, David R. 2008. "The 'I' in Libraries." *American Libraries* 39 (January/February 2008): 42.

Franks, Rachel. "Grey Matter: The Aging Librarian Workforce, with a Focus on Public and Academic Libraries in Australia and the United States." *Aplis* 25 (September 2012): 104–110.

Garrison, Dee. "The Tender Technicians: The Feminization of Public Librarianship." *Journal of Social History* 6 (winter 1972–1973): 131–159.

Gorman, Michael. "Whither Library Education?" *New Library World* 105 (2004): 376–380.

Graybill, Jolie O. "Millennials among the Professional Workforce in Academic Libraries: Their Perspective on Leadership." *The Journal of Academic Librarianship* 40 (2014): 10–15.

Helmick, Catherine, and Keith Swigger. "Core Competencies of Library Practitioners." *Public Libraries* 45 (March–April 2006): 54–69.

Jaeger, Paul T., John Carlo Bertot, and Mega Subramaniam. "Preparing Future Librarians to Effectively Serve Their Communities." *The Library Quarterly* 83 (2013): 243–248.

Jordan, Mary Wilkins. "All Stressed Out, But Does Anyone Notice? Stressors Affecting Public Libraries." *Journal of Library Administration* 54 (2014): 291–307.

Keer, Gretchen, and Andrew Carlos. "The Stereotype: Our Obsession with Librarian Representation." In *The Librarian Stereotype: Deconstructing Perceptions and Presentations of Information Work*, edited by Nicole Pagowsky and Miriam E. Rigby. Chicago: ALA, 2014, pp. 63–83.

Kelley, Michael. "Can We Talk About the MLS?" *Library Journal* 138 (May 1, 2013): 8.

Keiser, Barbie. "Professional Development and Continuing Education." *Online* (May–June 2012): 20–27.

Kendall, Joshua. "Melvil Dewey, Compulsive Innovator." *American Library* 45 (March/April 2014): 52–54.

Kim, Kyung-Sun, and Sei-Ching Joanna Sin. "Increasing Ethnic Diversity in LIS: Strategies Suggested by Librarians of Color." *Library Quarterly* 78 (April 2008): 153–177.

King, John Leslie. "Identity in the I-School Movement." *Bulletin of ASIST* 32 (April/May 2006): 13–15.

Latham, Joyce M. "Clergy of the Mind: Alvin S. Johnson, William S. Learned, the Carnegie Corporations, and the American Library Association." *Library Quarterly* 80 (2010): 249–265.

Maack, Mary Niles. "Women in Library Education: Down the Up Staircase." *Library Trends* 34 (winter 1986): 401–432.

Matteson, M. L., S. Chittock, and D. Mease. "In Their Own Words: Stories of Emotional Labor from the Library Workforce." *The Library Quarterly* 85 (2015): 85–105.

Matteson, Miriam L, Elizabeth Schleuter, and Morgan Hidy. Continuing Education in Library Management: Challenges and Opportunities." *Library Management* 34 (2013): 219–235.

Miksa, Francis L. "Library and Information Science: Two Paradigms." In *Conceptions of Library and Information Science: Historical, Empirical and Theoretical Perspectives*, edited by Pertti Vakkari and Blaise Cronin. London: Taylor Graham, 1992, 229–252.

Mulvaney, John Philip, and Dan O'Connor. "The Crux of Our Crisis." *American Libraries* 37 (June/July 2006): 3840.

Mulvaney, Phil, and Dan O'Connor. "Most Likely to Succeed: Opinion: Rethinking How We Rate and Rank MLIS Programs." *Library Journal.* 139: (June 15, 2014): 37.

Munde, Gail. "Considerations for Managing an Increasingly Intergenerational Workforce in Libraries." *Library Trends* 59 (2010): 88–108.

Murray, Adam. "Mind the Gap: Technology, Millennial Leadership and the Cross-Generational Workforce." *The Australian Library Journal* 60 (February 2011): 54–64.

Nardini, Robert F. "A Search for Meaning: American Library Metaphors: 1876–1926." *Library Quarterly* 71 (April 2001): 111–149.

Park, Jung-ran, Caimei Lu, and Linda Marion. "Cataloging Professionals in the Digital Environment: A Content Analysis of Job Descriptions." *Journal of the American Society for Information Science and Technology* 60 (2009): 844–857.

Seavey, Charles A. "The Coming Crisis in Education for Librarianship." *American Libraries* 36 (October 2005): 54–56.

Singer, Paula, and Jeanne Goodrich. "Retaining and Motivating High-Performance Employees." *Public Libraries* 45 (January–February 2006): 58–63.

Stoffle, Carla J., and Kim Leeder. "Practitioners and Library Education: A Crisis of Understanding." *Journal of Education for Library and Information Science* 46 (fall 2005): 312–319.

Van House, Nancy, and Stuart A. Sutton. "The Panda Syndrome." *Journal of Education for Library and Information Science* 41 (winter 2000): 52–68.

Vassilakaki, Evgenia, and Valentini, Moniarou-Papaconstantinou. "Identifying the Prevailing Images in Library and Information Science Profession: Is the Landscape Changing?" *New Library World* 115 (2014): 355–375.

Westbrook Lynn. "I'm Not a Social Worker! An Information Service Model for Working with Patrons in Crisis." *The Library Quarterly* 85 (2015): 6–25.

Wiegand, Wayne. "Dewey Declassified: A Revelatory Look at the 'Irrepressible Reformer.'" *American Libraries* 27 (January 1996): 54–60.

Wiggins, Andrea, and Steven Sawyer. "Intellectual Diversity and the Faculty Composition of iSchools." *Journal of the American Society for Information Science and Technology* 63 (2012): 8–12.

Wu, Dan, Daqing He, Jiepu Jiang, Wuyi Dong, and Kim Thien Yo. "The State of iSchools: An Analysis of Academic Research and Graduate Education." *Journal of Information Science* 38 (2011): 15–36.

6

The Organization
of Knowledge
Techniques and Issues

I. INTRODUCTION

Considering the quantity of information available today, and the inevitable and explosive growth of information in the future, the challenge of organizing all this information and making it accessible is daunting. A library's primary purpose is to acquire, store, organize, preserve, disseminate, or otherwise provide access to materials and information already produced. In this sense, a library is itself a type of information retrieval system, among other things. In the computerized world, the library catalog, indexes, etc. are systems that facilitate retrieval.

Any retrieval system has at least two parts: a database and a system for retrieving the information in the database. Traditionally, a library's database included all of its physical contents: the books, periodicals, audiovisual materials, and other items in the collection. Systems to organize all this content could be simple and straightforward, such as organization by the type of media used to record the information (e.g., print, sound, or image), by type of user (e.g., children, adults, vision impaired), by genre (e.g., westerns, jazz, impressionism), or even by size (e.g., oversize, large print). Obviously, except in the smallest of collections, such general forms of organization will not be sufficient to locate most materials effectively without more subtle ways to distinguish and locate each item within each category. Historically, a primary tool in the library's retrieval system has been the library catalog, governed by a sophisticated classification scheme with both alphabetical and numerical rules. Although sometimes it was difficult to locate information or items using the catalog, what is truly remarkable is that despite the incredible range and diversity of materials in libraries, the correct information or item has often been located in a relatively short period of time. This is due in large part to the intricate systems and techniques developed over hundreds of years to organize and retrieve the content of the library collection.

In the twenty-first century, those traditional systems no longer suffice. The ubiquity of the Internet and highly sophisticated search engines to explore its content has changed everything. The concept of the library's "collection" far exceeds its physical space and the retrieval system includes the hardware, software, rules, policies, and management practices by which content can be accessed over sophisticated computer networks. In fact, the concept of retrieval has been replaced by "discovery systems." Discovery is about finding what is "out there." Today people expect their libraries to make available to them the wealth of the world's information and to find that information with the same ease as searching the Internet in their home or office. They want the library catalog to be as efficient as Google. In sum, today's library users expect their libraries to be a one-stop shop—where all the information they need is found, described, *and* delivered to them, quickly, accurately, and conveniently. The challenges are daunting.

This chapter explores both the traditional modes of organization employed by libraries and some of the new emerging techniques and trends for knowledge organization. A complete discussion of knowledge organization is not practical, nonetheless, seven foundational areas will be explored: (1) traditional library classification systems, (2) controlled vocabularies including thesauri and subject headings such as the LOC Subject Headings, (3) the traditional library catalog including discussion of the Anglo-American Cataloging Rules (AACR2) and RDA, (4) newer developments such as the Functional Requirement for Bibliographic Records (FRBR), (5) indexes, abstracts, and bibliographies, (6) the organization of knowledge within electronic retrieval systems including the coding systems of MARC and MARC21, and (7) the organization of knowledge on the Internet including discussions of the next-generation catalogs, Linked Open Data and the Semantic Web.

In some ways, many of these topics are interdependent. For example, searching on the Internet and searching in traditional catalogs relies on controlled vocabularies to render the searches most efficient, and many aspects of the new search schemes depend in part on the principles behind the MARC format developed over 50 years ago. Nonetheless, each of the seven areas selected requires our attention if we are to understand how knowledge has been organized for many decades and how the changing information environment dictates that we find new ways to organize our rapidly growing knowledge. How well we succeed will determine whether libraries will remain important partners in the information infrastructure.

II. TRADITIONAL CLASSIFICATION SYSTEMS

Retrieval by subject and discipline is fundamental to information access. Subject and discipline are closely related but distinct concepts. In general terms, a subject is what something is about; a discipline is a related body of knowledge that defines a particular approach. Take, for example, the subject of the origin of the human species. A book that examines that subject from a scriptural perspective is placed within the discipline of religion; a book that focuses on physical processes and evolution is placed in the biosciences: same subject, different disciplines. Despite these differences, disciplines and subjects share many similarities when it comes to searching for information. Two tools that provide access to subjects and disciplines are considered here: classification systems and controlled vocabularies.

A. Classification Systems

One of the primary intellectual technologies or organizing principles used by LIS professionals is called classification, "the process of organizing knowledge into some systematic order" (Chan 2007, p. 309). Classification provides "a descriptive and explanatory framework for ideas and a structure of the relationships among the ideas" (Kwasnik 1992, p. 63). Classification schemes attempt to identify knowledge and the interrelationships among knowledge. In this way, one is connected not only to a specific item, but also to other items on the same subject, or items on related subjects. Good classification systems reflect the interconnectedness of ideas; they not only help individuals locate specific material on a shelf but also help them to think about related aspects of their topic. By placing items addressing the same or related subjects in the same physical or digital space, a concept called collocation, people can discover items of similar interest through browsing. Two classification systems dominate in American libraries: Dewey Decimal Classification (DDC) and Library of Congress Classification (LCC). These tools were devised originally to organize books—the traditional medium for information. In more recent times they have been adapted for use with other media. Suffice it to say, these systems are quite complex, and the following discussion is meant only to highlight a few of their major characteristics.

1. Dewey Decimal Classification (DDC)

The most widely used classification system in the world is DDC, which has formed the foundation of knowledge organization in American libraries since 1876, when it

FIGURE 6.1
Dewey Decimal Classification Main Classes

000	Generalities
100	Philosophy and Psychology
200	Religion
300	Social Sciences
400	Language
500	Natural Sciences and Mathematics
600	Technology (Applied Sciences)
700	The Arts
800	Literature (Belle Lettres) and Rhetoric
900	Geography, History, and Auxiliary Disciplines

was first proposed by Melvil Dewey. It is used in 200,000 libraries around the globe and in 95% of all U.S. public and school libraries, a quarter of all college and university libraries, and one-fifth of all special libraries. It is produced in 30 languages and is available in an abridged version for libraries with collections of less than 20,000 titles (OCLC 2004, 2015).

DDC arranges items and collections of items in a logical fashion using Arabic numerals. It divides knowledge into ten main classes representing traditional academic disciplines that were intended to encompass the universe of knowledge. Each class is assigned a specific numerical range. The main classes are shown in figure 6.1.

Each item that falls within the scope of a class is assigned a number within the designated numerical range, called a class number. The internal logic within a main classification is hierarchical: that is, within a main discipline or class there are subclasses or subdivisions, and the subclasses are further subdivided with greater and greater specificity. Each subclass is assigned a range of numbers within the range of the main class. For example, items about the home and family management are classed in the 640s. Items assigned a number in the 641s deal with food and drink, while those dealing with household furnishings are classed in the 645s (Mitchell et al. 1996). The class number becomes longer as the subclass of the discipline becomes more specific. To this end, decimals are used. Hence, the number 795 applies to games of chance, 795.4 to card games, 795.41 to "games in which skill is a major element," and 795.412 to poker (Mitchell et al. 1996, pp. 731–732). The length of the decimal notation can extend many digits, reflecting highly detailed subdivisions of a discipline.

DDC is a remarkable system for organizing both physical and intellectual materials and has served library users for more than a century. Interestingly, although DDC affects the physical location of items, a key feature is that it provides for a relative location rather than a fixed one. Before DDC, books in libraries were numbered based on a specific, fixed physical location. In DDC, the numbers are related not to a particular place, but to other books (Chan 2007). Hence, the physical location of materials can change as long as the books remain in appropriate relation to each other (any shelver shifting books will tell you this). In online library catalogs, the same function remains for locating and exploring library materials in virtual spaces.

This is not to say that DDC is without problems. One major problem is that the system is closed; the range of numbers is limited between 000 and 999, and the disciplines they designate have already been assigned. New disciplines must be accommodated within the existing ten classes, and in many cases this is not easy. Disciplines that were just emerging or unknown a hundred years ago today must be crowded into narrow ranges. For example, the growth of the social sciences in the twentieth century and, more recently, the introduction of computers have necessitated considerable modifications. DDC has been revised many times, and the changes can entail substantial work on the part of library staff. A second problem is that DDC places heavy emphasis on knowledge created and disseminated in European and North American culture, reflecting the nineteenth-century biases from which the system emerged. There has been a concerted effort to remove Christian and Western biases from the system, and the latest edition (the twenty-third) continues this effort. Most other classification systems also share these difficulties.

2. LCC

LCC developed at the turn of the century to deal with the ever-growing collection at the LOC. Other libraries that adopt LCC tend to be academic libraries or research libraries with large collections. Although DDC and other existing classification systems influenced its development, LCC is unique. LCC is an alphanumeric system. Each class number begins with one to three letters followed by one to four integers. Decimals can be used to expand the class. The letters represent the main class and subclass divisions followed by the integers that further subordinate the discipline. Hence a notation that begins with the letter P deals with language and literature, while PT stands for German literature. There are twenty main classes, as shown in figure 6.2, with specific subclasses under the main classes. For example, under class

FIGURE 6.2
Library of Congress Main Classes

A	General Works	L	Education
B	Philosophy, Psychology, Religion	M	Music
C	Auxiliary Sciences of History	N	Fine Arts
D	General and Old World History	P	Language and Literature Tables
E–F	American History	Q	Science
G	Geography, Maps, Anthropology, Recreation	R	Medicine
		S	Agriculture
H	Social Sciences, Economics, Sociology	T	Technology
		U	Military Science
J	Political Science	V	Naval Science
K	Law	Z	Bibliography, Library Science

K (law), there are specific schedules for laws of the United States, Germany, United Kingdom, and Ireland, Latin America, and Canada.

3. Classification and Shelf Arrangement

The manner in which a library physically arranges its collection plays a critical role in the ability of the user to retrieve the desired information and browse related materials. The arrangements must take into account a wide variety of subjects, formats, and uses. Theoretically, a library could assign accurate and highly precise classification numbers to items but arrange the materials on the shelf randomly, ignoring the benefits of the classification system. Such randomness might promote serendipity but it is hardly efficient retrieval. Fortunately, shelf arrangement in libraries is not random and reflects a variety of organizational models, predominately alphabetical, numerical, and disciplinary.

Most library collections begin with the premise that items on the same subject or from the same discipline should be shelved together. Because disciplines are designated by numerical notations (DDC) or alphanumeric notations (LCC), subject proximity is created through the alphabetical/numerical sequences arranged hierarchically from broader to narrower within disciplines or topics. Alphabetical arrangement predominates in fiction collections in public libraries, which are usually arranged in alphabetical order by author's last name and not generally classified by number. It should also be noted that discipline affects the arrangement even when the numbers for the disciplines are not sequential. For example, one might place language materials and literature together (grouping 800s and 400s in Dewey), because users of one are also frequent users of the other. Other models of knowledge organization are usually more general, but certainly quite common. For example, collections might be organized by (1) type of materials (indexes, general reference materials, periodicals), (2) format (videocassettes, audiocassettes, computer software, microforms, print materials), or (3) user (children's, young adult, adult, vision impaired).

B. Controlled Vocabularies

A second crucial technique for knowledge organization is controlled vocabulary. Controlled vocabulary is "a list of terms that have been enumerated explicitly. This list is controlled by and is available from a controlled vocabulary registration authority. All terms in a controlled vocabulary must have an unambiguous, non-redundant definition" (NISO 2005, p. 5). Vocabulary control is "the process of organizing a list of terms (1) to indicate which of two or more synonymous terms is authorized for use, (2) to distinguish between homographs, and (3) to indicate hierarchical and associate relationships among terms in the context of a controlled vocabulary or subject heading list" (NISO 2005, p. 10).

Decisions about which terms will be used to refer to authors, titles, or subjects are referred to as authority control. With authority control, one term is selected for use. The list of accepted terms used in a controlled vocabulary is referred to as an authority list. Authority control extends beyond the words or vocabulary itself; it also includes the rules for assigning terms, methods for describing relationships among terms, and a means for changing and updating terms (Meadows 1992).

Controlled vocabularies are critical, especially when seeking subject-related information, because they provide consistency in the assignment and use of subject terms or headings, as well as name and title terms. Controlled vocabularies, such as lists of subject headings and thesauri, are vital for effective searching and for the collocation function of the library catalog. People use a controlled vocabulary when consulting subject headings in a catalog, when consulting the index terms in a periodicals index, or when searching a computerized bibliographic database. The following are some of the issues addressed by controlled vocabularies:

> **Synonymy:** A variety of terms can mean the same thing. Organizers of informa-
> tion must select and consistently apply the same term so that people can

retrieve information effectively. Those selecting such terms also can c
additional access points by using terms synonymous with the one se
for use, such as "see" references in the catalog. For example, if t
selected is "guns," there might also be a "see firearms" reference

Hierarchical relationships: Controlled vocabularies can reveal wl
identified by a particular term is part of a larger concept or whe
narrowed further, such as references to broader terms or narrov

Associative relationships: Controlled vocabularies help identify r
(concepts) that can broaden and enrich an information searc¹

Homographs: Sometimes terms spelled the same way might represent different
concepts. Controlled vocabularies reveal this ambiguity and refer information seekers to the appropriate terms, such as "China (country)" versus
"china (table setting)."

It is easy to see why controlled vocabularies are important. Consider the problem of
synonymy. Suppose there was no vocabulary control for the subject headings related
to entries on aircraft. Catalogers could choose any number of terms such as aircraft,
airplanes, planes, or flying machines to describe various items on this subject. A
person would then need to look in at least four places in the catalog to find all the
material, if he or she could think of each of these terms. Clearly, if different terms
are assigned to describe the same content in different items, it becomes very difficult
to retrieve those items. Controlled vocabularies reduce error and ambiguity and
guide people to the proper place by showing relationships between terms. For example, when someone consults a given term, the controlled vocabulary might suggest
additional terms that are broader or narrower, or give the equivalent term used by
the controlled vocabulary. Examples of these relationships are discussed further in
the context of the Library of Congress Subject Headings below.

1. Thesauri

A critical tool intended to promote retrieval of information through the use of a
controlled vocabulary is the thesaurus, (not to be confused with the glossary type of
thesaurus such as *Roget's Thesaurus*). A library thesaurus is a "controlled vocabulary
arranged in a known order and structured so that the various relationships among
terms are displayed clearly and identified by standardized relationship indicators"
(NISO 2005, p. 9). Indexers and catalogers use thesauri to determine precisely what
terms to assign as access points to a record or document. Individuals can also refer to
these thesauri to identify the proper terms for searching or to discover related terms

and subjects prior to using indexes, catalogs, and databases. According to NISO, thesauri and other types of controlled vocabularies accomplish five purposes:

> (1) Translation: Provide a means for translating the natural language of authors, indexers, and users into a controlled vocabulary that can be used for indexing and retrieval; (2) Consistency: Promote uniformity in term format and in the assignment of terms; (3) Indication of relationships: Indicate semantic relationships among terms; (4) Label and browse: Provide consistent and clear hierarchies in a navigation system to help users locate desired content objects; (5) Retrieval: Serve as a searching aid in locating content objects. (NISO 2005, p. 11)

Thus thesauri play critical roles in structuring access as well as information retrieval. Thesauri list core index terms, usually single words referred to as descriptors, but sometimes combinations of words, phrases, or names. The list of core terms indicates the preferred terms to represent and provide access to concepts in the catalog, index, or database. In addition, many equivalent, but non-preferred terms are also identified, which will direct a user to the preferred term. These are sometimes referred to as lead-in terms. Lead-in terms are critical because most people trying to gain access to a particular information system are often unaware of the preferred terms. They come with their own vocabulary and ideas about which terms describe the subject matter. The value of the thesaurus is also enriched by suggesting associated concepts and their relationships. Although thesauri have existed for many years, they have become especially important in conjunction with automated information retrieval systems, such as the ERIC Thesaurus and INSPEC Thesaurus.

2. Subject Heading Lists

Subject headings provide another critical access point for finding information. The list of subject headings of greatest importance for American libraries is the Library of Congress Subject Headings (LCSH). LCSH serves as an authoritative source not only for library catalogs but also for many indexes around the world. Among its significant advantages is that they control terms for both the information organizer (e.g., cataloger or indexer) and the information seeker (the user or librarian).

Subject headings have a special relationship to the classification system. As noted earlier, classification puts subjects into the context of disciplines. For example, information on horses can appear in an animal class (zoology), in sports (horse racing), and in pets. Subject headings, in contrast, list subjects outside a disciplinary context, so a search on horses retrieves items about horses regardless of disciplinary context. Subject headings act as a kind of index to the classification scheme. That

FIGURE 6.3
Sample Library of Congress Subject Headings

Life-saving apparatus USE: Lifesaving—Equipment and supplies	**Life sciences—Bibliography** RT: Life sciences literature
Life-saving at fires USE: Lifesaving at fires	**Life sciences—Moral and ethical aspects** USE: Bioethics
Life-saving nets USE: Lifesaving nets	**Life sciences and philosophy** USE: Philosophy and the life sciences
Life-saving stations USE: Lifesaving stations	**Life sciences ethics** USE: Bioethics
Life science engineering USE: Bioengineering	**Life sciences in literature (Not Subd Geog)**
Life science publishing (May Subd Geog) UF: Life sciences literature—Publishing BT: Science publishing NT: Medical publishing	**Lifeboats (May Subd Geog)** [VK1473] UF: Life-boats [Former heading] UF: Surf boats BT: Boats and boating BT: Lifesaving—Equipment and supplies
Life sciences (May Subd Geog) UF: Biosciences UF: Sciences, Life BT: Science NT: Agriculture NT: Biology NT: Immunology NT: Medical sciences NT: Medicine NT: Philosophy and the life sciences	**Lifeboats—Crew members** USE: Lifeboat crew members Lifeboats—Crews USE: Lifeboat crew members **Lifeboats—Motors** BT: Marine engines

is, by identifying a subject through a subject heading, one also discovers the various classification number or numbers assigned to that subject.

The LOC developed LCSH to provide access to its own collections, but it is widely used, in part, because they are one of the few general (nondisciplinary) controlled vocabularies in English. LOC uses these headings in MARC bibliographic records (discussed below), which means that any organization that uses MARC records also benefits from the LCSH.

LCSH is arranged alphabetically (figure 6.3). Among the types of headings used are (1) single noun or term (e.g., Lifeboats), (2) adjective with a noun (e.g., Life-saving stations), (3) prepositional phrases (e.g., Lifesaving at fires), (4) compound or conjunctive phrases (Philosophy and the life sciences), and (5) phrases or sentences (Life sciences in Literature). The headings can also include subheadings by time (e.g., nineteenth century), geography (e.g., France), or form of the item (e.g., dictionary).

The dominance of these subject headings highlights their importance in providing effective and complete access to library collections. As with all controlled vocabularies, LCSH employs a syndetic structure that links related terms as discussed earlier in relation to thesauri. For example, for the subject heading "life sciences" there is a reference to a broader term (BT), "science," and a narrower term (NT), "biology." If someone began a search using "life science engineering," she would learn that there is an equivalent term," bioengineering," which is the preferred LCSH, indicated by the notation (USE). Indexers and catalogers use this structure to provide the helpful "see" and "see also" references in catalogs and indexes.

LCSH is not the only subject headings in common use. Many smaller public libraries, for example, use the Sears List of Subject Headings, whose terms and structure are less complex. On the other end of the spectrum is the highly technical Medical Subject Headings (MeSH) created by the National Library of Medicine for searching Medline, a database of medical materials.

Over the years, critics have expressed concern that some LCSH is inadequate or that it reflects a cultural bias. Sanford Berman (1971) argued for many years that the "LC list can only 'satisfy' parochial, jingoistic Europeans and North Americans, white-hued, at least nominally Christian (and preferably Protestant) in faith . . . and heavily imbued with the transcendent, incomparable glory of Western civilization" (p. ix). Berman repeatedly exposed subject headings that suggested racial or religious prejudices and stereotypes and subsequently, LC modified some headings considered discriminatory (Menchaca 1997). Berman also suggested that many of the headings were too formal and that there were not nearly enough "people helping descriptors" or popular terms. As a consequence, people coming to the catalog with a popular term often could not find that term, and therefore were at a loss to find the desired information. Other criticisms included the complaint that many of the headings had an academic bias that was not helpful in public libraries. Another problem was that some of the headings were outdated, and therefore newer items listed under outdated terms might not be located because the user was searching for the more modern term. More recently, O'Neill and Chan (2003) observed that "LCSH's complex syntax and rules for constructing headings restrict its application by requiring highly skilled personnel and limit the effectiveness of automated authority control" (p. 1). Finally, there is concern that the concept of pre-assigned subject headings restricts the search process, and that keyword searching is a better process.

Despite these criticisms, LCSHs have proved to be an invaluable tool for searching and will likely serve as a foundation for new systems that can provide more flexibility for accessing information on the Internet. To this end, a collaboration involving OCLC, LOC, and the Association for Library Collections and Technical Services of the ALA developed the Faceted Application of Subject Terminology (FAST), a simplified vocabulary based on LCSH. FAST was designed for use in the Web environment and was intended to meet three goals: "it should be simple in structure (easy to assign and use) and easy to maintain; it should provide optimal access points; [and] it should be flexible and interoperable across disciplines and in various knowledge discovery and access environments including the online public access catalog" (O'Neill and Chan 2003, p. 2). FAST retained over two million subject headings in an authority file, but simplified the rules for syntax, so that they can be used by individuals with little training and experience. Hopefully it will provide effective access in the Internet environment.

III. THE TRADITIONAL LIBRARY CATALOG

The library catalog, whether physical cards in a manual catalog or electronic records, is an intellectual technology that represents the knowledge contained in a library in a systematic fashion. A catalog lists all the materials that comprise a library's physical collection. The records are considered surrogates for the physical materials. A catalog that arranges records in one alphabetical file is called a dictionary catalog. Catalogs that have separate subject catalogs are called divided catalogs. Catalogs that arrange their records by classification number are called classified catalogs. While card catalogs might have separate physical files, one electronic catalog can provide even more search options and perform the search far more efficiently. Classification numbers on the cataloging record, combined with the classification number on the material itself, effect retrieval of the materials. The contemporary library catalog also provides access to electronic indexes and other information retrieval tools that expand a library's resources far beyond its own collection.

Charles Ami Cutter was among the earliest and most influential developers to define the purpose of the catalog. He developed what he called the "objects" of the

FIGURE 6.4
Cutter's Objects of the Catalog

Objects

1. To enable a person to find a book which either
   a. the author
   b. the title   }is known
   c. the subject

2. To show what the library has
   d. by a given author
   e. on a given subject
   f. in a given kind of literature

3. To assist in the choice of a book
   g. as to its edition (bibliographically)
   h. as to its character (literary or topical)

catalog in his *Rules for a Dictionary Catalog* (Cutter 1904). As shown in figure 6.4, Cutter's first two items describe the two basic access functions of catalogs: the finding function and the collocation function. The catalog was designed to help locate items and to bring similar identifiers together: "a library catalog should facilitate finding a desired item and should enlighten us about related items by displaying, in one place, all items that share a common characteristic, be it author, title, or subject" (Tillett 1991, p. 150).

These purposes were affirmed in 1961 by IFLA, which included fifty-three countries, at the International Conference on Cataloguing Principles. At the conference, a statement of Principles (or "Paris Principles") was adopted, which established basic principles for access (see figure 6.5).

The goal of a catalog, therefore, is not only to permit individuals to find items that they already know exist, but also to help them find items of which they were previously unaware (Layne 1989, p. 188). Some of the descriptive functions of the catalog include the following:

- to state significant features of an item; to identify an item
- to distinguish one from other items by describing its scope, contents, and bibliographic relation to other items
- to present descriptive data that respond best to the interests of most catalog users

FIGURE 6.5
Functions of the Catalog

2.
Functions of the Catalogue
The catalogue should be an efficient instrument for ascertaining
2.1
whether the library contains a particular book specified by
   a. its author and title, or
   b. if the author is not named in the book, its title alone, or
   c. if the author and title are inappropriate or insufficient for identification, a suitable substitute for the title, and
2.2
   a. which works by a particular author and
   b. which editions of a particular work are in the library

Source: International Federation of Library Associations. 1971. "Statement of Principles: Adopted at the International Conference on Cataloguing Principles, Paris, October 1961." Annotated edition by Eva Verona. London: IFLA, Committee on Cataloguing, p. xiii.

- to provide justification for access points, that is, to make clear to users why they have retrieved an item; for example, to discover that a particular person authored, illustrated, or adapted a particular work (Carlyle 1996)

These descriptive functions provide valuable information about an item and ensure that the item is actually the one sought. This leads naturally to a discussion of a key element of catalogs—the bibliographic record itself.

A. Bibliographic Records (For Print or Machine-Readable Catalogs)

An essential aspect of designing information retrieval systems is creating records that represent the items needed. The content in a record is called the bibliographic description and the entire record is the bibliographic record. Bibliographic records can be found in the library catalog, bibliographies, indexes, and abstracts. Each record consists of a series of data elements (author, title, place and date of publication, subject heading, etc.). Elements created specifically for retrieval are called access points or index terms.

Sometimes the bibliographic record alone can provide the information needed, without the necessity of actually retrieving the object for which it is a surrogate. In this sense the record itself can be seen as part of the body of knowledge to be retrieved. Some bibliographic records contain just a little information, while others might be quite detailed, but their purpose is always the same: to represent and distinguish a unique item. For example, there are many versions of *Alice in Wonderland*. A bibliographic record must provide sufficient information to distinguish one version, or manifestation, from others and yet relate the particular item to the other related items, a concept referred to as bibliographic families. Smiraglia (2001) defined a bibliographic family as "all texts of a work that are derived from a single progenitor" (p. 75). These texts have a "derivative bibliographic relationship" to the original. To illustrate this concept, Smiraglia identified some of the possible manifestations of a novel that include but are not limited to these:

- the first edition of the published novel
- subsequent editions with changes
- translated editions of the first or subsequent editions of the novel
- a screenplay of the novel
- a motion picture

Other manifestations might include radio versions, abridgements, or adaptations including musical works or plays. Smiraglia observed that even the smallest bibliographic families are complex, but the largest families are those most often found in academic research libraries. If information retrieval systems could effectively identify common bibliographic relationships among family members, the results could be used to collocate the family members and increase access to this complexly related group of materials. As Smiraglia and Leazer (1999) pointed out, "The development of direct and explicit control of bibliographic families would greatly enhance the user's ability to navigate the bibliographic universe" (p. 494).

Creating bibliographic records is a complex task, and there is considerable discussion as to how much and what type of information is needed to represent an item. In fact, each surrogate must reflect subtle intellectual distinctions. For example, there is a distinction between a particular book (the physical object) and the "work," which is embodied not only in a particular book but in many books. Hence, the work *Moby Dick* is embodied in many books of the same name, including many editions or translations. Creating a bibliographic record, called descriptive cataloging, requires that the physical and intellectual character of each manifestation of the work are properly described and differentiated. Lubetzky (1985) observed, "A book is not an independent entity but represents a particular edition of a particular work by a particular author" (p. 190).

The creation of bibliographic records is guided by codes that provide standards or rules. Standardization has been occurring on the international level for many years. In 1971, IFLA promulgated the International Standard Bibliographic

Description for Monographs or ISBD(M) (revised in 2002). In the years following, standards were developed for serials, the ISBD(S), printed music, maps, and other non-book materials that identified the key components for bibliographic description, the punctuation, and the preferred order for the components. These standards were incorporated in many other cataloging codes, including the Anglo-American Cataloguing Rules (AACR). IFLA continued standardization activities through its Universal Bibliographic Control (UBC) program. This program went through a variety of changes and restructuring over the years, but the ideal of coordinating bibliographic description and control on an international level remains a priority for IFLA (IFLA 2012).

Similarly, major constituencies involved in the creation of cataloging records are also working to improve bibliographic access. Most notably, in 1992 the LOC, OCLC, and the Research Libraries Group formed the Cooperative Cataloging Council to "facilitate an increase in the number of mutually acceptable bibliographic records available for use by the cooperative community" (Cromwell 1994, p. 415). The cooperative was succeeded by the Program for Cooperative Cataloging (PCC) in 1995 which is administered by the LOC. The mission of the PCC is to focus "on efficiently creating and refining metadata that meet user needs for effective resource discovery" (PCC 2015). Collaboration is occurring in a variety of areas including cooperative work on the bibliographic record, name and subject authority, and serials. The PCC supports activities such as

- developing, adopting, and adapting standards for resource discovery
- providing continuing education and training for metadata creators
- enabling the extension, iterative, enhancement, reuse, and open exchange of metadata
- facilitating the automated generation of metadata
- developing tools and templates for metadata creation
- leveraging emerging technologies, such as linked data
- encouraging work at the network level
- registering controlled vocabularies
- employing technology creatively
- collaborating with scientific and cultural heritage institutions, publishers, and vendors
- partnering with professional organizations in areas of mutual interest (PCC 2015)

Of course, perfect standardization might not be possible, or even desirable, as variations in languages, cultural values, types of users, and purposes of institutions might be sufficiently great to create a need for variation in bibliographic description.

B. Anglo-American Cataloguing Rules (AACR) and Resource Description and Access (RDA)

Anglo-American Cataloguing Rules (AACR) are widely used to create bibliographic descriptions. AACR descend from the rules first proposed by Antonio Panizzi for the British Museum library in 1841. In 1908, the ALA promulgated its own rules for descriptive cataloging and revised them several times. The LOC used its own internal rules for description until the 1960s, when there was a strong interest in developing international standards and in accommodating the use of computers. The first code designed specifically to respond to these needs was AACR1, promulgated in 1967 and developed following the Paris Principles noted earlier. AACR1 included rules for choosing access points for description and for cataloging nonbook materials.

Although the intention was to create international standards, in reality the practices of American, Canadian, and British libraries varied in significant ways (a separate edition was issued for British libraries), and required constant revision and enhancement. This ultimately led an international committee comprising representatives from various national library associations and representatives from Canada, Great Britain, and the United States to undertake a major revision of AACR1 in 1974. The resulting revision was called the Anglo-American Cataloguing Rules, 2nd ed. (AACR2), which incorporated International Standard Book Description (ISBD) standards. AACR2 set the international standard for bibliographic description and continues to be revised.

The growth of the Internet and the ever-increasing diversity of electronic resources challenged the adequacy of AACR2. In 1997, the Joint Steering Committee for Revision of AACR (JSC) sponsored a conference in Toronto to review the underlying principles of AACR2 (JSC 2009). The JSC began work on a new version, AACR3, in 2004 and in April 2005 distributed a first draft of a section. The response to the draft confirmed for the committee a need for a new approach that more closely corresponded to the emerging digital environment. The new approach, Resource Description and Access (RDA), provided a "comprehensive set of guidelines and instructions on resources description and access covering all types of content and media" (RDA 2009). RDA was developed as a cooperative effort of the ALA, the Canadian Library Association, other national libraries, and the Chartered Institute of Library and Information Professionals. RDA provides a framework to describe both analog and digital data, and adapts to database structures and existing online catalogs. It focuses both on the *attributes* of an entity (e.g., author, title, or concept) and *relationships* (e.g., between concepts, people, other works, or places). It was designed originally for libraries and uses the entity model established by FRBR (see below) as its foundation. RDA focuses on resource description only; it does not provide guidelines for subject headings. It is compatible with MARC21 and the Dublin Core (see below).

This large-scale rethinking of AACR2 has not been without controversy. The LOC Working Group on the Future of Bibliographic Control (2008) argued that "the business case for moving to RDA has not been made satisfactorily" (p. 27). Broad-based concerns included potential financial implications, impact on workflow and supporting systems, and the lack of evidence of improved navigation or enhanced description of electronic records. Nonetheless, RDA is being used broadly in many different environments and plays a critical role in the Linked Data Initiative discussed below. Those interested in the critical area of bibliographic control will need to monitor the developments in RDA for years to come.

C. Functional Requirements for Bibliographic Records (FRBR)

Because the complexity of the bibliographic universe increases daily, cataloging practices and applications have been inconsistent. In an attempt to provide a more concise conceptual model, IFLA created a study group in 1992 to establish a common understanding of the aims of the information provided in the bibliographic record. The group developed an "entity relationship" model, the Functional Requirements for Bibliographic Records (FRBR). Although FRBR is not associated with any particular cataloging code, it provides an opportunity for organizers of information to take a new look at cataloging rules and principles (Tillett et al. 2004). FRBR "does not state *how* to structure data elements nor how to display them . . . Instead, FRBR provides an intellectual framework to typify data elements and to show how they are interrelated among distinct records" (Tillett et al. 2008, p. 134). The model is designed to help users, who can be professional organizers of information such as catalogers, consumers, or library patrons, or someone involved in developing bibliographic systems. FRBR is user focused and emphasizes four user tasks: find, identify, select, and obtain (figure 6.6).

FRBR shifts attention away from concerns about cataloging per se toward viewing the catalog as a whole and to its navigational aspects. It also places greater

FIGURE 6.6
FRBR User Tasks

- To *find* entities that correspond to the user's stated search criteria (i.e., to locate either a single entity or a set of entities in a file or database as the result of a search using an attribute or relationship of the entity

- To *identify* an entity (i.e., to confirm that the entity described corresponds to the entity sought or to distinguish between two or more entities with similar characteristics)

- To *select* an entity that is appropriate to the user's needs (i.e., to choose an entity that meets the user's requirement with respect to content, physical format, etc. or to reject an entity as being inappropriate to the user's needs)

- To acquire or *obtain* access to the entity described (i.e., to acquire an entity through purchase, loans, etc. or to access an entity electronically through an online connection to a remote computer

Source: IFLA Study Group, 1998, p. 82.

emphasis on the content of a resource and somewhat less emphasis on the container. Focus is on how the data elements function to assist the user (Riva 2007). In addition, FRBR examines these principles as they apply to three groups. Group 1 comprises the products of creative or artistic endeavors and includes four, often confounded entities: work, expression, manifestation, and item. Tillett et al. (2004) explained how these entities were related:

> When we say "book" to describe a physical object that has paper pages and a binding . . . FRBR calls this an "item." When we say "book" we also might mean a "publication" as when we go to a bookstore to purchase a book. We might know its ISBN but the particular copy does not matter. . . . FRBR calls this a "manifestation." When we say "book" as in "who translated that book," we have a particular text in mind and a specific language. FRBR calls this an "expression." When we say "book" as in "who wrote that book" we could mean a higher level of abstraction, the conceptual content that underlies all of the linguistic versions. . . . FRBR calls this a "work." (pp. 2–3)

Group 2 entities are related to Group 1 entities. They include people or corporate bodies responsible for the creation, production, and distribution of Group 1 entities. Group 3 entities are the subjects of works. According to Tillett et al. (2004), "these can be concepts, objects, events, places, and any of the 'Group 1' or 'Group 2' entities" (p. 3). For example, there can be works about another work or about a person or corporate body. Subjects are related at the level of the work.

For FRBR, the concept of relationships is critical; the more people understand those relationships, the greater chance they have to encounter the entire family of works that will meet their needs. FRBR helps clarify not only the hierarchical relationships among Group 1 entities but also the complex content relationships of works. This family of works lies along a continuum. At one end of the continuum are works that are expressed in the same way, as in a reprint, facsimile edition, or copy. That same work moving along this continuum might be modified in some way to produce a new expression of the work, as in an abridgement, arrangement, revision, or translation. At some point, however, an entirely new work is created based on the original work but transformed into something new—for example, if a novel is turned into a play or movie or is parodied. Works that are very different but still members of the same family reside at the end of the continuum. Examples might be reviews, criticism, or commentaries on a given work. The cataloging rules for how an item is cataloged depend, in part, on where an item fits on this continuum. This conceptual model allows catalogers to place a given expression on this continuum and provides an important tool for consistent decision making in ordering the bibliographic universe.

The potential benefits of FRBR are many: improved searching for staff and users, easier catalog navigation, more effective insertion of data into bibliographic records, and easier copy cataloging and sharing of records. Because FRBR is particularly sensitive to the many manifestations and expressions of a given work, it should be particularly useful for sophisticated collections that possess many different forms of a given work (Salaba and Zhang 2007). Dudley (2006) provided a simple example of how FRBR could be useful:

> A "FRBR-ized" database (one constructed using FRBR concepts) would present results in a more hierarchical manner. For example, a search for Jane Austen . . . might first give us a result with two choices: works *by* Jane Austen or works *about* Jane Austen. A click on the works by Jane Austen would take us to a list of titles, without specifying particular editions. Then, a click on a title would lead us to specific editions of that work. In this example, detailed information about individual publications is hidden or kept back until needed by the searcher.
>
> In the same hypothetical FRBR-ized database, a search for *Pride and Prejudice* might first give us a display that lists the various formats of this Jane Austen work. A click on motion pictures would lead us to a listing of all the motion pictures. And, a click on the 2005 version would result in a list of all various editions and material types (e.g. VHS, DVD) available for last year's motion picture. (pp. 1–2)

FRBF shifts focus away from the bibliographic record as a whole to component pieces of data; once the record is disaggregated, each component is available for search and re-aggregation that greatly increases the opportunity for sharing and novel reuse of the data (Howarth 2012).

FRBR is in the early stages of implementation and considerable room remains for interpretation and improvement. For example, the concept of "entity" has been criticized for its level of abstraction, ambiguity, and applicability (Smiraglia 2012; Peponakis 2012). Nonetheless, a variety of types of materials is currently being subjected to "FRBRization," including artworks, classical texts, fiction, film and video, live performing arts, music, and serials. It is also being applied in a variety of organizational settings including traditional libraries, consortia, digital libraries, institutional repositories, museums, Internet archives, and Web portals (Salaba and Zhang 2007). In addition, functional requirements have also been created for authority data (FRAD) and for subject authority data (FRSAD).

There is also limited evidence that a library catalog based on FRBR might be perceived by users as superior. Zhang and Salaba (2012) compared the attitudes of students after performing a set of entity-related searching tasks using a prototype FRBR catalog and a regular catalog. A large majority of students preferred using the prototype FRBR catalog especially when looking for a specific author or title. A slight majority also preferred it when looking for a generic topic.

Despite growing interest, Zumer (2007) identified a variety of factors that might inhibit broad acceptance of FRBR, including (1) legacy data, which makes transition to a new model difficult, (2) conservative attitudes of librarians, (3) ambiguities of the model including clearly differentiating between works and expressions, (4) absence of the necessary cataloging rules, although they might be developed in the near future, and (5) the fact that only 20% of all works in catalogs have more than one manifestation. Nonetheless, FRBR has "provided a unifying framework and a common terminology for discussion" on cataloging standards (Riva 2007, p. 9). Zumer (2007) summed up the potential of FRBR this way:

> After a relatively slow start, FRBR has recently gained some momentum. To foster further development, we have to emphasize the model's biggest potential: access to distributed bibliographic information in union catalogs and portals. . . . For such portals, FRBR offers meaningful clustering of search results and navigation. The same approach could then be applied to access all cultural information. (p. 29)

IFLA continues to develop this model though its review groups.

IV. BIBLIOGRAPHIES, INDEXES, AND ABSTRACTS

In addition to classification and bibliographic description, there are other knowledge organization tools. These tools not only help identify and locate materials in a library; they also extend retrieval capabilities beyond those of the classified collection or catalog. Among these are bibliographies, indexes, and abstracts, which can come in print, microform, and electronic formats. The effectiveness of these tools relies heavily on their ability to apply many of the intellectual technologies previously described, most notably the principles involved in controlled vocabulary, including the assignment of subject headings or descriptors.

A. Bibliographies

Bibliographies, as lists with the purpose of defining the literature of a particular topic, first appeared in the Renaissance around 1500 (Krummel 1984). A bibliography is usually restricted in some way, such as by subject, form (e.g., periodicals), or coverage (e.g., items published before 1900). There are basically two types of bibliographies: systematic and analytical. Systematic bibliographies generally focus on a particular subject or are designed for a particular purpose. They are sometimes further subdivided into enumerative bibliographies and subject bibliographies. The latter is self-explanatory; it is a bibliography in a particular subject area. Enumerative bibliography is designed to provide an extensive list of items, but not necessarily on a specific subject. A catalog is an enumerative bibliography, as is a national bibliography. Analytical bibliography (also known as descriptive bibliography) is a list of items that carefully focuses on the physical aspects of an item so that historical and comparative analyses can be affected. In such bibliographies, careful attention is paid to the physical characteristics of various editions, and they identify any characteristics of the item that would permit a scholar to place the item in its historical or aesthetic context (Bates 1976). As a rule, bibliographies are intended to lead the user to the sources they identify. Bibliographies centralize bibliographic information: they are another form of collocation. Some, which include a brief note or summary of the contents of each item, are referred to as annotated bibliographies.

B. Indexes

An index is "a systematic guide designed to indicate topics or features of documents in order to facilitate retrieval of documents or parts of documents" (NISO 1997, p. 8). This very broad characterization is especially appropriate for automated indexes, which consist of five components: terms, rules for combining terms, cross-references,

a method for linking headings, and a particular order of headings, or search procedure (NISO 1997). More simply, an index can be viewed as an alphabetized list of
items that direct the searcher to further information. It can point to content within
a given work (e.g., an index in the back of a book) or to items located outside the
work (such as a periodical index). For example, when a searcher uses a book index,
the index term provides the appropriate section or page numbers within the work
where information denoted by the term is provided. Indexes can provide retrieval
information for most types of materials, including books, periodical articles, and
dissertations. Other indexes have features much the same as bibliographies such
as indexes to the periodical literature. . These tools provide bibliographic citations
arranged under various index terms, which might include, but are not limited to,
subject terms, author names, article, or book titles. Some indexes are devoted to a
specific discipline such as art or the social sciences, or be of a general nature indexing popular periodicals. Given the proliferation of journals and published articles
over the years, the periodical indexes, especially those contained in electronic databases, provide an essential pathway for the location of up-to-date material.

There are two major methods of indexing: precoordinate and postcoordinate.
In precoordinate indexing, the indexer organizes all the indexing terms as items are
being indexed. That is, the control over how terms can be combined or how terms
are related to each other is done for the user in advance of using the retrieval system.
(A book index is an exemplar of a precoordinated index). Postcoordinate indexing
allows users to select index terms of their own choosing (within the bounds of the
controlled vocabulary) at the time of searching. This method is most common in
(although not exclusively restricted to) electronic information retrieval systems in
which the searcher selects combinations of search terms and connects them by logical operators, such as the Boolean terms "and," "or," and "not." Obviously, postcoordinate indexing permits great flexibility when using electronic indexes.

C. Abstracts

An abstract is "a brief and objective representation of the contents of a document or
an oral presentation" (NISO 1997, p. 1). Whether prepared by the author or not, it
is a type of surrogate that summarizes the contents of a document so that readers can
determine if the document is appropriate for their purposes. Because of their abbre-
viated character, abstracts can serve many useful purposes. For example, abstracts
allow readers to quickly scan a large body of literature, including material in foreign
languages (Pao 1989). An abstract usually includes a bibliographic citation indicating where the entire text of an item can be located. It can be quite detailed or brief,
but at a minimum it attempts to describe key aspects of the document.

There are two varieties of abstracts: informative and indicative. Informative abstracts represent and summarize the content of all major aspects of the material. Indicative abstracts briefly summarize what the document is about and include results when they are significant. Abstracts, however, are neither critical nor evaluative (Pao 1989). This aspect differentiates an abstract from an annotation or a review. An annotation is a "brief explanation of a document or its contents, usually added as a note to clarify a title" (NISO 1997, p. 1). A review generally provides a more extensive summary of a document including an evaluation and comment.

Tools that arrange abstracts, often by broad classifications or subjects, so that they can be accessed by index terms are especially useful for knowledge location. The tools operate like periodical indexes except that they also contain abstracts, providing the searcher with even more information to help decide if consulting the full text would be helpful. Examples of such tools might be *Psychological Abstracts* or *Library and Information Science Abstracts*.

The intention of bibliographies, abstracts, and indexes is to centralize bibliographic information on materials that might exist in a variety of physical or digital spaces, to arrange that information in a systematic way, and to help users locate the items. As such, they represent important finding tools for both LIS professionals and the library user. However, such tools have their limitations. For example, they often reflect the cultural or theoretical biases of their authors or, because of economic limitations, are not complete. Some tools, notably those published as books, can quickly become outdated, especially in disciplines that change or produce new information rapidly. Few periodical indexes and abstracts are comprehensive; they seldom index all periodicals that might have a relevant article. Hence, some journals might not be indexed or might be only partially indexed. This is not to underestimate the importance of these tools; rather, it highlights the complexity of trying to control and organize large bodies of knowledge. Information professionals must understand that all intellectual technologies and tools have their deficiencies; our confidence should not be placed entirely in any one item.

V. THE ORGANIZATION OF KNOWLEDGE WITHIN ELECTRONIC INFORMATION RETRIEVAL SYSTEMS

Electronic information retrieval systems include a wide variety of tools. The online catalog is one example, as are online databases. Understanding their basic structure is critical, because these systems are integral components of information access in libraries and other information centers and will continue to grow in importance.

A. Records, Fields, and Files

Electronic retrieval systems are in many ways similar to a card catalog; they contain records, stored information concerning a particular item. Each electronic record is divided logically into fields. There is a field for the author, a field for title information, and so on. These fields are subdivided into one or more "subfields" where a specific attribute or characteristic is added. For example, there might be fields for author, title, issue or volume, subject heading or descriptor, an abstract or special comments or notes. A file is a group or collection of records that share common characteristics. Electronic files are referred to as databases, and there are literally thousands of such databases. The way files are arranged within a database is referred to as file organization. Generally, files are stored and organized around a key field such as the record number or the author's name. This results in a linear or sequential file. Files arranged by key field make up the main file but there are many other types of files. Just like in a physical file, the logical organization within an electronic file determines how well the information can be retrieved.

Today's complex and sophisticated databases require more flexible searching capability than just being searchable by a key field. This is certainly true of online catalogs and databases used by LIS professionals. Most file searching is supplemented by the use of inverted files, which serve as indexes to the main file. An inverted file consists of particular fields associated with particular records within the database. For example, if the key field is an author field, the inverted files might contain title words or subject heading terms or descriptors. Searching on any of these terms leads to the identification of items associated with that term. Although there are other ways to organize electronic files such as list chains and clustered files, the inverted file is usually the fundamental organization for information storage and retrieval systems (Bawden and Robinson 2013).

Database designers create the records and fields, but they do not necessarily select the access points by which the information can be retrieved. Although LIS professionals might suggest which fields should be searchable, it is usually the database vendors who determine which fields can be searched and which ones will simply be displayed. In general, it is always desirable to maximize the searchable fields.

B. MARC

One of the most important advances in the creation of electronic records occurred in the mid-1960s at the LOC. Machine-Readable Cataloging was created to standardize bibliographic description in a computerized or online environment. The MARC format was developed initially for cataloging books but there are formats for a wide variety

FIGURE 6.7
Selected MARC Fields

010	LC card number
020	International Standard Book Number
050	Library of Congress Call Number
082	Dewey Decimal Classification Number
100	Personal name main entry
245	Title proper, subtitle, and statement of responsibility
246	Varying form of title
250	Edition statement
260	Publication information
300	Physical description
440	Series
500	General note
505	Contents note
650	Subject heading
700	Personal author added entry

of materials. For example, the organization of knowledge in abstracting and indexing databases can be quite different in terms of the fields available or the type and number of searchable fields. Fortunately, some database producers in related subject areas have agreed to use substantially the same formats. For example, Chemical Abstracts Services (CAS) and Biosciences Information Services (BIOSIS) use standardized record formats. Nonetheless, there is definitely a need for greater standardization.

MARC provided a consistent format within the record labeled to identify what information goes in a particular field. These labels or content designators (tag, indicator, subfield) are represented by three-digit numeric codes that serve as guideposts to assist the cataloger in creating the bibliographic record (see figures 6.7 and 6.8).

The effect of the MARC format cannot be overestimated. MARC made possible the first substantive use of computer technologies for libraries—the centralized preparation of catalog cards—as well as the founding of bibliographic utilities such as OCLC. The impact on collection development and resource sharing has been tremendous.

C. MARC21

MARC21 is the latest version of the MARC format maintained by the LOC and should greatly improve global access and sharing of bibliographic records. In fact,

FIGURE 6.8
Sample MARC Record with Fields

(Abridged without Coding by Author)

The record contains the basic bibliographic information fields (fields 100, 245, 260, and 300) as well as additional fields (e.g., fields 020 (International Standard Book Number), 050 (Library of Congress Call Number), 082 (Dewey Decimal Classification Number), 246 (Varying Form of Title), 500 (General Note), and 650 (Subject Added Entry—Topical Term)).

020	(pbk.)
040	[organization code]$c[organization code]
050	1991
082	$219
100	Terrace, Vincent,1948-
245	Fifty years of television guide to series and pilots, 1937-1988 /Vincent Terrace.
246	50 years of television
260	New York :Cornwall Books,1991.
300	864 p. ;24 cm.
500	Includes index.
650	Television pilot programs United States Catalogs.
650	Television serials United States Catalogs.

Source: www.loc.gov/marc/bibliographic/examples.html. October 2003.

MARC21 is now being used not only in the United States and Canada, but also in Australia, New Zealand, many Latin American countries, the Middle East, and Asian countries, including China (Radebaugh 2003). The British Library adopted MARC21 in June 2004. MARC21 brings together the U.S. and Canadian MARC formats. It also updates MARC to include access to Web pages in library catalogs and makes accommodations for the data created using RDA. There are now fields to add URLs, FTP sites, and other computer addresses. In addition, hypertext links can now be embedded into the bibliographic record so that a link to a website can be accomplished directly from the record. Although some have questioned the applicability of the MARC21 format in the Web environment, others believe it can be used effectively (Radebaugh 2003).

FIGURE 6.9
NISO Standards Relevant to Libraries

Z39.2	Information for Interchange Format
Z39.4	Guidelines for Indexes and Related Information Retrieval Devices
Z39.9	International Standard Serial Numbering
Z39.14	Guidelines for Abstracts
Z39.18	Scientific and Technical Reports—Organization, Elements, and Design
Z39.41	Printed Information on Spines
Z39.48	Permanence of Paper for Publications and Documents in Libraries and Archives
Z39.50	Information Retrieval: Application Service Definition and Protocol Specification
Z39.63	Interlibrary Loan Data Elements
Z39.84	Syntax for the Digital Object Identifier
Z39.85	Dublin Core Metadata Element Set

D. Standardization of Records

With the ever-expanding volume of documents, the need to standardize the format and organization of records has become critical. Considerable help in this direction is provided by the National Information Standards Organization (NISO), which is accredited by the American National Standards Institute (ANSI) to create and maintain technical standards for information organizations and others that exchange data. NISO develops standards only after a considerable process of consultation and participation by the individuals and organizations that would be affected by the standard under development. When NISO believes a consensus has been reached, a standard is issued (although sometimes not all participants agree with a standard, even when it is issued in its final form) (see figure 6.9). Compliance with the standard is voluntary, but the use of standardized formats can be of considerable value, both financial and instrumental.

VI. KNOWLEDGE ON THE INTERNET:
Structure, Organization, and Access

A current and growing problem facing all seekers of knowledge is how to deal with the deluge of information available on the Internet and World Wide Web. The

Internet was developed as a decentralized system with minimal content control or organization and from the perspective of producing and making information widely available. Such a system has great advantages. However, from the perspective of standardization of information organization it offers significant disadvantages. Standardization could make vast amounts of information more accessible. Unfortunately, this standardization is not available on the Web.

A. Standard Generalized Markup Language (SGML)

With the growth of information retrieval through online computer systems and the Web, alternative techniques for describing, organizing, and retrieving electronic documents are being developed. Most notable has been the Standard Generalized Markup Language (SGML), originally developed in 1970 as the Generalized Markup Language (GML) (Gaynor 1996). SGML provides a standardized means to describe various classes of documents and to identify the elements that comprise each class. Classes are characterized by document-type definitions or schemas, which also identify the structure of the document by identifying the necessary and optional elements. Each element for a class is assigned a code number. For example, one class of documents might be poems, and among the elements might be lines, stanzas, couplets, and an author (Gaynor 1996). SGML can describe content as well as structure. For example, it can identify phone numbers, chemical structures, and citations within a document. It also permits the addition of nonbibliographical elements that can provide evaluative and analytical information. Overall, the use of SGML permits a hierarchical structure in which the bibliographical information, analytical information, and the full text itself can be tagged for retrieval. In this environment, retrieval can be very flexible and informative: each element or combination of elements, including whole documents, can be manipulated electronically and retrieved.

The consistent application of SGML in the creation or processing of documents, has substantial implications for effective retrieval not only of individual documents, but of the individual elements. SGML is now accepted as both a national and international standard (ISO 8879). In addition, items in MARC format can be translated into SGML, making the application even broader for library use.

Perhaps the most far-reaching application of SGML has been the development of Hypertext Markup Language (HTML), which has been the fundamental language used to create Web documents. It allows the designer to structure a Web page, display images, and create links to other pages or documents so that individuals can navigate the Web. HTML was described by Miller and Hillman (2002) as the "first layer or first tier" (p. 57) of a three-tiered Web. HTML assigned a simple set of tags to describe a Web document and allowed document sharing based on these tags. The extent of sharing, however, was limited, especially when the document was rich in information.

B. Extensible Markup Language (XML)

A second tier was established through the creation of XML (Extensible Markup Language) files, which allowed a greater degree of document sharing. Approved by the World Wide Web Consortium (W3C) in 1998, XML is a subset of SGML and is compatible with both SGML and HTML. Where HTML focuses on how information is displayed, XML describes the information content of an electronic document. Although it was first conceived for use on the World Wide Web, it can be used for general electronic publication as well. XML

> is not a single, fixed format like HTML, nor is it a replacement for HTML. XML is a meta-language that lets users design their own markup languages to meet specific applications or industry needs. It provides a standard way for describing and exchanging data regardless of its nature, how the sending system stored it, or how the receiving system will use it (Desmarais 2000, p. 10).

A particular advantage of XML documents is that they can be created in one application but used in others without conversion; as such, XML has encouraged open-source solutions and stimulated the development of products that cross operating systems. XML is expected to be widely used and advantageous to help describe and organize Web contents. Indeed, with the development of XML, a new version of HTML, called XHTML, has been developed. XHTML is written in XML and can be viewed on current browsers and also used for XML documents (Lemight and Colburn 2003).

XML, through its linking features, can reveal *that* two or more documents are related to one another, but it cannot describe *how* one document is related to another. The tags used in XML do not have meaning in and of themselves unless linked to the XML schema that defined them. Understanding how objects on the Web are connected or related requires that the system actually understand the meaning within the tags, and by understanding the meaning within the tags, the system goes a long way to understanding the meaning of the Web pages themselves and how their meanings relate.

C. The Semantic Web

Establishing a World Wide Web that allows computers to relate websites on the basis of their meaning, referred to as the Semantic Web, was a fundamental aim of the early Web creators. The Semantic Web "is not a separate Web but an extension of the current one, in which information is given well-defined meaning, better enabling computers and people to work in cooperation" (Berners-Lee et al. 2001, p. 40). The Semantic Web moves beyond the notion of "link to" and builds relationships to richer connections such as "Works for," "is Author of," or "Depends on." The Semantic Web, according to Miller and Swick (2003), "is based on the idea of having data on the Web defined and linked such that it can be used for more effective discovery, automation, integration and reuse across various applications" (p. 11). Currently, meaning is absent except for the basic notion that one page is linked to another. Similarly, the Semantic Web links are designed to be accessed by machines as well as people, and the content accessed includes datasets as well as documents. There is much data being added to the Web that can be of great value if individuals and computers can access and massage it. Library catalogs themselves are datasets for possible access. The Semantic Web makes such access a reality (Coyle 2012).

Creating the tools to develop this semantic relationship is the third layer of the Web, and much of the activity involves the World Wide Web Consortium (W3C). A key component in the development of the Semantic Web is the Resource Description Framework (RDF). RDF is an application of XML used as a standard model for exchanging data on the Web and provides a model for creating metadata (W3C 2014). "In RDF, a document makes assertions that particular things (people, Web pages or whatever) have properties (such as 'is a sister of,' 'is the author of') with certain values (another person, another Web page)" (Berners-Lee et al. 2001, p. 40). In other words, RDF can express general relationships between entities. The basic building block of RDF is a statement that consists of three components (semantic units) a subject, a predicate, and an object. The subject might be J. K. Rowling, the predicate might be "Author of," and the object might be "Harry Potter and the Goblet of Fire." These statements are known as "triples." Each semantic unit has a unique identifier–a Uniform Resource Identifier (URI). Hence each part of the statement, "J. K. Rowling is the author of Harry Potter and the Goblet of Fire" can be disaggregated and re-aggregated with semantic units in other statements in other records. The URIs are critical because they permit each unit to be searched, combined, and recombined by computer.

What is particularly important is that RDF is very amenable to machine processing, compared to other metadata approaches and has been used as part of the

Dublin Core, FRBR, and MARC21 (Kroeger 2013). As Semantic Web research-ers develop the necessary rules and logic to expand the potential of RDF, exciting opportunities to exploit the knowledge represented on the Web are becoming reality.

D. Open Government Data and the Linked Open Data Initiative

1. Open Government Data (OGD)

One of the most exciting developments moving in the direction articulated by the concept of the Semantic Web was the OGD movement. Underlying this initiative was the conviction that as much data as possible should be widely available not just to be accessed but also to be applied and massaged in ways different from the initial purposes of the data. In particular, the basic idea of OGD was "to open up government/public administration data, information and content to both human and machine-readable, non-proprietary formats for reuse by civil society, economy, media and academic as well as by politicians and public administrators" (Bauer and Kaltenböck 2012, p. 10.) In 2007, 30 open government advocates from several nations met in Sebastopol, California, to discuss how government could make elec-tronically stored information available for public use. Led by Carl Malamud and Tim O'Reilly, the conference resulted in eight principles that if implemented, could achieve more open government and public use of government data. The principles (abridged below) were subsequently updated and expanded to ten by the Sunlight Foundation:

> *Completeness:* Datasets released by the government should be as com-plete as possible, reflecting the entirety of what is recorded about a particular subject . . .

> *Primacy:* Datasets released by the government should be primary source data. This includes the original information collected by the government, details on how the data was collected and the original source documents recording the collection of the data. . . . .

> *Timeliness:* Datasets released by the government should be available to the public in a timely fashion. Whenever feasible, information collected by the government should be released as quickly as it is gathered and collected. Priority should be given to data whose utility is time sensitive . . .

> *Ease of Physical and Electronic Access:* Datasets released by the government should be as accessible as possible with accessibility

defined as the ease with which information can be obtained, whether through physical or electronic means. . . .

Machine Readability: . . . Information should be stored in widely used file formats that easily lend themselves to machine processing . . .

Non-discrimination: "Non-discrimination" refers to who can access data and how they must do so. Barriers to use of data can include registration or membership . . . At its broadest, non-discriminatory access to data means that any person can access the data at any time without having to identify him/herself or provide any justification for doing so.

Use of Commonly Owned Standards: Commonly owned (or "open") standards refers to who owns the format in which data is stored . . . Freely available alternative formats often exist by which stored data can be accessed without the need for a software license. Removing this cost makes the data available to a wider pool of potential users.

Licensing: The imposition of "Terms of Service" attribution requirements, restrictions on dissemination and so on acts as barriers to public use of data. Maximal openness includes clearly labeling public information as a work of the government and available without restrictions on use as part of the public domain.

Permanence: The capability of finding information over time is referred to as permanence. Information released by the government online should be sticky: It should be available online in archives in perpetuity . . . For best use by the public, information made available online should remain online, with appropriate version-tracking and archiving over time.

Usage costs: . . . Most government information is collected for governmental purposes, and the existence of user fees has little to no effect on whether the government gathers the data in the first place. Imposing fees for access skews the pool of who is willing (or able) to access information. It also may preclude transformative uses of the data that in turn generates business growth and tax revenues. (Wonderlich 2010)

Added impetus was provided by President Obama who in 2009 issued "The Memorandum on Transparency and Open Government" which bolstered the political clout of the movement.

2. Linked Open Data Initiative (LOD)

To satisfy the goals and principles of open government data or any other type of data, it is not enough simply to publish data on the Web; the data must be structured appropriately and standards established so that the data can be linked. The data, if properly prepared, could not only be used and reused by other individuals and organizations, but it could be "massaged" by other machines. In this sense, the Semantic Web becomes a "Web of Data."

This recognition formed the impetus for the creation of the Linked Open Data initiative (LOD). LOD confronts the fact that historically many creators perceived their databases as data "silos" to be protected and used selectively by experts, and to be administered only by IT professionals (Bauer and Kaltenböck 2012). This protective attitude might have been logical at one time but this perspective is out-of-date today. In addition, because of the techniques used to create those early databases, it was often difficult for others to reuse or reorganize the data and databases in valuable and important ways, what today we would call a "mash-up."

In the LOD, "data is open to any kind of application and this can be achieved if we use open standards . . . to describe metadata" (Bauer and Kaltenböck 2012, p. 22). Mitchell (2013) identified two central concepts that form the foundation of LOD:

> . . . the first being that data published on the Web should connect readily with related information ("linked") and that in doing so should be as accessible to computers as it is to humans ("data"). The second concept . . . is that in order for data to be linked and reused, it must be open and free from legal and copyright restrictions ("open"). (p. 12)

Fortunately, many of the open standards established for the Semantic Web by the World Wide Web Consortium (W3C) comport with and promote this initiative. The implications for a truly open data environment are great. Tim Berners-Lee (2009, 2009a) described what is necessary to link data published on the Web. First, all data items representing any type of object or concept (including documents, people, places, products, events) start with "Http." This is what distinguishes LOD from the hypertext environment that links documents written in HTML only. Second, if an item is retrieved, it comes in a standard format and contains substantive information. Third, the information provided should be more than just facts, but should also identify relationships and these relationships also start with "http." In other words, an information seeker can browse and make further connections.

The LOD initiative is still in its early stages. As more and more individuals and agencies in government, industry, and education publish their data using these protocols, the Web of Data will grow. Linked open data has obvious implications for libraries as well and is discussed below (see Catalog 2.0).

E. Metadata

The information environment grows more complex every year. As the amount, types, and formats of information proliferate it becomes increasingly more difficult to organize and access it. The problem is magnified particularly by the Web. Zeng and Qin (2014) observe that

> Along with the rise of the Internet, Web-based technologies have enabled mass information creation and publication through a low entry barrier platform—anyone who is able to use a text or image editor or capturer is now able to create digital documents or objects and publish them directly on the Web. This has greatly democratized the publication and dissemination of information and has resulted in an exponential increase in the volume and complexities of digital resources . . . the Internet and Web have in many ways, become the new library catalogs, indexing databases, dictionaries, encyclopedias, newspaper, schools, museums, entertainment centers, travel agencies, shopping centers, and many other sources and places we used to *physically* access only. (chp. 1)

This situation presents new challenges for those who want to control this ever-expanding information universe. Metadata is the key to this control. Metadata is sometimes referred to as data about data. More precisely, metadata "is structured information that describes, explains, locates, or otherwise makes it easier to retrieve, use, or manage an information resource" (NISO 2004, p. 1). Metadata can be applied to a single resource, an aggregation of resources, or parts of a single resource. Metadata is everywhere. Metadata does not have to exist in a digital environment. For example the nutrition label on a package of food is metadata (Zeng and Qin 2014).

In a traditional library environment, metadata traditionally focused on describing physical documents: books and journals. For example, metadata on a book might tell us the author name, title, publisher, date of publication, and the subject headings assigned to it. Metadata has always been central aspect of cataloging: subject headings, classification numbers, indexing, and bibliographic description. It was originally designed for human use; machine processing was unknown. Today, because we are in a rich, digital, Web environment, many other parties—database producers, website creators, publishers, vendors, scientific, technical, social science and humanities organizations, software developers, and general or expert Web users—all contribute metadata to the digital content of the Web. This is not to say that librarians have lost any role in metadata creation; their expertise remains important, but they are now only a part of a much larger domain of metadata creators. These other players not only create metadata but can also play a major role in creating the standards and practices for metadata creation.

To some extent, metadata performs functions similar to those provided in a traditional library catalog; they create access points for resources. Metadata facilitates discovery in at least four ways:

- allowing resources to be found by relevant criteria
- identifying resources
- distinguishing dissimilar resources
- giving location information (NISO 2004, p. 1)

But metadata in the digital environment has more than discovery functions; it also attempts to help manage that information. NISO (2004) describes three main types of metadata:

1. *Descriptive metadata* describes a resource for purposes such as discovery and identification. It can include elements such as title, abstract, author, and keywords.
2. *Structural metadata* indicates how compound objects are put together, for example, how pages are ordered to form chapters.
3. *Administrative metadata* provides information to help manage a resource, such as when and how it was created, file type and other technical information, and who can access it. (p. 1)

Descriptive metadata describe "what a digital resource is and what it is about." (Zeng and Quin 2014, chp. 1). Structural metadata might describe the volume or issue number of the resource. Examples of administrative metadata include rights management information identifying a copyright owner, access permission, licensing rules.

When taken as a whole, metadata should be able to perform the following functions (NISO 2004):

- Describe what the resources are and what they are about, and organize them according to controlled criteria.
- Allow resources to be found by relevant criteria, aggregate similar resources, and provide pathways to the location of the desired information.
- Facilitate metadata exchange and enable interoperability.

FIGURE 6.10
The Dublin Core Metadata Element Set

Element name	Definition
Contributor	An entity responsible for making contributions to the resource
Coverage	The spatial or temporal topic of the resource, the spatial applicability of the resource, or the jurisdiction under which the resource is relevant
Creator	An entity primarily responsible for making the resource
Date	A point or period of time associated with an event in the life cycle of the resource
Description	An account of the resource
Format	The file format, physical medium, or dimensions of the resource
Identifier	An unambiguous reference to the resource within a given context
Language	A language of the resource
Publisher	An entity responsible for making the resource available
Relation	A related resource
Rights	Information about rights held in and over the resource
Source	A related resource from which the described resource is derived
Subject	The topic of the resource
Title	A name given to the resource
Type	The nature or genre of the resource

Source: DCMI 2014.

- Provide digital identification and description for archiving and preserving resources.

There is a variety of metadata schemes created for specific purposes. The most prominent and influential exemplar was developed by the Dublin Core Metadata Initiative (DCMI) and is known as the Dublin Core Metadata Element Set (DCMES). The DCMI is a nonprofit corporation whose purpose is to support "shared innovation in metadata design and best practices across a broad range of purposes and business models" (DCMI 2014). The Dublin Core defines a set of elements for resource description in the online environment. (See figure 6.10.)

It is considered a "general purpose" scheme and was developed primarily through the impetus of the LIS community. Their activities promote broad-based, and open international consensus, neutrality, and a cross-disciplinary focus promoting discovery and effective management of resources through metadata on a worldwide basis (DCMI 2014). In fact, the DCMES has been used as a basis for describing resources and promoting discovery around the world, and its elements have been incorporated in many specialized schemes (Zeng and Qin 2014). As a consequence, the DCMI is a major player in promoting interoperabililty among the various schemes. A metadata system with these standardized elements makes it possible for many individuals who lack the expertise of a professional cataloger to describe their digital objects and assign terms that could significantly aid others in accessing them.

A variety of individuals and organizations participate in this initiative, including the LOC, the National Science Foundation, OCLC, the National Center for Supercomputing Applications, the national libraries of Australia and Canada, archives and museums, educational institutions, digital libraries, governmental agencies, networks, publishers, and knowledge managers.

The Dublin Core Metadata elements were formally endorsed as a NISO Standard (Z39.85–2007) and establish the basis for the international standard (ISO 15836:2009). The Dublin Core provides the basic elements for resource description in an electronic environment, as well as for specialized applications and standards for describing particular types of objects. These include, for example, the Content Standards for Digital Geospatial Metadata (CSDGM) for objects such as maps and gazetteers, Categories for the Description of Works of Art (CDWA) for describing art objects, Visual Resources Association (VRA) Core Categories for Visual Resources, and Learning Object Metadata (LOM) for learning objects such as syllabi, lecture notes, simulations, and educational kits.

As digitization becomes commonplace and digital repositories are created, additional standards are being developed. For example, under the sponsorship of the Digital Library Federation with the support of the LOC, an XML schema, the Metadata Encoding and Transmission Standard (METS), was created to encode digital library materials and assist institutions in sharing the digital objects. In 2004, the new standard was registered by NISO. The METS framework allows the incorporation or linking of metadata from different resources in one structure. This means a METS record can package descriptive, administrative, and structural metadata in one XML document. METS can be particularly useful in the context of digital repositories. As LOC noted:

> The Metadata Encoding and Transmission Standard (METS) is a data encoding and transmission specification, expressed in XML, that provides the means to convey the metadata necessary for both the management of digital objects within a repository and the exchange of such objects between repositories (or between repositories and their users). . . . When a repository of digital objects intends to

share metadata about a digital object, or the object itself, with another repository or with a tool meant to render the object, the use of a common data transfer syntax between repositories and between tools greatly improves the facility and efficiency with which the transactions can occur. METS was created and designed to provide a relatively easy format for these kinds of activities during the life-cycle of the digital object. (p. 5)

There are many other common metadata schemes as well covering areas such as learning objects, archival materials, geospatial, and biodiversity data. The selected list of schemes below demonstrates the broad scope of the metadata community (Zeng and Qin 2014):

> Dublin Core Metadata Element Set (DCMES, or DC)
>
> Categories for the Description of Works of ART (CDWA)
>
> Visual Resources Association (VRA) Core Categories (VRA Core)
>
> Learning Object Metadata (LOM)
>
> Encoded Archival Description (EAD)
>
> Metadata Object Description Schema (MODS)
>
> PREMIS: PREservation Metadata Implementation Strategies
>
> Online Information eXchange (ONIX)
>
> Digital Object Identifier (DOI)
>
> The Friend of a Friend (FOAF) (Describes individuals, organizations, etc, and their relationship to others, their experience, other connections.)
>
> MPEG-7 (the standard for description and search of audio and visual content)
>
> Public Broadcasting Metadata Dictionary (PBCore)
>
> Darwin Core (for sharing information about biological diversity)

Although metadata in the digital environment performs many of the same functions as traditional cataloging, the administrative aspects and the ability to navigate directly from the metadata to the resource on the Internet provides additional and important flexibility. The metadata, if created subject to accepted standards, can be machine processed so that computer processes can message the information without human intermediation (Zeng and Qin 2014).

F. Catalog 2.0

The library catalog has a long and distinguished history. The traditional catalog provided access primarily to a library's local collection of mostly print materials (focused heavily on books) or to the mostly print collections of nearby libraries in the region. One used other sources to locate journal articles. Catalogs were always designed to assist users, but they also provided significant administrative and management support for library processes. For example, they served as the basis for cataloging, circulation, serials management, and acquisition activities. Sometimes, these internal functions outweighed the needs of users as evidenced by the many users over the years, both expert and novice, who struggled with the catalog's organization and rules. But library users in the past were a captive audience dependent on library resources and subject to the library's practices and methods of access. The catalog did change and evolve, however incrementally, as needs and technologies changed, one of the more recent changes being the evolution to the online catalog.

But today, catalogs are experiencing a "transformative evolution" (Breeding 2013, p.xi). The library world has changed because the information world has changed. Today's knowledge seekers have a multitude of sources to choose from, and their experience with information seeking has been heavily influenced by powerful search engines that provide easy navigation through vast amounts of digital information. Google provides much more access and flexibility than the library catalog; it provides access to many different formats, electronic and print, from a multitude of sources. It offers results in seconds. It not only identifies and locates the source, but *delivers* the information. Quality and accuracy issues notwithstanding, even academics and researchers appreciate this type of service and often prefer search engines to the library catalog (Calhoun 2013).

These changes have not gone unnoticed by some LIS professionals who have been calling for a next-generation catalog, or Catalog 2.0, that can meet the expectations of twenty-first-century digital natives. This new catalog "decouples" the catalog from its internal management functions and focuses on a "presentation layer facing the users of the library" (Breeding 2013a, p. 37). Catalog 2.0 reconceptualizes the catalog as a single point of entry for all the information, regardless of format, contained within a library as well as the world of information beyond the library's walls. As an entry point, Catalog 2.0 becomes what is referred to as a "discovery layer," "discovery tool," or "discovery system" that gives the knowledge seeker a critical starting point for their search. It transforms the catalog into a user-focused, all-purpose, value-added tool that searches the world of information, discovers desired items, and delivers them to the user. Obviously, to compete with Google, Catalog 2.0 must offer something different. Below are some considerations that might generate added value (Christensen 2013; Calhoun 2013; Breeding 2013a):

> **Guidance:** The traditional catalog operates using an inflexible "exact match paradigm" (Kinstler 2013, pp. 22). The user has to input the search term

or phrase without any error to produce the desired results. Popular search engines, in contrast, are much more tolerant of error and try to minimize user effort. Library users, although they like their independence, also appreciate unobtrusive assistance. Catalog 2.0 might offer suggestions such as search terms or employ autocomplete or spell check to reduce user effort. It might also clarify search queries by asking "Did you mean?" All these functions would improve user-catalog interface.

Enriched Content and Comprehensive Scope: Traditional catalogs are mostly limited to whole items, mostly books in print form. Today's users want access to everything that is available and they want it in one place: both electronic and print materials including books, journals, documents, archival materials, digital images, and access to digital libraries and special collections along with enriched bibliographic content such as tables of contents, excerpts, reviews, abstracts, and annotations. Catalog 2.0 might also link with LIS professionals and other experts who are part of the library or who are partners with the library.

Search Flexibility: There are many ways Catalog 2.0 could provide flexible search options. For example, it could limit searches to certain formats, to electronic items only, or to items only available in the local library. It could offer discovery browsing that encourages serendipity or search for related titles. It could also offer "faceted navigation" that breaks up the search results into categories or clusters such as personal names, subject headings, journal titles, publication dates and ranges, publishers, languages, and formats. The displayed number of results for each category would allow users to narrow their search (Kinstler 2013). This function is currently available with search engines, e-commerce sites, and vendor sites.

Evaluation: Many popular search engines generally use relevance rankings to display the closest matches to the search query. Catalog 2.0 might use circulation data to identify the most popular items among users or include reviews or user comments. Borrowing from Amazon, circulation data could be used to suggest items, "Patrons reading this item, also read . . . ."

Delivery: The catalog has to deliver items in the same way that Google delivers them—in digital format.

User Experience/Presentation: The catalog should have the look and feel of a high-quality search engine; users should enjoy using and looking at the catalog. It should have a user-centered design that encourages repeat use. Important evaluative information such as relevance rankings must be presented in a clear, easily readable format.

End-user Services: Catalog 2.0 should provide users with ways to manipulate the found material such as using bookmarks, the ability to export items to a citation manager, and full text delivery of digital items, albeit within the bounds of licensing requirements.

Access to Hidden Collections: It is a given that next-generation catalogs will reach beyond the walls of the library. However, many libraries also have special collections of their own, sometimes referred to as "hidden collections." These materials might not currently appear in the catalog and can only be accessed locally. Once digitized, however, such materials should be accessible through the local catalog.

The next-generation catalogs will also be mobile. Dempsey observed, "The boundary between mobile and fixed has dissolved into multiple connection points . . ." (2013, p. 182). A mobile catalog "is a view of a library's collection with corresponding services, targeted at customers using mobile devices" (Koster and Heesakkers 2013, p. 65). Because of the expanding number and types of mobile devices, making the catalog accessible to them makes the library accessible anytime and anywhere. Although this type of access tends to reduce the emphasis of the library as a physical space, such ubiquitous access should also generate new users and added support for library services and resources.

The potential of next-generation catalogs cannot be fully realized until the data available in them becomes an integral part of the Web. Currently, most online catalogs remain part of the "deep Web," which means they cannot be reached by outside search engines. They remain, for most part, data silos. Bermes (2013) observed that initiatives like the Semantic Web and LOD

> could empower the catalogue's interoperability way beyond what it is today. They could make library data really open, available, and reusable in a global information space not restricted to libraries and their community. They could make library data really a part of the Web. (p. 118)

In such an environment, the library's access to knowledge outside its walls expands greatly, but it also makes the resources of the library available to others on a global scale. Using the Resource Description Framework and following the guidelines and best practices of the Linked Open Data Initiative, library digital collections, archives and records, insofar as licensing requirements are met, could become accessible on a Web-level network.

G. BIBFRAME

The LOC and other members of the library community quickly recognized the potential of the Linked Open Data model. In May 2011 LOC launched its own Bibliographic Framework Initiative and on November 21, 2012, released a draft document describing a new bibliographic control model for libraries: BIBFRAME. Using W3C's Resource Description Framework (RDF) and encoded in XML, the model was also influenced by the conceptual work of IFLA's FRBR. BIBFRAME is intended as a transition and ultimate replacement of MARC21. It was designed to respond to the needs, expectations, and practices of the worldwide, networked community that seeks information. According to LOC (2012) the purpose of BIB-FRAME was "to re-envision and, in the long run, implement a new bibliographic environment for libraries that makes 'the network' central and makes interconnections commonplace . . . the BIBFRAME model is the library community's formal entry point for becoming part of a much larger Web of data" (pp. 3–4). Consistent with LOD, BIBFRAME emphasizes the exploration of relationships (links); one of BIBFRAME's major objectives is to "leverage and expose relationships between and among entities" (p. 1). These relationships might be other documents, but they might also be people, topics, places, etc. The BIBFRAME model is graphically illustrated in figure 6.11 and consists of four main classes:

Creative work—a resource reflecting a conceptual essence of the cataloging item

Instance—a resource reflecting an individual, material embodiment of the Work

Authority—a resource reflecting key authority concepts that have defined relationships reflected in the Work and the Instance (e.g., Authority Resources include People, Places, Topics, Organizations, etc.)

Annotation—a resource that decorates other BIBFRAME resources with additional information. Examples of such annotations including Library Holdings information, cover art, and reviews. (LOC 2012, p. 8)

The model is in its early stages of testing and is admittedly not complete. Much further discussion and dialog within the library community will be needed. Unfortunately, despite its potential, it is not clear whether BIBFRAME will be fully implemented. Kroeger (2013) identified several reasons, including the fact that MARC21 has been an enduring and deeply entrenched form of bibliographic control for decades and it is closely bound with other accepted cataloging practices such as

FIGURE 6.11
The BIBFRAME Model

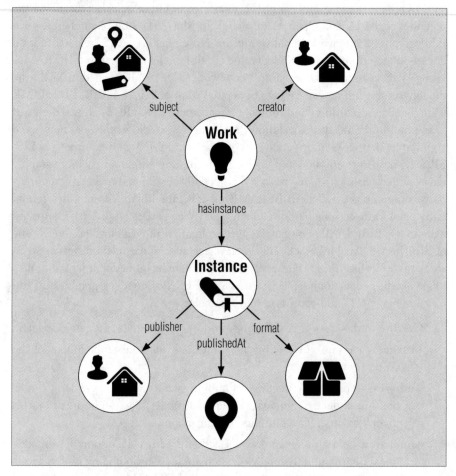

AACR2. In addition, current library systems do not support BIBFRAME, and there is little motivation from vendors to integrate it into their systems unless there is a broad-based library movement to accept BIBFRAME. On the latter point, the influence of the LOC might be considerable. Despite these barriers, BIBFRAME has the potential to expand the reach of library catalogs and the resources contained within them. It is clear that in the networked era there is a critical need for rethinking bibliographic description. If libraries are to be important participants in the Web of Data, BIBFRAME, or some other model will play an important role.

VII. SUMMARY

The information space is now global; information is ubiquitous. Knowledge now arrives as discrete units of data and metadata. The Web dominates access to both popular and academic knowledge. Knowledge is available in many forms and even traditional packages such as books and journals are now available in digital form as e-books and e-journals. What LIS professionals organize today is not only documents and records of documents, but digital objects, including people, events, places, things, and relationships. Many of the traditional means of knowledge organization continue to serve us well when dealing with traditional formats. But as people use the Web to seek information outside these traditional domains, LIS professionals need new means of organizing and accessing information. These new tools will continue to allow access to local holdings while enabling libraries to link with archives, museums, and the global community. Development of these systems thus far has advanced without significant involvement of LIS professionals. Going forward the library community must play a more active role as a full partner with the broader Web community in ensuring quality data, in helping to develop the standards necessary to tame the information chaos, and in promoting open access to that data. These are important values of the LIS community and they help ensure that both traditional and new types of knowledge will be available to all who desire it.

REFERENCES

Bates, Marcia. 1976. "Rigorous Systematic Bibliography." *RQ* 16 (fall): 2–26.

Bauer, Florian, and Martin Kaltenböck. 2012. *Linked Open Data: The Essentials*. Vienna, Austria: edition mono/monochrome.

Bawden, David, and Lyn Robinson. 2013. *Introduction to Information Science*. Chicago: ALA.

Bellanger, Terry. 1977. In *Book Collecting: A Modern Guide*, edited by Jean Peters. New York and London: R. R. Bowker, 97–101.

Berman, Sanford. 1971. *Prejudices and Antipathies: A Tract on the LC Subject Headings Concerning People*. Metuchen, NJ: Scarecrow.

Bermes, Emmanuelle. 2013. "Enabling Your Catalogue for the Semantic Web." In *Catalogue 2.0*, edited by Sally Chambers. Chicago: ALA, pp. 117–142.

Berners-Lee, Tim. 2009. "Linked Data." www.w3rg/Design/Issues/LinkedData.html. Retrieved September 25, 2014.

_____. 2009a "The next Web." Transcript. www.ted.com/talks/tim_berners_lee_on_the _next_Web/transcript?language=en. Retrieved September 25, 2014.

Berners-Lee, Tim, James Hendler, and Ora Lassila. 2001. "The Semantic Web." *Scientific American* 284: 34–43.

Breeding, Marshall. 2013. "Foreward." In *Catalogue 2.0*, edited by Sally Chambers. Chicago: ALA, pp. xi–xiii.

———. 2013a. "Next-Generation Discover: An Overview of the European Scene." In *Catalogue 2.0*, edited by Sally Chambers. Chicago: ALA, pp. 37–64.

Calhoun, Karen. 2013. "Supporting Digital Scholarship: Bibliographic Control, Library Co-operatives and Open Access Repositories." In *Catalogue 2.0*, edited by Sally Chambers. Chicago: ALA, pp. 1–15.

Carlyle, Allyson. 1996. "Descriptive Functions of the Catalog." Unpublished class materials. Kent, OH: Kent State University, SLIS.

Chan, Lois Mai. 2007. "Classification and Categorization." In *Cataloging and Classification: An Introduction*, 3rd ed. Lanham, MD: Scarecrow, 309–319.

Christensen, Anne. 2013. "Next-Generation Catalogues: What Do Users Think?" In *Catalogue 2.0*, edited by Sally Chambers. Chicago: ALA, 1–15.

Coyle, Karen. 2010. *RDA Vocabularies for a Twenty-First Century Data Environment*. *Library Technology Reports* 46, no. 2. Chicago: ALA.

———. 2012. *Linked Data Tools: Connecting on the Web*. *Library Technology Reports* 48, no. 4. Chicago: ALA.

Cromwell, Willy. 1994. "The Core Record: A New Bibliographic Standard." *Library Resources and Technical Services* 38 (October): 415–424.

Cutter, Charles Ami. 1904. *Rules for a Dictionary Catalog*. Washington, DC: GPO, 1904.

Delsey, Tom. 1989. "Standards for Descriptive Cataloguing: Two Perspectives on the Past Twenty Years." In *The Conceptual Foundations of Descriptive Cataloging*, edited by Elaine Svenonius. San Diego: Academic Press, 51–60.

Dempsey, Lorcan. 2013. "Thirteen Ways of Looking at Libraries, Discovery and the Catalogue: Scale, Workflow, Attention." In *Catalogue 2.0*, edited by Sally Chambers. Chicago: ALA, 179–202.

Desmarais, Norman. 2000. *The ABCs of XML: The Librarian's Guide to the eXtensible Markup Language*. Houston: New Technology.

Dublin Core Metadata Initiative. 2014. "About Us." www.dublincore.org/about.

Dudley, Virginia. 2006. "What's All the Fuss about FRBR?" Messenger Extra. Minitex Library Information Network (June 30): 1–3.

Gaynor, Edward. 1996. "From MARC to Markup: SGML and Online Library Systems." *ALCTS Newsletter* 7 (Supplement): A–D.

Howarth, Lynne C. 2012. "FRBR and Linked Data: Connecting FRBR and Linked Data." *Cataloging & Classification Quarterly* 50, 763–776.

IFLA. 2012. "IFLA Professional Statement on Universal Bibliographic Control." www.ifla.org/publications/ifla-professional-statement-on-ubc.

JSC (Joint Steering Committee). 2009. "International Conference on the Principles and Future Development of AACR." www.collectionscanada.gc.ca/jsc/intlconf.html.

Kinstler, Till. 2013. "Making Search Work for the Library User." In *Catalogue 2.0*, edited by Sally Chambers. Chicago: ALA, 17–36.

Koster, Lukas, and Driek Heesakkers. 2013. "The Mobile Library Catalogue." In *Catalogue 2.0*, edited by Sally Chambers. Chicago: ALA, 65–91.

Kroeger, Angela. 2013. "The Road to BIBFRAME: The Evolution of the Idea of Bibliographic Transition into a Post-MARC Future." *Cataloguing & Classification Quarterly* 51: 873–890.

Krummel, D. W. 1984. *Bibliographies: Their Aims and Methods*. New York: Mansell.

Kwasnik, Barbara H. 1992. "The Role of Classification Structures in Reflecting and Building Theory." In *Advances in Classification Research: Proceedings of the 3rd ASIS SIG/CR Classification Research Workshop*, vol. 3. Medford, NJ: Learned Information, 63–81.

Layne, Sara Shatford. 1989. "Integration and the Objectives of the Catalog." In *The Conceptual Foundations of Descriptive Cataloguing*, edited by Elaine Svenious. San Diego: Academic Press, 185–195.

Lemight, Laura, and Rafe Colburn. 2003. *Web Publishing with HTML and XHTML in 21 Days*, 4th ed. Indianapolis: Sams.

LOC. November 21, 2012. *Bibliographic Framework as a Web of Data: Linked Data Model and Supporting Services*. Washington DC: LOC.

Lubetzky, Seymour. 1985. "The Objectives of the Catalog." In *Foundations of Cataloging: A Sourcebook*. Littleton, CO: Libraries Unlimited, 186–191.

Meadows, Charles T. 1992. *Text Information Retrieval Systems*. San Diego: Academic Press.

Menchaca, Deirdre. 1997. "Robert B. Downs Award." http://lists.Webjunction.org/wjlists/publib/1997-February/078039.html.

Miller, Eric, and Diane Hillmann. 2002. "Libraries and the Future of the Semantic Web: RDF, XML, and Alphabet Soup." In *Cataloging the Web: Metadata, AACR, and MARC21: ALCTS Papers on Library Technical Services and Collections*. Edited by Wayne Jones, Judith R. Ahronheim, and Josephine Crawford. Lanham, MD: Scarecrow, 57–64.

Miller, Eric, and Ralph Swick. 2003. "An Overview of W3C Semantic Web Activity." *Bulletin of the American Society of Information Science and Technology* 29 (April–May): 8–11.

Mitchell, Erik T. 2013. *Library Linked Data: Research and Adoption*. ALA: Chicago.

Mitchell, Joan S., et al., eds. 1996. *Dewey Decimal Classification and Relative Index*, 22nd ed. Albany: Forest Press.

NISO (National Information Standards Organization). 1997. "Guidelines for Indexes and Related Information Retrieval Devices" (TR-02–1997). Bethesda, MD: NISO.

———. 2004. *Understanding Metadata*. Bethesda, MD: NISO.

———. 2005. "Guidelines for the Construction, Format, and Management of Monolingual Controlled Vocabularies" (Z39.19–2005). Bethesda, MD: NISO.

OCLC. 2004. "Dewey Services." www.oclc.org/dewey/default.htm.

———. 2015. "Dewey Services." www.oclc.org/dewey/features.en.html.

O'Neill, Edward T., and Lois Mai Chan. 2003. "FAST (Faceted Application of Subject Terminology): A Simplified LCSH-Based Vocabulary." World Library and Information Congress: 69th IFLA General Conference and Council, August 1–9, 2003, Berlin, Germany.

Pao, Miranda. 1989. *Concepts of Information Retrieval*. Englewood, CO: Libraries Unlimited.

PCC (Program for Cooperative Cataloging). February 4, 2015. "Vision, Mission, and Strategic Directions." www.loc.gov/aba/pcc/about/PCC-Strategic-Plan-2015–2017.pdf.

Peponakis, Manolis. 2012. "Conceptualizations of the Cataloging Object: A Critique of Current Perceptions of FRBR Group 1 Entities." *Cataloging & Classification Quarterly* 50 (June): 587–602.

Radebaugh, Jackie. 2003. "MARC Goes Global—and Lite." *American Libraries* 34 (February): 43–44.

RDA. 2009. "RDA: Resource Description and Access." www.rdaonline.org.

Riva, Pat. 2007. "Introducing the Functional Requirements for Bibliographic Records and Related IFLA Developments." *Bulletin of the American Society for Information Science and Technology* 33 (August/September): 7–11.

Salaba, Athena, and Yin Zhang. 2007. "From a Conceptual Model to Application and System Development." *Bulletin of the American Society for Information Science and Technology* 33 (August/September): 17–23.

Smiraglia, Richard P. 2001. *The Nature of "A Work": Implications for the Organization of Knowledge*. Lanham, MD: Scarecrow.

———. 2012. "Be Careful What You Wish For: FRBR, Some Lacunae, A Review." *Cataloging & Classification Quarterly* 50: 360–368.

Smiraglia, Richard P., and Gregory H. Leazer. 1999. "Derivative Bibliographic Relationships: The Work Relationship in a Global Bibliographic Database." *Journal of the American Society for Information Science* 50: 493–504.

Tillett, Barbara B. 1991. "A Taxonomy of Bibliographic Relationships." *Library Resources and Technical Services* 35 (April): 150–158.

Tillett, Barbara B., et al. 2004. *What Is FRBR? A Conceptual Model for the Bibliographic Universe*. Washington, DC: LOC.

———. 2008. *IFLA Cataloging Principles: Steps Towards an International Cataloging Code*. Berlin/Munich: De Gruyter/Saur.

Wonderlich, John. 2010. "Ten Principles for Opening Up Government Information." www.sunlightfoundation.com/policy/documents/ten-open-data-principles.

Zeng, Marcia Lei, and Jian Qin. 2014. *Metadata*, 2nd ed. Chicago: ALA.

Zhang, Yin, and Athena Salaba. 2012. "What Do Users Tell Us about FRBR-Based Catalogs?" *Cataloging & Classification Quarterly* 50: 705–723.

Zumer, Maja. 2007. "FRBR: The End of the Road or a New Beginning?" *Bulletin of the American Society for Information Science and Technology* 33 (August/September): 27–31.

SELECTED READINGS: Intellectual Organization of Libraries
Books/Monographs

Anderson, Richard L., Brian C. O'Connor, and Jodi Kearns. *Doing Things with Information: Beyond Indexing and Abstracting*. Westport, CT: Libraries Unlimited, 2008.

Bauer, Florian, and Martin Kaltenbuck. *Linked Open Data: The Essentials*. Vienna, Austria: edition mono/monochrome, 2012.

Bawden, David, and Lyn Robinson. *Introduction to Information Science*. Chicago: ALA, 2013.

BIBFRAME. www.loc.gov/bibframe/faqs.

Calhoun, Karen, Joanne Cantrell, Peggy Gallagher, and Janet Hawk. *Online Catalogs: What Users and Librarians Want: An OCLC Report*. Dublin, OH: OCLC Online Computer Library Center, 2009.

Chambers, Sally. *Catalog 2.0: The Future of the Library Catalogue*. Chicago: ALA, 2013.

Chan, Lois Mai. *Cataloging and Classification: An Introduction*. Metuchen, NJ: Scarecrow, 2007.

Coyle, Karen. *Linked Data Tools: Connecting on the Web.*" *Library Technology Reports* 48, no. 4. Chicago: ALA, 2012.

———. *Understanding the Semantic Web: Bibliographic Data and Metadata. Library Technology Reports* 46, no. 1. Chicago: ALA, 2010.

Eden, Bradford. *More Innovative Redesign and Reorganization of Library Technical Services*. Westport, CT: Libraries Unlimited, 2009.

El-Sherbini, Magda. *RDA: Strategies for Implementation*. Chicago, ALA, 2013.

Juodrey, Daniel N., Arlene G. Taylor, and Devaid P. Miller. *Introduction to Cataloging and Classification*. Santa Barbara, CA: Libraries Unlimited, 2015.

Kneale, Ruth. *You Don't Look Like a Librarian: Shattering Stereotypes and Creating Positive New Images in the Internet Age*. Medford, NJ: Information Today, 2009.

LOC. *Bibliographic Framework as a Web of Data: Linked Data Model and Supporting Services*. Washington, DC: LOC, 2012.

LOC Working Group on the Future of Bibliographic Control. *On the Record: Report of the Library of Congress Working Group on the Future of Bibliographic Control.* Washington, DC: LOC, 2008.

Marcum, Deanna. "A Bibliographic Framework for the Digital Age." www.loc.gov/bibframe/hews/framework-10320111.html.

Mitchell, Erik T. *Library Linked Data: Research and Adoption.* ALA: Chicago, 2013.

Nagy, Andrew. *Analyzing the Next-Generation Catalog. Library Technology Reports* 47, no. 7. Chicago: ALA, 2011.

Oliver, Chris. *Introducing RDA: A Guide to the Basics.* Chicago, ALA, 2010.

Taylor, Arlene. *Understanding FRBR.* Westport, CT: Libraries Unlimited, 2007.

Taylor, Arlene G., and Daniel N. Joudrey. *The Organization of Information.* 3rd ed. Westport, CT: Libraries Unlimited, 2008.

Tillett, Barbara. *What Is FRBR?* www.loc.gov/cds/downloads/FRBR.PDF.

Van Hooland, Seth, and Ruben Verborgh. *Linked Data for Libraries, Archives and Museum.* Chicago: ALA, 2014.

Weihs, Jean. *Metadata and Its Impact on Libraries.* Westport, CT: Libraries Unlimited, 2005.

Zeng, Marcia Lei, and Jian Qin. *Metadata.* 2nd ed. Chicago: ALA, 2014.

Zhang, Yin, and Athena Salaba. *Implementing FRBR in Libraries: Key Issues and Directions.* New York: Neal-Schuman, 2009.

Articles

Baker, Thomas. "Libraries, Languages of Description, and Linked Data: A Dublin Core Perspective." *Library Hi Tech* 30 (2012): 116–133.

Bermes, Emmanuelle. "Enabling Your Catalogue for the Semantic Web." In *Catalogue 2.0*, edited by Sally Chambers. Chicago: ALA, 2013, pp. 117–142.

Breeding, Marshall. "Next-Generation Discover: an Overview of the European Scene." In *Catalogue 2.0*, edited by Sally Chambers. Chicago: ALA, 2013, pp. 37–64.

Calhoun, Karen. "Supporting Digital Scholarship: Bibliographic Control, Library Co-operatives and Open Access Repositories." In *Catalogue 2.0*, edited by Sally Chambers. Chicago: ALA, 2013, pp. 1–15.

Christensen, Anne. "Next-Generation Catalogues: What Do Users Think?" In *Catalogue 2.0*, edited by Sally Chambers. Chicago: ALA, 2013. pp. 1–15.

Coyle, Karen. *Linked Data Tools: Connecting on the Web. Library Technology Reports* 48, no. 4. Chicago: ALA, 2012.

———. "FRBR, the Domain Model." *Library Technology Reports* (February/March 2010): 20–25.

———. "Understanding Metadata and Its Purpose." *Journal of Academic Librarianship* 31 (2005): 160–163.

Dempsey, Lorcan. "Thirteen Ways of Looking at Libraries, Discovery and the Catalogue: Scale, Workflow, Attention." In *Catalogue 2.0*, edited by Sally Chambers. Chicago: ALA, 2013, pp. 179–202.

Howarth, Lynne C. "FRBR and Linked Data: Connecting FRBR and Linked Data." *Cataloging & Classification Quarterly* 50 (2012) 763–776.

Kinstler, Till. "Making Search Work for the Library User." In *Catalogue 2.0*, edited by Sally Chambers. Chicago: ALA, 2013, pp. 17–36.

Koster, Lukas, and Driek Heesakkers. "The Mobile Library Catalogue." In *Catalogue 2.0*, edited by Sally Chambers. Chicago: ALA, 2013, pp. 65–91.

Kroeger, Angela. "The Road to BIBFRAME: The Evolution of the Idea of Bibliographic Transition into a Post-MARC Future." *Cataloging& Classification Quarterly* 51 (2013): 873–890.

LOC. *Bibliographic Framework as a Web of Data: Linked Data Model and Supporting Services.* Washington DC: LOC, November 21, 2012.

Marcum, Deanna B. "The Library of Congress and Cataloging's Future." *Cataloging & Classification Quarterly* 45 (2008): 3–15.

Moore, Matt. "The Semantic Web: An Introduction for Information Professionals." *The Indexer* 30 (March 2012): 38–43.

Picco, Paola, and Virginia Ortiz Repiso. "The Contribution of FRBR to the Identification of Bibliographic Relationships: The New RDA-Based Ways of Representing Relationships in Catalogs." *Cataloging & Classification Quarterly* 50 (2012): 622–640.

Pisanski, Jan, and Maja Zumer. "User Verification of the FRBR Conceptual Model." *Journal of Documentation* 68 (2012): 582–592.

Smiraglia, Richard P. "Be Careful What You Wish For: FRBR, Some Lacunae, A Review." *Cataloging & Classification Quarterly* 50 (2012): 360–368.

Tennant, Roy. "MARC Must Die!" *Library* Journal 127 (October 15, 2002): 26–28.

Wonderlich, John. "Ten Principles for Opening Up Government Information." 2010. Sunlightfoundation.com/policy/documents/ten-open-data-principles.

Zabel, Diane, and Liz Miller "Resource Description and Access (RDA): An Introduction for Reference Librarians." *Reference and User Services Quarterly* 50 (2011). http://rusa .metapress.com/content/wrg1501514721g7n/fulltext.pdf.

Zhang, Yin, and Athena Salaba. "Critical Issues and Challenges Facing FRBR Research and Practice." *Bulletin of the American Society for Information Science and Technology* 33 (August–September 2007): 30–31.

———. 2012. "What Do Users Tell Us about FRBR-Based Catalogs?" *Cataloging & Classification Quarterly* 50:705–723.

7

Information Science
A Service Perspective

I. INTRODUCTION

Over the centuries, librarians systematically organized knowledge, primarily contained in books. Innovations such as the Dewey Decimal System greatly increased efficiency. However, with the proliferation of scientific and technical information in the twentieth century, often stored in media other than books, came considerable interest in the theoretical and practical aspects of how to organize nonprint information and improve access to the new media. From this need, a new field emerged. Developed first in Europe and known originally as "documentalism," it focused on the creation, organization, and dissemination of information in all formats. Library schools quickly recognized the value of documentalism, and Case Western Reserve University in Ohio and Columbia in New York offered the first two courses in 1950 and 1951 respectively (Taylor 1966). Organizations to promote the field were established, most notably the Federation Internationale de Documentation (FID) and its U.S. counterpart, the American Documentation Institute, which continues today as the American Society for Information Science and Technology (ASIS&T).

The foundation of contemporary information science rests heavily on the development of computers, which increased the capacity to store information without the need for a physical object. Early articles on the potential of computers following World War II predicted great things. Vannevar Bush's (1945) seminal article "As We Might Think," in which he forecast a machine for the storage and retrieval of documents that he dubbed "Memex," was a prominent exemplar of the hopes raised by computerized information technologies. Interestingly, Veith (2006) noted that in today's environment, Memex might look like a combination of the iPod design and a tablet computer. Only five years after Bush's article, the phrase "information retrieval" was first used (Wellisch 1972, p. 161).

Some have described the period 1950–1970 as the "golden age" of information science in the United States (Burke 2007, p. 13). The growth of computers, combined with technology needs stemming from the cold war, an increased number of well-funded applied research projects at large universities, and the resulting need for sophisticated indexing and information retrieval tools provided a fertile ground for the growth and development of the field. Given the broad-based needs of business, government, military, and research demands for information properly organized and stored, the evolution of documentalists (pre–World War II) into information scientists (post–World War II) focusing on indexing and retrieving information was inevitable. One might argue that this period reified the professional identity of information science (Burke 2007).

II. THE CHARACTER OF INFORMATION SCIENCE

Information science (IS) has many definitions, but Taylor (1966, p. 19) captured the essential elements:

> Information Science: The science that investigates the properties and behavior of information, the forces governing the flow of information, and the means of processing information for optimum accessibility and usability. The processes include the origination, dissemination, collection, organization, storage, retrieval, interpretation, and use of information. The field is derived from or related to mathematics, logic, linguistics, psychology, computer technology, operations research, the graphic arts, communications, library science management and some other fields.

Three features of this definition stand out: (1) a focus on the phenomenon of information regardless of the format (e.g., a book, database, or website) or context (e.g., government, business, or personal), (2) attention to the entire information cycle from creation to use, and (3) recognition of the interdisciplinary nature of the field, drawing from scientific, social scientific, and psychological disciples as well as library science. Also notable was what was *not* included in the definition: IS is not institution based. Information science comprises a library without walls; its collection is the entire world of information and the information scientist, a term attributed to Farradane in the early 1950s (Summers et al. 1999), was the agent who acquired, organized, and disseminated that information to help people meet their needs, whether practical, theoretical, religious, or aesthetic. In fact, this purpose can be seen as a defining characteristic of both librarianship and IS. Brittain (1980) observed, "It might be that information science is a different way of looking at many of the problems and tasks that have confronted librarians for many decades" (p. 37). Indeed, IS has sometimes been characterized as deinstitutionalized library science.

Summers et al. (1999) identified three core concerns of information science: "storage (digital libraries); communication (information retrieval and intelligent agent interaction), and use (knowledge management) of information" (p. 1159). For them, IS exhibited traditional scientific, social scientific, and humanistic attributes.

> It is not surprising that information science, which is dependent upon human activities such as writing articles, having information needs, creating search strategies, and making relevance judgments, shows itself to have a mixture of science-like and nonscience-like characteristics. (p. 1156)

On the other hand, Bates (2007) speculated that IS was quite different from the traditional disciplines characterized with the arts and humanities on one end and the social and natural sciences on the other. She suggested that information science might be orthogonal to the conventional disciplines—that is, its concerns cut across them. Orthogonal disciplines focus on a particular social purpose and draw from the various traditional disciplines as needed. Bates identified these orthogonal professions as information disciplines (including information science and librarianship), communication/journalism, and education (see figure 7.1).

In Bates's (2007) characterization, information science was more related to scientific disciplines while library science was associated more with the use and preservation of the cultural record, even though both fields share a concern for recorded information. Bates (1999) identified three "Big Questions" addressed by information science:

1. *The physical question*: What are the features and laws of the recorded-information universe?
2. *The social question*: How do people relate to, seek, and use information?
3. *The design question*: How can access to recorded information be made most rapid and effective? (p. 1048)

The breadth and variety of fields explored by information science are considerable. *Information Science and Technology Abstracts*, for example, lists among the subject areas covered bibliometrics, cataloging, classification, electronic publishing, information management, online information retrieval, printed and electronic

FIGURE 7.1
The Spectrum of the Information Disciplines

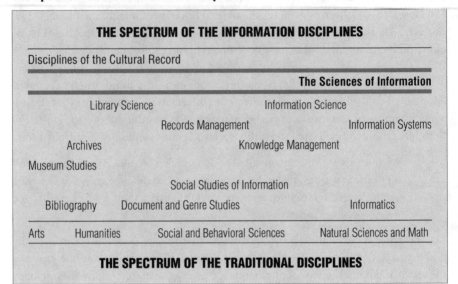

Source: Bates 2007. Reprinted with permission.

information, search engines, scholarly communication, and the information industry (EBSCO 2015). A more detailed list of subfields and contributing disciplines is
found in figure 7.2.

III. DEFINING THE NATURE OF INFORMATION

A. Distinguishing between data, information, and knowledge.

Perhaps the most conspicuous debate in information science deals with distinguishing among three basic constructs: data, information, and knowledge. From time to
time, a fourth construct, wisdom, is added. The discussion that follows provides a
brief overview.

1. Data

Data are the building blocks of information and knowledge. In this sense, data are
numbers, letters, or symbols. Some data are more readily processed by a computer

FIGURE 7.2
Information Science: Subdisciplines and Contributing Fields

Subdisciplines of Information Science	Contributing Fields
• Information technology	• Archival science
• Informatics	• Cognitive science
• Classification	• Commerce
• Bibliometrics	• Communications
• Preservation	• Computer science
• Cultural studies	• Law
• Categorization	• Library science
• Data modeling	• Museology
• Memory	• Management
• Computer storage	• Philosophy
• Intellectual property	• Public policy
• Intellectual freedom	• Social sciences
• Privacy	
• Censorship	

Source: Wikipedia. http://en.wikipedia.org/wiki/outline_of_information_science#Sub-disciplines_of_information_science.

than others. The term often implies that meaning is as yet absent, or unassigned, as in raw data. The numbers stored in a computer file are referred to as a data set. Although the terms *data* and *information* are often used synonymously, a greater understanding can be gained by noting their distinctive characteristics.

2. Information

Information has a very long etymological history. Early senses of the term suggested that information involved a "forming" or "moulding of the mind" (*Oxford English Dictionary* 1989, p. 944). In this early sense, the soul might be "informed." Although not a current usage of the term, it is suggestive of the power of information. The verb form of the term, "the action of informing" or the "communication of the knowledge or 'news' of some fact or occurrence" (*OED*, p. 944) suggests both an active process and the object being communicated. It is the "knowledge communicated concerning some particular fact, subject, or event; that which one is apprised of or told; intelligence, news" (*OED*, p. 944). LIS professionals both inform their users and provide them with information.

In fact, there are numerous definitions of information, many of them highly technical. Summers et al. (1999) noted that information "sometimes seems to be the prototypical 'weasel' word: one, the dictionary tells us, that is intentionally ambiguous or misleading" (p. 1153). Bates (2006) identified eighteen types or forms of information, the most general of which was "the pattern of organization of matter and energy" (p. 1036). Other definitions were highly specific, relating to such things as genetics, expressed information including speech, and recorded information including in durable media.

LIS professionals commonly see information as an aggregation, organization, or classification of data, and perhaps more importantly, as data that has been assigned meaning. This also seems to imply that some type of human understanding and processing has occurred. Somewhat more restrictive definitions hold not only that information must contain meaning, but that the meaning must be previously unknown to the recipient; in other words, it is something new. Some argue that the information must also be true or accurate, or that it must be conveyed from one person to another. One might argue that libraries and information centers hold data that are then processed either by staff or users, creating information.

3. Knowledge (and Wisdom)

Knowledge is defined as a cohesive body of information or information that is integrated into a larger body of knowledge. Knowledge is applied or potentially applicable to some end. From our perspective, one presumes that knowledge as well as information is gained through libraries—that users can gain an understanding of the interrelationship of the information obtained and its applicability to a particular setting. Such a view recognizes the potential of libraries and LIS professionals to help make connections whenever possible so that people can translate information into knowledge.

Wisdom, although not always part of the discussion, is also an important notion. Wisdom can be appreciated as knowledge applied to human ends to benefit the world. In this sense, wisdom is imbued with values. One can apply knowledge to immoral ends, but there is a beneficial end to the application of wisdom. The goal of LIS professionals as agents of an important social institution is to provide the data that becomes information that increases knowledge that results in wisdom to benefit society. In sum, there appears to be a conceptual ladder: data are raw and unprocessed; information is processed data from which meaning arises and is communicated; and knowledge is further processed information that is organized and interrelated and more broadly understood and applied. Wisdom is knowledge applied to the benefit of humanity. Despite the seeming simplicity of this hierarchy, one should accept these distinctions with great caution. For LIS professionals, the question of what constitutes knowledge is very important, because we rely on bodies of knowledge, or knowledgeable works, to perform many of our question-answering functions. That is, although the library and the Web are full of information, when LIS professionals attempt to respond to someone's question, we prefer to use knowledgeable or authoritative works to provide the most dependable responses.

But how does something come to be accepted as knowledge? Wilson (1983) observed that most of the knowledge people acquire does not come from direct experience (firsthand knowledge), but from secondhand knowledge: "We mostly depend on others for ideas, as well as for information about things outside the range of direct experience. . . . Much of what we think about the world is what we have second hand from others" (p. 10). What leads us to infer that one item is more authoritative than another is referred to as cognitive authority. LIS professionals trust those sources they think have greater cognitive authority. Do LIS professionals censor materials, or authors, or publishers they regard as low in cognitive authority, although other groups might not agree? Are there new cognitive authorities on the Web? Can we assess the cognitive authority of a website in the same way we do other publications?

Savolainen (2007) observed that although people were aware of the Web's many credibility issues, it was still seen as a "relatively credible source of information. . . . In particular, factual information was perceived to be equally credible in the Internet and in the printed newspaper" (p. 9). Morville (2005) noted that search engines rank websites based on the number of hits they receive and therefore he cautioned that authority on the Web can be based as much on popularity as other characteristics. The fact is that the Web is redefining what people identify as authoritative. For example, people with a medical condition are likely to visit the Web to learn about their condition, whether they see a doctor or not. In the end, this places greater responsibility on the individual to discern high-quality information and less reliance on a particular authority such as the doctor. As Morville noted, "As we take responsibility for our own decisions, our relationship with authority changes" (p. 163). This presents a dilemma for LIS professionals who, on the one hand, highly value authority, but at the same time recognize that the Web offers many opportunities for helping people find the information they need.

B. The Value of Information and Value-Added Processes

Part of understanding the nature of information is appreciating its value. Over the centuries, attempts to determine its monetary value have increased. With the industrial society evolving into an information-based society, a new concept emerged—that information was a product, a commodity with its own value. Accepting this concept led to the assumption that those people, organizations, and countries that possessed the highest-quality information were more likely to prosper economically, socially, and politically.

Investigations into the economics of information encompass a variety of categories including the costs of information and information services, the effects of information on decision making, the savings from effective information acquisition, the effects of information on productivity sometimes referred to as "downstream productivity," and the benefits of specific agencies (such as corporate, technical, or medical libraries) on the productivity of organizations. Obviously many of these areas overlap, but it is clear that information has taken on a life of its own outside the medium in which it is contained. Information has become a recognized entity to be measured, evaluated, and priced.

LIS professionals are becoming more sophisticated in assigning value to their information services. For example, libraries have been shown to have a positive economic impact on the community generating a return on investment of between $4 and $6 for every dollar spent (Matthews 2013). Although more difficult to measure quantitatively, we know that providing the right information to meet peoples' needs can save time, it can help them more easily accomplish a particular project or activity, it can help solve problems, it can educate them or make them feel better, or simply entertain them. The information provided by LIS professionals helps parents and their children, brings together all segments of a community, and fosters partnerships among other community organizations (Matthews 2013). The library creates this value because LIS professionals structure easy access to the requested information—all these are "value-added" functions.

Much of the early research in value-added functions was conducted by Robert Taylor (1986), who viewed libraries as document-based systems within broader information systems. He identified a variety of value-added functions related to information systems in general and to libraries in particular (figure 7.3).

Although published over 25 years ago, Taylor's work still applies in the digital world; in fact, the discovery systems of today have many of the value-added functionalities he identified. The irony is that because these value-added services make information access so easy, they are frequently taken for granted and often underestimated. If information seekers aren't frustrated or don't struggle to find information, they tend to underestimate the complex design of the system that makes the search so easy. This highlights the need for LIS professionals to enlighten the community regarding the value they bring to managing the wealth of information available.

FIGURE 7.3
Taylor's Value-Added Functions

(Updated by the Author)

Access processes narrow the search for information and include classification systems, indexes, subject headings, and discovery systems. Additional processes reduce larger amounts of information into manageable quantities for summary and review such as abstracts, summaries, and graphs.

Accuracy processes decrease the possibility of error in the data or information provided. These processes include the use of standards, including national and international standards, to ensure consistency, completeness, and accuracy of bibliographic records; the use of high-quality sources to select materials; and weeding processes to remove inaccurate materials.

Browsing processes permit the patron to browse a "neighborhood" of information. Such processes include classification systems that group items of a similar subject or author together and discovery systems that permit browsing. Physical book arrangements can also foster browsing, as do book displays or special exhibitions of materials. These processes also encourage the serendipitous discovery of related information.

Currency processes ensure that the materials and information services are up to date and include weeding and ordering later editions, acquiring new digital resources, using the most recent indexing and abstracting terms, and subject headings that reflect current thinking.

Flexibility (adaptability) processes provide a variety of methods or techniques, adapted to the needs and abilities of users, to help them find reliable information and analyze, interpret, and evaluate it.

Formatting processes affect the physical arrangement and presentation of information, including the effective formatting of electronic records and presentation on discovery systems. They also include signage and graphics to guide patrons to the appropriate information or services.

Interfacing processes provide assistance to the user in understanding and using the system, including navigation and help systems on computers. Most important, they include the librarians who are often essential for interpreting and providing orientation and advice concerning the library's collection and services, both physical and digital.

Ordering processes organize the physical collection by subject area, format, or type of user, and the digital collection through its discovery system.

Physical access processes improve access to library collections or computer databases and include circulation systems, checkout desks, study areas, shelving, and spaces for computer access. They also include offering remote and mobile access to library resources and sources.

IV. INFORMATION STORAGE AND RETRIEVAL

Research into information retrieval systems in the 1960s constituted the "first flowering of information science as a science" (Rayward 1983, p. 353). Harter (1986) defined an information retrieval system as "a device interposed between a potential end-user of an information collection and the information collection itself. From a service perspective, the purpose of an information storage and retrieval system is to capture wanted items and filter out unwanted items from the information collection" (p. 2). This definition highlights a central concept of information retrieval: relevance. There are at least two aspects of relevance: relevance to the user and relevance to the topic. In the former, the user defines the context for relevance; an item is relevant if the user believes it helps meet the information need. In the latter case, an item is relevant if it is about the subject regardless of a given user (Pao 1989). Relevance is a critical variable in much of the evaluation of information systems. Effective systems retrieve relevant items and avoid irrelevant items, also called false hits or false drops.

A. Precision, Recall and Relevance

By what criteria should information retrieval systems be evaluated? Two frequently used measures are recall and precision defined as the following:

> **Recall**: Total number of relevant documents retrieved divided by the total number of relevant documents in the file.

> **Precision**: Total number of relevant documents divided by the total number of documents retrieved.

Within any given system, it is critical to know if all the available items relevant to a particular search were found; the degree of success is a measure of recall. With poor recall, items that might have been useful were not located. On the other hand, it is also important to weed irrelevant items from relevant ones. This weeding is difficult and time consuming if the searcher has to read through all of the items to identify the useful information. The degree to which a system finds *only* relevant items is a measure of precision. These quantitative measures have been criticized by some as too limiting. Froehlich (1994) observed that relevance judgments are made dynamically and often involve multiple criteria, not just one. More recent approaches to evaluation place greater emphasis on a searcher's knowledge, cognitive process, and the problem to be solved.

B. Searching Tools

Information storage and retrieval systems are not useful unless information can be quickly and effectively retrieved. The search approach can make a big difference. Since the development of electronic databases, the search strategy most often used in library settings was Boolean logic which combined search terms with various operators such as "and," or," or "not." Multiple terms could be used simultaneously, permitting highly flexible search strategies, compared to manual searches. Other operators could be used to limit searches by author, title, year of publication, or a range of years, journal title, and article type (feature articles, reviews). Sometimes the search process was enhanced by guidance the system itself might provide such as suggested terms, error correction (e.g., spelling correction), or identification of the most popularly searched items. Some search systems employed text mining and displayed patterns in the texts retrieved or displayed retrieved information sorted into categories such as dates of publication, types of articles, or sub-topics. With the rise of powerful Internet search engines, the searching became much more flexible as the search engines did not require exact matches with predetermined terms. Without qualifiers or limiting terms, however, the retrieved materials could number in the millions. The search engines today attempt to sort and rank by the most probable matches.

C. Database and File Structure

Davis and Shaw (2011) defined a database as "a collection of data that is stored to facilitate addition, updates, deleting, and access (p. 101). Stephens (2009) identified four basic functions that a database must satisfy using the mnemonic CRUD: create, read, update, and delete. Databases can be structured in many ways. Four of the more common types are listed below:

Flat files: These files contain text only. They have no special features and they don't provide any support for searching them. These files store simple data that are not often altered.

Relational: These are the most common databases searched in libraries because they can provide answers for complicated queries. They permit searching based on specific criteria (Davis and Shaw 2011).

Spreadsheets: LIS professionals also frequently use spreadsheets. Rows and columns of data are displayed and users can massage the data using formulas and other analytical tools. Updating is expected and generally easy to do. When new data is entered the entire spreadsheet is updated to reflect the new values entered. Unlike relationship databases, the database can respond only to simple queries. In addition, due to the high probability of input errors, the output might be less reliable.

Object-Relational: These databases are relational but with extra features. In object-oriented databases "data is stored as objects" (Davis and Shaw 2011, p. 101). This type of storage simplifies the search process and enhances the searches based on complex queries.

The database structure determines the types of information (numerical, textual, video, audio) available. It determines the nature of the vocabulary (highly restricted or relatively open) that must be used in the search process. It identifies the fields and subfields that can be searched—author, title or keyword, or subject. It also directs what can be retrieved—abstracts, full text, or images—and can restrict the search by date, language, or publisher. In short, database design, the structure of the information, and how it is presented, significantly affect the ability to retrieve information.

D. Human-Computer Interaction (HCI)

Many information-seeking activities today involve the use of computers. LIS professionals must make every effort to make people's interactions with computers comfortable and efficient. To accomplish these ends, designers of information retrieval systems must understand how people use computers and how they search for information.

Human-Computer Interaction (HCI) is the field within information science that specifically focuses on the point of contact between people and computers. HCI is "a discipline concerned with the study, design, construction and implementation of human-centric interactive computer systems" (Webopedia 2014). The field is interdisciplinary and incorporates knowledge and research from computer science, sociology and anthropology, ergonomics, psychology, and linguistics. In fact, there are numerous specialties with HCI, each within its own focus:

> HCI is a very broad discipline that encompasses different specialties with different concerns regarding computer development: computer science is concerned with the application design and engineering of the human interfaces; sociology and anthropology are concerned with the interactions between technology, work and organization and the way that human systems and technical systems mutually adapt to each other; ergonomics is concerned with the safety of computer systems

and the safe limits of human cognition and sensation; psychology is concerned with the cognitive processes of humans and the behavior of users; linguistics is concerned with the development of human and machine languages and the relationship between the two. (Webopedia 2014)

Historically, HCI developed during the period when people used individual computers with CRTs. During that time many devices and developments arose from HCI research, including the mouse, windows, the desktop metaphor, and point-and-click functionality (Hewett et al. 2009). Studies examined screen display features such as color, speed of response, interactive functions such as commands and menus, post-processing functions such as downloading, help systems and messages, graphics capabilities, training time required, user satisfaction, and error rates (Shaw 1991). Other research studied font type and size, screen brightness, screen layout, spatial arrangement, organization of text, and graphic organization (Chalmers 2003). Some of these areas remain pertinent, but they are now redefined in terms of the dramatically evolved technologies of the Internet, networks, databases, and digital libraries. HCI activities today are shaped by many of the following developments (Hewett et al. 2009):

The widespread use of computers. As noted elsewhere, a large percentage of the U.S. population, including young people, own or have access to computers of one type or another. HCI must take into account the vast heterogeneity of these users from a variety of perspectives including demographic characteristics, sociological, economic, psychological, and physical abilities.

The heterogeneity of devices. Life was simpler when a personal computer was the only device people were using to find information. Today, personal computers, laptops, tablets, cell phones, and other mobile devices each present their own HCI challenges.

Widespread access to the Internet. The Internet is filled with a variety of content: print, sound, visual/graphic, streaming, alpha and numeric, and interactive. HCI must address each of these.

The growth of group activities. The traditional model of computer use was one person seeking information from a particular source or sources. Today, social networking and groupware permit hundreds or even thousands of people to engage in personal and professional interactions, meetings, e-conferences, e-projects, and gaming. In addition, online education offers tremendous opportunities for classroom education and training of millions of people (e.g., MOOCs), but it also presents a variety of HCI problems to create an interface and online environment conducive to effective teaching and learning.

Demand for flexibility. In the self-service world of search engines, people expect their technologies to be responsive to their particular wants and needs. The world of applications, "apps," has grown to meet this demand. Each app has its own HCI challenges, and with the ever-growing number of mobile devices with different platforms and screen sizes, HCI professionals must adequately address each issue for all the intended devices.

Networked communications and "the cloud." Interfaces are no longer confined to the screen design and functionality of an individual computer. They are part of an increasingly networked and distributed computing world that is itself continuing to evolve. HCI must concern itself with how people interact in these new environments.

The rise of effective natural language processing (NLP). The goal of NLP is to create user interfaces that allow people to search using their natural language. In other words, using NLP, a person should be able to query the system in the same way they might ask a reference librarian a face-to-face question. This is no small task. Lee and Olsgaard (1989) identified several major challenges for NLP:

Speech recognition: A computer needs a voice-recognition system that allows it to hear and understand a question.

Command recognition: A computer should be able to understand the command without use of an artificial language or vocabulary.

Content analysis and representation: To respond to a question, a computer must first interpret the question's meaning, which requires understanding its context. Given the subtleties and ambiguities of language, content analysis represents a major challenge.

System interaction: The system has to be able to take the natural language query and relate it to the database so that correct information can be retrieved.

For many, NLP was a *Star Trek* dream. Yet, today we "Ask Google" or "Ask Siri." This is not to say that NLP has been perfected, but HCI activities in this area have made tremendous progress and there will be continued focus in the years ahead.

Much attention in HCI is focused specifically on humans' interaction with the Internet. There are many reasons for this, including the popularity and ubiquity of Internet access, the impact of Internet use for major social functions such as business and education, the rapid evolution of the Internet requiring careful attention to changes, and the relative ease of developing a Web presence enabling websites to proliferate easily and rapidly (Ashman et al. 2012). There are many challenges to website use that are subjects for HCI. Among them are difficulties in browsing and linking on the Web (e.g., broken links, large numbers of sites retrieved), difficulty in effective searching and querying (e.g., uncertain information needs or difficulties expressing the need), and challenges to effective navigation of the Web (e.g., wasted time performing unhelpful searching strategies) (Ashman et al. 2012).

Despite the complexity and challenges these various issues present, and the distinctive perspectives taken by each HCI specialty, their common purpose is to integrate their findings to create a unified, positive, and beneficial experience for the information seeker. HCI is an important and necessary discipline that only increases in significance as most of the affairs of daily life are integrated into networks. LIS professionals need to be conversant with HCI developments and participate in HCI research and applications whenever possible.

V. BIBLIOMETRICS AND CITATION ANALYSIS

A. Bibliometrics

Wallace (1989) defined bibliometrics as "the application of quantitative methods to the study of information resources" (p. 10). The field explores patterns in the production of knowledge as well as its use. Bibliometric studies provide a broader understanding of entire disciplines, revealing which authors are most productive or which countries or languages produce greater amounts of material. Sometimes these studies reveal consistent patterns to the extent that bibliometric laws can be established. One of the most common of these is Lotka's law, named after Alfred Lotka (1926), who observed that there are a few authors who contribute a large number of publications, a larger number of authors who contribute smaller numbers of publications, and many authors who contribute a few or only one. He expressed this relationship as $1/n^2$, where n is the number of contributions. Hence, the number of authors making three contributions in a field would be one-ninth ($1/3^2$) of the total number of authors. The number of authors making four contributions would be one-sixteenth ($1/4^2$). Lotka's law is not a perfect description of how authors and publications are related within a discipline, but generally it is a good estimate.

Another frequently mentioned bibliometric law is Bradford's law or the Bradford distribution, based on the work of Samuel Bradford (1934). Bradford's law deals with the concept of scatter, which describes in a quantitative manner how articles within a particular field are distributed among periodical titles. Bradford found that given a body of journal literature in a particular area (such as engineering), the distribution throughout the various journals is not even, nor is the literature consulted equally. Although the distribution is not even, it is predictable. Most notably, he found that the spread of journal articles could be placed into three zones. The first zone was the nucleus of the field in which most articles appeared, generally in a relatively small number of journal titles. A second zone contained the same number of articles spread out in a substantially larger number of journals. The third zone contained the same number of articles but scattered among even more titles. This relationship was expressed as $1{:}n{:}n^2$. That is, if there were a total of 1,500 articles, the first 500 might be found in 10 journals (Zone 1); the next 500 might be found in 50 journals (Zone 2). This produced a ratio of Zone 1 to Zone 2 of 1:5. The next 500 articles should therefore be of a ratio of 1:25. This means that Bradford's law would predict that the 500 articles of Zone 3 would be scattered among (10×25) or 250 journal titles. This regularity suggests a predictable scatter. Therefore, in selecting materials for library collections, the crucial selections would be those found in the nucleus, or Zone 1. As with Lotka's law, Bradford's law has its exceptions, but nonetheless, it holds for many disciplines and represents an important bibliometric contribution to the field.

LIS professionals use bibliometrics to study a variety of issues in libraries including, but not limited to, the following:

Analysis of circulation patterns: Studies of which items circulate or fail to circulate provide valuable information for future purchases or reveal deficiencies in the library's organization or practices.

Studies of in-house use: How materials are used inside libraries provides valuable insights into people's information-seeking behavior and the use of reference materials.

Aging studies: Review of the obsolescence (aging) of library materials can reveal the currency of library collections and how people use older materials.

Collection overlap: Studies comparing the collections of two or more libraries can reveal duplications and help in planning cooperative collection development, reveal unique features of different library collections, and reduce unnecessary expenditures for materials.

B. Citation Analysis

A related area of bibliometrics is citation analysis, which deals with the frequency and pattern of citations in articles and books. Citations can be analyzed various ways: direct citation, bibliographic coupling, and co-citation. Direct citation analyzes the items cited by authors. Bibliographic coupling and co-citation are closely related but distinct concepts:

> Two documents are bibliographically coupled if their reference lists share one or more of the same cited documents. Two documents are co-cited when they are jointly cited in one or more subsequently published documents. Thus in co-citation earlier documents become linked because they are later cited together; in bibliographic coupling later documents become linked because they cite the same earlier documents. The difference is that bibliographic coupling is an association intrinsic to the documents (static) while co-citation is a linkage extrinsic to the documents, and one that is valid only so long as they continue to be co-cited (dynamic). (Smith 1981, p. 85)

Citation studies can identify which works and authors are most often cited within a given discipline and why items are cited. This tool can be very useful in libraries for collection development or selection because it helps identify influential works or authors who are likely to be requested. Citation analysis can also help explain which ideas and thinkers influence conceptual development within a discipline or which disciplines appear to be active and whose work is playing a central role.

VI. THE IMPACT OF INFORMATION SCIENCE IN LIBRARIES

As noted above, information science and librarianship have similar, complementary interests. The following discussion examines some of significant findings in information science research that informs practice in libraries.

A. Understanding Information Behavior: Information Needs and Information Seeking

Information behavior is a concept that encompasses a wide range of activities related to how people interact with information. Case (2012) defined it in the following way:

> Information Behavior . . . encompasses information seeking as well as the totality of other *unintentional* or *passive* behaviors (such as glimpsing or encountering information), as well as purposive behaviors that do not involve seeking, such as actively *avoiding* information. (p. 5)

Approaches to studying information behavior vary considerably. Case (2012) identified three broad approaches as common: studies by occupation, by social role, and by demographics. Many different occupations have been studied, including scientists and engineers, social scientists, humanities scholars, health-care providers (physicians and nurses), managers, journalists, lawyers, and farmers. In terms of social role, studies have been conducted on citizens/voters, consumers, hobbyists, patients, and students. Among the demographic groups were studies by age, race and ethnicity, and socioeconomic status (Case 2012).

1. Information Needs

The concept of an information need can be understood generally as an uncertainty that arises in an individual and which that person believes can be satisfied by information (Krikelas 1983). Case (2012) described an information need as "a recognition that your knowledge is inadequate to satisfy a goal that you have" (p. 5). But the concept can also be separated into information wants (or desires) and information needs. An information want is a desire for information to satisfy an uncertainty; an information need is the condition, whether recognized by an individual or not, in which information is required to resolve a problem. Such a distinction is especially important for LIS professionals if they intend to satisfy individuals' wants and needs. Merely answering someone's question might not be enough; the individual might want a particular piece of information, only to discover that something different is needed. If LIS professionals are to perform their jobs well, they must find out what is wanted as well as what is needed. Interestingly, they must also be careful not to find too much information. Studies reveal, for example, that there is "an inverted-U relationship between the volume of information and decision quality" (Morville 2005, p. 165). In other words, too much information reduces decision quality as does too little.

Effectively assessing information wants and needs requires understanding how people learn, how they search for information, and how they use information. The LIS professional must also know how to interview effectively, how to evaluate the person's need, and how to determine the degree to which the proffered information satisfied the need. In addition, the LIS professional must have a thorough and current knowledge of the available digital, print, and human resources and how to access them. This places a serious responsibility on LIS professionals, beyond merely locating requested pieces of information.

2. Information Seeking

There have been many studies on information seeking. Below is a summary of some of the major findings pertinent to LIS professionals.

a. There is a Difference between Information Seeking and Information Gathering

Krikelas (1983) defined information seeking as "an attempt to satisfy an *immediate* need by searching for relevant information. Information gathering is an attempt to satisfy a *deferred* need" (p. 8, emphasis added). In information gathering there is no immediate need, but a search is expected to yield useful information for future use. For example, someone might be looking for a specific item, or need information within a specific time requirement. Alternatively, a person might browse a collection or explore a variety of links in the electronic environment without need for specific information or time pressure. Similarly, newspaper and magazine collections might be most often consulted, albeit not exclusively, by information gatherers, while reference materials might be most often consulted by information seekers.

b. Information Seeking Proceeds in Stages

Information seeking generally begins with an undefined notion of need, sometimes referred to as an "anomalous state of knowledge" (Belkin et al. 1982, p. 62). As the search process proceeds, the need becomes more defined, and the area explored narrows. The search strategy varies depending on the nature of the inquiry, and as the query becomes narrowed, the strategy and type of information sought varies as well (Rouse 1984). Bates (1989) described the process as "berrypicking"; berries are usually scattered on bushes, not found in one clump.

Kuhlthau (1991) described six stages in the information search process (figure 7.4). Kuhlthau's model reveals the essentially personal nature of information seeking. The problem context provides its own frame of reference, and the information's meaning and relevance, rather than some objective measure, is based on that frame. Kuhlthau (1993) suggested that the six stages can help LIS professionals identify the appropriate "zone of intervention" when "a user can do with guidance and assistance" (p. 176). The personal context also involves emotions in the search process. Lopatovska and Arapakis (2011) note that numerous studies associate success and satisfaction with search results and strategies with positive emotions (fun, control, optimism) and poor strategies and search tasks with negative emotions (anxiety, uncertainty, frustration). These results were found for both adults and children.

c. People Usually Search for Information in Some Context

As Case (2012) noted, "information needs do not arise in a vacuum, but rather owe their existence to some history, purpose, and influence" (p. 279). People seldom

FIGURE 7.4
Kuhlthau's Six Stages of the Information Search Process

Stage 1: Initiation. This stage is characterized by uncertainty, as the individual realizes an un-focused need for some knowledge or understanding. The topic and the search approach are undefined. Alternative courses of action might be discussed with others.

Stage 2: Selection. The topic comes into focus, and various search strategies are considered. Tentative searching begins.

Stage 3: Exploration. The seeker obtains preliminary information on the topic to provide an orientation for further searching. Considerable confusion or doubt might remain if the information appears contradictory or provides little direction. At this point, the seeker still might not be able to articulate precisely the type of information required.

Stage 4: Formulation. The seeker begins to establish a clear focus, and feelings of uncertainty diminish. Rather than just collecting information, the seeker begins to evaluate critically the information obtained, accepting some and discarding what appears to be irrelevant. The seeker experiences increased confidence both in the direction of the search and in the methods used.

Stage 5: Collection. The focus is now clear, and the seeker collects only information related to the defined topic. The seeker can articulate clearly the type of information needed. The search process becomes more effective, uncertainty is reduced, and the seeker's confidence is increased further.

Stage 6: Presentation. The search is complete. Its success might vary depending on factors such as the availability of information, the effectiveness of the information system used, and the skills of the searcher. Some of the information might duplicate previous results, so the seeker's attention is turned to summary, synthesis, and reporting of the information gathered.

seek information as an end in itself; it is usually needed within a particular context or "problem environment" (Durrance 1989, p. 162). For example, part of the context of information seeking is the seekers own memories, personality, and motivations—an "internal environment of influence" (Case 2012, p. 279). In addition, the seekers' role—their profession, for example, affects the context. Contexts will vary: a scientist might seek information on a technical procedure; an English teacher might look for a particular essay; an electrician might need directions for repairing a refrigerator; or a minister might want quotations for a sermon.

Context was a central feature of an important information-seeking model developed by Brenda Dervin (1983). According to Spink and Cole (2006), in this model "the information user is conceptualized as constructing information based on the values and specific environment of the 'small world' in which the user exists concurrently apart from and as a member of the larger society" (p. 27). The model anticipated the complex and subtle relationships that form the environment of today's information seekers.

The fact that people seek information within a context is particularly pertinent to libraries: people ask questions for a purpose. Historically, however, reference librarians were instructed not to probe why a particular question was asked for fear of violating the person's privacy and thus deterring someone from seeking help. Today we know this practice is not consistent with research on information seeking. When someone seeks information to solve a problem, LIS professionals can help only if they can distinguish between wants and needs. Therefore, the interview must extend beyond "What do you want to know?" to "How and why is the information needed? How is the requested information likely to help? What does the user know already? What is expected? What are the parameters of the problem?" (Durrance 1989, p. 163). This is not to suggest that LIS professionals should pry, but merely answering questions without understanding the underlying issues can be problematic. Wilson (1986) offered an approach that he called the "face value rule," which emphasized "clarifying the question" (p. 469). The importance of context also highlights the point that evaluating the success of providing information to a user cannot simply be based on the objective "correctness" of the answer; rather, it must be evaluated in terms of how the answer successfully resolves the problem for the user in the context of his or her situation. Finally, research suggests that people often do not require the most complete answer to their queries. In fact, they often find the amount of information available daunting. They tend to filter out information whenever possible and to gather just enough information to satisfy them; a concept referred to as *satisficing* behavior (Case 2012).

d. People Seek Information from People First

When an information need arises, people first scan their memory for ready solutions. If this fails, they attempt to use their powers of observation (Krikelas 1983). Failing this, they seek information from external sources: first from nearby individuals such as their family, friends, coworkers, neighbors, doctors, or clergy. Bawden and Robinson (2014) note that information seeking is often unstructured, depending on serendipitous discovery rather than seeking information from formal sources using structured search processes. Case (2012) in summarizing the research on information-seeking behavior found that people still turn to other people for information before using mass and/or specialized media, or before seeking help from institutions like libraries. The Internet, however, is challenging this overall pattern, and is, for some, a first or equal choice. The changes in information-seeking behavior are complex involving both an appreciation of the new, electronic information channels available, but also a continued desire to interact with people. As Connaway et al. (2013) observe in their study of the information-seeking behavior of high school and college students:

> When talking about places they went for information interviewees mentioned Internet resources, such as search engines and social media sites, far more often than physical places. *This reliance on digital spaces coexists with a persistent need to be in contact with other people both online and face to face.* Personal networks, and the relationship that comprise them, were more important factors in participants' information-seeking strategies across educational stages. (Italics mine, p. 7)

Nonetheless, the desire to seek electronic information sources first might have much to do with the factor of convenience discussed below.

e. Convenience above All: The Principle of Least Effort

The Principle of Least Effort, which has been the subject of research since 1950, has direct application for LIS professionals. It predicts that information seekers "will minimize the effort required to obtain information, even if it means accepting a lower quality or quantity of information (Case 2012, p. 178). In other words, people seek the most convenient source to meet their needs, even when they know the information might not be as good. The recognition of such a principle, although not surprising, can be disconcerting when considering the amount of time and energy LIS professionals devote to trying to provide the highest quality information.

One hopes that people prefer authoritative to nonauthoritative sources. In fact, one would hope that as the importance of the question increases, individuals would insist on the highest quality information. Research by Xu, Tan, and Yang (2006), however, belies this point. Although they found a positive relationship between the quality of a personal source and its use, they also noted that "as the task becomes more important, seekers pay less attention to source quality, and they look for closer rather than more remote sources. . . . They resort to the local network for problem solving" (p. 1675). Connaway et al. (2011) explored convenience among information seekers and found that convenience was "central to information-seeking behaviors" (p. 186) across all demographic characteristics—age, gender, academic role and use/nonuse of virtual reference services. Convenience was particularly important among millennials. People use the Internet because it is much easier to search from home, from one's office, or on a mobile device than to physically visit the library. The Principle of Least Effort should be a constant reminder that people are not necessarily looking for the most complete or best answer, but one that is "good enough" (satisficing) to deal with their information need. As Case (2012) presciently observed:

> Some investigators complain that *least effort seeking* is too common. Yet, there are inherent efficiencies in least effort behavior—for instance, searching takes no longer than is necessary to produce, on average, a satisfactory result. Thus, it is wrong to interpret least effort information seeking as "irrational." Such behavior can be both satisfying and successful. (p. 375)

f. Internet Searching Behavior

Bilal (2002) identified at least three ways Internet searching differs from traditional information seeking: the Internet is an extraordinarily large system that often produces information overload and disorientation; it is constantly changing; and it is not indexed. Rose (2006), citing the work of Broder (2002), identified three types of Internet-based searches: navigational searches to locate a specific website, information searches to obtain specific information, and transactional searches to locate an online service that allows additional interaction, such as a map database. Approximately 30% of all Internet searches are unsuccessful and people frequently stop looking after the first page of hits. Alternatively, many people use a "spoke-and-hub" approach to searching; that is, they begin at a certain point, search, return to the original point, and start a search again. This style relies heavily on the back button and is sometimes called "backtracking" which is particularly common among young children (Slone 2002; Gossen and Nurnberger 2013). Because it is easy to lose one's place on the Internet, returning to an original page provides a stable point of reference.

Although some people assume that individuals searching the Web are looking for a particular piece of information or subject, in reality, the process is far more complex and often involves multiple searches, multitasking, and coordination of strategies and topics. Throughout this process the thinking and strategies of the searcher can change (Du and Spink 2011). Xie and Joo (2010) identified ten search tactics that searchers employ alone or in combination (figure 7.5).

Xie and Joo found that searchers might use multiple search tactics, but that few tactics were used frequently. In fact, only two tactics accounted for nearly half of all tactics used: accessing forward (27%) (e.g., typing a URL directly) and evaluating an individual item (22%). Creating or modifying search statements occurred only a small number of times (4% and 3%, respectively), and even fewer were involved in organizing results, monitoring the search process, learning about the system, or

FIGURE 7.5
Web Search Tactics

Identifying search leads to get started	Discover information as search leads at the beginning of the search process.
Creating search statement	Come up with a search statement for searching
Modifying search statement	Change a previous search statement (e.g., narrow search results, broaden search results.)
Evaluating an individual item	Assess relevance/usefulness of an item, or authority of an item.
Evaluating search results	Quickly assess the relevance of search results.
Keep a record	Keep records of metadata of an item(s) before accessing it/them.
Accessing forward	Go to a specific item or Web page that has not been accessed in the search by using direct location, tracking meta-information or hyperlinks.
Accessing backward	Go back to a previous page by using direct location, tracking meta-information, or hyperlinks.
Learning	Gain knowledge of system features, system structure, domain knowledge, and database content.
Exploring	Survey information/items in a specific site
Organizing	Sort out a list of items with common characteristics
Monitoring	Keep track of the search process or check the current status.
Using/obtaining	Use relevant information to satisfy information needs or obtain information in physical or electronic formats

Source: Xie, Iris and Soohyung Joo. 2010. "Transitions in Search Tactics During the Web-Based Search Process." *Journal of the American Society for Information Science and Technology* 61 (November): 2193.

keeping a record of the results (1% or less for each). Xie and Joo suggested that information retrieval systems might focus less on helping people formulate queries and more on helping users evaluate the items they discover.

i. Search Abilities Vary among Individuals

The more varied a users' abilities, the more flexible the search systems must be to accommodate those variations. For example, although information-seeking ability improves with age, older individuals often find information technologies less friendly. Other differences affecting search abilities include intelligence, analytical ability, and manual dexterity. Other personal attributes such as cognitive style, level of anxiety related to searching, and previous experience with Internet searching can also influence search behavior.

Historically women tended to encounter more difficulty than men, believed they were less competent in searching, used the Internet less frequently, and used fewer Internet applications (Hsieh-Yee 2001). However, new evidence suggests that the gender gap has narrowed. Dresang (2005) noted that "studies consistently used to find males were more interested and involved with technology than females; this is often no longer the case" (p. 182). She further noted that a 2004 study revealed that "girls and boys, ages nine to thirteen, were equally positive about computers and their ability to use them" (p. 182).

Research on adults, sometimes called "digital immigrants," revealed that many depend on hyperlinks to find documents, seldom use Boolean search strategies, rely heavily on keyword searching, limit their explorations to specific sections within a site, use a few pages frequently, and spend considerable time scrolling, reading Web pages, and waiting for Web pages to load (Hsieh-Yee 2001). Novice users made more errors, retrieved irrelevant hits, avoided the use of advanced features, or quickly became frustrated and stopped the search (Slone 2002). On the other hand, despite these problems, novice searchers sometimes exhibited very high and even "frenetic levels of effort throughout the process" (Debowski 2001, p. 378).

Searchers with domain expertise had significantly greater success and were faster at searching (Lazonder et al. 2000). One would assume that academics had domain expertise. However, the British Library (2008) found that academic user behavior was diverse and that certain academic disciplines were more reliant on electronic access than others. Niu and Hemminger el al. (2010) for example, found that academic researchers in the natural sciences, engineering, and medicine strongly favored the use of electronic searching for access to scholarly content. Searchers with domain expertise tended to exhibit the following behaviors:

> **Horizontal information seeking:** A skimming activity where people viewed just one or two pages from an academic site and then bounced out, perhaps never to return.
>
> **Navigators:** People spent as much time finding their way around a digital environment as they did actually viewing what they found.
>
> **Viewers:** The average time spent on e-book and e-journal sites was very short: typically four and eight minutes respectively.

Squirreling behavior: Academics saved information for future use by downloading content, especially when downloads were free.

Checkers: Users assessed authority and trust in a matter of seconds by dipping and cross-checking across different sites, and by relying on favored brands (e.g., Google).

Heinstrom (2006) studied the search strategies of master's-level students and found three patterns:

- fast surfing dominated by minimal effort, easy access, and easily digestible material;

- broad scanning using an exploratory search pattern and spontaneous planning, using wide searches among many types of information sources; and

- deep diving involving substantial effort, structured searches, and a preference for high-quality information sources.

Interestingly, Heinstrom used a standardized personality measure with each group and found that fast surfing was associated with a lack of conscientiousness and positive associations with openness to experience and sensitivity. Extroversion was positively associated with broad scanning. Personality traits had little effect on deep diving.

ii. Internet Searching by Children and Youth

Adolescents and young adults search quite differently than their parents. Known variously as millennials, the Net generation, or "digital natives," these individuals have grown up with the Internet and are adept at its use. Griffiths and Brophy (2005) summarized the research of Cmor and Lippold (2001), who found:

- Students use the Web for everything.
- They might spend hours searching or just a few minutes.
- Searching skills vary and students will often assess themselves as being more skilled than they actually are.
- They will give discussion list comments the same academic weight as peer-reviewed journal articles. (p. 541)

Griffiths and Brophy also noted that students preferred search engines, especially Google, over other means of locating materials; used fewer academic resources and found it difficult to locate other resources; sacrificed quality to save time and effort; and set their expectations of other electronic resources based on their experience with search engines. These findings are consonant with the principle of least effort discussed above.

The research behavior of the "Google generation" was a special focus of a study by the British Library (2008). Among their findings was that young people spent little time evaluating information for accuracy or authority; employed poor search strategies because they did not have a good grasp of their own information needs; preferred natural language rather than using keywords; had difficulty discriminating relevant hits from a long list of sites; and had a poor conception of the Internet and therefore relied on search engines such as Google and Yahoo.

Younger children have fewer problem-solving and mechanical skills as well as less developed cognitive abilities than adults. Despite these shortcomings, Spink et al. (2010) found

> . . . young children engage in complex Web searches, including keyword searching and browsing, query formulation and reformulation, relevance judgments, successive searches, information multitasking and collaborative behaviors. (p. 191)

This, of course, is not to say that they are particular good at these strategies. In fact the evidence is otherwise. Hsieh-Yee found, for example, that children preferred to browse the Web and did not search systematically (2001). They had difficulty evaluating the quality of websites, developing search strategies, using correct search syntax, typing in the proper search terms, and locating relevant hits. According to Gossen and Nurnberger (2013) children's queries tended to be shorter than adults, and they clicked on the first items presented regardless of quality. Children had greater difficulty than adults formulating precise queries probably due to deficiencies in vocabulary and cognitive skills. Similarly, younger children tended to use natural language queries probably because they have difficulty conceptualizing keywords. In terms of interface design, young children sometimes had difficulty navigating sites and used a "loopy" (p. 745) browsing strategy often returning to the first page. In addition, children preferred websites with many pictures with high-quality colors, graphics, and animation. Relevance judgments were difficult for them. Despite these handicaps, children felt confident about their Web searches. Dresang (2005) also found some exploratory studies suggesting that children prefer to do their searching collaboratively with other children. This might explain the roots of older children's heavy use of social networks and computer games that involve group activity, which dominate many young peoples' lives today.

iii. Information Behavior: A Summary

Understanding information-seeking behavior is fundamental for LIS profession-als. It is a complex and subtle phenomenon examined in a large and wide-rang-ing body of research trying to describe and explain it. Case (2012) attempted to characterize this research in "eight lessons," which are summarized below:

> *Formal sources and rationalized searches reflect only one side of human information behavior.* In fact, formal sources are less frequently con-sulted compared to how often people consult their families, friends, and colleagues.

> *More information is not always better.* People cope with information overload by filtering it to save time and energy. Ignoring informa-tion can be a sensible strategy.

> *Context is central to the transfer of information.* People's perception of their situation, accurate or not, affects their information behavior. In addition, the meaning of the information they receive is often evaluated based on factors that have little to do with the informa-tion package itself. Information that is not connected to their world, which does not seem relevant, or which might produce anxiety might be ignored.

> *Sometimes information doesn't help.* People usually gather and seek information for a purpose, usually related to a basic need. People look for information that helps them cope with their own particular situation. Often the information received from books, articles, or Websites by itself, is not adequate.

> *Sometimes it is not possible to make information available or accessible.* Sometimes, formal information systems are simply unable to deal with the multiplicity and variety of important human needs. The digital divide exacerbates this problem.

> *Information seeking is a dynamic process.* A person's information needs can change over time and in the middle of the information seek-ing process. Satisfying one information need might produce other information needs. We must not adopt a service model that focuses only on the first query, but one that can deal with the dynamic nature of the information seeking process.

> *Information seeking is not always about a "problem" or "problematic sit-uations."* Certainly, much information seeking is done to solve a

problem, find pertinent facts, or make a decision, but not always. Sometimes it is for entertainment, distraction, or the satisfaction of simple, spontaneous curiosity.

Information behavior is not always about "sense-making" either. Although there is much to be said that a good deal of information behavior arises out of trying to make sense of one' own world, there is still much value in exploring the sources and channels that people use to seek information. Understanding the situation and understanding how sources and channels of information are used are complementary activities. (pp. 375–377)

VII. EMERGING INFORMATION SCIENCE AREAS AFFECTING LIS PROFESSIONALS

As noted earlier, there are many specialties within the discipline of Information Science. Many of these fields are becoming increasingly important as information services evolve. Four of these areas will be briefly discussed here: informatics, big data, user experience design, and knowledge management.

A. Informatics

The growth of the Internet and the World Wide Web, the ubiquity of computers, and the ever-expanding quantities of information stored in the digital environment have challenged peoples' ability to organize, locate, evaluate, and use information in a timely and effective manner. A number of disciplines including library and information science, cognitive sciences, business, computer sciences, medicine, nursing, and communications have contributed insights, research, and methods for resolving this challenge—giving rise to a new interdisciplinary field called informatics. Etymologically, informatics is a combination of the science of information and automated information processing (Wikipedia 2009). Still not clearly defined, informatics has been variously described as "the art, science, and human dimensions of information technology" or "the study, application, and social consequences of technology" (Wikipedia 2009). In its broadest sense, its focus is on "information and how it is represented in, processed by, and communicated between a variety of systems" (Fourman 2002, p. 2). Informatics emphasizes aspects of computerization and technology and its relationship to information creation, processing, organization, and transfer. Indeed, informatics has become a subspecialty in a number of disciplines. For example, Hersh (2008) defined medical informatics as "the integrative discipline that arises from the synergistic application of computational, information, cognitive, organizational, and other sciences whose primary focus is the acquisition, storage, and use of information in the health/biomedical domain" (p. 1). Kling (1999) defined social informatics as "the interdisciplinary study of the design, uses and consequences of information technologies that take into account their interaction with institutional and cultural contexts" (p. 1). Sawyer (2005) viewed social informatics as "the trans-disciplinary study of the design, deployment and uses of information and communication technology (ICT) that account for their interaction with institutional and cultural contexts, including organizations and society" (p. 9). Several LIS schools in the United States and internationally currently offer both degrees and specializations in informatics, and the number is expected to grow.

B. Big Data

A recent development related to informatics is the rise of" Big Data." Big data is the product resulting from the rapidly increasing amount of digital information and the growing capacity of computers to store it. Bertot and Choi (2012) reviewed several definitions from the literature and identified four features that characterize big data:

- Vast datasets that cannot be analyzed using conventional software and analytic tools;
- Require significant processing power (such as via a supercomputer);
- Span a range of data types such as text, numeric, image, video; and
- Can cross multiple data platforms such as from social media networks, Web log files, sensors, location data from smart phones, digitized documents, and photograph and video archives. (p. 4)

As Dumbill (2012) put it, "the data is too big, moves too fast, or doesn't fit the structures of your database architectures" (p. 1). According to the Executive Office of the President (2014), big data is characterized informally as the result of dramatic changes in the "3 Vs": *volume, variety,* and *velocity* of data. In terms of *volume,* it is estimated, for example, that in 2013 alone, four zetabytes of data were generated worldwide A zetabyte is 1,000,000,000,000,000,000,000 bytes of information. From the perspective of *variety,* the variety of networks from which digital information can be drawn now has dramatically increased. These sources can include "the public Web; social media; mobile applications; federal, state and local records and databases; commercial databases that aggregate individual data for a spectrum of commercial transactions, and public records; geospatial data; surveys; and traditional offline documents scanned by optical character recognition into electronic form" (p. 5). The databases that form this network themselves draw their data from heterogeneous sources including "instruments, sensors, Internet transactions, emails, video, click streams, and /or all other digital sources available today . . ." (Executive Office 2014, p. 3).

In fact, data can now be drawn from "things" as well as traditional databases. This new environment is known as the "Internet of Things."

> The "Internet of Things" is a term used to describe the ability of devices to communicate with each other using embedded sensors that are linked through wired and wireless networks. These devices could include your thermostat, your car, or a pill you swallow so the doctor can monitor the health of your digestive tracts. These connected devices use the Internet to transmit, compile, and analyze data. (Executive Office 2014, p. 2)

The digital nature of all these sources allows increased *velocity* of data production — that is, transmission of large volumes at very high speed. The potential opportunities and challenges of harnessing and using this vast amount of data are unlimited. In fact, the complexity of handling and analyzing such large datasets has spawned a new field related directly to these challenges: "Data Analytics."

Manyika et al. ("Insights . . ." 2011) identified five ways that big data creates value:

> First, big data can unlock significant value by making information transparent and usable at much higher frequency. Second, as organizations create and store more transactional data in digital form, they can collect more accurate and detailed performance information on everything from product inventories to sick days . . . Third, big data allows ever-narrower segmentation of customers and therefore much more precisely tailored produce or services. Fourth, sophisticated analytics can substantially improve decision making. Finally, big data can be used to improve the development of the next generation of products and services. For instance, manufacturers are using data obtained from sensors embedded in products to create innovative after-sales service offerings such as proactive maintenance (preventive measure that take place before a failure occurs or is even noticed.) (p. 1)

Indeed the benefits of big data are present in numerous sectors of society already. For example, banks use big data techniques to improve fraud detection. We all benefit when credit card companies can quickly detect atypical transactions or behaviors to prevent fraudulent credit card use. Beyond business and industry, other areas using big data include education, law enforcement; military and national security;

medicine and health, social services, and scientific, technical, social science and cultural research.

> Health care providers are leveraging more detailed data to improve patient treatment. Big data is being used by manufacturers to improve warranty management and equipment monitoring, as well as to optimize the logistics of getting their products to market. Retailers are harnessing a wide range of customer interactions, both online and offline, in order to provide more tailored recommendations and optimal pricing. (Executive Office 2014, p. 39)

The potential magnitude and impact of Big Data is hard to overestimate:

> It's not just increased amounts and types of data; it's also improved tools to store, aggregate, combine, analyze, and extract new insights. Put Big Data together with big analytics, and it becomes possible to spot business trends, uncover ways to prevent diseases, combat crime, add economic value, gain new insights in scientific research, and make government more transparent. (Gordon-Murnane 2012, p. 1)

Despite the positive benefits, with all such large-scale, technological developments, there are potential problems as well. For example, although big data can enable a company to track individual consumers' buying practices and allow them to provide better customer service, at the same time, many people prefer not to be "tracked" and want to constrain this type of data collection. Certainly, privacy concerns come quickly to the surface when big data is involved. Ironically, many of us willingly, albeit innocently, contribute to the great pool of data. As a recent Executive Office of the President Report noted (2014) noted:

> More than 500 million photos are uploaded and shared every day, along with more than 200 hours of video every minute. But the volume of information that people create themselves—the full range of communications from voice calls, emails, and text to uploaded pictures, video and music—pales in comparison to the amount of digital information created *about* them each day. (p. 2)

Many of the existing laws and regulations providing privacy protection to citizens were created at a time when there was little computer access and the Internet was in its infancy. Given the exponential growth of digital information, the advances in computer and networking technologies, and the dramatic shift in use, the need for a deliberate review of this issue is essential. The rise of big data demands a shift in focus to

> . . . put our attention more squarely on the hard questions we mush reckon with: how to balance the socially beneficial uses of big data with the harms to privacy and

other values that can result in a world where more data is inevitably collected about more things. (Executive Office 2014, p. 56)

There are many additional policy concerns that arise. The Executive Office Report (2014) identified five such areas:

1. *Preserving Privacy Values*: Maintaining our privacy values by protecting personal information in the marketplace, both in the United States and through interoperable global privacy frameworks;
2. *Educating Robustly and Responsibly*: Recognizing schools—particularly K-12—as an important sphere for using big data to enhance learning opportunities, while protecting personal data usage and building digital literacy and skills;
3. *Big Data and Discrimination*: Preventing new modes of discrimination that some uses of big data might enable;
4. *Law Enforcement and Security*: Ensuring big data's responsible use in law enforcement, public safety, and national security; and,
5. *Data as a Public Resource*: Harnessing data as a public resource, using it to improve the delivery of public services, and investing in research and technology that will further power the big data revolution. (p. 59)

Gordon-Murnane (2012) suggested that LIS professionals can play a significant role as big data increases in importance because they "have the skills, the knowledge, and the service mentality to help our businesses, government, universities, and non-profits capitalize on all that Big Data has to offer" (p. 1). Librarians can help people in all sectors of our economy and government extract the information they need from these large datasets; train people in discovery methods to locate information and resources; and contribute to the organization, archiving, preservation and management of the data that is discovered.

The ultimate impact of Big Data is unknown. Anderson and Rainie from Pew Research (2012) queried experts in a variety of areas to help assess its potential. Many felt that Big Data would produce an improved understanding of ourselves and the world; and that it would be very useful for "nowcasting" (using real-time data to predict important social and economic trends). Others were concerned that big data will not be developed in an open environment and that the technological barriers will be very difficult to overcome. In addition, there is concern that big data will be harnessed primarily for profit motive and not for social goods. There is little disagreement however that big data will have a significant impact and LIS professional need to watch these developments carefully.

C. User-Experience Design (UXD)

Businesses, government agencies, and every service-oriented organization, particularly libraries, place a high priority on making people's experience with them useful and enjoyable. People are much more likely to repeat their interaction if they have a positive experience. This is not an easy task; it requires a deliberate and ongoing commitment to customer service. If the organization wants to promote user loyalty, then good customer service is essential.

As these organizations transition to a digital environment, they must develop a digital presence with a "user-centered design" that can communicate that same ethos. In fact, as websites proliferate and become integrated into nearly every aspect of people's lives, it is clear that how information is organized and presented on a website has substantial impact on people's ability to get the information they need and therefore on their satisfaction. Lindgaard and colleagues (2006) found that people form their first impressions of a website in as little as fifty milliseconds. Robins, Holmes, and Stansbury (2010) found that the initial perceptions of a site's credibility were determined within two seconds.

Garrett (2011) described "user-centered design" as the practice of creating engaging, efficient websites that take the user into account every step of the way, what Morville (2005) described as "the vital importance of empathy for the users" (p. 31). The concept of "user-centered design" has been embraced as integral to an emerging field known as "user experience design" (UXD). Although its boundaries are not yet clearly delineated, UXD borrows from HCI, human factors engineering, and user interface design (Paluch 2006). At the heart of UXD is the user's experience. The International Organization of Standards (ISO 1998) defines "user experience" as a

> person's perceptions and responses resulting from the use and/or anticipated use of a product, system or service . . . User experience includes all the users' emotions, beliefs, preferences, perceptions, physical or psychological responses, behavior and accomplishments that occur before, during and after use.

A site is more likely to provide a positive user experience if it meets six criteria according to Morville (2005). It must be:

Useful: The content should make a genuine contribution to fulfilling a need.

Usable: The site should be intuitive and easy to navigate.

Desirable: The elements of the site should produce satisfaction and appreciation in the user.

Findable: The site should be locatable and navigable.

Accessible: The site should be usable by people with disabilities.

Credible: The site should contain trusted content.

Beyond these criteria there are other considerations. Functionality is another factor that can determine the user experience. Three areas in particular contribute to functionality: the information architecture, the site's usability, and its visual design. Below are some of the tasks comprising each of these areas:

Information Architecture

- Creating effective navigation techniques so that users can move easily throughout the site (e.g., menus, hyperlinks, guided tours, site maps, buttons, and indexes)
- Establishing a logical site structure that is easily understood and intuitive for the user
- Employing effective search systems, such as Boolean or natural language
- Labeling for improved information access (links, terms in indexes, choices in drop-down lists, and product names)
- Linking relevant external sources by hyperlinks
- Enabling users to personalize or customize their own preferences for a site, or provide filters for site content
- Using metadata effectively to improve access
- Ensuring the scalability of the website, that is, making sure that it can grow and still retain its effectiveness and usability
- Ensuring that content is structured in such a way that it meets standards for accessibility.

Usability

- Making the site usable in terms of language and terminology employed
- Providing effective orientation for users within the site
- Assessing the efficiency and effectiveness with which users can accomplish necessary tasks.
- Providing quantitative and qualitative evidence to support changes.

Visual Design

- Developing an aesthetically pleasing site
- Maintaining portability, a consistent look and feel across different platforms, different browsers, screen resolutions and devices

- Producing a brand for the organization.
- Promoting credibility through sophisticated and effective design.
- Adapting the design for use by various constituencies such as children and adults.

1. Usability Testing

UXD employs a comprehensive and systematic development process that begins by identifying the goals of both the site developers and the goals of the users of the site and continues to the site's aesthetic or surface design (Garrett 2011). Determining whether a particular site meets the needs of both the user and the creator requires testing—known as "usability testing." A variety of research methods are employed: questionnaires, surveys, interviews, focus groups, and intrusive and unobtrusive observation. Occasionally ethnographic and field studies, journals, eye tracking, and "think aloud" protocols might be used. In think-aloud studies, a user is observed or videotaped while engaged in a particular task and is asked to talk aloud, expressing his or her feelings, thoughts, opinions, and strategies through the process. The responses are recorded for subsequent analysis. Another technique employs a question-asking protocol. In this case, the researcher asks questions to get feedback from the user, who is using a website (Norlin and Winters 2002). Software packages, including site usage logs that collect information on the sites visited and search strategies employed, are also helpful. Although usability testing is not perfect—the studies frequently use small samples that might or might not represent the many users who might visit a particular website—the field is establishing some valid and reliable criteria for evaluation.

2. Responsive Design

The complexity of UXD is obvious, but it has increased even more in the last few years. The proliferation of electronic devices including laptops, tablets, and smartphones with different screen sizes and built to different standards has created a particular challenge for UX designers. Traditionally, different screens had to be prepared for different devices. The need to design highly flexible interfaces that adapt to the requirements of a user's particular device generated the concept of "responsive design." Wisniewski (2014) defined responsive design as "a set of tools . . . and techniques . . . that allow Web designers to create a single website that responds to context" (p. 74). A responsively designed site, for example, will resize type and images or raise or lower image resolution based on the device being used. The result

FIGURE 7.6
User-Centered Design Touchpoints in Libraries

Websites	Telephone	Programs/events, classes
Catalog	Parking lot	Computers
Databases	Building	Brochures/posters
E-mail	Library workers	Library card
Instant messaging	Signage	Print newsletters
Online reference	Materials	Advertisements
Furniture/shelving		

Source: Schmidt, Aaron and Amanda Etches. 2014. *Useful, Usable, Desirable: Applying User Experience Design to Your Library.* Chicago: ALA, p. 2.

is that users have quality access to a site no matter what device they are using, and it simplifies the webmaster's work because only one website is needed across all platforms (Wisniewski 2013).

3. UXD in Libraries

Although many people associate UXD with websites, its principles can be applied more broadly to any activity that involves people. This concept is particularly useful to service organizations such as libraries. Schmidt and Etches (2014) identified the many aspects of a library that affect a user's experience which they refer to as "touchpoints" (figure 7.6).

For them, the user experience is defined simply as "how someone feels when using a product or service" (p. 3). They remind us that our users might see things differently than we do; that we must be empathetic and not assume that functional problems relate to the inadequacy of the user, but perhaps to the inadequacy of our system. UXD plays an increasingly important role in ensuring that websites are designed not for the designer but for the people who use them. It comports well with the underlying community orientation that drives all library services today.

D. Knowledge Management

Knowledge is dynamic because it evolves as it is influenced by people's thoughts, feelings, and experience (McInerney 2002). Some knowledge can be *explicit*, such as knowledge in a database or document; but a vast quantity of organizational knowledge is *tacit*, consisting of the values, beliefs, and perspectives of the individuals within the organization who create the context for the explicit knowledge. Organizations themselves can have values, history, unwritten laws, and ways of doing things that also constitute tacit knowledge. Knowledge that is currently tacit, but could become tangible, is known as *implicit* knowledge (Koenig 2012).

Effectively managing both explicit and tacit knowledge in an organization is likely to achieve the best results. When important knowledge is not accessible or unused, it degrades decision processes, reduces decision quality, and impairs organizational effectiveness. Similarly, organizations rely on inventiveness and innovation to survive and prosper. This means that they rely on their employees' knowledge, skills, and ideas (sometimes referred to as human capital, one of the main components of the organization's intellectual capital) to create new services and products. Innovation and inventive thinking often require collaboration and the sharing of information, and a work environment that encourages both activities on a formal and informal level. Individuals engaged in these activities or in similar work often form "communities of practice" (Wenger 1998). These communities define authority and work goals within them based on the expertise of the participants rather than formal assignments. Organizations structured to facilitate collaborative activities, information sharing, and communities of practice are likely to progress more quickly and leverage the talents of their people effectively. In the for-profit environment this can mean a competitive advantage and increased profitability. In the nonprofit environment it can mean better service and stronger political support.

The field of knowledge management (KM) emerged to help build human and intellectual capital and diminish the impact of poor knowledge use within organizations. KM focuses specifically on understanding and structuring organizations so that knowledge can be best accessed, communicated, and used. Davenport, De Long, and Beers (1997) identified four objectives of KM: creating repositories, improving access, enhancing the environment, and managing knowledge as an asset. The assets involved include databases, policies and procedures, documents, and undocumented expertise (Koenig 2012). Overall, KM is concerned with planning, capturing, organizing, interconnecting, and providing access to organizational knowledge through both intellectual and information technologies. It is an interdisciplinary field which as a consequence is sometimes described as "theoretically eclectic" (Martin 2009, p. 388) drawing from a variety of disciplines including psychology, sociology, business, economics, expert systems, information science, and computer science.

Although information and information technologies remain important, KM places considerable emphasis on people. As Blair (2002) noted, "knowledge management is largely the management and support of expertise. . . . It is primarily the management of individuals with specific abilities, rather than the management of repositories of data and information" (p. 1022). For Blair, people are the repositories of the knowledge. Koenig (2012) agreed observing—"Perhaps the most central thrust in KM is to capture and make available, so it can be used by others in the organization, the information and knowledge that is in people's heads as it were, and that has never been explicitly set down" (p. 1). Martin (2009) pointed out that although the processes that make tacit knowledge explicit focus on people-oriented activities such as face-to-face meetings and mentoring, technology can play an important supporting role. Among the applications he identified as most common were groupware, document management, data warehousing, portals and intranets, workflow, information retrieval technologies and search engines.

Koenig (2012) identified three types of databases that are instrumental parts of KM within an organization. One is a "community of practice" which was discussed above. The other two are Lessons Learned databases, which contain information about the strengths and weaknesses of a given project collected by the KM manager from all staff involved in the project while the knowledge was still fresh, and Expertise locator databases which identify expert knowledge in the organization that can be called upon as needed. Lessons Learned activities can be tricky. Martin (2009) noted, "The collection and compilation of lessons require the right combination of infrastructure, technological and structural, and of staff skills in eliciting and reporting the information" (p. 384).

Given the tremendous range of functions involved in KM and its inherent value, McInerney (2002) suggested that organizations should spend less time trying to extract "knowledge artifacts" from workers and spend more time developing a "knowledge culture" in which opportunities for knowledge creation are optimized and there is encouragement for learning and sharing. Sharing is a particularly thorny aspect in stimulating a knowledge management culture and knowledge hoarding is commonplace. There is a variety of reasons why important information might not be shared. Martin (2009) noted that on the organization's part, disseminating critical information widely might invite industrial espionage; for individual employees, if the organization has a pay for performance system, sharing information might provide coworkers with a competitive advantage (Martin 2009). Hoarding information might also increase ones' status as a possessor of vital knowledge. Interestingly, Aharony (2011) also reported that the disposition of librarians as knowledge managers is also important: librarians with high levels of self-efficacy (control) and self-esteem are more likely to support knowledge sharing and collaboration within their organization. Martin (2009) notes that the organizational environment is critical:

Sharing can be induced where there are perceived benefits to individuals, groups, or the organization. The organizational climate is very important here, including such elements as trust, an open exchange of information, tolerance of failure, and infusion of the organization with pro-social norms (p. 392).

Although KM practices would logically appear to justify significant investment by organizations, it is not a panacea for organizational inefficiencies, and there is some evidence that KM investments are not always justified in terms of organizational outcomes (McIver et al. 2013). Whether formal KM activities are required depends greatly on the particular work situation. Nonetheless, KM contributes significantly to our understanding of how to elicit, store, and transfer knowledge throughout an organization. Like other information professions it values knowledge in an instrumental role in improving individual and organizational growth, health, and productivity.

VIII. SUMMARY

Information science is devoted to understanding information in all its forms: its creation, nature, organization, storage, retrieval, evaluation, and use. Although information might be difficult to define, it clearly plays a central role in our society; it is inextricably linked to our everyday life: our problems, challenges, and aspirations. There are few topics as important to LIS professionals as information, and it behooves all of us to be familiar with the pertinent research and developments that arise from this field.

The field of information science is broad and interdisciplinary. Its dimensions are technological, economic, psychosocial, educational, political, cultural, and philosophical. Libraries, albeit not exactly in the same way, share these dimensions and although not every activity in libraries concerns itself with information, much of what takes place in them relies on information to assist library users. In this sense, librarians and information science professionals share numerous common values related to making information accessible and usable, and satisfying individuals' information needs. In particular, we share a need to understand how to distinguish information needs and wants, how to understand individuals' behavior when they search for information, and how information systems, including the Internet, can best be designed and used to satisfy needs. To a large extent, librarians depend on information scientists for this understanding. Information science is an important partner to libraries and LIS professionals, and much of the research and knowledge acquired in information science can improve the contributions libraries and LIS professionals make to their users.

REFERENCES

Aharony, Noa. 2011. "Librarians' Attitudes toward Knowledge Management." *College & Research Libraries* 72 (March): 111–126.

Anderson, Janna Quitney, and Lee Rainie. 2012. *Big Data.* www.pewInternet.org/Files/Reports/2012/PIP_Future_of_Internet_2012_Big_Data.pdf.

Ashman, Helen, Declan Dagger, Tim Brailsford, James Goulding, Declan O'Sullivan, Jan-Felix Schmakeit, and Vincent Wade. 2012. "Human-Computer Interaction and the Web." In *The Human-Computer Interaction Handbook,* edited by Julie A. Jacko. Boca Raton: CRC, pp. 565–587.

Bates, Marcia J. 1989. "The Design of Browsing and Berrypicking Techniques for the Online Search Interface." *Online Review* 13 (October): 407–424.

———. 1999. "The Invisible Substrate of Information Science." *Journal of the American Society for Information Science* 50: 1043–1050.

———. 2006. "Fundamental Forms of Information." *Journal of the American Society for Information Science and Technology* 57: 1033–1045.

———. 2007. "Defining the Information Disciplines in Encyclopedia Development." *Information Research* 12 (October). http://informationr.net/ir/12–4/colis/colis29.html.

Bawden, David, and Lyn Robinson. 2014. *Introduction to Information Science.* Chicago: ALA.

Belkin, Nicholas J., Helen M. Brooks, and Robert N. Oddy. 1982. "ASK for Information Retrieval." *Journal of Documentation* 38: 61–71.

Bertot, John Carlo, and Heeyon Choi. 2012. *Big Data: Strategies, Issues, & Recommendations.* http://ipac.umd.edu/publications/big-data-strategies-issues-and-recommendations.

Bilal, Dania. 2002. "Children's Use of the Yahooligans! Web Search Engine." *Journal of the American Society for Information Science and Technology* 53: 1170–1183.

Blair, David C. 2002. "Knowledge Management: Hype, Hope, or Help?" *Journal of the American Society of Information Science and Technology* 53: 1019–1028.

Bradford, Samuel C. 1934. "Sources of Information on Specific Subjects." *Engineering* 85–86.

British Library. 2008. *Information Behaviour of the Researcher of the Future.* London: University College London. www.jisc.ac.uk/media/documents/programmes/reppres/gg_final_keynote_11012008.pdf.

Brittain, J. M. 1980. "The Distinctive Characteristics of Information Science." In *Theory and Application of Information Research: Proceedings of the Second International Research Forum on Information Science,* edited by Ole Harbo and Leif Kajberg. London: Mansell.

Broder, Andrei. 2002. "A Taxonomy of Web Search." *SIGIR Forum* 36, no. 2 (fall): 3–10.

Burke, Colin. 2007. "History of Information Science." In *Annual Review of Information Science and Technology,* vol. 41, edited by Blaise Cronin. Medford, NJ: Information Today, 3–53.

Bush, Vannevar. 1945. "As We Might Think." *Atlantic Monthly* 176 (July): 101–108.

Case, Donald O. 2012. *Looking for Information: A Survey of Research on Information Seeking, Needs, and Behavior,* 3rd ed. Bingley, Eng.. Emerald Group. San Diego: Academic Press.

Chalmers, Patricia A. 2003. "The Role of Cognitive Theory in Human-Computer Interface." *Computers in Human Behavior* 19: 593–607.

Chatman, Elfreda A. 1996. "The Impoverished Life-World of Outsiders." *Journal of the American Society for Information Science* 47: 193–206.

Chen, Ching-Chih, and Peter Hernon. 1982. *Information Seeking: Assessing and Anticipating User Needs.* New York: Neal-Schuman.

Cmor, Dianne, and Karen Lippold. 2001. "Surfing vs. Searching: The Web as a Research Tool." Presented at the 21st Annual Conference of the Society for Teaching and Learning in Higher Education, June 2001.

Connaway, Lynn Silipigni, Donna M. Lanclos, and Erin M. Hood. 2013. "'I Always Stick with the First Thing That Comes up on Google . . .' Where People Go for Information, What They Use, and Why." *Educause Review Online.* www.educause .edu/ero/article/i-always-stick-first-thing-comes-google-where-people-go-information -what-they-use-and-why.

Connaway, Lynn Silipigni, Timothy J. Dickey, and Marie L. Radford. 2011. "'If It Is Too Inconvenient, I'm Not Going After It': Convenience as a Critical Factor in Information-Seeking Behaviors." *Library and Information Science Research* 33: 179–190.

Davenport, Thomas, David De Long, and Michael Beers. 1997. "Building Successful Knowledge Management Projects." Center for Business Innovation Working Paper, Ernst & Young.

Davis, Charles H., and Deborah Shaw. 2011. *Introduction to Information Science and Technology.* Medford, NJ: Information Today.

Debowski, Shelda. 2001. "Wrong Way: Go Back! An Exploration of Novice Search Behaviors While Conducting an Information Search." *The Electronic Library* 19: 371–382.

Dervin, Brenda. 1983. "An Overview of Sense-Making: Concepts, Methods, and Results to Date." Paper presented at the International Communication Association Annual Meeting, May 1983, Dallas, Texas.

Dresang, Eliza T. 2005. "The Information-Seeking Behavior of Youth in the Digital Environment." *Library Trends* 54 (fall): 178–196.

Du, Jia Tina, and Amanda Spink. 2011. "Toward a Web Search Model: Integrating Multitasking, Cognitive Coordination, and Cognitive Shifts." *Journal of the American Society for Information Science and Technology* 62: 1466–1472.

Dumbill, Edd. 2012. "What Is Big Data? An Introduction to the Big Data Landscape." http://radar.oreilly.com/2012/01/what-is-big-data.html.

Durrance, Joan C. 1989. "Information Needs: Old Song, New Tune." In *Rethinking the Library*. Washington, DC: GPO, 159–178.

EBSCO. 2015. "EBSCO host." www.ebscohost.com/corporate-research/information -science-technology-abstracts.

Executive Office of the President. 2014. *Big Data: Seizing Opportunities, Preserving Values*. Washington DC: The White House. www.whitehouse.gov/sites/default/files/docs/ big_data_privacy_report_may_1_2014.pdf.

Farnum, Chris. 2002. "Information Architecture: Five Things Information Managers Need to Know." *Information Management Journal* (September/October): 33–40.

Fourman, Michael. 2002. "Informatics." July. www.informatics.ed.ac.uk.

Froehlich, Thomas J. 1994. "Relevance Reconsidered—Towards an Agenda for the 21st Century." *Journal of the American Society of Information Science* 45 (April): 124–134.

Garrett, Jesse James. 2011. *The Elements of User Experience: User-Centered Design for the Web and Beyond*, 2nd ed. www.proquest.safaribooksonline.com/book/Web-design-and -development/9780321688651.

Gordon-Murnane, Laura. 2012. "Big Data: A Big Opportunity for Librarians." *Online* 36 (September/October): 1–4. .

Gossen, Tatiana, and Andreas Nurnberger. 2013. "Specifics of Information Retrieval for Young Users: A Survey." *Information Processing and Management* 49: 739–756.

Griffiths, Jillian R., and Peter Brophy. 2005. "Student Searching Behavior and the Web: Use of Academic Resources and Google." *Library Trends* 53 (spring): 539–554.

Harter, Stephen. 1986. *Online Information Retrieval*. Orlando, FL: Academic Press.

Hawkins, Donald T., Signe E. Larson, and Bari Q. Cato. 2003. "Information Science Abstracts: Tracking the Literature of Information Science. Part 2: A New Taxonomy for Information Science." *Journal of the American Society for Information Science and Technology* 54: 771–781.

Heinstrom, Jannica. 2006. "Broad Exploration or Precise Specificity: Two Basic Information Seeking Patterns among Students." *Journal of the American Society for Information Science and Technology* 57: 1440–1450.

Hersh, William. 2008. "What Is Medical Informatics?" www.ohsu.edu/ohsuedu/academic/ som/dmice/about/whatis.cfm.

Hewett, Baecker, Carey Card, Mantei Gasen, Strong Perlman, and William Verplank. 2009. *Chapter 2: Human-Computer Interaction*. ACM SIGCHI Curricula for Human-Computer Interaction. http://old.sigchi.org/cdg/cdg2.html.

Hsieh-Yee, Ingrid. 2001. "Research on Web Search Behavior." *Library and Information Science Research* 53:167–185.

ISO (International Standards Organization). 1998. *Ergonomics of Human-System Interaction—Part 210*. www.iso.org/obp/ui/#iso:std:iso:9241:-210:ed-1:v1:en.

Kling, Rob. 1999. "What Is Social Informatics and Why Does It Matter?" *D-Lib Magazine* 5 (January): 1.

Koenig, Michael. 2012. "What Is KM? Knowledge Management Explained." www .kmworld.com/Articles/Editorial/What-Is- . . . /What-is-KM-Knowledge-Management _Explained-82405.aspx.

Krikelas, James. 1983. "Information-Seeking Behavior: Patterns and Concepts." *Drexel Library Quarterly* 19 (spring): 5–20.

Kuhlthau, Carol C. 1991. "Inside the Search Process: Information Seeking from the User's Perspective." *Journal of the American Society of Information Science* 361–371.

———. 1993. *Seeking Meaning: A Process Approach to Library and Information Services.* Westport, CT: Libraries Unlimited.

Lazar, Jonathan, Mega Subramaniam, Paul Jaeger, and John Bertot. 2014. "HCI Policy Issues in U.S. Libraries." (Interactions.) 21 (September/October 2014): 78–81.

Lazonder, Ard W., Harm J. A. Biemans, and Iwans G. J. H. Wopereis. 2000. "Differences between Novice and Experienced Users in Searching Information on the World Wide Web." *Journal of the American Society for Information Science* 51: 576–581.

Lee, Chingkwei Adrienne, and John N. Olsgaard. 1989. "Linguistics and Information Science." In *Principles and Applications of Information Science for Library Professionals*, edited by John N. Olsgaard. Chicago: ALA, 27–36.

Lindgaard, Gitte, Gary Fernandes, Cathy Dudek, and J. Brown. 2006. "Attention Web Designers: You Have 50 Milliseconds to Make a Good First Impression!" *Behavior and Information Technology* 25 (March–April): 115–126.

Lopatovska, Irene, and Ioannis Arapakis. 2011. "Theories, Methods, and Current Research on Emotions in Library and Information Science, Information Retrieval and Human-Computer Interaction." *Information Processing and Management* 47: 575–592.

Lotka, Alfred J. 1926. "The Frequency Distribution of Scientific Productivity." *Journal of the Washington Academy of Sciences* 16: 317–323.

Matthews, Joseph R. 2013. "Valuing Information, Information Services, and the Library: Possibilities and Realities." *Portal: Library and the Academy* 13: 91–112.

McInerney, Claire. 2002. "Knowledge Management and the Dynamic Nature of Knowledge." *Journal of the American Society for Information Science and Technology* 53: 1009–1018.

McIver, Derrick, Cynthia A. Lengnick-Hall, Mark L. Lengnick-Hall, and Indu Ramachandran. 2013. "Understanding Work and Knowledge Management from a Knowledge-in-Practice Perspective." *Academy of Management Review* 38: 597–620.

Manyika, James et al. 2011. *Big Data: The Next Frontier for Innovation, Competition, and Productivity.* www.mckinsey.com/insights/business_technology/big_data_the_next _frontier_for_innovation.

———. "Insights & Publications: Big Data: The Next Frontier for Innovation, Competition, and Productivity." www.mckinsey.com/insights/business_technology/ big_data_the_next_frontier_for_innovation.

Martin, Bill. 2009. "Knowledge Management." *Annual Review of Information Science and Technology* 42: 369–424.

Morville, Peter. 2005. *Ambient Findability: What We Find Changes Who We Become.* Sebastopol, CA: O'Reilly.

Niu, Xi, Bradley M. Hemminger et al. 2010. "National Study of Information Seeking Behavior of Academic Researchers in the United States." *Journal of the American Society for Information Science and Technology* 61: 869–890.

Norlin, Elaina, and C. M. Winters. 2002. *Usability Testing for Library Web Sites: A Hands-On Guide.* Chicago: ALA.

Oxford English Dictionary, 2nd ed. 1989. Oxford: Clarendon Press.

Paluch, Kimmy. 2006. "What Is User Experience Design." www.montparnas.com/articles/what-is-user-experience-design.

Pao, Miranda Lee. 1989. *Concepts of Information Retrieval.* Englewood, CO: Libraries Unlimited, 54–55.

Rayward, Boyd. 1983. "Library and Information Sciences." In *The Study of Information: Interdisciplinary Messages,* edited by Fritz Machlup and Una Mansfield. New York: Wiley, 343–363.

Robins, David, Jason Holmes, and Mary Stansbury. 2010. "Consumer Health Information on the Web: The Relationship of Visual Design and Perceptions of Credibility." *Journal of the American Society for Information Science and Technology* 61: 13–20.

Rose, Daniel E. 2006. "Reconciling Information-Seeking Behavior with Search User Interfaces for the Web." *Journal of the American Society for Information Science and Technology* 57: 797–799.

Rosenfeld, Louis, and Peter Morville. 2002. *Information Architecture for the World Wide Web.* Sebastopol, CA: O'Reilly.

Rouse, William B. 1984. "Human Information Seeking and Design of Information Systems." *Information Processing and Management* 20.

Savolainen, Reijo. 2007. "Media Credibility and Cognitive Authority. The Case of Seeking Orienting Information." *Information Research* 12 (April). http://informationr.net/ir/12–3/paper319.html.

Sawyer, Steve. 2005. "Social Informatics: Overview, Principles, and Opportunities." *Bulletin of the American Society for Information Science and Technology* 31 (June/July): 9–12.

Schmidt, Aaron and Amanda Etches. 2014. *Useful, Usable, Desirable: Applying User Experience Design to Your Library.* Chicago: ALA

Shaw, Debora. 1991. "The Human-Computer Interface for Information Retrieval." *Annual Review of Information Science and Technology (ARIST)* 26: 155–195.

Slone, Debra J. 2002. "The Influence of Mental Models and Goals on Search Patterns during Web Interaction." *Journal of the American Society for Information Science and Technology* 53: 1152–1169.

Smith, Linda C. 1981. "Citation Analysis." *Library Trends* 30 (summer): 83–106.

———. 1987. "Artificial Intelligence and Information Retrieval." *Annual Review of Information Science and Technology (ARIST)* 22: 41–77.

Spink, Amanda, and Charles Cole. 2006. "Human Information Behavior: Integrating Diverse Approaches and Information Use." *Journal of the American Society for Information Science and Technology* 57: 25–35.

Spink, Amanda, Susan Danby, Kerry Mallan, and Carly Butler. 2010. "Exploring Young Children's Web Searching and Technoliteracy." *Journal of Documentation* 66: 191–206.

Stephens, Rod. 2009. *Beginning Database Design Solutions.* Indianapolis: Wiley.

Summers, Ron, Charles Oppenheim, Jack Meadows, Cliff McKnight, and Margaret Kinnell. 1999. "Information Science in 2010: A Loughborough University View." *Journal of the American Society for Information Science* 50:1153–1162.

Taylor, Robert S. 1966. "Professional Aspects of Information Science and Technology." In *Annual Review of Information Science and Technology*, vol. 1, edited by Carlos A. Cuadra. New York: Wiley, 15–40.

———. 1986. *Value-Added Processes in Information Systems.* Norwood, NJ: Ablex.

Veith, Richard H. 2006. "Memex at 60: Internet or iPod?" *Journal of the American Society for Information Science and Technology* 57: 1233–1242.

Wallace, Danny P. 1989. "Bibliometrics and Citation Analysis." In *Principles and Applications of Information Science for Library Professionals*, edited by John N. Olsgaard. Chicago: ALA, 10–26.

Webopedia. 2014. "HCI-human-computer Interaction." www.webopedia.com/TERM/H/HCI.html.

Wellisch, Hans. 1972. "From Information Science to Informatics: A Terminological Investigation." *Journal of Librarianship* 4 (July): 157–187.

Wikipedia. 2009. "Informatics." http://en.wikipedia.org/wiki/Informatics.

Wilson, Patrick. 1983. *Second-Hand Knowledge.* Westport, CT: Greenwood.

———. 1986. "The Face Value Rule in Reference Work." *RQ* 25 (summer): 468–475.

Wisniewski, Jeff. 2013. "Responsive Design." *Onlinesearcher.net* (January/February): 74–76.

Xie, Iris, and Soohyung Joo. 2010. "Transitions in Search Tactics during the Web-Based Search Process." *Journal of the American Society for Information Science and Technology* 61 (November): 2188–2205.

Xu, Yunjie, Bernard Cheng-Yian Tan, and Li Yang. 2006. "Who Will You Ask? An Empirical Study of Interpersonal Task Information Seeking." *Journal of the American Society for Information Science and Technology* 57: 1666–1677.

SELECTED READINGS: Information Science

Books

Bawden, David, and Lyn Robinson. *Introduction to Information Science*. Chicago: ALA, 2014.

Case, Donald O. *Looking for Information: A Survey of Research on Information Seeking, Needs, and Behavior*. 3rd ed. Bingley, Eng.: Emerald Group. San Diego: Academic Press, 2012.

Davis, Charles H., and Deborah Shaw. *Introduction to Information Science and Technology*. Medford, NJ: Information Today, 2011.

Garrett, Jesse James. *The Elements of User Experience: User-Centered Design for the Web and Beyond*, 2nd ed. 2011. http://proquest.safaribooksonline.com/book/Web-design -and-development/9780321688651.

Lester, June, and Wallace C. Koehler Jr. *Fundamentals of Information Studies*. New York: Neal-Schuman, 2003.

Machlup, Fritz, and Una Mansfield, eds. *The Study of Information: Interdisciplinary Messages*. New York: Wiley, 1983.

Schmidt, Aaron, and Amanda Etches. *Useful, Usable, Desirable: Applying User Experience Design to Your Library*. Chicago: ALA, 2014.

Srikantaiah, Kanti T., and Michael E. D. Koenig. *Knowledge Management in Practice: Connections and Context*. Medford, NJ: Information Today, 2008.

Wenger, Etienne. *Communities of Practice: Learning, Meaning, and Identity*. Cambridge University Press, 1998.

Articles

Aharony, Noa. "Librarians' Attitudes toward Knowledge Management." *College & Research Libraries* 72 (March 2011): 111–126.

Alfino, Mark, and Linda Pierce. "The Social Nature of Information." *Library Trends* 49 (winter 2001): 471–485.

Anderson, Janna Quitney, and Lee Rainie. *Big Data*. 2012. www.pewInternet.org/Files/ Reports/2012/PIP_Future_of_Internet_2012_Big_Data.pdf.

Ashman, Helen, Declan Dagger, Tim Brailsford, James Goulding, Declan O'Sullivan, Jan-Felix Schmakeit, and Vincent Wade. "Human-Computer Interaction and the Web." In *The Human-Computer Interaction Handbook*, edited by Julie A. Jacko. Boca Raton: CRC, 2012, pp. 565–587.

Bates, Marcia J. "The Design of Browsing and Berrypicking Techniques for the Online Search Interface." *Online Review* 13 (October 1989): 407–424.

———. "The Invisible Substrate of Information Science." *Journal of the American Society for Information Science* 50 (1999): 1043–1050.

————. "Fundamental Forms of Information." *Journal of the American Society for Information Science and Technology* 57 (2006): 1033–1045.

Bertot, John Carlo, Ursula Gorham, Paul T. Jaeger, and Lindsay C. Sarin. "Big Data, Libraries, and the Information Policies of the Obama Administration." In *Library and Book Trade Almanac*, 59th ed. Medford, NJ: Information Today, 2014, pp. 5–23.

Borko, H. "Information Science: What Is It?" *American Documentation* 19 (December 1968): 3–5.

Bush, Vannevar. "As We Might Think." *Atlantic Monthly* 176 (July 1945): 101–108.

Case, Donald O. "Information Behavior." *Annual Review of Information Science and Technology (ARIST)* 40 (2006): 327.

Connaway, Lynn Silipigni, Donna M. Lanclos, and Erin M. Hood. "'I Always Stick with the First Thing That Comes up on Google . . .' Where People Go for Information, What They Use, and Why." *Educause Review Online.* 2013. www.educause.edu/ero/article/ i-always-stick-first-thing-comes-google-where-people-go-information-what-they-use -and-why.

Connaway, Lynn Silipigni, Timothy J. Dickey, and Marie L. Radford. "'If It Is Too Inconvenient, I'm Not Going After It': Convenience as a Critical Factor in Information-Seeking Behaviors." *Library and Information Science Research* 33 (2011): 179–190.

Courtright, Christina. "Context in Information Behavior Research." *Annual Review of Information Science and Technology (ARIST)* 41 (2007): 273–306.

Dresang, Eliza T. "The Information-Seeking Behavior of Youth in the Digital Environment." *Library Trends* 54 (fall 2005): 178–196.

Du, Jia Tina, and Amanda Spink. "Toward a Web Search Model: Integrating Multitasking, Cognitive Coordination, and Cognitive Shifts." *Journal of the American Society for Information Science and Technology* 62 (2011): 1466–1472.

Dumbill, Edd. "What Is Big Data? An Introduction to the Big Data Landscape." 2012. radar.oreilly.com/2012/01/what-is-big-data.html.

Executive Office of the President. *Big Data: Seizing Opportunities, Preserving Values.* Washington DC: The White House, 2014. www.whitehouse.gov/sites/default/files/ docs/big_data_privacy_report_may_1_2014.pdf.

Gordon-Murnane, Laura. "Big Data: A Big Opportunity for Librarians." *Online* 36 (September/October 2012): 1–4.

Gossen, Tatiana, and Andreas Nürnberger. "Specifics of Information Retrieval for Young Users: A Survey." *Information Processing and Management* 49 (2013): 739–756.

Herner, Saul. "Brief History of Information Science." *Journal of the American Society for Information Science* 35 (May 1984): 157–163.

Hupfer, Maureen, and Brian Detlor. "Gender and Web Information Seeking: A Self-Concept Orientation Model." *Journal of the American Society for Information Science and Technology* 57 (2006): 1105–1115.

Kalbach, James. "'I'm Feeling Lucky': The Role of Emotions in Seeking Information on the Web." *Journal of the American Society for Information Science and Technology* 57 (2006): 813–818.

Koenig, Michael. "What Is KM? Knowledge Management Explained." 2012. www .kmworld.com/Articles/Editorial/What-Is- . . . /What-is-KM-Knowledge-Management _Explained-82405.aspx.

Lazar, Jonathan, Mega Subramaniam, Paul Jaeger, and John Bertot. "HCI Policy Issues in U.S. Libraries." (Interactions.) 21 (September/October 2014): 78–81.

Lindgaard, Gitte, Gary Fernandes, Cathy Dudek, and J. Brown. "Attention Web Designers: You Have 50 Milliseconds to Make a Good First Impression!" *Behaviour and Information Technology* 25 (March–April 2006): 115–126.

Lopatovska, Irene, and Ioannis Arapakis. "Theories, Methods, and Current Research on Emotions in Library and Information Science, Information Retrieval and Human-Computer Interaction." *Information Processing and Management* 47 (2011): 575–592.

McInerney, Claire. "Knowledge Management and the Dynamic Nature of Knowledge." *Journal of the American Society for Information Science and Technology* 53 (2002): 1009–1018.

Manyika, James, et al. *Big Data: The Next Frontier for Innovation, Competition, and Productivity.* 2011. www.mckinsey.com/insights/business_technology/big_data_the _next_frontier_for_innovation.

———. "Insights & Publications: Big Data: The Next Frontier for Innovation, Competition, and Productivity." www.mckinsey.com/insights/business_technology/ big_data_the_next_frontier_for_innovation.

Martin, Bill. "Knowledge Management." *Annual Review of Information Science and Technology* 42 (2009): 369–424.

Matthews, Joseph R. "Valuing Information, Information Services, and the Library: Possibilities and Realities." *Portal: Library and the Academy* 13 (2013): 91–112.

Nui, Xi, Bradley M. Hemminger, et al. "National Study of Information Seeking Behavior of Academic Researchers in the United States." *Journal of the American Society for Information Science and Technology* 61 (2010): 869–890.

Robins, David, Jason Holmes, and Mary Stansbury. "Consumer Health Information on the Web: The Relationship of Visual Design and Perceptions of Credibility." *Journal of the American Society for Information Science and Technology* 61 (2010): 13–20.

Spink, Amanda, and Charles Cole. "Human Information Behavior: Integrating Diverse Approaches and Information Use." *Journal of the American Society for Information Science and Technology* 57 (2006): 25–35.

Vaidhyanathan, Siva, and Chris Bulock. "Knowledge and Dignity in the Era of "Big Data." *The Serials Librarian* 66 (2014): 49–64.

Veith, Richard H. "Memex at 60: Internet or iPod?" *Journal of the American Society for Information Science and Technology* 57 (2006): 1233–1242.

Warner, Julian. "W(h)ither Information Science." *Library Quarterly* 71 (2001): 243–255.

Wisniewski, Jeff. "Responsive Design." *Onlinesearcher.net* (January/February 2013): 74–76.

Xie, Iris, and Soohyung Joo. "Transitions in Search Tactics During the Web-Based Search Process." *Journal of the American Society for Information Science and Technology* 61 (November 2010): 2188–2205.

8

Information Policy
Stakeholders and Agendas

As printed and electronic information have become the lifeblood of government, commerce, education, and many other daily activities, information policy has come to influence most interactions in society. Further, the importance of information means that information policy now has considerable impact on other forms of public policy. (Jaeger and Fleischmann 2007, p. 843)

I. INTRODUCTION

Information policy is any law, regulation, rule, or practice (written or unwritten) that affects the creation, acquisition, organization, dissemination, or evaluation of information. Information policy can be discussed from the perspective of information technologies for educational and industrial uses, telecommunications, privacy issues, computer regulations and crimes, copyright and intellectual property, and government information systems (Burger 1993). Not surprisingly, a variety of stakeholders in the information policy process are deeply concerned about information from both legal and political perspectives. These stakeholders include business and industry, government, and information producers and disseminators, as well as individual citizens and various organizations that represent their interests.

A. Business and Industry

In American society, the discussion of information policy highlights a fundamental tension between entrepreneurship and democracy. Under capitalism, information can be viewed as a form of private property that provides a competitive edge. Insofar as it can be held privately, there is a strong incentive for individuals to discover information and use it to create new products and services. On the other hand, the democratic values of American society promote the free flow of information and access to it both as a right and as essential to a free society. This is not to say that capitalism and democracy are incompatible; it is to suggest that information policy in a democratic society requires a balancing of social, economic, and political interests. Because information is critical to competition, business and industry actively lobby to influence policies that will affect its dissemination and restriction. Business and industry have special interests in both protecting new knowledge, and accessing and organizing current knowledge.

1. Protecting New Knowledge to Improve Productivity and Profits

Business and industry invest considerable sums in pursuit of new inventions or discoveries and have legitimate needs to protect their proprietary information. Patent, copyright, and trademark laws, otherwise known as intellectual property laws, offer protection, as do laws that restrict an employee's use of protected knowledge even after separation from employment. Employers can use a no-competition clause in contracts that prevents former employees from working for a competitor so that they cannot reveal information about the employer's processes or inventions. Such restrictions allow businesses to maintain a competitive edge with domestic and foreign competitors and help ensure organizational survival. Similarly, laws governing and regulating computer programs and codes that modify an organization's products are important protections for software designers.

2. Access to Information and Its Organization

The extent to which government policies permit easy and inexpensive access to technical and scientific information can have a substantial effect on an organization's ability to function effectively in competitive national and international environments. Similarly, the way information is created, organized, stored, made accessible, distributed, communicated, and discarded within a government or within a company can affect the ability to use it efficiently and effectively. Having free access to computer code alone can have a tremendous impact on the development of new systems and applications. The emergence of "open source" software is testimony to the significance of this influence.

B. Government

Local, state, and federal governments collect, organize, and evaluate vast quantities of information. The federal government holds numerous hearings, departments generate volumes of data, and agencies like the FBI or the CIA constantly acquire information both print and digital. Also, federally funded research especially in the sciences and medicine generates a significant amount of data and findings for potential use. The federal government controls how that information is disseminated by promulgating regulations that specify what information is restricted, such as information affecting national security, or released to the public (or the press) and what information must be publically available. Laws such as the Freedom of Information Act, the National Security Act, and the USA PATRIOT Act form part of the policy framework that defines the dissemination and control of information from government sources.

C. Information Producers and Disseminators

Stakeholders in information policy also include members of the telecommunications industry, including the telephone, television, cable, and radio industry; producers of DVDs; publishers of both print and electronic information; Internet content providers, database producers and vendors; and technology giants such as Microsoft and Google. All of these stakeholders have a special interest in information policy because of its direct and profound effect on their operations. For example, a number of laws and regulations either promote or diminish their effectiveness, such as laws affecting competition, pricing and availability of services, taxation, postal rates, royalties, copyright, and laws concerning libel or privacy rights. This sector also includes libraries. Libraries have a special role and exercise a special interest because they are among the few stakeholders in this group whose motivations are not profit oriented.

D. American Citizens and Organizations That Represent Their Interests

Every citizen in a democratic society is a major stakeholder in laws and policies dealing with information. The way information flows in a society directly affects each person's ability to make informed decisions. The subtlest shift in policy can affect the extent to which the public receives accurate, up-to-date, and sufficient information, as well as who receives this information. Individual citizens, however, seldom have the ability to influence these policies. Consequently, a variety of organizations try to represent the public's interests, including the American Library Association (ALA), the American Civil Liberties Union, and Computer Professionals for Social Responsibility.

II. THE POLITICAL CLIMATE AND POLICY MAKING THAT AFFECTS LIBRARIES

Libraries have always been affected by public policies and the public perceptions that shape those policies. The current political situation is no exception; in fact, it might well be that public policy and perception affects library services now more than ever. To some extent, this situation is ironic. As the country continues to recover from the major recession of 2008, people have increasingly relied on the services that libraries provide. Over the same time, public tax support for libraries has continued to decline—as demand for library services increases, support for them decreases. This disjunction is also reflected in the fact that many people highly value public library services, but many are also unaware of what specific services libraries provide (Jaeger et. al. 2014).

In addition, the current political climate is generally not conducive to the types of compromises that produced salutary results in the past. Jaeger et al. (2014) observed that the current climate is "defined by hyperpartisanship and entrenched ideology . . ." (p. 101). Despite these difficulties, LIS professional must accept that political attitudes and policies will continue to have substantive impact on library missions and operations and it is useful to identify a few of the factors affecting them:

Taxpayer resistance: For several decades, there has been increasing reluctance of citizens to maintain or increase levels of taxation for public services. Certainly, the recession of 2008 exacerbated this situation, but the movements opposing taxation were occurring long before it. The result has been declining funding for many publicly funded libraries, most notably public libraries, but also school and academic libraries.

Declining confidence in public institutions: For years, people placed confidence in major public institutions, such as local, state, and national government, public schools, and universities. Over the last few decades, this confidence has declined.

Some have argued that some of these institutions can be replaced: Google can replace libraries; charter schools can replace public schools. Citizens are less likely to provide either fiscal or political support for public institutions if they believe that they are not accomplishing the goals for which they were designed.

Political ideologies that favor private enterprise over public good: As public institutions declined in favor among some policy makers and influencers, they advanced an alternative belief suggesting that private enterprise was a more appropriate model for structuring such institutions. Some even argued that public libraries should be privatized. Those who favor an entrepreneurial model use a new vocabulary of accountability where "return on investment" (ROI) becomes a central measure of worth. Following this framework, only those services that can pay for themselves or produce measurable benefits (in economic terms) to the private sector deserve support. Traditionally, institutions have been assumed to be public goods such as education, public health, police and fire services, and libraries have not based their value on the economic advantages that might accrue from their services, but on the social, cultural, and educational benefits assumed to be valued in-and-of-themselves. Today, this assumption, albeit a noble and appropriate one, is being sorely challenged (Jaeger et al. 2014).

Lack of effective advocacy on the part of libraries: In the past, libraries seldom engaged in advocacy on their own behalf based on a belief, at least in part, that they should remain *neutral* when it comes to political activities (Jaeger et al. 2014). As a result, libraries failed to communicate to legislators and other influential citizens the critical role that libraries play in their communities. Among the many library services that provide significant social and economic benefits to the community are the following: assisting with job hunting strategies (reducing unemployment); helping individuals apply for social services or interact with government agencies; providing spaces for meetings and group activities; offering educational and digital literacy programming (skill development); providing information services, access to digital and print books, and other materials, as well as free Internet access; offering specialized programs for various segments of the population, including children and teens, immigrants, those with low incomes, and the homeless. In too many cases, legislators and other critical stakeholders remain unaware of these many valuable services. Although some organizations, such as the American Library Association, have been more active in lobbying and advocacy in recent years, the depth and breadth of their efforts have been limited and not based on strong data-based evidence but on generalities about the value of libraries in a democratic society. In the future, in order for libraries to move forward they will have to become more engaged in the political process, with better data and more articulate arguments (Jaeger et al.

2014). The stakes are high. Below are some of the major information policy issues that must be addressed.

III. SELECTED INFORMATION POLICY ISSUES

There are many information policy issues that, in one way or another, significantly impact library services. Below is a brief discussion of some of the major issues. (Issues related to intellectual freedom will be discussed in chapter 9):

A. Protecting the Privacy of Citizens

Judith Krug, the late Executive Director of the Office of Intellectual Freedom of the American Library Association, in the foreword to *Privacy in the 21st Century*, described the issues facing LIS professionals:

> Privacy is the issue of the moment in librarianship, brought forward by relentless changes in technology, law, and social attitudes. Whether it is the question of adopting Radio Frequency Identification Devices (RFIDs) to track book inventory, devising policy to deal with law enforcement inquiries under the USA PATRIOT Act, or addressing a library user's concerns about the use of her personal information, each day finds librarians confronting new questions and new challenges concerning privacy and confidentiality. (2005 p. ix)

Although there is no explicit right to privacy in the U.S. Constitution, the Supreme Court recognized that the amendments in the Bill of Rights have "penumbras" or implied powers. In common usage, a penumbra is "a space of partial illumination between the perfect shadow (as in an eclipse) on all sides and the full light" (*Merriam-Webster's Collegiate Dictionary* 1996). The legal meaning of the term is best known from the Supreme Court decision *Griswold v. Connecticut* (381 US 479, 1965). In this case, appellants Estelle Griswold, executive director of the Planned Parenthood League (PPL) of Connecticut, and Dr. C. Lee Buxton, a professor at Yale Medical School and director of the New Haven PPL office, were convicted for prescribing contraceptive devices and giving contraceptive advice to married people in violation of a Connecticut statute that made it unlawful to use any drug or medicinal article for the purpose of preventing conception. They challenged the constitutionality of the statute and the Supreme Court held that the Connecticut statute was unconstitutional because it violated a person's right to privacy implied in the due process rights outlined in Fourteenth Amendment. In his opinion, Justice

William O. Douglas stated that the specific guarantees of the Bill of Rights have penumbras "formed by emanations from those guarantees that help give them life and substance." The right to privacy exists within this area (Gale Group 1998).

Magi (2011) argued that protecting privacy provides benefits in three broad categories: benefits to the individual, to personal relationships, and to society-at-large. From an individual's perspective, protecting privacy provides a sense of solitude which permits relaxation and concentration; it increases one's sense of self and autonomy; it increases opportunity for freedom of choice and reduces the need for unnecessary conformity; it protects a person's sense of personal space; and preserves the opportunity for people to make a fresh start in life. From the perspective of personal relationships, it supports the building of intimate relationships by allowing people to share personal information or exchange controversial ideas without fear. From the perspective of the society-at-large, supports the common good by building trust and protecting confidentiality; it reduces over-categorization of people into groups and reduces improper collection and misuse of data; helps maintain the equilibrium of power between the State and the individual; promotes free speech and association; and creates a fertile environment for discussion of controversial issues.

Today, many Americans express growing concerns that the ubiquity of information technologies makes personally identifiable information on citizens' health, financial affairs, or buying habits too vulnerable to unauthorized access. In response, the federal and many state governments have passed legislation to protect privacy in specific areas such as the Right to Financial Privacy Act of 1978, which protects financial records; the Electronic Communications Privacy Act of 1986, which deals with the privacy of cellular phones; and the Communications Assistance for Law Enforcement Act of 1994, which, in part, deals with the privacy of cellular phones and data communications (Science Applications International Corporation 1995). Other acts, such as the Health Insurance Portability and Accountability Act (HIPAA) and the Family Educational Rights and Privacy Act (FERPA), deal with the confidentiality of health and education records. In addition, many states have passed statutes on the confidentiality of library circulation records that provide fairly complete protection against third-party access to borrowers' records, while still providing limited access by governmental agencies for specific reasons. These protections are not, however, complete. For example, the PATRIOT Act can compel libraries to provide information about their users.

Privacy issues arise in many instances in libraries. For example, to ensure authorized and proper use of library materials, LIS professionals must often access databases and digital services that can make individuals vulnerable to personal identification and monitoring. As a rule, libraries seek to limit that vulnerability by "engaging in limited tracking of user activities, instituting short-term data retention policies, and generally enabling the anonymous browsing of materials" (Zimmer 2014, p. 123). Nonetheless, e-books have raised particular concerns because they rely on third-party vendors to supply downloaded books. Privacy issues are also raised when libraries consider adopting new discovery systems. Vendors of such systems can collect personal data, create profiles, or record the articles or topics searched (Zimmer 2014; Rubel 2014). Without appropriate contractual and policy protections, the reading habits of these users could be subject to inappropriate scrutiny (Chmara 2012; Rubel 2014). Interestingly, Rubel (2014) suggested that although privacy issues remain a concern, such databases increase intellectual freedom by increasing the autonomy people have in their intellectual pursuits, what Rubel refers to as "positive intellectual freedom" (p. 183). In other words, such databases open the possibility of exploring ideas to which an individual might not otherwise have access.

The privacy of reference transactions, whether virtual or in-person, has also raised issues because individuals might not seek information if they believe their queries might be subject to public or governmental scrutiny. Although it would be useful if librarians could assert a privileged relationship during reference transactions, similar to a doctor-patient or lawyer-client privilege, it is unlikely that the courts would uphold such a claim. Although sympathetic to the desirability of such a privilege, Austin cited eight reasons why it would not be supported (2004):

- The client does not directly pay for the service.
- No permanent records are maintained.
- Patrons can perform many of the functions themselves.
- The relationship is usually ephemeral.
- In general, the importance of the transaction is minimal.
- In general, disclosure of the information would have minimal impact.
- Most reference queries are of minor significance.
- Much of the transaction takes place in public.

LIS professionals take seriously the need to protect a citizen's privacy from third-party intrusions—from individuals or governments. The ALA Library Bill of Rights and the ALA Code of Ethics both take a strong stance on privacy protections. In general, librarians' attitudes toward privacy reflect those of the norms of the profession. Most are concerned about privacy protections and believe that access to personal information should be controlled. Regarding library users, there is also very strong support for maintaining the confidentiality of users' personal information, including circulation and Internet records (Zimmer 2014). Regarding the Internet, the ALA adopted "Privacy: An Interpretation of the Library Bill of Rights," in 2002 (discussed further below). Internet communication involves many different activities including sending and receiving e-mail messages, transmitting and downloading files, participating in social networking, and the purchase and sale of goods and services. Many Internet users are still under the erroneous assumption that their identities are private because these activities usually take place in the privacy of one's home or work setting. In reality, they can usually be discovered easily as websites attach "cookies" to the hard drives of personal computers or install spyware or adware to track an individual's use.

The issue of privacy will continue to be an important issue for LIS professionals. The digital environment creates increasing opportunities for personal data to be collected, aggregated, and analyzed. On the one hand, this allows us to analyze trends, improve our organizations and practices, and respond to our users' needs. In other instances, it might have the chilling effect of impairing people's ability to explore ideas and express opinions openly and frankly. Privacy is not a simple concept. Solove (2008) summarized the issues nicely:

> Privacy thus involves more than keeping secrets—it is about how we regulate information flow, how we ensure that others use our information responsibly, how we exercise control over our information, and how we should limit the way others can use our data." (p. 59)

B. Promoting Freedom of Information

Protecting privacy is vital, but it is equally important that citizens have a right to information regarding governmental activities. As James Madison wrote in 1822, "A popular government without popular information, or the means of acquiring it, is but a Prologue to a Farce or a Tragedy or perhaps both" (Madison 1973). This balance between privacy and public records is constantly being tested and redefined. Ironically, some of the same acts that protect an individual's privacy are also ones that ensure public rights of access to information when legitimate interests arise. The most prominent of these acts is the federal Freedom of Information Act (FOIA) of 1966, which applies to "all records held by all executive branch agencies, creates a presumption in favor of release, permits only defined reasons for withholding information, and authorizes a requester to invoke judicial review" (Strickland 2005, p. 548). The act was meant to ensure that government records that were not specifically protected for national security or other valid reasons would be available for inspection by members of the public. The intent was to prevent government officials from withholding information because they thought it might be embarrassing or a political liability. The federal act was followed by many state acts defining which records the public could access. Restricted records might include law enforcement investigation records, adoptions, and personnel or medical records.

1. Internet (Network) Neutrality

Early Internet transmissions were carried by telephone lines that were governed by the Communications Act of 1934. This act had a nondiscrimination requirement for "common carriers" such as telephone companies and cable operators:

> It shall be unlawful for any common carrier to make any unjust or unreasonable discrimination in charges, practices, classifications, regulations, facilities, or services for or in connection with like communication service, directly or indirectly, by any means or device, or to make or give any undue or unreasonable preference or advantage to any particular person, class of person, or locality, or to subject any particular person, class of person, or locality to any undue or unreasonable prejudice or disadvantage.

However, as Internet access moved away from its dependence on telephone lines toward broadband and other forms of access, the courts were less inclined to apply the common carrier provisions.

From the beginning, participation and access to the Internet has been open. For example, if someone wanted to create a website or an application (app), once certain protocols were observed, the developer could make that product available to all. Similarly, individuals can move throughout the Internet without barriers or restrictions from an Internet service provider (ISP), such as Verizon or AT&T. In fact, "The *sine qua non* of the Internet is the ability for everyone to connect and have their traffic routed to the desired location" (Weitzner 2006, p. 10). This concept is known as network neutrality:

> Network neutrality . . . is the idea that an Internet provider (ISP) should treat all the data that travels through its network equally, regardless of the source, destination, or content of that data. In practice, this means that the data packets that make up streaming video, images from a digital archive, massively multiplayer online games, and class material in a course management system are all delivered from service to user indiscriminately, with minor modifications for network optimization. Discriminating against or blocking content from reaching an end user (e.g. slowing down

certain Websites like Netflix or blocking access to a service like Apple's Face Time) violates the principle of net neutrality. (ALA 2014)

The notion of ISP neutrality has been essential in promoting rapid development and innovation on the Internet. In fact, companies such as Google and Yahoo! depend in large part on Internet neutrality to preserve the value of their search engines. Internet neutrality is also grounded in legislative history. However, in March 2002, the Federal Communications Commission (FCC) ruled that broadband Internet services provided by cable companies were to be treated as "information services," not "telecommunication services," a decision upheld by the U.S. Supreme Court in 2005. Hence, telephone or cable companies that provide broadband services, essentially the "pipes" for Internet use, do not need to comply with the common carrier provisions (Gilroy 2006; Windhausen 2009).

This decision caused great consternation and there was a movement for additional legislation to preserve the neutrality of ISPs and to reestablish the common carrier approach to broadband Internet services. As might be expected, those who believed that such legislation would stifle entrepreneurial activities and impose excessive costs on ISP providers were opposed to that idea. They argued that the forces of the marketplace should price Internet use. Ed Whitacre of AT&T made the following case:

> Now what they would like to do is use my pipes free, but I ain't going to let them do that because we have spent this capital and we have to have a return on it. So there's going to have to be some mechanisms for these people who use these pipes to pay for the portion they're using. Why should they be allowed to use my pipes? The Internet can't be free in that sense, because we and the cable companies have made an investment and for a Google or Yahoo! or Vonage or anybody to expect to use these pipes free is nuts! (Weitzner 2006)

These comments conjure a world in which ISPs block or otherwise obstruct some content. If network providers were allowed to prioritize traffic, the results might be chilling. The ALA (2007) noted, "'Pipe' owners (carriers) should not be allowed to charge some information providers more money for the same pipes, or establish exclusive deals that relegate everyone else . . . to an Internet 'slow lane'" (p. 1). Gilroy (2006) observed that the "consolidation and diversification of broadband providers into content providers has the potential to lead to discriminatory behaviors which conflict with net neutrality principles" (p. 2). An ISP might, for example, make its own content more readily available. Similarly, the ability to move throughout the Internet might be restricted since some links might not be available. This could produce serious and adverse effects on social networking activities. Access to a blog, for example, might be substantially limited if a poster's network operators did not have an agreement with a particular ISP (Weitzner 2006).

ALA responded to continued concerns about network neutrality and its possible impact on libraries by adopting their own resolution in 2006—"*Resolution Affirming 'Network Neutrality*.'" This statement "affirms the right of all library users to enjoy equal and equitable Internet access free from commercial bias, whether provided in the library, or through remote access to library resources" (ALA 2010). In 2010, the FCC also responded to the problems and issues created by excepting broadband from common carrier obligations by promulgating new "Open Internet" rules (FCC 2010). This action was an attempt to "preserve the Internet as an open platform for innovation, investment, job creation, economic growth, competition, and free expression (p. 17906). Three basic rules were adopted:

> *Transparency*. Fixed and mobile broadband providers must disclose the network management practices, performance characteristics, and terms and conditions of their broadband services;
>
> No *blocking*. Fixed broadband providers might not block lawful content, applications, services, or non-harmful devices; mobile broadband providers might not block lawful Websites, or block applications that compete with their voice or video telephony services; and
>
> No *unreasonable discrimination*. Fixed broadband providers might not unreasonably discriminate in transmitting lawful network traffic.
> (p. 17906)

These rules went a long way to reestablishing the underlying values that were part of the common carrier provisions. However, ISP providers were not disposed to accept them and Verizon challenged the authority of the FCC in court. The U.S. Court of Appeals for the District of Columbia in *Verizon v. FCC* (U.S. Court . . . 2014) determined that the FCC had overstepped its authority and threw out the Open Network rules, although it did retain rules related to disclosure of ISP management practices to those they serve. Not surprisingly, the ALA was deeply troubled by this decision and on the day of the ruling issued a critical press release stating:

> The court's decision gives commercial companies the astounding legal authority to block Internet traffic, give preferential treatment to certain Internet services or applications, and steer users to or away from certain Web sites based on their own commercial interests. This ruling, if it stands, will adversely affect the daily lives of Americans and fundamentally change the open nature of the Internet,

where uncensored access to information has been hallmark of the communication medium since its inception. (ALA "ALA Troubled . . . 2014)

Under this ruling access to academic databases or content could receive lower priority or that libraries would have to pay additional fees to receive faster speeds. Similarly, websites might become available on a "tiered access" model, like cable channels are currently packaged (ALA 2014).

In response to the Verizon ruling, in July 2014 representatives from the higher education and library community adopted a set of "Net Neutrality Principles" (see figure 8.1). The principles reaffirm that "preserving an open Internet is essential to our nation's freedom of speech, educational achievement, and economic growth."

FIGURE 8.1
Net-Neutrality Principles

Ensure Neutrality on All Public Networks. Neutrality is an essential characteristic of public broadband Internet access. The principles that follow must apply to all broadband providers and ISPs that provide service to the general public, regardless of underlying transmission technology (e.g., wireline or wireless) and regardless of local market conditions.

Prohibit Blocking. ISPs and public broadband providers should not be permitted to block access to legal websites, resources, applications, or Internet-based services.

Protect against Unreasonable Discrimination. Every person in the United States should be able to access legal content, applications, and services over the Internet without "unreasonable discrimination" by the owners and operators of public broadband networks and providers or discrimination against particular Internet services based on the identity of the user, the content of the information, or the type of service being provided. "Unreasonable discrimination" is the standard in Title II of the Communications Act of 1934; the FCC has generally applied this standard to instances in which providers treat similar customers in significantly different ways.

Prohibit Paid Prioritization. Public broadband providers and ISPs should not be permitted to sell prioritized transmission to certain content, applications, and service providers over other Internet traffic that shares the same network facilities. Prioritizing certain Internet traffic inherently disadvantages other content, applications, and service providers—including those from higher education and libraries that serve vital public interests.

Prevent Degradation. Public broadband providers and ISPs should not be permitted to degrade the transmission of Internet content, applications, or service providers, either intentionally or by failing to invest in adequate broadband capacity to accommodate reasonable traffic growth.

Enable Reasonable Network Management. Public broadband network operators and ISPs should be able to engage in reasonable network management to address issues such as

(cont.)

FIGURE 8.1
Net-Neutrality Principles (cont.)

congestion, viruses, and spam as long as such actions are consistent with these principles. Policies and procedures should ensure that legal network traffic is managed in a content-neutral manner.

Provide Transparency. Public broadband network operators and ISPs should disclose network management practices publicly and in a manner that (1) allows users as well as content, application, and service providers to make informed choices and (2) allows policy makers to determine whether the practices are consistent with these network-neutrality principles. This rule does not require disclosure of essential proprietary information or information that jeopardizes network security.

Continue Capacity-Based Pricing of Broadband Internet Access Connections. Public broadband providers and ISPs might continue to charge consumers and content, application, and service providers for their broadband connections to the Internet, and might receive greater compensation for greater capacity chosen by the consumer or content, application, and service provider.

Adopt Enforceable Policies. Policies and rules to enforce these principles should be clearly stated and transparent. Any public broadband provider or ISP that is found to have violated these policies or rules should be subject to penalties, after being adjudicated on a case-by-case basis.

Accommodate Public Safety. Reasonable accommodations to these principles can be made based on evidence that such accommodations are necessary for public safety, health, law enforcement, national security, or emergency situations.

Maintain the Status Quo on Private Networks. Owners and operators of private networks that are not openly available to the general public should continue to operate according to the long-standing principle and practice that private networks are not subject to regulation. End users (such as households, companies, coffee shops, schools, or libraries) should be free to decide how they use the broadband services they obtain from network operators and ISPs.

Endorsed by:

American Association of Community Colleges (AACC)
American Association of State Colleges and Universities (AASCU)
American Council on Education (ACE)
American Library Association (ALA)
Association of American Universities (AAU)
Association of Public and Land-Grant Universities (APLU)
Association of Research Libraries (ARL)
Chief Officers of State Library Agencies (COSLA)
EDUCAUSE
Modern Language Association (MLA)
National Association of Independent College and Universities (NAICU)   Adopted: July 2014

Source: www.ala.org/news/press-releases/2014/07/higher-education-library-groups-release-net-neutrality-principles.

In February 2015, the FCC issued new rules that comports substantially with these principles by reclassifying broadband Internet access service as a telecommunications service and issued additional rules that banned blocking of legal content, applications, and services as well as paid prioritization of Internet traffic (ALA 2015).

Threats to net neutrality and their implications will require LIS professionals' attention for years to come. It is essential that libraries continue to foster the greatest freedom on the Internet because of its vital importance to the exchange of ideas. As Hutton (2014) observed:

> Those that don't pay—or can't—could instead be stuck sending their content through crowded, low-speed lanes. And more, importantly, their users would be stuck waiting, too.

2. Broadband Access

Broadband access was an issue of particular interest to President George W. Bush and on October 10, 2008, he signed the Broadband Data Improvement Act. Availability of broadband service was considered critical to the information infrastructure, and overall access was increasing rapidly primarily using DSL or cable connections. Among the act's provisions was a requirement to identify geographical areas not yet served by broadband access and to conduct periodic surveys in urban, suburban, and rural areas to determine current levels of broadband capability. In early 2009, Congress expressed the desire for every American to have access to high speed broadband capability and directed the Federal Communications Commission (FCC) to develop a national plan for broadband access (FCC 2010). The FCC commenced a thorough national examination of broadband needs and in 2010 created the *National Broadband Plan* (FCC 2010). The FCC admitted that the task was great and likened the development of broadband infrastructure as similar in magnitude as the development of an infrastructure for electricity a century before—it was, the FCC observed, "the great infrastructure challenge of the early 21st century" (p. xi). The FCC further noted that although nearly 200 million Americans had some access to broadband at home, there remained nearly 100 million Americans without access. The plan made many recommendations in several major areas including (1) promoting and protecting competition in broadband markets, (2) ensuring that government assets such as broadband spectrum are allocated efficiently, (3) developing incentives to increase private sector investment and innovation in broadband access that could improve areas identified as critical national priorities such as health, education, and national security, and (4) creating the incentives needed for universal availability and adoption of broadband.

Regarding universal availability, the plan recommended the creation of a Connect America Fund (CAF) "to support the provision of affordable broadband and voice . . ." (p. xiii). The work of the CAF, created in 2012, was supported by shifting funds from the Universal Service Fund that had been devoted to subsidizing voice telephone networks in rural or remote areas (Connected Nation 2012). In phase I, $115 million was allocated to connect 7 million unserved rural Americans over a six-year period in 37 states. By 2014, over $438 million had been spent to connect 1.6 million people with broadband service (FCC 2012; Buckley 2014). Phase II, referred to as "Rural Broadband Expansion Experiments" was launched in 2014 with a focus on "how to expand robust broadband in rural America in the most cost-effective way . . ." (FCC 2014a). The FCC allocated up to $100 million in the hopes of not only expanding broadband, but also dramatically increasing download speed for rural communities (Buckley 2014; FCC 2014).

Providing broadband access to citizens is a critical component in equalizing access to information, but the political challenges can be formidable. For example, some cities attempted to create their own broadband services for their citizens, but were met with resistance from commercial providers. Responding to pressures from commercial interests, approximately twenty states passed laws prohibiting their cities from competing with private broadband vendors. Cities, in their struggle against what they felt was an overreaching of the state, appealed to the FCC for assistance. States, on the other hand, believed that cities were subdivisions of the state and that any federal intervention would be overreaching on their part (Kim 2014). This situation is a good example of why balancing federal, state, local, and commercial interests is critical.

LIS professionals will need to follow developments in broadband access closely. Currently approximately 90% of public libraries offer wireless Internet access, but they share their bandwidth with other library services such as computer workstations. The result is that about 40% of libraries report having insufficient speed to meet patron needs (iPac 2014). And despite increasing use of broadband along a wide spectrum of the U.S. population, broadband access is still significantly lower among lower-income, older, and less-educated Americans, as well as among African-American, Hispanic/Latino, and rural Americans (Horrigan 2013). As more library services are provided through broadband access, LIS professionals will have to increase their involvement in the political discourse. Certainly, the new technologies are opening up the real possibility of universal and affordable access to digital information for millions, but it must be more than mere access, it must be high-quality access. LIS professionals must be willing to engage their constituencies and political representatives to ensure quality access for all.

C. The Digitization of Government Information and the Rise of E-government

1. Digitization of Government Information

By the 1990s, ever-increasing amounts of government information were available either directly on the Internet or through CD-ROMs. The movement toward digitization was stimulated by the Paperwork Reduction Act of 1995 and the Government Paperwork Elimination Act of 1998, which required government agencies to develop "alternative information technologies that provide for electronic submission, maintenance, or disclosure of information as a substitute for paper" (Robertson and Vatrapu 2010, p. 329). The Clinton administration continued this initiative by ensuring that many of the forms used by major government services were available online and could be processed using the Internet. The digitization movement also prompted the development of GPOAccess—"a collection of online searchable databases of government information" (Mason 2008).

By the end of 1998, "about 34 percent of the titles received by the Federal Depository Library at the end of the fiscal year were in electronic format" (Jorgensen 2006, p. 153). Although 9/11 constricted the amount of government information freely available on the Internet, the general trend of digitally available government information continued through the first decade of the twenty-first century. For example, the E-Government Act of 2002 encouraged cross-agency initiatives, increased e-participation in making government rules and regulations, and improved interoperability of systems with state, local, and tribal governmental units (Robertson and Vatrapu 2010).

The impact of these efforts on libraries was significant. Shuler (2005) observed that as more and more information was digitized and made available through GPO-Access and searchable databases, the need for physical collections was substantially reduced. As a result, he suggested that it was more important for LIS professionals to understand how government works in general, how government information was accessed and used by individuals, and how this information influences the lives of citizens and their communities. Shuler's observations were prescient as the digitization of government information has in turn spawned the rise of e-government.

2. The Rise of E-government

E-government, sometimes referred to as "digital government," has many definitions but it can be characterized generally as "the use of information and communication technologies to enable citizens, politicians, government agencies, and other organizations to work with each other and to carry out activities that support civic life" (Roberson and Vatrapu 2010, p. 319). The federal government recognized the centrality of e-government when it passed the E-government Act of 2002 (reauthorized in 2007). The original act defined electronic government as

> the use by the Government of Web-based Internet applications and other information technologies, combined with the processes that implement these technologies, to—(A) enhance the access to and delivery of Government information and services to the public, other agencies, and other Government entities; or (B) bring about improvements in Government operations that might include effectiveness, efficiency, service quality, or transformation. (U.S. Congress 2002)

The act's definition emphasized the mechanical aspects of e-government. Alternatively, Bertot, Jaeger, and McClure (2008) characterized e-government with a more political orientation:

> The promise of E-government (and its more recent spin-offs of E-Democracy, E-Participation, E-Procurement, and a range of other "E's") is to engage citizenry in government in a citizen-centered manner, but also to develop quality government services and delivery systems that are efficient and effective. (p. 137)

In fact, e-government has evolved over decades from static websites to interactive, two-way communication between citizens and government, as well as increased citizen participation in governmental life. Today, the types of interactions involved in e-government include but are not limited to the following:

- simple gathering of information about government programs and services
- active citizen involvement in public decision making
- administrative functions such as paying taxes online
- use of and application to government social services
- law enforcement and court activities such as jury duty registration and access to court opinions
- digital democracy, including access to laws, ballot issues, candidate information, and voting technologies
- access to regulations and forms for businesses
- access to educational resources and applications for funding
- emergency management such as FEMA applications
- community and neighborhood activities

- government-to-government communication to improve internal operations (Roberson and Vatrapu 2010)

It is clear that e-participation in the political and electoral process has increased substantially. For example, in the 2004 presidential election campaign, 37% of the adult population and 61% of adults online employed the Internet for political news and discussion about the candidates and issues. Campaign contributions could be given over the Internet and people could also participate in chats and discussion forums (Roberson and Vatrapu 2010). These trends continued and grew during the 2008 campaign when Obama staffers used a variety of e-communications (not just the Internet) to interact with people to increase awareness, energize constituencies, and raise funds.

Originally, e-government was conceived as an improved way for government to communicate directly with citizens usually through websites. It was soon discovered, however, that many citizens were unable to use electronic channels easily or successfully. Unsurprisingly, it became increasingly clear that librarians, particularly public librarians, were serving as critical intermediaries in the information, communication, and navigation process (Taylor et al. 2014). Librarians became involved in facilitating communication in both directions: from government to citizen and from citizen to government (Taylor et al. 2014). As the Information Policy and Access Center (2014) has observed:

> Public libraries provide an essential link between government and people. As government information, services, and resources move online, public libraries serve as critical community gateways to electronic government . . . The E-government roles public libraries play are particularly important for those who do not have high speed Internet, or computer access in the home; lack the technology skills that E-government Websites require; or have difficulty understanding and using E-government services. (iPAC 2014, p. 1)

Many people continue to rely on public libraries to help them locate and understand e-government. Bertot et al. (2008) reported that individuals access e-government in libraries for four reasons: (1) lack of computer and Internet technology access, (2) lack of technology skills, (3) inability to understand government services and resources, and (4) the need to ask for assistance from an individual rather than a website or seldom-answered phone help service (p. 138). The public library is still perceived as an important place to get assistance when navigating the maze of e-government websites or completing complicated government forms such as Medicare, immigration, or tax forms, among others (Jaeger 2008; Jaeger and Fleischmann 2007). The most common government information on public library websites includes links to state and federal tax websites (Burke and Boggs 2015). The Public Library Funding and Technology Access Survey (iPAC 2012) provided solid evidence that public libraries are, in fact, performing considerable service related to e-government. It reported,

- 92% of public libraries provided assistance with government Websites;
- 97% provided assistance with government services;
- 71% provided assistance with government forms;
- 50% provided assistance in understanding government services;
- 31% partnered with other government agencies to assist library users. (IPAC 2012, p. 4)

Similarly, Becker et al. (2010) found that public libraries "served as the neighborhood-based extension of a government agency linking users to government officials, programs and services" (p. 7). Among these users:

> 60 percent logged on to learn about laws and regulations, 58% reported using a library computer to download government forms, and 56 percent reported logging on to find out about a government program or service. Fifty-three percent of these users (over 13 million people) reported that they sought help from [a] specific government official or agency. Approximately 83 percent of the people who looked for help from a specific government official or agency reported that they got the help they needed. (p. 7)

Despite the overwhelming evidence of library involvement in e-government, libraries receive little if any financial assistance to provide these services (Bertot et al. 2006b). The ALA, in a 2007 statement to the U.S. Senate Committee on Homeland Security and Governmental Affairs, noted that the federal Library Services and Technology Act (LSTA) provided only 1% of all public library funding for operations. ALA explicitly urged greater support, noting:

> When government moves to save costs by E-government, they pass the costs to public libraries, yet the library community has seen little collaboration or support from federal agencies for the significant increase in services public libraries provide on their behalf. (ALA 2007, p. 1)

Despite these significant limitations, LIS professionals continue to develop e-government services for their users. Bertot et al. (2012a) noted a variety of best practices that characterize the most effective e-government services (see figure 8.2).

FIGURE 8.2
Best Practices of Effective E-Government Programs in Libraries

---

Effective e-government programs

- incorporate e-government service provision into their institutional mission

- form partnerships with government agencies and nongovernmental organizations that are already providing assistance to members of the public with e-government services in a particular area (such as immigration or taxation)

- create user-friendly websites and information resources that function as a gateway between e-government services and the individuals who need these services but struggle with how to access them

- provide users with opportunities to improve their language, digital literacy, and other skills through collection development, programs, and services

- create linkages to other library services to facilitate meeting the e-government needs of the public (i.e., holding storytime while parents are in language or civics classes)

- look to create a continuum of e-government services (i.e.. becoming a passport center and incorporating voter registration as part of a larger immigration service set)

- build infrastructures (e.g., information resources technology training, staff assistance) to support e-government services (p. 2)

Source: Bertot, John Carlo, Jessica McGilvray, Paul T. Jaeger. 2012. "E-Government Partnerships Projects: Executive Summary." Internet Policy and Access Center. http://ipac.umb.edu/sites/default/files/publications/ EGOVT_Exec_SummaryJan2012_0.pdf. Project sponsored by the ALA and the IMLS.

In addition, Bertot et al. (2006b) made a number of policy recommendations aimed at recognizing the importance of libraries in e-government:

- Recognize public libraries as outlets for E-government services in legislation, policy initiatives, and program literature

- Provide training for state library and public library staff regarding E-government service provision in a public library context.

- Provide direct support from federal, state, and local agencies to public libraries for the services that libraries offer on behalf of the agencies.

- Educate government officials regarding the roles public libraries play in relation to E-government, the effect of agency referrals to public libraries, and the need to support the public library.

- Coordinate and update federal, state, and local information policies to support better the role of public libraries as agents of E-government.

- Expand the responsibilities and funding of state library agencies to assist and support public libraries in their E-government role.

- Develop, through a collaborative process that includes key library profession-al associations, public librarians, policymakers, and LIS researchers, a set of best practices and practical guides that provide public libraries with insight into how to serve as providers of E-government services, issues associated with serving as E-government providers, and ways in which libraries can develop E-government services and resources. (p. 4)

Despite the concerns of some that libraries are irrelevant in the age of the Internet, e-government presents a clear opportunity to demonstrate the library's concrete role in a democracy and illustrates how the library continues its mission to ensure access to and a voice in government for all people.

D. National Security Issues

As a matter of policy, governments restrict information that could threaten national security. Yet in a democracy, the government's need to protect the nation's security interests must be balanced with the rights of citizens to obtain information. This complex issue was brought into bold relief by the events occurring on 9/11.

1. The USA PATRIOT Act (P.L. 107–56)

As a direct consequence of the terrorist attack, Congress passed the Uniting and Strengthening America by Providing Appropriate Tools Required to Intercept and Obstruct Terrorism Act, better known as the PATRIOT Act. The act, signed by President George W. Bush on October 26, 2001, amended at least fifteen different statutes dealing with tracking and intercepting communications, conducting for-eign intelligence investigations, money laundering, and dealing with alien terrorists and victims. The law created a broadly defined new crime of "domestic terrorism," expanded the authority of domestic investigative agencies such as the FBI, and broadened their powers related to wiretaps, search warrants, and subpoenas.

The ALA and other library organizations quickly expressed serious concerns about potential violations of First Amendment and privacy rights. Although the PATRIOT Act contained no provisions specifically directed at libraries or their patrons, several elements were worrisome, particularly the provisions that amended the Foreign Intelligence Surveillance Act (FISA). This act created a Foreign Intelli-gence Surveillance Court (Court), composed of selected federal judges, which had the power to authorize wiretaps, searches, or the use of pen/trap devices that could secretly identify the source of telephone calls to and from a particular phone by FBI agents involved in foreign intelligence investigations. It also authorized "roving wiretaps" that could trace an individual's communication on a variety of devices, regardless of place. This meant the FBI could track an individual's communication from a public phone or an e-mail to a friend's computer, or track that individual's activity on a public library computer. In other words, it focused on the person, not the place. Not surprisingly, this raised serious Fourth Amendment search and seizure concerns.

The PATRIOT Act significantly expanded the Court's power. For example, originally, the types of business records that could be routinely searched included common transportation carriers such as airlines or bus companies, vehicle rental agencies, or businesses that provided public accommodations such as hotels. Section 215 of the PATRIOT Act expanded this definition to include searching for "any relevant tangible item." Broadly interpreted, this could include books, circulation records, or electronic records of Internet searches in libraries. Further, if a request for such a record was made under the PATRIOT Act, librarians were required to keep the request secret. In addition, the individuals who were the subject of the request could not be informed of the search request, and there could be no discussion of the incident with other librarians. Similarly, there was concern that requests for library records authorized under the PATRIOT Act were not subject to the traditional requirement of probable cause. Rather, the FBI merely needed to assert to the Court that the information was needed as part of an ongoing investigation into terrorism. Such an assertion could be made in a secret proceeding.

Although chilling in its potential, the actual impact of the PATRIOT Act on libraries has been unclear. In May 2003 the House Judiciary Committee reported that the FBI had visited about fifty libraries ("FBI Has Visited" 2003), although Attorney General Ashcroft stated that no Section 215 requests were made. The Justice Department confirmed that as of March 2005 the authority had been used on thirty-five occasions, but not to acquire library, bookstore, gun sale, or medical records (Doyle 2005). The ALA and other organizations remain vigilant.

The overall fear concerning the PATRIOT Act was that the normal checks and balances that protect individual rights had been seriously eroded, and could significantly violate public trust in libraries. Of primary concern was that (1) innocent patrons might be subjected to surveillance regarding their reading habits, their use of electronic resources, or program attendance, (2) librarians might be unduly tempted to monitor patrons, and (3) libraries might be reluctant to collect and maintain data that were traditionally used for planning and management purposes for fear the data might be used as part of an investigation (Jaeger et al. 2004). In response to these concerns the ALA adopted the "*Resolution on the USA PATRIOT Act and Related Measures That Infringe on the Rights of Library Users*" in addition to a series of resolutions and procedures to deal with the PATRIOT Act, including "*Resolution Reaffirming the Principles of Intellectual Freedom in the Aftermath of Terrorist Attacks*," and "*Privacy: An Interpretation of the Library Bill of Rights*." These resolutions condemned the use of governmental power to suppress the free and open exchange of information and free inquiry, and exhorted librarians to support open access and user privacy. ALA continues to work with such organizations as the American Civil Liberties Unions, the ARL, and the Coalition for Reader Privacy to enact reforms of the act (Terry 2011).

Because several critical sections of the PATRIOT Act, including Section 215, had sunset provisions that required reauthorization, several attempts have been made to address civil liberty concerns. Most notably, an amendment introduced by Senator Leahy, the "Sunset Extension Act of 2009," attempted to significantly modify the PATRIOT Act including changes to Section 215. This amendment was not successful and in 2011, President Obama signed a four-year reauthorization of the act with no significant changes. However, in recognition of the civil liberties implications of some of the provisions, President Obama indicated that the Department of Justice would, as a procedural matter, implement certain measures that reflected the concerns of Senator Leahy, a requirement that "when library or bookseller records are sought via a Section 215 order for business records, a statement of specific and articulable facts showing relevance to an authorized investigation must be produced" (Taylor 2011, p. 3).

2. Homeland Security

The events of 9/11 clearly demonstrated that the United States was vulnerable to attack and precipitated a reevaluation of the nation's security systems, especially its critical infrastructure. As defined in the PATRIOT Act, the critical infrastructure of the United States includes "systems and assets, whether physical or virtual, so vital to the United States that the incapacity or destruction of such systems, and assets would have a debilitating impact on security, national economic security, national public health or safety, or any combination of those matters." The information and telecommunications sector was identified as part of that vital infrastructure. President Bush created a Critical Infrastructure Protection Board (CIPB), composed of representatives from government and the private sector and charged the CIPB with creating a national strategy to secure the "critical information infrastructure"; it issued its report in February 2003. Viewing cyberspace as the "nervous system" of our infrastructure (CIPB 2003, p. vii), the CIPB noted, "Without a great deal of thought about security, the Nation shifted the control of essential processes in manufacturing, utilities, banking, and communication to networked computers" (CIPB 2003, p. 5). This shift left the U.S. cyber-infrastructure vulnerable despite concerted efforts to install virus protections, firewalls, and intrusion detection devices. The CIPB urged a new national strategy to secure cyberspace and to "prevent cyber attacks against America's critical infrastructures; reduce national vulnerability to cyber attacks; and, minimize damage and recovery time from cyber attacks that do occur" (CIPB 2003, p. viii). The CIPB recommended a comprehensive national plan overseen by the Office of Homeland Security (OHS) for securing information technology and telecommunications systems, including the following recommendations:

- quick and efficient sharing of information regarding the cyber-infrastructure (with concomitant limitations of the same information to the public)
- improving information sharing among intelligence and law enforcement (OHS 2002, p. 48)
- integrating information sharing across the federal government
- integrating information sharing among federal, state, and local government and law enforcement
- adopting common metadata standards for data related to homeland security (OHS 2002, pp. 55–58)

The OHS was concerned that the considerable amount of scientific, technical, and economic information generally available either directly from the federal government on its websites or through government documents in local libraries could be used by terrorists to damage critical infrastructure. For this reason, the federal government quickly recalled or removed from public access vast quantities of information, including Department of Energy reports and risk management plans from the Environmental Protection Agency (ALA 2003a). For example, in October 2001 the OHS and the U.S. Geological Survey requested government depository libraries to destroy a CD-ROM on U.S. water supplies. Since depository documents remain the property of the U.S. government, compliance was expected (Smith 2002). Similarly, in March 2003, local Homeland Security agents removed hazmat and emergency-plan documents from local libraries (ALA 2003a).

The ALA and other organizations were deeply concerned about the withdrawal or restriction of government information and the effects of broad and indiscriminate application of a protected status to a wide range of material that would otherwise be available to the public. The "Resolution on Withdrawn Electronic Government Information" and the "Resolution on Security and Access to Government Information" speak to these issues. In addition, the ALA appointed a task force on Restrictions on Access to Government Information (RAGI) to review government policy on dissemination of government information (ALA 2003b). The task force's report expressed serious reservations:

> While acknowledging the need on the part of government to consider potential security risks when making public information available for access, it is the conclusion of the Task Force that recent federal government actions limiting access promote a climate of secrecy tending to upset the delicate balance between the public's need to access government information and perceived national security concerns. (ALA 2003b, p. 4)

The RAGI task force issued ten recommendations that exhorted ALA to oppose vigorously any attempts to restrict access to government information on the basis of national security assertions, to monitor activities that lead to restrictions, and to stimulate advocacy on the part of librarians to protect the rights of patrons to government information (ALA 2003b). In particular, the RAGI task force expressed concern about two memoranda. The first, issued by Attorney General Ashcroft, instructed executive agencies to interpret narrowly the Freedom of Information Act (FOIA) and its emphasis on the legal authority to withhold information. The second memo, issued to all agency and department heads by White House Chief of Staff Andrew Card in March 2002, was titled "Action to Safeguard Information Regarding Weapons of Mass Destruction and Other Sensitive Documents Related to Homeland Security." The memo instructed agency administrators to review their records management procedures with an eye to protecting information that could be misused to harm national security such as unclassified documents that should be classified and other information that should be treated as sensitive, even if not classified. He attached to his request a memorandum from the government's top FOIA classification officers that said agencies should proceed on a case-by-case basis to evaluate sensitivity and the benefits of information sharing. Card's memo stated that this "sensitive but unclassified" (SBU) homeland security information could include records that dealt with the agency, public infrastructure that the agency might regulate or monitor, some internal databases (reports, data the agency collected, maps, etc.), vulnerability assessments, and information provided to the government by private firms such as chemical companies. It said that SBU information could be withheld using exemptions that protected personnel rules and practices and involved proprietary information. It also suggested that some classifications should be extended beyond their ten- or twenty-five-year limits, and that some sensitive information should be classified.

> In making decisions about this category of information—such as whether to make it available on agency Web sites—agencies must weigh the benefits of certain information to their customers against the risks that freely available sensitive homeland security information might pose to the interests of the Nation. (OHS 2002, p. 56)

One effect of the Card memo was that a number of agencies reviewed their website postings and by one estimate, more than 6,000 pages were withdrawn (Coalition of Journalists for Open Government 2009). For example, the Federal Aviation Administration removed several databases from public access, the Office of Pipeline Safety discontinued access to its National Pipeline Mapping System, and the U.S. Geological Survey requested that depository libraries destroy information on CD-ROMs dealing with surface water (Hammitt 2005). In some cases, the information removed had little or no clear relationship to terrorism (Jaeger and Fleischmann 2007). It is likely that little of this information was archived or saved.

Another effect of the Card memo was the government's claim that it could restrict information requested under the FOIA if agency administrators believed that it might be used in a manner that "could," although not necessarily "would," be harmful to the American people (Feinberg 2004). These FOIA exemptions were used with increasing frequency by the military. For example, use of the executive privilege exemption by the DoD increased 42% from 2000 to 2005 (Cochran and Davenport 2006). Although the military claimed it used the exemption primarily to protect employees, others argued that the exemption privileges were abused. At the same time, the percentage of approved FOIA requests declined significantly, dropping from 54% in 2000 to 44% in 2004 (Cochran and Davenport 2006). The reliance on administrative discretion, rather than statutory guidance, significantly undermined the intent of FOIA. One review of SBU activity by the Information Sharing Environment Program Office of the GAO revealed that 81% of the SBU assignments were based on department or agency policies, rather than on formal regulations (OpenTheGovernment 2007).

Of course, federal agencies have a responsibility to safeguard information that might be damaging to national security, but, as Hammitt (2005) observed:

> Part of the dismantling of electronic information sources after 9/11, was because agencies had made too much information available without much thought about the potential consequences. However, in taking down large chunks of information, there was never any sense that agencies were going through a thoughtful process in

analyzing whether information should be taken down and balancing the legitimate societal value of the information against the heightened sensitivity of some information after 9/11. (p. 431)

Feinberg (2004) noted that categories such as SBU or "for official use only" or "sensitive security information" sometimes collided with other important ideals such as the right of the public to be informed. In addition, she observed that access to government information is now in a "nether world" (p. 439), with each agency adopting its own definitions, resulting in a lack of consistency in their application. Such *ad hoc* directives have complicated the policies on information protection and bring into relief the larger issue: a significant lack of an underlying theory that balances openness and secrecy within a consistent U.S. information policy (Strickland 2005). Fortunately, access to some government information increased under the Obama administration. Attorney General Eric Holder promulgated new rules for government officials related to FOIA that emphasized the importance of transparency in government and encouraged openness in the provision of government information, even if there might be a plausible rationale for exemption (Sanchez 2009). Similarly President Obama issued Executive Order 13526 on December 29, 2009, which tended to reduce over-classification and encourage the release of previously classified ones. The Executive Order restored earlier standards that indicated that if there is "significant doubt" about the need to classify an item then it should not be classified; it also noted that no information should be classified indefinitely. The Order created the National Archives and National Declassification Center to ensure an efficient declassification process (Siefert 2011).

3. The Library Awareness Program

ALA's strong reactions to the PATRIOT Act and subsequent activities were grounded in specific, historical experiences. Beginning in the early 1960s, Soviet intelligence systematically collected unclassified information in U.S. libraries using Soviet agents as well as innocent university students. When this activity became known to the FBI, they recruited clerks and other staff in the New York City area in the scientific and other technical libraries that were the likely Soviet targets. The FBI initiative was called the Library Awareness Program. Librarians became aware of the program in June 1987, when two FBI agents came to the Math and Science Library at Columbia University and asked a clerk about foreigners using the library (Schmidt 1989). A librarian who overheard the conversation referred the agents to the library director, who reported this exchange to the New York Library Association's Intellectual Freedom Committee, who in turn reported it to the ALA. This led to an ALA investigation and subsequent congressional hearings. The FBI agreed to discontinue the program but did not guarantee that it would not be started again.

National security is an important issue, but so is the concern that it not be used as a rationale to suppress embarrassing information or to impede unnecessarily the free flow of ideas in a democratic society. Balancing these important interests will remain a challenge for all.

E. Other Channels of Information Control

1. Transborder Data Flow (TDF)

In a world in which satellites instantaneously transmit information around the globe, and in which substantial electronic computer storage is both practical and economical, the globalization of information raises a number of issues. The international exchange of information is sometimes referred to as transborder data flow (TDF). Although there might be many reasons to control the international dissemination of information, the UN asserted an underlying principle familiar to all Americans. In its Universal Declaration of Human Rights, Article 19, it states,

> Everyone has the right to freedom of expression and opinion. This right includes freedom to hold opinions without interference and to seek, receive, and impart information and ideas through any media regardless of frontiers. (United Nations 1948)

Transborder data flow affects people on at least four levels—personal, economic, national, and sociocultural.

a. Personally Identifiable Information

Computers and computer networks store in the cloud or in large data networks vast amounts of personal information which can be transmitted via the Internet throughout the world. Although this capacity can be quite useful for law enforcement, it also makes vulnerable to exploitation and abuse much medical, financial, educational, and other personal information. The European Union, in particular, has made attempts to protect individual rights by controlling the unnecessary transmission of personal information while permitting the transmission of approved information.

b. Economic Implications

In a world of transnational corporations and international economic alliances, TDF is essential yet often problematic. Businesses and nations compete for information that will give them an economic edge. The information industry alone (e.g.,

Google) is worth billions of dollars, and nations naturally compete for this and other markets. Countries are particularly concerned about the theft of industrial secrets or business strategies or sabotage by outside hackers as well as those who could cause damage to business operations, including financial institutions and markets. Today, hackers can be individuals, members of organizations, or agents of other national governments.

c. National Implications

Some nations attempt to jump ahead of their neighbors by importing technologies, software, and information from other countries. However, when importing technology, hardware, software, and language from other places many people rightly express serious concerns about foreign nationals or multinational corporations controlling their information resources and/or infrastructure. Sovereignty can be threatened when nations become increasingly dependent on the technologies of other nations. Such actions also inhibit development of an indigenous information infrastructure. In addition, not all countries define public and private information the same. For example, some information on topics such as sexuality or civil disobedience might be readily available in one country but not in another. A related issue is protecting national security information from electronic intrusion. Electronic storage of highly sensitive government information is now common, and the fear that this information might be accessed and transmitted across international borders is an important consideration. It is not uncommon today for countries to protest that their computer systems have been "hacked" not only by individuals, but by other countries. The recent case of Edward Snowden is a prime example of how sensitive national security information can be downloaded by an individual and made available to other nations or the world.

d. Sociocultural Consequences

Technologies can transform values, fundamental assumptions, and traditional activities within a society. This issue was highlighted in recent political uprisings in Egypt and the Middle East by the effective use and power of mobile devices and social networks that instantaneously transmitted images and sounds around the world. Xue (2005) noted that countries with well-developed policies regarding information technology were more likely to have access to the Internet, which in turn resulted in a free flow of information, expanded education and training, and the ability to diffuse the benefits of the Internet in the general population. He cautioned, however,

> While the Internet brings visible economic, social, and cultural benefits to nations, it also brings quick idea diffusion, and therefore has a huge impact on social values and political ideology in developing and non-democratic countries. (p. 238)

Clearly, using these technologies can create social and cultural dislocations. As a result, the response from some countries has been to monitor Internet traffic and block what they feel violates social or political norms or that could create social and political unrest.

On the other hand, access to information can bring many social benefits. IFLA has been instrumental in promoting the relationship between open information access, universal literacy, and sustainable development. In August 2014, for example, IFLA adopted, along with other organizations, the "Lyon Declaration on Access to Information and Development" (IFLA 2014) which argues that the right to information is "transformational" to national development and notes that:

> Information intermediaries such as libraries, archives, civil society organizations (CSOs), community leaders and the media have the skills and resources to help governments, institutions and individuals communicate, organize, structure and understand data that is critical to development.

2. Other Types of Restricted Information

Many governments, including the United States, attempt in a variety of ways, to control information assumed to be harmful to national security, libelous or slanderous, or that could incite individuals to violence. Among the many categories of information the U.S. government has tried to control, currently or at one time or another, are various forms of artistic expression, expressions of opposition to the U.S. government, and sexually explicit materials.

a. Artistic Expression

Historically, to regulate objectionable materials the government used obscenity statutes, postal regulations, or the withholding of funds. For example, the National Endowment of the Arts withheld funding because certain staff members objected to the content of some citizen-approved projects. Although some suppressed books, plays, and other art forms were of questionable artistic merit, many others are now considered literary classics, including James Joyce's *Ulysses* and J. D. Salinger's *Catcher in the Rye*.

b. Political Opposition

A variety of State Department, postal, and import regulations have also been used to bar individuals and information from entering the country when the information or the person was considered contrary to the interests of the U.S. government. For example, foreign nationals, such as members of certain ethnic or political groups, have been prevented from speaking at conferences. Similarly, the importation of films and videos considered to be propaganda has been prohibited.

c. Sexually Explicit Materials

Federal, state, and local laws prohibit the production, importation, and mailing of "obscene" materials. These laws have created a complex, often opaque, *de facto* national policy. For example, our society clearly does not permit child pornography. On the other hand, books that are obviously intended to educate minors about puberty but might depict nude children could also be construed as obscene under these laws. Policy on sexual information remains confused because court interpretations of obscenity laws are often based on community standards, making it difficult to know what materials can be restricted and what cannot. The issues have become much more complicated with access to explicit materials on the Internet. Today, although obscenity laws still persist, given the ubiquity of "adult" materials on the Internet and its ease of access, attention has shifted primarily to child pornography or on exposure of explicit materials to minors.

IV. COPYRIGHT LEGISLATION AND ISSUES

A. Characteristics of the Copyright Law

The U.S. Constitution grants to the federal government the power to "promote the Progress of Science and useful Arts, by securing for limited Times to Authors and Inventors the exclusive Right to their respective Writings and Discoveries" (U.S. Constitution, Article I, Section 8, Clause 8). The underlying foundation of this right is the idea that by rewarding individuals for their creative efforts, the whole society benefits. The original intent of copyright focused on its application as a social good and not on protecting creative property (Bailey 2006).

1. What Is Protected?

The most recent version of the Copyright Act, reauthorized in 1976, does not protect ideas themselves, but on ideas once they are fixed in some form. Copyright protects numerous categories of works including

- literary works
- musical works, including any accompanying words
- dramatic works, including any accompanying music
- pantomimes and choreographic works
- pictorial, graphic, and sculptural works
- motion pictures and other audiovisual works
- sound recordings
- architectural works (U.S.C. 1988, 1993).

Copyright interpretation is increasingly complicated because so many works are now available electronically. Central to these issues for LIS professionals is determining to what extent the creator or publisher of information can control copying and use by others. This dilemma has been further complicated by the Internet, which has changed our notion of publication. Does something become a publication once it is available on the Internet? Given the ease with which electronic material can be changed, which version is copyrighted and how can it be protected? ALA considers this such a serious issue that one provision of its code of ethics is specifically devoted to respect for intellectual property rights, and the ARL has its own statement on this issue as well.

From a constitutional perspective, information policies must balance several interests—the individual creators who deserve to profit from their works, the rights of individuals to access and use information, and the benefit to society as a whole. This tension creates considerable controversy, and LIS professionals often find themselves caught in the center:

> Librarians face a dilemma when it comes to copyright. On the one hand, if content providers disappeared, libraries and our patrons would suffer. By doing our part to eliminate copyright violations, we help keep publishers in business. On the other hand, we understand that "information wants to be free." We resent license agreements that prevent us from sharing information. Who hasn't bent the rules or seen others do so? We became librarians in order to help people find information; we don't want to be gatekeepers or copyright cops. (Skala et al. 2008, p. 28)

Works in digital format are not explicitly protected by the 1976 Copyright Act and therefore legal interpretation has been complicated. However, the act does state:

> Copyright protection subsists, in accordance with this title, in original works of authorship fixed in any tangible medium of expression, now known or later developed, from which they can be perceived, reproduced, or otherwise communicated, either directly or with the aid of a machine or device. (17 U.S.C. 102)

In addition, a House report that accompanied the proposed legislation in 1976 noted that the concept of a literary work should be broadly interpreted, including "computer databases and computer programs to the extent that they incorporate authorship in a programmer's expression of original ideas" (House Report 1976, p. 566). This language suggests that ideas fixed in media such as DVDs or on a website have copyright protections.

Once a creative work is in a fixed form, the individual who created the work does not have to do anything to obtain the copyright; it resides with the creator; the creator does not have to affix a copyright notice or register the work with the Copyright Office. This was not true for many works published before 1978. When two or more people produce a work they might own it jointly. When a work is produced within the scope of one's employment, it is considered a "work for hire" and the employer generally holds the copyright in this circumstance. Copyright can be transferred by written agreement of the copyright owner (Crews 2012). This is often what happens, for example, when an author publishes a book and copyright is transferred to the publisher. The length of time the work is protected is determined by a variety of factors. In general, works published in the United States before 1923 are now in the public domain; they can no longer be privately owned. Works created after January 1, 1978, are protected from the point of creation until the creator dies plus seventy additional years. Between 1923 and 1978 copyright protection varied based on whether the material was registered with the Copyright Office or otherwise claimed, but it could be for as long as 95 years (Crews 2012).

2. What Are the Rights and Limitations of the Copyright Owner?

Five exclusive rights belong to a copyright owner, the right to:

- Reproduce the copyrighted work;
- Prepare derivative works based upon the copyrighted work;
- Distribute copies of the copyrighted work to the public by sale or other transfer of ownership, or by rental, lease, or lending;
- Perform literary, musical, dramatic, and choreographic works, pantomimes, motion pictures and other audiovisual works; and
- Display literary, musical, dramatic, and choreographic works, pantomimes, and pictorial, graphic, or sculptural works, including the individual images of a motion picture or other audiovisual work (U.S.C. 1988, 1993).

Generally, people who produce original works, or who purchase the rights to reproduce them, want to restrict copying privileges. LIS professionals, on the other hand, seek to disseminate information as freely as possible. Librarians do this by loaning a copy of the work, making additional copies, or permitting others to make copies. The library's right to do this is defined under two doctrines in the copyright law: the first sale doctrine and the doctrine of fair use.

a. First Sale Doctrine

The first sale doctrine (codified at 17 U.S.C. § 109 [a]) permits libraries and others to loan copyrighted materials. Under the doctrine, the holder of a lawfully owned copy is authorized "without the authority of the copyright owner, to sell or otherwise dispose of the possession of that copy." Libraries exercise this right when they purchase an item (first sale) and then subsequently loan the book, periodical, or film without remunerating the copyright owner further. The first sale doctrine supports the notion of subsidized browsing, a critical concept in librarianship. That is, libraries spend public dollars to purchase an item, essentially subsidizing its use by members of the community. It is critical to keep this in mind, because electronic dissemination of information substantially alters this notion. The implications of this change are discussed below.

The right of first sale was recently challenged when the publisher Wiley & Son argued that books purchased in the United States but manufactured overseas were not covered by the first sale doctrine. The Supreme Court rejected this notion in *Kirtsaeng v. Wiley & Sons, Inc.* Although libraries were not directly involved, the ruling ensures that libraries purchasing books made overseas may be loaned to the public freely (Sheketoff and Wright 2014).

b. Fair-Use Doctrine

The doctrine of fair use evolved over many years and as a result of a substantial number of court decisions. It is a fundamental doctrine protecting the dissemination of ideas. ARL (2012) notes,

> Fair use is a user's right. In fact, the Supreme Court has pointed out that it is fair use that keeps copyright from violating the First Amendment; without fair use and related exceptions, copyright would create an unconstitutional constraint on free expression. (p. 6)

Section 107 of the copyright law contains a list of the various purposes for which reproduction of a particular work might be considered fair use, such as criticism, comment, news reporting, teaching, scholarship, and research. When an individual makes a copy under the fair use doctrine, he or she is not required to get permission from the copyright owner. However, Section 107 also sets out four criteria that should be considered when determining whether or not a particular use is fair:

- The purpose and character of the use, including whether such use is for commercial or for nonprofit educational purposes;
- The nature of the copyrighted work;
- The amount and substantiality of the portion used in relation to the copyright work as a whole;
- The effect of the use upon the potential market for, or value of, the copyrighted work (U.S.C. 1988, 1993).

Generally, when the use is noncommercial (educational or research purposes) and would have little effect on the profits of the copyright owner, the fair-use doctrine applies (Lipinski 2011). Librarians depend heavily on the fair-use doctrine when making copies or permitting individuals to make copies for themselves.

Loss of subscription income is a reasonable concern of publishers who often take issue with librarians who make liberal numbers of copies for interlibrary loan purposes, especially copies of periodical articles. The librarian does not want to risk "contributory copyright infringement," which in one court case was described as "one who, with knowledge of the infringing activity, induces or causes, or materially contributes to the infringement of another" (*Gershwin Publishing Corp* 1971; Lipinski 2005, p. 2). Nor does the library want to be liable for encouraging others to violate the Copyright Act. The copyright law permits libraries to make individual copies of most copyrighted works, but not "in such aggregate quantities as to substitute for a subscription to or purchase of" a copyrighted item (17 U.S.C. § 108 [g][2]). Russell (2005a) characterized the conditions for making copies under Section 108:

> If the following three things are true—your library is open to the public, and you do not make a copy (of an article or a portion of a copyright work) in order to seek "commercial advantage," and you include the copyright notice on the copy or a legend that states the work might be protected by copyright—you can make reproductions without the prior authorization of the copyright holder. (p. 275)

There are restrictions, however. Russell warned that "these allowances do not apply to musical works; pictorial, graphic, or sculptural works; motion pictures; and other audiovisual works" (p. 275).

The introduction of electronic access magnifies the complexities and subtleties of interpreting fair use. Although copyright for digital materials remains somewhat unclear, Russell suggested that libraries should consider them covered by copyright law, keeping in mind that databases and online sources are often purchased with licensing agreements that might limit copying (see discussion below). If patrons copy excessively, libraries might consider time restrictions for computer use or charge for printing.

Unfortunately, from the standpoint of daily operations, the law does not clearly identify how much copying is too much. Fortunately, this issue was addressed by the National Commission on New Technological Uses of Copyrighted Works (CONTU), a group created when the 1976 Copyright Act was being drafted, comprising representatives from the legal profession, librarians, journalists and writers, consumer organizations, publishers, business executives, and officials of the LOC and the Copyright Office. The commission was formed primarily to deal with the effects of computers on copyrighted works but it agreed to address the issue of photocopying as well (CONTU 1978). The result of their deliberations is known as the "CONTU Guidelines on Photocopying under Interlibrary Loan Arrangements" (CONTU 1978, p. 54). CONTU attempted to balance the interest of periodical publishers with those of libraries and to clarify what was meant by "aggregate quantities as to substitute for a subscription" (17 U.S.C. § 108 [g][2]). The guidelines apply to requests for periodical articles published within the past five years and permit libraries to make as many as five copies of a given periodical in a given calendar year (CONTU 1978). The guidelines were subsequently incorporated as part of the legislative history of the 1976 Copyright Act, and they continue to play an important role in guiding photocopying practices for interlibrary loans (CONTU 1978). Unfortunately, they provide no guidance concerning journal articles published more than five years ago; that is left to the library's judgment (Crews 2012).

A related area of concern affects academic libraries. When faculty request that a portion of a book be placed on reserve for student use, LIS professionals must determine how much of a book can be copied under the fair use doctrine, an issue fraught with problems. However, a court decision involving Georgia State University provided some clarification. In the case of *Cambridge University Press et al. v. Patton et al.* the court determined that for books of nine chapters or less, 10% of the total page count could be copied; for books of 10 chapters or more, only one complete chapter could be copied (Educause 2012).

For copying of print materials that might exceed the fair use guidelines, the Copyright Clearance Center (CCC) was created to help pay royalties to publishers. The CCC creates agreements with a wide variety of journal publishers. Royalty payments are made to the CCC, which then grants the right to copy material to corporations and other institutions.

The growth of electronic publication on the Web brought new issues about interpreting fair use. In 1994, the Working Group on Intellectual Property Rights, a committee of the Information Infrastructure Task Force (1995) created by President Clinton, published a report called the Green Paper that suggested that the traditional interpretations of fair use were difficult to apply in the digital environment. Consequently, the working group convened a Conference on Fair Use (CONFU), which brought together information users and copyright owners to review and discuss how fair use might be applied and to determine what new guidelines might be needed. These deliberations lasted over four years but regrettably produced mixed success (U.S. Patent and Trademark Office 1998). Guidelines for educational multimedia were developed, and guidelines related to digital images and some aspects of distance learning were proposed. Many other issues were deferred. Over time, a variety of additional fair use guidelines have been developed—some based on the CONFU discussions. These include guidelines for educational uses of music; off-air recording of broadcast programming for educational purposes; college and university photocopying for classroom, research, and library reserve use; library and classroom use of copyrighted videotapes and computer software; electronic reserves; digital images; distance learning; and educational media. It is important to remember that none of these guidelines has the power of law (Crews 2012); they merely serve as informed advice. Crews (2012) noted that, in fact, many of the guidelines are deficient in that they misinterpret fair use, create rigidity instead of flexibility, and tend toward unnecessarily narrow interpretations of the law to gain consensus. Russell (2005b) cautioned libraries not to serve as "copyright police" (p. 339), which might ultimately increase the library's liability and violate the basic notions of privacy and confidentiality that form the foundation of library service.

B. File Sharing

Today's technologies allow the digitalization and storage of all types of information—visual, audio, and print. File sharing software permits the copying of files with little or no loss of quality. The files can then be uploaded or downloaded over electronic networks to any individual who has also downloaded the file sharing software. Games and movies have been common objects for downloading. Music has been a particularly attractive object for such treatment and over the past two decades, peer-to-peer (P2P) music file sharing has become quite popular. File sharing is not in itself unlawful; what is unlawful is the sharing of copyrighted files without copyright permission. Although separate instances of sharing one file might present few problems, the magnitude of the impact increases substantially when some individuals establish services that identify and aggregate a large number of links to sites that provide copyrighted music without copyright permission. Napster and Grokster were examples of such sites. The music industry claimed these sites substantively affected their bottom lines. Not surprisingly, the recording industry responded aggressively. Its advocacy organization, the Recording Industry Association of America (RIAA) took several courses of action:

Taking individuals to court: some individuals who shared a large volume of music files were taken to court with mixed results. The industry believed that such actions would punish individual offenders and create a deterrent for others. However, in some cases the suits caused public ire over the appearance that some individuals were being victimized by a wealthy and large adversary;

Taking file sharing services to court: This technique resulted in the desired goal of putting the targeted service out of business, but it did not stop new services from starting;

Threatening law suits against universities: colleges and universities are common locations for file-sharing abuse. Digitally savvy students used the university's computer network to download copyrighted files. As a consequence, many universities now have strict policies concerning unlawful file sharing and when necessary they warn students who are involved in this activity.

Providing public education: The RIAA attempted to educate the public concerning the rights of copyright owners and the legal and ethical responsibilities of those who download music in an unauthorized fashion.

Overall, the threat of litigations had little impact on file-sharing behavior. As Ned (2014) observed:

> The reality is that there are millions of infringers throughout the world spanning a multitude of jurisdictions. Therefore, a lawsuit against hundreds or even thousands of infringers is unlikely to have a strong impact on online infringement. (p. 399)

Fortunately, generally affordable alternatives to infringement have been developed: Apple, iTunes, Amazon Music, and a reformed Napster now charge a modest fee to download the music legally. With increasing broadband access and the rise of YouTube, similar issues have been raised with video productions. Pew reported that 72% of adults who are online video viewers watched or shared videos and 36% downloaded video files to their computer or cell phone (Purcell 2013). On the international level, Pirate Bay, a "bittorrent indexer," established in 2003 in Sweden, provides links to a significant amount of digital content, including audio, video, games, and applications, providing means for the rapid downloading and sharing of large digital files (Pirate Bay 2015). The services provided, however, are controversial, and Pirate Bay has been the object of numerous legal challenges.

C. Digital Rights Management

Historically, fair use was determined by the user; that is, the copyright holder placed faith in the individuals using the material to ask for copyright permission when it was required. In reality, it was nearly impossible to monitor how people used copyrighted material. Such vulnerability was especially problematic in the digital environment where copies could be quickly created, disseminated widely, and altered by anyone with access. For example, book piracy was becoming acute with the Association of American Publishers estimating that publishers were losing $80–$100 million each year (Springen 2014).

Producers and distributors attempted to control use with DRM systems. "Digital rights management" is defined as "the documentation and administration of rights for the access to and use of digital works" (Agnew and Martin 2003, p. 267). DRM covers a broad spectrum of activity including accessing, viewing, copying, printing, editing, or transferring digital data. DRM uses a variety of means to control digital information, most notably sophisticated encryption technologies. The technology creates "trusted systems" often focused on two areas: authentication and authorization. Authentication verifies that a user is in fact a valid user—for example, the user paid the required fee or the user is a faculty member at a university. Authorization ensures that a valid user has the right to access a particular system and determines the degree of access—is access limited, or can the user manipulate or alter the digital data?

Another trusted system is the Digital Object Identifier (DOI). The DOI identifies content objects in the digital environment and assigns names for use on digital networks (DOI Foundation 2009). Although information about a digital object might change over time, including where to find it, its DOI name does not change. The system is managed by the International DOI Foundation, an open-membership consortium that includes both commercial and noncommercial partners. DOI was recently accepted for standardization within the International Organization for Standardization (ISO). Over 100 million names were assigned worldwide by 2014 (DOI 2014).

DOI names make managing intellectual property in a networked environment much easier and more convenient and allow the construction of automated services and transactions. Although DOI was developed as a DRM system, it has much broader potential to assist in organizing objects on the Web. The DOI identifies the digital object itself, not its address, and is therefore independent of location and can be searched independently. It is sometimes compared to a bar code for physical objects.

It seemed for a short time that the need for DRM was diminishing as publishers found new ways to distribute content through services such as iTunes—the items were purchased lawfully usually at low cost. But as digital content moved to the cloud and DRM systems charged monthly fees for access, the arguments were reinvigorated (Swartz 2013). Those who produce digital information certainly have rights to protect the fruits of their labors. The problem resides in DRM controls that inhibit what would normally be considered fair use of such material. In other words, the digital technologies can subvert types of access normally considered beneficial and permitted. In fact, such technologies are intended to inhibit sharing of digital information, thus controverting the underlying principle of the first sale doctrine. If there is a cost every time digital information is shared, the costs will become prohibitive for libraries:

> The protections afforded by these systems need not bear any particular relationship to the rights granted under, say, U.S. copyright law. Rather, the possible technological restrictions on what a user might do are determined by the architects themselves and thus might (and often do) prohibit many other legal uses. . . . Libraries that subscribe to electronic material delivered through copyright management systems might find themselves technologically incapable of lending out that material the way a traditional library lends out a book, even though the act of lending is a privilege—a defense to copyright infringement for unlawful distribution—under the first sale doctrine. (Zittrain 2006, p. 1998)

Interestingly, Lipinski (2011) noted that the use of DRM systems does not stop someone from copying portions of a text by other means, such as the old-fashioned way of hand-copying or otherwise word-processing the text so long as the DRM system is not compromised and so far as the use is otherwise a fair use.

The restrictive aspects of DRM systems have been particularly problematic for the adoption of e-books in academic libraries. Academic libraries routinely restrict access to their databases, requiring special passwords or other controls to authenticate the user. Students view the restrictions as inflexible; they "want a more immersive experience with e-books, in which they can download and interact with the content" (Van Arnhem and Barnett 2014, p. 64). Lacking this flexibility, students return to the print version if available.

LIS professionals clearly have a stake in DRM. Libraries themselves use DRM systems as they increasingly digitize their own collections and provide access to large amounts of digital content. Even public libraries might need to control access to certain materials which would mean that users might be identifiable and the nature of their use might be recorded. Such record keeping undermines some of the fundamental principles of librarianship. In line with these concerns, Puckett (2010) argued that DRM was philosophically problematic for librarians:

> Digital rights management (DRM) technology creates intentional and artificial information usage barriers. In doing so, it compromises libraries' mission of providing free access to information—"free" in the sense that users can make their own determination about how to use that information appropriate and ethically. By providing and supporting information that incorporates DRM, we choose to privilege a system that allows the publisher or vendor to intervene in the reader's freedom of information use. It has become increasingly apparent that libraries must adopt a position on the issue of DRM and begin advocating for DRM-free information systems. (p. 11)

Whether one agrees entirely with Puckett or not, there is no doubt that DRM raises many important issues for LIS professionals.

D. The Open Source Initiative

Traditionally, when a software company creates a product they carefully guard their source code and they closely scrutinize for copyright violations products produced by others who claim they have enhanced the original product or created a new product that can be used with the original product. The open source movement began in the 1980s as a countervailing force to these proprietary interests protected by copyright. The Open Source Initiative (OSI) describes open source software in the following way:

> Open source software is software that can be freely used, changed, and shared (in modified or unmodified form) by anyone. Open source software is made by many people, and distributed under licenses that comply with the Open Source Definition. (OSI 2014, p 1)

Although there are many different types of open source licenses, the General Public License (GPL) is used with approximately 70% of open source products (Corbly 2014). The license extends to the owner four rights:

- The freedom to use the software for any purpose.
- The freedom to change the software to suit your needs.
- The freedom to share the software with your friends and neighbors, and
- The freedom to share the changes you make. (Smith 2014)

The defining characteristic of open source software is that the license encourages people to modify or improve the software and make the resulting changes available to others for further enhancement. Open source products, including their source code, become public rather than private property.

Open source software has numerous applications for a range of library services, including library automation, website management, knowledge management, digital library management, and document editing (Barve and Dahibhate 2012). The Linux operating system, Apache Web server, MySQL, PHP, and Firefox are well-known examples of open-source operating systems (Barve and Dahibhate 2012). Additional open-source software that might be useful in libraries includes but is not limited to:

> DSpace: useful for creating and managing institutional repositories; Evergreen and Koha, and OpenBiblio: open source integrated library systems (ILS); Wordpress and Drupal for management of Websites, blogs and other applications; Open Journal Systems (OJS): a journal management and publishing system including refereeing, submission management, and online publication and indexing; and Moodle: a teaching and learning management system for the online environment. (Creative Librarian 2014)

Dorman (2002) predicted correctly that open-source software might well become a significant computing trend because it has strong ethical, economic, and technical foundations. Certainly, any movement that welcomes open access to critical technical information and that, in turn, could lead to significant progress for all rather than serving proprietary interests, is consonant with librarianship's values. In fact, libraries have significant potential to employ open-source systems, especially given the high costs of online systems purchased from traditional vendors.

E. Creative Commons Movement

Like the open source movement, the Creative Commons movement offered an alternative to the "all rights reserved" perspective of the Copyright Act. Creative Commons (CC) is a nonprofit organization established in 2001 with funding from the Center for the Public Domain. Its stated mission is that it "develops, supports, and stewards legal and technical infrastructure that maximizes digital creativity, sharing, and innovation" (Creative Commons 2014). CC's vision is ambitious:

> Our vision is nothing less than realizing the full potential of the Internet—universal access to research and education, full participation in culture—to drive a new era of development, growth, and productivity.

In large part it accomplishes this mission by providing less restrictive copyright license templates at no cost to the public. Using a Web application platform, six options allow creators to protect their works in a variety of ways (Creative Commons 2014a):

Attribution: This license lets others distribute, remix, tweak, and build upon the work, even commercially, as long as they credit the creator for the original version.

Attribution:NoDerivs: This license allows for redistribution, commercial and noncommercial, as long as it is passed along unchanged and in whole, with credit to the creator.

Attribution:ShareAlike: This license lets others remix, tweak, and build upon the work even for commercial purposes, as long as they credit the creator and license new creations under the identical terms. This license, often called "copyleft," is free and open-source software. All new works based on the original will carry the same license, so any derivatives will also allow commercial use.

Attribution:Non-Commercial: This license lets others remix, tweak, and build upon the work noncommercially, and although new works must be non-commercial and also acknowledge the creator, they do not have to license their derivative works on the same terms.

Attribution:Non-Commercial-ShareAlike: This license lets others remix, tweak, and build upon the work noncommercially, as long as they credit the creator and license their new creations under the identical terms.

Attribution:NonCommercial-NoDerivs: This license is the most restrictive, only allowing others to download the original and share it as long as they credit the creator, but they cannot change it in any way or use it commercially.

Creative Commons licenses have gained considerable popularity worldwide. As of 2014, there were 882 million Creative Commons licenses (37% from North America, 34% from Europe, and 16% from the Asia-Pacific) compared to 400 million in 2010 and 50 million in 2006. Sixty percent of these licenses were among the least restrictive; 56% permitted commercial use or adaptations, compared to 40% in 2010. More than 9 million websites now use Creative Commons licenses, including users of Wikipedia, Flickr, and YouTube (Creative Commons 2014b).

F. Contract and Licensing Laws versus Fair Use

Today, online access to intellectual property in electronic format is regulated as much, if not more, by licensing and leasing agreements than by copyright. As Gregory (2011) observed:

> Electronic vendors rarely, if ever, offer to sell their electronic products outright today. Rather, they simply provide to libraries something that is far short of the

ownership that the collection development process implies—a mere license of the right to use the products, not a copy thereof—and for good measure a license might be revocable under certain conditions . . . The contrast to a collection development librarian's traditional permanent book acquisition process could not be more stark. Licensing and DRM systems have shifted the focus from reliance on copyright laws to the provisions of the contracts between the rights holder and the user to determine what can be done with a work. (p. 146)

Because these contracts are based on mutual agreement, they are governed by state contract laws rather than copyright law. Unlike copyright law, which had idealistic motives to advance social progress, contract law has no such objective. Once a contract is signed, copyright law does not apply if it conflicts with the contract. Contracts are written to benefit the parties to them; benefits to society-at-large are incidental. For the producers and distributors, there is no need to consider social issues at all—merely economic ones. Because libraries must sign a licensing agreement before they can gain access to information, they have less control over the material's dissemination than under the doctrine of first sale. In fact, if a library discontinues its lease on an information product, it can lose access to both current and retrospective information files. Bailey (2006) described these developments as moving from a "permissive culture" to a "permission culture."

More recently, librarians and publishers have sought to avoid the burdensome, costly, and time-consuming complexities of licensing with individual libraries, especially in the area of e-resources, through what is referred to as "shared e-resource understandings" (SERUs). SERUs eliminate the need to negotiate separate contracts for each library and are based on a sense of trust, goodwill, and mutuality, but in some circumstances a license might remain the best practice (NISO 2009). McKee et al. (2012) noted that

SERU does not do away with contracts; it just provides a mutually accepted set of terms and conditions for those who chose to forego the long process of negotiating a full license agreement . . . SERU has succeeded in making transactions of electronic resource subscriptions easier to manage, acquire, and access, saving time and costs for libraries and publishers. (p. 105)

The extent to which information producers control access to electronic information in the future will depend on the policies and practices regarding use of information on electronic networks. The National Information Standards Organization (NISO) identified best practices in the implementation of such agreements (NISO RP-7–2008). These guidelines outline commonly accepted practices and expectations for use of e-resources and rely on existing copyright law as a foundation. In the absence of such policies, six library associations—the ALA, the ARL, the American

Association of Law Libraries, the Association of Academic Health Sciences Libraries, the Medical Library Association, and the Special Libraries Association collaboratively developed a set of principles to be considered when negotiating licenses for electronic resources (ARL 1997). Among the key areas addressed is the need for clear statements concerning the nature of the access rights obtained, liability or lack thereof for unauthorized use, protection of users' privacy and confidentiality, rights to make archival copies, and protection of rights under current copyright law.

G. International Copyright Issues

Control over intellectual property was recognized as an international issue in early international treaties such as the Rome Convention for the Protection of Performers, Producers of Phonograms and Broadcasting Organizations (1961) and the Berne Convention for the Protection of Literary and Artistic Works (1971). Developments in networked communication technologies, however, made it clear that these treaties were inadequate for the dramatically changed information environment. Thus, in December 1996, members of the World Intellectual Property Organization (WIPO), an agency of the United Nations, adopted a new copyright treaty for literary and artistic works, including electronic works. Among its central features was the extension of copyright protection to computer programs, including their copying, distribution, and rental (WIPO 1996). Interestingly, a major issue debated at the conference was whether accessing a Web page, which requires a computer to store data in RAM on a temporary basis, constituted making a copy—hence requiring permission from the copyright owner. After much debate and controversy, the treaty did not grant copyright to this type of use. In other words, the copy still must be fixed or distributable in a tangible form (Blum 1997).

Although, in general, nations were expected to comport with the internationally recognized standards of copyright protections, WIPO also recognized the need for "limitations and exceptions" to these standards when necessary. Among the important exceptions recently addressed were issues affecting individuals with disabilities. Of particular concern was the problem referred to as the "book famine" for visually disabled individuals. Only about 5% of all books published worldwide are accessible in formats for disabled individuals (Sinodinou 2013). To deal with this problem, in 2013 WIPO convened representatives from 186 member states with an intent to increase access to works published in formats such as Braille, large-print text and audio books (WIPO 2013). The result was the *Marrakesh Treaty to Facilitate Access to Published Works for Persons who are Blind, Visually Impaired, or otherwise Print Disabled* adopted in June 2013. According to WIPO (2013), the treaty requires WIPO members to adopt national law provisions that permit the reproduction, distribution and making available of published works in accessible formats through limitations and exceptions to the rights of copyright holders. It also provides for the exchange of these accessible format works across borders by organizations that serve the people who are blind, visually impaired, and print disabled . . . This sharing of works in accessible formats should increase the overall number of works available because it will eliminate duplication and increase efficiency. Instead of five countries producing accessible versions of the same work, the five countries will each be able to produce an accessible version of a different work, which can then be shared with each of the other countries. (p. 2)

The WIPO treaty deals primarily with the important rights of copyright owners but pays less attention to the rights of users especially in regard to the expanding digital environment. This has created an imbalance in favor of copyright holders over information consumers and there is a need for an international mandate to redress this imbalance. IFLA observed that

. . . libraries and archives work under a patchwork of provisions that differ in scope and effect from country to country, and which increasingly fail to address the legal and policy challenges of the global digital environment. The world's common information platform is now the Internet, operating across invisible national borders, so to play their full part libraries and archives now need minimum international copyright norms so they can continue to provide full access to information and cultural heritage in the global digital environment. (2013 pp. 1–2)

Consequently IFLA and other like-minded organizations proposed a "Draft Treaty on Copyright Exceptions and Limitations for Libraries and Archives" to address public interest considerations. The provisions of the treaty apply only to noncommercial organizations and focus on the needs of promoting information flow, knowledge, and scholarship across national boundaries. Among the areas addressed were the promotion of information sharing, parallel importation (i.e., buying books from other nations); library lending, cross-border uses of works reproduced under the exception; preservation and conservation, use of works for individuals with disabilities, use of works for educational, research, or private purposes; use of orphan works; ability of libraries and archives to circumvent technological protection measures (TPMs) for specific purposes; limitations on liabilities for activities performed in good faith, and the obligations of nations to respect exceptions to copyright with regard to the terms of contracts and licenses that are inconsistent with those exceptions (IFLA 2013, 2013a). Unfortunately, disagreements among member states, including the United States, South American, and African nations prevented the adoption of the treaty (TWN 2014).

Nonetheless, three U.S. library associations—ALA, ARL, and ACRL—joined together to form the Library Copyright Alliance (LCA)

> to work toward a unified voice and common strategy for the library community in responding to and developing proposals to amend national and international copyright law and policy for the digital environment. The mission is to foster global access and fair use of information for creativity, research, and education. (LCA 2014)

LCA acts in a variety of way to implement this mission by filing Friend of the Court briefs in lawsuits related to copyright and libraries, testifying to Congress, and submitting comments to WIPO on library-related initiatives.

H. Copyright Legislation Related to Digital Access and Dissemination

Copyright issues in the international, digital environment have become particularly complicated. Two laws are particularly pertinent in terms of their effect on libraries: the Digital Millennium Copyright Act (DMCA), and the Technology, Education and Copyright Harmonization Act (TEACH).

1. DMCA

The DMCA, signed into law on October 28, 1998, was designed to make copyright protections around the world more consistent. Sections 1201 and 1202 were most pertinent to libraries. Section 2101 provided protections against individuals who attempted to disable a copyright owner's technological protection mechanisms designed to prevent people from accessing the content for non-approved uses. Section 1202 protected copyrighted management information such as the title of a work, author's name, copyright owner, and terms and conditions of use (Crews 2012). The manufacture, sale, or distribution of devices or services that would circumvent these protections was unlawful. The goal of these provisions was to prevent the piracy of copyrighted material and prohibit the dissemination of information that might help others violate copyright restrictions.

DMCA has significant implications for LIS professionals and educators, innovators, and scientific researchers. For example, making a single copy of an article is a common practice in libraries and other educational agencies and is protected under fair use provisions. Yet in a digital environment, this type of copying might be impossible because of software protections. If a library should attempt to disable those protections, it would violate the DMCA. These mechanisms present serious barriers to libraries' efforts to disseminate new knowledge.

In fact, the DMCA can limit innovation and the creation of new knowledge. For example, large corporations have used the law to hinder competitors who, by breaking computer protection codes, were able to engineer products that could be used with a corporation's product. Although this form of reverse engineering is generally lawful, the ability to bring lawsuits under the DMCA creates a significant burden for smaller companies. This issue was highlighted in 2009 when some independent software developers modified Apple iPhone software to create unauthorized applications. Apple argued that this was a violation of the DMCA in a statement to the U.S. Copyright Office (Kane 2009). In another case, concern about civil and criminal liability for disseminating information on copyright protection devices led researchers and others to delimit both their investigations of copyright protection systems and their publication of research on security protocols. The result was a chilling effect on research related to encryption technologies and a stifling of innovation.

The act did provide some exemptions for law enforcement and for libraries under very limited conditions (U.S. Copyright Office 1998). The DMCA empowers the Librarian of Congress to create special, temporary exceptions to the DMCA's anti-circumvention provisions by promulgating regulations that remain in effect for a three-year period and then lapse pending their renewal or issuance of new regulations. Among the exemptions as of 2012 were the following:

- Unlocking literary works to permit "read aloud" functions for individuals who are blind or otherwise disabled;
- Engaging computer programs that enable wireless telephone handsets to execute lawful software applications for the sole purpose of enabling interoperability or moving to a different wireless network (but only for a brief period after purchase of the phone);
- Disabling the content scrambling system of a motion picture or DVD so that a short portion might be used for the purpose of criticism or comment if the use is of noncommercial or documentary files, or for educational purposes. The educational purposes exclusion includes educators K–12, and college and university faculty and students (LOC 2012).

These exceptions, although useful, do not eliminate the onerous climate. Because the exceptions are created and re-created every three years, LIS professionals must monitor constantly which activities are permitted and which might constitute violations of the law. Interestingly, in Europe, the balance favors the user rather than the copyright owner and circumvention is explicitly permitted for bona fide uses (Gregory 2011). Although U.S. courts have generally been sympathetic to copyright owners, they have also indicated that if the intent of the circumventing access was for a purpose that is itself lawful, then circumvention might be possible. For example, the

Court in *Chamberlain Group Inc. v. Skylink Technologies, Inc.* seemed sympathetic to protecting fair use and resisting its erosion by the anticircumvention provisions of the DMCA. Subsequent U.S. cases should help define how libraries will deal with this law in the future.

2. The Technology, Education, and Copyright Harmonization Act (TEACH)

Section 110(1) of the U.S. Copyright Act extended to educators the right to display and perform copyrighted works in the classroom. This right applied to any work, regardless of the medium. However, when teaching remotely through a distance education program, the law's generous terms shrank dramatically (Section 110[2]). These severe limitations prompted Congress to ask the Copyright Office in 1998 for help in facilitating distance education. The Copyright Office recommended significant changes, which were incorporated into a bill passed in November 2002. The pertinent provisions of the TEACH Act apply only to accredited, nonprofit institutions. They must develop and enforce appropriate copyright policies and provide information on copyright responsibilities to faculty, students, and staff. In particular, students must receive special notification regarding copyright protections and only enrolled students can use copyrighted materials. This last point places special responsibilities on the technology officers of schools, colleges, and universities to ensure that access is limited only to appropriate individuals, that only authenticated people can use digital materials, and then only for a designated period of time. Educational institutions must also ensure that DRM safeguards are protected from interference. Faculty can only disseminate materials that are an integral part of the course content, and they must control or supervise the dissemination of the material (Crews 2012).

The TEACH Act expanded the scope of educators' rights to perform and display copyrighted works and to make copies necessary for distance education. However, significant inequities remained between face-to-face teaching and distance education. For example, as part of the face-to-face classroom curriculum, an educator could use any copyrighted work, including still images, music, and movies, with no limits and no permissions required. Under 110(2), however, even as revised and expanded, the same educator must limit what can be shown to students in remote locations. In particular, only "reasonable and limited portions" of audiovisual works and dramatic musical works could be shown. In addition, the act covered only those materials provided as part of "mediated instructional activities"; that is, materials that an instructor uses in a classroom. It does not cover digital dissemination of supplemental reading materials, and it might restrict the ability to store and consult teaching materials after a short, prescribed time period (Crews 2012). Although, overall, the act liberalized the opportunities to use and distribute copyrighted material, it also set significant restrictions and required educational institutions to take a more active role in controlling access and developing and enforcing the necessary copyright protections.

LIS professionals were not specifically mentioned in the act, but the role of libraries in distance learning is substantial. Functions such as digital reserves and services that deliver electronic information to students are closely related concerns. Crews (2012) observed that librarians might be involved in a number of areas:

- active participation in developing copyright policies
- locating and preparing electronic materials for dissemination
- locating alternative materials when copyright restrictions prohibit some materials
- assisting others in the interpretation of fair use in the digital environment
- monitoring enforcement and interpretation of the TEACH Act

The Association of College and Research Libraries (ACRL) noted that TEACH did not, nor was it intended to, cover e-reserves. Consequently, ACRL issued a "Statement on Fair Use and Electronic Reserves" identifying important considerations when determining fair use for digitally stored documents (2003). In effect, the ACRL policy interpreted the four basic criteria for fair use: the character of the use, the nature of the work, the amount used, and the effect of the use on the market in the e-reserve environment. For example, fair use of e-reserves is more likely to be appropriate when the use is nonprofit, when it serves the interests of faculty and students, where there is a clear relationship of the amount used to the course objectives, and when access is restricted to registered students and materials are unavailable after the course is completed. The relationship of e-reserves and copyright law remains unclear. Band (2008) suggested that insofar as instructors use digital material in a transformative manner, that is, repurposing it by integrating it into the course in a special way, recent court decisions on fair use would support them.

3. Legislation and the Dissemination of Scientific Information

By the turn of the twenty-first century, the digital age was fully integrated into the global scientific community. The potential for collaborative activities among U.S. scientists as well as international colleagues was quickly realized. A good example is the international *Human Genome* Project in which an openly accessible scientific repository was responsible for mapping the entire human genome. Put simply, scientific innovation and research now relies on digital data, stored in digital format, accessible around the globe. Digital access has become the cornerstone of scientific progress.

Understandably, the stewardship of this data and all publically funded research are a major focus of the U.S. government and cooperating partners. In 2006, the Organization for Economic Cooperation and Development (OECD), comprising 30 democratic nations, including the United States, Canada, France, Germany, the United Kingdom, and Japan, published its *Principles and Guidelines for Access to Research Data from Public Funding* (2007). The principles explore a wide variety of access issues including openness, flexibility, transparency, legal conformity, protection of intellectual property, formal responsibility, professionalism, interoperability, quality, security, efficiency, accountability, and sustainability (OECD 2007). Significantly, the document recognized the need for open access to scientific research data across national borders and affirmed the important, inherent advantages of open access (OA) and sharing, including the following:

- Reinforces open scientific inquiry;
- Encourages diversity of analysis and opinion;
- Promotes new research;
- Makes possible the testing of new or alternative hypotheses and methods of analysis;
- Supports studies on data collection methods and measurement;
- Facilitates the education of new researchers;
- Enables the exploration of topics not envisioned by the initial investigators;
- Permits the creation of new data sets when data from multiple sources are combined. (OECD 2007, p. 10)

In the United States, leadership in the movement toward OA was assumed by the National Institutes of Health (NIH), which created a "Public Access Policy" codified in Section 217 the *Omnibus Appropriations Act of 2009* (NIH 2009). The law states,

> The Director of the National Institutes of Health ("NIH") shall require in the current fiscal year and thereafter that all investigators funded by the NIH submit or have submitted for them to the National Library of Medicine's PubMed Central an electronic version of their final, peer-reviewed manuscripts upon acceptance for publication, to be made public available no later than 12 months after the official

data of publication: Provided, that the NIH shall implement the public access policy in a manner consistent with copyright law.

Certain members of the U.S. scientific community viewed this law so favorably that in 2012, they drafted and widely disseminated a petition to the Obama administration to "require free access over the Internet to scientific journal articles arising from taxpayer-funded research" (We the People 2012). In response, in February 2013 the Director of the Office of Science and Technology, John Holdren, issued a "Memorandum for the Heads of Executive Departments and Agencies" directing "Federal agencies with more than $100M in R&D expenditures to develop plans to make the published results of federally funded research freely available to the public within one year of publication and requiring researchers to better account for and manage the digital data resulting from federally funding scientific research" (OSTP 2013).

Both the law and the memorandum granted commercial publishers a year in which to profit, implicitly recognizing the benefits of the peer review process that accompanies publication in scientific journals. However, Reichman and Okediji (2012) argued that global copyright laws present serious barriers to OA because they "automatically confer exclusive propriety rights on authors of scientific literature who routinely transfer those rights to commercial publishers" (p. 1369). Commercial publishers then attach technological protection measures to the digital content thus restricting access. Reichman and Okediji (2012) suggested that radical reforms will be needed to copyright and database protection laws if the potential for sharing scientific information is to be fully realized. They called for a serious rebalancing of interests: reducing the power of intellectual property rights owners and increasing the access rights of public science researchers.

V. TELECOMMUNICATIONS LEGISLATION

A. Telecommunications Act of 1996

The Telecommunications Act of 1996, signed by President Clinton on February 8, contained an important provision that directly affected libraries. The Snowe-Rockefeller-Exon-Kerry provision authorized reduced rates to access the Internet for libraries, schools, and health care providers. The Schools and Libraries Universal Service Support Mechanism, more commonly known as the E-Rate, provided a significant discount that enabled most U.S. schools and libraries to obtain affordable access in four service categories: telecommunications services, Internet access, internal connections other than basic maintenance, and basic maintenance of internal connections. Discounts ranged from 20%–90% of the costs of these services, depending on the urban or rural status of the population served and its level of poverty. Eligible schools, school districts, and libraries could apply individually or as part of a consortium. The E-Rate supported connectivity—the conduit or pipeline for communications; the school or library was responsible for providing the end-user equipment (computers, telephones, etc.), software, professional development, and other necessary elements. The Universal Service Administrative Company administers the program under the direction of the FCC. Disbursements to schools and libraries had an annual cap in 2014 of $2.4 billion. In 2014 the FCC adopted the E-Rate Modernization Order, expanding Wi-Fi networks and broadband connectivity to schools and libraries. (FCC 2014b).

B. The Communications Decency Act (CDA)

A provision of the Communications Decency Act (CDA), subjected to fines and criminal penalties a person who knowingly transmitted or displayed to minors materials that might be construed as indecent. Indecency was construed very broadly to include words as well as images. Challenged by the ACLU, the ALA, and other organizations, the Supreme Court declared this section of the law unconstitutional and a violation of the First Amendment. Justice John Paul Stevens, writing for the majority of the Court, noted that

> the CDA lacks the precision that the First Amendment requires when a statute regulates the content of speech. . . . As a matter of constitutional tradition, in the absence of evidence to the contrary, we presume that governmental regulation of the content of speech is more likely to interfere with the free exchange of ideas than to encourage it. The interest in encouraging freedom of expression in a democratic society outweighs any theoretical but unproven benefit of censorship. (*Janet Reno v. American Civil Liberties Union et al.* 1997)

C. Child Online Protection Act (COPA)

The Supreme Court ruling on the CDA delayed, but did not deter Congress from attempting to control content that it deemed inappropriate on the Internet. In 1998, it passed the Child Online Privacy Protection Act. In part, the act stated:

> Whoever knowingly and with knowledge of the character of the material, in interstate or foreign commerce by means of the World Wide Web, makes any communication for commercial purposes that is available to any minor and that includes

any material that is harmful to minors shall be fined not more than $50,000, imprisoned not more than 6 months, or both. (Section 231)

The law attempted to restrict the viewing of sexually explicit or other adult materials to adults only by requiring commercial distributors to obtain credit card certifications and adult access codes or personal identification numbers. The law was again challenged on constitutional grounds. The federal district court determined that the law was unconstitutional and issued a permanent injunction against its enforcement. Eventually, the Supreme Court heard the case and sent the case back. The law remains unconstitutional and unenforced at this time.

D. Children's Internet Protection Act (CIPA)

The Children's Internet Protection Act (CIPA) was enacted by Congress to address concerns about access on school and library computers to offensive content over the Internet. In early 2001, the FCC issued rules implementing CIPA for schools and libraries receiving E-Rate discounts. CIPA imposed the following requirements:

- They must include on computers that are available for use by minors technology protection measures that block or filter Internet access to pictures that are: (a) obscene, (b) child pornography, or (c) harmful to minors.

- Schools and libraries must certify that they educate minors about appropriate online behavior, including cyber bullying awareness and response, and using social networking sites and chat rooms.

- Schools were also required to adopt and enforce a policy to monitor online activities of minors.

- Schools and libraries could not receive the discounts offered by the E-Rate program unless they certified that they had an Internet safety policy.

A complementary piece of legislation, the Neighborhood Children's Internet Protection Act (NCIPA) required that the Internet safety policy addressed the following five components:

- Access by minors to inappropriate matter on the Internet and Web
- The safety and security of minors when using e-mail, chat rooms, and other forms of direct electronic communications (including instant messaging)
- Unauthorized access, including so-called hacking and other unlawful activities by minors online

- Unauthorized disclosure, use, and dissemination of personal identification information regarding minors
  - Measures designed to restrict minors' access to materials harmful to minors (not just visual depictions) (E-Rate Central, 2009)

Schools and libraries were required to certify that their safety policies and technology were in place before receiving E-Rate funding. CIPA did not affect E-Rate funding for schools and libraries receiving discounts only for telecommunications, such as telephone service. In addition, an authorized person could disable the blocking or filtering measures during any use by an adult to enable access for bona fide research or other lawful purposes. Although schools were required to monitor use, CIPA did not require actual electronic tracking of use.

In 2002, responding to First Amendment concerns, the ACLU, ALA, and other organizations challenged CIPA on constitutional grounds, focusing on the fact that filters are imperfect tools for at least two reasons. First, filters block constitutionally protected sites as well as those that might be considered obscene. Second, filters block sites that might be considered obscene for young people but not adults, thus reducing Internet access to only materials available to children. Although a federal district court agreed that the CIPA provisions for filtering were unconstitutional, on June 23, 2003, the Supreme Court reversed the federal district court decision in a 5–4 vote. The majority, recognizing a compelling state interest in protecting young people from inappropriate materials, held that CIPA did not impose an unconstitutional condition on libraries, and that Congress has broad powers to define limits on how its funds might be used. In fact, the Court held that Congress, in making such limitations, was actually aiding the selection activities of libraries in their "traditional role of obtaining materials of requisite and appropriate quality for educational and informational purposes" (*United States et al. v. American Library Association* 2002, p. 3). It is notable, however, that the Supreme Court did not deny that filters remove constitutionally protected speech as well as obscenity, but the majority argued that the filters could easily be removed at the request of an adult. The Court left open the possibility of a subsequent challenge if libraries were unable to disable filters easily or if Internet access to constitutionally protected speech was otherwise burdened in a substantial way. This decision raised numerous intellectual freedom concerns for libraries:

1. Although the intent of CIPA was to block materials deemed harmful to minors, the filters inevitably block sites that contain material that is

constitutionally protected when viewed by adults, a concept known as "overblocking." The blocking of constitutionally protected speech is anathema to the ALA Library Bill of Rights.

2. The Supreme Court did not deny that filters overblock; rather, the justices argued that as long as a filter was easily disabled, there was little or no constitutional problem. From the library profession's perspective, however, this assumption does not diminish the intellectual freedom issue—the need to request that a filter be disabled. Although seemingly straightforward, the necessity of requesting that a filter be disabled places a barrier between the person and the information as many patrons would be reluctant to make such a request because it might imply that they wished to see sexual or otherwise sensitive material. This situation is analogous to the time when individuals had to ask a librarian for sexual materials stored in closed stacks. Such barriers are specifically proscribed in the ALA document "Restricting Access to Library Materials." In her analysis of the Supreme Court decision, Smith (2013) noted that the Court did not sufficiently take into account the widely accepted right-to-receive doctrine in which the right to receive information is recognized as a necessary corollary of the First Amendment right to produce it. In addition, they misunderstood the role of the Internet as a public forum and underestimated the difficulty of disabling filters.

3. Filters block access to speech that is constitutionally protected, even for minors. The Supreme Court was silent on the rights of minors and instead emphasized the compelling interest of the state to protect them from harmful materials. The ALA Library Bill of Rights affirms that age should not be considered when access to information is involved. There is substantial evidence that filters block sites totally unrelated to harmful material and blocks sites that are constitutionally protected for minors, a violation of our profession's intellectual freedom principles.

A recent ALA report titled *Fencing Out Knowledge* reviewed the impact of CIPA over the last ten years. Among the findings were that (1) filtering in libraries causes patron needs to go unmet, (2) filtering in schools goes far beyond the legal mandate of CIPA, (3) there is a disproportionate negative impact on the acquisition of digital and media literacy skills and on low-income communities, and (4) there are better alternatives to complying with CIPA than over filtering (Batch 2014).

VI. EDUCATION LEGISLATION

A. Elementary and Secondary Education Act of 1965, Improving America's Schools Act of 1994, and the No Child Left Behind Act of 2001

The Elementary and Secondary Education Act (ESEA) was signed into law in 1965 by President Lyndon Baines Johnson, who believed that "full educational opportunity" should be "our first national goal." The law was intended to improve the quality of education in both public and private schools by supplementing state and local funding. Much of the act supported programs for low-income children (Title I) or those with special needs. Title II was designed to enhance school library collections. At the time the law was passed, nearly one-third of the nation's students attended schools without libraries. ESEA provided monies for textbooks, library resources including monographs, periodicals, and AV materials; staff training and development; and media demonstration programs, special education programs, programming for at-risk children, materials for bilingual studies, and support for the acquisition of materials in areas of social problems (Krettek 1975).

In 1994, ESEA was reauthorized as the Improving America's Schools Act. It contained a variety of provisions focused on issues such as equal access to a quality education, especially for children in poverty; parental participation in schooling; and professional development programs for teachers, administrators, and other school staff (U.S. Department of Education 1994).

On June 8, 2002, the law was reauthorized as the No Child Left Behind Act (NCLB) (Public Law 107-110), a sweeping revision of ESEA that redefined the role of the federal government in K–12 education. Then–Secretary of Education Margaret Spellings noted,

> The law . . . signaled a fundamental and common-sense change to American education. Academic standards would be set by states, schools would be held accountable for results, and the federal government would support both with increased resources and flexibility. (U.S. Department of Education 2007)

According to the U.S. Department of Education (2010), NCLB was based on four pillars: stronger accountability for results, more freedom for states and communities, more choices for parents, and implementation of programs and practices that had been proven effective through rigorous scientific research. Under NCLB, states were required to ensure that all students achieved academic proficiency, including students who were disadvantaged. Schools that did not make adequate yearly progress (AYP) were required to take corrective actions. Parents of children in low-performing schools that did not meet state standards for at least two consecutive years could transfer their children to a better-performing public school, including a public charter school, within their district. The district must provide transportation, using Title I funds if necessary. Students from low-income families in schools that failed to meet state standards for at least three years were eligible to receive supplemental educational services, including tutoring, after-school services, and summer school. If a school did not make AYP after five years, the school could be restructured, including removal and replacement of all staff.

Part B of NCLB emphasized reading skills and literacy in four subparts: Reading First, Early Reading First, Even Start Family Literacy, and Improving Literacy through School Libraries. Whelan (2004) described NCLB as a golden opportunity and recommended that school librarians become experts on their state curriculum standards and then partner with classroom teachers to meet those standards. If school library media specialists can demonstrate that they help meet their state curricular standards, they can become substantial beneficiaries of the act.

In 2010, the Obama administration submitted a "Blueprint for Reform" for the reauthorization of ESEA. The Blueprint focused on four areas originally enunciated in the American Recovery and Reinvestment Act of 2008 (discussed below):

> (1) Improving teacher and principal effectiveness to ensure that every classroom has a great teacher and every school has a great leader; (2) Providing information to families to help them evaluate and improve their children's schools, and to educators to help them improve their students' learning; (3) Implementing college- and career-ready standards and developing improved assessments aligned with those standards; and (4) improving student learning and achievement in America's lower-performing schools by providing intensive support and effective interventions (U.S. Dept. of Ed. 2010, p. 3).

Unfortunately, due to serious partisan political disagreements in Congress, the ESEA has not been reauthorized and it is very difficult to predict when a reauthorization will occur. In 2012 the Obama administration began offering flexibility to states regarding specific requirements of NCLB in exchange for rigorous and comprehensive state-developed plans designed to close achievement gaps, increase equity, improve the quality of instruction, and increase outcomes for all students. However, there are significant disagreements not only among political parties but also interested stakeholders like school superintendents, teachers, and civil rights organizations. Issues such as how much testing should be involved and how much flexibility school districts and states should have remain sources of considerable debate (Klein 2013; Maxwell 2014). LIS professionals will need to stay abreast of this uncertain situation.

B. Higher Education Act of 1965/1992/1998/2008

The Higher Education Act of 1965 (HEA) supported colleges and universities. It focused on four areas: improving student financial assistance; supporting services and activities that help students, especially disadvantaged students, to graduate from high school, enter a postsecondary institution, and complete its program; providing aid to academic institutions; and improving K–12 teacher training at a postsecondary institution (Almanac of Policy Issues 2003). HEA was reauthorized in 1986, 1992, 1998, and 2008. The current law, the Higher Education Opportunity Act (PL 110-315) was enacted on August 14, 2008, and includes titles and sections dealing with a variety of issues in higher education, including

- improving teacher quality through grants for professional development coupled with increased accountability and evaluation of teachers
- promoting international education
- improving financial aid and student assistance processes
- monitoring tuition costs and the total costs of a higher education

In addition, the act has specific provisions regarding peer-to-peer file sharing and protection of student speech and association rights. Recent amendments encourage the development of distance learning programs and create new reporting requirements for academic institutions on the costs of higher education.

The Act is subject to renewal every five years which would have been in 2013, but, as with the ESEA there was considerable disagreement in Congress, so funding remains dependent on continuing resolutions until a reauthorization is passed. There does seem to be general agreement from both parties regarding making higher education more affordable for students and their parents. President Obama proposed a comprehensive bill which included developing new performance measures for colleges and students that would impact federal aid; promoting affordable options to the traditional college model; encouraging innovations by reducing regulations; and making debt repayment less burdensome by creating flexible options for repayment and capping payments at 10% of a student's monthly income. The Republicans also addressed many of these issues, but in separate bills rather than one comprehensive one (White House 2013; Field 2014, Bidwell 2014).

VII. LIBRARY LEGISLATION

A. The Library of Congress

In 1800, when President John Adams signed a bill transferring the seat of government from Philadelphia to the new capital city of Washington, the legislation also created a reference library for Congress. The LOC was established; the closest thing the United States has to a national library in conjunction with the National Library of Medicine, the National Agricultural Library, and the National Archives. Its mission is "to support the Congress in fulfilling its constitutional duties and to further the progress of knowledge and creativity for the benefit of the American people" (LOC 2014). The library service's mission is

> to develop qualitatively the Library's universal collections, which document the history and further the creativity of the American people and which record and contribute to the advancement of civilization and knowledge throughout the world, and to acquire, organize, provide access to, maintain, secure, and preserve these collections. (LOC 2014)

The size and scope of the collection are formidable: LOC is one of the great repositories of the world, with more than 158 million items, including 36 million books and other print materials, 3.5 million records, 13.7 million photographs, 5.5 million maps, 6.7 million pieces of sheet music, and 69 million manuscripts. Approximately 470 languages are represented. It is the largest law library in the world (2.9 million volumes) and the largest rare-book collection in North America (more than 700,000 volumes); it holds more than 3.5 million sound records and 1.7 million film, TV, and video items. LOC had a budget in 2013 of nearly $600 million and it employs more than 3,200 permanent staff. It welcomed nearly 1.6 million visitors on-site in 2013 alone (LOC "Year" 2014).

The programs funded by Congress and implemented by the LOC are many and varied. Historically, some of its programs have had a profound influence on librarianship. For example, as developers of MARC, LOC transformed and made uniform the bibliographic record, which in turn greatly accelerated the development of bibliographic utilities. Similarly, the Copyright Office, which is part of the LOC, requires that publishers deposit two copies of each item published. Although LOC is not required to retain material sent to it, the law created a central repository for much of the material printed in the United States. The historical and research implications are manifest.

The LOC's highest priority is service to Congress through its Congressional Research Service (CRS), which was created in 1914 under President Woodrow Wilson. CRS "serves as shared staff to congressional committees and Members of Congress. CRS experts assist at every stage of the legislative process—from the early considerations that precede bill drafting, through committee hearings and floor debate, to the oversight or enacted laws and various agency activities" (LOC 2014). The reports of CRS are intended to be confidential, authoritative, objective, and non-partisan. CRS, in 2013, responded to more than 500,000 reference requests in-person, telephone, or through written and electronic communications (LOC 2014).

LOC provides services to the public through its reading rooms and website. It provides an online reference service—Ask a Librarian Service—which provides responses to queries submitted online within five business days. It also provides limited services to the general citizenry, such as materials to the blind and physically handicapped. In addition, LOC cooperates with OCLC, to provide an online reference service called "Question-Point," a collaborative network of reference librarians throughout the United States, available twenty-four hours a day.

LOC also places considerable emphasis on U.S. history through its American Memory Project, a part of the National Digital Library Program. Originally begun as a CD-ROM project in 1990, the American Memory Project's purpose is to provide "free and open access through the Internet to written and spoken words, sound recordings, still and moving images, prints, maps, and sheet music that document the American experience" (LOC 2014). The project partners with a variety of collecting institutions and includes primary source and archival materials. These collections represent a critical contribution to the National Digital Library. Photographs and documents can be searched full text by keyword. To date, over 9 million items have been scanned, representing access to more than 100 thematic historical collections (LOC 2014a, under "About . . ."). In a related area, LOC also partnered with a variety of organizations, including the Pew Internet and American Life Project, to create the September 11 Web Archive. The archive is intended to preserve "Web expressions of individuals, groups, the press and institutions in the United States and from around the world in the aftermath of the attacks in the United States of September 11, 2001." Access is provided directly to more than 2,300 sites with access by URL to more than 30,000 additional sites (LOC 2014b).

A related program is the National Digital Information Infrastructure and Preservation Program (NDIIPP), created by Congress in 2000. For some time LOC recognized that digital technologies produce information that is often impermanent and fragile but nonetheless of significant historical value. Consequently, LOC has been aggressive in preserving it. According to LOC,

NDIIPP is based on an understanding that digital stewardship on a national scale depends on public and private communities working together. The program has engaged hundreds of organizations and partners across the United States and around the world to preserve at-risk digital collections and build a distributed digital preservation infrastructure. (LOC 2014c)

Over the years, NDIIPP has invested in numerous initiatives such as establishing digital preservation partnerships, digital archiving and long-term preservation, technical architecture, digital preservation policy, preserving creative works, preserving state government information, and creating strategic partnerships (LOC 2014c). A major current initiative is the National Digital Stewardship Alliance:

> Founded in 2010, the National Digital Stewardship Alliance (NDSA) is a consortium of institutions that are committed to the long-term preservation of digital information. NDSA's mission is to establish, maintain, and advance the capacity to preserve our nation's digital resources for the benefit of present and future generations. The NDSA comprises over 160 participating institutional members. These members come from 45 states and include universities, consortia, professional societies, commercial businesses, professional associations, and government agencies at the federal, state and local level. (NDSA 2014, p. 7)

NDSA's mission is accomplished through working groups of experts, guided by a National Agenda. Among the Agenda's areas of focus are collecting data on current at-risk, large-scale digital content and how to ensure access to it; sharing information on what digital content is currently being collected and the type of access to it; creating partnerships with owners and creators of digital content; advocating for resources to manage digital content and promoting multi-institutional collaboration; fostering best practices; and improving research on and practice of digital stewardship (NDSA 2014).

B. The Federal Depository Library Program (FDLP)

Access to information collected or produced by the government is critical if the citizenry is to be engaged and make informed judgments. The FDLP was established in the mid-1800s to serve this purpose. Managed by the Government Printing Office, the FDLP makes government information available to 1,350 libraries designated as depository libraries. About half of these libraries are academic, 20% are public, with the remaining in community colleges and state, federal, and special libraries. The mission of depository libraries is to provide local, free access to information from the Federal government in an impartial environment. Federal depository libraries select materials from lists of subjects provided by the Government Printing Office. The depository library must then provide the public with free and uninhibited access to these selected materials. (FDLP 2014)

The FDLP performed its function very well for many years. However, as noted many times previously, the emergence of the electronic information environment has radically transformed all library services. Traditionally government information was distributed in the form of physical documents. Today, government agencies, prompted by the E-Government Act of 2002, publish their reports and data in electronic form and the FDLP provides direct access to the online versions of some of these publications. It also developed a powerful search engine to search for documents with basic and advanced search options, and delivers search results through e-mail (FDLP 2014). Nonetheless, Jaeger et al. (2010) suggested that the FDLP needs to adapt more quickly to the Internet age, making "changes in both concept and practice in the provision of information . . ." (p. 469). They identified six factors that challenge depository libraries because they exist in an Internet environment that

- Increasingly chooses digital over print and paper;
- Offers multiple access points other than those traditional search tools offered by libraries;
- Follows user preferences rather than traditional library bibliographic control technologies;
- Creates new knowledge management tools that enables users direct and independent access to content;
- Fosters non-librarian organizations (that are often competitive with libraries) to create access points and dissemination mechanisms for government information; and
- Pushes users [sic] expectations to expect immediate access to information beyond the confines of a library's physical collection housed within a particular building. (p. 474)

In this environment, Jaeger et al. contend that depository libraries will need to find new ways to collaborate using broadband networks and social software in order to sustain and provide access to the vast quantities of digital content produced by the government.

C. The Library Services Act and the Library Services and Construction Act (LSA, LSCA)

Since 1956 the federal government has passed legislation to improve library services in the United States. The Library Services Act (LSA) was meant originally to redress the considerable inequalities evident in cities compared to rural areas and funneled monies through state library agencies to address the needs of public libraries serving fewer than 10,000 people. This restriction was removed in 1964 and the legislation's name was changed to the Library Services and Construction Act (LSCA). Administered by the Department of Education, LSCA was the largest single provider of federal assistance to support library services (Title I) for many years (Molz 1990). As the law and its name changed funding was expanded to include not only library services, but also library construction (Title II). Over the years, other titles were added: Title III for interlibrary cooperation; Title IV for services to Indian tribes; Title V for foreign-language materials acquisition; Title VI for library literacy programs. LSCA was a major contributor to the improvement of library services and facilities until it was repealed when the Museum and Library Services Act and the Library Services and Technologies Acts were passed.

D. National Commission on Libraries and Information Science Act of 1970 (P.L. 94–345)

The National Commission on Libraries and Information Science (NCLIS) was established as an independent commission within the executive branch by the National Commission on Libraries and Information Science Act on July 20, 1970. The role of the commission was to advise the president and Congress on matters relating to library and information policies and plans. It was responsible for developing or recommending overall plans for the provision of library and information services adequate to meet the needs of the people of the United States.

The commission was authorized to conduct studies, appraise the state of library resources and services and evaluate their effectiveness, develop national plans for library services, and promote research and development activities that would improve the nation's libraries. It was responsible for sponsoring influential major conferences involving multiple national constituencies on library services. The commission's activities and concerns were quite varied, including the creation, dissemination, and access to government information on the part of the public, particularly information in electronic form; the role of school library media centers in educational achievement and literacy and advocacy for more certified media specialists; mass digitization and its implications for the Copyright Act; and advocacy for health information distribution centers. Following 9/11 the commission also examined the potential role that libraries could play after a terrorist attack or natural disaster. In addition, the commission developed a Library Statistics Program in cooperation with the National Center for Education Statistics (NCES), the IMLS, and NISO. The program encouraged national collection of library data and helped develop models of data collection, particularly in the area of network statistics and performance measures for public libraries.

Because national information policy was a major focus of the commission, it advocated for the value of public information as a foundation for a free society. Public information was defined by NCLIS as "information created, compiled and/or maintained by the Federal Government." In 1990, the commission promulgated eight principles of public information that it hoped would serve as a foundation for information policy in the federal government:

- The public has a right of access to public information.
- The Federal Government should guarantee the integrity and preservation of public information, regardless of its format.
- The Federal Government should guarantee the dissemination, reproduction, and redistribution of public information.
- The Federal Government should safeguard the privacy of persons who use or request information, as well as persons about whom information exists in government records.
- The Federal Government should ensure a wide diversity of sources of access, private as well as governmental, to public information.
- The Federal Government should not allow costs to obstruct the people's access to public information.
- The Federal Government should ensure that information about government information is easily available and in a single index accessible in a variety of formats.
- The Federal Government should guarantee the public's access to public information, regardless of where they live and work, through national networks and programs like the Depository Library Program. (NCLIS 2008, p. 21)

Today, the functions of the NCLIS are integrated into the Institute for Museum and Library Services.

E. The Museum and Library Service Act of 1996 and the Library Services and Technology Act (LMSA, LSTA)

In 1996, President Clinton signed the Museum and Library Services Act (PL 104-208) (MLSA) which established the Institute of Museum and Library Services (IMLS) within the National Foundation on the Arts and Humanities. IMLS operates through two offices: the Office of Museum Services, which authorized grants to museums to increase and improve museum services and the Office of Library Services. Subtitle B of the MLSA, known as the Library Services and Technology Act (LSTA), was established for the following purposes:

- to consolidate federal library service programs
- to stimulate excellence and promote access to learning and information resources in all types of libraries for individuals of all ages
- to promote library services that provide all users access to information through state, regional, national, and international electronic networks
- to provide linkages among and between libraries
- to promote targeted library services to people of diverse geographic, cultural, and socioeconomic backgrounds, to individuals with disabilities, and to people with limited functional literacy or information skills

The Museum and Library Services Act was reauthorized in 2003 and 2010 (PL 111-340). The stated mission of IMLS (2015) is "to inspire libraries and museums to advance innovation, lifelong learning, and cultural and civic engagement. We provide leadership through research, policy development, and grant making." IMLS's vision is to foster a democratic society "where communities and individuals thrive with broad public access to knowledge, cultural heritage, and lifelong learning." The strategic plan for 2012–2016, titled *Creating a Nation of Learners*, identified five strategic goals:

- IMLS places the learner at the center and supports engaging experiences in libraries and museums that prepare people to be full participants in their local communities and our global society.
- IMLS promotes museums and libraries as strong community anchors that enhance civic engagement, cultural opportunities, and economic vitality.
- IMLS supports exemplary stewardship of museum and library collections and promotes the use of technology to facilitate discovery of knowledge and cultural heritage.

- IMLS advises the President and Congress on plans, policies, and activities to sustain and increase public access to information and ideas.

- IMLS achieves excellence in public management and performs as a model organization through strategic alignment of IMLS resources and prioritization of programmatic activities, maximizing value for the American public. (p. 5)

IMLS supports all types of libraries and museums serving all populations. Special priorities for 2015 are "science, technology, engineering and math (STEM) learning, early childhood learning, and expanding access to federal information through libraries" (IMLS 2014). IMLS remains an important source of funding for research and innovation, underserved populations, children, and the general public.

VIII. SUMMARY

As the value of information increases, more and more stakeholders attempt to shape information policies to serve their needs. Because LIS professionals generally serve the public interest, value service rather than profit, and uphold fundamental democratic principles, they serve as critical advocates for an open, free exchange of ideas and information. A long legislative tradition supports this role. However, the growth of electronic technologies has created competitors—many more interested in gain than in universal access. This might be both just and natural in an entrepreneurial society, but it makes it doubly important that LIS professionals have a place in the information policy debate. LIS professionals must actively monitor the information policy climate and aggressively make the case for their values.

REFERENCES

ACRL. 2003. "Statement on Fair Use and Electronic Reserves." November. www.ala.org/ala/mgrps/divs/acrl/publications/whitepapers/statementfair.cfm.

Adler, Prudence. 2001. "Copyright and Intellectual Property Legislation and Related Activities: New Challenges for Libraries." In *Impact of Digital Technology on Library Collections and Resource Sharing*, edited by Sul H. Lee. Binghamton, NY: Haworth Press, 107–118.

Agnew, Grace, and Mairead Martin. 2003. "Digital Rights Management: Why Libraries Should Be Major Players." In *The Bowker Annual: Library and Book Trade Almanac*, 48th ed., edited by Dave Bogart. Medford, NJ: Information Today, 267–278.

Almanac of Policy Issues. 2003. "Higher Education Act: Reauthorization Status and Issues." www.policyalmanac.org/education/archive/crs_higher_education.shtml.

————. 2003a. "Homeland Security Agents Pull Ohio Libraries' Haz-Mat Documents." *American Libraries*. www.ala.org/ala/alonline/currentnews/newsarchive/2003/april2003/homelandsecurity.htm.

————. 2003b. *Restrictions on Access to Government Information (RAGI) Report*. Chicago: ALA.

————. 2007. "E-government 2.0: Improving Innovation, Collaboration and Access." www.ala.org/advocacy/sites/ala.org.advocacy/files/content/advleg/federallegislation/govinfo/egovernment/ALAEGovernmentStatem.pdf.

————. 2010. "Network Neutrality." Chicago: ALA. www.ala.org/ala/issuesadvocacy/telecom/netneutrality/index.cfm.

————. 2014. "ALA Troubled by Court's Net Neutrality Decision." Press Release. www.ala.org/news/press-releases/2014/01/ala-troubled-court-s-net-neutrality-decision.

————. 2014a. "Keeping Up with . . . Net Neutrality." www.ala.org/acrl/publications/keeping_up_with/net_neutrality.

————. 2015. "ALA Applauds FCC Vote to Protect Open Internet." Press Release. www.ala.org/news/press-releases/2015/02/ala-appaluds-fcc-vote-protect-open-internet.

ARL. 1997. "Principles for Licensing Electronic Resources." www.arl.org/sc/marketplace/license/licprinciples.shtml.

————. 2012. *Code of Best Practices in Fair Use for Academic and Research Libraries*. www.arl.org/storage/documents/publications/code-of-best-practices-fair-use.pdf.

Austin, Brice. 2004. "Should There Be 'Privilege' in the Relationship between Reference Librarian and Patron?" *Reference Librarian* 42: 301–311.

Bailey, Charles W., Jr. 2006. "Strong Copyright + DRM + Weak Net Neutrality = Digital Dystopia?" *Information Technology and Libraries* 25 (September): 116–127.

Band, Jonathan. 2008. "Educational Fair Use Today." In *Library and Book Trade Almanac: The Bowker Annual*, 53rd ed., edited by Dave Bogart. Medford, NJ: Information Today.

Barve, Sunita and N.B. Dahibhate. 2012. "Open Source Software for Library Services." *DESIDOC Journal of Library & Information Technology* 32 (September): 401–408.

Batch, Kristen R. 2014. *Fencing Out Knowledge: Impacts of the Children's Internet Protection Act 10 Years Later*. Policy Brief No. 5. Chicago: ALA.

Becker, Samantha, Michael D. Crandall, Karen E. Fisher, Bo Kinney, Carol Landry, and Anita Rocha. 2010. *Opportunity for All: How the American Public Benefits from Internet Access at U.S. Libraries*. (IMLS-2010-RES-01). Institute of Museum and Library Services. Washington, D.C.

Bertot, John Carlo, Paul T. Jaeger, Lesley A. Langa, and Charles R. McClure. 2006a. "Drafted: I Want You to Deliver E-government." *Library Journal* 131 (August 1): 34–37. www.libraryjournal.com/index.asp?layout=articlePrint&articleID=CA6359866.

————. 2006b. "Public Access Computing and Internet Access in Public Libraries: The Role of Public Libraries in E-government and Emergency Situations." *First*

Monday 11 (September 4). www.uic.edu/htbin/cgiwrap/bin/ojs/index.php/fm/rt/printerFriendly/1392/1313.

Bertot, John Carlo, Paul T. Jaeger, and Charles R. McClure. 2008. "Citizen-Centered E-government Services: Benefits, Costs, and Research Needs." Proceedings of the 9th Annual International Digital Government Research Conference, Montreal, Canada, May 18–21, 2008, pp. 137–142.

Bidwell, Alice. 2014. "Senate Higher Education Bill Focuses on Affordability." www.usnews.com/news/articles/2014/20/senate-higher-education-act-sekks-to-tackle-college-cost-transparency.

Blum, Oliver. 1997. "The New WIPO Treaties on Copyright and Performers' and Phonogram Producers' Rights." www.educause.edu/Resources/ThenewWIPOTreatieson Copyright/153941.

Buckley, Sean. 2014. "FCC's Connect America Fund II Receives Mixed Response." www.fiercetelecom.com/story/fccs-connect-america-fund-ii-receives-mixed-response/2014-04-25.

Burger, Robert H. 1993. *Information Policy: A Framework for Evaluation and Policy Research*. Norwood, NJ: Ablex.

Burke, Susan, and Erin M. Boggs. 2015. "E-Government on Public Library Websites." *Public Libraries* (March-April): 42–51.

Chmara, Theresa. 2012. "Privacy and E-Books." *Knowledge Quest* 40 (January/February): 62–65.

Coalition of Journalists for Open Government. 2009. "The Card Memo." www.cjog.net/background_the_card_memo.html.

Cochran, Wendell, and Coral Davenport. 2006. "'Executive Privilege' Used by More Federal Agencies to Withhold Information." *The IRE Journal* 29 (October): 9–10.

Communications Act of 1934, 47 U.S.C. Section 202(a).

Connected Nation. 2012. "FCC Begins Implementation of Connect America Fund: Price Cap and Rate of Return Carriers: A Connected Nation Policy Brief." www.connectednation.org/sites/default/files/bb-pp/connected_nation_usf_update_2012_04_27.pdf.

CONTU (National Commission on New Technological Uses of Copyrighted Works). 1978. *Final Report*. July 31, 1978. Washington, DC: GPO.

Corbly, James E. 2014. "The Free Software Alternative: Freeware, Open-Source Software, and Libraries." *Information Technology and Libraries* (September): 65–75.

Creative Commons. 2014. "About." creativecommons.org/about.

———. 2014a. "Licenses." creativecommons.org/licenses.

———. 2014b. "State of the Commons." https://stateof.creativecommons.org/?utm_campaign=2014fund&utm_source=carousel&utm_medium=Web.

Creative Librarian. 2014. "Open-Source Software for Libraries." www.creativelibrarian.com/library-oss.

Crews, Kenneth D. 2012. *Copyright Law for Librarians and Educators*, 3rd ed. Chicago: ALA.

Critical Infrastructure Protection Board. 2003. *National Strategy to Secure Cyberspace.* Washington, DC: White House.

DOI. 2014 "Frequently Asked Questions about the DOI System." www.doi.org/faq.html.

DOI Foundation. 2009. "Welcome to the DOI System." www.doi.org.

Dorman, David. 2002. "Open Source Software and the Intellectual Commons." *American Libraries* 33 (December): 51–54.

Doyle, Charles. 2005. *Libraries and the USA PATRIOT Act.* CRS Report for Congress. Updated July 6, 2005. www.fas.org/sgp/crs/intel/RS21441.pdf.

Educause. 2012. *A Case for Fair Use: The Georgia State Decision.* www.educause.edu/library/resources/case-fiar-use-georgia-state-decision-51512.

E-Rate Central. 2009. "Internet Safety Policies and CIPA: An E-Rate Primer for Schools and Libraries." www.e-ratecentral.com/CIPA/cipa_policy_primer.pdf.

"FBI Has Visited about 50 Libraries." 2003. www.libraryjournal.com/article/CA302414.html.

FCC (Federal Communications Commission). 2010. "In the Matter of Preserving Open Internet Broadband Industry Practices." FCC 10–201. Washington, DC.

———. 2010. *Connecting America: The National Broadband Plan.*

———. 2012. "Connect America Fund (CAF) Phase I." www.fcc.gov/maps/connect-america-fund-caf-phase-i.

———. 2014. "FCC Launches Rural Broadband Expansion Experiments." Press Release (July 14). https://apps.fcc.gov/edocs_public/attachmatch/DOC-328470A1.pdf.

———. 2014a. "Rural Broadband Experiments Draw Interest from Almost 200 Applicants." Press Release (November 2014).

———. 2014b. "E-Rate—Schools & Libraries USF Program." www.fcc.gov/encyclopedia/e-rate-schools-libraries-usf-program.

FDLP (Federal Depository Library Program). 2014. "U.S. Federal Depository Library Program." www.doi.gov/library/collections/federal-documents.cfm.

Feinberg, Lotte. 2004. "FOIA, Federal Information Policy, and Information Availability in a Post-9/11 World." *Government Information Quarterly* 21: 439–460. www.sciencedirect.com/science/article/pii/S0740624X04000577.

Field, Kelly. 2014. "Senate Democrats' Bill to Renew Higher Education Act: Many Ideas, Little Hope of Passing." chronicle.com/article/Senate-Democrats-Bill-to/150175.

Gale Group. 1998. "Penumbra" *West's Encyclopedia of American Law.* www.answers.com/topic/penumbra.

Gershwin Publishing Corp. v. Columbia Artists Management, Inc., 443 F.2d 11 59, 1162 (2d Cir. 1971).

Gilroy, Angela A. 2006. *Net Neutrality: Background and Issues.* Washington, DC: LOC, Congressional Research Service, May 18, 2006.

Gregory, Vicki. 2011. *Collection Development and Management for 21st Century Library Collections: An Introduction.* Neal-Schuman/ALA: Chicago.

Griswold v. Connecticut, 381 U.S. 479, 85 S. Ct. 1678, 14 L. Ed. 2d 510 (1965).

Hammitt, Harry. 2005. "Less Safe—The Dismantling of Public Information Systems after 9/11. *Social Science Computer Review* 23 (winter): 429–438.

Horrigan, John B. 2009. "Home Broadband Adoption 2009." Pew Internet and American Life Project, July. www.pewInternet.org/~/media/Files/Reports/2009/Home-Broadband -Adoption-2009.pdf.

———. 2013. *Narrowing Gaps, New Challenges*. www.knightfoundation.org/media/ uploads/media.pdfs/DigitalAccessUpdateFeb2014.pdf.

House Report. 1976. "House Report No. 94–1476, Copyright Act." In *United States Code: Congressional and Administrative News*. 94th Congress—Second Session 1976. St. Paul, MN: West, 5659–5823.

Hutton, Susan. 2014. "Nothing Neutral about Net Neutrality." www.lsa.mich.edu/lsa/ ci.nothingneutralaboutnetneutrality_ci.detail.

IFLA. 2014. "Lyon Declaration on Access to Information and Development." www.lyondeclaration.org/content/pages/lyon-declaration.pdf.

———. 2013. "TLIB—Frequently Asked Questions." www.ifla.org/node/5775.

———. 2013a. "Treaty Proposal on Copyright Limitations and Exceptions for Libraries and Archives." www.ifla.org/node/5856.

IMLS. 2013. *Creating a Nation of Learners: Strategic Plan 2012–2016*. Institute of Museum and Library Services. www.imls.gov/assets/1/AssetManager/StrategicPlan2012–16.pdf.

———. 2014. "President's FY 2015 Budget Request Includes $226,448,000 for the Institute of Museum and Library Services." www.imls.gov/president's_fy_2015_budget_request _includes_226448000_for_the_institute_of_museum_and_library_services_aspx.

Information Infrastructure Task Force. 1995. *Intellectual Property and the National Information Infrastructure*. Washington, DC: IITF.

iPAC (Internet Policy and Access Service). 2014. "E-government & Public Libraries." www.plInternetsurvey.org/analysis/public-libraries-and-E-government.

———. 2012. "2011–2012 Public Library Funding and Technology Access Survey: Executive Summary." http://ipac.umd.edu/publicatos/2011–2012-public-library -funding-and-technology-access-survey-executive-summary.

———. 2012a. "E-government Partnership Projects: Executive Summary." ipac.umb.edu/ sites/default/files/publications/EGOVT_Exec_SummaryJan2012_0.pdf.

———. 2014. "Broadband and Public Libraries" http://ipac.umd.edu/survey/analysis/ broadband-public-libraries.

Jaeger, Paul T. 2008. "Building E-government into the Library and Information Science Curriculum: The Future of Government Information and Services." *Journal of Education for Library and Information Science* 49 (summer): 167–179.

Jaeger, Paul T., John Carol Bertot, and John A. Shuler. 2010. "The Federal Depository Library Program (FDLP), Academic Libraries, and Access to Government Information." *The Journal of Academic Librarianship* 36 (November): 469–478.

Jaeger, Paul T., and Kenneth R. Fleischmann. 2007. "Public Libraries, Values, Trust, and E-government." *Information Technology and Libraries* 26 (December): 34–43.

Jaeger, Paul, Ursula Gorham, John Carlo Bertot, and Lindsay C. Sarin. 2014. *Public Libraries, Public Policies, and Political Processes.* New York: Rowman & Littlefield.

Jaeger, Paul T., Ursula Gorham, Lindsay C. Sarin, and John Carlo Bertot. 2013. "Libraries, Policy, and Politics in a Democracy: Four Historical Epochs." *Library Quarterly* 83 (April): 166–181.

Jaeger, Paul T., Charles R. McClure, John Carlo Bertot, and John T. Snead. 2004. "The USA PATRIOT Act, the Foreign Intelligence Surveillance Act, and Information Policy Research in Libraries: Issues, Impacts, and Questions for Libraries and Researchers." *Library Quarterly* 74: 99–121.

Janet Reno v. American Civil Liberties Union et al. 1997. "Supreme Court Opinion." Cited in Citizen Internet Empowerment Coalition. www.ciec.org/SC_appeal/opinion.shtml.

Jorgensen, Jan. 2006. "The Online Government Information Movement: Retracing the Route to DigiGov Through the Federal Documents Collection." *Reference Librarian* 45:139–162.

Kane, Yukari Iwatani. 2009. "Breaking Apple's Grip on the iPhone." *Wall Street Journal* (March 6): B1.

Kim, Anne L. 2014. "Cities Ask FCC to Fight Restrictive Broadband Laws." *Roll Call.* www.rollcall.com/news/cities_ask_fcc_to_fight_restrictive_broadband_laws-236151-1 .html?zkPrintable-true.

Klein, Alyson. 2013. "Stark Partisan Split Persists on ESEA Renewal." *Education Week.* www.edweek.org/ew/articles/2013/07/37esea_ep.h32.html.

Krettek, Germaine. 1975. "Library Legislation, Federal." In *Encyclopedia of Library and Information Science.* Vol. 15. New York: Marcel Dekker, 337–354.

Krug, Judith. 2005. "Foreword." In *Privacy in the 21st Century.* By Helen R. Adams, Robert F. Bocher, Carol A. Gordon, and Elizabeth Barry-Kessler. Westport, CT: Libraries Unlimited, ix–x.

La Porte, Todd M. 2005. "Being Good and Doing Well: Organizational Openness and Government Effectiveness on the World Wide Web." *Bulletin of the American Society for Information Science and Technology* (February/March): 23–27.

LCA (Library Copyright Alliance). 2014. "About." www.librarycopyrightalliance.org/about/ index.shtml.

LOC. 2012. "Exemption to Prohibition on Circumvention of Copyright Protection System for Access Control Technologies." 37 CFR Part 201. Washington, DC: LOC.

———. 2014. "About the Library." www.loc.gov/about.

———. 2014a. "About the Collections" (American Memory). http://memory.loc.gov/ ammem/about/index.htm.

———. 2014b. "Collection Overview." http://lcWeb2.10c.gov/diglib/lcwa/html/sept11/ sept11-overview.html.

————. 2014c. "National Digital Stewardship Alliance." www.digitalpreservation.gov/ndsa.

Lipinski, Tomas A. 2005. "The Legal Landscape after *MGM v. Grokster*: Is It the Beginning of the End or the End of the Beginning?" *Bulletin of the American Society for Information Science and Technology* 32 (October/November). www.asis.org/Bulletin/Oct-05/lipinski.html.

————. 2011. "Toward a Functional Understanding of Fair Use in U.S. Copyright Law." In *Annual Review of Information Science and Technology* 45: 523–621.

Madison, James. 1973. "Letter to W. T. Barry, August 4, 1822." In *The Mind of the Founder: Sources of the Political Thought of James Madison.* Indianapolis: Brandeis, 437.

Magi, Trina J. 2011. "Fourteen Reasons Privacy Matters: A Multidisciplinary Review of Scholarly Literature." *Library Quarterly* 81: 187–209.

Mason, Marianne. 2008. "Providing Access to Electronic Government Information to Diverse Populations." In *Managing Electronic Government Information in Libraries: Issues and Practices,* edited by Andrea M. Morrison. Chicago: ALA, 44–59.

Maxwell, Lesli A. 2014. "Superintendents Push Vision for Next Version of ESEA." *Education Week.* www.edweek.org/ew/articles/2014/02/19/21districts.h33.html.

McKee, Anne, Margaret Donahue Walker, and Jose Luis Andrade. 2012. "Shaping, Streamlining, and Solidifying the Information Chain in Turbulent Times." *The Serials Librarian* 62: 103–111.

Merriam-Webster's Collegiate Dictionary. 1996. Springfield, MA: Merriam-Webster, Inc.

Molz, R. Kathleen. 1990. *The Federal Roles in Support of Public Library Services: An Overview.* Chicago: ALA.

NCLIS (National Commission on Libraries and Information Science). March 2008. *Meeting the Information Needs of the American People: Past Actions and Future Initiatives.* Washington, DC: NCLIS.

NDSA (National Digital Stewardship Alliance). 2014. *2015 National Agenda for Digital Stewardship.* www.digitalpreservation.gov/ndsa/documents/2015NationalAgendaExecSummary.pdf.

Ned, Brionna N. 2014. "Unenforceable Copyrights: The Plight of the Music Industry in a P2P File-Sharing World." *The Review of Litigation* 33: 397–426.

NIH (National Institutes of Health). 2009. "NIH Public Access Policy Details." http://public.access.nih.gov/policy.htm.

NISO (National Information Standards Organization). 2009. "Shared E-Resource Understanding (SERU)." www.niso.org/workrooms/seru.

OECD (Organisation for Economic Co-operation and Development). 2007. *OECD Principles and Guidelines for Access to Research Data from Public Funding.* www.oecd.org/sti/sci-tech/38500813.pdf.

Office of Homeland Security. 2002. *National Strategy for Homeland Security.* Washington, DC: White House.

Open Source Initiative. 2014. "Open Source Initiative." www.opensource.org/osd.

OpenTheGovernment.org. 2007. "Secrecy Report Card 2007." Washington, DC: Open The Government. www.openthegovernment.org/otg/SRC2007.pdf.

OSTP (Office of Science and Technology). 2013. "Memorandum for the Heads of Executive Departments and Agencies." www.whitehouse.gov/sites/default/files/ microsites/ostp/ostp_public_access_memo_2013.pdf.

Pirate Bay. 2015. "About." https://piratebay.host/about.

Puckett, Jason. 2010. "Digital Rights Management as Information Access Barrier." *Progressive Librarian* 34: 11–24. www.progressivelibrariansguild.org/PL_Jnl/pdf/PL34– 35-fallwinter2010.pdf.

Purcell, Kristen. 2013. "Online Video: 2013." www.pewInternet.org/2013/10/10/online -video-2013.

Reichman, Jerome H., and Ruth L. Okediji. 2012. "When Copyright Law and Science Collide: Empowering Digitally Integrated Research Methods on a Global Scale." *Minnesota Law Review* 96: 1362–1480.

Robertson, Scott P., and Ravi K. Vatrapu. 2010. "Digital Government." In *Annual Review of Information Science and Technology* 44: 317–364.

Rubel, Alan. 2014. "Libraries, Electronic Resources, and Privacy: The Case for Positive Intellectual Freedom." *Library Quarterly* 84: 183–208.

Russell, Carrie. 2005a. "Copyright Concerns: Photocopies, Scanners, and Downloads: Is the Library Liable? (Part 1)." *Public Libraries* 44 (September/October): 275–276.

———. 2005b. "Copyright Concerns: Photocopies, Scanners, and Downloads: Is the Library Liable? (Part 2)." *Public Libraries* 44 (November/December): 339.

SAIC (Science Applications International Corporation). 1995. *Information Warfare: Legal, Regulatory, Policy and Organizational Considerations for Assurance*. Washington, DC: Pentagon.

Sanchez, Julian. 2009. "New FOIA Rules Official—Let the Data Flood Begin." www.arstechnica.com/tech-policy/news/2009/03/will-new-foia-rules-yield-a-data -flood.ars.

Schmidt, James C. 1989. "Rights for Users of Information: Conflicts and Balances among Privacy, Professional Ethics, Law, National Security." *Bowker Annual: Library and Book Trade Almanac 1989–90*, 34th ed. Medford, NJ: Information Today, 83–90.

Sheketoff, Emily, and Jazzy Wright. 2014. "Legislation and Regulations Affecting Libraries in 2013." In *Library and Book Trade Almanac*, 59th ed. Medford, NJ: Information Today, pp. 253–260.

Shuler, John. 2005. "The Political and Economic Future of Federal Depository Libraries." *Journal of Academic Librarianship* 31 (July): 377–382.

Siefert, Jeffrey W. 2011. "Sharing and Safeguarding Government Information: Evolving Postures and Rising Challenges." In *Library and Book Trade Almanac*, 56th ed. Medford, NJ: Information Today, pp. 17–35.

Sinodinou, Tatiana. April 19, 2013. "On Copyright and Rights of Persons with Disabilities: WIPO Treaty for the Blind." www.kluwercopyrightblog.com/2013/04/19/on-copyright-and-rights-of-persons-with-disabilities-wipo-treaty-for-the-blind.

Skala, Matthew, Brett Bonfield, and Mary Fran Torpey. 2008. "Enforcing Copyright." *Library Journal* 133 (February 15): 28–30.

Smith, Barbara H. 2013. "The First Amendment Right to Receive Online Information in Public Libraries." *Communications Law & Policy* 18 (winter): 63–89.

Smith, Brett. 2014. "A Quick Guide to GPLv3." www.gnu.org/licenses/quick-guide-gplv3.html.

Smith, Ted D. 2002. "Security versus Freedom of Information: An Enduring Conflict in Federal Information Policy." *OLA Quarterly* 8 (winter): 2–6.

Solove, Daniel J. 2008. "The Future of Privacy." *American Libraries* 39 (September): 56–59.

Springen, Karen. 2014. "The Piracy Problem." *Publishers Weekly* (July 21): 1–5.

Strickland, Lee S. 2005. "The Information Gulag: Rethinking Openness in Times of National Danger." *Government Information Quarterly* 22: 546–572.

Swartz, Mark. 2013. "Shifting Tides: How the Re-emergence of DRM Impacts Libraries." *Feliciter* 59: 3–5.

Taylor, David G. 2011. "No Official Oversight, but a Few Voluntary Measures." *The Obameter* (July 21). www.politifact.com/truth-o-meter/promises/obameter/promise/179/revise-the-patriot-act-to-increase-oversight-on-go.

Taylor, Natalie Greene, Paul T. Jaeger, Ursula Gorham, John Carlo Bertot, Ruth Lincoln, and Elizabeth Larson. 2014. "The Circular Continuum of Agencies, Public Libraries, and Users: A Model of E-Government in Practice." *Government Information Quarterly* 31: 518–525.

TWN (Third World Network). 2014. "WIPO: Divide Over New Treaty on Exceptions for Libraries/Archives." www.twnside.org.sg/title2/intellectual_property/info.service/2014/ip140702.htm.

United Nations. 1948. "Universal Declaration of Human Rights." www.un.org/en/documents/udhr.

United States et al. v. American Library Association, Inc. et al. "Syllabus." Supreme Court of the United States. October Term, 2002.

U.S.C. (United States Code). 17 U.S.C. Section 102(a) [1988 & Supp V 1993].

U.S. Congress. 2002. E-government Act of 2002 (Public Law 107-347). 107th Congress. www.archives.gov/about/laws/egov-act-section-207.html.

U.S. Copyright Office. 1998. *The Digital Millennium Copyright Act of 1998: U.S. Copyright Office Summary.* Washington, DC: Copyright Office, December.

———. 2008. *The Section 108 Study Group Report.* Washington, DC: Copyright Office, March.

U.S. Court of Appeals for the District of Columbia Circuit. 2014. *Verizon v. Federal Communications Commission.* www.cadc.uscourts.gov/Internet/opinions. nsf/3AF8B4D938CDEEA685257C6000532062/$file/11-1355-1474943.pdf.

U.S. Department of Education. 1994. "HR 6: Improving America's Schools Act of 1994." www.ed.gov/legislation/ESEA/toc.html.

———. 2007. Building on Results: A Blueprint for Strengthening the No Child Left Behind Act. Washington, DC: U.S. Department of Education.

———. 2010. ESEA Blueprint for Reform. Washington, DC: U.S. Department of Education, Office of Planning Evaluation and Policy Development. www2.ed.gov/policy/elsec/leg/blueprint/blueprint.pdf.

———. 2010. "Overview: Four Pillars of NCLB." www2.ed.gov/nclb/overview/intro/4pillars.html.

U.S. Patent and Trademark Office. 1998. "The Conference on Fair Use: Final Report to the Commissioner on the Conclusion of the Conference on Fair Use." www.uspto.gov/sites/default/files/document/confurep_0.pdf.

Van Arnhem, Joland-Pieta, and Lindsay Barnett. 2014. "Is Digital Rights Management (DRM) Impacting E-Book Adoption in Academic Libraries?" *The Charleston Advisor* (January): 63–66.

We the People. 2012. "Require Free Access Over the Internet to Scientific Journal Articles Arising from Taxpayer-Funded Research." https://petitions.whitehouse.gov/response/increasing-public-access-results-scientific-research.

Weitzner, Daniel J. 2006. "The Neutral Internet: An Information Architecture for Open Societies." http://dig.csail.mit.edu/2006/06/neutralnet.html.

Whelan, Debra Lau. 2004. "A Golden Opportunity." *School Library Journal* (January): 40–42.

White House. 2013. "Fact Sheet on the President's Plan to Make College More Affordable: A Better Bargain for the Middle Class." www.whitehouse.gov/the-press-office/2013/080/22/fact-sheet-president-s-plan-make-college-more-affordable-better-bargain.

Windhausen, John, Jr. 2009. A Plan to Extend Super-Fast Broadband Connections to All Americans. New York: Century Foundation.

WIPO (World Intellectual Property Organization). 1996. "WIPO Copyright Treaty." www.wipo.int/treaties/en/ip/wct/trtdocs_w0033.html.

———. 2013. "Historic Treaty Adopted, Boosts Access to Books for Visually Impaired Persons Worldwide." www.wipo.int/pressroom/en/articles/2013/article_0017.html.

Xue, Susan. 2005. "Internet Policy and Diffusion in China, Malaysia and Singapore." *Journal of Information Science* 31: 238–250.

Zimmer, Michael. 2014. "Librarians' Attitudes Regarding Information and Internet Privacy." *Library Quarterly* 84: 123–151.

Zittrain, Jonathan L. 2006. "The Generative Internet." *Harvard Law Review* 119 (May): 1974–2040.

SELECTED READINGS: Information Policy
Books/Monographs

Association of College and Research Libraries. *Code of Best Practices in Fair Use for Academic and Research Libraries.* 2012. www.arl.org/storage/documents/publications/code-of-best-practices-fair-use.pdf.

Batch, Kristen R. *Fencing Out Knowledge: Impacts of the Children's Internet Protection Act 10 Years Later.* Policy Brief No. 5. Chicago: ALA, 2014.

Cloonan, Michèle Valerie. *Preserving Our Heritage.* Chicago: ALA, 2015.

Crews, Kenneth D. *Copyright Law for Librarians and Educators*, 3rd ed. Chicago: ALA, 2012.

Horrigan, John. *Narrowing Gaps, New Challenges.* 2013. www.knightfoundation.org/media/uploads/media.pdfs/DigitalAccessUpdateFeb2014.pdf.

Jaeger, Paul, Ursula Gorham, John Carlo Bertot, and Lindsay C. Sarin. *Public Libraries, Public Policies, and Political Processes.* New York: Rowman & Littlefield, 2014.

Mossberger, Karen, Caroline Tolbert, and Mary Stansbury. *Virtual Inequality: Beyond the Digital Divide.* Washington, DC: Georgetown University Press, 2003.

National Digital Information Infrastructure and Preservation Program. *Preserving Our Digital Heritage: Plan for the National Digital Information Infrastructure and Preservation Program.* Washington, DC: LOC. www.digitalpreservation.gov/library/resources/pubs/docs/ndiipp_plan.pdf.

Thompson, Kim M., Paul T. Jaeger, Natalie Greene Taylor, Manimegalai M. Subramaniam, and John Carlo Bertot. *Digital Literacy and Digital Inclusion: Information Policy and the Public Library.* Lanham: Rowman & Littlefield, 2014.

Articles

Ahlbrand, Ashley. "'Free' Access to Government Information: How the Current Budget Crisis May Affect Government Publishing and Access to Government Information." *DTTP: Documents to the People* 39 (winter 2011): 26–31.

Burke, Susan, and Erin M. Boggs. "E-Government on Public Library Websites." *Public Libraries* (March–April 2015): 42–51.

Casper, Scott. "Promoting Electronic Government Documents: Part One: Direction." *DTTP: Documents to the People* 41 (spring 2013): 15–17.

———. "Promoting Electronic Government Documents: Part Two: Interconnection." *DTTP: Documents to the People* 41 (summer 2013): 18–20.

Chmara, Theresa. "Privacy and E-Books." *Knowledge Quest* 40 (January/February 2012): 62–65.

Corbly, James E. "The Free Software Alternative: Freeware, Open-Source Software, and Libraries." *Information Technology and Libraries* (September 2014): 65–75.

Hutton, Susan. "Nothing Neutral about Net Neutrality." 2014. www.lsa.mich.edu/lsa/ ci.nothingneutralaboutnetneutrality_ci.detail.

Jaeger, Paul T. "Building E-government into the Library and Information Science Curriculum: The Future of Government Information and Services." *Journal of Education for Library and Information Science* 49 (summer 2008): 167–179.

Jaeger, Paul T., John Carol Bertot, and John A. Shuler. "The Federal Depository Library Program (FDLP), Academic Libraries, and Access to Government Information." *The Journal of Academic Librarianship* 36 (November 2010): 469–478.

Jaeger, Paul T., and Kenneth R. Fleischmann. "Public Libraries, Values, Trust, and E-government." *Information Technology and Libraries* 26 (December 2007): 34–43.

Jaeger, Paul T., Ursula Gorham, Lindsay C. Sarin, and John Carlo Bertot. "Libraries, Policy, and Politics in a Democracy: Four Historical Epochs." *Library Quarterly* 83 (April 2013): 166–181.

Janning, Nicholas. "A Delicate Balance: National Security, Government Transparency, and Free Speech." *DttP: Documents to the People* 40 (winter 2012): 10–14.

———. "Toward a Functional Understanding of Fair Use in U.S. Copyright Law." In *Annual Review of Information Science and Technology* 45 (2011): 523–621.

Lor, P., and J. Britz. "Is a Knowledge Society Possible, Without Freedom of Access to Information?" *Journal of Information Science* 33 (2007): 387–397.

Magi, Trina J. "Fourteen Reasons Privacy Matters: A Multidisciplinary Review of Scholarly Literature." *Library Quarterly* 81 (2011): 187–209.

McKee, Anne, Margaret Donahue Walker, and Jose Luis Andrade. "Shaping, Streamlining, and Solidifying the Information Chain in Turbulent Times." *The Serials Librarian* 62 (2012): 103–111.

Neal, James G. "Copyright Is Dead . . . Long Live Copyright." *American Libraries* 33 (December 2002): 48–51.

Ned, Brionna N. "Unenforceable Copyrights: The Plight of the Music Industry in a P2P File-Sharing World." *The Review of Litigation* 33 (2014): 397–426.

Puckett, Jason. "Digital Rights Management as Information Access Barrier." *Progressive Librarian* 34 (2010): 11–24. Available: www.progressivelibrariansguild.org/PL_Jnl/pdf/ PL34–35-fallwinter2010.pdf.

Reichman, Jerome H., and Ruth L. Okediji. "When Copyright Law and Science Collide: Empowering Digitally Integrated Research Methods on a Global Scale." *Minnesota Law Review* 96 (2012): 1362–1480.

Robertson, Scott P., and Ravi K. Vatrapu. "Digital Government." In *Annual Review of Information Science and Technology* 44 (2010): 317–364.

Rubel, Alan. "Libraries, Electronic Resources, and Privacy: The Case for Positive Intellectual Freedom." *Library Quarterly* 84 (2014): 183–208.

Siefert, Jeffrey W. "Sharing and Safeguarding Government Information: Evolving Postures and Rising Challenges." In *Library and Book Trade Almanac*. 56th ed. Medford, NJ: *Information Today*, 2011, pp. 17–35.

Solove, Daniel J. "The Future of Privacy." *American Libraries* 39 (September 2009): 56–59.

Swartz, Mark. "Shifting Tides: How the Re-emergence of DRM Impacts Libraries." *Feliciter* 59 (2013): 3–5.

Taylor, Natalie Greene, Paul T. Jaeger, Ursula Gorham, John Carlo Bertot, Ruth Lincoln, and Elizabeth Larson. 2014. "The Circular Continuum of Agencies, Public Libraries, and Users: A Model of E-Government in Practice." *Government Information Quarterly* 31: 518–525.

Zimmer, Michael. "Librarians' Attitudes Regarding Information and Internet Privacy." *Library Quarterly* 84 (2014): 123–151.

Intellectual Freedom

I. INTRODUCTION

Intellectual freedom is both a fundamental professional value and an inherent aspect of library policy and practice. However, it is one thing to endorse intellectual freedom as a concept; it is another thing to make it a reality in the day-to-day life of a library. In this chapter, intellectual freedom and its opposite — censorship — will be examined from the perspective of their characteristics and how libraries have dealt with both in policy and practice.

The roots of intellectual freedom in American society are first and foremost connected to the First Amendment of the Constitution with its strong support of freedom of expression and religion. In addition, from a philosophical perspective, the contemporary roots of intellectual freedom were articulated by the work of the nineteenth-century British philosopher John Stuart Mill in his essay, *On Liberty*, published in 1859. To Mill, the importance of individual liberty of thought was of great importance and it was inextricably tied to "liberty of the press":

> This, then, is the appropriate region of human liberty. It comprises, first, the inward domain of consciousness, demanding liberty of conscience in the most comprehensive sense, liberty of thought and feeling, absolute freedom of opinion and sentiment on all subjects, practical or speculative, scientific, moral, or theological. The liberty of expressing and publishing opinions may seem to fall under a different principle, since it belongs to that part of conduct of an individual which concerns other people, but, being almost of as much importance as the liberty of thought

itself and resting in great part on the same reasons, is practically inseparable from it (Mill p. 16).

The need for open discussion of ideas, some of which may be heretical and anathema to the majority or the society-at-large, is essential according to Mill if one is to understand what is right and to guard against the tyranny of the majority or against tyrannical government. Many of Mill's arguments are still used today in defense of intellectual freedom.

In contemporary terms, Dresang (2006) defines intellectual freedom as "freedom to think or believe what one will, freedom to express one's thoughts and beliefs in unrestricted manners and means, and freedom to access information and ideas regardless of the content or viewpoints of the author(s) or the age, background, or beliefs of the receiver" (p. 169). In other words, it is freedom *from* government oversight or undue regulation, public scrutiny, and invasion of one's privacy regarding what one reads, views, or hears; it is also freedom *to* access information unimpeded, to learn through discovery of new ideas, to interact with others including library staff, to have access to controversial issues, and to engage others on diverse issues in a constructive and hospitable environment (Stripling 2013). It is also freedom to create one's own content in blogs, wikis, and social media (Johnson 2013). Intellectual freedom is based on a fundamental belief that the health of a democratic society is maintained and improved when ideas can be created and disseminated without governmental, political, or social impediment.

Librarians have not always been in the forefront of preserving intellectual freedom and defending against censorship. Throughout most of the nineteenth century and most of the first half of the twentieth, librarians perceived themselves primarily as preservers of the public good and protectors of the predominant social mores. As such, they wanted to expose people to "good" books and not purchase "bad" ones. Even when books of lesser quality were selected they were intended to attract new library users so they could be led from the popular books to the best reading materials. It was not until totalitarianism overtook Germany in the late 1930s, when the world first witnessed books burning, that intellectual freedom rose to a prominent role in the profession.

During that dark period the profession solidified its commitment to intellectual freedom in three ways: by codification, by institutionalization, and by investigation (Knox, 2014). Codification began in 1939, when the ALA adopted a Library Bill of Rights that provided guidance and important ethical foundations for supporting open access to library materials and resisting censorship. Institutionalization occurred a year later when the ALA established its Intellectual Freedom Committee (IFC) whose purpose was to collect data on censorship attempts, to recommend policies concerning intellectual freedom issues, and to promote intellectual freedom among librarians. The IFC also began to provide interpretations to further explicate the policies presented at conferences on censorship and intellectual freedom. Investigations explored the attitudes of librarians toward censorship, and researchers examined how best to deal with censorship issues (ALA 2010). Asato (2014) studied the American Library Association's response to challenges involving LIS professionals over a fifty-year period. He identified three categories when intellectual freedom rights were at stake: (1) when librarians acted in a professional capacity (e.g., defending against censorship of materials), (2) when librarians exercised their rights inside the workplace (e.g., whistle-blowing or expressing religious or political speech), and (3) when librarians exercised their rights outside the workplace (e.g., expressed a personal—unrelated to the library—or unpopular point-of-view in their community). Not surprisingly, Asato found that ALA's response was uneven over the years.

In those early years, the ALA exhorted librarians to protect the intellectual freedom rights of the citizenry, but the Association was reluctant to defend individual librarians involved in censorship cases, citing local administrative jurisdiction (Bushman 2009). For many years, there was little tangible support for the librarians and library directors who defended intellectual freedom, many of whom became victims of punitive actions on the part of library trustees or other government officials.

The importance of supporting librarians during censorship challenges was placed in high relief in the late 1940s and early 1950s when people both within and outside the government feared that our society was being infiltrated by subversives who were undermining not only our federal, state, and local governments, but our civic organizations and institutions as well. As Robbins (2000) observed:

> The nation perceived itself as threatened, not only by foreign military might, but also by an insidious foreign ideology that appeared to be spread, like rumors and the common cold, through casual contact. (p. 6)

These were the early years of the Cold War, and in 1947, President Truman issued an executive order requiring loyalty oaths from federal employees. Soon thereafter other government agencies and private and public institutions, including some libraries, also demanded them. Some libraries dismissed librarians who refused to take the oath (Robbins 1995).

Fueling these fears, in 1949 the Soviet Union exploded its first atomic bomb and Mao Tse Tung assumed leadership in China. By the early 1950s, the United States was fighting the Korean War and the search for communists became a national mania. There were systematic attempts to discredit individuals and institutions for their real or imagined subversive political beliefs or activities. In the name of patriotism, various organizations—the American Legion, the Veterans of Foreign Wars, and the Daughters and Sons of the American Revolution (DAR, SAR)—attempted to expose anti-patriotic activities and those who participated in them. Most notably, the House Un-American Activities Committee under the leadership of Senator Joe McCarthy began its investigations of citizens suspected of subversive activities, launching what came to be known as the "McCarthy Era." Organizations prepared lists—blacklists—of authors or titles (and actors) suspected of subversive thinking, including Langston Hughes, Sherwood Anderson, Pearl Buck, Norman Mailer, John Steinbeck, Lillian Hellman, Richard Wright, and Dashiell Hammett.

Librarians across the United States came under attack. The U.S. Chamber of Commerce recommended a variety of watchdog activities including monitoring teachers and librarians whose classrooms or collections either intentionally or naively allegedly promoted communist ideas or denigrated American values. Organizations and sometimes a single individual challenged not just books, but films and periodicals that at least in their minds were sympathetic to communism and the Soviet Union (Francoeur 2006). The attacks focused on three areas of concern: the libraries' materials collection, individual staff members, and library services and exhibits. The collection was the primary area of attack (Francoeur 2006). For example, books that mentioned discrimination, urban decay, unfair labor practices, dishonest politicians, and crime were considered anti-American (Mediavilla 1997). Of particular interest were books that promoted intergroup or international understanding such as books that portrayed the United Nations in a favorable light. Another focus was books for children and young adults who were considered especially vulnerable to subversive ideas (Jenkins 2001).

As might be expected, libraries responded in a variety of ways as they struggled to maintain balanced collections while coping with community and national hysteria. Some librarians continued to use the recognized standard selection and reviewing tools as the best means to protect them in case of attack. Many others were reticent to collect authors, titles, or films that had been blacklisted. Other libraries collected some of the works, but did not promote them. Many maintained a low profile and attempted to handle any challenges quietly; few actually reported attacks to the ALA. Even major libraries, such as the New York Public Library, sometimes compromised their intellectual freedom principles when challenges arose (Jenkins 2001; Francoeur 2011; Wiegand 2005).

Although the ALA was also under suspicion for subversive activity, the profession took a stand in 1950. After much debate, and under the leadership of David Berninghausen, chair of the Intellectual Freedom Committee, the ALA adopted a resolution opposing loyalty oaths. The resolution condemned attempts to investigate and punish individuals because of what they read or because they belonged to particular organizations. The Resolution also insisted on due process when an employee was accused of un-American activities. In response to efforts to make libraries put labels on books judged to promote communism, in 1951 ALA adopted the "Statement on Labeling." Perhaps ALA's proudest moment was in 1953, when, in cooperation with the American Book Publisher Council, it adopted the Freedom to Read Statement which was a complete repudiation of censorship and the suppression of intellectual freedom and an affirmation of an individual's right to choose what one reads. This remarkable Statement is discussed in more detail below.

In December 1954 the U.S. Senate censored McCarthy for his excesses and abuses but by then much damage had been done. Unfortunately, the end of the McCarthy era was not the end of censorship in libraries. As concerns for rooting out political subversives subsided, censors soon turned their attention to upholding America's religious and moral values. Librarians were soon forced to defend themselves for collecting "indecent" literature (Francoeur 2006). The McCarthy period clearly revealed the insidious forces that can be unleashed against the free flow of ideas and the significant challenges that face libraries and LIS professionals in defending intellectual freedom.

Today, the commitment to intellectual freedom continues to have far-reaching implications because it permeates a variety of critical library activities including selecting, weeding, and classifying materials; physically locating materials in the library; providing information services; confidentiality; and access policies. For example, it might lead to selecting or providing access to materials containing ideas considered heinous, for example, Hitler's *Mein Kampf*. A commitment to intellectual freedom presupposes that the best way to combat a bad idea is not to suppress it, but to produce a better idea, and that the only alternative to censorship is free expression. It also presumes people are more likely to generate better ideas when there is unimpaired freedom to produce them. Individuals who fear that some ideas might be so harmful that they should be suppressed or restricted are prone to acts of censorship. Censorship is an act or set of acts by government, groups, or individuals (including librarians) to restrict the flow of information or ideas.

On its surface, it seems intuitively obvious that librarians should inhibit censorship and promote intellectual freedom, but the protection of intellectual freedom is, in fact, one of the most difficult aspects of library work and the focus of considerable professional debate. At the root of the problem are conflicting moral, ethical, personal, and social values, and legal obligations. Some of these factors form powerful motivators to restrict access to some materials, while other elements serve as countervailing forces, encouraging unrestricted access. By making these forces more explicit, it becomes clear why LIS professionals sometimes have difficulty making policy decisions on this issue.

II. FACTORS THAT INHIBIT OR ENCOURAGE INTELLECTUAL FREEDOM

A. Factors That Tend to Restrict Access

1. Personal Values

Each of us, through childhood training and experience, develops certain moral precepts. LIS professionals do not surrender those values when they go to work. While it is understood that LIS professionals should not impose their personal beliefs on their practice, certain circumstances are more likely to evoke a desire to apply personal values than others. For example, librarians might be tempted to restrict access to materials that promote bigotry, especially to young people. The conflict between holding certain social values and advocating for open access to ideas that might be inimical to those values is a constant tension that some might feel is professionally irreconcilable (Dresang 2006).

2. Community Values

Quite naturally, LIS professionals perceive the library as part of the community. Many live, as well as work, in the community and participate in its many social, political, recreational, and cultural activities. Similarly, most libraries, public and school libraries in particular, depend on their local communities for funding support and it is a fundamental tenet of the profession that a library's collection and services should reflect the community's needs and desires. Consequently, there might be some hesitation on the part of the LIS professional when purchasing materials that represent viewpoints and perspectives substantially different from the community's, or that might offend a significant number of community members.

3. The Desire to Protect Children from Harm

Few obligations are as indisputable as the commitment of all members of a society to protect from exploitation those who are defenseless or vulnerable. What group falls more clearly into this category than children? Society even legally requires that certain groups dealing with children—teachers, health care workers, social workers, and university researchers—monitor potential harm to children and report suspected harm to the authorities. Although most LIS professionals are not required to do this, it is unreasonable to presume that they have no stake in caring for and protecting children. Indeed, a central tenet of librarianship historically has been nurturing children's growth and development through exposure to books and other materials. Can one reasonably believe that books and information can improve children, but that they cannot also harm them; a common argument by those who wish to restrict materials for young people?

4. The Need to Ensure the Survival of the Library

Few obligations are dearer to LIS professionals than the preservation of the library as an institution. The survival of a major cultural and social institution is an important factor in ethical decisions. Therefore, the selection, organization, and dissemination of materials that might threaten the fiscal and political support of the community give librarians pause. Those who wish to restrict materials often threaten to campaign against funding for library services, thus threatening the survival of the library itself.

B. Factors That Tend to Increase Access

The factors that tend to restrict access are not trivial; in fact, they enlighten us about the realistic pressures that many LIS professionals face. But there are other counterbalancing elements that help LIS professionals resist the temptation to restrict access.

1. The Need to Educate Future Generations

Public libraries educate children and youth through careful collection development, access to digital content, responsive reference services, entertaining and educational programming, and cooperation with outside agencies such as schools and social service agencies. Although some might feel that public libraries should prevent exposure to certain ideas, others would argue that children and youth who are free to explore ideas become healthy adults and better-educated citizens. Most public libraries adopt policies clarifying that the choice to restrict access rests with parents alone.

School library media centers, on the other hand, are more subject to the views and beliefs of the educational community in which they are embedded. Some

educators see the library as a means of inculcating the young with only particular values and behaviors. Others contend that a comprehensive education involves
exposing students to many different points of view and teaching them the critical
thinking skills necessary to make well-reasoned decisions. This argument was a
fundamental issue in one of the most important Supreme Court cases on school
censorship, *Island Trees v. Pico* (1982) discussed in more detail in chapter 3. The
perspective of the ALA generally has been that access to information should be
unrestricted and this has been outlined in a variety of formal statements. As the
strategic plan of the Association for Library Service to Children (ALSC, ALA) states:

> Through free, public, and equal access to library services, children develop a love
> of reading, and become responsible citizens contributing to a global society. As a
> result of positive library experiences, children remain library users throughout their
> lives and pass this engagement on to future generation. (ALSC 2014)

2. Professional Standards

Through formal education and on-the-job training, LIS professionals assimilate the
professional standards of behavior and service best expressed in the ALA's Library
Bill of Rights and the Code of Ethics of both the ALA and the American Society
for Information Science and Technology. These documents guide our professional
judgments using reasonably objective criteria, as opposed to our personal biases. A
good example of this distinction came from Lester Asheim (1954) more than sixty
years ago, who succinctly characterized the difference between censorship and the
professional selection of library materials:

> To the selector, the important thing is to find reasons to keep the book. Given such
> a guiding principle, the selector looks for values, for virtues, for strengths, which
> will overshadow minor objections. For the censor, on the other hand, the important
> thing is to find reasons to reject the book. His guiding principle leads him to seek
> out the objectionable features, the weaknesses, the possibilities for misinterpreta-
> tion. . . . The selector says, if there is anything good in this book let us try to keep it;
> the censor says, if there is anything bad in this book, let us reject it. And since there
> is seldom a flawless work in any form, the censor's approach can destroy much that
> is worth saving. (pp. 95–96)

Although Asheim lived when books were preeminent, the point remains: adherence
to professional values and standards requires a broad and representative collection.

3. The Obligation to Protect the Rights of Citizens in a Democratic Society

The First Amendment of the U.S. Constitution plays a central role in the establishment, maintenance, and protection of libraries and their patrons. The First Amendment not only provides Americans with the right to express their ideas, it establishes a corollary right to access the ideas of others. A value held dear by many LIS professionals, both personally and professionally, is the importance of providing information to all those who seek it. This view corresponds with a number of beliefs about democracy:

- It is the most effective form of government.
- Citizens should be able to obtain information about a variety of viewpoints in order to make informed choices.
- Opposing points of view are aired, not suppressed.
- The untrue should be heard as well as the true because falsehoods can often be quite useful in the learning process.

Indeed, sometimes what is considered false in one generation becomes the truth of another (Swan 1986). Restricting access to materials contravenes the letter and spirit of the First Amendment and diminishes its authority and effect. LIS professionals as a group, affirm their obligation to protect the First Amendment.

The struggle of librarians to balance these competing forces has led to much tension and ambivalence within the profession over the years.

III. MAJOR CONCERNS OF THOSE WHO WISH TO CENSOR MATERIALS

There are many reasons offered for censorship attempts, including sexual explicitness, violence, offensive language, satanic themes, content developmentally inappropriate for a particular age group, antifamily content, antidemocratic content, or content "promoting" homosexuality (ALA 2014; Anderson 2014). From 2000–2009, the Office of Intellectual Freedom (OIF) reported more than 5,000 challenges to library materials: 1,577 for sexual explicitness; 1,291 for offensive language; 989 for age unsuitability; 619 for violence; 361 for homosexuality (ALA 2014a). Assuming that only a modest percentage of censorship attempts were reported to the OIF, the total number was likely considerably larger. Among the books challenged during this period were some of the most celebrated or widely read works in modern

American literature, including the *Harry Potter* series by J. K. Rowling, *The Chocolate War* by Robert Cormier, *Of Mice and Men* by John Steinbeck, *Beloved* by Toni Morrison, *Forever* by Judy Blume, *To Kill a Mockingbird* by Harper Lee, and *The Adventures of Huckleberry Finn* by Mark Twain. Books, of course, were just one target for censors; sex and violence in movies or music lyrics were also sources of frequent complaints. Some of the targets included *Snow White*, *The Little Mermaid*, and *My Friend Flicka*.

Although recent trends indicate a decline in the number of reported challenges, there were still 311 reported challenges in 2014, including *The Absolutely True Diary of a Part-Time Indian* by Sherman Alexie for being antifamily, culturally insensitive, and containing drugs, alcohol, smoking, and gambling; *Persepolis* by Marjan Satrapi for offensive language, gambling, and being politically and socially offensive; *And Tango Makes Three* by Justin Richardson and Peter Parnell for antifamily, homosexuality, political and religious offensiveness; *The Bluest Eye* by Toni Morrison for sexual explicitness; *It's Perfectly Normal* by Robie Harris for nudity, sex education, sexual explicitness; *Saga* by Brian Vaughan and Fiona Staples for being antifamily and containing nudity, offensive language, sexual explicitness; *The Kite Runner* by Khaled Hosseini for offensive language and being unsuitable for young people; and *The Perks of Being a Wallflower* by Stephen Chbosky for containing drugs, alcohol, smoking, homosexuality, and offensive language (ALA 2015). Recently, the Office of Intellectual Freedom (OIF) of ALA has noticed increasing challenges that focus on "diverse titles." Diverse titles focus on certain characteristics:

- nonwhite main or secondary characters
- LGBT main or secondary characters
- disabled main or secondary characters
- issues about race or racism
- LGBT issues
- issues about religion, which encompass in this situation the Holocaust and terrorism
- issues about disability or mental illness
- non-Western settings in which the West is North America and Europe

Over the last ten years, 52% of the top 100 books challenged or banned included diverse content and 80% of the top ten banned in 2014 contained diverse content (ALA 2015, Lo 2014). Regarding LGBT materials Downey (2013) suggested that librarians were employing many of the standard self-censorship rationales: hard to find materials on the subject; lack of potential circulation; no LGBT individuals in the community or lack of budget.

Other recent concerns emerged with the publication of the *50 Shades of Grey* trilogy described by one observer as "Lady Chatterley's Lover of 2012" (IFC 2012). The book caused much consternation and debate among public libraries and librarians. Hill and Harrington (2014) described the trilogy as a "unique event where an erotic novel series became openly read and widely discussed" (p. 62).

Challenges are initiated by many sources. In 2014, for example, parents represented the largest group (35%) followed by patrons (23%) and administrators (6%). Librarians and Board members each represented 1% of challengers.

The following discussion highlights some of the most common concerns, regardless of format or whether the item is digital or physical.

A. Sexual Content

Some individuals believe that sexual subject matter of any type should not be in libraries, especially if it is available to minors. Such people often believe that sexuality education should be provided only by parents and that children's access to sexually related informational materials in the library should be restricted. Similarly, some argue that certain materials promote "perverse" sexual behaviors and adversely affect the attitudes of young people. Clearly, sexuality is a topic that triggers strong passions. Sometimes even a single word might cause a problem. For example, the 2007 Newbery Medal award winner, *The Higher Power of Lucky*, was challenged by both patrons and some librarians because the word "scrotum" appeared in the book (Schultz 2007). The pervasiveness of the Internet raises considerable concern that young people might locate sexually explicit sites or be inadvertently subjected to such sites by adult library users. Consequently, there is considerable interest by individuals, groups, and policy makers concerning the filtering of library computers and placing responsibility for control over explicit content on Internet content providers.

B. Violence

Does exposure to violent themes in books, music, and films promote unacceptable behavior? Some evidence suggests a relationship between exposure to violence and subsequent aggressive behavior. Kunkel and Zwarun (2006) reviewed the literature on TV violence and youth behavior and noted:

> It is well established by a compelling body of scientific evidence that television violence is harmful to children. These harmful effects include (1) children's learning of aggressive attitudes and behaviors; (2) desensitization, or an increased callousness toward victims of violence; and (3) increased or exaggerated fear of being victimized by violence. (p. 203)

At the same time, the researchers point out that the relationship is complex; not all children are negatively affected by what they see or read. In addition, they noted that although television violence might be pervasive, it is not necessarily the most potent factor in subsequent violent behavior. Evidence on the relationship of violent lyrics in music and subsequent aggressive behavior is modest, but a few studies confirmed a relationship between exposure to rap and heavy metal music and aggressive attitudes and behavior (Wilson and Martins 2006). Other research suggested that exposure to violent themes in music, linked with sexual content, can affect young people. Martino et al. (2006), for example, conducted a three-year study of 12–17-year-olds and found that young people in the United States listen to music 1.5 to 2.5 hours a day, not including music videos. They found a complex relationship between certain types of music and subsequent sexual activity:

> Youth who listened to more degrading sexual content . . . were more likely to subsequently initiate intercourse and to progress to more advanced levels of non-coital sexual activity, even after controlling for 18 respondent characteristics that might otherwise explain these relationships. In contrast, exposure to non-degrading sexual content was unrelated to changes in participants' sexual behavior. (p. 431)

It does seem obvious that constantly watching people get shot, stabbed, and brutalized, or listening to music that promotes violence of one kind or another diminishes the shock of these disturbing actions. Clearly, as a society, we are less shocked by such explicit violence than we were in the past. Are libraries promoting this insensitivity or contributing to the violence by making available materials with violent themes?

As American society grows more concerned about violence, people search for factors that might promote or foster it. Some people believe that certain materials in libraries contribute to this problem. On the other hand, freedom of expression, even violent speech, is protected by the First Amendment. Efforts to limit exposure to violence might rest more effectively on educational efforts by parents and the media industry than attempts to control it by legal means (Ross 2006). Nonetheless, concerns over censorship were sufficient that the ALA, along with eight other national organizations, including the American Society of Journalists and Authors and the Association of American Publishers, adopted "Violence in the Media: A Joint Statement" (ALA 2001). This statement acknowledged that the community has legitimate reasons to be concerned about violence in the media, including the Internet, but that some of the proposed solutions had a deleterious effect on freedom of expression. It noted that "concern for our children and fundamental speech freedoms are not mutually exclusive." The statement identified six principles:

- Censorship is not the answer to violence in society.
- The First Amendment protects the widest range of expression.
- It is not properly the role of government to evaluate the merits of expression.
- Evaluating the worth of expression is subjective.
- Portrayals of violence in the media reflect a violent world.
- Individuals, not the government, bear responsibility for determining what materials are appropriate for themselves and their children. (ALA 2001)

C. Offensive Language

Language used in print, AV materials, music, and digital content has become progressively more "colorful" over the years. Today, explicit sexual slang and profanity are parts of many works especially in the movie and music industries. Many fear that improper language provides an unhealthy model and influences subsequent behavior, especially for young people, and like violence, there is concern that we become used to profane language in everyday speech. Coyne et al. (2012) studied profanity in young adult novels. Based on a selection of 40 best-selling adolescent works, they found that although some novels (12%) contained no profanity, in the remainder about half of the profanity was "mild." Other works, usually targeted at older adolescents, contained a large amount including strong profanity. Coyne observed with concern that there was no age guidance or warnings concerning the content on the covers of the books. Although stopping short of recommending that such warning labels be required, some serious attention to possible rating systems or warnings was implied. Coyne's concern was that parents needed more information so that they could make informed decisions about the books their children read (Hill 2013).

D. Concern with Formats and Types of Access

Although print materials have been censored for centuries, new concerns focus on audiovisual materials including DVDs, streaming videos, and images from the Internet as well as video games. Visually oriented media are particularly powerful as people are more deeply and immediately affected by what they see on a screen than by what they read in a book. Audio materials have also come under attack. Rap music has been a frequent target for censors using the argument that the combination of words and music makes the offensive lyrics more powerful than the use of the words alone. It is hard to deny that music can intensify an experience, as anyone who has been to the movies can attest.

E. Concern for Children

Our fear of the harmful effects of ideas on youth goes back to classical Greece—recall that Socrates was put to death for corrupting the youth of Athens. Every society seeks to protect its young from undesirable influences. The first obscenity case in English law occurred around 1860 when the English court was concerned with the effects of "obscene" materials on "vulnerable minds" including children. Interestingly, the obscene materials in this case were anti-Catholic pamphlets.

People who abhor censorship, in general, might still experience qualms when it comes to circulating materials with adult themes to the young. Librarians often feel ambivalent: they believe in intellectual freedom, but they also recognize the legitimate interest of parents to control and monitor their children's reading or viewing habits (Isajlovic-Terry and McKechnie 2012). In fact, defending unrestricted access to such materials is probably the most difficult intellectual freedom task that LIS professionals perform, and the matter is further complicated by legal concerns. Almost all states now have "harmful to juvenile" statutes that create obscenity standards for youth that are easier to meet than those for adults. The librarian is confronted not just with people's natural concerns that certain materials might negatively affect children and adolescents, but with the real possibility that an irate citizen or public official might employ legal means to restrict or eliminate library materials. On the other hand, when it comes to the type of materials found in libraries, there is no substantive evidence that such laws actually protect children and, ironically, such laws "might have detrimental effects on their imaginations, their psychological development, and their ability to cope with various challenges in life" (Dresang 2006, p. 180). Nonetheless, concern for the welfare of the young is a powerful motivator for some who believe that some library materials have negative effects on children.

If one steps back and considers the five concerns mentioned above, one can acknowledge that people's concerns are not irrational—albeit the intensity of their response and the solutions proposed might not always be the best. Knox (2014) pointed out that LIS professionals base their defense of intellectual freedom, at least in part, on their belief that it is extremely difficult to predict how library materials might affect a particular individual. The relationship between exposure and behavior is not simple or direct as many other factors play a role in influencing how people actually behave.

IV. THE INTERNET AND THE DEBATE OVER FILTERING

The ubiquity of the Internet and its relative ease of use permit millions of individuals, including minors, to access countless websites, some of which might be objectionable.

There is an understandable desire to limit children's exposure to these sites. As noted earlier, federal legislation, especially the Children's Internet Protection Act (CIPA) and the subsequent Supreme Court decision upholding its constitutionality, made some type of Internet filtering mandatory in libraries receiving federal E-Rate or LSTA monies. Similarly, state "harmful to juvenile" laws prompted some libraries to implement filtering to protect themselves from potential legal liabilities.

Although filtering technologies have improved, they remain imperfect. Houghton-Jan (2010) observed that "filters today employ artificial intelligence, image recognition, and complex keyword analysis algorithms to an extremely granular level." Yet, she also warns,

> Filters still cannot successfully evaluate and determine the actual content, context, and intent of Web content of various media types—text, still images, video, audio, and more. As a result filter performance is highly dependent on the program's artificial intelligence content recognition and any possible administrative human intervention, as well as the chosen settings and features. (p. 26)

The types of filters used in libraries are usually a combination of URL-based filtering (site blocking) and content-based filtering using key words or phrases. In the former case, the filter uses a database of predetermined websites that are then compared against the website being accessed. In the latter case, the filter uses an algorithm that balances such factors as keywords, ads, metadata, and the types of numbers or links. This is especially useful because large numbers of new websites are constantly being added which makes it impossible to maintain a wholly current list of blocked URLs. Filters can also block by bandwidth consumption and file type. Although some filters can selectively block out parts of a website (e.g., images), most simply block the entire website. The categories most commonly blocked include sexuality, nudity, profanity, and violence.

Batch (2014) examined the impact of Internet filters on access and found that the filters selected for use often had significant technical and performance limitations; often went far beyond what was mandated by law; and most important, filtered out information, websites, and platforms needed by teachers and young people. In some cases, particularly in schools systems, subjects considered controversial or sensitive, such as information about Iran or teen suicide, have been blocked.

Houghton-Jan (2010) noted that performance studies conducted between 2001 and 2009 reported an average accuracy of around 78%. Since that time, performance on average has increased to around 83%. When text and image are separated, performance on text is considerably higher but performance is poor on about one in five cases involving text and more than half the cases involving images. The technical reasons for this imprecision are difficult to determine because the vendors who create and sell filtering software consider their algorithms and lists of blocked URLs proprietary. A variety of issues make filtering problematic:

Overblocking: The unintentional blocking of desired sites. Overblocking deprives individuals of access to constitutionally protected information. An ironic example of overblocking was the case of the Flesh Public Library in Ohio, whose filter blocked access to its own website. More seriously, Batch (2014) reported on a variety of important subjects that were blocked, including information on genocide, safe sex, and public health. Other sites that have been blocked include the American Civil Liberties Union (ACLU), People for the Ethical Treatment of Animals (PETA), National Organization for Marriage, and Planned Parenthood (Batch 2014). Filters have also blocked the Declaration of Independence, *Moby Dick*, and "The Owl and the Pussy Cat." On average, the filters overblock legitimate sites about 17% of the time (Batch 2014).

Underblocking: Filters often fail to block a significant percentage of the sites they were intended to block. Batch (2014) reported that, like overblocking, about 17% of the time the filter underblocks problematic sites and, as noted above, underblocking appears to be even more of a problem with images.

Subjective and discriminatory judgment: The filter developers use subjective criteria that might not satisfy the needs of teachers or librarians. This is problematic because the line between what meets legally prescribed parameters and what some might find offensive can be thin, and it is not clear that software developers make these important distinctions. This problem is exacerbated by the refusal of many filter manufacturers to provide information on the blocked subjects or sites. Houghton-Jan (2010) reported on the subjective judgment of one vendor whose filter blocked pro-choice websites but not pro-life, and another vendor that blocked the National Organization for Women. Maycock (2011) reported similar problems with LGBT sites: Many filtering companies—private entities with no obligation to disclose how and why they blacklist particular sites—set their product to default blocking of LGBT sites, including those featuring political issues, educational content, and support groups for LGBT youth. This is not only ethically and constitutionally unacceptable, but also makes libraries that use such tools potential targets of litigation. (p. 9)

Such "blacklists" should be of great concern to LIS professionals.

Susceptibility to errors: Producers of filtering products often rely on automated systems for making content decisions. This type of "mindless mechanical blocking" inevitably leads to many mistakes (Heins and Cho 2001). Artificial intelligence programs are simply not yet sufficiently refined to make subtle distinctions necessary to screen out only the sites that were intended to be screened. The impact of these errors in some cases could be small; in others it could deprive users of important information. Filters on local computers tend to be less reliable than filters installed on servers, and they have more problems involving conflicting software.

Vulnerability to dismantling: Knowledgeable users, particularly young people, can often bypass filtering software. There are, in fact, sites specifically designed to aid people in overriding filters.

Computer problems: Blocking software can affect computer performance during installation, maintenance, upgrades, and removal.

Privacy: Filtering software raises significant issues regarding the privacy of personal information and privacy related to one's information needs. When a computer is used with a filter installed, the users' identity and search are tracked. What type of information is collected, who retains that information and for how long, and how the data will be used and maintained are all critical intellectual freedom concerns that a library needs to address before selecting a particular filter.

Despite these problems, several arguments support the need for some filtering. The Internet permits access to sites that are extremely violent, hateful, or sexually explicit. Although adults should be able to view such material freely, most would argue that such imagery is not appropriate for young people. Proponents argue that filters, although imperfect, are the most feasible way to provide protection. It is true that libraries have for years explicitly or implicitly chosen not to collect pornographic materials, and it could be argued that filters are simply a logical extension of those policies. Perhaps the most avid defense of filters came from David Burt, a librarian working in the filtering industry who expressed particular concern that the level of exposure to pornography in public libraries was significantly greater than librarians admitted. His arguments (1997) included the following:

- Although keyword blocking has its problems, the better filters can have this feature disconnected, leaving the more accurate site-blocking feature to govern access.
- Better filters are increasing in their refinement so that fewer non-pornographic sites related to sexuality are blocked.
- Libraries have always restricted the choices of patrons to some extent to material deemed appropriate. Restricting sites that are pornographic is neither new nor undesirable.

- Although filters do perform some type of preselection activity before librarians can review the material, this feature is not new; publisher approval plans have been preselecting materials for years.
- The claim that filters are unconstitutional misconstrues what filtering is; filters restrict access to materials that are not yet part of the library collection. This process is no different from deciding not to select some materials, and as such it is not ipso facto censorship or a violation of constitutional rights.

Auld (2003) observed, "Despite the onslaught of reports denying their effectiveness, filters, when managed properly, can and do achieve a virtually pornography-free online environment while only minimally affecting access to constitutionally protected speech" (p. 38). He made the following four points (Auld 2005):

- Filtering materials on the Internet does not go against our intellectual freedom principles.
- Filters are effective.
- Communities, including staff and patrons, are complaining about pornography on computer screens in their public libraries.
- The U.S. Supreme Court ruled that there are circumstances in which filtering is constitutional. (p. 197)

Numerous organizations find these arguments convincing and many lobby for libraries to install filters if they have not done so already. The ALA, however, does not view these arguments as compelling; rather, they recognize the Internet as another forum for speech that requires First Amendment protection. The following are among the pertinent resolutions and policies passed by the ALA regarding filtering: "Resolution on Opposition to Federally Mandated Internet Filtering," "Guidelines and Considerations for Developing a Public Library Internet Use Policy," and "Resolution on the Use of Filtering Software in Libraries." Of particular concern to the ALA is that filters deprive both young people and adults of constitutionally protected speech, and that libraries have a special obligation to protect such access. Many filters were intended to reduce access to certain sites only for minors. In response, the ALA has suggested other less restrictive means for ensuring that children do not use the Internet inappropriately, in particular parents' supervision of their children's Internet use while in the library.

The Supreme Court decision supporting CIPA did not settle the issue of filtering for libraries. Although filtering was not considered an unconstitutional violation of patron rights, the Court indicated that filters must be easily disabled for adult patrons, and that if adults believed their First Amendment rights were violated, they might find a sympathetic ear in the Court. There is evidence that some libraries are not disabling filters for adults and one might see in the future a return to the courts on the First Amendment impacts of filtering on library users (Caldwell-Stone 2013; Smith 2013).

V. RESEARCH ON CENSORSHIP AND INTELLECTUAL FREEDOM IN LIBRARIES

Although intellectual freedom is a strong value generally within LIS professions, some LIS professionals find it difficult to practice the principles in the real world. This ambivalence is not without historical roots; in the nineteenth and well into the twentieth century, librarians were admonished to obtain only the most "wholesome" materials. Dewey himself exhorted that "only the best books on the best subjects" were to be collected (Dewey 1989, p. 5). Librarians were expected to represent the values of polite middle-class society and to steer individuals to "better" books (Garrison 1972–1973). In the 1950s, Serebnick (1979) found that censorship in schools and public libraries was not just due to the complaints of principals and parents, but came largely from the librarians themselves, often without prompting, based on widely held beliefs that certain books could harm children. In many cases, they simply did not buy books they thought might be controversial, or they restricted access to them (Eakin 1948; Fiske 1959). Subsequent research confirmed this finding. Numerous studies of librarians in high schools and public libraries in the Midwest in the 1960s and 1970s revealed that a significant proportion of them had weak or wavering views about censorship and that there was little correlation between asserting a belief in intellectual freedom and censoring materials (Farley 1964; Busha 1971). The librarians tended to censor materials with pictures more than those that were not illustrated. In general, throughout this period, the propensity to restrict materials was greatest among school librarians, followed by public librarians, and then academic librarians. Librarians with the strongest educational backgrounds were least likely to restrict materials (Pope 1973).

Budd (2006–2007) investigated the claim sometimes made by conservative groups that library collections tend to have a liberal bias. He analyzed popular titles in the collections of 416 public libraries looking for both conservative and liberal political points of view. He found, to the contrary, that library collections tended toward the conservative side. Given the strength of community values, in general, this should not be surprising.

A number of studies focused on censorship in schools. One study, titled *Limiting What Students Shall Read,* sampled 1,891 librarians in public elementary and secondary schools, library supervisors, principals, and district superintendents using mail and telephone surveys. Nearly one-third of the librarians reported at least one challenge in the previous year, and in 30% of the cases, the material was altered, restricted, or removed. More than 50% of the challenges came from parents, about 10% from teachers, and 6% from school-board members (Association of American Publishers 1981). Another study sampled more than 6,500 U.S. school systems and found that challenges came from both within and outside the libraries (Hopkins, 1993). Librarians were found to be most supportive of intellectual freedom when they had a high level of confidence in their own abilities. Challenges from within, especially by principals, were the most problematic because the item was least likely to be retained in this circumstance. This particular study also highlighted the political aspect of protecting library materials as Hopkins noted that support from media and outside groups played a significant role in protecting materials. Dresang (2006), in reviewing the censorship literature between 2000 and 2004, found that 75% of all book challenges reported to the ALA were in schools, with 44% involving the school library.

Aiken (2007) examined the commitment of public library directors to the Library Bill of Rights. He surveyed 400 directors nationally, asking about any restrictions the library imposed that might be considered a violation of the age discrimination prohibitions in the Library Bill of Rights. He found that more than 50% of the 110 respondents failed to conform to the open-access policies prescribed by the Library Bill of Rights. Nearly 20 percent did not permit access to social networking sites. He surmised that the ALA was not responding to the changes in family structure that made it difficult for parents to accompany their children to the library and suggested that it might be time to revisit the potential role public librarians might play in serving *in loco parentis.* At the least, Aiken concluded that the ALA was out of touch with the library community and needed to communicate more effectively with library directors and increase public awareness of the Library Bill of Rights.

Burke (2010) examined the attitudes of librarians and the public regarding the removal of racist materials in a public library. Using data from 1976–2009 obtained from the General Social Survey (GSS), a biennial national opinion poll, he found that one-third of the respondents would support removing racist books. Those least likely to support censorship tended to be younger and had higher levels of formal education. As might be expected, race was also a factor with African-Americans much more inclined than whites to remove the materials (50% compared to 33%). People from the South were also more likely to remove the materials. From a religious perspective, Protestants provided the most support for removal (39.5%) followed by Catholics (32.3%) and Jews (20.5%). Librarians as a group exhibited very low support with only 6.5% supporting removal; library staff also exhibited a reluctance to remove the materials but at a somewhat higher rate of 19.4%. Both librarians and library staff, however, were less supportive of removal than teachers (26.6%).

Sloan (2012) studied the inclusion of atheist or "freethought" materials in public libraries by region. Libraries in New England were most likely to demonstrate collection balance in contrast to the East South Central portion of the United States (Alabama, Kentucky, Mississippi, and Tennessee) which had significantly fewer such materials. Sloan posited that the religiosity of the region and the fact that atheism was not an accepted part of discourse were potential reasons for the differences.

Whelan conducted a study of self-censorship among school librarians for *School Library Journal* (2009). A questionnaire on the prevalence and rationale for self-censorship in school libraries was sent to more than 650 school libraries across the United States. Eighty-seven percent of the respondents said that they had not purchased at least one book because of sexual content, language (61%), violence (51%), homosexuality (47%), and racism (34%). Seventy percent cited the potential reaction from parents as the primary factor influencing their decision. Potential reactions from administrators or from the community-at-large played a much smaller role (29% and 28% respectively).

Latham (2014) reexamined the self-censorship found among librarians in the 1959 Fiske study noted above. She argued that criticisms of those self-censoring librarians (mostly women) lack an understanding of their limited power to act against community and societal expectations. She asserted that any tendency for self-blame or criticism from the professional community must be tempered by acknowledgment of the historical limitations imposed on female librarians.

Knox (2014) examined the differences in perception of censorship between librarians and challengers to library materials by examining one particular censorship case in West Bend, Wisconsin. While librarians perceived any form of depriving access to a book as censorship, the challengers believed that only outright banning of a book constituted censorship. For the challengers, actions such as relocating books (e.g., from the youth section to the adult section), labeling books, and employing "common sense" majority values did not constitute censorship.

Although most censorship studies focus on public and school libraries, Ingolfsland (2009) examined potential selection bias among academic librarians from 100 libraries. He focused on books about the historical Jesus, dividing them into two groups: those that supported an evangelical perspective and those that were nontraditional. Ingolfsland found that libraries as a whole were "four times more likely to hold one or more of the non-evangelical Jesus books than one or more of the evangelical Jesus books" (p. 1). The author contended, however, that the imbalance was less likely from overt censorship and more likely from lack of attention to collection balance—a critical element in ensuring intellectual freedom.

VI. THE POLICIES OF THE AMERICAN LIBRARY ASSOCIATION

Clearly, LIS professionals frequently struggle with their perceived obligations—personal, professional, and organizational—regarding intellectual freedom and First Amendment rights. To guide librarians in protecting the rights of their patrons, ALA adopted a variety of policies developed by the Intellectual Freedom Committee (IFC) and approved by ALA Council. The ALA policies and their interpretations can be found in the Office of Intellectual Freedom's *Intellectual Freedom Manual*, 9th ed., and also at the ALA website (www.ala.org). The following is a brief discussion of some of the major IFC policies organized into four areas: philosophical foundations, access issues, modification of materials, and administrative aspects.

A. Philosophical Foundations

1. The Library Bill of Rights

The fundamental obligations of libraries and library professionals are clearly defined by the central document of the ALA: the Library Bill of Rights (LBR) adopted in 1939 (see figure 9.1).

Some have argued that adoption of the LBR occurred in response to attempts to ban Steinbeck's *The Grapes of Wrath* (Krug and Morgan 2010). Although a climate of censorship might well have produced an increased interest in the LBR, Campbell (2014) argued that *The Grapes of Wrath* had only been published in March of 1939 and was therefore too close in time to the adoption of the LBR to really be the primary impetus. Rather, he notes that throughout the 1930s librarians had been identifying the need for libraries to serve as forums for the exchange of ideas and to provide books from all perspectives. The LBR was therefore a result of an emerging professional consensus, rather than a particular event. Campbell suggested that the debate around *The Grapes of Wrath* had a more direct connection to the creation of the Intellectual Freedom Committee in 1940, than to the LBR.

The obligations of libraries in the LBR include selecting materials for the entire community and rejecting censorship based on characteristics of an author (Section

FIGURE 9.1
ALA Library Bill of Rights

The American Library Association affirms that all libraries are forums for information and ideas and that the following basic policies should guide their services.

I. Books and other library resources should be provided for the interest, information, and enlightenment of all people of the community the library serves. Materials should not be excluded because of the origin, background, or views of those contributing to their creation.

II. Libraries should provide materials and information presenting all points of view on current and historical issues. Materials should not be proscribed or removed because of partisan or doctrinal disapproval.

III. Libraries should challenge censorship in the fulfillment of their responsibility to provide information and enlightenment.

IV. Libraries should cooperate with all persons and groups concerned with resisting abridgment of free expression and free access to ideas.

V. A person's right to use a library should not be denied or abridged because of origin, age, background, or views.

VI. Libraries which make exhibit spaces and meeting rooms available to the public they serve should make such facilities available on an equitable basis, regardless of the beliefs or affiliations of individuals or groups requesting their use.

Adopted June 19, 1939, by the ALA Council; amended October 14, 1944; June 18, 1948; February 2, 1961; June 27, 1967; January 23, 1980; inclusion of "age" reaffirmed January 23, 1996.

A history of the Library Bill of Rights is found in the latest edition of the *Intellectual Freedom Manual*.

1); selecting materials with a wide array of viewpoints and rejecting censorship due to doctrinal disapproval of content (Section 2); rejecting censorship in general and cooperating with others to fight the abridgement of free speech (Sections 3 and 4); providing library materials and services to all individuals regardless of their characteristics (Section 5); and permitting equitable access to library facilities (Section 6). Upholding the Library Bill of Rights is not easy, especially when attempting to balance the entire range of obligations noted above.

2. The Freedom to Read Statement

The Freedom to Read Statement was originally adopted in 1953 and revised several times, the most recent being 2004. It was jointly prepared by ALA and the American Book Publishers Council and directed at both publishers and librarians. Its origin, in part, was a concern for the climate created by the McCarthy Era when there was an obsessive preoccupation with possible subversive activities and materials in the United States. The statement concerns the importance of reading to a democratic society and the inadvisability of suppressing of ideas due to perceived controversial or immoral content. There are seven key propositions (ALA 2015a):

- It is in the public interest for publishers and librarians to make available the widest diversity of views and expressions, including those that are unorthodox, unpopular, or considered dangerous by the majority.

- Publishers, librarians, and booksellers do not need to endorse every idea or presentation they make available. It would conflict with the public interest for them to establish their own political, moral, or aesthetic views as a standard for determining what should be published or circulated.

- It is contrary to the public interest for publishers or librarians to bar access to writings on the basis of the personal history or political affiliations of the authors.

- There is no place in our society for efforts to coerce the taste of others, to confine adults to the reading matter deemed suitable for adolescents, or to inhibit the efforts of writers to achieve artistic expression.

- It is not in the public interest to force a reader to accept the prejudgment of a label characterizing any expression or its author as subversive or dangerous.

- It is the responsibility of publishers and librarians, as guardians of the people's freedom to read, to contest encroachments upon that freedom by individuals or groups seeking to impose their own standards or tastes upon the community at large; and by the government whenever it seeks to reduce or deny public access to public information

- It is the responsibility of publishers and librarians to give full meaning to the freedom to read by providing books that enrich the quality and diversity of thought and expression. By the exercise of this affirmative responsibility they can demonstrate that the answer to a "bad" book is a good one, the answer to a "bad" idea is a good one. (pp. 203–207)

Perhaps the Freedom to Read Statement's most notable assertion was the recognition of the importance of the freedom to read, its promise, and its dangers:

> We do not state these propositions in the comfortable belief that what people read
> is unimportant. We believe rather that what people read is deeply important; that

ideas can be dangerous; but that the suppression of ideas is fatal to a democratic society. Freedom itself is a dangerous way of life, but it is ours. (p. 206)

3. Privacy: An Interpretation of the Library Bill of Rights

The ALA has a long tradition of affirming library patrons' right to privacy. Its statements often focus on protecting personally identifiable information, such as the identification of a particular patron with a specific item, but it also includes resources consulted, questions asked, records of database searches, records regarding use of facilities, and interlibrary loan records. In 1999, with the ever-increasing sophistication of new electronic technologies and the growing potential for privacy intrusions using those technologies, the association began a reexamination of its policies on privacy protections (ALA 2010).

Underlying the ALA's position is the belief that patrons will not use materials or make inquiries regarding controversial topics if they believe such actions are not free from public exposure or governmental intrusion. Such exposure and criticism create a chilling effect on First Amendment rights. Adopted in 2002, "Privacy: An Interpretation of the Library Bill of Rights" reaffirms that protecting the privacy rights of patrons is an ethical obligation of libraries and librarians, and that patrons have a right to be free from unreasonable intrusion or surveillance of their library use. The interpretation also emphasizes that patrons have a right to know about library policies and procedures regarding records that contain their personal information, such as circulation records. Collection of personal information should be limited to only what is necessary to accomplish the mission of the library.

Since its adoption in 2002, libraries have been visited by federal, state, and local law enforcement agencies requesting information on the library use habits of individuals. These activities prompted ALA in 2004 to revise a 1991 version of the "Policy Concerning Confidentiality of Personally Identifiable Information about Library Users" (ALA 2010). Noting the potential threats to individuals' First Amendment rights, the policy states, "The government's interest in library use reflects a dangerous and fallacious equation of what a person reads with what that person believes or how that person is likely to behave" (p. 270). Recognizing that legitimate national security interests must be respected, the policy also observed that "there has been no showing of a plausible probability that national security will be compromised by any use made of unclassified information available in libraries" (p. 270).

The ALA privacy interpretation was further enhanced by a set of guidelines titled, "RFID in Libraries: Privacy and Confidentiality Guidelines" (ALA 2015a). This policy guides librarians in selecting and implementing RFID technologies, identifies best practices, and makes suggestions regarding how to work with vendors. Key issues address educating the public and staff about RFID technologies; permitting alternatives to RFID borrowing processes if desired by patrons; ensuring that the personally identifiable information collected is protected and used appropriately; and protecting library users' privacy whenever possible.

4. Intellectual Freedom Principles for Academic Libraries: An Interpretation of the Library Bill of Rights

Although the Library Bill of Rights was written with many types of libraries in mind, it has most often been associated with public libraries. "Intellectual Freedom Principles for Academic Libraries" adopted in 2000 and amended in 2014 provides a specific application of the Library Bill of Rights to academic libraries. Among its provisions, the interpretation affirms the critical importance of intellectual freedom in the development of academic library collections and services, and emphasizes the necessity of (1) protecting patron privacy, (2) developing collections and services that meet the institutional mission, (3) preserving and replacing materials on controversial topics, and (4) providing open, equal, and unfiltered access to the collection and information.

B. Access Issues

1. Restricted Access to Library Materials

As noted above, some librarians practice censorship when they choose not to select certain materials they consider offensive. Should a library restrict access to materials it believes are problematic? The ALA interpretation stated in "Restricted Access to Library Materials," indicates that when libraries use techniques such as closed or restricted shelving (materials available only to staff) or create "adults-only" sections, it is a de facto suppression of ideas (ALA 2015). But aren't there legitimate reasons to restrict access to some materials? The ALA recognizes that it is acceptable to restrict access to materials for special reasons, such as protection from mutilation or theft, but these should not be used as a pretense for censorship.

The interpretation also addresses the use of filters. Emphasis is on making sure that filters even if legally mandated in public libraries and schools do not violate the principles of intellectual freedom by restricting access to speech protected by the First Amendment. The interpretation also addresses schools that employ computerized reading management programs that assign reading levels to books and other materials, which often confines reading to the program's reading lists. The interpretation states "Organizing collections by reading management program level, ability, grade, or age level is another example of restricted access (ALA 2015a, p. 66)" and fails to consider the reading abilities of many library users.

2. Access to Library Resources and Services for Minors

The right of access to library collections by minors has been a matter of considerable debate for many years. The original LBR did not contain a provision related to age. A provision related to age was not adopted until 1967 and a subsequent interpretation "Free Access to Libraries for Minors" was not adopted until 1972. The interpretation has been revised numerous times, most recently in 2014, when it was renamed "Access to Library Resources and Services for Minors." (ALA 2015a). The interpretation clearly states that the needs of library users vary and access to information, library materials, and services are not to be restricted on the basis of a patron's age. Equality of access is the guiding principle regardless of the age of the library user. The interpretation also strongly asserts that children and young adults possess First Amendment rights and that librarians are obligated to respect them. ALA (2015a) asserts that parents have the critical role of determining their children's exposure to library materials:

> Librarians and library governing bodies should maintain that only parents and guardians have the right and the responsibility to determine their children's—and only their children's—access to library resources. Parents and guardians who do not want their children to have access to specific library services, materials, or facilities should so advise their children. (p. 119)

In other words, the library (except for school libraries) does not serve *in loco parentis* (in the place of the parent), and the responsibility for controlling the reading, viewing, or listening habits of children is vested with the parent alone.

3. Economic Barriers to Information Access

Over the years, some libraries charged minimal fees for a variety of reasons. The issue became particularly problematic in the early 1990s when government was becoming increasingly reluctant to provide sufficient revenues to finance public services including libraries (ALA 2010). At the same time budgets were shrinking, libraries were experiencing increased costs from the growing number of formats and expanding demands for new technologies. Under these circumstances, libraries were tempted to charge substantial fees for their services. The ALA statement, adopted in 1993, affirmed that free access to information is a fundamental mission of publicly funded libraries, and that fees ipso facto create barriers to access. The policy states unequivocally that access to information in all formats should be provided equitably and that charging fees for materials, services, and programs is anathema to the concept of free and equal access. Ability to pay should not govern ability to know.

4. Access to Library Resources and Services Regardless of Sex, Gender Identity, Gender Expression, or Sexual Orientation

Originally passed in 1993 and revised most recently in 2008, the policy "Access to Library Resources and Services Regardless of Sex, Gender Identity, Gender Expression or Sexual Orientation" affirms that the rights of LGBT individuals to services, materials, and information on these subjects are protected by the Library Bill of Rights, and that the nonselection of materials or access to information because of the sexual orientation of the creator is prohibited. In addition, librarians must actively resist any attempts to suppress materials in these areas.

5. Services to People with Disabilities

Passed in January 2009, this interpretation reemphasized the library's responsibility to provide the highest levels of service to all users to support "their full participation in society." The interpretation supports a proactive approach to individuals with disabilities and places a responsibility on LIS professionals to be aware of assistive technologies that could improve library services. In addition, libraries should train staff to ensure that individuals with disabilities are treated sensitively and should make sure that accommodations are available when requested to provide full access to library services and programs.

6. Access to Digital Information, Services, and Networks

The potential and real problems arising from the Internet prompted ALA in 1996 to create a new interpretation of the Library Bill of Rights, "Access to Digital Information, Services, and Networks." The most recent revision was in 2009. The interpretation reflects the consistent position of ALA that access to information empowers library users and that libraries, in furtherance of this goal, should act to promote, not restrict digital access whenever possible—"Libraries should use technology to enhance, not deny, digital access" (ALA 2015a p. 55). In addition, the interpretation emphasizes the rights to privacy and confidentiality in the use of digital resources and that restrictive licenses and contracts with vendors that deprive users of these rights should be avoided. The interpretation also emphasized equality of access and that restrictions by age, economic status, or controversial content were not appropriate so long as the speech was constitutionally protected. As with other ALA policies, minor's access should not be abridged and that the decision to deny access rests with parents. The interpretation acknowledged that in some instances the law might require filtering, but in doing so, the library was to employ the "least restrictive level" to maximize access to constitutionally protected speech.

7. Minors and Internet Activity

As learning tools have increased in sophistication, some libraries have considered limiting students' use of interactive Web tools such as social networking sites. This situation became sufficiently problematic that ALA passed "Minors and Internet Interactivity" in 2009 and amended it in 2014. The interpretation notes that the digital environment provides a genuine opportunity for accessing, creating, and sharing information, and that access to the Internet is an extension of a student's First Amendment rights (ALA 2015a). The policy notes that access to social networking sites and interactive Web tools can enhance student learning and constructive personal interactions. Restricting interactive Internet tools inhibits students from being part of a community of learners and inhibits free expression.

8. Access to Resources and Services in the School Library

Schools are frequently involved in censorship efforts because of their *in loco parentis* responsibilities. Parents expect schools to protect their children from harm; indeed, schools are legally obligated to do so. Some parents believe that this harm extends to exposure to "unhealthy" materials. Access to the Web has exacerbated the issue. The ALA recognizes the importance of specifically addressing the needs of school library media centers. "Access to Resources and Services in the School Library," adopted first in 1986 and most recently revised in 2014, notes that the underlying value of intellectual freedom should be sustained by school libraries and librarians and that the ALA Library Bill of Rights applies in these settings (ALA 2015a). ALA also affirmed that school libraries have a unique role in that they serve as a learning laboratory that promotes critical thinking and problem solving in a pluralistic society. Collections should be developed broadly on the basis of educational criteria and promote diverse points of view. Access to the collection and facilities should be free and open and attempts to restrict materials by limiting use, restricting by age, charging fees, and creating closed or restricted shelving should be resisted. Access to digital content should be open. The interpretation also notes that while English is the customary language of the United States, library collections should also recognize the "linguistic pluralism" of those the library serves. It places the responsibility for creating broad collections that reflect diverse points of view directly in the hands of the school librarian.

9. Internet Filtering

Internet access is now widely available in all types of libraries. However, concern for some Internet content as well as prevailing state and federal laws, most notably the Children's Internet Protection Act (CIPA), have required in some instances the installation of content filters especially in public and school libraries. The relationship of Internet filters to the *Library Bill of* Rights (LBR) and the First Amendment have raised important concerns for libraries regarding access to constitutionally protected speech. Although the American Library Association has expressed its reservations regarding filtering for some years, many complex issues are involved and it was not until 2015 that the Association adopted a specific interpretation of the LBR, *Internet Filtering*.

The interpretation notes that filters consistently block constitutionally protected speech (overblocking) and fail to block content they were designed to prevent (underblocking). Filtering policies are particularly problematic in schools where filtering systems may also block access to videos, graphics, music, and original content generated by students. Similarly, because the filters are often designed for broader purposes than libraries, they often filter out controversial or unpopular points of view and questionable language. In addition, the introduction of filters enables third-party vendors to make decisions related to what resources and services (e-mail, social media, websites) are available through the library. Although some aspects of filtering can be overridden by librarians or library administrators, in practice, overriding filters is cumbersome. In other instances, library users may be reluctant to ask that a particular site be unblocked for privacy reasons.

The interpretation recognizes that in some instances filters are required by law, but in such cases the library should implement policies and procedures that mitigate as far as possible the negative effects of filtering. In addition, the library should make it easy and fast for individuals to unblock desired sites while maintaining the user's privacy.

10. Resolution Reaffirming the Principles of Intellectual Freedom in the Aftermath of Terrorist Attacks

The shocking events of September 11, 2001, understandably disturbed and frightened people. In their aftermath, Congress passed a variety of legislation such as the PATRIOT Act. Although many of the provisions of these acts were important to restore confidence and security, the ALA and other groups concerned about individuals' civil liberties grew concerned that certain elements of these laws promoted potentially oppressive behavior on the part of governmental officials. The fear that the legitimate exercise of free speech might be compromised led to the passing of the "Resolution Reaffirming the Principles of Intellectual Freedom" in January 2002. In it, ALA reaffirmed its opposition to government censorship and suppression of news and government information, exhorted libraries to protect the privacy and confidentiality of their users, and affirmed the importance of dissent and timely provision of information to the citizenry.

11. Resolution on the U.S.A. PATRIOT Act and Related Measures that Infringe on the Rights of Library Users

Similar to the previous statement, this resolution, passed in January 2003, expressed concern that some of the provisions of the PATRIOT Act inappropriately expanded the authority of the federal government to investigate citizens and noncitizens. Such authority threatens the privacy rights of patrons using libraries and impedes the dissemination of knowledge. As such, ALA declared that the act is "a present danger to the constitutional rights and privacy rights of library users." Without unimpeded access to libraries and free inquiry within them, the purpose of libraries and their democratic mission cannot be fulfilled. The resolution exhorts libraries to educate patrons about the possible excesses of the PATRIOT Act and to take action to ensure that the privacy rights and the rights of inquiry of library users are not adversely affected.

C. Modification of Materials

1. Expurgation of Library Resources

Rather than restricting potentially controversial items, some librarians might attempt to alter library materials. In 1971, several libraries attempted to censor Maurice

Sendak's children's book, *In the Night Kitchen*, by "diapering" the unclothed little boys using paint. This prompted an examination of the issue by the IFC, which resulted in the interpretation "Expurgation of Library Materials" adopted in 1973 (ALA 2010). The policy was renamed in 2014, "Expurgation of Library Resources." The interpretation defines expurgation as "any deletion, excision, alteration, editing, or obliteration of any part of a library resource by administrators, employees, governing authorities, parent institutions (if any), or third-party vendors when done for the purpose of censorship" (p. 82). Expurgation is considered a form of restricted access and as such is a violation of the ALA Library Bill of Rights. The policy encourages opposition to the expurgation of materials available through licensed digital collections.

2. Labeling Systems

In 1951 a chapter of the Sons of the American Revolution (SAR) tried to pressure a public library in New Jersey to place prominent labels on materials which the organization believed favored or advocated communism. The matter was reported to the ALA, and the result was the first Statement on Labeling adopted that same year. The policy has been amended over the years, the most recent in 2015 as more materials became subject to labeling. More recent attempts to label materials include audio recordings for their lyrics, DVDs for violent contents and language, video games and websites. The policy on Labeling Systems notes that libraries contain materials and provide access to digital information on many subjects, representing many points of view. This does not mean that the library advocates or endorses the ideas expressed in the content, but the library does have to make professional judgments about how to organize content to make it available—essentially labeling them for the purpose of organization. Examples of such labels are the Dewey Decimal or LOC call numbers; it may also include labeling books as "fiction" or "reference." Such "viewpoint-neutral" directional aids are designed to facilitate access and are not violations of intellectual freedom principles. However, labels that have the intent of prejudicing or discouraging use of content are violations since they are designed to restrict access. Prejudicial labeling assumes that the library has the institutional wisdom to decide what is appropriate or not appropriate for users to access; such decisions should be placed in the user not the library.

3. Rating Systems

The Rating Systems policy was originally part of the policy on labeling, but in 2015, it was separated into its own policy. Rating systems became prominent as an intellectual freedom issue when the Motion Picture Association of America (MPAA) began its voluntary rating systems for films. Ratings for sound recordings soon followed. Some individuals and organizations wanted public libraries to employ the rating systems in the distribution of its films and recordings, but the ALA recommended that libraries resist such attempts because the use of such systems are forms of labeling. Recently, rating systems have been developed for a variety of different sources of digital content, including websites, electronic games, and other items. The issue has been further complicated by the passing of laws in some states requiring the use of such systems in libraries. The Rating Systems policy notes that (1) the use of rating systems violates the Library Bill of Rights and in some cases may be unconstitutional, (2) if rating systems are mandated by law, the library should seek legal advice on exactly what the library must do to comply, (3) when ratings are included as part of the packaging of an item, the library cannot remove it, because this would constitute expurgation, (4) libraries are not required to include a rating in the bibliographic record, but if they do include it, a disclaimer must be added that the library does not endorse rating systems, (5) if a library user asks about the rating of a particular item, it is consonant with professional practice to answer the question as any question would be answered.

D. Administrative Aspects

1. Challenged Resources

The "Challenged Materials" interpretation was first adopted in 1971 after several attempts to ban materials containing sexual content. It was last amended in 2014 and the name was changed to "Challenged Resources." Resources are to be understood in the broadest sense, including "digital resources such as databases, e-books and other downloadable and streaming media" (ALA 2015a, p. 81). Challenging resources is often an attempt to censor the material and such attempts threaten the dissemination of ideas and as such, challenge the basic principles of intellectual freedom. Nonetheless, the interpretation recognizes the right of all individuals to raise objections to resources owned by a library and to request that the material be removed or restricted. The statement asserts that libraries should have a clear materials selection and collection development policy, including criteria for the selection of websites and a procedure for challenging resources. Resources that conform to that policy should not be removed simply because individuals challenge them. The procedure for challenging resources should be clear and transparent and should be designed to protect freedom of expression. This is not to say that a library should never remove materials or websites, but doing so under pressure should be avoided and based solely on the adopted selection criteria. These policies have been quite useful particularly because such requests are often stressful to libraries and their Boards and they sometimes involve political and legal pressures accompanied by unpleasant media exposure.

2. Guidelines for the Development and Implementation of Policies, Regulations, and Procedures Affecting Access to Library Materials, Services, and Facilities

In the early 1990s, a homeless person was removed from a public library for inappropriate behavior. There was much debate over this issue, which came to be known as the *Kreimer* case (*Kreimer v. Bureau of Police* 1991). Although the library community wanted to ensure the rights of each individual, even one who might behave differently, they also wanted to maintain control of the library environment for the safety and access of others. Because the case was so controversial, the library community looked to ALA for guidance on the development of rules and regulations regarding patron behavior. The guidelines adopted in 1994 and revised in 2005, make it clear that rules for patron behavior should be no more restrictive than absolutely necessary, should be consistent with constitutional protections of citizens, be clearly written, and should be consistent with the ALA Library Bill of Rights and the mission of the library (ALA 2010). The guidelines further condemn restrictions placed on specific groups of people, such as children or the homeless, and assert that local guidelines should include an appeal procedure.

After more than a decade, Kelly (2006) analyzed the impact of *Kreimer* and several other court decisions regarding hygiene and patron behavior in public libraries and concluded:

- Libraries are considered public forums and removing individuals on the basis of a particular political message violates an individual's right to freedom of speech.
- The First Amendment is applicable when considering an individual's right to receive information in libraries.
- A disruptive individual can be removed.
- Personal hygiene can be a reason for removal as long as the standards for removal are clear and reasonable.

The long-term implications of *Kreimer* have also been a focus of the Hunger, Homelessness, and Poverty Task Force (2005) of ALA's Social Responsibility Roundtable. The task force was particularly concerned about the growth of "odor policies" in some public libraries. The task force felt that some librarians were ignoring the underlying dynamics of poverty and that homelessness and poor hygiene were being treated as forms of behavior, rather than as a symptom of extreme poverty. As a result, the homeless were being ignored as a service population and denied access. These issues are likely to grow in intensity during periods of economic distress.

VII. AN INTERNATIONAL PERSPECTIVE ON FREEDOM OF EXPRESSION

Although the ALA Library Bill of Rights is the centerpiece that guides library practice in the United States, it is instructive to remember that the battle for freedom of expression and against censorship is a concern throughout the world. In 2002, the International Federation of Library Associations celebrated its seventy-fifth anniversary. At this meeting, it passed the Glasgow Declaration (see figure 9.2). It is a fitting expression of the universal concern for the free flow of ideas and the ability of all to express those ideas. The close kinship with the ALA Bill of Rights is manifest.

FIGURE 9.2
The Glasgow Declaration on Libraries,
Information Services, and Intellectual Freedom

> **Meeting in Glasgow on the occasion of the 75th anniversary of its formation, the International Federation of Library Associations and Institutions (IFLA) declares that:**
>
> IFLA proclaims the fundamental right of human beings both to access and to express information without restriction.
>
> IFLA and its worldwide membership support, defend and promote intellectual freedom as expressed in the United Nations Universal Declaration of Human Rights. This intellectual freedom encompasses the wealth of human knowledge, opinion, creative thought and intellectual activity.
>
> IFLA asserts that a commitment to intellectual freedom is a core responsibility of the library and information profession worldwide, expressed through codes of ethics and demonstrated through practice.
>
> IFLA affirms that:
>
> - Libraries and information services provide access to information, ideas and works of imagination in any medium and regardless of frontiers. They serve as gateways to knowledge, thought and culture, offering essential support for independent decision-making, cultural development, research and lifelong learning by both individuals and groups.
>
> (cont.)

- Libraries and information services contribute to the development and maintenance of intellectual freedom and help to safeguard democratic values and universal civil rights. Consequently, they are committed to offering their clients access to relevant resources and services without restriction and to opposing any form of censorship.

- Libraries and information services shall acquire, preserve and make available the widest variety of materials, reflecting the plurality and diversity of society. The selection and availability of library materials and services shall be governed by professional consider-ations and not by political, moral and religious views.

- Libraries and information services shall make materials, facilities and services equally accessible to all users. There shall be no discrimination for any reason including race, national or ethnic origin, gender or sexual preference, age, disability, religion, or political beliefs.

- Libraries and information services shall protect each user's right to privacy and confiden-tiality with respect to information sought or received and resources consulted, borrowed, acquired or transmitted.

IFLA therefore calls upon libraries and information services and their staff to uphold and promote the principles of intellectual freedom and to provide uninhibited access to information.

Statement prepared by the International Federation of Library Associations and Institutions (IFLA), Free Access to Information and Freedom of Expression (FAIFE) Committee and approved by the Governing Board of IFLA 27 March 2002, The Hague, Netherlands. Proclaimed by the Council of IFLA 19 August 2002, Glasgow, Scotland. Available: www.ifla.org/en/publications/the-glasgow-declaration-on-libraries-information-services-and-intellectual-freedom.

In addition, IFLA has an ongoing initiative, Committee on Freedom of Access to Information and Freedom of Expression (FAIFE) that is intended to promote and defend human rights. FAIFE works with other international organizations includ-ing UNESCO. In 2014, IFLA adopted its "Internet Manifesto 2014," promoting unhindered access to the Internet and exhorting libraries to defend free expression regardless of format or geography (figure 9.3).

VIII. SUMMARY

LIS professionals play a critical role in the advancement of knowledge, the exchange of ideas, and the provision of information. The library provides a physical and virtual forum for a democratic society; it supports and sustains our institutions and our citi-zenry. There will always be those who believe that open access to ideas is dangerous

FIGURE 9.3
IFLA Internet Manifesto 2014

---

1. Library and information services and the Internet

1.1. Library and information services are vibrant institutions that connect people with global and local information resources. They provide access to ideas and creative works and make the richness of human expression and cultural diversity available to everyone.

1.2. The Internet enables individuals and communities throughout the world, whether in the smallest and most remote villages or in the largest cities, to have greater equality of access to information to support personal development, education, cultural enrichment, economic activity, access to government and other services, and informed participation in a democratic society as an active citizen. At the same time the Internet creates opportunities for all to share their own ideas, interests and culture with the world.

1.3. Library and information services should be essential gateways to the Internet, its resources and services. Their role is to act as access points which offer convenience, guidance and support, whilst helping overcome barriers created by differences in resources, technology and skills.

2. Freedom of access to information and freedom of expression are essential to equality, global understanding and peace.

Therefore IFLA asserts that:

2.1. Freedom of access to information and freedom of expression, regardless of format and frontiers, is a central responsibility of the library and information profession.

2.2. The provision of unhindered access to the Internet by library and information services forms a vital element of the right to freedom of access to information and freedom of expression, and supports communities and individuals to attain freedom, prosperity and development.

2.3. Access to the Internet and all its resources should be consistent with the United Nations Universal Declaration of Human Rights, and especially Article 19: Everyone has the right to freedom of opinion and expression; this right includes freedom to hold opinions without interference and to seek, receive and impart information and ideas through any media and regardless of frontiers.

2.4. Barriers to the flow of information should be removed, especially those that prevent individuals from taking advantage of opportunities that will improve their quality of life and can result in inequality and poverty. An open Internet is essential, and access to information and freedom of expression should neither be subject to any form of ideological, political, or religious censorship, nor to economic or technological barriers.

3. The role and responsibilities of library and information services

Library and information services have a vital role in ensuring freedom of access to information and freedom of expression, and have a responsibility to:

- serve all of the members of their communities, regardless of age, race, nationality, religion, culture, political affiliation, physical or mental abilities, gender or sexual orientation, or other status

- provide access to the Internet in an appropriate environment for all users

(cont)

523

FIGURE 9.3
IFLA Internet Manifesto 2014 (cont.)

- support users, including children and young people, to ensure they have the media and information literacy competencies they need to use their chosen information resources freely, confidently and independently
- support the right of users to seek and share information
- strive to ensure the privacy of their users, and that the resources and services that they use remain confidential
- facilitate and promote intellectual, cultural and economic creativity through access to the Internet, its resources and services.

4. Implementing the manifesto

4.1. IFLA encourages all governments to support the unhindered flow of Internet accessible information and freedom of expression, to ensure openness and transparency by opposing attempts to censor or inhibit access, and ensure that surveillance and data collection are demonstrably legal, necessary and proportionate.

4.2. IFLA calls upon library and information services to work with states, governments, or religious or civil society institutions, to develop strategic policies and plans that support and implement the principles expressed in this manifesto through the development of public access to the Internet in library and information services across the world, and especially in developing countries.

Endorsed by IFLA Governing Board, August 2014.

and that libraries should reflect the opinions of the majority—the safe and orthodox. This viewpoint was shared by librarians in the nineteenth century and into the early part of the twentieth century. But for many years now, LIS professionals have realized that restricting knowledge is the practice of totalitarian societies not democracies. They recognize that they have a special responsibility to secure for all individuals the right to receive knowledge as well as to create it. In fact, intellectual freedom and resistance to censorship are core values of our profession; few policies are as important. The intellectual freedom policies adopted by the ALA serve as both a philosophical and instrumental foundation for library service.

Defending intellectual freedom and resisting censorship are not easy tasks. LIS professionals have often been subjected to intense pressures and there is little reason to believe that these pressures will dissipate. On the contrary, as the world shrinks and the use of communication technologies increases, they will likely increase. Only a firm understanding of the principles of our profession can provide the necessary tools to protect all individuals' rights to read, view, and hear what they choose, and to obtain the library's services in their search for knowledge.

REFERENCES

Aiken, Julian. 2007. "Outdated and Irrelevant? Rethinking the Library Bill of Rights—Does It Work in the Real World?" *American Libraries* 38 (September 1): 54–56.

American Libraries. 2001 (April): 23.

ALA. 2001. "Violence in the Media: A Joint Statement." Chicago: ALA.

_____. 2006. "RFID in Libraries: Privacy and Confidentiality Guidelines." Chicago: ALA.

_____. 2014. "Top 100 Banned/Challenged Books: 2000–2009." www.ala.org/advocacy/banned/frequentlychallenged/challengedbydecade/2000_2009.

_____. 2015. "Frequently Challenged Books of the 21st Century." www.ala.org/books/frequentlychallengedbooks/top10.

_____. 2015a. *Intellectual Freedom Manual.* Chicago: ALA.

ALA (Office of Intellectual Freedom). 2010. *Intellectual Freedom Manual.* Chicago: ALA.

ALSC (Association for Library Service to Children [ALA]). 2014. "ALSC Strategic Plan, 2012–2017." www.ala.org/alsc/aboutalsc/stratplan.

Anderson, Jaclyn Lewis. 2014. "The Classification of Censorship: An Analysis of Challenged Books by Classification and Subject Heading." *Endnotes: The Journal of the New Members Round Table* 5 (June): 1–18.

Asato, Noriko. 2014. "Librarians' Free Speech: The Challenge of Librarians' Own Intellectual Freedom to the American Library Association, 1946–2007." *Library Trends* 63: 75–108.

_____. 2011. "The Origins of the Freedom to Read Foundation: Public Librarians' Campaign to Establish a Legal Defense against Library Censorship." *Public Library Quarterly* 30: 286–306.

Asheim, Lester. 1954. "The Librarian's Responsibility: Not Censorship but Selection." In *Freedom of Book Selection*, edited by Frederic Mosher. Chicago: ALA, 95–96.

Association of American Publishers, American Library Association, and Association for Supervision and Curriculum Development. 1981. *Limiting What Students Shall Read.* Washington, DC: Association of American Publishers.

Auld, Hampton. 2003. "Filters Work: Get Over It." *American Libraries* 34 (February): 38–41.

_____. 2005. "Do Internet Filters Infringe upon Access to Materials in Libraries?" *Public Libraries* (July/August): 196–198.

Batch, Kristen R. 2014. *Fencing Out Knowledge.* Chicago: ALA.

Bowers, Stacey L. 2006. "Privacy and Library Records." *Journal of Academic Librarianship* 32 (July): 377–383.

Budd, John. 2006–2007. "Politics & Public Library Collections." *Progressive Librarian* 28 (winter): 78–86.

Burke, Susan K. 2010. "Social Tolerance and Racists Materials in Public Libraries." *Reference & User Services Quarterly* 49: 369–379.

Burt, David. 1997. "In Defense of Filtering." *American Libraries* 28 (August): 46–48.

Busha, C. H. 1971. "The Attitudes of Midwestern Public Librarians toward Intellectual Freedom and Censorship." Unpublished dissertation. Indiana University. Cited in Serebnick (1979).

Bushman, John. 2009. "Who Defends Intellectual Freedom for Librarians?" *Academe* (September/October). www.aaup.org/article/who-defends-intellectual-freedom-libraries#.VIS-xNLF98E.

Caldwell-Stone. 2013. "F-ltering and the First Amendment: When Is It Okay to Block Speech Online?" *American Libraries* (March/April 2013): 58–61.

Campbell, Douglas. 2014. "Reexamining the Origins of the Adoption of the ALA's Library Bill of Rights." *Library Trends* 63: 42–56.

Coyne, Sarah M., Mark Callister, Laura A. Stockdale, David A. Nelson, and Brian M. Wells. 2012. "'A Helluva Read: Profanity in Adolescent Literature." *Mass Communication and Society* 15: 360–383.

Dewey, Melvil. 1989. "The Profession." *Library Journal* (June 15): 5. Reprint of article in *American Library Journal* 1 (September 1876): 5.

Downey, Jennifer. 2013. "Self-Censorship in Selection of LGBT-Themed Materials." *Reference & User Service Quarterly* 53 (winter): 104–107.

Doyle, Tony, and John L. Hammond. 2006. "Net Cred: Evaluating the Internet as a Research Source." *Reference Services Review* 34: 56–70.

Dresang, Eliza T. 2006. "Intellectual Freedom and Libraries: Complexity and Change in the Twenty-First Century Digital Environment." *Library Quarterly* 76: 169–192.

Eakin, M. L. 1948. "Censorship in Public High School Libraries." Master's thesis. Columbia University. Cited in Serebnick (1979).

Farley, J. J. 1964. "Book Censorship in the Senior High Libraries of Nassau County, N.Y." Unpublished dissertation. New York University. Cited in Serebnick (1979).

Fiske, Marjorie. 1959. *Book Selection and Censorship: A Study of School and Public Libraries in California.* Berkeley: University of California Press. Cited in Serebnick (1979).

Francoeur, Stephen. 2006. *McCarthyism and Libraries: Intellectual Freedom Under Fire, 1947–1954.* Master's thesis. New York: Hunter College.

———. 2011. "Prudence and Controversy: The New York Public Library Response to Post-War Anti-Communist Pressures." *Library & Information History* 27 (September): 140–160.

Garrison, Dee. 1972–1973. "The Tender Technicians: The Feminization of Public Librarianship." *Journal of Social History* 6 (winter): 131–156.

Heins, Marjorie, and Christina Cho. 2001. *Internet Filters: A Public Policy Report.* Free Expression Policy Project, National Coalition Against Censorship, fall.

Hill, Heather, and Marni Harrington. 2014. "Beyond Obscenity: An Analysis of Sexual Discourse in LIS Educational Texts." *Journal of Documentation* 70: 62–73.

Hill, Rebecca A. 2013. "Content without Context: Content Ratings for Young Adults Books." *School Library Monthly* 29 (February): 35–37.

Hopkins, Dianne McAfee. 1993. "A Conceptual Model of Factors Influencing the Outcome of Challenges to Library Materials in Secondary School Settings." *Library Quarterly* 63 (January): 40–72.

Houghton-Jan, Sarah. 2010. "Internet Filtering." In *Privacy and Freedom of Information in 21ˢᵗ-Century Libraries*. Libraries Technology Report. Chicago: ALA.

Hunger, Homelessness, and Poverty Task Force. 2005. "Are Public Libraries Criminalizing Poor People?" *Public Libraries* 44 (May/June): 175.

IFC (Intellectual Freedom Committee). 2012. "Fifty Shades of Censorship?" *Newsletter on Intellectual Freedom* 61 (July): 146–148.

Ingolfsland, Dennis. 2009. "Books on the Historical Jesus as a Test Case for Selection Bias in American Academic Libraries." *Journal of Religious & Theological Information* 8: 1–12.

Isajlovic-Terry, Natasha, and Lynne (E. F.) McKechnie. 2012. "An Exploratory Study of Children's Views of Censorship." *Children and Libraries* 10 (spring): 38–43.

Island Trees Union Free School District v. Pico. 102 S. Ct. 2799 (1982).

Jenkins, Christine. 2001. "International Harmony: Threat or Menace? U.S Youth Services Librarians and Cold War Censorship, 1946–1955." *Libraries & Culture* 36 (winter): 116–130.

Johnson, Doug. 2013. "The Neglected Side of Intellectual Freedom." *Library Media Connection* (March/April): 98.

Kelly, James. 2006. "Barefoot in Columbus: The Legacy of Kreimer and the Legality of Public Library Access Policies Concerning Appearance and Hygiene." *Public Libraries* 45 (May/June): 42–49.

Knox, Emily. 2014. "Intellectual Freedom and the Agnostic-Postmodernist View of Reading Effects." *Library Trends* 63: 11–26.

———. 2014. "Supporting Intellectual Freedom: Symbolic Capital and Practical Philosophy in Librarianship." *Library Quarterly* 84 (July): 8–21.

———. 2014. "'The Books Will Still Be in the Library': Narrow Definitions of Censorship in the Discourse of Challenges." *Library Trends* 62: 740–749.

Knox, J. M. Emily. 2015. *Book Banning in the 21st Century.* Lanham, MD: Rowman & Littlefield.

Kreimer v. Bureau of Police for the Town of Morristown, et al. 765 F. Supp. 181 (D.N.J. 1991).

Krug, Judith F., and Candace Morgan. 2010. "ALA and Intellectual Freedom: A Historical Overview." In *Intellectual Freedom Manual.* Chicago: ALA.

Kunkel, Dale, and Lara Zwarun. 2006. "How Real Is the Problem of TV Violence?" In *Handbook of Children, Culture and Violence*, edited by Nancy E. Dowd, Dorothy G. Singer, and Robin Fretwell Wilson. Thousand Oaks: Sage, 203–224.

Latham, Joyce M. 2014. "Heat, Humility, and Hubris: The Conundrum of the Fiske Report." *Library Trends* 63: 57–73.

Lo, Melinda. 2014. "Book Challenges Suppress Diversity." www.diversityinya.com/2014/09/book-challenges-suppress-diversity.

Martino, Steven C., Rebecca L. Collins, Marc N. Elliott, Amy Stachman, David E. Kanouse, and Sandra H. Berry. 2006. "Exposure to Degrading Versus Nondegrading Music Lyrics and Sexual Behavior among Youth." *Pediatrics* 118: 430–441.

Maycock, Angela. 2011. "Issues and Trends in Intellectual Freedom for Teacher Librarians." *Teacher Librarian* 39 (October): 8–12.

Mediavilla, Cindy. 1997. "The War on Books and Ideas: The California Library Association and Anti-Communist Censorship." *Library Trends* 46 (fall): 331–347.

Mill, John Stuart. 1956. *On Liberty*, edited by Currin V. Shields. Indianapolis: Bobbs-Merrill.

Pope, M. J. 1973. "A Comparative Study of the Opinions of School, College, and Public Librarians Concerning Certain Categories of Sexually Oriented Literature." Doctoral dissertation, Rutgers University, Rutgers, NJ.

Robbins, Louise S. 1995. "After Brave Words, Silence: American Librarian Responds to Cold War Loyalty." *Libraries & Culture* 30 (fall): 345–365.

———. 2000. *The Dismissal of Miss Ruth Brown*. Normal, OK: University of Oklahoma.

Ross, Catherine J. 2006. "Constitutional Obstacles to Regulating Violence in the Media." In *Handbook of Children, Culture and Violence*, edited by Nancy E. Dowd, Dorothy G. Singer, and Robin Fretwell Wilson. Thousand Oaks, CA: Sage, 291–310.

Schultz, Connie. 2007. "One Word Ignites Some Librarians' Ire." *Cleveland Plain Dealer*, February 20.

Serebnick, Judith. 1979. "A Review of Research Related to Censorship in Libraries." *Library Research* 1: 95–118.

Sloan, Stephen. 2012. "Regional Differences in Collecting Freethought Books in American Public Libraries: A Case of Self-Censorship." *Library Quarterly* 82: 183–205.

Smith, Barbara H. 2013. "The First Amendment Right to Receive Online Information in Public Libraries." *Communication Law & Policy* 18 (winter): 63–89.

Stripling, Barbara K. 2013. "Intellectual Freedom: Moving Beyond Freedom from . . . to Freedom to . . ." *Indiana Libraries* 32: 8–12.

Swan, John. 1986. "Untruth or Consequences." *Library Journal* 111 (July 1): 44–52.

Wiegand, Wayne. 2005. "Collecting Contested Titles: The Experience of Five Small Public Libraries in the Rural Midwest, 1893–1956." *Libraries & Culture* 40 (summer): 368–384.

Wilson, Barbara J., and Nicole Martins. 2006. "The Impact of Violent Music on Youth." In *Handbook of Children, Culture and Violence*, edited by Nancy E. Dowd, Dorothy G. Singer, and Robin Fretwell Wilson. Thousand Oaks, CA: Sage, 179–202.

SELECTED READINGS

Books/Monographs

Adams, Helen R. *Protecting Intellectual Freedom and Privacy in Your School Library*. Santa Barbara, CA: Libraries Unlimited. 2013.

ALA. *Intellectual Freedom for Teens*. Chicago: ALA, 2014.

_____. *Intellectual Freedom Manual*. 9th ed. Chicago: ALA, 2015.

_____. *Privacy and Freedom of Information in 21st-Century Libraries. Library Technology Reports* 46, no. 8. Chicago: ALA, 2010.

Batch, Kristen R. *Fencing Out Knowledge*. Chicago: ALA, 2014.

Samek, Toni. *Librarianship and Human Rights: A Twenty-First Century Guide*. Oxford: Chandos, 2007.

Swan, John C., and Noel Peattie. *The Freedom to Lie: A Debate about Democracy*. Jefferson, NC: McFarland, 1989.

Whelan, Debra Lau. "SLJ Self-Censorship Survey." *School Library Journal*. 2009. www.slj .com/2009/02/collection-development/slj-self-censorship-survey.

Woodward, Jeannette. *What Every Librarian Should Know about Electronic Privacy*. Westport, CT: Libraries Unlimited, 2007.

Articles

Anderson, Jaclyn Lewis. "The Classification of Censorship: An Analysis of Challenged Books by Classification and Subject Heading." *Endnotes: The Journal of the New Members Round Table* 5 (June 2014): 1–18.

Asato, Noriko. "Librarians' Free Speech: The Challenge of Librarians' Own Intellectual Freedom to the American Library Association, 1946–2007." *Library Trends* 63 (2014): 75–108.

_____. "The Origins of the Freedom to Read Foundation: Public Librarians' Campaign to Establish a Legal Defense against Library Censorship." *Public Library Quarterly* 30 (2011): 286–306.

Budd, John. "Politics & Public Library Collections." *Progressive Librarian* 28 (winter 2006–07): 78–86.

Burke, Susan K. "Social Tolerance and Racists Materials in Public Libraries." *Reference & User Services Quarterly* 49 (2010): 369–379.

Bushman, John. "Who Defends Intellectual Freedom for Librarians?" *Academe* (September/October 2009). www.aaup.org/article/who-defends-intellectual-freedom -libraries#.VIS-xNLF98E.

Caldwell-Stone. "Filtering and the First Amendment: When Is It Okay to Block Speech Online?" *American Libraries* (March/April 2013): 58–61.

Campbell, Douglas. "Reexamining the Origins of the Adoption of the ALA's Library Bill of Rights." *Library Trends* 63 (2014): 42–56.

Coyne, Sarah M., Mark Callister, Laura A. Stockdale, David A. Nelson, and Brian M. Wells. "A Helluva Read: Profanity in Adolescent Literature." *Mass Communication and Society* 15 (2013): 360–383.

Downey, Jennifer. "Self-Censorship in Selection of LGBT-Themed Materials." *Reference & User Service Quarterly* 53 (winter 2013): 104–107.

Francoeur, Stephen. *McCarthyism and Libraries: Intellectual Freedom Under Fire, 1947– 1954.* Master's Thesis. New York: Hunter College, 2006.

_____. "Prudence and Controversy: The New York Public Library Response to Post-War Anti-Communist Pressures." *Library & Information History* 27 (September 2011): 140–160.

Hahn, Trudi Bellardo. "Impacts of Mass Digitization Projects on Libraries and Information Policy." *Bulletin of the American Society for Information Science and Technology* 33 (October/November 2006): 20–24.

Hill, Heather, and Marni Harrington. "Beyond Obscenity: An Analysis of Sexual Discourse in LIS Educational Texts." *Journal of Documentation* 70 (2014): 62–73.

Hill, Rebecca A. "Content without Context: Content Ratings for Young Adults Books." *School Library Monthly* 29 (February 2013): 35–37.

_____. "The Problem of Self-Censorship." *School Library Monthly* 28 (November 2010): 9–12.

Houghton-Jan, Sarah. "Internet Filtering." In *Privacy and Freedom of Information in 21st-Century Libraries.* Libraries Technology Report. Chicago: ALA, 2010.

Ingolfsland, Dennis. "Books on the Historical Jesus as a Test Case for Selection Bias in American Academic Libraries." *Journal of Religious & Theological Information* 8 (2009): 1–12.

Isajlovic-Terry, Natasha, and Lynne (E. F.) McKechnie. "An Exploratory Study of Children's Views of Censorship." *Children and Libraries* 10 (spring 2012): 38–43.

Jenkins, Christine. "International Harmony: Threat or Menace? U.S Youth Services Librarians and Cold War Censorship, 1946–1955." *Libraries & Culture* 36 (winter 2001): 116–130.

Johnson, Doug. 2013. "The Neglected Side of Intellectual Freedom." *Library Media Connection* (March/April 2013): 98.

Knox, Emily. "Intellectual Freedom and the Agnostic-Postmodernist View of Reading Effects." *Library Trends* 63 (2014): 11–26.

_____. "Supporting Intellectual Freedom: Symbolic Capital and Practical Philosophy in Librarianship." *Library Quarterly* 84 (July 2014): 8–21.

_____. "'The Books Will Still Be in the Library': Narrow Definitions of Censorship in the Discourse of Challenges." *Library Trends* 62 (2014): 740–749.

Knox, J. M. Emily. 2015. *Book Banning in the 21st Century*. Lanham, MD: Rowman & Littlefield.

Kranich, Nancy. "Why Filters Won't Protect Children or Adults." *Library Administration and Management* 18 (winter 2004): 14–18.

Latham, Joyce M. "Heat, Humility, and Hubris: The Conundrum of the Fiske Report." *Library Trends* 63 (2014): 57–73.

Maycock, Angela. "Issues and Trends in Intellectual Freedom for Teacher Librarians." *Teacher Librarian* 39 (October 2011): 8–12.

Mediavilla, Cindy. "The War on Books and Ideas: The California Library Association and Anti-Communist Censorship." *Library Trends* 46 (fall 1997): 331.

Robbins, Louise S. "After Brave Words, Silence: American Librarian Responds to Cold War Loyalty." *Libraries & Culture* 30 (fall 1995): 345–365.

_____. "Champions of a Cause: American Librarians and the Library Bill of Rights in the 1950s." *Library Trends* 45 (summer 1996): 28–49.

_____. "The Library of Congress and Federal Loyalty Programs, 1947–1956: No 'Communists or Cocksuckers.'" *Library Quarterly* 64 (1994): 365–385.

Schmidt, Cindy M. "Those Interfering Filters! How to Deal with the Reality of Filters in Your School Library." *Library Media Connection* (March 2008): 54–55.

Sloan, Stephen. "Regional Differences in Collecting Freethought Books in American Public Libraries: A Case of Self-Censorship." *Library Quarterly* 82 (2012): 183–205.

Smith, Barbara H. "The First Amendment Right to Receive Online Information in Public Libraries." *Communication Law & Policy* 18 (winter 2013): 63–89.

Stripling, Barbara K. "Intellectual Freedom: Moving Beyond Freedom from . . . to Freedom to . . ." *Indiana Libraries* 32 (2013): 8–12.

Wiegand, Wayne. "Collecting Contested Titles: The Experience of Five Small Public Libraries in the Rural Midwest, 1893–1956." *Libraries & Culture* 40 (summer 2005): 368–384.

10

The Values and Ethics of Library and Information Science

But if indeed we have no philosophy, then we are depriving ourselves of the guiding light of reason, and we live only a day-to-day existence, lurching from crisis to crisis, and lacking the driving force of an inner conviction of the value of our work. (Foskett 1962)

I. INTRODUCTION

Librarians and information professionals are moral agents, responsible to themselves, to others, and to society as a whole. This chapter is devoted to the values and ethics of librarians and other LIS professionals, as well as libraries as organizational entities. We will examine professional and institutional values defined by the norms, culture, and history of the profession, the statements of professional organizations, and by written professional codes. Our professional values and ethics provide a framework for our conduct, policies, and services, and to a large extent, they are the same values and ethics that we hold in everyday life as people, but not always. Sometimes, albeit rarely, one's personal values and ethics conflict with professional codes. At such times, LIS professionals must attempt to balance them. There is no magic formula when such instances arise; much depends on the specific issue and on the potential consequences for the people being served, for the organization, for the profession as a whole, and for the individual making the ethical choices. Suffice it to say that the values and ethics of our profession are critical to accomplishing our mission.

II. THE VALUES OF LIBRARY AND INFORMATION SCIENCE

Without values we are, as Foskett observed, merely lurching about, stumbling in the dark. Values are strongly held beliefs that serve to guide our actions. When we think of values, we associate them with words like convictions or principles, more than just opinions. Values structure our experiences and provide insight when we must make important decisions. Our values provide for institutional and professional stability and consistency even though society and the library are constantly changing. The next section examines some of the basic values integral to our professional work.

A. Seven Values of Library and Information Science

The discussion that follows identifies seven critical values for LIS professionals that have been tested and endured over time: service, reading and the book, truth and the search for truth, tolerance, the public good, justice, and aesthetics.

1. The First Value: Service

Perhaps the most distinctive feature of library and information science, in contrast, for example, to computer science, is that the purpose of the field is to communicate knowledge to people. This is more than just "meeting an information need." Underlying the value of service is a belief in the betterment of the individual and the community as a whole. Bringing knowledge to people and to society is the sine qua non of the profession. Pierce Butler (1951) characterized this notion succinctly over sixty years ago:

> The cultural motivation of librarianship is the promotion of wisdom in the individual and the community . . . to communicate, so far as possible, the whole of scholarship to the whole community. The librarian undertakes to supply literature on any and every subject to any and every citizen, for any and every purpose. . . . [These actions], in the long run, will sharpen the understanding, judgment, and prudence of the readers and thus sustain and advance civilization. (pp. 246–247)

Service to others has been the foundation of American librarianship for more than a hundred years, and this value applies to LIS professionals no matter what type of library or information service is involved.

> Our natural reaction to the approach of a patron is not irritation at being interrupted, but delight at another chance to help someone pick his or her way through

our beloved maze. It is, we should admit, a noble urge, this altruism of ours, one that seems both morally and psychologically good. (Finks 1991, p. 353)

Librarianship emerged as one of the service-oriented professions of the nineteenth century in part as a reaction to the profit-centered, entrepreneurial excesses of the industrial revolution (Winter 1988). As such, librarianship arose from the same American wellspring as nursing, social work, teaching, medicine, law, and the clergy. This service orientation might also be related to the fact that American libraries, at least since the latter half of the nineteenth century, have been numerically dominated by women. When women entered the workforce during this period, their activities were expected to conform to the stereotypes of appropriate behavior for their gender (Garrison 1972–1973). Women occupied professions distinguished by their nurturing characteristics: teaching, nursing, social work, and librarianship among them. Garrison (1972–1973) referred to nineteenth-century librarians as "tender technicians" (p. 131). Serving others, usually at a sacrificial wage one might add, was part and parcel of librarianship.

As fiscal resources dwindled, libraries have been pressured more and more to act as businesses. Although some feared that a business-oriented approach would emphasize increased productivity, pricing information as a commodity, and repackaging information services as products for sale, essentially changing the very nature of library service (Estabrook (1982), this does not seem to have occurred. Most libraries today, regardless of type, use management techniques, technologies, and marketing strategies often borrowed directly from the private sector while continuing to provide quality service—testimony to the persistence of service as a fundamental value.

The reason for the tenaciousness of the service value might be because it has been explicit in the philosophical foundations of librarianship for a very long time. Many of these philosophical tenets were articulated by one of the most notable figures in the history of librarianship, S. R. Ranganathan. Ranganathan (1892–1972) conducted much of his work and study in India, beginning its first school of library science. But his contributions were international in scope, influencing librarianship in America as well as other countries. He explored a number of philosophical and theoretical issues, most notably classification theory, and developed critical principles for libraries and librarianship.

Ranganathan proposed five laws that remain central to our understanding of libraries, and that reflected his deeply held conviction that the library was "an instrument of universal education" dedicated to the service of all people (Ranganathan 1963, p. 354). Although promulgated at a time when books dominated libraries and knowledge dissemination, the laws remain applicable in a digital world. In fact, a brief review of the laws provides a surprisingly contemporary perspective on libraries.

a. Books Are for Use

Ranganathan observed that in earlier times, books were often chained to prevent their removal, and libraries emphasized storage and preservation rather than use. He acknowledged that before the invention of the printing press, materials were rare and difficult to produce and therefore preservation and storage were important. Nonetheless he asserted that if stored and preserved materials were not used, libraries had little value. By emphasizing use, Ranganathan focused the attention of the profession on access-related issues. This law maintains its currency as today's libraries emphasize quality customer service and community engagement.

b. Every Reader His/Her Book

Ranganathan believed that all individuals from all social levels were entitled to an education and that libraries were essential instruments to provide that education. He understood that to accomplish the library's goals, society must contribute. He argued that the state was obligated to provide financial resources through taxation and legislation so that all people could be served by libraries. In addition, the state's obligation extended to creating a library authority such as a state librarian, whose duty it would be to create local libraries and ensure that those institutions provided service to all individuals in the local area. Librarians were not without obligations as well. For example, he believed that librarians should have excellent firsthand knowledge of the people the library served, that collections should meet the special interests of the community, and that libraries should extensively promote and advertise their services to attract a wide range of users. He also felt that the materials selected should be well written and well illustrated. The obligations of library users, on the other hand, were to advocate for library service, follow the rules and regulations, keep the library in good order, and borrow only needed materials so that others could also use the library's resources.

c. Every Book Its Reader

Ranganathan believed that the library should employ many methods to ensure that each book found its appropriate reader. He saw open shelving as particularly helpful because it gave people a chance to examine the collection freely. According to Ranganathan (1963), "In an open access library, the reader is permitted to wander among the books and lay his hands on any of them at his will and pleasure" (p. 259). How the collection was arranged could also make a difference; he suggested arranging by subject matter for the most effective access, though he was not dogmatic about this. He also possessed a very modern sense of marketing. For example, he suggested setting up displays that showcased certain collections, such as newly acquired materials, and providing special reading areas for popular materials. Other avenues for matching books with readers included surveying library users, providing readers' advisory services, offering a variety of programs such as story hours, providing extension services, and selecting good books. Finally, he urged libraries to promote and market their services through publicity, displays, publications, and public activities such as festivals.

d. Save the Time of the Reader

Ahead of his time, Ranganathan recommended using appropriate business methods to improve library management. He observed that centralizing a library collection in one location provided distinct advantages for saving time. He also noted that excellent library staff possessed strong reference skills, as well as strong technical skills in cataloging, cross-referencing, ordering, accessioning, and circulation. All of these functions contribute to timely service. In a way he anticipated, although not necessarily predicted, today's more competitive environment in which the seeker has more than one option for finding material and information.

e. The Library Must Be a Growing Organism

Ranganathan described this law as fundamental: "It is an accepted biological fact that a growing organism alone will survive. An organism which ceases to grow will petrify and perish" (p. 326). He argued that libraries must accommodate growth in staff, in the physical collection, in patron use, and in the facility. As collections grew, he anticipated increased need for security against theft and traffic flows that permitted easy movement. He recognized that growth would also affect personnel structure, anticipating an increased division of labor among administrative, technical, and reference staff. He recommended the formation of an administrative staff council to assist in decision making regarding operations and library organization. This clearly anticipated the participatory management styles of the 1960s and beyond.

Ranganathan's laws are central to LIS and they make explicit many of the principles that guide our practices for structuring library collections, services, and staff even today. Gorman (1995) revisited Ranganathan's work and advanced five new laws:

> **Libraries serve humanity.** This is a restatement of the service ethic that permeates librarianship, recognizing that the "dominant ethic of librarianship is service to the individual, community, and society as a whole" (p. 784).

Respect all forms by which knowledge is communicated. In Ranganathan's time, print materials dominated. For this reason, his principles talk of books and readers. But today, knowledge can be found in libraries in many more forms. According to Gorman, "each new means of communication enhances and supplements the strengths of all previous means" (p. 784). This new principle suggests that LIS professionals should not fear that new forms of communication will replace print; rather, librarians should exploit all media to advance library service.

Use technology intelligently to enhance service. The obligation of LIS professionals is neither to resist new technologies nor to use technology uncritically. Rather, it is to recognize the potential of some technologies to help libraries accomplish their missions. To the extent that new technologies can offer advantages to library service, they should be applied in a constructive and intelligent manner.

Protect free access to knowledge. The historical role of the library as one of the foundations of democratic institutions remains as important today as ever. The controls and centralization that some new technologies require can exacerbate many of the problems involved in protecting intellectual freedom. The knowledge of the world's cultures must be freely transmitted to all; otherwise freedom is threatened and tyranny promoted.

Honor the past and create the future. A central value of librarianship is the recognition that the past serves as a guide to the future. The library has been a central institution for archiving humankind's cultural record. To this end the library must continue to protect the historical record and perhaps use it as a guide, while adapting to the needs of the future.

2. The Second Value: The Importance of Reading and the Book

A central value of both libraries and LIS professionals has been and continues to be a deep and abiding respect for both reading and the book:

> The first presupposition associated with the appearance of libraries is a faith in the power and use value of books, as repositories of practical, technical and theoretical knowledge, of wisdom and truth, of a particular state of the language and a social memory. (Jacob 2002, p. 42)

Of course, today, we have both physical books and virtual books (e-books). Although the e-book is rising rapidly in popularity, it is still worth noting the many advantages of the physical book: Books . . .

- Are generally lightweight and very portable, easy to take to the beach or to bed
- Require no electricity (except when it's dark)
- Require little maintenance and repair, and when repair is needed it is usually quite inexpensive and can be accomplished by an individual with minimal training; no service contract is needed
- Require no diagrams or documentation to use
- Can get pretty damp and dusty and still function
- Can be dropped on the floor with little damage
- Are comparatively cheap
- Can be browsed easily and contain finding aids, such as an index, that are relatively easy to use
- Provide a large number of thoughtful and interconnected ideas in one place that can be read from start to finish or scanned in sections
- Are an excellent source for stimulating the imagination
- Store easily
- Can be written in and text can be easily underlined for emphasis during later reading and study
- Require little knowledge to operate
- Can last a very long time, especially when printed on acid-free paper

This is not to say that each of these features is unique to books but in combination they represent an impressive technology. The book, whether virtual or physical, offers other advantages as well. For example, Neill (1992) argued that books stimulate more active intellectual involvement than television or movies. Books can convey more complex concepts and more closely approximate real life thus often leading to improved understanding, discovery, and growth in our personal lives.

> Reading is a visual, vocal and auditory process which also requires the reader's thoughts to follow the thread of an argument or meditation, to share a vision. A book is a tool of learning and stimulator of thought, a kind of cognitive prosthesis which, when consulted, provides information, ideas, coherent logic, knowledge or wisdom. (Jacob 2002, p. 43)

Given that reading has been associated with success in school, in careers, and in life in general, LIS professionals work hard to promote it. Reading, although primarily associated with the book, occurs in other domains as well, and librarians have a deep commitment to reading regardless of the format. For example, often underestimated are the library's efforts to promote reading as an aural activity. The physical (DVD) and virtual versions of "books-on-tape" are very popular and provide an additional important dimension for exposing individuals to the benefits of books and reading. The most obvious efforts focus on children and youth with well-developed children's collections, in-library reading programs that begin in infancy (lap-sit programs) and extend through the teen years, as well as outreach programs to daycare centers and schools. In addition, libraries offer literacy programs for adults and those for whom English is a second language.

3. The Third Value: Respect the Search for Truth

When individuals seek answers to questions, they expect LIS professionals to provide timely and accurate information and library professionals would consider themselves remiss if they failed in that task. With the growth of the Internet and the vast amount of information available, some accurate, some not, Wengert (2001) argued that librarians' responsibility to provide access to accurate information is greater than ever. However, people often seek information on issues that are too complex to answer with a simple response. The third value requires LIS professionals to remove or reduce barriers that might frustrate a person's search. For example, if individuals believed that their circulation records could be made public or that their search for digital content would be exposed, they might not look for information considered controversial. LIS professionals reduce this barrier by protecting individuals' privacy rights, and by refusing to supply information to third parties concerning users' circulation records or search activities.

4. The Fourth Value: Tolerance

Tolerance has a complementary relationship to truth; tolerance admits of the possibility that our ability to judge truth is flawed, that there might be many truths, or that the truth in some cases might not be known. It presumes that more than one perspective on a subject might be reasonable and that exposure to many ideas might help us understand and approach the truth. The value of tolerance thus suggests that library collections should possess a variety of perspectives on a wide array of topics. Swan (1986) argued that librarians must have the untrue on their shelves as well as the true. For example, Hitler's *Mein Kampf* contains ideas that are clearly false, but analyzing these ideas helps individuals to know the truth of our past and the dangers that might lie in the future. If such material were unavailable it might impede one's understanding of the truth. Tolerance suggests that LIS professionals should be nonjudgmental when someone seeks information. Without such a value, library collections would be little more than the dogmatic assertions of the majority.

5. The Fifth Value: A Public Good

The notion that libraries are a public good has roots that begin in the nineteenth century. It was common at that time to refer to libraries metaphorically as "colleges" "schools" and "a people's university." But there were other metaphors that were less common but still reflected the library as a public good: they were referred to as "churches," "workshops" "laboratories" "gift shops"—even a public utility such as the water department but providing a reservoir for drinking knowledge (Nardini 2001). The concept of the library as a public good assumes that people and society as a whole are changed and, in the long run, improved by the ideas found in libraries. There is little reason for libraries to exist if we do not believe that they make a positive contribution to society. A list of those contributions might include promoting literacy, reading, and education; preserving the cultural record; serving as a community center; and providing entertainment and pleasure, an implicit acknowledgment of peoples' right to enjoy life. The presence of copious fiction, romance, travel, and popularized science and history attests to LIS professionals' strong feelings about this last contribution. Another implication of the public good is that LIS professionals actively reach out to the "public" regardless of age, economic status, or ethnic or racial group in order to provide library service to all.

6. The Sixth Value: Justice

McCook (2001) pointed out that information equity is an underlying goal of our profession. "Inherent in this goal is social justice—working for universal literacy, defending intellectual freedom, preserving and making accessible the human record to all" (p. 81). In part, this means that every person should have equal access to knowledge and be respected as an individual; providing inadequate service to anyone violates this value. The philosopher John Rawls (1958) noted however, that justice cannot be understood solely as equality; it must also include fairness. Equality implies the same amount for everyone; fairness implies an amount that is needed or deserved. This is an important distinction for LIS professionals because it might mean that some services provided are fair rather than equal. For example, services to children might not be equal to the services provided to adults because their needs are different. The sixth value requires LIS professionals to recognize when equality is required, such as when ensuring access, and when fairness is at issue, such as serving those with extenuating or special circumstances.

7. The Seventh Value: Aesthetics

Many libraries create their collections in order to ensure that those they serve will have access to the works of genius that epitomize the best of the world's cultural achievements—great music, art, literature, and philosophy even when their circulation levels are low. These works often receive special consideration for preservation.

Although one might debate which of these seven values is most important, there is general agreement that they are consistent among LIS professionals around the world. Koehler (2003), for example, in an international survey of nearly 1,900 librarians, found that patron service was the highest-rated value and that information literacy, equality of access, preservation of the intellectual record, and intellectual freedom were also among the top-rated values. Trushina (2004) examined the ethical codes adopted by library associations in thirty countries and found the greatest emphasis placed on the importance of free access, confidentiality of users, and intellectual freedom. These values inform the actions of LIS professionals and account for their misgivings and resistance when these values are threatened.

B. Core Values and the American Library Association (ALA)

Although the ALA promulgates a variety of policies reflecting its values, such as policies on intellectual freedom and ethical conduct, for a long time there was no single document that clearly enunciated all the critical values of the field. The need for such a document was first voiced in 1999 at the ALA's first Congress on Professional Education. In response, a Core Values Task Force was appointed and a *Statement on Core Values* was released in 2000. The following values were cited:

- connection of people to ideas
- assurance of free and open access to recorded knowledge, information, and creative works
- commitment to literacy and learning
- respect for the individuality and the diversity of all people
- freedom for all people to form, to hold, and to express their own beliefs
- preservation of the human record
- excellence in professional service to our communities
- formation of partnerships to advance these values (ALA 2000)

Reaction from the profession was mixed; one editorial writer described it as "a bland homogenization of euphemisms" (Buschman 2000), and it was not adopted by ALA. In the meantime, the Association of College and Research Libraries, a division of ALA, adopted its own core values for academic libraries (Spaulding 2002):

- Equitable and open access to information
- Service
- Intellectual freedom
- Cooperation, collaboration, and sharing of resources
- Commitment to the profession of librarianship
- Fair use
- Education and learning
- Commitment to the use of appropriate technology
- Knowledge as an end in itself
- Conservation and preservation of knowledge
- Diversity
- Scholarly communication and research
- Global perspective

In 2004, the ALA made another, successful attempt to identify and adopt core values:

Access: ensuring that all information resources are provided equally regardless of format and technology.

Confidentiality/privacy: ensuring that all interactions with library users are private and confidential and that the principles of intellectual freedom are upheld.

Democracy: ensuring that the First Amendment rights of users are protected so that the citizenry can be appropriately informed.

Diversity: ensuring that a broad range of services are provided to all populations.

Education and lifelong learning: ensuring that all types of libraries and library services support the education of users throughout their lifetime.

Intellectual freedom: ensuring that the principles of intellectual freedom are upheld.

The public good: ensuring that libraries support the public good and promote democratic institutions.

Preservation: ensuring that all types of information are preserved.

Professionalism: ensuring that library services are supported by professionally educated staff members from graduate programs in higher education.

Social responsibility: ensuring that libraries participate in the amelioration of the substantive social problems of the day. (ALA 2004)

These values, although they tend to focus on public libraries, fairly represent the values of LIS professionals in general and provide a sensible framework for how LIS professionals should conduct themselves.

There are many other ways to characterize our values. Gorman (2014), for example, advanced nine "enduring" or "central" values of the profession: stewardship, service, intellectual freedom, rationalism, literacy and learning, equity of access to recorded knowledge and information, privacy, democracy, and the greater good. Interestingly, using Gorman's values, Foster and McMenemy (2012) studied thirty-six national codes for librarians around the world. They found that the codes differed significantly in many ways, but that three of Gorman's values were common to all or most: service, privacy, and equity of access. Central to our work are the concepts of ensuring free and open access to knowledge, serving the public interest, and protecting the intellectual freedom of users. They are values that ennoble our profession and give it purpose.

III. THE ETHICS OF LIBRARY AND INFORMATION SCIENCE

Ethical deliberations are complex because they deal with fundamental questions of right and wrong. Central to ethical issues is how people should be treated and how one should act, if one wishes to act rightly. To help make ethical decisions, people draw on philosophical, religious, and legal sources, and the divergent points of view offered in these various perspectives account for lively discussion. These debates are not explicated here as we cannot determine once and for all what is right or wrong in a given instance. Rather, my purpose is to identify some of the major principles, codes, obligations, and ethical dilemmas that accompany our professional responsibilities.

The focus of ethical debates in librarianship has varied over the years. For example, DuMont (1991) examined three historical periods and found that each dealt with different ethical issues. In the years prior to 1930, American librarianship was engaged in building and maintaining collections and the ethical questions concerned whether to include materials with potentially corrupting attributes. From 1930 to 1950, the ethical discussions focused on how people in libraries, including staff, should be treated. Debate centered on issues such as job security, safe working conditions, education, and training. Another ethical concern was related to the free access to information, perhaps due, at least in part, to the rise of fascism in Nazi Germany (Harris 1973). Since 1960, the ethical issues centered on improving the public good, promoting social justice, and taking socially progressive political positions. Other issues included affirmative action, the needs of the underserved, and the ethical responsibilities of the reference librarian in answering questions. In regard to the latter, for example, Hauptman (1976) questioned whether reference librarians should provide information on building a car bomb, and Dowd (1989) explored whether they should provide information on freebasing cocaine. The underlying ethical question was whether reference librarians can be totally neutral in the performance of their duties, or whether social consequences of the information should be considered.

Although there have been several conferences on ethical issues, and the *Journal of Information Ethics* regularly offers thoughtful discussions, the reality is that for most LIS professionals, today's work environment allows very little time for reflection on values and ethical practice. That is unfortunate for almost every LIS professional at some time will be confronted with an ethical issue. Hoffman (2005) for example, surveyed Texas librarians in public libraries and schools and found that more than one-third had experienced an ethical dilemma related to censorship, copyright, or patron privacy. Interestingly, only a third of the respondents indicated that they applied the ALA Code of Ethics to their daily work situations, and school librarians were more likely to report a tension between the Code and their day-to-day responsibilities.

In some circumstances, concern for ethical behavior arises not because particular actions might be unethical, but because certain actions, even when ethical, might result in undesired outcomes for some. These circumstances highlight the need for examining how the ethical actions of LIS professionals affect and are affected by a number of factors and stakeholders. Froehlich (1992) identified at least seven stakeholders in the information dissemination process who might be affected by our actions, including authors, publishers, database producers, database vendors or networks, information professionals, the organization and managers, and the end users or consumers. He proposed an ethical model addressing professional conduct from three perspectives: self, organization, and environment. The self is a moral agent, the person who must act or suffer the consequences of the actions; the organization is the institution, also a moral agent, that acts in an autonomous manner and directs the actions of others; the environment includes the standards of the community or professional societies that create the ethical context in which the self and the organization operate. Ethical stresses arise from the interactions and imperatives of each of these perspectives, which are not always easily balanced. Hence, there might be a conflict between the self as an individual and the self as an employee or a member of an organization. For example, a librarian might have a personal belief that certain content is morally offensive and should not be disseminated. At the same time, there are organizational and professional standards of conduct that dictate that the material should be available for others. Such conflicts might be infrequent for some and commonplace for others, but they are from time to time inevitable for LIS professionals.

A. Factors in Ethical Deliberations

Most of the time, LIS professionals do not think consciously about the ethical ramifications of what they do; our behavior follows from training and habit. It is only in special situations that ethical dissonance arises. In such situations, there is general agreement that we need standards of professional conduct to proscribe unethical actions and promote ethical ones. In addition, ethical constraints apply not only to individuals but to organizations. Libraries and other information organizations are not value neutral; they act, make choices, affect human beings, and receive, allocate, and disseminate resources in ways analogous to individuals. They too have ethical obligations. In fact, ethical practices apply to all occupations, although some professions are more likely to confront ethical issues than others. In order for LIS professionals to take informed and appropriate actions, they must anticipate and understand the nature of ethical dilemmas likely to occur in libraries, be familiar with the ethical prescriptions of the field, and know the factors that should be considered when deliberating ethical issues. At least four considerations factor into ethical deliberations: social utility, survival, social responsibility, and respect for the individual. These factors are not ethical principles in themselves, but they are critical variables to consider in arriving at a decision. In fact, it is the constant attempt to balance these factors that often makes ethical decisions so difficult.

1. Social Utility

Public organizations are intended to serve important social ends. Libraries are certainly among those institutions that have a socially desirable purpose. Academic libraries advance society by educating students and supporting research that will improve society; public libraries meet the educational, recreational, informational, and cultural needs of the general public; and school libraries help students succeed

[handwritten annotation: what is the library's social purpose]

in learning. The extent to which an organization accomplishes its social purpose is its social utility. Decisions and actions that aid the organization in accomplishing its social purpose are ethically desirable but not always easy to make. For example, suppose a supervisor needed to release a personable employee who made an earnest effort but was simply unable to meet the demands of the job and serve the library users adequately. The decision to terminate the employee might produce considerable discomfort despite the fact that keeping the employee would impair the library's function. Another example might be that in order for one's own worthy organization to succeed, other worthy institutions might be disadvantaged. For example, the library might compete with city parks, law enforcement, or schools for a limited amount of public monies. *[handwritten annotation: library funding + taxes]*

2. Survival

Organizations, like individuals, need to survive if they are to accomplish their mission. When people are threatened and they act in self-defense, it is generally presumed that they are acting correctly. Libraries regularly confront issues that challenge their survival. Perhaps the most obvious example is when some members of a community object to something in the collection or when the library allows library users to access controversial material on the Internet. In a censorship case, the need to survive might conflict with the social utility factor. Censors often threaten the library's funding. Under these circumstances, the library's leadership might consider bowing to these pressures because the continued existence of the library is considered more important than the retention of a few items in the collection. On the other hand, there seems little value in protecting the library's fiscal survival if it can no longer meet its social purpose: free access to all types of ideas, even objectionable ones.

3. Social Responsibility

Organizations have an obligation not only to survive and fulfill their specific purposes but to serve the larger society. Public organizations, in particular, must meet this obligation because their survival depends in large measure on society's fiscal support. LIS professionals recognize that they have social responsibilities to their communities as well as responsibilities to help the library survive and perform their professional functions. For example, a policy promoting equal employment opportunity ensures that all members of the society have an equal opportunity for library positions. Another example might be a policy of sustainability that saves on energy consumption and acquires materials on acid-free paper to reduce pollution. As in the previous examples, there might be conflicts with other factors.

4. Respect for the Individual

People have a right to act as they choose, insofar as they do not violate the dignity and respect of others. LIS professionals strive to respect individuals in many ways. For example, libraries are open to all people and LIS professionals pay special attention to building collections and providing digital services that serve a diverse set of interests and reflect diverse perspectives. Libraries protect the privacy of library users' circulation records and user searches and ensure that the rules and policies treat employees fairly and respect their privacy as well. Again, balance is important. For example, library administrators might choose to purchase more materials with popular appeal and fewer materials that might create controversy. They might reason that users will be more inclined to support the library in these circumstances. Such a choice puts greater emphasis on survival and less on respect for the individual. Other conflicts might occur between social responsibility and respecting the individual. For example, the former factor might be used to justify compliance with law enforcement authorities who request the circulation record of a patron who allegedly committed a serious crime.

All of the factors mentioned above are important. Nonetheless, even when LIS professionals think they have made the best decision after weighing all of the various factors, there is often a residue of dissatisfaction. This ambivalence arises, in part, because of the often-competing interests of the public, board members, administrators, staff, and professional norms. Attempts to arrive at decisions that will satisfy all of these parties frequently result in frustration. Balancing them is a complex and challenging task. There is no simple formula for determining which factor weighs more heavily in a given situation. Rubin and Froehlich (1996) suggested four questions that might be helpful in these deliberations:

1. To what extent is the survival of the organization threatened?
2. To what extent will the purpose of the organization be harmed?
3. To what extent is the organization or employee socially responsible or irresponsible when acting in a particular manner?
4. To what extent are the actions of the organization or individuals acting in its behalf harming or benefiting other individuals, organizations, or the profession? (p. 41)

Recently, Wilkinson (2014) argued that most ethical codes in the library profession lack the specificity needed when specific ethical issues arise at the point of service. He proposed a "rational decision procedure" based on three values and six principles inherent in the library profession. The three values are expertise, service, and social service. The value of expertise produces two ethical principles: a *principle of competence* and a *principle of diligence*. (Librarians are expected to be both knowledgeable and thorough in their practices.) The value of service produces two principles: *a principle of fidelity* and *a principle of respect for autonomy*. (Librarians must be faithful to the trust library users place in them; they must respect the users as an individuals, serve their interests, and protect their privacy.) The value of social service produces two principles: a *principle of respect for community* and *a principle of justice*. (Librarians must be committed to the various communities they serve including the society as a whole, the profession, the library user, and themselves. In addition, they must be committed to protecting the rights of all their users to open access to information.) Wilkinson believes that if librarians are cognizant of these principles while engaged in library practice, they can more ably assess specific situations than attempting to refer to ethical codes.

B. Categories of Ethical Concern

Ethical situations in LIS generally arise in relation to two issues. One issue is information ethics, concerned with the use and misuse of information. Concerns include the ownership of information, intellectual property rights, free or restricted access, use of government information, ensuring privacy and confidentiality, data integrity, and the international flow of information. The second issue deals with professional behavior, including how we apply ethical principles to our decisions and actions as information professionals (Smith 1993a). These two issues are closely related and often overlap—more a matter of emphasis rather than unique content—and often discussion of one cannot proceed satisfactorily without discussing the other. The following is a more detailed discussion of some of the many categories of ethical concern within the library and information context.

1. Free Access to Information and the Effects of Information

The freedom of information tenet touches virtually all activities and policies of LIS professionals. Primary guidance comes from the ALA Code of Ethics and the American Society for Information Science and Technology's (ASIS&T) Professional Guidelines, which refer to "free and equal access" (ALA 1995; ASIS&T 1994). But we need to consider other issues as well, such as the tension that comes from the need to protect individual rights and the imperative to act in a socially responsible manner. Smith (1993b) characterized this tension as a dynamic relationship between three components: (1) freedom, meaning intellectual freedom, (2) information democracy, that is, promoting the need for social equity in information, and

(3) responsibility, or the obligation to promote the social good. Some might argue, for example, that inappropriate and potentially harmful content should be restricted either by prohibiting, filtering, or monitoring access, particularly if young people are involved. Others would argue that it is the ethical duty of LIS professionals to provide access to all, including young people, and that we should not violate library users' privacy rights by acting as watchdogs. Internet use further complicates matters. Wyatt (2006) argued that the ethics of monitoring Internet use are a matter of degree. For example, constantly monitoring computer activities would constitute unethical conduct because it is a serious privacy intrusion, but periodically monitoring to provide assistance, which also allows a check on appropriate computer use, is not.

From an ethical perspective, the duty to provide access does not free us from assessing potential harms. Baker (1992) articulated this consideration as "Do no harm" (p. 8). She was referring specifically to the activities of library administrators, but the underlying notion applies in other instances as well. It suggests that library activities should minimize harm to others. Ethical behavior not only protects the rights of others but also considers their welfare. The tension between providing access and doing harm is revealed in the debate over whether LIS professionals should disseminate materials about suicide to minors. Similarly, there is some evidence that exposure to violent materials might lead to levels of increased aggressive behavior; as a consequence, some librarians are concerned about the dissemination of violent materials to minors (Green and Thomas 1986). It is not being suggested here that LIS professionals should act as censors, but rather that they should consider the effects of information on a particular patron. Intellectual freedom issues, although intimately related, do not exhaust other important considerations when making ethical decisions. Of course, trying to predict the effects of a particular item or resource on a particular individual is certainly problematic in most cases and might lead to inappropriate, censorious behavior. Such conduct is its own harm.

2. Selection and Acquisition Decisions

The decisions made by LIS professionals determine, at least in part, who receives information and who does not. Selection and acquisition decisions determine the nature of the library's collection and services both physical and digital. There is an ethical obligation to meet the needs of library users, to use appropriate selection criteria, to hire qualified selectors, and to establish an efficient system for procuring items and services. Ethical conflicts arise when selectors choose items or services of particular interest to them rather than their users, or acquire services because of undue influences of vendors, board members, or administrators. Perhaps even more common, sometimes selectors fear that a particular selection will be controversial and therefore they opt not to select it even when the item will be heavily used. In each of these cases, ethics are a factor.

3. Privacy

Respect for privacy is a fundamental concept in a democratic society. As the amount of personally identifiable information stored in computer networks increases, privacy issues are magnified. This has been particularly true because of the increasing popularity of e-books. Vendors, for a variety of reasons, track the use of particular e-books with the particular user. Hence, the reading habits of library users are now stored and potentially available for inspections. Similarly, with the passage of the PATRIOT Act, the government increased its powers of surveillance to prevent terrorism (discussed in more detail in chapter 8). Suffice it to say here that the government now has a surveillance capability that was unavailable previously and can track someone's activities on the Internet.

Given the significance of privacy issues today, both LIS professionals and library staff remain resolute regarding their commitment to protect the privacy of library users. Zimmer (2014) in a survey of librarians and library staff found that 90% or greater strongly agreed or agreed that: (1) individuals should be able to control who sees their personal information, (2) companies are collecting too much personal information, (3) government agencies should not share personal information with third parties unless authorized by the individual or a court of law, (4) when people give personal information to a company for a specific purpose, they should use the information only for that purpose, and (5) business should not share personal information with third parties unless they first get specific permission. Seventy percent or greater believed that government agencies collect too much personal information.

Zimmer also explored the attitude of LIS professionals toward the roles libraries and librarians should play in protecting privacy. Overall, 75% believed that librarians do all they can to prevent unauthorized access to individual's personal information and circulation records. However, this finding also suggests that one in four believe they should be doing more. Ninety-seven percent believed that libraries should never share personal information, circulation records, or Internet use records with third parties unless authorized by the individual or by a court; 75% or more believed that librarians should play a role in educating the public on privacy risks from the

Internet and on privacy issues in general. In addition, LIS professionals perceived significant privacy dangers from search engines such as Google, Yahoo, and Bing. More than 90% believed that policies on how users' information is treated should be prominently displayed on such sites and more than 80% were concerned that these sites share search records with the government.

4. Copyright

Although copyright is fundamentally a legal concept subsumed under the broader notion of intellectual property, it can also be an ethical issue. In many ways, librarians find themselves caught between two competing obligations. The ALA Library Bill of Rights affirms a central ethical tenet of librarianship—to provide free and open access to information. This is reiterated in the Code of Ethics (Principle I) exhorting librarians to provide the highest level of service and equitable access to information. On the other hand, the ALA Code of Ethics (Principle IV) specifically directs librarians to respect the intellectual property rights of authors, publishers, and creators—which can result in restricting an individual's access to content, to copy it, or otherwise use or integrate it into new content. To some extent this situation is ameliorated by the provision of fair use (discussed in chapter 8); but Aulisio (2013) noted that in recent years court decisions and legislation have tended to broaden the rights of copyright owners and diminished fair use rights—a situation referred to as "copyright creep." Aulisio (2013) warns that we must not "play into the culture of copyright creep . . ." (p. 570), that it is a form of censorship unduly restricting access to information, a violation of the ALA Bill of Rights. At the same time, copyright is the law; LIS professionals must respect it for both legal and ethical reasons. After all, if unlawful copying reduces the incentive for authors to produce works, then the library will have nothing to disseminate. LIS professionals want authors to profit, but they do not want authors and publishers to restrict and control the flow of information.

These issues are exacerbated in the digital environment. Balancing the application of fair use, with a plethora of limiting provisions in vendor licenses, navigating digital rights management systems, educating library users on copyright issues, and providing high quality service at the same time makes the job of LIS professionals very difficult. The ethical environment for copyright will remain complex for the foreseeable future. The central obligations of LIS professionals—to provide free and open access to information and to provide the highest quality of service to all—must always be the touchstone of our ethical and professional conduct.

5. The Organization of Information

Organizing information has been a fundamental task of librarianship since its beginnings. Usually this task was considered from a strictly conceptual and procedural perspective, largely a question of techniques: which ones were best, and which were the easiest to understand and use? However, how information is organized is not without ethical implications. For example, a cataloger might classify as adult some materials that were written for young people because the cataloger believed they were inappropriate. These biases, whether intentional or not, deprive or inhibit access to information, inappropriately silencing the voices of authors or producers who have a right to be heard. Such actions violate several fundamental values of librarianship, particularly excellence in service.

How knowledge is organized often reflects a society's attitudes. For example, the Dewey Decimal Classification System has been criticized for diminishing the importance of contributions from non-Western cultures. When organizing information we must consider what values, prejudices, or preconceptions we might bring to this process. Too often people believe that technical services have only an oblique relationship to the library user but they can play a critical role in executing professional values. In fact, the library user has a direct relationship with technical services, because they determine, to a considerable extent, how access is accomplished. As Bierbaum (1994) noted, "The mission of technical services is to provide bibliographical and physical access to collections and information" (p. 13). Among other things, this implies that technical services professionals have an ethical obligation to maintain high bibliographic standards, to process materials efficiently and effectively, to reduce barriers to information, to keep up with technical and professional issues in technical services, and to resist censorship. In the digital world, technical services play an even greater important role of ensuring that discovery systems are designed to maximize access. The role of technical services is the same as all other library functions: to provide the highest-quality service.

6. Information Policy

Information policies of all types: international, national, state, and organizational have ethical implications. When addressing information policies expressed in laws and regulations, it is easy to confound legal issues and ethical ones. They often appear linked, but they are also distinct. For example, a law that has the impact of producing equality of access to information conforms to the ethical value of equality, while laws that create unequal access are problematic for LIS professionals. Some

laws and regulations, such as public records acts, encourage democratic participation and facilitate citizen oversight of public conduct; similarly, education laws
may increase equality of access to resources and services in libraries. On the other
hand, laws that require filtering can deprive individuals of constitutionally protected
speech; copyright and contract laws can unduly restrict access to digital content. LIS
professionals must assess information policies in light of the consequences that result
and determine if the basic values of our profession are supported or contravened.

7. Information Quality

Ethical obligations extend to the quality of information LIS professionals provide. To
the extent that a library can ensure the information it provides is timely and accurate,
it preserves its service values. When libraries cannot ensure quality, they might well
have an obligation to inform library users that there might be deficiencies, limitations, or biases in the information provided, and to educate library users on how they
can evaluate the quality of information for themselves. These obligations become
especially relevant when library users use automated databases and the Internet. LIS
professionals have ethical duties, if not legal ones, to ensure that library users understand that these systems do not access all relevant information and that some information, especially information on the Internet, might be of low quality.

 If one assumes that information professionals are just that—professionals—
then they have an ethical obligation to maintain high professional standards in their
work. We certainly expect that a doctor's recommendations are based on the most
scientifically accurate information and best practices; the same assumption applies
to attorneys. When they fail to meet the standards of practice in their fields, they
are subject to charges of malpractice. Although Diamond and Dragich (2001) suggested that LIS professionals might be subject to malpractice suits, thus far there is
no evidence that any legal actions have occurred. Nonetheless, they suggest that
LIS professionals should focus on "what constitutes good practice in librarianship"
(p. 395). LIS professionals might not have the same legal obligations as some other
professionals, but their ethical obligations to maintain the highest standards of service are similar to those of any profession. For example, Ulvik and Salvesen (2007)
suggested that if reference librarians conducted inadequate interviews, they would
not be acting in the best interest of their library users. Other activities that would fail
to meet the highest standards of practice might include the following:

- Opening reference queries that do not help to clarify questions or obtain
  sufficient information to answer the question
- Inadequate inclusion of the patron in the search process

- Lack of empathy
- Showing discomfort with questions of a sensitive nature
- Using communication strategies that foreclose the process prematurely
- Giving insufficient opportunity for young people to choose materials on their own

Isaacson (2004) suggested that sometimes reference librarians provide answers that satisfy or please a patron, but are not necessarily the best answers—ones that the patron might not want to hear. McKinzie (2002) argued that libraries fail to provide the highest quality service when they permit paraprofessionals to perform reference services that should be the responsibility of degreed staff. All of these examples serve to highlight the need to consider our activities from the standpoint of best practice.

8. Ethical Issues in the Workplace

The management and administration of the library workplace raise a variety of ethical issues outside of the ethical obligation to provide high-quality service. Among them are actions involving business dealings with vendors and consultants; and allocation of fiscal and staff resources. Cihak and Howland (2012) identified several workplace situations with ethical aspects: (1) use of public funds for social events (staff lunches, celebrations), (2) supervisors who ignore an employee's poor performance or policy infringements, (3) development and enforcement of dress codes, (4) acceptance of gifts from staff members, (5) tolerating gossip or speaking falsely about another employee, (6) failure to assist another employee when the opportunity arises, (7) failure to promote a harmonious workplace.

Human resource management staff confront ethical dilemmas frequently. Figure 10.1 identifies a variety of behaviors which, except in extraordinary cases, constitute unethical conduct involving staff.

Although all library employees are responsible for their own actions, it is the responsibility of leadership to create a workplace culture in which ethical conduct is modeled, supported, and rewarded. Institutional approaches that can help promote ethical conduct include the following:

- establishing rules and regulations that clearly identify the ethical obligations of employees and management and clearly state the penalties for ethical violations
- developing training and education programs that sensitize staff to ethical issues
- disciplining individuals for ethical violations

FIGURE 10.1
Ethical Issues in the Fair Treatment of Personnel

Violations of Privacy

- Revealing information about employees to individuals who do not need to know such information or revealing information that might unnecessarily damage the reputation of an employee
- Misusing personnel records or files, including inappropriate access to computer files
- Collecting any personal information about employees that is not related to the necessary function of the organization
- Conducting inappropriate investigations of an individual's personal history or using irrelevant personal information to make a personnel decision
- Conducting drug, alcohol, HIV, or other testing unless it is essential to the safe operation of the job or is directly related to the safety of others
- Monitoring employees with video cameras or recording devices without their knowledge or consent, unless significant and specific job-related reasons make such monitoring necessary
- Using a polygraph unless there is clear and substantial reason for its use
- Attempting to censor the writing or speech of employees unless such speech or writing would significantly damage the institution's ability to perform its essential functions

Misuses of Authority

- Showing favoritism to employees who are friends or relations
- Making personnel decisions out of anger or spite
- Writing inaccurate job references for employees to prevent them from gaining other employment, or for increasing their chance for employment elsewhere
- Collecting job-related information from employees without informing them of the potential consequences (e.g., for disciplinary action)
- Retaliating against employees who are outspoken or who have merely exercised their legal rights
- Withholding information from an individual to ensure or promote job failure

Organizational Inadequacies

- Designing a system of rewards that fosters cheating, sabotaging the work of others, or withholding important information, or that places emphasis only on quantity rather than quality (e.g., providing substantial financial rewards for higher library circulation)
- Paying wages and benefits that do not give minimal protection and security to employees
- Creating a personnel system that discriminates or is unfair in administering essential personnel functions
- Permitting the hiring and placement of individuals with a master of library and information science degree in support staff positions
- Misusing behavior-modification techniques to manipulate employees
- Knowingly allowing employees to work in unsafe or unhealthy working conditions, especially without their knowledge or consent

- establishing an ethics code within the organization
- hiring and promoting individuals who demonstrate ethical behavior and understanding
- developing a system of rewards that provides recognition and incentives for ethical actions and disincentives for inappropriate behavior

9. Impact of Technology on Ethical Behavior

Today's technological environment might by its very nature promote unethical behavior. For example, Hauptman (2001) observed that "technology changed the ways in which we create, store, and access data and information so dramatically that a real qualitative difference emerges" (p. 434). Rubin (1995) noted that the very nature of these technologies might encourage or even promote unethical conduct. If this is true, then relying solely on professional codes of ethics might not be sufficient. It is, therefore, worthwhile to consider some of the qualities associated with new technologies that might promote unethical behavior.

a. Computers Promote a Sense of Anonymity

Although some computer use occurs in public areas, most people use their computers privately in an office, at home, or while mobile. Even if people are in the same room or proximate to the individual using the technology, it is relatively difficult for them to observe exactly what the individual is doing on the device. The feeling that one cannot be found out tends to increase one's propensity to commit unethical acts.

b. Theft Can Be Accomplished from Great Distances with Comparative Ease

Prior to the advent of computers, stealing generally required the thief to be present physically when something was stolen. Wireless technologies and computers, on the other hand, allow people to stealthily abscond with data or files in another city, state, or country with relative ease. Even with high levels of data security, detection can be quite difficult; there have been numerous examples of data theft which remained undetected for considerable periods of time.

c. Potential Audiences Are Large and Easily Reached

Because of the nature of the Internet, messages and files can now be sent to millions of individuals simultaneously. One common unhappy example is the transmission of "spam." This capacity presents an opportunity for the unscrupulous to exploit large numbers of unwitting victims. In a world where social interaction is increasingly integrated into the digital environment, the opportunities for unethical behaviors increase dramatically.

d. Copying Is Easy

The electronic medium is highly flexible, allowing someone to download or make a copy of an electronic file while leaving the original unchanged. Under these circumstances, one might be tempted to rationalize that nothing was actually taken. Perhaps this is why individuals seem to have fewer misgivings about copying music and video files.

e.   Everyone Does It

Historically, we defined stealing as the removal of a person's property without their permission. When someone visits an electronic site and downloads music or videos that were not properly obtained from the copyright owner, that person is stealing. However, as noted above, copying music and video content has been commonplace for more than a decade, especially for young people. Such "piracy" becomes more acceptable when it is perceived that friends, neighbors, and family members are doing it as well (Gray 2012). Gray observes,

> While there are many studies that intend to create an ethical profile of digital pirates, attempting to prove that they are influenced by social situations and personal ethical shortcoming such as poor self-control, these same studies often point out that the reason digital piracy is so widespread is that it is *not* viewed as morally wrong. The data support the hypotheses that digital pirates have certain traits that may be considered ethically undesirable, but it also paints a picture of a social atmosphere where the piracy is totally accepted as a norm. If we are going to describe digital pirates as unethical, we would first have to condemn the society that created them and allows them to exist without knowing that they are committing a crime. (p. 293)

C. Professional Codes of Ethics

As noted earlier, LIS professionals seldom have the time or opportunity to think about ethics. When conflicts arise, we respond automatically without taking much time to reflect on the implications of our acts. The fact that people generally act out of habit highlights the importance and power of our early professional training. Once the ethics of one's profession are ingrained, acting in accordance with them should follow as an integral element of our everyday behavior. This is not to say that one's personal ethics cannot vary from one's professional ethics. In most cases, however, one would hope that professional ethics can be seen as a specialized example of our personal ethical practices although from time to time, they might conflict.

Although many schools of LIS indicate that they include ethics as part of the curriculum and cover such topics as privacy, censorship, and intellectual freedom, Buchanan (2004) reported that there are no standard readings or content for inculcating professional ethics in LIS curricula. Instead, most schools rely on early exposure to various codes of ethics including ALA's Code of Ethics, the Society of American Archivists' (SAA's) Code of Ethics for Archivists, and the ASIS&T Professional Guidelines. Other information-based disciplines also have codes of ethics, such as the Special Libraries Association, Association for Computing Machinery's Code of Ethics and Professional Conduct, and the Society of Competitive Intelligence Professionals' Code of Ethics for CI Professionals. Professional codes are important for at least four reasons:

- They represent a statement of the fundamental values of the profession.
- They are useful in teaching new professionals about fundamental values.
- Reading (and rereading) them, listening to others discuss them, and seeing them applied promote their assimilation.
- When particularly knotty ethical issues arise, the professional code can serve as a decision-making guide and as a jog for one's conscience.

Unfortunately, simply reading the codes will not inculcate them into professional practice. Because only a small number of people actively participated in the discussions that created the codes, some of the provisions might seem obscure or unnecessarily arbitrary. LIS students should debate and internalize the meaning and rationale behind the codes if they are to be fully prepared to act appropriately in a crisis. Unless students can articulate a solid understanding of the code's rationale, the explanation is likely to sound dogmatic rather than like a thoughtful justification of professional conduct.

Koehler (2002, p. 327) described most ethical codes related to the information professions as "prescriptive" and "aspirational" in that they recommend conduct and also tend to identify the greater purposes that they serve. Sturgeon (2007) noted that the codes are "a way of enhancing the profession's reputation and professional trust, and of defining and sensitizing persons to their professional responsibility." Well-written codes "reveal the tension among the various values that the profession represents" (p. 57). Despite differences in professional focus, the various codes are often consistent in their themes. Koehler and Pemberton (2000) examined the ethical codes of various information organizations and identified five shared themes:

- Whenever possible, place the needs of clients above all other concerns.
- Understand the roles of the information practitioner and strive to meet them with the greatest possible skill and competence.
- Support the needs and interests of the profession and the professional associations.
- Insofar as they do not conflict with professional obligations, be sensitive and responsive to social responsibilities appropriate to the profession.
- Be aware of and responsive to the rights of users, employers, fellow practitioners, one's community, and the larger society. (p. 329)

Obviously, ethical codes are only as good as the willingness of individuals to follow them. For professions such as law and medicine, violations of the codes are enforced through loss of licensure and disciplinary actions, certainly appropriate when one's life or liberty might be affected. In library and information science, the codes are enforced through social norms and social expectations that they will be followed; they represent consensus on appropriate behavior. Unethical conduct in the LIS professions is subject to peer criticism and disapproval but not sanctions.

1. ALA Code of Ethics

There was little demand for an ethical code for librarians before the twentieth century. The earliest discussions took place between 1903 and 1909. Two individuals were particularly influential and contributed significantly to these early discussions: Mary Wright Plummer, director of the Pratt Institute Library School, and Charles Knowles Bolton, librarian of the Boston Athenaeum. The ALA considered a code in 1928, but it was not formally adopted until 1938 (Lindsey and Prentice 1985). The ALA Library Bill of Rights was adopted a year later. Together, these two documents form the ethical foundation for the LIS professions.

The Code of Ethics (figure 10.2) explicitly recognizes the potential conflicts in values inherent in LIS and establishes one overriding value: "commitment to intellectual freedom and freedom of access to information" (ALA 1995). Although not formally subdivided, the eight provisions of the code focus on three general areas: access issues, rights of authors and creators, and employment issues.

a. Access Issues

Consistent with the overriding value cited in the preamble, three of the eight provisions deal directly with the issue of access. The first provision emphasizes the obligation to treat all equally, emphasizing equal treatment and access. The second

FIGURE 10.2
Code of Ethics of the American Library Association

As members of the American Library Association, we recognize the importance of codifying and making known to the profession and to the general public the ethical principles that guide the work of librarians, other professionals providing information services, library trustees and library staffs.

Ethical dilemmas occur when values are in conflict. The American Library Association Code of Ethics states the values to which we are committed, and embodies the ethical responsibilities of the profession in this changing information environment.

We significantly influence or control the selection, organization, preservation, and dissemination of information. In a political system grounded in an informed citizenry, we are members of a profession explicitly committed to intellectual freedom and the freedom of access to information. We have a special obligation to ensure the free flow of information and ideas to present and future generations.

The principles of this Code are expressed in broad statements to guide ethical decision making. These statements provide a framework; they cannot and do not dictate conduct to cover particular situations.

   I.   We provide the highest level of service to all library users through appropriate and usefully organized resources; equitable service policies; equitable access; and accurate, unbiased, and courteous responses to all requests.
   II. We uphold the principles of intellectual freedom and resist all efforts to censor library resources.
   III. We protect each library user's right to privacy and confidentiality with respect to information sought or received and resources consulted, borrowed, acquired, or transmitted.
   IV. We respect intellectual property rights and advocate balance between the interests of information users and rights holders.
   V.   We treat coworkers and other colleagues with respect, fairness, and good faith, and advocate conditions of employment that safeguard the rights and welfare of all employees of our institutions.
   VI. We do not advance private interests at the expense of library users, colleagues, or our employing institutions.
   VII. We distinguish between our personal convictions and professional duties and do not allow our personal beliefs to interfere with fair representation of the aims of our institutions or the provision of access to their information resources.
   VIII. We strive for excellence in the profession by maintaining and enhancing our own knowledge and skills, by encouraging the professional development of coworkers, and by fostering the aspirations of potential members of the profession.

Adopted at the 1939 Midwinter Meeting by the ALA Council;
amended June 30, 1981; June 28, 1995; and January 22, 2008.

suggests that there is an obligation to promote intellectual freedom and to resist attempts to censor library materials. The third recognizes the special nature of librarian-patron interactions. It highlights the privileged character of that relationship, albeit not necessarily in the legal sense. To this end, the librarian is exhorted to protect the privacy of all library users and to ensure that their interactions remain confidential.

b. Rights of Authors and Creators

Although the Code of Ethics places great emphasis on service to library users, one provision recognizes that the producers or creators of information are critical participants in this process and also deserve ethical treatment. Obviously, failure to recognize this aspect of information transfer and dissemination could seriously restrict the distribution of information products to libraries, with unhappy consequences for library service. To this end, Section IV of the code recognizes that authors and creators have the right to benefit from their creativity but a balance must be respected to ensure that library users have access to those ideas.

c. Employment Issues

Employment issues comprise more provisions of the code than any other issue. Section V suggests that treating fellow employees ethically is itself part of the ethical obligation to respect the rights and welfare of all employees. Section VI recognizes the essentially altruistic nature of the professional obligation and reminds us that our personal or private interests are not to be served above the interests of library users, the employer, or other employees. Section VII focuses on a very delicate aspect of professional work. Each of us brings to the workplace a set of values, beliefs, and moral perspectives that govern our everyday behavior, but sometimes, acting in our professional capacity, we should act in the best interests of our clients. Section VII suggests that we act to serve the patron, even if the material provided might violate our own values. Finally, Section VIII emphasizes the professional obligation to improve one's skills continuously. In an increasingly complex information and technological environment, this is certainly vital. Interestingly, the obligation as set forth in this provision is broader than just self-improvement; it extends to the development of others. As such, it is especially pertinent to library decision makers and managers who have the capacity to create opportunities for training and development for their staff.

d. Additional Interpretative Statements

For many years, the ALA Code of Ethics, unlike the ALA Library Bill of Rights, had no interpretive documents to assist librarians in applying the principles espoused. However, in 2001, ALA adopted its first "explanatory statement." Many questions had arisen regarding the rights of library staff to speak in the workplace. "*Questions and Answers on Speech in the Workplace*" attempted to address the ethical issues involved. It encouraged library employers to solicit the ideas and opinions of all staff on matters of importance to the library, but it also reminded employees that the First Amendment does not generally apply to employees and that they are governed by other laws and contracts that limit their freedom of speech. This explanatory statement was followed in 2009 by the explanatory statement, "*Enforcement of the Code of Ethics of the American Library Association*" and in 2013 by "*Questions and Answers on Ethics and Social Media*" (ALA 2010; ALA 2013).

2. American Society for Information Science & Technology (ASIS&T) Guidelines for Professional Conduct

The ethical guidelines from the American Society for Information Science & Technology ASIS&T (figure 10.3) are more broadly written because they are aimed at information workers in all types of occupations, not just librarianship.

These guidelines acknowledge that some information services are part of private organizations and that the proprietary interests of employers must be taken into account in the dissemination of information. Nonetheless, many of the underlying principles are similar to the ALA Code of Ethics. The ASIS&T Code identifies three basic areas of ethical responsibility: (1) responsibilities to employers, clients, and system users, (2) responsibilities to the profession, and (3) responsibilities to society. Like the ALA code, these guidelines consider the right to privacy, confidentiality, and fair treatment of clients, users, and employers. The guidelines, under a more general notion of protecting privacy and confidentiality, also highlight a critical obligation of those who design and administer information systems—to provide security for those systems. In addition, as in the ALA code, the responsibility to the profession includes the promotion of continuing education. The guidelines add, however, the responsibility not to misrepresent one's qualifications or the information system being used. The responsibility to the society also echoes the ALA code in the emphasis on free and equal access to information (ASIS&T 2014).

FIGURE 10.3
ASIS&T Professional Guidelines

Dedicated to the memory of Diana Woodward

ASIS&T recognizes the plurality of uses and users of information technologies, services, systems, and products as well as the diversity of goals or objectives, sometimes conflicting, among producers, vendors, mediators, and users of information systems.

ASIS&T urges its members to be ever aware of the social, economic, cultural, and political impacts of their actions or inaction.

ASIS&T members have obligations to employers, clients, and system users, to the profession, and to society to use judgement and discretion in making choices, providing equitable service, and in defending the rights of open inquiry.

Responsibilities to Employers/Clients/System Users

- To act faithfully for their employers or clients in professional matters

- To uphold each user's, provider's, or employer's right to privacy and confidentiality and to respect whatever proprietary rights belong to them, by limiting access to, providing proper security for, and ensuring proper disposal of data about clients, library users, or users

- To treat all persons fairly

Responsibility to the Profession

To truthfully represent themselves and the information systems which they utilize or which they represent, by

- not knowingly making false statements or providing erroneous or misleading information

- informing their employers, clients, or sponsors of any circumstances that create a conflict of interest

- not using their position beyond their authorized limits or not using their credentials to misrepresent themselves

- following and promoting standards of conduct in accord with the best current practices

- undertaking their research conscientiously, in gathering, tabulating, or interpreting data; in following proper approval procedures for subjects; and in producing or disseminating their research results

- pursuing ongoing professional development and encouraging and assisting colleagues and others to do the same

- adhering to principles of due process and equality of opportunity

3. Society of American Archivists

Although some of the ethical issues confronted by archivists overlap with those noted above, the special function of archives—the storage and dissemination of cultural records of long-term value—has some special ethical burdens. Members of the SAA recognized this in the creation of two documents: "Statement of Core Values of Archivists" most recently revised in 2011 and "Code of Ethics for Archivists" most recently revised in 2012 (SAA 2014). These two documents are intended to be used together as complementary guides for professional conduct (figure 10.4).

FIGURE 10.4
SAA Core Values Statement and Code of Ethics

Introduction

Statements of ethics emerge from the core values of a profession. The *Core Values of Archivists* and the *Code of Ethics for Archivists* are intended to be used together to guide archivists, as well as to inform those who work with archivists, in shaping expectations for professional engagement. The former is a statement of what archivists believe; the latter is a framework for archivists' behavior.

In addition, case studies drawn from real life that address one or more of the areas covered by the *Code of Ethics for Archivists* have been published by the Committee on Ethics and Professional Conduct (CEPC).

■ ■ ■ ■ ■

Core Values of Archivists
(Approved by the SAA Council May 2011)

Purpose

Archivists select, preserve, and make available primary sources that document the activities of institutions, communities, and individuals. These archival sources can be used for many purposes including providing legal and administrative evidence, protecting the rights of individuals and organizations, and forming part of the cultural heritage of society. The modern archives profession bases its theoretical foundations and functions on a set of core values that define and guide the practices and activities of archivists, both individually and collectively. Values embody what a profession stands for and should form the basis for the behavior of its members.

Archivists provide important benefits and services such as: identifying and preserving essential parts of the cultural heritage of society; organizing and maintaining the documentary record of institutions, groups, and individuals; assisting in the process of remembering the past through authentic and reliable primary sources; and serving a broad range of people who seek to locate and use valuable evidence and information. Since ancient times, archives have afforded a fundamental power to those who control them. In a democratic society such power should benefit all members of the community. The values shared and embraced by archivists enable them to meet these obligations and to provide vital services on behalf of all groups and individuals in society.

This statement of core archival values articulates these central principles both to remind archivists why they engage in their professional responsibilities and to inform others of the basis for archivists' contributions to society. Archivists are often subjected to competing claims and imperatives, and in certain situations particular values may pull in opposite directions. This statement intends to provide guidance by identifying the core values that guide archivists in making such decisions and choices. Core values provide part of the context in which to examine ethical concerns.

Core Values of Archivists

Access and Use: Archivists promote and provide the widest possible accessibility of materials, consistent with any mandatory access restrictions, such as public statute, donor contract, business/institutional privacy, or personal privacy. Although access may be limited in some instances, archivists seek to promote open access and use when possible. Access to records is essential in personal, academic, business, and government settings, and use of records should be both welcomed and actively promoted. Even individuals who do not directly use archival materials benefit indirectly from research, public programs, and other forms of archival use, including the symbolic value of knowing that such records exist and can be accessed when needed.

Accountability: By documenting institutional functions, activities, and decision-making, archivists provide an important means of ensuring accountability. In a republic such accountability and transparency constitute an essential hallmark of democracy. Public leaders must be held accountable both to the judgment of history and future generations as well as to citizens in the ongoing governance of society. Access to the records of public officials and agencies provides a means of holding them accountable both to public citizens and to the judgment of future generations. In the private sector, accountability through archival documentation assists in protecting the rights and interests of consumers, shareholders, employees, and citizens. Archivists in collecting repositories may not in all cases share the same level of responsibility for accountability, but they too maintain evidence of the actions of individuals, groups, and organizations, which may be required to provide accountability for contemporary and future interests.

Advocacy: Archivists promote the use and understanding of the historical record. They serve as advocates for their own archival programs and institutional needs. They also advocate for the application of archival values in a variety of settings including, to the extent consistent with their institutional responsibilities, the political arena. Archivists seek to contribute to the formation of public policy related to archival and recordkeeping concerns and to ensure that their expertise is used in the public interest.

Diversity: Archivists collectively seek to document and preserve the record of the broadest possible range of individuals, socio-economic groups, governance, and corporate entities in society. Archivists embrace the importance of identifying, preserving, and working with communities to actively document those whose voices have been overlooked or marginalized. They seek to build connections to under-documented communities to support: acquisition and preservation of sources relating to these communities' activities, encouragement of community members' use of archival research sources, and/or formation of community-based archives. Archivists accept and encourage a diversity of viewpoints on social, political, and intellectual issues, as represented both in archival records and among members of the profession. They actively work to achieve a diversified and representative membership in the profession.

History and Memory: Archivists recognize that primary sources enable people to examine the past and thereby gain insights into the human experience. Archival materials provide surrogates for human memory, both individually and collectively, and when properly maintained, they serve as evidence against which individual and social memory can be tested. Archivists preserve such primary sources to enable us to better comprehend the past, understand the present, and prepare for the future.

Preservation: Archivists preserve a wide variety of primary sources for the benefit of future generations. Preserving materials is a means to this end, not an end in itself. Within prescribed law and best practice standards, archivists may determine that the original documents themselves must be preserved, while at other times copying the information they contain to alternate media may be sufficient. Archivists thus preserve materials for the benefit of the future more than for the concerns of the past.

(cont.)

FIGURE 10.4
SAA Core Values Statement and Code of Ethics (cont.)

Professionalism: Archivists adhere to a common set of missions, values, and ethics. They accept an evolving theoretical base of knowledge, collaborate with colleagues in related professions, develop and follow professional standards, strive for excellence in their daily practice, and recognize the importance of professional education, including lifelong learning. They encourage professional development among their coworkers, foster the aspirations of those entering the archival profession, and actively share their knowledge and expertise. Archivists seek to expand opportunities to cooperate with other information professionals, with records creators, and with users and potential users of the archival record.

Responsible Custody: Archivists ensure proper custody for the documents and records entrusted to them. As responsible stewards, archivists are committed to making reasonable and defensible choices for the holdings of their institutions. They strive to balance the sometimes competing interests of various stakeholders. Archivists are judicious stewards who manage records by following best practices in developing facilities service standards, collection development policies, user service benchmarks, and other performance metrics. They collaborate with external partners for the benefit of users and public needs. In certain situations, archivists recognize the need to deaccession materials so that resources can be strategically applied to the most essential or useful materials.

Selection: Archivists make choices about which materials to select for preservation based on a wide range of criteria, including the needs of potential users. Understanding that because of the cost of long-term retention and the challenges of accessibility most of the documents and records created in modern society cannot be kept, archivists recognize the wisdom of seeking advice of other stakeholders in making such selections. They acknowledge and accept the responsibility of serving as active agents in shaping and interpreting the documentation of the past.

Service: Within the mandates and missions of their institutions, archivists provide effective and efficient connections to (and mediation for) primary sources so that users, whoever they may be, can discover and benefit from the archival record of society, its institutions, and individuals. Archivists serve numerous constituencies and stakeholders, which may include institutional administrators, creators and donors of documentary materials, rights holders, un/documented peoples, researchers using the archives for many distinct purposes, corporate and governmental interests, and/or citizens concerned with the information and evidence held in archival sources. Archivists seek to meet the needs of users as quickly, effectively, and efficiently as possible.

Social Responsibility: Underlying all the professional activities of archivists is their responsibility to a variety of groups in society and to the public good. Most immediately, archivists serve the needs and interests of their employers and institutions. Yet the archival record is part of the cultural heritage of all members of society. Archivists with a clearly defined societal mission strive to meet these broader social responsibilities in their policies and procedures for selection, preservation, access, and use of the archival record. Archivists with a narrower mandate still contribute to individual and community memory for their specific constituencies, and in so doing improve the overall knowledge and appreciation of the past within society.

■ ■ ■ ■ ■

Code of Ethics for Archivists

(Approved by the SAA Council February 2005; revised January 2012)

Archives are created by a wide array of groups and provide evidence of the full range of human experience. Archivists endeavor to ensure that those materials, entrusted to their care, will be accessible over time as evidence of human activity and social organization. Archivists embrace principles that foster the transparency of their actions and that inspire confidence in the profession. A distinct body of ethical norms helps archivists navigate the complex situations and issues that can arise in the course of their work.

The Society of American Archivists is a membership organization comprising individuals and organizations dedicated to the selection, care, preservation, and administration of historical and documentary records of enduring value for the benefit of current and future generations.

The Society endorses this *Code of Ethics for Archivists* as principles of the profession. This Code should be read in conjunction with SAA's "Core Values of Archivists." Together they provide guidance to archivists and increase awareness of ethical concerns among archivists, their colleagues, and the rest of society. As advocates for documentary collections and cultural objects under their care, archivists aspire to carry out their professional activities with the highest standard of professional conduct. The behaviors and characteristics outlined in this Code of Ethics should serve as aspirational principles for archivists to consider as they strive to create trusted archival institutions.

Professional Relationships

Archivists cooperate and collaborate with other archivists, and respect them and their institutions' missions and collecting policies. In their professional relationships with donors, records creators, users, and colleagues, archivists are honest, fair, collegial, and equitable.

Judgment

Archivists exercise professional judgment in appraising, acquiring, and processing materials to ensure the preservation, authenticity, diversity, and lasting cultural and historical value of their collections. Archivists should carefully document their collections-related decisions and activities to make their role in the selection, retention, or creation of the historical record transparent to their institutions, donors, and users. Archivists are encouraged to consult with colleagues, relevant professionals, and communities of interest to ensure that diverse perspectives inform their actions and decisions.

Authenticity

Archivists ensure the authenticity and continuing usability of records in their care. They document and protect the unique archival characteristics of records and strive to protect the records' intellectual and physical integrity from tampering or corruption. Archivists may not willfully alter, manipulate, or destroy data or records to conceal facts or distort evidence. They thoroughly document any actions that may cause changes to the records in their care or raise questions about the records' authenticity.

(cont.)

FIGURE 10.4
SAA Core Values Statement and Code of Ethics (cont.)

Security and Protection

Archivists protect all documentary materials for which they are responsible. They take steps to minimize the natural physical deterioration of records and implement specific security policies to protect digital records. Archivists guard all records against accidental damage, vandalism, and theft and have well-formulated plans in place to respond to any disasters that may threaten records. Archivists cooperate actively with colleagues and law enforcement agencies to apprehend and prosecute vandals and thieves.

Access and Use

Recognizing that use is the fundamental reason for keeping archives, archivists actively promote open and equitable access to the records in their care within the context of their institutions' missions and their intended user groups. They minimize restrictions and maximize ease of access. They facilitate the continuing accessibility and intelligibility of archival materials in all formats. Archivists formulate and disseminate institutional access policies along with strategies that encourage responsible use. They work with donors and originating agencies to ensure that any restrictions are appropriate, well-documented, and equitably enforced. When repositories require restrictions to protect confidential and proprietary information, such restrictions should be implemented in an impartial manner. In all questions of access, archivists seek practical solutions that balance competing principles and interests.

Privacy

Archivists recognize that privacy is sanctioned by law. They establish procedures and policies to protect the interests of the donors, individuals, groups, and institutions whose public and private lives and activities are recorded in their holdings. As appropriate, archivists place access restrictions on collections to ensure that privacy and confidentiality are maintained, particularly for individuals and groups who have no voice or role in collections' creation, retention, or public use. Archivists promote the respectful use of culturally sensitive materials in their care by encouraging researchers to consult with communities of origin, recognizing that privacy has both legal and cultural dimensions. Archivists respect all users' rights to privacy by maintaining the confidentiality of their research and protecting any personal information collected about the users in accordance with their institutions' policies.

Trust

Archivists should not take unfair advantage of their privileged access to and control of historical records and documentary materials. They execute their work knowing that they must ensure proper custody for the documents and records entrusted to them. Archivists should demonstrate professional integrity and avoid potential conflicts of interest. They strive to balance the sometimes-competing interests of all stakeholders.

a. Statement of Core Values of Archivists

The statement notes that core values are "'what archivists believe." They "define and guide the practices and activities of archivists, both individually and collectively" (SAA 2014). There are eleven core values that can be summarized as follows:

1. encourage the greatest possible open access subject to legal and contractual limitation and matters of privacy
2. ensure accountability by documenting the activities of public and private agencies and officials
3. actively promote the use of archival records and advocate for the creation of public policies that promote responsible use of such records
4. promote collections representing the broadest range of individuals and groups, including encouraging the development of collections related to under-represented groups and providing the broadest range of viewpoints
5. emphasize the importance of collecting and maintaining primary sources as a way to better understand the past and counterbalance individual and social memory
6. pursue a variety of preservation strategies to ensure that records will be preserved for future generations
7. conform to professional standards of practices and share common mission, values, and ethics
8. steward records and documents according to the best practices of the profession
9. take into account long-term challenges such as cost and accessibility when selecting records and documents and consult with third parties when appropriate to assist in making selection decisions
10. provide the highest quality mediation in making available and interpreting archival records and documents to a wide constituency of potential users
11. view services and collections as a public good; the mission is not only to serve the organization, but also to preserve the cultural heritage of society

b. SAA Code of Ethics for Archivists

The SAA Code of Ethics is "a framework for archivists' behavior" (SAA 2014). Seven areas are discussed: professional relationships, judgment, authenticity, security and protection, access and use, privacy, and trust.

There is an inherent ethical tension associated with the primary purpose of archival services. The archivist is obligated to safeguard and protect materials of lasting value by applying best-practice preservation techniques. Ethical conflicts arise due to the concomitant responsibility to promote access to these materials by ensuring that only reasonable restrictions be placed on their use. It is a natural temptation for an archivist to do everything possible to preserve the human record, but archives are of little value if they cannot be consulted relatively easily. The archivist is ethically bound to minimize restrictions and to create the necessary finding aids so that the collection can be used. This tension is especially challenging when the works are rare and fragile.

Another ethical consideration in archival work is the issue of privacy related to the donation of letters and correspondence. Sometimes those who wrote the letters or who are the subject of the correspondence might not know that this material was donated. Archivists are exhorted to protect the privacy of such individuals, especially if they had no control over the provision of such records to the archives. This highlights the careful balancing of interests required of archivists who must consider both the rights of access to information and the protection of the privacy of others.

Finally, archivists often find themselves in competition with other archives to obtain certain materials. Archivists are expected to act ethically in procuring materials, accurately representing the capacity of the archive to store and maintain them. Similarly, archivists must avoid competition that might work against preservation of the materials, and they should not attempt to appropriate records already archived in other organizations.

IV. SUMMARY

Although organizations have a significant responsibility to promote ethical behavior, in the final analysis, ethical conduct rests first and foremost on individual behavior. Each of us, as professionals, is an individual moral agent, and we do not give up our ethical obligations when we become employees. The ethical codes of the profession are helpful, although sometimes they do fail us with their lack of specificity. Others have restated or supplemented these codes with additional principles (Baker 1992; Rubin and Froehlich 1996). For example, Froehlich (1992) offered the following five principles: minimize harm, respect the autonomy of others, act justly and fairly, seek social harmony, and comport with organizational, professional, and public trust. In general, the most basic principles for ethical conduct for LIS professionals would include the following:

- Promote open, unbiased access to information;
- Maintain professional skills and knowledge;
- Act honestly with colleagues and consumers of information;

- Respect the privacy and confidentiality of others; and
- Provide the best service possible.

No matter which principles or codes we examine, it is clear that LIS professionals embrace the notion that our duties and obligations extend far beyond just doing a job. Our professional behavior follows from fundamental principles of respect for individuals and the desire to benefit both the organization and the society. These precepts are not new; on the contrary, they are quite old.

Ethical situations arise in many contexts during the execution of our professional responsibilities. The resulting ethical deliberations are complex and often require a balancing of many interests and considerations: individual, organizational, and societal. If LIS professionals abide by the fundamental ethical tenets expressed in our Code of Ethics and the ALA Bill of Rights, the mission and values that underlie American libraries can be preserved and sustained. Although it might not be possible to find one statement that encompasses all the ethical obligations of LIS professionals, the American Library Association promulgated a statement titled "Libraries: An American Value" (ALA 1999) (figure 10.5) that goes a good way toward accomplishing this goal and could easily be adapted to a variety of information settings.

FIGURE 10.5
Libraries: An American Value

Libraries in America are cornerstones of the communities they serve. Free access to the books, ideas, resources, and information in America's libraries is imperative for education, employment, enjoyment, and self-government.

Libraries are a legacy to each generation, offering the heritage of the past and the promise of the future. To ensure that libraries flourish and have the freedom to promote and protect the public good in the twenty-first century, we believe certain principles must be guaranteed.

To that end, we affirm this contract with the people we serve:

- We defend the constitutional rights of all individuals, including children and teenagers, to use the library's resources and services.

- We value our nation's diversity and strive to reflect that diversity by providing a full spectrum of resources and services to the communities we serve.

- We affirm the responsibility and the right of all parents and guardians to guide their own children's use of the library and its resources and services.

(cont.)

FIGURE 10.5
Libraries: An American Value (cont.)

- We connect people and ideas by helping each person select from and effectively use the library's resources.
- We protect each individual's privacy and confidentiality in the use of library resources and services.
- We protect the rights of individuals to express their opinions about library resources and services.
- We celebrate and preserve our democratic society by making available the widest possible range of viewpoints, opinions, and ideas so that all individuals have the opportunity to become lifelong learners—informed, literate, educated, and culturally enriched.

Change is constant, but these principles transcend change and endure in a dynamic technological, social, and political environment.

By embracing these principles, libraries in the United States can contribute to a future that values and protects freedom of speech in a world that celebrates both our similarities and our differences, respects individuals and their beliefs, and holds all persons truly equal and free.

Adopted February 3, 1999, by the Council of the American Library Association.

NOTE

I am indebted to Dr. Thomas Froehlich, Kent State University, for many discussions on the ethical factors that affect deliberations in library and information science. The factors presented here were a product of those discussions.

REFERENCES

American Library Association. 1995. "Code of Ethics." www.ala.org.

———. 2009. "Libraries: An American Value." www.ala.org.

———. 2000. "Librarianship and Information Service: A Statement on Core Values." Fifth draft, April 28, 2000. www.pla.org/ala/educationcareers/education/1stcongressonpro/1stcongressstatement.cfm.

———. 2004. "Core Values of Librarianship." www.ala.org/ala/aboutala/offices/oif/statementspols/corevaluesstatement/corevalues.cfm.

———. 2010. *Intellectual Freedom Manual*. Chicago: ALA.

———. 2013. "Questions and Answers on Ethics and Social Media." www.ala.org/advocacy/proethics/questions-and-answers-ethics-and-social-media.

ASIS&T (American Society for Information Science and Technology). 1994. "ASIS&T Professional Guidelines." www.asis.org/AboutASIS/professional-guidelines.html.

———. 2014. "ASIS&T Professional Guidelines." www.asis.org/AboutASIS/professional-guidelines.html.

Aulisio, George J. 2013. "Copyright in Light of Ethics." *Reference Services Review* 41: 566–575.

Baker, Sharon L. 1992. "Needed: An Ethical Code for Library Administrators." *Journal of Library Administration* 16: 1–17.

Bierbaum, Esther Green. 1994. "Searching for the Human Good: Some Suggestions for a Code of Ethics for Technical Services." *Technical Services Quarterly* 11: 1–18.

Buchanan, Elizabeth A. 2004. "Ethics in Library and Information Science: What Are We Teaching?" *Journal of Information Ethics* 13 (spring): 51–60.

Buschman, John. 2000. "Editorial: Core Wars." Progressive Librarian 17 (summer). www.libr.org/PL/17_Editorial.html.

Butler, Pierce. 1951. "Librarianship as a Profession." *Library Quarterly* 21 (October): 235–247.

Cihak, Herbert E., and Joan S. Howland. 2012. "Temptations of the Sirens: Ethical Issues in Libraries." *Law Library Journal* 104: 531–551.

Diamond, Randy, and Martha Dragich. 2001. "Professionalism in Librarianship: Shifting the Focus from Malpractice to Good Practice." *Library Trends* 49 (winter): 395–414.

Dowd, Robert. 1989. "I Want to Find Out How to Freebase Cocaine; or Yet Another Unobtrusive Test of Reference Performance." *Reference Librarian* 25–26: 483–493.

DuMont, Rosemary. 1991. "Ethics in Librarianship: A Management Model." *Library Trends* 40 (fall): 201–215.

Estabrook, Leigh. 1982. "The Library as a Socialist Institution in a Capitalist Environment." In *The Economics of Information*, edited by Jana Varlys. Jefferson, NC: McFarland, 3–16.

Finks, Lee W. 1991. "Librarianship Needs a New Code of Professional Ethics." *American Libraries* 22 (January): 84–92.

Foskett, D. J. 1962. "The Creed of a Librarian: No Politics, No Religion, No Morals." Paper given at North Western Group, Reference, Special, and Information Section, Manchester Literary and Philosophical Society House, Manchester, England, March 27, 1962.

Foster, Catherine, and David McMenemy. 2012. "Do Librarians Have a Shared Set of Values? A Comparative Study of 36 Codes of Ethics Based on Gorman's *Enduring Values*." *Journal of Librarianship and Information Science* 44: 249–262.

Froehlich, Thomas J. 1992. "Ethical Considerations of Information Professionals." *Annual Review of Information Science and Technology* (ARIST) 27: 292.

Garrison, Dee. 1972–1973. "The Tender Technicians: The Feminization of Public Librarianship." *Journal of Social History* 6 (winter): 131–156.

Gorman, Michael. 1995. "Five New Laws of Librarianship." *American Libraries* 26 (September): 784–785.

———. 2014. *Our Enduring Values: Librarianship in the 21st Century.* 2nd ed. (Forthcoming) (Typescript) Chicago: ALA.

Gray, Kate. 2012. "Stealing from the Rich to Entertain the Poor? A Survey of Literature on the Ethics of Digital Piracy." *The Serials Librarian* 63: 288–295.

Green, Russell G., and Susan L. Thomas. 1986. "The Immediate Effects of Media Violence on Behavior." *Journal of Social Issues* 42: 7–27.

Harris, Michael. 1973. "The Purpose of the American Public Library." *Library Journal* 98 (September 15): 2509–2514.

Hauptman, Robert. 1976. "Professionalism or Culpability? An Experiment in Ethics." *Wilson Library Bulletin* 50: 626–627.

———. 2001. "Technological Implementations and Ethical Failures." *Library Trends* 49 (winter): 433–440.

Hoffman, Kathy. 2005. "Professional Ethics and Librarianship." *Texas Library Journal* (fall): 96–98.

Isaacson, David. 2004. "Is the Correct Answer the Right One?" *Journal of Information Ethics* 13 (spring): 14–18.

Jacob, Christian. 2002. "Gathering Memory: Thoughts on the History of Libraries." *Diogenes* 49 (April): 41–57.

Koehler, Wallace. 2002. "Trends of Library Associations and Ethics in the US." In *The Ethics of Librarianship: An International Survey*, edited by Robert Vaagan. IFLA Publications 101. Munich: K. G. Saur, 323–336.

———. 2003. "Professional Values and Ethics as Defined by 'The LIS Discipline.'" *Journal of Education for Library and Information Science* 44 (spring): 99–112.

Koehler, Wallace, and Michael Pemberton. 2000. "A Search for Core Values: Towards a Model Code of Ethics for Information Professionals." *Journal of Information Ethics* 9: 26–54.

Lindsey, Jonathan A., and Ann E. Prentice. 1985. *Professional Ethics and Librarians.* Phoenix, AZ: Oryx.

McCook, Kathleen de la Peña. 2001. "Social Justice, Personalism, and the Practice of Librarianship." *Catholic Library World* 72 (December): 80–84.

McKinzie, Steve. 2002. "For Ethical Reference, Pare the Paraprofessionals." *American Libraries* 33 (October): 42.

Nardini, Robert F. 2001. "A Search for Meaning: American Library Metaphors, 1876–1926." *The Library Quarterly* 71 (April): 111–140.

Neill, Sam D. 1992. "Why Books?" *Public Library Quarterly* 12: 19–28.

Ranganathan, S. R. 1963. *The Five Laws of Library Science.* New York: Asia, 1963. First published 1931.

Rawls, John. 1958. "Justice as Fairness." *Philosophical Review* 67: 164–194.

Rubin, Richard. 1990. *Human Resources Management in Libraries: Theory and Practice.* New York: Neal-Schuman.

Rubin, Richard E. 1995. "Moral Distancing and the Use of Information Technologies: The Seven Temptations." In *Proceedings of the Ethics in the Computer Age Conference, November 11–13, 1994.* New York: Association for Computing Machinery.

Rubin, Richard E., and Thomas J. Froehlich. 1996. "Ethical Aspects of Library and Information Science." *Encyclopedia of Library and Information Science.* Vol. 58 (Supplement). New York: Marcel Dekker, 33–52.

SAA (Society of American Archivists). 2014. "SAA Core Values Statement and Code of Ethics." www2.archivists.org/statements/saa-c0re-values-statement-and-code-of-ethics.

Smith, Martha M. 1993a. "Editorial." *North Carolina Libraries* 51 (spring): 4.

———. 1993b. "Information Ethics: Freedom, Democracy, Responsibility." *North Carolina Libraries* 51 (spring): 6–8.

Spaulding, Helen H. 2002. "New Realities, New Relationships." www.ala.org/ala/mgrps/divs/acrl/publications/crlnews/2002/sep/newrealities.cfm.

Sturgeon, Roy L. 2007. "Laying Down the Law: ALA's Ethics Codes." *American Libraries* 38 (November): 56–57.

Swan, John. 1986. "Untruth or Consequences." *Library Journal* 111 (July 1): 44–52.

Trushina, Irina. 2004. "Freedom of Access: Ethical Dilemmas for Internet Librarians." *Electronic Library* 22: 416–421.

Ulvik, Synnøve, and Gunhild Salvesen. 2007. "Ethical Reference Practice." *New Library World* 108: 342–353.

Wengert, Robert G. 2001. "Some Ethical Aspects of Being an Information Professional." *Library Trends* 49 (winter): 486–509.

Wilkinson, Lane. 2014. "Principlism and the Ethics of Librarianship." *The Reference Librarian* 55: 1–25.

Winter, Michael F. 1988. *The Culture and Control of Expertise: Toward a Sociological Understanding of Librarianship.* Westport, CT: Greenwood.

Wyatt, Anna. 2006. "Do Librarians Have an Ethical Duty to Monitor Library Users' Internet Usage in the Public Library?" *Journal of Information Ethics* 15 (spring): 70–79.

Zimmer, Michael. 2014. "Librarians' Attitudes Regarding Information and Internet Privacy." *The Library Quarterly* 84 (April): 123–151.

SELECTED READINGS: Ethics and Values

Books

Adams, Helen. *Ensuring Intellectual Freedom and Access to Information in the School Library Media Program.* Westport, CT: Libraries Unlimited, 2008.

ALA. *Intellectual Freedom Manual*, 8th ed. Chicago: ALA, 2010.

Buchanan, Elizabeth A., and Kathrine A. Henderson. *Case Studies in Library and Information Science Ethics.* Jefferson, NC: McFarland, 2009.

Gorman, Michael. *Our Enduring Values: Librarianship in the 21st Century.* 2nd ed. Chicago: ALA, 2015.

McMenemy, David, Alan Poulter, and Paul F. Burton. *A Handbook of Ethical Practice: A Practical Guide to Dealing with Ethical Issues in Information and Library Work.* Oxford: Chandos Publishing, 2007.

Preer, Jean. *Library Ethics.* Westport, CT: Libraries Unlimited, 2008.

Articles

Aiken, Julian. "Outdated and Irrelevant?" *American Libraries* 38 (September 2007): 54–56.

Aulisio, George J. "Copyright in Light of Ethics." *Reference Services Review* 41 (2013): 566–575.

Cihak, Herbert E., and Joan S. Howland. "Temptations of the Sirens: Ethical Issues in Libraries." *Law Library Journal* 104: (2012): 531–551.

Crowley, Bill, and Deborah Ginsberg. "Professional Values: Priceless." *American Libraries* 36 (January 2005): 52–55.

Doyle, Tony. "Should Web Sites for Bomb-Making Be Legal?" *Journal of Information Ethics* 13 (spring 2004): 34–37.

Duthe, Fiona. "Libraries and the Ethics of Censorship." *The Australian Library Journal* (August 2010): 86–94.

Finks, Lee W. "What Do We Stand For? Values without Shame." *American Libraries* 20 (1989): 352–356.

Foster. Catherine, and David McMenemy. "Do Librarians Have a Shared Set of Values? A Comparative Study of 36 Codes of Ethics Based on Gorman's *Enduring Values.*" *Journal of Librarianship and Information Science* 44 (2012): 249–262.

Fox, M. J. "Which Ethics? Whose Morality? An Analysis of Ethical Standards for Information Organization." *Knowledge Organization* 39 (2012): 377–383.

Fricke, Martin, Kay Mathiesen, and Don Fallis. "The Ethical Presuppositions behind the Library Bill of Rights." *Library Quarterly* 70 (2000): 468–491.

Gray, Kate. "Stealing from the Rich to Entertain the Poor? A Survey of Literature on the Ethics of Digital Piracy." *The Serials Librarian* 63 (2012): 288–295.

Homan, Philip A. "Library Catalog Notes for 'Bad Books': Ethics vs Responsibilities." *Knowledge Organization* 39 (2012): 347–355.

Houston, Rondal D. "Archival Ethics and the Professionalization of Archival Enterprise." *Journal of Information Ethics* 22 (fall 2013): 46–60.

Koehler, Wallace. "Professional Values and Ethics as Defined by 'The LIS Discipline.'" *Journal of Education for Library and Information Science* 44 (spring 2003): 99–119.

Miltenoff, Plamen, and Robert Hauptman. "Ethical Dilemmas in Libraries: An International Perspective." *Electronic Library* 23 (2005): 664–670.

Trushina, Irina. "Freedom of Access: Ethical Dilemmas for Internet Librarians." *Electronic Library* 22 (2004): 416–421.

Ulvik, Synnøve, and Gunhild Salvesen. "Ethical Reference Practice." *New Library World* 108 (2007): 342–353.

Watstein, Sarah B. "Do Libraries Matter?" *Reference Services Review* 34 (2006): 181–184.

Wengwert, Robert G. "Some Ethical Aspects of Being an Information Professional." *Library Trends* 49 (winter 2001): 486–509.

Wilkinson, Lane. "Principlism and the Ethics of Librarianship." *The Reference Librarian* 55 (2014): 1–25.

Willingham, Taylor L. "Libraries as Civic Agents." *Public Library Quarterly* 27 (2008): 97–110.

Wyatt, Anna. "Do Librarians Have an Ethical Duty to Monitor Library Users' Internet Usage in the Public Library?" *Journal of Information Ethics* 15 (spring 2006): 70–79.

Zaiane, Jane Robertson. "Global Information Ethics in LIS." *Journal of Information Ethics* 20 (fall 2011): 25–41.

Appendix A

Major Library and Information Science Associations and List of Additional Associations

AMERICAN ASSOCIATION OF LAW LIBRARIES (AALL)

The American Association of Law Libraries was established in 1906 to support law libraries and the professional legal community. The association's mission "advances the profession of law librarianship and supports the professional growth of its members through leadership and advocacy in the field of legal information and information policy (aallnet.org)." Today, there are approximately 5,000 members. A wide variety of libraries are represented, including law firms, legal departments, local, state, and federal courts, other government agencies, and law schools. Its core values include

- lifelong learning and intellectual growth
- equitable and permanent public access to legal information
- continuous improvement in access to justice
- community and collaboration
- the essential role of law librarians within their organizations and in a democratic society (aallnet.org)

AALL focuses on three key areas: promoting the role of the law librarian as an essential contributor to the legal profession, advocating for legal and government information policies and promoting private and public goods, and providing high quality education to law librarians and other law information professionals. Continuing education is provided through annual meetings, webinars, a leadership academy, and a management institute. Aside from an executive board, much of the work of AALL is performed by thirty committees focusing on a variety of areas including continuing professional education, copyright, diversity, economic value of law libraries, government policy, leadership development, and legal research. The association publishes *Law Library Journal*, its official publication since its creation in 1906. It also publishes *AALL Spectrum*, a monthly magazine, and the *AALL E-newsletter* (aallnet.org).

AMERICAN LIBRARY ASSOCIATION (ALA)

Founded in 1876, the American Library Association is the oldest and largest library association in the world. Any individual or organization that has an interest in libraries can join. A wide variety of types of libraries participate in ALA membership and activities, including state, public, school, and academic libraries, as well as libraries in government, commerce, the arts, the armed services, hospitals, and prisons. In 2014, the organization had more than 55,300 personal members; the number of members has been slowly declining since 2008 when it reached a peak of nearly 65,000 members. The stated mission of the organization is "to provide leadership for the development, promotion, and improvement of library and information services and the profession of librarianship in order to enhance learning and ensure access to information for all."

The association has identified eight key action areas to which it is devoting substantial energies:

Advocacy for Libraries and the Profession

Diversity

Education and Lifelong Learning

Equitable Access to Information and Library Services

Intellectual Freedom

Literacy

Organizational Excellence

Transforming Libraries

ALA is an impressive bureaucracy with 19 round tables, 11 divisions, 57 state and regional chapters, 25 affiliated organizations, and a headquarters staff of approximately 270 employees. ALA is operated by a council, an executive director, and an executive board. A large number of committees composed primarily of ALA members play a critical role in reflecting the professional and political interests of the association. Round tables focus on such areas as continuing library education, armed forces libraries, ethnic materials, library history, and government documents. Divisions focus on services for children and adults, public libraries, and academic libraries. Standing committees include accreditation of programs of library and information studies, literacy and outreach, pay equity, diversity, development and recruitment, research and statistics, the status of women in librarianship, and membership. The organization also maintains Membership Initiative Groups (MIGs), which consist of ALA members with a common concern or interest in an area of librarianship that falls outside the responsibilities of other designated ALA units. MIGs are intended to be of short-term duration.

The primary political lobbying is effected by the Washington office of the American Library Association. The office monitors political legislation and other activities that could affect the well-being of libraries and attempts to influence legislation to conform to the goals of the ALA.

The association authors many publications, including books and journals focusing on a variety of aspects of the profession. These include *Reference and User Services Quarterly*, a publication of the Reference and User Services Association (RUSA); *Public Libraries*, from the Public Library Association (PLA); *Library Administration and Management*, from the Library Leadership and Management Association (LLAMA); *Young Adult Library Services*, from the Young Adult Library Services Association (YALSA); *Children and Libraries*, from the Association for Library Service to Children (ALSC); *College and Research Libraries*, from the Association of College and Research Libraries (ACRL); and *American Libraries*, the official organ of the American Library Association. Such publications not only provide news and information on library activities, but also serve as sources for published research, analysis, and continuing education in professional practice. The association also holds two major conferences a year: the Midwinter Meeting, which is primarily devoted to committee activities, and the Annual Conference, where there are major program presentations.

AMERICAN SOCIETY FOR INFORMATION SCIENCE AND TECHNOLOGY (ASIS&T)

The American Society for Information Science and Technology was established in 1937 and was originally known as the American Documentation Institute. In 1968 its name was changed to the American Society for Information Science. In

2000 the name was again altered to its current one. ASIS&T was founded in 1937 by the Science Service and the microfilm services of the Bibliofilm Service of the U.S. Department of Agriculture. The money to finance the institute originally came from a grant from the Chemical Foundations, and the purpose of the institute was to produce scientific bibliographies, develop microphotography devices, and generally explore other mechanisms for improving the communication of recorded knowledge. At first, only institutional members were permitted, but in 1952 changes were made to the bylaws of the organization to permit individual membership. Membership consists of approximately 4,000 individuals and 300 institutional members. ASIS&T has twenty-one special interest groups (SIGs), which are designed to bring together members with common interests. For example, there are SIGs on digital libraries, bioinformatics, knowledge management, social informatics, human-computer interaction, arts & humanities, information policy, and library technologies. ASIS&T also has 56 regional and student chapters throughout the United States.

Today, the focus of ASIS&T is on all aspects of the information transfer process, including organization, storage, retrieval, evaluation, and dissemination. Its stated mission is "to advance the information sciences and related applications of information technology by providing focus, opportunity, and support to information professionals and organizations" (www.asis.org). Its membership includes, but is not limited to, computer scientists, linguists, librarians, engineers, medical practitioners, chemists, and educators. The society also functions as an instrument of professional development through conferences, continuing education programs, professional development workshops, and publications. Among its major publications are the *Journal of the American Society for Information Science and Technology*, *Bulletin of the Association for Information Science and Technology*, and *Annual Review of Information Science and Technology*. ASIS&T also publishes its conference proceedings.

ASSOCIATION OF RESEARCH LIBRARIES (ARL)

The Association of Research Libraries was founded in December 1932 as a not-for-profit organization. It is governed by a board of directors, executive director, and a small headquarters staff. Unlike most other library organizations, membership is restricted to North American institutions; many of these are university libraries, although some are major public libraries, special libraries, and national libraries. There are approximately 125 members.

The mission of ARL is as follows:

> The Association of Research Libraries influences the changing environment of scholarly communication and the public policies that affect research libraries and

the diverse communities they serve. ARL pursues this mission by advancing the goals of its member research libraries, providing leadership in public and information policy to the scholarly and higher education communities, fostering the exchange of ideas and expertise, and shaping a future environment that leverages its interests with those of allied organizations. (www.arl.org)

ARL conferences provide a useful opportunity to exchange information on topics related to research libraries' survival. As with other types of libraries, among it "guiding principles" are the protection of intellectual freedom and the promotion of diversity. Similarly, the organization has identified a number of important "focus areas":

- Accessibility
- Copyright and Intellectual Property
- Court Cases
- E-Research
- Federal Funding
- Open Scholarship
- Planning and Visioning
- Privacy, Security and Civil Liberties
- Public Access Policies
- Research Collections
- Scholarly Communication
- Shared Access Research Ecosystem (SHARE)
- Space, Facilities and Services
- Statistics and Assessment
- Telecommunications Policies
- Workforce

In 1970 ARL created the Office of Management Services (OMS)—now known as the Office of Leadership and Management Services (OLMS)—which is intended to improve the leadership and management of human resources and the collections of research and academic libraries. This office collects statistics, prepares reports, and provides training and staff development in a variety of areas of management. Among the major publications of ARL are the *ARL Annual Salary Survey* and the *ARL Statistics Survey*, which produce annual data on research library performance and expenditures for ARL libraries as a whole and for law and medical libraries individually.

INTERNATIONAL FEDERATION OF LIBRARY ASSOCIATIONS AND INSTITUTIONS (IFLA)

The International Federation of Library Associations and Institutions was founded in 1927, primarily to create a place for the leading librarians of Europe and America to meet and discuss contemporary issues of mutual interest. Today it is "the leading international body representing the interest of library and information services and their users. It is the global voice of the library and information profession (ifla.org). It has more than 1,500 members from approximately 150 nations. Membership consists of associations and institutions. It also has corporate partners such as OCLC. It is headquartered in The Hague.

IFLA describes its core values as:

1. the endorsement of the principles of freedom of access to information, ideas and works of imagination and freedom of expression embodied in Article 19 of the Universal Declaration of Human Rights
2. the belief that people, communities and organizations need universal and equitable access to information, ideas and works of imagination for their social, educational, cultural, democratic and economic well-being
3. the conviction that delivery of high quality library and information services helps guarantee that access
4. the commitment to enable all Members of the Federation to engage in, and benefit from, its activities without regard to citizenship, disability, ethnic origin, gender, geographical location, language, political philosophy, race or religion (ifla.org).

Many of the major American library associations are members, including ALA, the Association of Research Libraries, and the American Association of Law Libraries (AALL). IFLA is organized into five divisions: Library Collections, Library Services, Library Types, Regions, and Support for the Profession. In addition, much of the work is done by IFLA Sections of which there are 43. Examples of sections include Academic and Research Libraries, Classification and Indexing, Education and Training, Government Libraries, Information Technology, Libraries for Children and Young Adults, Literacy and Reading, Public Libraries. There are also fifteen special interest groups (SIGS) in such areas as Environment Sustainability, Indigenous Matters, Semantic Web, and Women, Information and Libraries.

IFLA has a variety of programs that represent the main interests of the association. They include the Action for Development through Libraries Programme (ALP), IFLA UNIMARC, IFLA Committee on Standards, Freedom of Access to

Information and Freedom of Expression (FAIFE), and the Committee on Copyright and other Legal Matters (CLM). Among their current initiatives are those relating to fostering digital information access, strengthening the voice of regional, national, and international library associations, promoting sustainable development, and promoting cultural heritage by protecting endangered collections.

IFLA issues a variety of monographs, professional reports, newsletters, and periodicals including *IFLA Journal*.

THE MEDICAL LIBRARY ASSOCIATION (MLA)

The Medical Library Association was founded in 1898 as the Association of Medical Librarians. It is the second oldest national library association in the United States and serves as the primary professional association for health sciences librarians in the United States and Canada. The purpose of the MLA is to promote the growth and development of medical libraries, to serve as an advocate for health information professionals, and to support the exchange of medical literature among its members. MLA also attempts to promote educational and professional growth among health sciences librarians and provides a considerable number of continuing education programs to meet this purpose.

There are more than 3,600 individual members, 1,100 institutional members, and a growing corporate membership. As of 2015, MLA had thirteen geographic regional chapters and twenty-four special interest groups (SIGs), including those for African-American Medical Librarians, Complementary and Alternative Medicine, Mental Health, Molecular Biology and Genomics, Pediatric Libraries, and Vision Science. There are also twenty-two sections, including Cancer Librarians, Collection Development, Corporate Information Services, Hospital Libraries, Medical Informatics, Public Health/Public Administration, Public Services, and Technical Services (www.mlanet.org).

In contrast to most other forms of librarianship, medical librarians can be credentialed. Credentialing is performed through the Academy of Health Information Professionals (AHIP). AHIP is a professional development program of MLA and was created in 1949. Credentialing differs from certification in that it is more than acquiring training and education; credentialing consists of three areas: academic preparation, professional experience, and professional accomplishment. It is recognition of achievement in knowledge, experience, and professional development. The association also produces monographic and periodical publications, including the *Journal of the Medical Library Association* (*JMLA*) and *MLA News*.

SPECIAL LIBRARIES ASSOCIATION (SLA)

The Special Libraries Association is a not-for-profit corporation founded in 1909 as a response to a growing number of special libraries. It is an international association of librarians who work in special libraries serving such areas as business, industry, research, government, universities, and cultural institutions. They are focused on the strategic use of information. There are more than 9,000 members. SLA has fifty-six regional chapters and twenty-six divisions representing various subject fields and interests, including biomedical and life sciences, business and finance, competitive intelligence, engineering, government information, legal, petroleum and energy resources, pharmaceuticals, social science, and transportation. There are also numerous caucuses, which are information groups that foster discussion and interaction among members with common interests. Caucus areas include archives and preservation, information futurists, natural history, and user experience. SLA is sustained by five core values: leadership, service, innovation and continuous learning, results and accountability, and collaboration and partnering.

SLA is engaged in a variety of activities to support special libraries, including providing continuing education programs and advocacy for special librarians within special libraries. The Association is also engaged in political advocacy externally regarding national and international information policies. The monthly magazine of SLA is *Information Outlook*, which serves as a major professional continuing education tool for special librarians (sla.org).

List of Additional Library Associations or Closely Related Organizations

A. General

American Indian Library Association
Canadian Library Association
Council on Library Resources
Friends of Libraries USA
Information Industry Association
National Information Standards Organization
National Librarians Association

B. Archives/Bibliographical

Bibliographical Society of America
Society of American Archivists

Arts

American Film and Video Association (formerly the Educational Film Library Association)

Art Libraries Society of North America

Music Library Association

Theatre Library Association

Asian American

Asian/Pacific American Librarians Association

Chinese-American Library Association

Government/Federal

Association for Federal Information Resources Management

Chief Officers of State Library Agencies

Federal Library and Information Center Committee

National Association of Government Archives and Records Administrators

Law

American Association of Law Libraries

Library Education

Association for Library and Information Science Education

Religion

American Theological Library Association

Association of Christian Librarians

Association of Jewish Libraries

Catholic Library Association

Church and Synagogue Library Association

Lutheran Church Library Association

Business/Science

Association of Academic Health Sciences

Library Directors Patent and Trademark Depository

Library Association Society for Competitive Intelligence Professionals

Visual Images

Association for Information and Image Management

Association of Visual Science Librarians

Appendix B

List of ALA-Accredited Programs

ALA-ACCREDITED PROGRAMS

Alabama

University of Alabama

Arizona

University of Arizona

California

University of California, Los Angeles
San José State University

Colorado

University of Denver

District of Columbia

The Catholic University of America

Florida

Florida State University
University of South Florida

Georgia

Valdosta State University

Hawaii

University of Hawaii

Illinois

Dominican University
University of Illinois,
    Urbana–Champaign

(As of July 2014)

Source: American Library Association, Office of Accreditation

Indiana

Indiana University

Iowa

University of Iowa

Kansas

Emporia State University

Kentucky

University of Kentucky

Louisiana

Louisiana State University

Maryland

University of Maryland

Massachusetts

Simmons College

Michigan

University of Michigan
Wayne State University

Minnesota

St. Catherine University

Mississippi

University of Southern Mississippi

Missouri

University of Missouri

New Jersey

Rutgers, The State University of New
Jersey

New York

University at Albany, State University of
New York
University at Buffalo, State University
of New York
Long Island University
Pratt Institute
Queens College
St. John's University
Syracuse University

North Carolina

North Carolina Central University
University of North Carolina at Chapel
Hill
University of North Carolina
at Greensboro

Ohio

Kent State University

Oklahoma

University of Oklahoma

Pennsylvania

Clarion University of Pennsylvania
Drexel University
University of Pittsburgh

Puerto Rico

University of Puerto Rico

Rhode Island

University of Rhode Island

South Carolina

University of South Carolina

Tennessee

University of Tennessee

Texas

University of North Texas
University of Texas at Austin
Texas Woman's University

Washington

University of Washington

Wisconsin

University of Wisconsin–Madison
University of Wisconsin–Milwaukee

Alberta

University of Alberta

British Columbia

University of British Columbia

Nova Scotia

Dalhousie University

Ontario

University of Ottawa
University of Toronto
University of Western Ontario

Quebec

McGill University
Université de Montréal

Appendix C

Standards for Accreditation of Master's Programs in Library and Information Studies

INTRODUCTION

Purpose of Accreditation

Accreditation in higher education is defined as a collegial process based on self- and peer assessment for public accountability and improvement of academic quality.[1]

Accreditation serves to ensure educational quality, judged in terms of demonstrated results in supporting the educational development of students. Judgments are made by carefully vetted, unbiased practitioners and faculty professionals at the expert level.

These experts judge how well:

- Accreditation standards are met (and can continue to be met) by the institution or program;
- Elements such as curriculum, evaluation methods, faculty, resources and admission requirements are suited to the overall mission and level of program offerings and objectives;
- Students can be expected to fulfill the knowledge and skills requirements for completion of their programs.[2]

Adopted by approval of the Council of the American Library Association, February 2, 2015
Committee on Accreditation of the American Library Association

Authority and Responsibilities of the ALA Committee on Accreditation

The Council of the American Library Association (ALA) has designated the Committee on Accreditation "to be responsible for the execution of the accreditation program of the ALA and to develop and formulate standards of education . . ."[3] for graduate programs of library and information studies leading to a master's degree. The American Library Association Committee on Accreditation is recognized by the Council for Higher Education Accreditation as the accrediting agency for these programs.[4]

The Committee on Accreditation protects the public interest and provides guidance for educators. Prospective students, employers recruiting professional staff, and the general public concerned about the quality of library and information services have the right to know whether a given program of education is of good standing. By identifying those programs meeting recognized standards, the Committee offers a means of quality control in the professional staffing of library and information services.

The Committee on Accreditation examines the evidence presented for each of the Standards; however, its final judgment is concerned with the totality of the accomplishment and the environment for learning. The decision regarding accreditation is approached from an evaluation of this totality rather than from a consideration of isolated particulars. Thus, failure to meet any particular component of a standard may not result in failure to meet that standard. Similarly, failure to meet a single standard may not result in failure to achieve accredited status for a program.

Evaluators of a program for accreditation purposes are vetted for bias, formally oriented, experienced, and capable.

Scope of Standards

These Standards are limited in their application to the assessment of graduate programs of library and information studies that lead to a master's degree. As a prerequisite to accreditation, the institution in which a program resides must be accredited by its appropriate accrediting agency.

The phrase "library and information studies" is understood to be concerned with recordable information and knowledge, and the services and technologies to facilitate their management and use. Library and information studies encompasses information and knowledge creation, communication, identification, selection, acquisition, organization and description, storage and retrieval, preservation, analysis, interpretation, evaluation, synthesis, dissemination, and management. This definition incorporates a field of professional practice and associated areas of study and research, regardless of a degree's name.

A unit's mission is relevant to master's program review; when the unit offers other educational programs, the contribution of those programs is also relevant. A unit may seek accreditation for more than one graduate program of education in library and information studies leading to a master's degree; when that is done, the goals, objectives, and learning outcomes of each program and their interrelationships are to be presented.

Terminology within the Standards

The academic unit that provides graduate education in library and information studies may be organized as an autonomous college within its university, as a department in a college, or otherwise, as appropriate within the institution. Within the Standards, the term "program" refers to an organization of people and educational experiences that comprise the degree.

The term "research" as used in the Standards is understood to be (1) broad in its inclusiveness of scholarly activities of a wide variety; and (2) inclusive of communication of results through appropriate means.

When the term "faculty" is used, the Standard applies to the faculty as a whole, including both full-time faculty members (tenured/tenure-track and non-tenure-track) and part-time faculty members. Reference to a subset of the faculty is designated by referring specifically to "full-time" or "part-time" faculty members, or to "each" or "individual" faculty members.

Systematic planning is an ongoing, active, broad-based approach to (a) continuous review and revision of a program's vision, mission, goals, objectives, and learning outcomes; (b) assessment of attainment of goals, objectives, and learning outcomes; (c) realignment and redesign of core activities in response to the results of assessment; and (d) communication of planning policies and processes, assessment activities, and results of assessment to program constituents. Effective broad-based, systematic planning requires engagement of the program's constituents and thorough and open documentation of those activities that constitute planning.

A glossary of accreditation terminology is available at the ALA Office for Accreditation website, www.ala.org/accreditedprograms/standards/glossary.

Nature of the Standards

These Standards identify the indispensable components of library and information studies programs while recognizing programs' rights and obligations regarding initiative, experimentation, innovation, and individual programmatic differences. The Standards are indicative, not prescriptive, with the intent to foster excellence through a program's development of criteria for evaluating effectiveness, developing and applying qualitative and quantitative measures of these criteria, analyzing data from measurements, and applying analysis to program improvement.

The Standards stress innovation, and encourage programs to take an active role in and concern for future developments and growth in the field.

The nature of a demonstrably diverse society is referenced throughout the Standards because of the desire to recognize diversity, defined in the broadest terms, when framing goals and objectives, designing curricula, and selecting and retaining faculty and students.

The requirements of these Standards apply regardless of forms or locations of delivery of a program.

Philosophy of Program Review

The Committee on Accreditation determines the eligibility of a program for accredited status on the basis of evidence presented by a program and by the report of a visiting external review panel. The evidence supplied by the program in support of the Standards is evaluated against the statement of the program's mission and its program goals and objectives. A program's evidence is evaluated by trained, experienced, and capable evaluators.

Program goals and objectives are fundamental to all aspects of master's degree programs and form the basis on which educational programs are to be developed and upon which they are evaluated. Program goals and objectives are required to reflect and support student learning outcomes and the achievement of these outcomes.

This update to the 2008 *Standards* resulted from a six-year public review process via weblog, direct surveying of practitioners and LIS faculty, and online and open meetings at conference venues.

This document supersedes the 2008 *Standards for Accreditation*. It is based upon a synthesis of the views solicited during the review and revision process of 2008–2014.

The *Accreditation Process, Policies and Procedures* (AP3) document guides the accreditation process. Both the *Standards* and AP3 are available online from the Office for Accreditation website, www.ala.org/offices/accreditation. Assistance in obtaining materials used by the Committee on Accreditation (COA) is provided by the Office for Accreditation. These materials consist of documents used in the accreditation process, as well as educational policy statements developed by relevant professional organizations that can be used to inform the design and evaluation of a master's degree program.

NOTES

1. CHEA Recognition of Accrediting Organizations, Policy and Procedures (1998, revised June 28, 2010); Appendix A: Accreditation Defined. Retrieved March 28, 2014, http://chea .org/pdf/Recognition_Policy-June_28_2010-FINAL.pdf.
2. Association of Specialized and Professional Accreditors (ASPA) (2013). "Quick Reference: Standards, Outcomes and Quality." Retrieved March 24, 2014, http://www.aspa-usa.org/ system/files/inserts/ASPA_Standards_Jun12.pdf.
3. *American Library Association Handbook of Organization.* (Chicago, IL: ALA 2013).
4. The Council for Higher Education Accreditation (CHEA) is a national recognizing agency of higher education accrediting bodies that emerged from the dissolution of the Council on Postsecondary Accreditation (COPA). ALA discontinued U.S. Department of Education recognition review when the 1992 Higher Education Act limited the scope of recognition to only those agencies whose accreditation plays a "gatekeeping role" to establish eligibility for federal funding.

STANDARD I: SYSTEMATIC PLANNING

I.1   A program's mission and goals, both administrative and educational, are pursued, and its program objectives achieved, through implementation of an ongoing, broad-based, systematic planning process that involves the constituencies that a program seeks to serve. Elements of systematic planning include:

I.1.1   Continuous review and revision of a program's vision, mission, goals, objectives, and student learning outcomes;

I.1.2   Assessment of attainment of program goals, program objectives, and student learning outcomes;

I.1.3   Improvements to the program based on analysis of assessment data;

I.1.4   Communication of planning policies and processes to program constituents. The program has a written mission statement and a written strategic or long-range plan that provides vision and direction for its future, identifies needs and resources for its mission and goals, and is supported by university administration. The program's goals and objectives are consistent with the values of the parent institution and the culture and mission of the program and foster quality education.

I.2   Clearly defined student learning outcomes are a critical part of a program's goals. These outcomes describe what students are expected to know and be able to do by the time of graduation. They enable a faculty to arrive at a common understanding of the expectations for student learning and to achieve consistency across the curriculum. Student learning outcomes reflect the entirety of the learning experience to which students have been exposed. Student learning outcomes address:

    I.2.1   The essential character of the field of library and information studies;

    I.2.2   The philosophy, principles, and ethics of the field;

    I.2.3   Appropriate principles of specialization identified in applicable policy statements and documents of relevant professional organizations;

    I.2.4   The importance of research to the advancement of the field's knowledge base;

    I.2.5   The symbiotic relationship of library and information studies with other fields;

    I.2.6   The role of library and information services in a diverse global society, including the role of serving the needs of underserved groups;

    I.2.7   The role of library and information services in a rapidly changing technological society;

    I.2.8   The needs of the constituencies that a program seeks to serve.

I.3   Program goals and objectives incorporate the value of teaching and service to the field.

I.4   Within the context of these Standards each program is judged on the extent to which it attains its objectives. In accord with the mission of the program, clearly defined, publicly stated, and regularly reviewed program goals and objectives form the essential frame of reference for meaningful external and internal evaluation.

    1.4.1   The evaluation of program goals and objectives involves those served: students, faculty, employers, alumni, and other constituents.

1.5   The program has explicit, documented evidence of its ongoing decision-making processes and the data to substantiate the evaluation of the program's success in achieving its mission, goals and objectives.

1.6   The program demonstrates how the results of the evaluation are systematically used to improve the program and to plan for the future.

STANDARD II: CURRICULUM

II.1 The curriculum is based on goals and objectives, and evolves in response to an ongoing systematic planning process involving representation from all constituencies. Within this general framework, the curriculum provides, through a variety of educational experiences, for the study of theory, principles, practice, and legal and ethical issues and values necessary for the provision of service in libraries and information agencies and in other contexts. The curriculum is revised regularly to keep it current.

II.2 The curriculum is concerned with information resources and the services and technologies to facilitate their management and use. Within this overarching concept, the curriculum of library and information studies encompasses information and knowledge creation, communication, identification, selection, acquisition, organization and description, storage and retrieval, preservation and curation, analysis, interpretation, evaluation, synthesis, dissemination, use and users, and management of human and information resources.

The curriculum

II.2.1 Fosters development of library and information professionals who will assume a leadership role in providing services and collections appropriate for the communities that are served;

II.2.2 Emphasizes an evolving body of knowledge that reflects the findings of basic and applied research from relevant fields;

II.2.3 Integrates technology and the theories that underpin its design, application, and use;

II.2.4 Responds to the needs of a diverse and global society, including the needs of underserved groups;

II.2.5 Provides direction for future development of a rapidly changing field;

II.2.6 Promotes commitment to continuous professional development and lifelong learning, including the skills and competencies that are needed for the practitioner of the future.

II.3 The curriculum provides the opportunity for students to construct coherent programs of study that allow individual needs, goals, and aspirations to be met within the context of program requirements established by the school and that will foster the attainment of student learning outcomes. The curriculum includes as appropriate cooperative degree programs, interdisciplinary coursework and research, experiential opportunities, and other similar activities. Course content and sequence relationships within the curriculum are evident.

II.4   Design of general and specialized curricula takes into account the statements of knowledge and competencies developed by relevant professional organizations.

II.5   Procedures for the continual evaluation of the curriculum are established with input not only from faculty but also representatives from those served. The curriculum is continually evaluated with input not only from faculty, but also representatives from those served including students, employers, alumni, and other constituents. Curricular evaluation is used for ongoing appraisal and to make improvements. Evaluation of the curriculum includes assessment of students' achievements.

II.6   The program has explicit, documented evidence of its ongoing decision-making processes and the data to substantiate the evaluation of the curriculum.

II.7   The program demonstrates how the results of the evaluation of the curriculum are systematically used to improve the program and to plan for the future.

STANDARD III: FACULTY

III.1   The program has a faculty capable of accomplishing program objectives. Full-time faculty members (tenured/tenure-track and non-tenure-track) are qualified for appointment to the graduate faculty within the parent institution. The full-time faculty are sufficient in number and in diversity of specialties to carry out the major share of the teaching, research, and service activities required for a program, wherever and however delivered. Part-time faculty, when appointed, balance and complement the competencies of the full-time tenured/tenure-track and non-tenure-track faculty and are integral to the program. Particularly in the teaching of specialties that are not represented in the expertise of the full-time faculty, part-time faculty enrich the quality and diversity of a program.

III.2   The program demonstrates the high priority it attaches to teaching, research, and service by its appointments and promotions; by encouragement of excellence in teaching, research, and service; and through provision of a stimulating learning and research environment.

III.3   The program has policies to recruit and retain faculty from diverse backgrounds. Explicit and equitable faculty personnel policies and procedures are published, accessible, and implemented.

III.4 The qualifications of each faculty member include competence in designated teaching areas, technological skills and knowledge as appropriate, effectiveness in teaching, and active participation in relevant organizations.

III.5 For each full-time faculty member, the qualifications include a sustained record of accomplishment in research or other appropriate scholarship (such as creative and professional activities) that contribute to the knowledge base of the field and to their professional development.

III.6 The faculty hold advanced degrees from a variety of academic institutions. The faculty evidence diversity of backgrounds, ability to conduct research in the field, and specialized knowledge covering program content. In addition, they demonstrate skill in academic planning and assessment, have a substantial and pertinent body of relevant experience, interact with faculty of other disciplines, and maintain close and continuing liaison with the field. The faculty nurture an intellectual environment that enhances the accomplishment of program objectives.

III.7 Faculty assignments relate to the needs of a program and to the competencies of individual faculty members. These assignments assure that the quality of instruction is maintained throughout the year and take into account the time needed by the faculty for teaching, student counseling, research, professional development, and institutional and professional service.

III.8 Procedures are established for systematic evaluation of all faculty; evaluation considers accomplishment and innovation in the areas of teaching, research, and service. Within applicable institutional policies, faculty, students, and others are involved in the evaluation process.

III.9 The program has explicit, documented evidence of its ongoing decision-making processes and the data to substantiate the evaluation of the faculty.

III.10 The program demonstrates how the results of the evaluation of faculty are systematically used to improve the program and to plan for the future.

STANDARD IV: STUDENTS

IV.1 The program formulates recruitment, admission, retention, financial aid, career services, and other academic and administrative policies for students that are consistent with the program's mission and program goals and objectives. These policies include the needs and values of the constituencies served by a program. The program has policies to recruit and retain students who reflect the diversity of North America's communities. The composition of the student body is such that it fosters a learning environment consistent with the program's mission and program goals and objectives.

IV.2   Current, accurate, and easily accessible information about the program is available to students and the general public. This information includes documentation of progress toward achievement of program goals and objectives, descriptions of curricula, information on faculty, admission requirements, availability of financial aid, criteria for evaluating student performance, assistance with placement, and other policies and procedures. The program demonstrates that it has procedures to support these policies.

IV.3   Standards for admission are applied consistently. Students admitted to a program have earned a bachelor's degree from an accredited institution; the policies and procedures for waiving any admission standard or academic prerequisite are stated clearly and applied consistently. Assessment of an application is based on a combined evaluation of academic, intellectual, and other qualifications as they relate to the constituencies served by a program, a program's goals and objectives, and the career objectives of the individual. Within the framework of institutional policy and programs, the admission policy for a program ensures that applicants possess sufficient interest, aptitude, and qualifications to enable successful completion of a program and subsequent contribution to the field.

IV.4   Students construct a coherent plan of study that allows individual needs, goals, and aspirations to be met within the context of requirements established by the program. Students receive systematic, multifaceted evaluation of their achievements. Students have access to continuing opportunities for guidance, counseling, and placement assistance.

IV.5   The program provides an environment that fosters student participation in the definition and determination of the total learning experience. Students are provided with opportunities to:

IV.5.1 Participate in the formulation, modification, and implementation of policies affecting academic and student affairs;

IV.5.2 Participate in research;

IV.5.3 Receive academic and career advisement and consultation;

IV.5.4 Receive support services as needed;

IV.5.5 Form student organizations;

IV.5.6 Participate in professional organizations.

IV.6 The program applies the results of evaluation of student achievement to program development. Procedures are established for systematic evaluation of the extent to which a program's academic and administrative policies and activities regarding students are accomplishing its objectives. Within applicable institutional policies, faculty, students, staff, and others are involved in the evaluation process.

IV.7 The program has explicit, documented evidence of its ongoing decision-making processes and the data to substantiate the evaluation of student learning outcomes, using appropriate direct and indirect measures as well as individual student learning, using appropriate direct and indirect measures.

IV.8 The program demonstrates how the results of the evaluation of student learning outcomes and individual student learning are systematically used to improve the program and to plan for the future.

STANDARD V: ADMINISTRATION, FINANCES, AND RESOURCES

V.1 The program is an integral yet distinctive academic unit within the institution. As such, it has the administrative infrastructure, financial support, and resources to ensure that its goals and objectives can be accomplished. Its autonomy is sufficient to assure that the intellectual content of its program, the selection and promotion of its faculty, and the selection of its students are determined by the program within the general guidelines of the institution. The parent institution provides both administrative support and the resources needed for the attainment of program objectives.

V.2 The program's faculty, staff, and students have the same opportunities for representation on the institution's advisory or policy-making bodies as do those of comparable units throughout the institution. Administrative relationships with other academic units enhance the intellectual environment and support interdisciplinary interaction; further, these administrative relationships encourage participation in the life of the parent institution. Decisions regarding funding and resource allocation for the program are made on the same basis as for comparable academic units within the institution.

V.3 The administrative head of a program has title, salary, status, and authority comparable to heads of similar units in the parent institution. In addition to academic qualifications comparable to those required of the faculty, the administrative head has leadership skills, administrative ability, experience, and understanding of developments in the field and in the academic environment needed to fulfill the responsibilities of the position.

V.4 The program's administrative head nurtures an environment that enhances the pursuit of the mission and program goals and the accomplishment of its program objectives; that environment also encourages faculty and student interaction with other academic units and promotes the socialization of students into the field.

V.5 The program's administrative and other staff support the administrative head and faculty in the performance of their responsibilities. The staff contributes to the fulfillment of the program's mission, goals, and objectives. Within its institutional framework decision-making processes are determined mutually by the administrative head and the faculty, who regularly evaluate these processes and use the results.

V.6 The parent institution provides continuing financial support for development, maintenance, and enhancement of library and information studies education in accordance with the general principles set forth in these Standards. The level of support provides a reasonable expectation of financial viability and is related to the number of faculty, administrative and support staff, instructional resources, and facilities needed to carry out the program's teaching, research, and service.

V.7 Compensation for a program's faculty, and other staff is equitably established according to their education, experience, responsibilities, and accomplishments and is sufficient to attract, support, and retain personnel needed to attain program goals and objectives.

V.8 Institutional funds for research projects, professional development, travel, and leaves with pay are available on the same basis as in comparable units of the institution. Student financial aid from the parent institution is available on the same basis as in comparable units of the institution.

V.9 A program has access to physical and technological resources that allow it to accomplish its objectives in the areas of teaching, research and service. The program provides support services for teaching and learning regardless of instructional delivery modality.

V.10 Physical facilities provide a functional learning environment for students and faculty; enhance the opportunities for research, teaching, service, consultation, and communication; and promote efficient and effective administration of the program.

V.11 Instructional and research facilities and services for meeting the needs of students and faculty include access to information resources and services, computer and other information technologies, accommodations for independent study, and media production facilities.

V.12 The staff and the services provided for a program by libraries, media centers, and information technology units, as well as all other support facilities, are appropriate for the level of use required and specialized to the extent needed. These services are delivered by knowledgeable staff, convenient, accessible to people with disabilities, and are available when needed.

V.13 The program's systematic planning and evaluation process includes review of its administrative policies, its fiscal and support policies, and its resource requirements. The program regularly reviews the adequacy of access to physical resources and facilities for the delivery of face-to-face instruction and access to the technologies and support services for the delivery of online education. Within applicable institutional policies, faculty, staff, students, and others are involved in the evaluation process.

V. 14 The program has explicit, documented evidence of its ongoing decision-making processes and the data to substantiate the evaluation of administration, finances, and resources.

V. 15 The program demonstrates how the results of the evaluation of administration, finances, and resources, are systematically used to improve the program and to plan for the future.

Appendix D

IFLA/UNESCO Public Library Manifesto 1994

Freedom, prosperity and the development of society and of individuals are fundamental human values. They will only be attained through the ability of well-informed citizens to exercise their democratic rights and to play an active role in society. Constructive participation and the development of democracy depend on satisfactory education as well as on free and unlimited access to knowledge, thought, culture and information.

The public library, the local gateway to knowledge, provides a basic condition for lifelong learning, independent decision-making and cultural development of the individual and social groups.

This Manifesto proclaims UNESCO's belief in the public library as a living force for education, culture and information, and as an essential agent for the fostering of peace and spiritual welfare through the minds of men and women.

UNESCO therefore encourages national and local governments to support and actively engage in the development of public libraries.

The Manifesto is prepared in cooperation with the International Federation of Library Associations and Institutions (IFLA).

THE PUBLIC LIBRARY

The public library is the local centre of information, making all kinds of knowledge and information readily available to its users.

The services of the public library are provided on the basis of equality of access for all, regardless of age, race, sex, religion, nationality, language or social status. Specific services and materials must be provided for those users who cannot, for whatever reason, use the regular services and materials, for example linguistic minorities, people with disabilities or people in hospital or prison.

All age groups must find material relevant to their needs. Collections and services have to include all types of appropriate media and modern technologies as well as traditional materials. High quality and relevance to local needs and conditions are fundamental. Material must reflect current trends and the evolution of society, as well as the memory of human endeavour and imagination.

Collections and services should not be subject to any form of ideological, political or religious censorship, nor commercial pressures.

MISSIONS OF THE PUBLIC LIBRARY

The following key missions which relate to information, literacy, education and culture should be at the core of public library services:

1. creating and strengthening reading habits in children from an early age;
2. supporting both individual and self conducted education as well as formal education at all levels;
3. providing opportunities for personal creative development;
4. stimulating the imagination and creativity of children and young people;
5. promoting awareness of cultural heritage, appreciation of the arts, scientific achievements and innovations;
6. providing access to cultural expressions of all performing arts;
7. fostering inter-cultural dialogue and favouring cultural diversity;
8. supporting the oral tradition;
9. ensuring access for citizens to all sorts of community information;
10. providing adequate information services to local enterprises, associations and interest groups;
11. facilitating the development of information and computer literacy skills;
12. supporting and participating in literacy activities and programmes for all age groups, and initiating such activities if necessary.

FUNDING, LEGISLATION AND NETWORKS

The public library shall in principle be free of charge.

The public library shall in principle be free of charge. The public library is the responsibility of local and national authorities. It must be supported by specific legislation and financed by national and local governments. It has to be an essential component of any long-term strategy for culture, information provision, literacy and education.

To ensure nationwide library coordination and cooperation, legislation and strategic plans must also define and promote a national library network based on agreed standards of service.

The public library network must be designed in relation to national, regional, research and special libraries as well as libraries in schools, colleges and universities.

OPERATION AND MANAGEMENT

A clear policy must be formulated, defining objectives, priorities and services in relation to the local community needs. The public library has to be organized effectively and professional standards of operation must be maintained.

Cooperation with relevant partners—for example, user groups and other professionals at local, regional, national as well as international level—has to be ensured.

Services have to be physically accessible to all members of the community. This requires well situated library buildings, good reading and study facilities, as well as relevant technologies and sufficient opening hours convenient to the users. It equally implies outreach services for those unable to visit the library.

The library services must be adapted to the different needs of communities in rural and urban areas.

The librarian is an active intermediary between users and resources. Professional and continuing education of the librarian is indispensable to ensure adequate services.

Outreach and user education programmes have to be provided to help users benefit from all the resources.

IMPLEMENTING THE MANIFESTO

Decision makers at national and local levels and the library community at large, around the world, are hereby urged to implement the principles expressed in this Manifesto.

About the Author

RICHARD E. RUBIN served as Director of the School of Library and Information Science at Kent State University, Kent, Ohio, from 1999–2010, and subsequently became Associate Provost for Extended (Online) Education at KSU until his retirement in 2013. He received his AB in Philosophy from Oberlin College, his MLS from Kent State University, and his PhD from the School of Library and Information Science at the University of Illinois Urbana-Champaign. He has spoken and presented at workshops throughout the United States, primarily on aspects of human resource management, including hiring, performance evaluation, discipline and termination, worker motivation, and ethics in the workplace. Dr. Rubin has been active in professional associations on the national and local level, including serving as a member and Chair of the ALA Committee on Accreditation.

Dr. Rubin is the author of numerous publications, including three books, *Human Resources Management in Libraries: Theory and Practice* (Neal-Schuman, 1991), *Hiring Library Employees* (Neal-Schuman, 1994), and three editions of *Foundations of Library and Information Science* (Neal-Schuman 2000, 2004, 2010). His articles have appeared in a variety of journals, including *Library Quarterly* and *Library and Information Science Research*.

Index